Wine and Ecstasy in Plato

SUNY series in Ancient Greek Philosophy
____
Anthony Preus, editor

Wine and Ecstasy in Plato

A Metaphor of Sorts and Its Early Reception

EVA ANAGNOSTOU-LAOUTIDES

EU GPSR Authorised Representative:
Logos Europe, 9 rue Nicolas Poussin, 17000, La Rochelle, France
contact@logoseurope.eu

For information, contact State University of New York Press, Albany, NY
www.sunypress.edu

Library of Congress Cataloging-in-Publication Data

Name: Anagnostou-Laoutides, Eva, author.
Title: Wine and ecstasy in Plato : a metaphor of sorts and its early
   reception / Eva Anagnostou-Laoutides.
Description: Albany : State University of New York Press, [2025]. | Series:
   SUNY series in ancient Greek philosophy | Includes bibliographical
   references and index.
Identifiers: LCCN 2025017851 | ISBN 9798855804850 (hardcover : alk. paper) |
   ISBN 9798855804874 (ebook) | ISBN 9798855804867 (pbk. : alk. paper)
Subjects: LCSH: Plato. Dialogues—Intoxication—Rome—History. | Intoxication—
   Egypt—History. | Drinking customs—Rome—History. | Drinking customs—
   Egypt—History.
Classification: LCC B395 .A557 2025 | DDC 184—dc23/eng/20250620
LC record available at https://lccn.loc.gov/2025017851

Για τα τραύματα που μας έθρεψαν

16–3–2002

Das, was an dir zehrt,
wird ein Starkes über dieser Nahrung.
Geh in der Verwandlung aus und ein.
Was ist deine leidendste Erfahrung?
Ist dir Trinken bitter, werde Wein.

. . . .

Und wenn dich das Irdische vergaß,
zu der stillen Erde sag: Ich rinne.
zu dem raschen Wasser sprich: Ich bin.

—Rainer Maria Rilke, *Die Sonette an Orpheus* II, 29, 1923

Contents

Preface and Acknowledgments

This project has been in the making since 2014. It is exhilarating and exhausting to be gripped by an idea for so long. The journey has been remarkably fruitful, resulting in two monographs: the first of these, the present volume, examines Plato's input to shaping the use of inebriation as a valid metaphor for achieving philosophical sublimity and traces its reception to the second century CE. Among Plato's heirs, I study his immediate successors in the Academy, Stoic thinkers, and other philosophically informed pagan writers, but also the Jewish thinker Philo of Alexandria. A second volume, with the title *Drunk with the Spirit: Inebriation from Plato to Christianity*, will explore the reception of inebriation as a distinctly Platonic metaphor by later Platonists, notably Plotinus and Proclus, and by Christian authors, from Clement of Alexandria and Origen, who shaped Christianity under Philo's influence, to Cristoforo Landino and Marsilio Ficino writing in quattrocento Florence. Along the way, my ideas found many supporters.

To start with, I would not be able to undertake this project without the support of the Australian Research Council (ARC), which afforded me four precious years of reading and thinking on the topic. Applying for an ARC Future Fellowship was a rigorous but gratifying exercise.[1] The first two colleagues to congratulate me on the award were Bronwen Neil and Ken Parry whom I joined at Macquarie University in early 2018. I am grateful to Bronwen for cheering on my progress, which subsequently led to our collaboration on an ARC Discovery project with the title *Crises of Leadership in the Eastern Roman Empire, 250–1000 CE.*[2] I am also hugely grateful to Ken for working with me on two related projects: one exploring the continuous interface of Christian and Platonic thinkers in the East from late antiquity to the Byzantine period and another extending the scope of Plato's reception from late antiquity to the Middle Ages and across all Abrahamic faiths.

Soon after securing the ARC grant, I was extremely fortunate to meet and have genuine, fruitful exchanges with Andrew Payne and Bart Van Wassenhove, leading to co-authored articles, one on "Drinking and Discourse in Plato" (with Andrew Payne, *Méthexis* 33, 2021) and one on "Drunkenness and Philosophical Enthusiasm in Seneca's *De Tranquillitate Animi*" (with Bart Van Wassenhove, *Scripta Classica Israelica* 39, 2020). Ideas from these articles feature in chapters 3 and 4, respectively, of the current book. Equally welcoming of my ideas were George Steiris and George Arabatzis of the National and Kapodistrian University of Athens, with whom I co-edited a journal special issue for *Religions*. I have incorporated my article from that issue, "Drunk with Wisdom: Metaphors of Ecstasy in Plato's *Symposium* and Lucian of Samosata," in chapter 4.

My greatest challenge in writing this book was formulating a theoretical model that would allow me to study inebriation as a figurative (but not fictional) mode of higher-level cognition. In this regard, I have benefited enormously from the generous and insightful advice of Yulia Ustinova, whose book on *Divine Mania and Altered Consciousness* (Routledge, 2017) I cite often in the Introduction and first chapter of this book. Thanks to Yulia, I came to study the philosophical aspects of metaphor and its reconceptualization in cognitive linguistics. I owe Yulia a heartfelt thank you for her guidance—and for an amazing tour of the Avdat and the Mamshit National Parks in the Negev Desert (with special thanks to the late Isaac Gilead). By the time I had finished the final edits to the volume, the *Theôria as Cognition in Plato* Conference was organized by Refik Güremen for the First Middle East Regional Meeting of the International Plato Society at the Middle East Technical University, 24–26 May 2023, Ankara, Turkey. The conference was a great opportunity to think along like-minded scholars who generously bolstered my confidence in my theoretical approach.

Moreover, I am also grateful to the International Institute of Education for the opportunity to spend three very productive months at the Kapodistrian and National University of Athens thanks to a Greek Diaspora fellowship, funded by the Stavros Niarchos Foundation and managed by the Fulbright Foundation. Finally, but certainly not least, I am very grateful to Hugo Branley, my patient and thorough research assistant, who has spent many hours trying to share my vision of this project, advising me on how to best tame my arguments.

Above all, this book would not have been possible without the love and steadfast support of my family. Throughout the Covid-19 pandemic, which struck Australia in late March 2020, we kept joking that with both parents working in academia we have always been in a kind of semi-permanent lockdown . . . Joking aside, however, I am very proud of the way we pulled through this experience as a family: Costas, Regas, and Rallou, upward and onward!

30 October 2024, Melbourne

Abbreviations and Citation Conventions

N.B.$_1$ Throughout the book, I quote ancient texts mostly from the *Loeb Classical Library* editions, unless otherwise specified. When a Loeb edition/translation merits further discussion, I cite it by the volume number rather than the author's name (for example, *Symposium* 194a is cited as L166: 148–149).

N.B.$_2$ All translations from other languages (French, Italian, Spanish) into English are mine, unless otherwise specified.

N.B.$_3$ Since my bibliography draws on several disciplines, I chose to write out all the journal titles in full.

N.B.$_4$ Titles of classical and late antique historical and literary texts and standard reference works are abbreviated in accordance with the *Oxford Classical Dictionary*, 4th edition revised, ed. S. Hornblower and A. Spawforth (Oxford, 2012).

- Works of ancient philosophy are abbreviated in accordance with the series *The Ancient Commentators on Aristotle*, ed. R. Sorabji, for which see *The Philosophy of the Commentators 200–600 AD Volume 1* (Ithaca, NY, 2005), 415–416.

- The works of Philo and Old Testament citations follow the *SBL Handbook of Style*, second rev. ed. J. M. LeMon and B. W. Breed, Atlanta, 2015.

- The works of Clement of Alexandria follow the SC editions = Sources chrétiennes.

  o *Les Stromates I*, ed. C. Mondésert, SC 30 (Paris, 1951).

  o *Les Stromates II*, ed. C. Mondésert, SC 38 (Paris, 1954).

  o *Les Stromates IV*, ed. A. van den Hoek, SC 463 (Paris, 2001).

  o *Les Stromates V*, 2 vols. ed. A. Le Boulluec, SC 278 and 279 (Paris, 1981).

  o *Les Stromates VI*, ed. P. Descourtieux, SC 446 (Paris, 1999).

  o *Le Pédagogue I*, ed. H.-I. Marrou and M. Harl, SC 70 (Paris, 1960).

  o *Le Protreptique*, ed. C. Mondésert and A. Plassart, SC 2 bis (Paris, 1949).

  o *Extraits de Théodote*, ed. F. Sagnard, SC 23 (Paris, 1970).

All remaining abbreviations are listed below.

BNJ   *Brill's New Jacoby: The Fragments of the Greek Historians I–III* (Jacoby Online), ed. I. Worthington, Leiden, 2006–

FGrH   *Fragmente der griechischen Historiker*, ed. F. Jacoby, Berlin/Leiden, 1923–1959 and continued by J. Bollansé; J. K. J. von Radicke; J. H. Brusuelas, D. Obbink, and Stefan Schorn; G. Verhasselt; et al., Leiden, 1998–

CMG   *Corpus Medicorum Graecorum*, ed. H. Diels et al., Berlin/Leipzig, 1907–

PG   *Patrologiae Cursus Completus: Series Graeca* (167 vols.), ed. J.-P. Migne, Paris, 1857–1866. [available online, https://patristica.net/graeca/]

Introduction

Raising a Glass

οἶνος πινόμενος πουλὺς κακόν· ἢν δέ τις αὐτὸν
πίνῃ ἐπισταμένως, οὐ κακὸν ἀλλ᾽ ἀγαθόν.

—Thgn. *El.* 509–510[3]

The Starting Point: Inebriation and Drunkenness

In this book I explore the role of wine consumption in Plato's dialogues, seeking to determine the cultural influences that shaped the metaphor of Socratic inebriation, its parameters, and its civic implications. To ascertain the dynamic character and continuous transformations of the metaphor, I follow its reception across Plato's pagan heirs to the second century CE but also in the works of Philo of Alexandria, his first century CE Jewish reader.[4] By engaging with the distinct categories of inebriation and drunkenness/intoxication,[5] I retrace the radical dichotomy in Greek culture between a negative evaluation of drunkenness as falling away from reason and losing self-control and the parallel development of a positive construal of inebriation as referring to the process of altering human consciousness and transcending the limitations of human reason. The difference(s) between inebriation and intoxication, evident not so much in the vocabulary employed by the Greeks and later the Romans but in the consequences of wine consumption, is/are exemplified by Plato who chose the context of the symposion—a term that etymologically signifies social occasions of drinking together[6]—to extol Socrates' philosophical aloofness as a form of *mania* and *baccheia* (*Symp.* 218b3–4); that is,

1

ecstasy achieved during celebrations in honor of Bacchus,[7] including the related Corybantic rites.[8] Still, although Plato celebrates inebriation as a metaphor for (the experience of) philosophical advancement, he also uses intoxication to signify negative mental states. Thus, he disproves of "getting drunk with pleasure,"[9] a state that characterizes the tyrannical man in the *Republic*,[10] and is exemplified in the *Symposium* by Alcibiades' drunken antics.[11] Nevertheless, human desires are "cognitively rich"[12] and, therefore, can be manipulated through education[13] until we learn to "get drunk with truth and knowledge," a state that ought to be determined by reason.[14] In this respect, Plato anticipates Aristotle and the Stoic moralists, who systematically criticize physical drunkenness and the irrational passions it arouses, prescribing sober restraint and temperance instead.[15]

Drawing on Plato's theory of the soul in the *Republic* (especially Books 4, 8, and 9),[16] and his analysis of how people of different psychic constitutions engage with the three different parts of the soul (the rational, the appetitive, and the spirited), Aristotle defined morality as the mean between excess and deficiency moderated by reason:[17] "Virtue then is a disposition to choose certain things (ἕξις προαιρετική), adjusted toward the mean relative to us, determined by reason (ὡρισμένη λόγῳ), and as the prudent man would determine it (ὡς ἂν ὁ φρόνιμος ὁρίσειεν)" (*Eth. Nic.* 1107a1–2). To illustrate the notion of failing to act in accordance with reason, Aristotle compared the "intoxication of desire" with alcoholic intoxication. Importantly, despite accepting the cognitive basis of desire,[18] Aristotle is aware that grasping the truth about the human good and plea-sure(s) cannot regulate human action unless our reasoning faculty—that is, our *phronēsis*, manages to convey the truth to the nonrational part of the soul in a persuasive manner.[19] Hence, in *Eth. Nic.* 1147a12–18, he acknowledges that there is "another way to gain knowledge" (ἔχειν τὴν ἐπιστήμην ἄλλον τρόπον)[20] in a subconscious state of mind, as is the case for "those asleep, or mad, or drunk" (οἷον τὸν καθεύδοντα καὶ μαινόμενον καὶ οἰνωμένον). Aristotle accepts that passions, including anger and sexual desire, have a similar effect with alcoholic intoxication since "they evidently alter the state of the body, and in some individuals even cause madness" (ἐπιδήλως καὶ τὸ σῶμα μεθιστᾶσιν, ἐνίοις δὲ καὶ μανίας ποιοῦσιν). Thus, he concludes, both types of intoxication, physical and emotional, cause a physically mediated corruption of perception that leads people to act voluntarily in a manner contrary to how they would if their deliberations were based on the *boulēsis* (wish) of reason.[21] Relying on his work, Stoic philosophers understood vice, of which intoxication is a typical symptom, as a rejection of reason.[22] Aristotle also wrote a treatise, *On Intoxication*,[23] which inspired several similar works by later Peripatetics such as Theophrastus but survives in fewer than a dozen citations.[24] While Aristotle, ever a pragmatist, admits the difficulty of maintaining control over desires,[25] alongside the inevitably individualistic character of self-realization,[26] Plato believed in education as the only way of taming the irrational aspects of the soul; in this context, handling the "fire" of wine offers a blueprint to imbibing/recalling the perpetual reality of virtue.

Wine Drinking and Plato

Despite its continuous popularity as a scholarly topic, the role of wine drinking in Greco-Roman antiquity has been studied in a polarized manner, either as part of ancient Greek material culture, or as a social phenomenon.[27] New research, however, in the past twenty years has proven scientifically that since the Neolithic period, when conditions in the upland regions of the Taurus and Zagros mountains enabled the development of viniculture and wine production,[28] our ancestors were inclined to experiment with wine by adding herbs, seeds, and other soluble substances to enhance not only its flavor but also its psychoactive effects.[29] The Greeks adapted this practice from an early time; our evidence indicates that by the second millennium wine production was introduced to Minoan Crete and later the Mycenaean mainland, while wine production in northern Greece appears to have been underway as early as 6,500 BCE.[30] Thus, not only was wine drinking a widespread phenomenon in ancient Greek societies, cutting across all social classes, but introducing and managing wine-induced ecstasy was an established practice, symptomatic of the ancient Greek preoccupation with reason and human perception. Although wine is one of many substances used by the ancient Greeks to stimulate human cognition,[31] wine drinking came to inform the most influential metaphor about altered states of mind thanks to Plato's comparison of inebriation with intellectual expansion.[32]

So far, scholarship has focused on the social and political implications of wine drinking, including its use in invective against tyrants (especially foreign tyrants) or political opponents.[33] Only a handful of contributions have touched upon the importance of wine drinking in Plato.[34] Among them, Rinella, drawing his inspiration from Foucault and Derrida and their interest in the history of madness,[35] perceives philosophy as Plato's attempt to neutralize and replace the negative effects of other prevalent forms of ecstasy, typically induced by wine and drugs during initiation rites or magic;[36] accordingly, he claims that for Plato, philosophy is meant to function as an(other) *pharmakon*, an antidote to the alcohol-induced experiences that contemporary Athenians were familiar with largely in the context of cult.[37] At the *polis* level the *pharmakon* of philosophy, a kind of beneficial "deceit" catering for the many, accommodates the "noble lie" of the ruler, discussed in the *Republic*.[38] Rinella's work on the pharmacology of wine introduces many astute arguments, which I revisit in my book;[39] my emphasis, however, lies on Plato's endorsement of ecstasy, notably wine-induced ecstasy, as a means of expanding human cognition and securing social harmony among citizens who share the same cultural values and the same cognitive horizon. Thus, I argue that in the *Laws* Plato revises the ideal polity of the *Republic* where the philosopher king is famously identified as the only individual worthy to be entrusted with ruling the city,[40] to accommodate wine-infused insight (*baccheia*) and philosophical contemplation (*theōria*) to the political life of Magnesia. In this respect, the *pharmakon* of philosophy functions as the elenctic mechanism that guides and regulates the interpretation of beneficial and keenly desired ecstatic events.

My analysis of the moral potential of ecstatic experiences in the *Laws* largely agrees with Pfefferkorn's recent work on the role of *choreia* in the dialogue, which builds on ideas previously teased out by Bartels.[41] Pfefferkorn discusses wine as a means of restoring the disposition of the elderly leaders of the Chorus who, having mastered the virtue of *sōphrosynē* (moderation), tend to find choric performances less enjoyable—what Slingerland describes as "temporarily but powerfully enhancing childlike creativity and receptiveness."[42] This return to a childlike disposition is required so that the leaders of the Chorus may build rapport with their young(er) students who are thus more likely to accept the social values of their teachers.[43] Pfefferkorn acknowledges the importance of accommodating nonrational elements in Magnesia's educational program,[44] though the thrust of her argument is the dynamic nature of this program, which enables citizens to acquire *sōphrosynē*[45] during all stages of human development. My work, focusing on Plato's use of inebriation as a metaphor for the nonrational aspects of philosophical engagement across his dialogues, stresses his attempt to cast philosophy as the means of imbibing an alternative, culturally determined cognitive model to which the *polis* must subscribe to ensure its coherence.

Symposiastic representations as a literary device for debating ancient identities, "ethnic and ethical, socio-political, and philosophical," have been also discussed by Hobden.[46] Her final chapter examines the catalytic function of the symposion in enabling philosophical discussions in Plato and Xenophon, establishing therefore a formidable tradition for later authors, from Aristotle, Epicurus, and Plutarch to Parmeniscus and Lucian.[47] Hobden takes the metaphors of symposiastic conduct at face value and does not engage with the problem of Socrates' *baccheia*, which is, seemingly at least, inconsistent with his symposiastic sobriety. Her analysis of the civic models that Plato and Xenophon negotiate through the structure of the symposion revolves around Socrates and his blatant contrast to the drunken Alcibiades, portrayed as a threat to democracy. Her work informs my discussion on the civic ramifications of the metaphor of *baccheia* in chapter 3: here, I draw attention to the drinking habits of the other participants in Plato's *Symposium* whom Hobden discusses as mainly speakers, not drinkers.

The cultural history of inebriation was also examined by Roth who discussed the twofold appreciation of the phenomenon as "potion and poison, *pharmakon* and catalyst,"[48] from antiquity to the twentieth century. Roth offers an accurate reading of Plato's *Symposium* and Euripides' *Bacchae* (his chapters 3 and 4) and points out the influence of Dionysiac worship on the Christian Eucharist (his chapter 6),[49] although his focus is explicitly on the aesthetic legacy of drunkenness in modern carnivalesque literature.[50] Equally, Roochnik considered Euripides' *Bacchae* and Dionysus in relation to altered states of consciousness that humans have always pursued, glossing over the metaphorical aspects of the Socratic symposion; however, his interest lies in juxtaposing food with drink, which he interprets vis-à-vis our tendency to "form maintenance and dissolution" in Nietzschean terms.[51]

Importantly, Ustinova has made a pivotal contribution with her work on *baccheia* as one of the types of *mania* that the ancient Greeks valued, situating the study of wine consumption in the wider context of our preoccupation with challenging ordinary human perception in favor of atypical mental states.[52] Yet, as she states,[53]

> The word *mania* refers to a range of multifarious conditions, which cannot be concisely described by the words "madness" or "frenzy" used in modern English translation. In Greek, *mania* also implies divine inspiration or revelation. Any deviation from

> an ordinary baseline state of consciousness, whether achieved
> voluntarily or involuntarily, deliberately sought or resulting
> from a disease, seen as a god-sent blessing or a curse could be
> dubbed *mania*. This variety of meanings reflects a wide range
> of experiences, from ecstatic prophesying to violent frenzy.

Thus, throughout the book, I translate *mania* as "madness" only when it is used in a medical/clinical context; I refer to *baccheia* when the term appears in the ancient source/s; and I use *frenzy* to describe the frantic behavior that marks ritual, poetic, and/or erotic inspiration.

The role of wine consumption in classical medical traditions about mental health and specifically in the diagnosis and/or treatment of *mania*[54] and related conditions such as *phrenitis, melancholy*, and epilepsy have been examined by Thumiger,[55] who provides an extensive list of the relevant vocabulary.[56] Plato's use of such vocabulary, also reflected in Aristotle as well as texts inspired by Aristotle, is discussed in chapter 2, where I seek to define the symptoms of Socratic inebriation and their cultural properties. Both Ustinova and Thumiger engage with the cognitive aspects of drunkenness but not its history as a conceptual metaphor. The works mentioned here provide invaluable insights for my analysis of Plato's reworking of inebriation to describe extraordinary mental states by means of which subsequent thinkers sought to ascertain truth (philosophical or theological) and the constitutional model(s) that reflected it. Still, it is crucial to situate this study in a theoretical setting that considers both ancient and modern attempts to articulate ecstatic experiences.

Thus, in chapter 1 I discuss the conceptual metaphor theory of Lakoff and Johnson and its ability to accommodate the kind of extended, organizing metaphor represented by Plato's use of inebriation as a proxy for philosophical ecstasy through which advanced cognition is secured. I exploit the theoretical resources of cognitive phenomenology (which overlap with Aristotle's appreciation of metaphors by analogy) and defend its potential to explain this kind of metaphorical thinking from a historical perspective that recognizes its development in culture-specific contexts. The human desire to enhance our perception originates in the Indo-European past, when mead was the main alcoholic drink.[57] Distinct from other types of irrationality, whether positive (poetic, religious) or negative (madness, pseudo-religious ecstasy), Plato understands philosophical ecstasy as the pathway to increasing awareness at both the individual and collective level. Despite appreciating the limits of language to render profound experiences,

Plato attempts to articulate the nature of philosophical insight and offer a blueprint to those wishing to emulate Socrates. Informed by early Greek poetry, which preserves accounts of ecstasy induced by both mead and wine, Plato employs the metaphor of Socratic inebriation in both the *Symposium* and the *Phaedrus*. This metaphor is, as I argue, particularly in dialogue with Euripides' description of Bacchic ecstasy.

Chapter 2 takes its start from the precarious nature of Plato's metaphor, seeking to identify its parameters: since the vocabulary that relates Socratic inspiration is also used to denote intoxication and madness, a tendency echoed in Aristotle's *Parva Naturalia* and the pseudo-Aristotelian *Problems*, Plato must defend his metaphor against misinterpretation. This chapter examines the medical and philosophical connotations of drunkenness on which Plato draws to clarify that, despite appearances, Socrates is neither intoxicated nor mad. A careful reading of the *Phaedrus*, together with insights from Euripides' *Bacchae*, reveals that Socrates regards ecstasy as a valuable experience of irrationality, which, however, must be subsequently subjected to sober analysis though reason. Plato also engages with contemporary medical advances as reflected in the influential Hippocratic *Regimen*[58] where intelligence, determined by the primacy of fire in the human constitution, is said to be influenced by the heat of wine. Similar ideas underpin Heraclitus' theory of fire as the cosmic principle still traceable in the hot and dry souls of the virtuous. These ideas, which have notable parallels in Sanskrit texts, help us explain Socrates' imperviousness in the *Symposium* to both wine *and* cold. Notably, although ancient clinicians agreed that drunkenness could cause madness, the therapeutic properties of wine were widely acknowledged and applied.

Chapter 3 examines the civic aspects of archaic *symposia*,[59] reflected in Plato's use of the symposion as a microcosm of the state.[60] In the *Laws*, Plato defends the civic benefits of philosophical reflection by envisaging the use of wine as part of an educational regime to assay and exercise civic ethos, nourished by the virtue of *sōphrosynē*.[61] The "Test of the Wine" is inspired by Solon's valorization of the symposion and his civic reading of traditional religious *theōria*.[62] Based on these educational tenets, also expounded in the *Republic* and the *Protagoras*, I revisit the negative representations of drunkenness in the *Symposium* where Plato explores the connection between wine drinking and various styles of discourse.[63] I argue that Plato compares the styles of the other speakers to the intellectual *and* moral haziness caused by intoxication. Thus, Socrates distances himself from drunken Alcibiades, whose profile corresponds to that of Critias,

Plato's cousin who became a leading member of the Thirty Tyrants and whom Xenophon cast as the epitome of the failed Socratic.[64] Drunkards *and* tyrants adopt a distorted version of *parrhēsia* (free speech), which is detrimental for civic values, as Plato reminds us in the *Laws*. Socrates also rejects the drunken carousals described in comedy, especially Aristophanes, since humor, like wine, is predicated on certain states of mind.[65] Socrates' ability to deliver sound, good-humored speeches in the *Symposium* and the *Phaedrus* reflects his outstanding ethos as a wine drinker *and* a citizen.[66]

Wine Drinking among Plato's Heirs to the Second Century CE

Finally, I examine the drinking cultures of the Hellenistic and Roman periods, during which Plato's metaphor of inebriation was adopted by other philosophical schools, notably the Stoics. The rapprochement of Platonic and Stoic views was paved by Arcesilaus in the third century BCE,[67] despite his rejection of the Stoic notion of καταληπτική φαντασία (conclusive or positive perception) as dogmatic and in essence un-Platonic and un-Socratic.[68] Following the production of Plato's first critical edition by Aristophanes of Byzantium in second century BCE Alexandria, Eudorus played a key role in the revival of Platonism to the Ptolemaic capital Eudorus' revision of Platonic ethics led to the development of the so-called Middle Platonism in Roman Alexandria (of the first BCE and CE centuries), to which the Jewish thinker Philo made a seminal contribution.[69]

In the Hellenistic period, images of drunkenness proliferated in art[70] and in literature, especially in epigrams,[71] which idealize drunkenness as the pinnacle of creative poetic compulsion while also detailing the gloomier aspects of alcoholism.[72] Drunkenness, however, never lost its appeal as a metaphor with important political connotations. Marked by the rise of Alexander and the inevitable dissolution of the classical *polis*, this was "an age of kings, political and philosophical, temporal and spiritual."[73] In the Hellenistic "symposion-feast,"[74] with its "new emphasis on food consumption and its consequent power dynamic," drunkenness was associated with extreme political power. The connection, already prominent in the context of the "rhetorical tyrant," as exemplified by Dionysius I of Syracuse and his son who famously resisted Plato's admonitions,[75] was now amplified with stories about Alexander's drunken antics. The topic became popular among Roman writers,[76] well-versed in both Plato and the Stoics; accordingly, drunkenness was adopted as a major tool of judging Roman political morality,[77] and the motif of drinking blood instead of wine, sealed by Vergil's portrayal of Polyphemus,[78] was increasingly employed to denote misplaced ambition.[79] Despite, however, the epic and tragic oeuvre of monstrous feasts,[80] Seneca's alleged endorsement of Platonic ecstasy[81] affirms the Roman eagerness to contribute to the debate on enhanced perception.

Hellenistic philosophers often acted as advisors of powerful kings.[82] Thus, Plato's philosopher king with his superior perception remained influential, although Aristotle proposed heroic virtue (not philosophy) as the key quality of the ideal king. This was the model of rule that Alexander abode by, prompting Onesicritus to refer to him as "philosopher in arms."[83] The concern with integrating political theory and practice, which goes back to Isocrates[84] and Xenophon,[85] continued under Alexander's successors, only to be resolved by Cicero and the Roman Stoics who stipulated that the wise man had a duty to participate in politics.[86] Similar ideas were also aired by Plutarch who sought to apply "his Platonic political philosophy to the concrete context of everyday municipal politics."[87] In this context, in agreement with Plato, the Stoics accepted moderate drinking but rejected intoxication, viewing it, as noted above, as a symptom of the soul's exposure to irrational passions,[88] which distract the Stoic philosopher from his training "for freedom from deception, hasty judgment, and wrong assents."[89] Plutarch, in the second century, and Athenaeus, taking us to the early part of the third century, employ the symposion mainly as the literary setting for discussing philosophical ideas,[90] although their style is forced to accommodate the political dimensions I have outlined here. These later *Symposia* reiterate and transmit Platonic notions of drunkenness to their audiences—a valuable service, if also enveloped in an aura of nostalgia (which reaches its peak during the Second Sophistic) for a long-gone intellectual elite.

In the meantime, however, Platonic inebriation underwent a powerful revision in the hands of Philo of Alexandria, who revamped the fiercely competitive intellectual arena of first century Alexandria by defending the superiority of Jewish religious truths. Philo identified YHWH (the name of God revealed to Moses in Ex 3:14) with the Platonic One[91] and employed Platonic allegory to harmonize scripture with philosophy.[92] He also advocated the doctrine of the Platonic Ideas as God's thoughts,[93] paving the way for the Neoplatonic reception of inebriation as an allegory of a mystic union with the divine. Importantly, Philo re-introduced drunkenness as the key quality of the charismatic leader whose alternative vision is rewarded with deification,[94] engaging anew with the Platonic telos of being "as godlike as possible" (*Tht.* 176b2: ὁμοίωσις θεῷ κατὰ τὸ δυνατόν).

Accordingly, chapter 4 discusses the criticism that Plato's metaphorical style drew in later periods, especially as ruthless philosophy teachers would often exploit inebriation as a ruse for attracting students.[95] Thus, philosophical drinking is treated humorously by Lucian and Horace, reflecting a renewed debate about the authenticity of ecstatic philosophical experiences. The topic is also examined by Seneca in his *De tranquillitate*, where he advises his young mentee Serenus, numb with worry about his ability to achieve intellectual growth, to drink liberally. Seneca does not deviate from the Stoic rejection of drunkenness, as often argued,[96] but accepts that the Stoic philosopher should aim at joy, a feeling emanating from his preoccupation with virtue. Seneca, therefore, endorses Plato's notion of exciting the intellect with wine to advance philosophical cognition in a practical manner, as recommended in the *Laws*.[97] Moreover, although ecstasy has no secure place in the Stoic cosmopolis, Philo's "sober inebriation,"[98] offers a spiritual pathway for achieving communion with God and participation in his House of Virtue, in Eden.[99] In due time, under the combined influence of later Platonists and Philo, the metaphor of inebriation informs Christian mysticism and the notion of becoming fellow citizens of God in the Heavenly Kingdom.[100] A huge part of human history, then, is indeed a history of inebriation as interpreted by Plato.[101]

Sobering Up: The Way Forward

Plato's metaphor of philosophical rapture as drunken revelry and *mania* through which the philosopher experiences the transcendent world of the Forms[102] reveals the central role of ecstasy in shaping and affirming identity and belonging, then and now, here and beyond. Overall, two common themes emerge from my examination: first, the effectiveness of inebriation as a metaphor for conveying ideas about our mental and ethical states; second, the anxiety Plato felt, in equal measure to later Platonists, to distinguish between his rejection of physical intoxication and the use of wine (partly to induce and mainly) to describe intellectual advancement. This, however, is not a testament to the limitations of the drinking metaphor. Rather, through a phenomenological perspective, we are reminded that approximating the highest good involves[103] "an understanding *not only* of how we as individuals are supposed to live our lives, *but also* of how we as social beings are supposed to live together and, even more generally, what the world we inhabit together is supposed to look like." In this framework, inebriation has been a uniquely pervasive "common language," across times and cultures that perfectly encapsulates our deepest existential fear, and perhaps, also our deepest hope: (we sense) that truth lies beyond reason.

Chapter 1

After Experience

Drunkenness and Metaphors of Mania in Plato

dans les chants, dans les rires, les danses, l' éroticism, l'ivresse, on cherche à la fois une exaltation de l'instant et une complicité avec les autres hommes.

—S. de Beauvoir, *Pour une morale de l'ambiguïté*, Gallimard, 1947, 176

This chapter examines the origins of Plato's use of inebriation as a metaphor to describe the states of consciousness induced by philosophy; it is informed by ancient and modern theoretical perspectives, notably that of cognitive phenomenology. Of course, a significant amount of research has been published to date on the role of drunkenness in Plato's *Symposium*, as well as on viticulture in ancient Greece and the eastern Mediterranean;[1] however, the role of wine in debating different types of inspiration in Platonism begs further study. Plato used wine and its psychoactive effects as a metaphor for validating and relating the experience of cognition, a need triggered by a deep-seated urge to challenge or second-guess our intellect.[2] I begin by explaining my theoretical considerations, starting with a definition of the key terms "consciousness" and "altered state of consciousness."

13

Drunkenness and Enhanced Cognition

Consciousness as a state of "mental alertness and awareness"—as defined in the 1994 report of the Committee on Techniques for the Enhancement of Human Performance of the US National Research Council, is notoriously difficult to explain.[3] It encompasses, at a minimum, the entirety of our subjective perception of ourselves and the world around us, our choices and aspirations, our thoughts, and our dreams. However, despite the myriad kinds of experience that go to make up consciousness, some states, typically induced by hypnosis, drugs, or ritual practice,[4] are singled out as distinct and atypical. Whether ascribed to drunkenness, ecstasy, or divine possession,[5] these "altered states of consciousness" are states in which one's awareness is in some way heightened or intensified beyond the norm. Importantly, this enhancement of one's consciousness can also manifest itself physically in the form of enhanced performance; for example, a person in a state of ecstatic reverie might display higher levels of pain tolerance, greater resistance to fatigue, or improved memory. Although the psychosomatic effects of ecstasy are undeniably real,[6] our brains are conditioned to recognize, experience, and understand incidents of spiritual elevation in culturally specific ways.[7] Thus, it was a pervasive trope throughout Greek antiquity that oracles, hierophants, and poets (who were divinely authorized to relate the tales of the gods) possessed superior knowledge; not only were they relied upon for guidance on personal matters, but every city-state's military, religious, and educational agenda depended on them.[8] The forms of ecstasy undergone by these figures were therefore not adventitious, but rather firmly institutionalized through rituals and customs and implicitly understood as resulting from extraordinary access to the gods. Furthermore, the kinds of physical symptoms associated with the ecstasies undergone by these figures exerted a normative effect on other claims to divine insight.[9] This cultural specificity, however, entails that societies must engage in a continual renegotiation, based both on cross-cultural interface and local ingenuity, of the ways in which altered states of consciousness are manifested and interpreted.

The Greeks employed various means to stimulate human perception: music, dance, hallucinogens, strong emotions, and wine were often described as requisites of poetic inspiration,[10] and all were incorporated to some degree in religious mysteries and divination rites.[11] However, the ubiquity of references to wine drinking and inebriation in archaic Greek poetry reflects the centrality of the symposion among them, a point I will return to in chapter 2.[12] Plato, who was steeped in the literary traditions of his time,[13] drew on this tradition of "drinking together" (συμπίνειν) as a chance to perform one's historical identity (ethnic, social, civic, gender, etc.), and used it to discuss the experience of achieving (higher) cognition, and accordingly to explicate the philosophical reveries of Socrates. By employing the metaphor of inebriation, Plato was able to borrow the set of cultural norms that explained and justified drinking and apply them to uphold the value of Socrates' well-known eccentricities. However, while this metaphor gave Socrates' behavior a culturally recognized shape, it also risked assimilating him to the mundane realities of drunkenness—an assimilation that Plato is at pains to avoid, defending Socrates' uniqueness (ἀτοπίαν) repeatedly in the *Symposium*. Hence, at 221d3–8, Socrates commands admiration because he is "unlike any man, whether among past ones or those who live now" (**μηδενὶ ἀνθρώπων** ὅμοιον εἶναι . . . **μήτε τῶν παλαιῶν μήτε τῶν νῦν** ὄντων), a notion reiterated at *Symp*. 221c6–8 (**οὔτε τῶν νῦν οὔτε τῶν παλαιῶν . . . ἀνθρώπων μὲν μηδενί**).[14] Accordingly, my analysis here is informed by two main considerations: firstly, Plato's need to resort to the imagery available in his culture to describe Socrates' intellectual and ethical superiority, and secondly, the equally pressing need to differentiate Socrates' state from all other states this imagery could be used to describe. Plato must determine the parameters of his metaphor,[15] a task he is most preoccupied with in the *Symposium* and the *Phaedrus*.

In investigating Plato's figurative use of inebriation to express the effects of philosophy, I am interested both in the way that this metaphor was first articulated and how it was subsequently received and repurposed. As it would be a grave omission to focus on later interpretations alone, without seeking to detect Plato's authorial intentions, I subscribe to Skinner's availability principle, which stipulates that historical research ought to rely on the understanding of past agents' actions and utterances.[16] I am also concerned, however, with the transformations that philosophical inebriation underwent in the hands of Plato's intellectual heirs, as it was absorbed and revised in new cultural circumstances. Given the textual focus of my investigation, engaging with the poststructuralist approach of thinkers like Foucault, Lacan, and Derrida[17] would seem like an obvious methodological approach. This approach, however, suffers from several drawbacks, central to which are its undertheorization of metaphor and its undervaluation of experience. Experiences are often cast in an ahistorical light in the poststructuralist context and are perceived with an immediacy that implies lack of reflection.[18]

As a result of its burdensome structuralist legacy, poststructuralism has a notable difficulty with accommodating metaphors; despite moving away from the structuralist fascination with antithetical lexical pairs that reveal a fixed, underlying structure to a text, poststructuralism is still preoccupied with distinguishing literal from metaphorical meanings, typically assuming the primacy of literal meaning over metaphor.[19] Hence, Derrida, despite recognizing the importance of metaphor, denies that it has a role in philosophy, which he sees as committed to examining non-metaphorical concepts.[20] Even Lacan, in his use of Saussurean structural linguistics to map out an unconscious that he saw as based on metaphors and metonymies operating at a symbolic level, largely maintained the association of metaphors with the poetic.[21] The results of this when applied to historical work are shown, for example, in Calame's analysis of ancient Greek poetic speech.[22] As Calame himself is aware, the artificial division he employs between *logos* and *mythos* is already challenged by Plato, making it unsuitable for the present endeavor.[23]

Our ability to appreciate similarities and to articulate them in a variety of genres and contexts makes metaphor the prevalent cognitive mechanism for analyzing complex concepts, and worthy of being investigated on its own terms.[24] In Ricoeur's words, "[T]here is no non-metaphorical place from which to consider metaphor,"[25] especially when trying to explain philosophical genius. In what follows, I will draw on the premises of cognitive phenomenology, as anticipated in Merleau-Ponty's work on perception as "a system of meanings which makes the concrete essence of the object immediately recognizable,"[26] and will argue that it accords with ancient accounts of metaphor and its ability to relate mental states. Regarding the role of sensations and associated images in conveying experience, Merleau-Ponty notes:[27] "If . . . we admit that all these 'projections,' all these 'associations,' all these 'transferences' are based on some intrinsic characteristic of the object, the "human world" ceases to be a metaphor and becomes once more what it really is, the seat and as it were the homeland of our thoughts." Importantly, I will not regard this filtering of real experience though images as less valid or less authentic. On the contrary, poetic images can become "a source of psychic activity,"[28] informing the way(s) in which we create realities.[29] Thus, for Merleau-Ponty, the style in art is an elaboration of a style that appears already in perception.[30] Since the processes of consciousness are open to reflection, phenomenology engages with the perception of both appearances and reality[31] with the intention of identifying metaphorical meaning(s).

Metaphors and the Phenomenology of Inebriation

It is often difficult to relate the experiences that accompany altered states of consciousness. The encounter with the greatness of the cosmos or the divine, like that which Plato claims is part of Socrates' philosophizing, is marked by an inexpressible sublimity and is often bound up in feelings of amazement, fear, and reverence.[32] As a result, Plato's descriptions of the inner experience of philosophy are full of lacunae and have a literary, almost poetic, quality[33]—perhaps best exemplified in the *Symposium*, where Diotima resorts to a series of negatives to convey the ineffable uniqueness of Beauty,[34] claiming that the beautiful "exists forever itself by itself with itself, unique in its kind" (*Symp.* 211b2: αὐτὸ καθ᾽ αὐτὸ μεθ᾽ αὑτοῦ μονοειδὲς ἀεὶ ὄν). Nevertheless, there is an obvious need to relate the experience of philosophy in some fashion—apophatic accounts can only be meaningful when combined with *some* attempt to characterize our experience. Thus, Plato sketches philosophical trance by drawing on culturally validated states of altered consciousness, associated with a range of sensory experiences. In this context, a careful examination of Plato's descriptions of philosophical inebriation readily confirms his metaphorical use of the language of *mania* and *baccheia* (as, for example, at *Symp.* 218b3–4) in full awareness of its creative potential but also its limitations, since metaphorical language, being distinct from real experience, can have a creative path of its own.[35]

Plato's use of this kind of extended metaphor[36] to express a complex philosophical meaning is not unique or without precedent in ancient Greece. Introducing apophatic discourse by means of metaphor is seen in both Heraclitus and Parmenides: Heraclitus' surviving fragments are rife with implicit analogies and oblique references to various customs and practices, while Parmenides' philosophical poem, in which the authorial persona is introduced to the paths of truth and opinion, functions as an extended allegory for philosophical inquiry.[37] Aristotle, however, was the first to thematize metaphor as a subject of inquiry.

According to Aristotle, metaphor refers to a generous range of linguistic phenomena, since "we all engage in conversation using metaphors" (*Rhet.* 1404b32–33: πάντες γὰρ μεταφοραῖς διαλέγονται).[38] Aristotle distinguishes metaphors from genus to species, species to genus, species to species, and metaphors by analogy (*Poet.* 1457b7–9: κατὰ τὸ ἀνάλογον), by far the most popular type of metaphor (*Rhet.* 1411a1–2: Τῶν δὲ μεταφορῶν . . . εὐδοκιμοῦσι μάλιστα αἱ κατ᾽ ἀναλογίαν),[39] since "it allows for creativity on the part of the speakers to denote new sets of similarities and coin new expressions, and that it generates pleasurable learning on the part of the audience."[40] All metaphors involve the transference of a word associated with one domain to another (*Poet.* 1457b7: **μεταφορὰ δέ ἐστιν ὀνόματος ἀλλοτρίου ἐπιφορά**).[41] Importantly, Aristotle insists, "the right use of metaphors is to perceive similarities" (*Poet.* 1459a7: **τὸ γὰρ εὖ μεταφέρειν τὸ ὅμοιον θεωρεῖν ἐστιν**), an exercise meant to achieve clarity (*Poet.* 1458b1: **εἰς τὸ σαφὲς τῆς λέξεως**)—alongside the pleasurable engagement of the audience who is also introduced to some element of novelty.[42] The success of these features of speech (that is, clarity, pleasure, and novelty) depends on the sociolinguistic background of the speakers, partly determined by their age among other factors. Thus, while discussing the role of hyperbole in creating successful analogies, Aristotle characterizes it as "childlike" (*Rhet.* 1413a28: <αἱ> ὑπερβολαὶ μειρακιώδεις), prompting Kotarcic to make two observations:[43]

> First, Aristotle is aware of and acknowledges that language is used differently by same-sex speakers of different ages. Second, Aristotle's qualification of hyperbole as μειρακιώδεις, "adolescent," implies that there is a close connection between people's personal development and the manner in which they use language.

Analogy can also function as an extended simile, in which the points of similarity between the two elements of the metaphor are refined and specified by using negation, or as he says, "by calling something by a name belonging to another to deny one of its characteristics" (*Poet.* 1457b30: προσαγορεύσαντα τὸ ἀλλότριον ἀποφῆσαι τῶν οἰκείων τι).[44] Crucially, Aristotle notes that by drawing on similar images, metaphors allow a writer to specify things that do not have proper names (*Rhet.* 1405a34–35: **ἐκ τῶν συγγενῶν καὶ τῶν ὁμοειδῶν μεταφέρειν ἐπὶ τὰ ἀνώνυμα**).[45] Aristotle's understanding of metaphor (and its common use in poetry and rhetoric)[46] underpins Ricoeur's appreciation of it as a figure of speech, which

> presents in an *open* fashion, by means of a conflict *between* identity and difference, the process that, in a *covert* manner, generates semantic grids by fusion of differences *into* identity.[47]

However, while Aristotle "recognises the importance of metaphor as adorning language," he is clear that it cannot be reduced to this function alone.[48] Successful, creative metaphors[49] allow speakers to achieve much more than similes:

> for while the latter only describes a similarity, metaphor becomes a symbol of that similarity by replacing the original ὄνομα with another ὄνομα . . . metaphor *is not* a likeness but *merely refers to* a likeness.[50]

By referring to our ability to appreciate similarities, Aristotle does not just mean similarities between words but also between concepts. As such, Aristotle embraces the cognitive function of metaphors, and specifically their role in philosophy since, as he asserts, "in philosophy too, it is characteristic of a well-directed mind to perceive the likeness even in things very different" (*Rhet.* 1412a11–12: **οἷον καὶ ἐν φιλοσοφίᾳ τὸ ὅμοιον καὶ ἐν πολὺ διέχουσι θεωρεῖν εὐστόχου**).[51] Aristotle had already aired this view earlier in his treatise, where we read:

> Fables are suitable in deliberative oratory (εἰσὶ δ᾽ οἱ λόγοι δημηγορικοί), and they have this advantage (ἔχουσιν ἀγαθὸν τοῦτο), that while it is difficult to find similar historical incidents that have really happened (ὅτι πράγματα μὲν εὑρεῖν ὅμοια γεγενημένα χαλεπόν), it is easier to invent fables (λόγους δὲ ῥᾷον); for they must be invented (ποιῆσαι γὰρ δεῖ), like comparisons (ὥσπερ καὶ παραβολάς), if a man is capable of seizing the analogy (ἄν τις δύνηται τὸ ὅμοιον ὁρᾶν); and this is easy if one studies philosophy (ὅπερ ῥᾷόν ἐστιν ἐκ φιλοσοφίας). (*Rhet.* 1394a2–6)[52]

Nonetheless, Aristotle's theory of metaphor has long been understood as aesthetic,[53] or as "a matter of words, not concepts."[54] In so interpreting metaphor, we fail to appreciate its creative power and the vital role that metaphor might play in the otherwise abstract endeavor of philosophy.[55] As Lakoff and Johnson observe,[56] "[A]lthough Aristotle's theory of how metaphors work is the classic view, his praise of metaphor's ability to induce insight was never carried over into modern philosophical thought."

With that in mind, let us turn to Plato who engages more systematically with demonstrating the influence of images on cognition[57] and the power of metaphors to make things "appear before the eyes" (Arist. *Rhet.* 1386b1: πρὸ ὀμμάτων ποιοῦντες, 1405b13–14, 1411b1).[58] In the *Republic,* Plato defends the "manic reason" of philosophy as a mind-bending force that impels[59] ". . . the true lover of learning (ὄντως φιλομαθής) . . . to move on without losing heart or ceasing from his passion (ἴοι καὶ οὐκ ἀμβλύνοιτο οὐδ' ἀπολήγοι τοῦ ἔρωτος) until he grasps the nature of each and every thing (πρὶν αὐτοῦ ὃ ἔστιν ἑκάστου τῆς φύσεως ἅψασθαι) through that part of the soul which is fitted to grasp something of that sort through its kinship with it (ᾧ προσήκει ψυχῆς ἐφάπτεσθαι τοῦ τοιούτου - προσήκει δὲ συγγενεῖ)" (*Resp.* 490a9–b5). Once the philosopher immerses himself in "what really exists" (490b5: μιγεὶς τῷ ὄντι ὄντως), he "gives birth to intelligence and truth" (490b6: γεννήσας νοῦν καὶ ἀλήθειαν), so "he may gain knowledge and a true life" (490b7: γνοίη τε καὶ ἀληθῶς ζῴη). However, Plato's illustration of philosophical insight through the metaphor of inebriation that occurs primarily in the *Symposium* but also throughout his dialogues offers a more accessible description, familiar to all regardless of their class, gender, or education.[60]

Plato's metaphor of inebriation can be articulated using Lakoff and Johnson's notion of "conceptual metaphor"; that is, the tendency to render abstractions consistently in terms of more concrete, practical areas of life. More specifically, Lakoff and Johnson coin the term "structural metaphor" to describe metaphors such as LOVE IS MADNESS,[61] in which "one concept is metaphorically structured in terms of another."[62] The pervasive use of expressions such as "I'm crazy about her" or "She drives me out of my mind" results from this kind of metaphorical structuring. My analysis here accepts Lakoff and Johnson's premise that metaphors are mainly conceptual[63] and "structure how we perceive, how we think, and what we do";[64] notably, conventional conceptual metaphors can be subjected to novel extensions, through which they "are capable of giving us a new understanding of our experience,"[65] beyond merely helping us to describe preexisting similarities. As Lakoff and Johnson argue,[66] "[N]ew metaphors have the power to create a new reality." By mapping drunkenness onto the experience of philosophy, Plato coins such a new or novel metaphor, which might be formalized, in the manner of Lakoff and Johnson, as PHILOSOPHY IS INEBRIATING.

I have chosen to call this metaphor "Platonic inebriation," and much like the influence other novel or creative metaphors have on general discourse, it exerts a pervasive effect on Plato's characterization of the experience of philosophy. Plato relies on this metaphor to render Socrates' unusual proclivities intelligible and justified in the eyes of a contemporary audience. Capturing the experience of being under the influence of philosophy, however, requires Plato to deepen and enrich his chosen metaphor, as the ecstatic experience is not easily described to those who have not experienced it. Plato admits as much in the *Meno*, where the eponymous character tries to put his experience of Socrates in words:[67]

> Socrates, I used to hear before meeting you, that you do nothing else but leading yourself and others to doubt. And now, as you seem to me, you are bewitching and poisoning and totally casting a spell on me (**γοητεύεις** με καὶ **φαρμάττεις** καὶ ἀτεχνῶς **κατεπᾴδεις**), so that I have become full of doubt. And you seem to me completely, if some banter is proper, that you are most similar, both in appearance and in other aspects, to the flat torpedo of the sea (ὁμοιότατος εἶναι τό τε εἶδος καὶ τἆλλα ταύτῃ τῇ πλατείᾳ νάρκῃ τῇ θαλαττίᾳ):[68] for it also makes numb whoever approaches and touches it (ναρκᾶν ποιεῖ), and you seem to have done something similar to me, to make me numb (ναρκᾶν). For truly I am numb both in my soul and my mouth (τὴν ψυχὴν καὶ τὸ στόμα ναρκῶ), and I do not know what to answer you. (*Meno* 79e7–80b2)

Unable to express himself, Meno resorts to banter. Plato, however, cannot take the same route;[69] just as Socrates claims that an expert should be able to give an account of his expertise—a claim he repeats often across the Platonic dialogues,[70] Plato strives to offer a satisfactory description of his master.[71]

The metaphorical character of Socratic inebriation is amply evident in the language of the *Symposium*, while as I argue in chapter 2, it corresponds closely to Plato's understanding of *mania* in the *Phaedrus*, especially to the extent that intoxication was understood to cause madness or aggravate cases of mental instability—thus, the philosophically inclined lovers of the *Phaedrus* are thoroughly familiar with the symptoms of those suffering from madness. Although the *Symposium* is most known for its comparison of philosophy to falling in love, it should not be forgotten that, as Roth notes, "drink is embedded in the very center of the text."[72] The events of the dialogue, narrated by Apollodorus as heard from Aristodemus, take place at the drinking party of Agathon, an Athenian tragic poet, who achieved his first dramatic victory at the festival of Dionysus Lenaius in 416 BCE.[73] This splendid celebration, filled with wine and Dionysiac merriment, allows Plato to explore the phenomenology of inebriation and the cultural tropes that surround it. Socrates' philosophical rapture is often linked in the dialogue with Dionysiac *mania* or *baccheia* (that is, behaving with maenadic frenzy),[74] a phenomenon widely represented in ancient myth, literature, and art.[75] Furthermore, Roth continues, even the account of Erōs' parenthood, related to Socrates in a life-altering exchange with the priestess Diotima[76]—one of the climaxes of the dialogue's exposition of our desire for the beautiful and the good—contains an often-missed extension of the metaphor of inebriation:[77] "The inset narrative about the birth of Love is a drunken narrative: Love is the child of blind intoxication."[78] Diotima states that Penia (Poverty) slept with Poros (Resource) after he got drunk on nectar during a feast in the garden of Zeus, in the days "before wine was known" (*Symp.* 203b6–7: οἶνος γὰρ οὔπω ἦν).[79] Although the role of Erōs in Diotima's tale undoubtedly also evokes the erotic nature of philosophy, her account firmly emphasizes inebriation as a metaphor for philosophical inspiration. Diotima's reference to intoxication by nectar invites some additional discussion, but wine, although not the only or most ancient means of intoxication, seems the main paradigm of altering consciousness.

In the context of the metaphorical articulation of lived experience, the intersection of phenomenology with cognitive linguistics can be especially fruitful.[80] As indicated above, part of what troubles Plato as he develops his account of Socratic inebriation is the inherent difficulty of soberly describing ecstatic states of consciousness. The new metaphor of inebriation and the ways in which Plato tried to delimit its meaning offers a unique lens for understanding the troubled relationship between perception, cognition, and epistemology. The communicative strategies employed in the Platonic dialogues, especially the *Symposium*, show that Plato holds that language, no matter how deficient, can still approximate this altered state of consciousness. Plato was deeply aware of the power of speech on the human mind, which Gorgias, the sophist whose reasoning Plato challenges in the homonymous Platonic dialogue, had described as a powerful *pharmakon* in his famous *Encomium of Helen*.[81] Admitting that "speech is a powerful ruler, who achieves most divine effects despite having a very small and invisible body" (*Hel.* 8: λόγος δυνάστης μέγας ἐστίν, ὃς σμικροτάτωι σώματι καὶ ἀφανεστάτωι **θειότατα** ἔργα ἀποτελεῖ·), Gorgias continues thus:

The power of speech bears the same relation to the ordering of the mind (τὸν αὐτὸν δὲ λόγον ἔχει ἥ τε τοῦ λόγου δύναμις πρὸς τὴν τῆς ψυχῆς τάξιν) as the ordering of *pharmaka* bears to the constitution of bodies (ἥ τε τῶν φαρμάκων τάξις πρὸς τὴν τῶν σωμάτων φύσιν). Just as different *pharmaka* expel different humours from the body (ὥσπερ γὰρ τῶν φαρμάκων ἄλλους ἄλλα χυμοὺς ἐκ τοῦ σώματος ἐξάγει), and some stop it from being ill but others stop it from living (καὶ τὰ μὲν νόσου τὰ δὲ βίου παύει), so too some speeches cause sorrow (οὕτω καὶ τῶν λόγων οἱ μὲν ἐλύπησαν), some cause pleasure (οἱ δὲ ἔτερψαν), some cause fear (οἱ δὲ ἐφόβησαν), some give the hearers confidence (οἱ δὲ εἰς θάρσος κατέστησαν τοὺς ἀκούοντας), some drug and bewitch the mind with an evil persuasion (οἱ δὲ πειθοῖ τινι κακῆι τὴν ψυχὴν **ἐφαρμάκευσαν** καὶ **ἐξεγοήτευσαν**). (*Hel.* 14, text and trans. MacDowell 1982, 27)

As Trabattoni argued, for Plato, truth is manifested in persuasion; if it can convince the soul to pursue and acquire certain knowledge, then speech is "sufficient."[82] Thus, Plato is keen to employ the enchanting power of metaphors to "add persuasion to his speech" so to "mould the minds of his audiences, as he wishes" (*Hel.* 13: ὅτι δ' ἡ πειθὼ προσιοῦσα τῶι λόγωι καὶ τὴν ψυχὴν ἐτυπώσατο ὅπως ἐβούλετο).[83] Similarly, Merleau-Ponty defends man's use of language "to establish a living relation with himself or with his fellows," a need which transforms it from a mere instrument, making it a means to "a manifestation, a revelation of intimate being and of the psychic link which unites us to the world and our fellow men."[84] "[I]n every successful work, the significance carried into the reader's mind exceeds language and thought. . . . In so far as we believe that, through thought, we are in direct communication with a universe of truth in which we are at one with others."[85] Even if one can only allude to the experience of philosophy metaphorically, if it can exercise a protreptic function on the reader, it is sufficient. The experience of the intangible, then, is nonetheless an experience—or, to draw on Wittgenstein, it is a "phenomenological problem,"[86] subject to our need to structure and give meaning to it.

As already mentioned, all metaphor is historically and culturally conditioned,[87] thus allowing for the metaphorical description of states of consciousness. Maturana and Varela who proposed neurophenomenology as "a programmatic endeavour to integrate the basic principles of Husserl's phenomenology with the findings of cognitive neuroscience,"[88] have aptly summarized the process as follows:[89]

> It is thus, then, how the appearance of language in man and of the entire social context in which it appears, generates this unprecedented phenomenon—as far as we know—of the mind and of self-consciousness as the most intimate experience of mankind. Without the historical development of the appropriate structures, it is not possible to enter this human domain. . . . Conversely . . . the mind is not something that exists in my skull, it is not a fluid of my brain: consciousness and the mind belong to the domain of social coupling and it is there that their dynamics occur.

This cultural conditioning, however, also means that metaphors risk freighting whatever they are attempting to characterize with unwanted associations. These unwanted associations force Plato to elaborate and delimit his metaphor. Plato was sorely aware that the symptoms of Socrates' recurrent philosophical trances could be mistaken for common drunkenness or even madness, and this apprehension is reflected in the apologetic character of the *Symposium*[90] and in Plato (and Xenophon's) insistence that Socrates' imperviousness to the effects of wine is a long-term behavioral choice symptomatic of his exceptional character. The interpretation of Plato's metaphor of inebriation therefore benefits from a post-phenomenological outlook, as defined by Adams:[91] "Whereas phenomenology was originally concerned with the philosophy of consciousness and the subject, post-phenomenological approaches emphasize the anthropic confrontation with the world—and its cultural articulation—as a trans-subjective context of meaning in need of permanent elucidation and interrogation." Plato's work captures a fundamental problem of transcendent states of consciousness.[92] While human societies have been preoccupied with attaining such states since the earliest days,[93] the thorny issue of the social and cultural processes through which altered states of consciousness come to be accepted and importantly, experienced and validated at both the personal and the collective levels, remains unresolved.[94] To communicate the experience of philosophy, one must stand in opposition to the public culture, where meaning is ordinarily created[95]—a view explicitly shared by Socrates (and already a *topos* in Heraclitus and Democritus).[96] Due to this preoccupation with the misapprehensions of the many, Plato adopts an apophatic approach, insisting on what *is not* true.[97] Thus, at stake is not just the experience of transcendent truth(s) and the role of wine in transforming human consciousness[98] but also the culturally ingrained images used to relate what this experience is *like* but can never be. Plato seems to appreciate that by naming things (by coining a novel or creative metaphor) one can at most attempt to point out the associations of the symbols employed,[99] or as Ricoeur observed,[100] "[T]he 'similar' is not the 'same.' To see the similar . . . is to apprehend the 'same' within and in spite of 'difference.'" Still, the risk of being misunderstood or the need to clarify the meaning of the images we employ does not dissuade us from the use of metaphors but rather fuels our zeal to reuse them.[101]

The Cultural History of Drunkenness

In early Greek poetry nectar is the exclusive drink of the gods;[102] thus, Sappho asks Aphrodite to appear to her in an idyllic grove (where apple trees, flowers, gurgling waters, and grazing horses further allude to the goddess's erotic potency) and to pour nectar in golden goblets.[103] Other early poets such as Philoxenus and Archilochus refer to strong or exceptional wine as nectar.[104] Nectar was often conflated in the ancient sources with honey,[105] commonly used to worship the gods[106] and honor the dead,[107] while honey and its compound adjectives were often used to signify inspired poets or prophets and their divine patrons, the Muses.[108] In Plato's *Ion*, poets are thus compared to bees who fly to honey-dripping springs in certain gardens and glades of the Muses to collect their poems (534b1: ὥσπερ αἱ μέλιτται, καὶ αὐτοὶ οὕτω πετόμενοι). Yet Archilochus famously attributes his poetic ingenuity to Dionysus and wine:[109] ". . . for I know how to take the lead in the dithyramb, the lovely song of lord Dionysus, my wits thunderstruck with wine (οἴνῳ συγκεραυνωθεὶς φρένας)" (fr. 120, ap. Ath. *Deipn.* 14.628a). Thus, honey, wine, and nectar were widely accepted as means of achieving or inviting divine inspiration, whether poetic or prophetic. Consequently, Bacchic *mania* was expressed with the imagery of honey; in Euripides' *Bacchae* the *thyrsoi* of the Maenads are described as "dripping with sweet streams of honey" (*ll.* 710–711: γλυκεῖαι μέλιτος ἔσταζον ῥοαί). The notion is again reflected in Plato's *Ion*, where enthused poets are compared to the Bacchants who "draw milk and honey from rivers when possessed (by the god)" (534a5: ὥσπερ αἱ βάκχαι ἀρύονται ἐκ τῶν ποταμῶν μέλι καὶ γάλα κατεχόμεναι).[110] Honey was also linked with Aphrodite and sexual pleasure. Although Sappho's description of Erōs as "bittersweet" was an influential paradigm in Greek poetry for the ambivalence of erotic experience,[111] in the ancient Near East, honey (a term further used to refer to syrup made from dates and other sweet fruits) was associated with the fertility goddess and the sexual bliss she could bestow.[112] For example, in the *Courtship of Inanna and Dumuzi*, the lover of the goddess is addressed repeatedly as "honey-man"—that is, as sweetening her with his honey. The image remains palpable even in considerably later works such as the ps.-Theocritean *Idyll* 19, where Aphrodite, interpreted as the Greek equivalent of eastern fertility goddesses such as Inanna and Ishtar,[113] compares Erōs' painful "sting" to that of the bees, and the *Anacreontea*, where the image of Erōs the honey-stealer gains prominence.[114]

The connection of honey with wine suggests an interpretation of the *Symposium* in which Poros was coaxed to have intercourse with Penia after getting drunk on mead, the alcoholic version of honey.[115] Mead enjoyed much popularity among the Indo-Europeans; in Sanskrit poetry honey is associated with eloquence, prefiguring the early Greek use of mead as a means of communicating with the gods.[116] The Indo-European word for mead is *medhu (cf. Sanskrit *mádhu, meaning "sweet")[117] from which the Greek μέθυ is derived, a noun used in poetry as a synonym of wine, otherwise known as (ϝ)οῖνος.[118] From this perspective, Diotima's tale points to Plato's awareness of the importance of alcohol consumption as an image already employed extensively in ancient times to give expression to the socially and culturally embedded "proneness to unusual mental and/or emotional experiences."[119] After all, wine and love (Dionysus and Aphrodite) are typically joined in Greek poetry, functioning as a supreme combination of forces, capable of overwhelming even the most strong-willed individuals.[120] In the case of Socrates, inebriation is both a means of achieving an altered state of consciousness and a new symbol of it, since falling in love was another metaphor/symbol for philosophical ecstasy.[121] The two states are interrelated; thus, in the *Phaedrus* (249e3–253c7 and 255a1–257b8) erotic attraction is the first stage of realizing one's philosophical potential.

Does this mean, then, that Socrates equates getting drunk (and falling in love) with philosophical inspiration? Here, we come across a major paradox. Plato insists that despite his Dionysiac exterior (*Symp.* 215b), despite suffering and causing others to suffer symptoms of Bacchic ecstasy (*Symp.* 215d–e and 218b), and despite advocating, as the most appropriate praise of the god, the tale of Erōs' drunken conception (*Symp.*

203b–204a), most amazingly (θαυμαστότατον) *"no one among men has ever seen Socrates drunk (Σωκράτη μεθύοντα οὐδεὶς πώποτε ἑώρακεν ἀνθρώπων)"* (*Symp.* 220a5–7). The task for any interpreter of Plato, then, is to examine the way Socrates' extraordinary perception, equated with his unique and remarkable ability to remain sober,[122] can be expressed in terms of ecstatic inebriation. The claim that no one had ever seen Socrates drunk is clearly intended to create a sharp contrast with the abundant references to drunkenness (μέθη) in the *Symposium*.[123] The *Phaedrus*, similarly, contains two explicit references to drunkenness, both clearly negative: as a distraction that causes the lovers to deviate from the path to philosophy[124] and as a symptom of the soul yielding to excess (*hubris*), the opposite of *sōphrosynē*.[125] This tension in Socratic inebriation between ecstasy and sobriety introduces an unmistakable level of complexity to the metaphor—precisely stressing its novelty and resisting its integration into the normative understanding of drinking or previous metaphors about wine and ecstasy.

As a social activity, inducing states of altered consciousness allows communities to introduce their members to self-awareness. In the *Phaedrus* (244a–245a), Plato famously identifies four modes of altered consciousness as the most beneficial types of *mania*:[126] next to the prophetic (associated with Apollo), telestic (associated with Dionysus), and poetic *mania* (inspired by the Muses), Plato added erotic frenzy (inspired by Aphrodite and Erōs), which can inspire exceptional lovers to devote themselves to the pursuit of wisdom—to become "lovers of wisdom," that is, philosophers.[127] Plato also defends a strange, fifth kind of altered consciousness—Socratic inebriation—as the most beneficial form of *mania* of all. This, however, is a metaphorical reinterpretation of the whole notion of altered consciousness, the competing revisions of which acquire different dimensions and expressions over the centuries. Every time the metaphor of Socratic inebriation is redeployed in a new milieu, it needs to be renegotiated vis-à-vis its past connotations and the way it is envisaged to serve the present-day cultural aspirations. Thus, the political context of the Hellenistic period in which the proximity of kings to God is promoted,[128] giving rise to the concept of kings as embodiments of the divine law that rules the universe,[129] must necessarily inform our study of Philo's reception of Socrates' drunken delirium, especially given the importance of Dionysus' cult in the royal ideology of Alexander and the Ptolemies.[130] Equally consideration must be given to Philo's authorial intention to engage with Plato in order to defend the intellectual pedigree of the Alexandrian Jewish community.[131]

Plato's Metaphor of *Baccheia* and Its Ritual Aspects

The history of the metaphor of Socratic inebriation is not simply the history of its progressive distortion as it was renegotiated in new cultural contexts and subsequent periods. Plato, too, needed to negotiate its place within his own culture; new metaphors are always reliant on a preexisting cultural background and must struggle to distinguish themselves against it. In striving to coin a new metaphor to describe Socrates' philosophical perceptiveness, Plato draws on Bacchic ecstasy as portrayed in Euripides' *Bacchae* and influential rites such as the Eleusinian and the Orphic mysteries.[132] Aware of the obvious drawbacks of attempting to delineate reality by relying on phenomenal appearances only,[133] Plato emulates Socrates' teasing style and, by inverting the metaphor, he encourages his audiences to consider Socrates' inebriating effect *and* total sobriety. By repeatedly inviting his audience to observe the falsity of Socrates' comparison to a drunken person, Plato seeks to problematize his metaphor, urging them to further unpack the basic/conventional structural metaphor he employs and become aware of the deeper conceptual domains his metaphor draws on. Given the deeply entrenched comparison of intellectual and physical sustenance,[134] Socratic inebriation is, then, revealed as a higher application of reason—the best reasoning is like the best wine.

Plato portrays Socrates as ever preoccupied with intangible notions, meditating for hours in full public view, lost in his thoughts and oblivious of his surroundings,[135] often talking to himself,[136] and candidly musing on his frequent divine visitations (his *daimonion*).[137] Socrates thus epitomizes intellectual eccentricity, the soft target of fifth century BCE Athenian anti-intellectualism.[138] Together with this, Socrates' reputation for quaffing considerable amounts of wine[139] could easily render him misunderstood, even ridiculed, for being drunk. In the *Symposium*, Alcibiades compares Socrates with the Silenoi[140] and Marsyas,[141] figures typically associated with the wine god,[142] who drove his followers "out of their mind" (cf. Eur. *Bacch.* 850: ἔκστησον φρενῶν)[143] stinging them with bouts of *mania*.[144] Framed by repeated references to drinking in the dialogue—that of the other guests, of Poros in Diotima's tale, and most notably, Alcibiades' own state of intoxication[145]—the comparison seems to rely on a false impression of Socrates as an unrepentant dipsomaniac. A close reading, however, dispels any notion that Socrates may be under the influence at all; rather, he is *as though* drunk.

Alcibiades' description of Socrates is rife with comparisons designed to construct a simile, a figure of speech that, as discussed, Aristotle identified as a species of the genus metaphor, insisting that "simile is also a metaphor, for it differs little" from it (Arist. *Rhet.* 1406b19–20: ἔστιν δὲ καὶ ἡ εἰκὼν μεταφορά: διαφέρει γὰρ μικρόν; cf. *Rhet.* 1413a14–15: αἱ δ᾿ εἰκόνες ὅτι μεταφοραί, εἴρηται πολλάκις).[146] He also believed that most successful are metaphors by analogy that function as extended similes.[147] Operating in the same cultural context, Plato indicates the basic level on which Socrates' identification with the followers of Dionysus applies, namely the contrast between Socrates' ridiculous, Satyr-like outer appearance and his inner wisdom. Thus, Alcibiades claims that Socrates is strikingly similar to Marsyas, who was reputed for his *sōphrosynē*,[148] and the Satyrs (*Symp.* 215b5–6: **ἐοικέναι** αὐτὸν τῷ σατύρῳ τῷ Μαρσύᾳ . . . τό γε εἶδος **ὅμοιος** εἶ τούτοις), and "is most similar to the Silenoi [statues]" (215b1: **ὁμοιότατον** αὐτὸν εἶναι τοῖς σιληνοῖς). Alcibiades revisits this simile at 215b8,[149] 216c8–10,[150] and 216d5–7 of the *Symposium*,[151] eventually revealing the extent of his comparison:[152] ". . . unless you *compare* him (**ἀπεικάζοι**), like I did, not with any human, but with the Silenoi and the Satyrs, both him and his speeches . . . his speeches are *most similar* (**ὁμοιότατοί εἰσι**) to the Silenoi statues when they are opened" (*Symp.* 221d6–e1). Alcibiades' figurative style is evident, as he forms his simile by employing the adjective ὅμοιος ("like, resembling") and the verb ἀπεικάζω ("make a representation; reproduce, convey; illustrate by means of a comparison").[153] His approach is suggestive of cognitive theories of metaphor that argue that similes and metaphors are integral means of devising and negotiating cognitive patterns, determined additionally by our physical experiences and the cultural context in which they occur.[154] Language can hardly capture every detail of inner experience;[155] nonetheless, Plato specifies that despite his exterior, Socrates is full of moderation internally—like the curious Silenoi statues that contained images of gods hidden in their interiors[156] and that Alcibiades describes as "divine and gold . . . and all-beautiful and marvellous" (216e7–217a2: θεῖα καὶ χρυσᾶ . . . καὶ πάγκαλα καὶ θαυμαστά).[157] Notably, he concludes his eulogy with a revision of the motif, now applied to Socrates' speeches: "[His speeches are] most divine (**θειοτάτους**)[158] and have in them countless "statues" [i.e., images/representations] of virtue (πλεῖστα ἀγάλματ᾿ ἀρετῆς),[159] covering mostly, or rather completely, every subject fitting for study by anyone who is going to become a fine, decent man (τῷ μέλλοντι καλῷ κἀγαθῷ ἔσεσθαι)" (*Symp.* 222a3–7).

Let us now see how this simile, drawing on ritual patterns linked to Bacchic *mania,* is integrated into the broader metaphorical framework of Socratic inebriation. In the Platonic corpus, there are two occasions on which Socrates is linked directly with the Dionysiac mysteries and the Corybantic rites. Importantly, neither of these instances involves wine consumption explicitly. Furthermore, our sources do not allow us to determine the role of wine drinking in Dionysiac madness in a straightforward manner;[160] for example, the nature of the "rite of the *crater,*" linked with both Dionysiac and Corybantic festivities, remains unclear, though it probably involved the ritual consumption of wine with symbolic character.[161]

The first instance of Socratic delirium occurs in the *Symposium* (215d6–e4) and focuses on the effects of Socrates' speeches. His audiences, including Alcibiades, experience frenzy like those celebrating the Corybantic rites. Plato's language is distinctly figurative as he relates the symptoms of this Socratic *cum* Corybantic type of delirium: Alcibiades experiences an array of symptoms, including heart palpitations and tears, that are said to be more intense than those experienced by the celebrants of the Corybantic rites (*Symp.* 215e1–2: πολύ μοι μᾶλλον ἢ τῶν κορυβαντιώντων ἥ τε καρδία πηδᾷ καὶ δάκρυα ἐκχεῖται . . .).[162] Socrates revisits this imagery in the *Ion,* where he compares poets to the divinely inspired[163] performers of Corybantic rites:[164] "*Like* those who celebrate the Corybantic rites (ὥσπερ οἱ κορυβαντιῶντες) dance without being sane (οὐκ ἔμφρονες ὄντες), *so* (οὕτω) the lyric poets compose their fine songs without being sane (οὐκ ἔμφρονες ὄντες), but when they step into harmony and rhythm they behave like Bacchants and are possessed (βακχεύουσι καὶ κατεχόμενοι)" (*Ion* 533e7–535a1). The choice of the ὥσπερ . . . οὕτω construction leaves no doubt about Plato's simile here. The poets are cast as possessed (κατεχόμενοι), just like Socrates' audiences in the *Symposium* (215d6: κατεχόμεθα). They are compared to both Corybants (κορυβαντιῶντες) and Bacchants (βακχεύουσι), in a conflation of the two rites.[165] Rather than being a symptom of the generic affinity of the rites discussed,[166] in my view Plato's accumulation of overarching similarities aims to make his broader metaphor compelling. The amassing of examples is typical of inductive reasoning,[167] and the systematic investment of the philosopher's experience in the *Symposium* with motifs associated with mystic initiation rites confirms this.[168] Thus, in accordance with the rhetoric of ancient mystery cults, which promised their devotees knowledge of holy things (often through psychosomatic experiences),[169] Diotima poses as a mystagogue,[170] while the philosopher is an initiate to "the rites of love."[171]

For a fuller appreciation of Socratic ecstasy, we must turn to the *Phaedrus* and Socrates' description of philosophical revelry. Plato's metaphorical approach to philosophical *mania* is signaled at the start of a lengthy description of the condition:[172]

> But these, when they see any *likeness* of the things over there (τῶν ἐκεῖ **ὁμοίωμα**), are stricken with amazement and can no longer control themselves (ἐκπλήττονται καὶ οὐκέτ᾽ ἐν αὐτῶν γίγνονται); but they do not understand their condition because they do not clearly perceive (τὸ πάθος ἀγνοοῦσι διὰ τὸ μὴ ἱκανῶς διαισθάνεσθαι). Now in the *copies* that exist here (ἐν τοῖς τῇδε **ὁμοιώμασιν**), of justice and *sōphrosynē* and the other ideas which are precious to souls, there is no light, but only a few, approaching the *images* (ἐπὶ τὰς **εἰκόνας** ἰόντε) through the blurred organs of sense, behold in them with difficulty the nature of that which is *represented* (θεῶνται τὸ τοῦ **εἰκασθέντος** γένος). (*Phdr.* 250a7–b5)

The wording here closely echoes Alcibiades' description of Socratic enthusiasm in the *Symposium*, while adding that, although a philosophical state of consciousness is demanding for the soul, its natural disinclination can be overcome by various means.[173] Hence, a few paragraphs later, while asserting his allegiance to Erōs, Socrates admits that: "Having *represented* (**ἀπεικάζοντες**) the passion of love in that way, *partly touching upon an aspect of truth* (ἴσως μὲν ἀληθοῦς τινος ἐφαπτόμενοι), yet partly being carried away to a different direction, having composed a rather plausible argument (οὐ παντάπασιν ἀπίθανον λόγον), we sang a playful hymn in the form of a story (**μυθικόν τινα ὕμνον προσεπαίσαμεν**), Phaedrus, both fittingly and fairly (μετρίως τε καὶ εὐφήμως) in honour of your master and mine, Love, the guardian of handsome boys" (*Phdr.* 265b7–c4). Socrates' reference to the praise of Love in the *Phaedrus* is evocative of the *Symposium*, where each guest is asked to deliver a eulogy to the god (177d2–4)—a pastime suggested by Phaedrus, who was a regular member of Socrates' inner circle.

Philosophical *mania* in the *Phaedrus* is expressed with motifs drawn from the sphere of ritual and language evocative of mystic initiation and Bacchic frenzy. Thus, in the *Phaedrus* Socrates repeatedly refers to himself and those philosophizing as initiates,[174] linking mystic *mania* squarely with Dionysiac *teletai* (265b4: Διονύσου . . . τελεστικήν . . . μανίαν). Lovers of beauty, we are told, partake at the peak of their initiation in the most perfect mystery, which they celebrate to fulfilment (250c1–2: **ὠργιάζομεν ὁλόκληροι μὲν αὐτοὶ ὄντες**). Furthermore, Socrates describes a "witnessing" of otherworldly truths in *Phaedrus* 250c3–5, where he specifies that the lovers of beauty "are initiated and behold in pure light perfect and simple and calm and blissful apparitions" (ὁλόκληρα δὲ καὶ ἁπλᾶ καὶ ἀτρεμῆ καὶ εὐδαίμονα φάσματα μυούμενοί τε καὶ ἐποπτεύοντες ἐν αὐγῇ καθαρᾷ). The wording evokes the rite of the *epopteia*, enacted as part of Dionysiac cults and the Eleusinian mysteries.[175] The Bacchic character of philosophical *mania* is palpable in the dialogue, and at *Phaedrus* 253a8–9, Socrates compares the lover who draws inspiration from Zeus to the Bacchants (text cited in n76). Furthermore, Socrates evokes Euripides' typical description of the rites in honor of Dionysus as *orgia* in the *Bacchae* by using the verb ὠργιάζομεν at *Phaedrus* 250c1–2 to describe the initiation of lovers of beauty.[176] Early in the *Phaedrus*, Socrates also associates *mania* with purification rites and prophecy,[177] a notion repeated in Euripides' play, where, high in the mountains, Dionysus' worshippers perform purifying rites. Hence, in *ll.* 73–82 of the *Bacchae* the chorus praises the blessed (μάκαρ) and fortunate (εὐδαίμων) followers of the god, who are skilled in divine rituals (τελετὰς θεῶν εἰδὼς) and lead a pious life (βιοτὰν ἁγιστεύει), "revelling in Bacchic frenzy at the holy purifications on the mountains" (ἐν ὄρεσσι βακχεύων ὁσίοις καθαρμοῖσιν); while in *ll.* 298–309 Teiresias praises the prophetic powers inspired by the god:[178]

> This god is also a prophet (μάντις δ' ὁ δαίμων) since celebrating in Bacchic frenzy and being manic involves a lot of prophetic power (τὸ γὰρ βακχεύσιμον καὶ τὸ μανιῶδες μαντικὴν πολλὴν ἔχει). When the god overtakes the human body completely, he makes those driven mad able to predict the future (λέγειν τὸ μέλλον τοὺς μεμηνότας ποιεῖ). . . . Such madness comes from Dionysus (μανία δὲ καὶ τοῦτ' ἐστὶ Διονύσου πάρα). One may even see him on the rocks at Delphi leaping on the plain between two mountain peaks holding fir-trees, waving and shaking his Bacchic wand (πηδῶντα . . . πάλλοντα καὶ σείοντα βακχεῖον κλάδον), a great god across Greece.

Like the Socratic lover who is reminded of Beauty by his beloved's earthly appearance, thus undergoing a profound change (*Phdr.* 251a9–10: ἰδόντα δ' αὐτὸν οἷον ἐκ τῆς φρίκης μεταβολή), the Bacchants experience a change of consciousness (*Bacch.* 1266: μεταβολή).[179] This change is manifested in their enhanced senses, which include sharper sight; hence, at *Bacchae* 1267, Agave is described as seeing a brighter, more translucent sky (λαμπρότερος ἤ πρὶν καὶ διειπετέστερος). Socrates elaborates on this theme in the *Phaedrus*, where he notes that sight stimulates our memory more than any other sense.[180] Socrates stresses the impasse felt by the lover,[181] using vocabulary that corresponds to Dionysus' ability to resolve such deadlocks in the *Bacchae*.[182] The verbs οἰστρέω and μαίνομαι and their respective nouns οἶστρος and μανία[183] are used to describe the Bacchants, just like the soul of the lover in the *Phaedrus*, which, raging with pain, smarts throughout (*Phdr.* 251d7–8: πᾶσα κεντουμένη κύκλῳ ἡ ψυχὴ οἰστρᾷ καὶ ὀδυνᾶται).[184] Notably, attaining an altered state of consciousness is here described as "the growing of the soul's feathers" (251c4: τοῦ πτεροφυεῖν ἀρχομένου ψυχή),[185] an image that alludes to Erōs and Dionysus' representations as winged.[186] In my view, this reference to flight also evokes Euripides' trope that possession by Dionysus or his liquid essence, wine,[187] liberates the souls and minds of the drinkers, who thereby achieve a form of sublimity.[188] Despite its symposiastic setting, however, Socratic *baccheia* does not rely on wine; equally, Socratic *mania*, whether inspired by Aphrodite or Dionysus, is a semantic vault that must be filled with new meaning as its limits as a metaphor are determined.

With this in mind, we turn to the second instance of Socrates posing as a celebrant of Bacchic rites. In the *Phaedo*, Socrates admits that he has tried everything to achieve wisdom,[189] again by means of a Bacchic metaphor: echoing the imagery of the *Symposium* and the *Phaedrus*,[190] Socrates refers at 69c3–d2 to those who "practice philosophy correctly" (οἱ πεφιλοσοφηκότες ὀρθῶς) as Bacchoi. Once more, these Bacchoi value sobriety and thus, a few sections later, Socrates assures us that the bodily senses "deceive, disturb, and confuse" the soul *"though it were drunk"* (*Phd.* 79c7: καὶ αὐτὴ πλανᾶται καὶ ταράττεται καὶ εἰλιγγιᾷ **ὥσπερ μεθύουσα**).[191] Immediately afterward, he advocates the importance of solitary reflection in which "the soul inquires alone by itself" departing "into the realm of the pure, the everlasting, the immortal and the changeless" (*Phd.* 79d1–2: ὅταν δέ γε αὐτὴ καθ᾽ αὑτὴν σκοπῇ, ἐκεῖσε οἴχεται εἰς τὸ καθαρόν τε καὶ ἀεὶ ὂν καὶ ἀθάνατον καὶ ὡσαύτως ἔχον).[192] Unlike Alcibiades, Socrates thus appreciates that Bacchic experience does not have to be frenetic,[193] just as Dionysus notably remains calm in his confrontation with hubristic Pentheus in the *Bacchae*, repeatedly advising the king to do likewise.[194]

The performative aspects of ritual frenzy alone are not enough to achieve an appropriately altered state of consciousness. The distinctions that thus arise about the proper use of rites and wine also allow Socrates to differentiate between true philosophers and their impostors.[195] This is especially fitting because Socrates is about to die, and thus his situation reflects that of initiates, who were often promised knowledge about the afterlife.[196] Socrates admits that he had recurrent premonitions about philosophy in dreams (60e–61b)—perhaps referring to out-of-body experiences—and proceeds to explain his epistemology in figurative terms: having rejected Anaxagoras' theory that the mind is the cause of all things (97c1–6) as "absurd"[197] because it does not ascribe ethical agency to the phenomena it identifies (98e), Socrates came to revise his methodology as follows:

> After these, he said, since I had given up on studying the things that exist, I thought I should be careful not to suffer what happens to those who look at the sun and study it (θεωροῦντες καὶ σκοπούμενοι) during an eclipse. For some of them ruin their eyes unless they look at its image in water or something similar. I thought about this and was afraid that my soul would be blinded totally if I looked at things with my eyes and tried to grasp them with each of my senses (ἑκάστῃ τῶν αἰσθήσεων ἐπιχειρῶν ἅπτεσθαι αὐτῶν). So, I thought I must resort to concepts and examine the truth of things through them (εἰς τοὺς λόγους καταφυγόντα ἐν ἐκείνοις σκοπεῖν τῶν ὄντων τὴν ἀλήθειαν). Now perhaps *my comparison*[198] is not suitable in some way (ἴσως μὲν οὖν ᾧ εἰκάζω τρόπον τινὰ οὐκ ἔοικεν); for I do not accept in the least that he who studies things by concepts, studies them in images any more than he who studies them in actions (τὸν ἐν τοῖς λόγοις σκοπούμενον τὰ ὄντα ἐν εἰκόσι μᾶλλον σκοπεῖν ἢ τὸν ἐν τοῖς ἔργοις). (*Phd.* 99d5–100a3)

Here, Socrates is not only indulging in metaphorical imagery but also clearly working through the parameters of his metaphor, debating its effectiveness. Although Plato is critical of poetry overall,[199] and has Socrates in the *Phaedrus* (269a8–10) refer to εἰκονολογίαι (figurative speech) as a trick (τέχνημα) associated with the deceptive art of rhetoric,[200] his objection relates mainly to the readiness of the audiences to grasp its meaning—a worry that likely became a conviction after Socrates' death sentence.[201]

The point is illustrated in the *Republic* (360e–362c) where Glaucon claims the people crave for the apparatus of justice but not for justice itself.

Taking as his example two polar opposites, Glaucon juxtaposes the most unjust man, who nevertheless has the means of acquiring the reputation of being just, with the perfectly just man who remains dedicated to the path of justice until his death (361c8: ἴτω ἀμετάστατος μέχρι θανάτου) despite suffering ill-repute and having to undergo a thorough test of his very sense of justice (361c6–7: βεβασανισμένος εἰς δικαιοσύνην . . . ὑπὸ κακοδοξίας). One might imagine that Socrates' trial looms in the background here,[202] especially since the unjust man is said to be engaging in lawsuits to deal with his enemies (362b5) while the just man is predicted to suffer all sorts of punishments for his devotion to justice, including imprisonment and corporal punishments (362a1–2), which lead him to realize that his goal ought to be the impression and not the essence of justice (362a3–4: γνώσεται ὅτι οὐκ εἶναι δίκαιον ἀλλὰ δοκεῖν δεῖ ἐθέλειν). When Adeimantus joins the discussion in support of Glaucon's argument he points out that indeed fathers advise their sons to gain reputation for justice so they can be counted among those whom the poets praise as favored by the gods both during their lifetime and after death. Following Musaeus and the Orphric tradition, Adeimantus points out, people imagine that just men are rewarded with an everlasting, splendid feast in Hades where they spend their time drinking, reclined on couches, and crowned with wreaths (363c4–8: εἰς Ἅιδου γὰρ ἀγαγόντες τῷ λόγῳ καὶ κατακλίναντες καὶ συμπόσιον τῶν ὁσίων κατασκευάσαντες ἐστεφανωμένους ποιοῦσιν τὸν ἅπαντα χρόνον ἤδη διάγειν μεθύοντας).[203] Here, Plato clearly rebukes the popular perception of mystery religions that Aristophanes also parodies in the *Frogs* where Dionysus' retinue of "holy mystics" (*l.* 326: ὁσίους . . . θιασώτας) invite him to join their merry dancing, shaking the myrtle garland around his head (*ll.* 328–330: τινάσσων περὶ κρατὶ σῷ βρύοντα στέφανον μύρτων). People's misgivings, however, that "the fairest reward of virtue is eternal drunkenness" (*Resp.* 363d1: ἡγησάμενοι κάλλιστον ἀρετῆς μισθὸν μέθην αἰώνιον), do not deter Plato from using the metaphor of inebriation but rather lead him to employ it self-consciously and to revise it carefully to avoid misleading or extraneous associations.

Concluding Remarks

Plato's description of philosophical trance in terms of *mania*, the divine source of our greatest blessings,[204] forms part of a new structural metaphor.[205] The truly inebriated or inspired thinker is not he who drinks wine, but he who has trained his soul by various means, including wine, to handle mental breakthroughs inspired by, in Foucauldian terms, unreason,[206] or, in Kierkegaardian terms, meta-reason, that is reason reflective of experience.[207] As a higher form of knowledge, meta-reason can be expressed through familiar images and experiences, such as falling in love, getting drunk, or suffering madness,[208] provided that the parameters of each comparison are clearly set out and observed. Therefore, after explaining why I chose conceptual metaphor theory and cognitive phenomenology as a theoretical angle for discussing Socratic inebriation, I read closely through the vocabulary of *mania* in the *Symposium* and the *Phaedrus*.[209] Plato appreciated the difficulty of communicating the experience of philosophical trance and found in Dionysiac revelry a relatable and long-established paradigm, the nature of which Euripides had already negotiated in the *Bacchae* in a remarkable and influential manner. Importantly, Euripides had already pointed out the need to differentiate the essence of Bacchic rites from their deceptive appearances. Accordingly, although in the *Symposium* Alcibiades compares Socrates to Dionysiac figures renowned for their excessive drinking and the effect of Socrates' speeches to frenzied Corybantic rites, insofar as they produce uncontrollable shaking and crying, Socrates himself gave a considerably different account of the Bacchoi, focusing on silent reflection. By repeatedly contrasting the metaphors of Alcibiades with their emphasis on drunkenness to the obvious sobriety of Socrates, Plato defends Socrates' intellectual authority and crucially offers us a blueprint for using and interpreting his metaphors. In the next chapter, I will further map out the medical, philosophical, and literary background of Plato's new structural metaphor.

Chapter 2

An "Other" Experience

The Milieu and New Parameters of Socratic *Baccheia*

> . . . a madness greatly different in its appearances from that which
> arose from grief and love.
>
> —J. Monro, *Remarks on Dr Battie's Treatment of*
> *Madness*, 1758, John Clarke, 33

As mentioned in chapter 1, the many examples of physical drunkenness found in the convivial setting of the *Symposium* aim to alert the reader to the existence of different types of inebriation, similar in appearance yet profoundly different. The state valorized by Plato in connection with those engaging with philosophy, although outwardly akin to ritual, erotic, poetic, or even to pathological irrationality, is nonetheless, to those partaking in the experience, clearly distinct from all of them. As Alcibiades notes, despite looking every bit like a follower of Bacchus, like Marsyas or the Silenoi, and despite inciting his audiences to Corybantic frenzy, Socrates is distinguished by extraordinary *sōphrosynē*, a virtue meaning "sound-mindedness" and/or "moderation" (*Symp.* 216d8–9).[1] Notably, Socratic *sōphrosynē* is the result of an innovative, virtue-bestowing application of reasoning that, enhanced by his *elenchus* (the Socratic cross-examination), embraces irrational feelings such as shame and honor that the rationalist sophists rejected. As Woodruff notes: "Plato's Socrates . . . redraws the conceptual map around rationality more strictly, shifting much of human thinking into the camp of the irrational."[2] Across the Platonic dialogues

37

Socrates insists on following the dictations of reason or rather the "best reason" or the "right reason," as for example, in *Crito* 46b4–6 where we read:[3] "For I am, not only now but always, a man who is persuaded by nothing else but the reason (μηδενὶ ἄλλῳ πείθεσθαι ἢ τῷ λόγῳ) which upon examination (μοι λογιζομένῳ) seems to me best." The concern with establishing Socrates' sanity and sobriety is remarkably evocative of the problem that Foucault faced when examining madness: the definition of unreason, as Foucault famously noted, is not just a matter of medical diagnosis but crucially an issue of perception.[4] Plato is thus forced to carefully navigate contemporary views (medical, philosophical, literary) on human cognition in order to foreclose attempts to collapse the distinction between forms of drunkenness that would allow Socrates' rivals to insinuate that he is intoxicated or mad. His effort, however, is complicated by the prevalence of the same language across the discourses of intoxication and madness. To support the credibility of his view, Plato engages thoroughly with contemporary medical views on human intelligence, including those of Alcmaeon of Croton[5] and opinions found in Hippocratic texts, especially the *Regimen*. This kind of intermixing of early Greek medicine and natural philosophy had a strong precedent in Heraclitus, whose definition of virtue in terms of the fiery material principle of the cosmos offered an influential paradigm for the metaphorical expression of philosophical insight. As well as distinguishing the symptomatology of inebriation in medical terms, Plato also grafted the metaphor of Socratic inebriation to an established idea of divine madness associated with cultic rituals in honor of Dionysus. Thus, in the last section of this chapter, I explore the intertextual affinities between the *Symposium* and Euripides' *Bacchae*, probably the most influential literary depiction of *baccheia* and its mental effects.

Defending Socrates' Sanity

In the *Symposium*, Alcibiades describes the inebriation of Socrates' audiences with the verb ἐκπλήττω, carefully repeated in his account of Socrates' typical mental state (*Symp.* 215d6: ἐκπεπληγμένοι ἐσμὲν and 216d4: ἐκπέπληκται) and at *Symp.* 211d5 where Diotima compares the experience of the good with that of enjoying the beauty of beautiful boys (οὓς νῦν ὁρῶν ἐκπέπληξαι; "who now leave you transfixed when you look at them"). The verb is also employed in the *Phaedrus* to relate the emotional and mental turmoil of enthused lovers, who find themselves "astounded" (250a7: ἐκπλήττονται). Plato's choice of word is of a piece with metaphors commonly used to encapsulate the wonder experienced by those who engage in philosophy.[6] In his cultural context, however, this appropriation of the metaphor risked introducing an ambiguity to his depiction of Socratic inebriation, since the verb πλήττω had been used since Homer to denote bouts of irrationality afflicting soldiers who had experienced intense fear at the battlefield.[7] Plato, well aware of this use of the verb, describes the Greeks, including the Athenians, in the *Laws* as fear struck (698d8: τούς τε ἄλλους Ἕλληνας καὶ δὴ καὶ Ἀθηναίους ἐξέπληττεν) upon hearing the terrible fate of the Eretrians at the hands of Datis, the leader of the Persian fleet.[8] Plato's portrayal of Socrates could thus be misunderstood as implying that philosophy had "struck mad" or otherwise rendered Socrates irrational.[9] To distinguish Socrates' condition from other forms of irrationality, Plato was required to engage with contemporary medical discourse around madness and drunkenness and their often overlapping symptoms.

Intellectuals were a safe source of laughter in contemporary comedy,[10] and Aristophanes, the only playwright named in the *Apology*, had etched Socrates on the minds of the Athenians as an exemplar of aloof eccentricity:[11] "For you witnessed these things yourselves in Aristophanes' comedy: a Socrates being carried around there, proclaiming that he is treading on air and uttering a great deal of other nonsense (ἄλλην πολλὴν φλυαρίαν φλυαροῦντα) about things of which I know nothing" (*Apol.* 19c4–7). Madness is mentioned around fifteen times in the *Clouds*.[12] Strepsiades, puzzled by Socrates' constant questioning of even basic concepts, admits that he "was mad to side with Socrates" (*l.* 1476: οἴμοι παρανοίας· ὡς ἐμαινόμην ἄρα) before blaming his momentary lapse on Socrates' garrulity (*l.* 1480: ἐμοῦ παρανοήσαντος ἀδολεσχία). In the *Frogs*, again, Socrates is explicitly characterized as a mad (παράφρων) blabber: "So what's stylish is not to sit beside Socrates and chatter (χαρίεν οὖν μὴ Σωκράτει/ παρακαθήμενον λαλεῖν), casting the arts aside and ignoring the best of the tragedian's craft (ἀποβαλόντα μουσικήν/ τά τε μέγιστα παραλιπόντα/ τῆς τραγῳδικῆς τέχνης). To hang around killing time in pretentious conversation and hairsplitting twaddle (τὸ δ' ἐπὶ σεμνοῖσιν λόγοισι/ καὶ σκαριφησμοῖσι λήρων,/ διατριβὴν ἀργὸν ποιεῖσθαι), is the mark of a man who's lost his mind (παραφρονοῦντος ἀνδρός)" (*Ran.* 1491–1499). Although comical exaggeration can hardly be equated with medical diagnosis, Aristophanes does draw here on ancient medical terminology.[13]

Talkativeness, a crucial quality for crafting Socratic arguments, was commonly recognized as a symptom of irrationality. Several medical treatises agree that the speech of the mad tends to be confused and garrulous,[14] not unlike the speech of the drunk. Hence, in the Hippocratic treatise *On the Sacred Disease*, written around 400 BCE, madness is described as an illness of the brain[15] caused "by abnormal heat, cold, moistness or dryness" (*morb. sacr.* 17: ἀλλ' ἢ θερμότερος τῆς φύσιος γένηται ἢ ψυχρότερος ἢ ὑγρότερος ἢ ξηρότερος). When madness, conveyed with the verbs *mainomai* and *paraphroneō* (μαινόμεθα καὶ παραφρονέομεν), is caused by moistness in the brain (μαινόμεθα . . . ὑπὸ ὑγρότητος), it affects the patients' vision and hearing (μήτε τὴν ὄψιν ἀτρεμίζειν μήτε τὴν ἀκοήν). Thus, patients end up "seeing and hearing one thing at one moment, and another at another moment" (ἀλλ' ἄλλοτε ἄλλα ὁρᾶν καὶ ἀκούειν), and this discrepancy is reflected in their speech patterns, since "the tongue reports what one sees and hears at these different times" (τήν τε γλῶσσαν τοιαῦτα διαλέγεσθαι οἷα ἂν βλέπῃ τε καὶ ἀκούῃ ἑκάστοτε). The perceptual interruption of the afflicted is so persistent that "they are visited by fears and terrors (καὶ δείματα καὶ φόβοι)—some by night and others by day (τὰ μὲν νύκτωρ, τὰ δὲ καὶ μεθ' ἡμέρην)—have nightmares (ἐνύπνια),[16] make inopportune mistakes (πλάνοι ἄκαιροι), become the prey of imaginary worries (φροντίδες οὐχ ἱκνεύμεναι), are unable to grasp reality (ἀγνωσίαι τῶν καθεστεώτων), and act contrary to habit (ἀηθίαι) (*morb. sacr.* 17 = 6.388.14 L.)." When, again, madness is caused by heating of the bile (*morb. sacr.*18 = 6.390.15 L.: ὁ ἐγκέφαλος διαθερμαίνηται· τοῦτο δὲ πάσχουσιν οἱ χολώδεες . . .), patients become "noisy, evil-doers, and restless, always carrying out something inopportune" (οἱ δὲ ὑπὸ χολῆς κεκράκταί τε καὶ κακοῦργοι καὶ οὐκ ἀτρεμαῖοι, ἀλλ' αἰεί τι ἄκαιρον δρῶντες), while they also have terrifying nightmares (ἐνύπνιον ὁρῶν φοβερόν). Patients suffering brain disorders from an overflow of bile are also discussed in *Diseases* 3 (*Morb.* 3.48 = 7.284 L.: ὅταν χολὴ ἐπὶ τὸ ἧπαρ ἐπιρρυῇ καὶ ἐς τὴν κεφαλὴν καταστῇ). Once more, those affected tend to have frightful dreams which disrupt their sleep (καὶ ὅταν καθεύδῃ, ἀναΐσσει ἐκ τοῦ ὕπνου ὅταν ἐνύπνια ἴδῃ φοβερά). After coming to their senses, patients can recount their dreams by reliving them, that is, they are hallucinating, as evident in the way they move their bodies and speak with their tongues (ἀφηγεῖται τὰ ἐνύπνια τοιαῦτα ὁρᾶν ὁποῖα καὶ τῷ σώματι ἐποίει καὶ τῇ γλώσσῃ ἔλεγε).[17]

Similarly, the victims of *phrenitis* or *frontis* ("anxiety"),[18] described in *Diseases* 2—one of the earliest Hippocratic treatises—are said to be afflicted with fear (*Morb.* 2.72 = 7.108 L.: φοβεῖται; cf. *Morb.* 3.48: φόβος αὐτὸν λάβῃ),[19] and therefore they "see terrible visions, frightful dreams, and sometimes the dead" (δείματα ὁρᾷ καὶ ὀνείρατα φοβερὰ καὶ τοὺς τεθνηκότας ἐνίοτε). In *On the Glands*, again, we hear that the brain suffers damage, when unable to purge its fluxes (12 = 8.566 L.: ὁ δὲ ἐγκέφαλος πῆμα ἴσχει καὶ αὐτὸς οὐχ ὑγιαίνων); in such cases, if irritated (εἰ μὲν δάκνοιτο), the brain suffers great disturbance (τάραχον πολὺν ἴσχει) and the mind becomes deranged (ὁ νοῦς ἀφρονεῖ). Further, "the brain pulls and convulses the whole person" (ὁ ἐγκέφαλος σπᾶται καὶ ἕλκει τὸν ὅλον ἄνθρωπον).[20] The cognitive impairment of these patients is also reflected in their distorted vision and incongruous laughter: "his intelligence is disturbed (ἡ γνώμη ταράσσεται), and he goes about thinking and seeing bizarre things (περίεισιν ἀλλοῖα φρονῶν καὶ ἀλλοῖα ὁρέων), bearing the characteristics of the disease with mocking grins and strange visions" (φέρων τὸ ἦθος τῆς νούσου σεσηρόσι μειδιήμασι καὶ ἀλλοκότοισι φαντάσμασιν). (*On Glands* 12 = 8.568 L.)[21] In the Hippocratic medical tradition irregularities of the black bile were associated with melancholy, as the name of the disorder suggests (*melaina chole*), which shared many of its symptoms with *phrenitis*. Thus, in *Diseases* 1.30, "patients suffering with *phrenitis*" are said to "resemble most the melancholics with regard to their derangement" (= 6.200,20–21 L.: προσεοίκασι δὲ μάλιστα οἱ ὑπὸ τῆς φρενίτιδος ἐχόμενοι τοῖσι μελαγχολώδεσι κατὰ τὴν παράνοιαν).[22] Black bile was also believed to be especially susceptible to the effects of wine[23] *and* hydromel (μελίκρητον = mead).[24] Hence, in the *Epidemics*, we hear about Timocrates from Elis, who "drank too much and went insane from black bile" (5.2 = 5.205 L.: . . . ἔπιε πλέον· μαινόμενος δὲ ὑπὸ χολῆς μελαίνης),[25] while according to a spurious part of the *Regimen*,[26] "if the patient is subject to dark bile (μελαγχολικὸς), or his hands tremble from drink (ἐκ πόσιος χεῖρες τρομεραὶ), it is good to predict derangement or convulsions (παραφροσύνην . . . ἢ σπασμόν) (*Acut. app.* 29 = 2.450.8 L.)." Earlier in the so-called Appendix to the *Regimen*, we also come across a report about "affluxes of dark bile and sharp fluids" (7 = 2.406 L.: μελαίνης χολῆς καὶ δριμέων ῥευμάτων ἐπιρρύσιες γίνονται), which cause "darkening of the vision, loss of speech, heaviness of the head, and even convulsions" (καὶ σκοτώσιες καὶ ἀφωνίη καὶ καρηβαρίη ἢ καὶ σπασμοί), leading to epilepsy or paralysis (ἔνθεν ἐπίληπτοι γίνονται ἢ παραπλῆγες).[27] Among the symptoms described here, καρηβαρίη ("heavy-headedness/headache")[28] is widely associated with drunkenness.[29]

The medical views about the causes and symptoms of madness are suggestive of a wider intellectual debate, going back to the pre-Socratic philosophers, on our ability to perceive knowledge through the senses; gradually, the subjective workings of perception and its sensory modalities came to the fore of this debate, as illustrated by the Sophistic interest in juxtaposing madness and wisdom. As Passavanti has pointed out,[30] in one of the surviving *Dissoi Logoi*, a sophistic exercise on *Truth and Falsehood*, written in the Doric dialect between 403 and 395 BCE, the basic distinction between the mad (τὼς μαινομένως) and the wise (τὼς σωφρονοῦντας), the learned (τοὶ σοφοί) and the ignorant (τὼς ἀμαθεῖς) who otherwise seem to "say and do the same things" (4.5.1: ταὐτὰ . . . καὶ λέγοντι καὶ πράσσοντι, Robinson 1979, 124.17–126.1), is to be found in their speech patterns. For, while "the wise speak at the right moment (ἐν τῷ δέοντι), the fools speak at random" (4.5.9 in Robinson 1979, 128.4–8), an observation that accords with the erratic speech patterns of the mad as described in the Hippocratic corpus.

In his wide-ranging discussions of melancholy,[31] Aristotle also associates the melancholics with the garrulous since both groups tend to experience visions and suffer from madness (*div. somn.* 463b17–18: ἀλλ᾽ ὅσων . . . λάλος ἡ φύσις ἐστὶ καὶ μελαγχολική, παντοδαπὰς ὄψεις ὁρῶσιν).[32] In his *On Memory and Recollection*, Aristotle observes that "the melancholics are especially affected by mental images" (453a20–21: μάλιστα τοὺς μελαγχολικούς· τούτους γὰρ φαντάσματα κινεῖ μάλιστα),[33] while in his *On Dreams*, he specifies that "the melancholic, the feverish, and the intoxicated" (461a23: οἷον τοῖς μελαγχολικοῖς καὶ πυρέττουσι καὶ οἰνωμένοις) tend to perceive "confusing and monstrous images" in "morbid dreams" (461a21–22: τεταραγμέναι φαίνονται αἱ ὄψεις καὶ τερατώδεις καὶ οὐκ ἐρρωμένα τὰ ἐνύπνια).[34]

Melancholy's association with black-bile irregularities and garrulity is reiterated in the pseudo-Aristotelian *Problems*,[35] which draws closely on Aristotle, as van der Eijk has argued.[36] According to the text, "[T]hose in whom it [the black bile] is very considerable and hot (λίαν πολλὴ καὶ θερμή) become mad, clever, erotic, and easily moved to spiritedness and desire (μανικοὶ καὶ εὐφυεῖς καὶ ἐρωτικοὶ καὶ εὐκίνητοι πρὸς τοὺς θυμοὺς καὶ τὰς ἐπιθυμίας), and some become more talkative (λάλοι μᾶλλον)" (*Pr.* 30.954a32–34). Furthermore, pseudo-Aristotle identifies a link between interrupted speech-patterns and drunkenness, noting that the tongue of the drunk tends to stumble (ps.-Arist. *Pr.* 3.875b20: τῶν μεθυόντων ἡ γλῶττα πταίει)—a reaction of their body that mirrors the imbalance of their souls.[37] Then, a few paragraphs later, he repeats the view that wine aggravates the symptoms of melancholy: "For more than anything else, a lot of wine (ὁ γὰρ οἶνος ὁ πολὺς) appears to produce those qualities that we say are melancholic (τοιούτους οἵους λέγομεν τοὺς μελαγχολικοὺς εἶναι), and when it has been drunk it induces most (kinds of) temperaments (πλεῖστα ἤθη ποιεῖν πινόμενος), namely, the irascible, the benevolent, the compassionate and the reckless" (*Pr.* 30.953a34–37). Pseudo-Aristotle goes on to argue that wine interferes with people's disposition, making those who are normally silent more talkative, even eloquent and bold (*Pr.* 30.953b3–4: λαλιστέρους ποιεῖ, ἔτι δὲ πλείων ῥητορικοὺς καὶ θαρραλέους); in due course, however, they become reckless, hubristic, and finally mad (μανικούς), like those who suffer epileptic attacks since childhood and those susceptible to melancholy (30.953b6–8). Crucially, pseudo-Aristotle posits that "wine and nature produce the character of each person by the same means" (30.953b21–24: διὰ τὸ αὐτὸ ποιεῖ ὅ τε οἶνος καὶ ἡ φύσις ἑκάστου τὸ ἦθος), that is by "the regulation of heat" (τῇ θερμότητι ταμιευόμενα)—a view that Plato was believed to share,[38] since "wine and the mixture (of black bile) are similar in nature" (30.953b26–27: τὴν φύσιν ὅμοια ὅ τε οἶνος καὶ ἡ κρᾶσις).[39] Indeed, in the Hippocratic tradition, drunkenness is often reported as a cause of fever and even madness.[40] Thus, pseudo-Aristotle says, the melancholics "because this heat occurs near the location of intelligence (διὰ τὸ ἐγγὺς εἶναι τοῦ νοεροῦ τόπου τὴν θερμότητα ταύτην), are taken ill by madness *or* inspiration (νοσήμασιν ἀλίσκονται μανικοῖς ἢ ἐνθουσιαστικοῖς), whence come the Sibyls and Bakides and all inspired persons (ὅθεν Σίβυλλαι καὶ Βάκιδες καὶ οἱ ἔνθεοι γίνονται πάντες)" (*Pr.* 30.954a35–38). The association of wine and heat, also found in Aristotle,[41] is reiterated in the Peripatetic *Supplementa Problematorum* (2.36: θερμαντικὸς δὲ ὁ οἶνος),[42] attributed to Alexander of Aphrodisias, Aristotle's commentator, who was active circa the late second or the early third century CE.[43] Here, we are told that "the great heat of the wine produces relaxation of the [bodily] parts" (1.17: τὴν γὰρ ἀπὸ τῆς πολλῆς θερμότητος τοῦ οἴνου γενομένην ἔκλυσιν τῶν μορίων), a condition explicitly associated with Dionysus and Bacchic dancing.[44]

However, despite defining melancholy as an unpredictable illness that affects patients by interrupting their normal behavioral patterns (*Pr.* 30.954b8–10: ἡ δὲ μελαγχολικὴ κρᾶσις, ὥσπερ καὶ ἐν ταῖς νόσοις ἀνωμάλους ποιεῖ, οὕτω καὶ αὐτὴ ἀνώμαλός ἐστιν), pseudo-Aristotle also refers to a category of exceptional individuals who are *melancholic by nature, not illness* (30.954b40–41: περιττοὶ μέν εἰσι πάντες οἱ μελαγχολικοί, οὐ διὰ νόσον, ἀλλὰ διὰ φύσιν); this category includes eminent philosophers, like Socrates and Plato,[45] politicians, poets, and heroes like Heracles, whose fiery temperament corresponds to his reputation for drunkenness and lust.[46] For, according to pseudo-Aristotle, both wine ("described as the juice of the grape") and the mixture of the black bile contain breath (*Pr.* 30.953b24–25: ὅ τε δὴ χυμὸς καὶ ἡ κρᾶσις ἡ τῆς μελαίνης χολῆς πνευματικά ἐστιν) that is necessary for sexual excitement. "For this reason, wine works as an aphrodisiac (ὅ τε οἶνος ἀφροδισιαστικοὺς ἀπεργάζεται), and Dionysus and Aphrodite are correctly said to be with each other (ὀρθῶς Διόνυσος καὶ Ἀφροδίτη λέγονται μετ᾽ ἀλλήλων εἶναι), and most melancholic people are lustful (οἱ μελαγχολικοὶ οἱ πλεῖστοι λάγνοι εἰσίν)" (*Pr.* 30.953b31–34). Plato's comparison, then, of the ecstatic philosopher with the frenzied drinker and the lover, as employed in the *Symposium* and the *Phaedrus*, is an attempt to contribute to the contemporary debate about perception with a view to subvert it in defense of Socrates' remarkable insight.

At this point, it is worth revisiting Socrates' description of philosophical inebriation in the *Phaedrus*. Its symptoms include shaking, sweating, and running unusually high temperatures (*Phdr.* 251a10–b1: καὶ **ἱδρὼς** καὶ **θερμότης ἀήθης** λαμβάνει), all suggestive of black-bile problems, affected by wine consumption. The soul that "gazes" upon physical beauty (249d6–7: ὁρῶν κάλλος),[47] Socrates claims, is constantly reminded of its heavenly prototype and is thus moistened and warmed up (251c8–d1: ἄρδηταί τε καὶ **θερμαίνηται**).[48] But when separated from the beloved, the soul becomes dry (*Phdr.* 251d2: **αὐχμήσῃ**)[49] and pulsates like veins do, overwhelmed with yearning (251d5–6: **πηδῶσα** οἷον τὰ σφύζοντα).[50]

Plato adopts the medical language about mixtures of elements (46b8: μίξεις) in the *Philebus* too,[51] where he discusses the so-called mixed pleasures that involve pain since it is their deficit that dictates our pursuit to replenish them.[52] Notably, the main goal of the dialogue is to debate "condition and disposition of the soul which can make life happy for all human beings" (11d4–6: ἕξιν ψυχῆς καὶ διάθεσιν . . . τὴν δυναμένην ἀνθρώποις πᾶσι τὸν βίον εὐδαίμονα παρέχειν). According to Plato, some of these pleasures belong only to the body and others only to the soul, although "we also find some mingled pains and pleasures belonging both to the soul and to the body" (*Phil.* 46b1–2: τὰς δ᾽ αὖ τῆς ψυχῆς καὶ τοῦ σώματος ἀνευρήσομεν λύπας ἡδοναῖς μιχθείσας). Describing pleasures and pains in terms of experiencing a change in temperature (46c6–7: ποτὲ ῥιγῶν **θέρηται** καὶ **θερμαινόμενος** ἐνίοτε ψύχηται), alongside being compared to a mixture of sweet and bitter (47d1: τὸ . . . λεγόμενον πικρῷ γλυκὺ μεμιγμένον), Plato refers to the prevalence of pain in the mixture as an "itch" or "tickling" (46d8–9: τὰς τῆς ψώρας . . . καὶ τὰς τῶν **γαργα-λισμῶν**), "when the burning inflammation is within, and is not reached by the rubbing and scratching" (46d8–e1: ὁπόταν ἐντὸς τὸ ζέον ᾖ καὶ τὸ φλεγμαῖνον, τῇ τρίψει δὲ καὶ τῇ **κνήσει** μὴ ἐφικνῆταί). The language is strikingly evocative of the condition of the lover in the *Phaedrus* whose soul experiences the same kind of confusion (251e1: ἀποροῦσα; also, 255d2; cf. *Phil.* 51a2–8: . . . ἀπορίας)[53] before being afflicted by *mania*; furthermore, the soul of the lover also suffers from high body temperature, irritation, and itching as its wings begin to grow (251c2–5: **κνῆσίς**[54] τε καὶ **ἀγανάκτησις** . . . ταὐτὸν δὴ πέπονθεν ἡ τοῦ πτεροφυεῖν ἀρχομένου ψυχή· **ζεῖ** τε καὶ **ἀγανακτεῖ** καὶ **γαργαλίζεται**; cf. chapter 1, n185). In the *Philebus*, Socrates stipulates that this condition can be treated by bring-ing the affected parts either to the fire or to something cold (*Phil.* 46e2: τοτὲ φέροντες εἰς πῦρ αὐτὰ καὶ εἰς τοὐναντίον); then, the patient may undergo a dramatic change "from being at a dead end to inexpressible joy" (46e3: **μεταβάλλοντες** ἐνίοτε ἀμηχάνους ἡδονάς), a phrase that evokes yet again the perceptual change that the lover undergoes in the *Phaedrus* (251a9–10: ἐκ τῆς φρίκης **μεταβολή**). In addition, the soul experiences a slightly painful tickling (*Phil.* 47a5–6: **γαργαλίζει** τε καὶ ἠρέμα **ἀγανα-κτεῖν** ποιεῖ) when pleasure is the predominant element in the mixture, which sometimes even makes a patient leap for joy (47a8: ἐνίοτε **πηδᾶν** ποιεῖ), while on other occasions "it produces in him all sorts of colours, expressions, and breathings, and even causes great amazement and foolish shouting" (47a8–9: καὶ παντοῖα μὲν χρώματα, παντοῖα δὲ σχήματα, παντοῖα δὲ πνεύματα ἀπεργαζόμενον πᾶσαν **ἔκπληξιν** καὶ βοὰς μετ᾽ ἀφροσύνης ἐνεργάζεται). Thus, Plato, playfully and bravely, describes philosophical delirium by employing consistently across his dialogues the medical symp-toms of *mania* that correspond to or manifest cognitive transformations.

Indeed, the interaction of body temperature and mood, akin to the state described by Socrates, remains the subject of medical research to this day: changes in blood circulation, for example, have been observed following exposure to pleasant music,[55] physical activity is known to cause our endogenous opioid system to induce a sense of euphoria,[56] and sweating often follows alcohol ingestion since alcohol interferes with our thermoregulatory ability.[57] Plato, however, relies on the explicit disapproval of excessive intoxication in ancient medicine, as well as its rejection of divine causes for disease[58] to help him delimit his metaphorical version of drunkenness. Thus, the physician Eryximachus unequivocally states at the start of the *Symposium* his medical opinion that "drunkenness is harmful to people" (176d1–2: κατάδηλον γεγονέναι ἐκ τῆς ἰατρικῆς, ὅτι χαλεπὸν τοῖς ἀνθρώποις ἡ μέθη ἐστίν),[59] while in the *Phaedrus*, Socrates states that his *mania* is not divine (*Phdr.* 256b7–8)[60] and indeed very different to the godsent madness of tragic figures.[61] Plato, fighting against the sophists and the rhetoricians, shared an affinity with the Hippocratics who similarly fought to establish true science against folk healers and medical quackery;[62] thus, in the *Phaedrus*, probably drawing on chapter 20 of the treatise *On Ancient Medicine*, where "certain doctors and philosophers" are portrayed as arguing in unison "that no one can know medicine who does not know what the human being is" (= 1.622 L.: ὡς οὐκ εἴη δυνατὸν ἰητρικὴν εἰδέναι ὅστις μὴ οἶδεν ὅ τί ἐστιν ἄνθρωπος), Plato explicitly states that his arguments follow Hippocrates' examination method.[63] Strikingly, the Hippocratic text uses drunkenness as an example of medicine's emphasis on establishing the truth:

> Undiluted wine, drunk in large quantity, produces a certain effect upon a person (οἶνος ἄκρητος πολλὸς ποθεὶς διατίθησί πως τὸν ἄνθρωπον).[64] All who know this would realize this to be a potency of wine, and that wine itself is to blame (ὅτι αὕτη ἡ δύναμις οἴνου καὶ αὐτὸς αἴτιος); we know, too, through which parts of a person wine chiefly exerts this power (οἷοί γε τῶν ἐν τῷ ἀνθρώπῳ τοῦτο δύναταί γε μάλιστα). Just such precision of truth I would wish to be evident in all other instances (οἴδαμεν τοιαύτην δὴ βούλομαι ἀληθείην καὶ περὶ τῶν ἄλλων φανῆναι). (*VM* 22 = 1.622 L.)

Thus, Plato's analogy between body and soul, in which the workings of the soul produce corresponding symptoms in the body, helps him demarcate philosophical inebriation.

Furthermore, while arguing against the view that perception is knowledge in the *Theaetetus* (151e3: καὶ ὥς γεννῖ φαίνεται, οὐκ ἄλλο τί ἐστιν ἐπιστήμη ἢ αἴσθησις),[65] Socrates unequivocally dismisses the validity of dreams and visions, typically ascribed to the melancholics and the enraptured, as a secure source of knowledge:

> We are yet to examine this claim in the case of dreams and illnesses, including *mania*, and everything else that is defined as deception regarding hearing, sight, and all the other senses (λείπεται δὲ ἐνυπνίων τε πέρι καὶ νόσων, τῶν τε ἄλλων καὶ

μανίας, ὅσα τε παρακούειν ἢ παρορᾶν ἤ τι ἄλλο παραισθάνεσθαι λέγεται). For you realize that in all these cases the definition we just put forward seems to be admittedly refuted (οἶσθα γάρ που ὅτι ἐν πᾶσι τούτοις ὁμολογουμένως ἐλέγχεσθαι δοκεῖ ὃν ἄρτι διῇμεν λόγον), because in them we certainly have false perceptions (ὡς παντὸς μᾶλλον ἡμῖν ψευδεῖς αἰσθήσεις ἐν αὐτοῖς γιγνομένας), and it is by no means true that everything is to each man as it appears to him (καὶ πολλοῦ δεῖ τὰ φαινόμενα ἑκάστῳ ταῦτα καὶ εἶναι); on the contrary, nothing is as it appears (ἀλλὰ πᾶν τοὐναντίον οὐδὲν ὧν φαίνεται εἶναι). (*Tht.* 157e1–158a3)

Additional evidence on Plato's metaphorical use of Socratic inebriation is found in Aristotle's discussion of the dreams of the melancholics, which, as he claims, are *not* godsent; rather it is their ability to perceive similarities between things that enables them to chance occasionally upon "images similar to events"[66] (*div. somn.* 463b19: ἐπιτυγχάνουσιν ὁμοίοις θεωρήμασιν). As van der Eijk has argued, Aristotle implicitly contrasts melancholics "with the group of the best and most intelligent" (462b21–22: τοῖς βελτίστοις καὶ φρονιμωτάτοις), who "would typically be expected to be the recipients of divine provision,"[67] assuming it exists. In this regard, Aristotle agrees with the author of the *Problems* that melancholy is an abnormal state that relates variably and unpredictably to the faculty of reason.[68] Only in exceptional cases, Aristotle insists, when inspiration is accompanied by a special aptitude (*Rhet.* 1362b15: εὐφυΐα),[69] melancholy enhances reason instead of preventing it.[70] We may infer, then, that this is the kind of melancholy Plato and Socrates are thought to suffer from.

Although Aristotle has been credited with the "secularization" of Plato's portrayal of *mania* in the *Phaedrus*,[71] in my view, he appears well-versed in Plato's metaphor of Socratic inebriation and its parameters. Thus, in the *Nicomachean Ethics*, Aristotle compares "the man who lacks self-control . . . with those who get drunk quickly, and with a small amount of wine, or with less than most men" (1151a38–40: ὅμοιος γὰρ ὁ ἀκρατής ἐστι τοῖς ταχὺ μεθυσκομένοις καὶ ὑπ' ὀλίγου οἴνου καὶ ἐλάττονος ἢ ὡς οἱ πολλοί). Aristotle makes a distinction here between lack of self-control from recklessness (*propeteia*) and lack of self-control from weakness (*astheneia*), claiming that the melancholics ". . . are the most liable to the reckless type of lacking self-control (μάλιστα δ' οἱ ὀξεῖς καὶ μελαγχολικοὶ τὴν προπετῆ ἀκρασίαν εἰσὶν ἀκρατεῖς), because . . . they are too intense to wait for rational deliberation (οἱ δὲ διὰ τὴν σφοδρότητα οὐκ ἀναμένουσι τὸν λόγον), being prone to follow their imagination (διὰ τὸ ἀκολουθητικοὶ εἶναι τῇ φαντασίᾳ)" (*Eth. Nic.* 1150b25–28).[72] As we saw, Aristotle also remarks on the exceptional susceptivity of the melancholics to mental images in his *On Memory*, while in the *Nicomachean Ethics* he ascribes the reckless type of person who lacks self-control to the *ekstatikoi* ("those prone to bouts of ecstasy," 1151a1). The two character types are also identified in 1145b10–11 where "the self-restrained man who abides by the results of his reckoning" (ἐγκρατὴς καὶ ἐμμενετικὸς τῷ λογισμῷ) is contrasted to "the unrestrained who goes out of his mind" (ἀκρατὴς καὶ ἐκστατικὸς τοῦ λογισμοῦ).[73] Furthermore, at 1154b9–11 Aristotle juxtaposes the melancholics with the drunk and the young: the latter, he argues, are very similar to the drunk because they both seek to quench their desire for bodily pleasures (ὁμοίως δ' ἐν μὲν τῇ νεότητι διὰ τὴν αὔξησιν ὥσπερ οἱ οἰνωμένοι διάκεινται, καὶ ἡδὺ ἡ νεότης)—the melancholics, however, are unable to get satisfaction and are permanently in need of therapy (1154b11–13: οἱ δὲ μελαγχολικοὶ τὴν φύσιν δέονται ἀεὶ ἰατρείας), though eventually they become dissolute and bad (1154b15: ἀκόλαστοι καὶ φαῦλοι γίνονται).[74] Indeed, in the *Philebus*, Plato compares humans to wine pourers tasked with the responsibility of mixing the drink of pleasure in a balanced way,[75] under the auspices of Dionysus or Hephaestus, which could be understood as an allegory to adding the appropriate amount of heat or "fire" to the wine.[76] Those who fail to do so, "the foolish and the dissolute," are overwhelmed by pleasure "even to the point of madness" (45e2–3: τὸ δὲ τῶν ἀφρόνων τε καὶ ὑβριστῶν μέχρι μανίας ἡ σφοδρὰ ἡδονὴ κατέχουσα).

Another Aristotelian text that exemplifies the difference between the melancholics and the philosophers despite their outward similarities, is the *Eudemian Ethics*. Here, the melancholics are praised for their direct connection to the divine,[77] characterized as that "demonic something" in us which we are probably meant to associate with the Socratic *daimonion*;[78] nevertheless, Aristotle claims that the well-directed or successful enthusiasm of the melancholics lacks reason:[79]

> those are called fortunate who although irrational succeed in whatever they start on. (εὐτυχεῖς καλοῦνται οἳ ἂν ὁρμήσωσι κατορθοῦσιν ἄλογοι ὄντες); for they have within them a principle of a kind that is better than mind and deliberation (ἔχουσι γὰρ ἀρχὴν τοιαύτην ἣ κρείττων τοῦ νοῦ καὶ βουλεύ-

σεως) (whereas the others have reason but have not this; οἱ δὲ τὸν λόγον, τοῦτο δ' οὐκ ἔχουσι): they have inspiration, but they cannot deliberate (καὶ ἐνθουσιασμόν, τοῦτο δ' οὐ δύνανται). For although irrational they attain even what belongs to the prudent and wise—swiftness of divination (ἄλογοι γὰρ ὄντες ἐπιτυγχάνουσι καὶ τοῦ τῶν φρονίμων καὶ σοφῶν ταχεῖαν εἶναι τὴν μαντικήν), **so that one could almost take it for the divination engendered by reasoning** (καὶ μόνον οὐ τὴν ἀπὸ τοῦ λόγου δεῖ ἀπολαβεῖν). But some of them [achieve it] through experience (ἀλλ' οἱ μὲν δι' ἐμπειρίαν), some through habituation (οἱ δὲ διὰ συνήθειαν), instead of using enquiry ([τε] ἀν<τὶ τοῦ> τῷ σκοπεῖν χρῆσθαι), and [the outcomes of] these are thanks to the divine in us (τῷ θεῷ δὲ αὗται). (*Eud. Eth.* 1248a31–39)[80]

Thus, as Rowe observed, despite their ability to claim happiness, the melancholics "simply behave—somehow—like good people, without the reasoning and the dispositions that being good and acting well requires."[81] Importantly, the melancholics share with the philosophers the ability to perceive similarities and use metaphors by analogy in successful, well-directed ways, as discussed in chapter 1.[82] However, this is a superficial similarity that ought not to fool us. Unlike the melancholics, only those who possess *euphuia* (that is, the philosophers) can validate their insights through the application of reason and thus come closer to knowledge and truth.[83] Aristotle, therefore, follows Plato in scrupulously differentiating the mental disorders that merely look like the manic longing of the philosopher for real pleasure that is only found in virtue.[84]

Intoxicated with this *other* type of madness, the philosopher almost looks like a tragic character, performing in the theatre of the mind. Plato's medically sophisticated description of madness could also have been inspired by literature, especially tragedy, which offers many scenes of "burning" with emotion, followed by manic sweating[85] and/or jumping. Among these, the episode of Heracles' madness, which Euripides punctuates with references to corrupt Bacchic rites, presents a notable parallel that Plato's audiences would have been familiar with.[86] While relating the symptoms of his madness, Heracles observes in bewilderment: "But I am fallen as if into a wave and into dread confusion of mind (ἐν κλύδωνι καὶ φρενῶν ταράγματι /πέπτωκα δεινῶι), and my breath comes hot (πνοὰς θερμὰς πνέω) and spasmodically, not steadily (μετάρσι, οὐ βέβαια) from my lungs" (*Her.* 1091–1093). Heracles' affliction is diametrically opposed to the pure Bacchic rites of Euripides' Bacchants on which Plato models the experience of philosophically inclined lovers of the *Phaedrus* and the dedicated philosophers of the *Phaedo*.[87] Thus, upon recovering, Heracles realizes that his vision was corrupted while in the throes of madness (*l.* 1089: δέδορχ᾽ ἅπερ με δεῖ: "I see the things I ought to see"). His madness, which draws on medical vocabulary but leads to murder, confusion, and death, is symptomatic of a city "sick with dissention" (*ll.* 34 and 273: στάσει νοσοῦσαν/ νοσοῦσα); on the contrary, Socrates' madness[88] liberates the mind, prompting it to reassess its perception of reality.

As we saw, fifth century BCE medical advances, especially Hippocrates' introduction of autopsy as the best way of affirming facts,[89] kindled a debate on the human ability to assess reality. Although some irrational figures in tragedy lay claim to a superior understanding of reality—for example, Cassandra in Aeschylus' *Agamemnon*[90]—in the *Bacchae*, Teiresias explicitly distances himself from his prophetic skill when predicting the disastrous fate that will befall Pentheus after his rejection of the Bacchic cult: "I do not say this by my prophetic art but by looking at the facts" (*ll.* 68–69: μαντικῇ μὲν οὐ λέγω, τοῖς πράγμασιν δέ).[91] Plato, of course, as Capra has argued,[92] was a deft "poet" of dramatic dialogues in his own right, or at least undeniably familiar with poetic techniques, which he employs in the *Phaedrus*, for instance, to steer the reader toward philosophical initiation. Despite the speculative aspects of Capra's argument,[93] in my view there is little doubt that Socrates looks to impersonate the types of irrationality he identifies (that of a poet, a prophet, a *mystes*, and a lover), aiming thus to provide his audiences with illustrations of the shortcomings of creative irrationality unexamined by reason.[94] Drunkenness is associated with all these personas, but as Socrates clarifies in the *Theaetetus*, wine is the means of revealing one's character, not of forging it. Medical *mania* represents misperception;[95] thus, as Vogt has noted,[96] throughout the *Phaedrus*, Plato refers to madness as τὸ ἄφρων and παράνοια. Similarly, in the *Theaetetus*, Socrates uses the example of a sick person who misperceives sweet wine as bitter because of his illness, while inspiration is the result of perceiving the true essence of the wine (that is, the sweetness), which happens when wine hits the tastebuds of a healthy person (*Tht.* 159d5–6: γλυκὺν τὸν οἶνον τῇ ὑγιαινούσῃ γλώττῃ ἐποίησεν καὶ εἶναι καὶ φαίνεσθαι). Since reality and dream are so strikingly similar (158c6: ἄτοπος ἡ ὁμοιότης τούτων ἐκείνοις), much like madness and sanity, our only guide to distinguishing between the two states is our ability to "investigate and try to refute one another's fancies and opinions" (161d8–9: τὸ γὰρ ἐπισκοπεῖν καὶ ἐπιχειρεῖν ἐλέγχειν τὰς ἀλλήλων φαντασίας τε καὶ δόξας).[97] The Socratic *elenchus* could be seen in this light as the equivalent of the Hippocratic autopsy and even as a cure.[98] Despite the antagonistic relationship between medicine and philosophy (as well as philosophy and poetry) in antiquity[99] and the clear division between the diseases of the body and those of the soul,[100] the vocabulary used to designate and evaluate mental states largely coincides,[101] pointing to an awareness of the role of the body and the senses in shaping experience.[102]

Wine and Intellect in the Medical Tradition

Our understanding of the body as a reflection of the soul lies at the heart of the comparison of pathologically irrational people with eccentric geniuses. Foucault articulated it thus:[103] "We should no longer try to situate passion in the course of a causal succession, or halfway between the bodily and the spiritual; it indicates, on a deeper level, that soul and body are in a perpetual metaphorical relationship where the qualities do not need to be communicated because they are already common." Plato's confidence in Socrates' authority introduces some additional methodological questions arising from the challenging affinity between mental illness and genius. Just like Plato draws on Hippocrates, many have been tempted to draw on the resources of modern neuroscience and the medical understanding of mental health disorders to explain Socrates' behavior. The speculation that Socrates suffered from a neurological disorder aims to explain his visions and odd behavior[104] and would allow us to classify him alongside other exceptional thinkers such as Da Vinci, who is conjectured to have suffered from attention-deficit/hyperactivity disorder (ADHD).[105] Here, I briefly review several medical theories about Socrates before turning to ancient theories about the structure of human cognition and the impact of wine upon it.

Attention deficits, hyperactivity, and impulsiveness, the three most reported symptoms of ADHD,[106] can perhaps be associated to some degree with the surviving accounts of Socrates' odd meditational habits. However, all descriptions of ADHD insist on patients' diminished academic competence and pronounced antisocial behavior, often marked by aggression,[107] which wine (or alcohol in general) would likely exacerbate.[108] In this context, an attempt to explain Socratic meditation as emotional self-regulation does not correspond to current accounts of adult ADHD.[109] Owing to his high functionality, there have also been suspicions that Socrates suffered from a disorder within the autism spectrum, with Asperger's syndrome being the most common suggestion.[110] Adults suffering from Asperger's can maintain their functionality while drinking, including their narrative ability, which could accommodate accounts of Socrates' use of wine. Yet Asperger's sufferers tend to fail advanced narrative tasks that involve deeper semantic content, which is clearly at odds with Socratic argumentation.[111] Another common feature of autism spectrum disorders is atypical sensory behavior, which might explain Socrates' ability to withstand cold temperatures—a remarkable ability noted in Alcibiades' praise of the philosopher (*Symp.* 220a6–c1).[112] Yet, atypical sensory perception is associated with increased intellectual disability and severe social behavior deficits that often involve aggression, which again clearly overshoots Socrates' mild eccentricity.[113] In sum, our knowledge of neuropathological defects does not explain Socrates' behavior unless we make several exceptions to current medical observations.

Just as we are tempted to employ a medical register to make sense of Socrates' unusual behavior, Plato's allusions to ancient medical theory show that this temptation existed in Socrates' own time, too. However, modern studies of Socrates' neurological constitution have not considered his relationship with alcohol; thus, Plato's use of medical vocabulary and its metaphorical function are overlooked in favor of psychological or neurological explanations of Socratic inebriation. As discussed, ancient medicine helps Plato clarify that Socrates is neither drunk, nor mad (in either a ritual or pathological manner)—hence, his meditation practices do not constitute evidence of him being unaware of his surroundings. Plato's analogy between a healthy body and a virtuous soul, evident in the *Phaedrus*[114] and prevalent in the *Republic,* relies on a then-common understanding of health as "harmony and absence of strife."[115] In the *Symposium,* Plato seems to draw on the views of Alcmaeon of Croton,[116] an influential fifth century BCE physician, who argued that health is achieved when opposing forces within the body are balanced (for example, wet and dry, cold and hot, bitter and sweet). Thus, in the *Symposium* Eryximachus argues that:[117] "The most opposite qualities are most hostile to each other—cold and hot, bitter and sweet, dry and moist, and all such qualities. It was by knowing how to foster love and unanimity in these (ἐπιστηθεὶς ἔρωτα ἐμποιῆσαι καὶ ὁμόνοιαν) that our forefather Asclepius . . . composed our science (συνέστησεν τὴν ἡμετέραν τέχνην)"

(*Symp.* 186d9–e2). Similar views, pointing to imbalances in the hot, the cold, the dry, and the wet, were also aired by other physicians, like Petron of Aegina and Philistion of Locri.[118] The latter, an authority on dietetics mentioned in the Platonic *Second Letter*, was presumed as a potential author of the treatise *On Regimen*, which relates the earliest surviving theory of intelligence,[119] allegedly determined by the balance of fire and water in the soul in emulation of cosmic principles.[120] According to the *Regimen*, human souls have a fiery nature, unlike our bodies, which are watery,[121] and comprise three vascular systems that mirror the orbits of the sun, the moon, and the stars. The soul is situated in the middle circuit, alongside νοῦς (mind), φρόνησις (thought), and sleep;[122] the middle circuit corresponds to the sun and contains the hottest and strongest fire (*Vict.* 1.10 = 6.486 L.: τὸ θερμότατον καὶ ἰσχυρότατον πῦρ), which protects the soul from the impact of the senses while it remains in its proper abode (ἄϊκτον καὶ ὄψει καὶ ψαύσει). However, the soul is tasked with moving around the body through the other two circuits; it collects sensory data through the outward circuit, which, being closest to the flesh, is susceptible to effluences of "hot and cold *pneuma*" (*Vict.* 1.10 = 6.484 L. and 1.23 = 6.496 L.: πνεύματος ψυχροῦ καὶ θερμοῦ) that enter the body through the skin, the eyes, the ears, the nostrils, and the tongue. The soul transports the sensory information to the middle circuit to be analyzed objectively by our mental faculties.[123]

Individual intelligence is structured along similar lines; therefore, in the first book of the *Regimen*, we read:[124] "When the moistest fire and the driest water (πυρὸς τὸ ὑγρότατον καὶ ὕδατος τὸ ξηρότατον) become combined in a body, they produce the greatest intelligence (φρονιμώτατον), because the fire has moisture from the water, and the water dryness from the fire. Each is thus most self-sufficient. . . . The soul which is combined from these is most intelligent and has the best memory (ἐκ τούτων δὲ ἡ ψυχὴ συγκρηθεῖσα φρονιμωτάτη καὶ μνημονικωτάτη)" (*Vict.* 1.35.2–14 = 6.512,21–514,7 L.). The text goes on to specify the results of any possible imbalances in the mixture of water and fire in the soul, how they are reflected in our sensory perception, and how some of them, at least, can be ameliorated by following a suitable regime. It also identifies fire and its heat, a quality akin to the μένος (ardor) of the wine,[125] with the seed of intelligence, arguing that "if the soul is not shaken by the fire as it falls upon it, it cannot sense of what sort it is" (*Vict.* 1.35, 65–66 = 6.516,17–18 L.: ἢν γὰρ μὴ σεισθῇ ἡ ψυχὴ ὑπὸ τοῦ πυρὸς πεσόντος, οὐκ ἂν αἴσθοιτο ὁκοῖόν ἐστιν).[126] Two scenarios in which the fire progressively gains control over the water element of the soul are identified. In the first, the soul becomes sharper and reacts with faster movement as fire strikes its senses more quickly.[127] Such a soul tends to pass rushed judgements because its attention becomes easily diverted, hence it lacks determination.[128] In the second scenario, the primacy of the fire element in the soul results in perception so enhanced that those who have such souls suffer from dreams, like Socrates,[129] and are called *half*-mad (ὑπομαινομένους):[130] "Such a state is the closest to madness (ἔγγιστα μανίης), and they go into frenzy (μαίνονται) even from a small inexpedient inflammation, whether arising from intoxication (ἐν τῇσι μέθῃσι), or overabundance of flesh, or eating meat . . . (for these people) it is best to drink water only, if possible; otherwise, the closest thing to this is soft (i.e., less acidic) white wine . . . from this diligence such a soul could be most intelligent (ἡ τοιαύτη ψυχὴ φρονιμωτάτη ἂν εἴη)" (*Vict.* 1.35.128–131 = 6.520,19–522,2 L.).

Drunkenness and irrationality are extensively linked in Hippocratic medicine, with a focus on the "pathologies that emerge as a consequence of wine abuse."[131] Alcohol interferes with our psychic constitution by affecting the balance of the elements of fire and water in our soul. However, warmth is also associated with increased mental agility. As a result, madness is related to (though not identical with) heightened perception.[132] This lore can also explain why, although ancient medicine condemned intoxication, it still recognized the therapeutic properties of wine.[133] Thus, in the *Laws* (672d7–9), one of his later dialogues,[134] Plato employs medical arguments to refute the view that Dionysus bestowed wine on people as punishment to drive them mad (ἵνα μανῶμεν), an argument we also come across in Euripides' *Bacchae*:[135] ". . . Semele's offspring discovered and brought to people the liquid drink of the grape (βότρυος ὑγρὸν πῶμ'), which releases miserable mortals from grief (ὃ παύει τοὺς ταλαιπώρους βροτοὺς λύπης), and gives them, when filled with the flow of the vine (ἀμπέλου ῥοῆς), sleep to forget their daily troubles (λήθην τῶν καθ' ἡμέραν κακῶν); nor is there another medicine for hardships (φάρμακον πόνων)" (*Bacch.* 278–283). Similarly, Plato argues that wine was given to us as a medicine that benefits both the soul, by helping us to acquire modesty, and the body, by keeping it healthy and strong (*Leg.* 672d: φάρμακον . . . αἰδοῦς μὲν ψυχῆς κτήσεως ἕνεκα δεδόσθαι, σώματος δὲ ὑγιείας τε καὶ ἰσχύος).[136]

Plato is not interested in pathological cases of irrationality, for which he prescribes confinement.[137] Rather, he focuses on the citizens whose irrationality (ἄνοια) can be healed through education.[138] Hence, in the *Laws* (934a) he explains irrationality as a symptom that afflicts two groups of people: the young, who are easily manipulated,[139] and those unable to control their emotions[140]—as I discuss in the next chapter, neither of these groups can be entrusted with wine. Furthermore, in the *Timaeus* (86b–90d), Plato uses the term ἄνοια to denote the "illnesses of the soul"[141] that may result from an illness of the body (86b2–3: τὰ δὲ περὶ ψυχὴν (νοσήματα) διὰ σώματος ἕξιν; cf. *Phil.* 46a2: νοσημάτων ἡδονάς), a scenario he also entertained in the *Theaetetus*, as we saw, where different states of health are said to produce different versions of reality.[142] Plato then rejects medical *mania* because the madman "is no longer capable of reasoning" (λυττᾷ δὲ καὶ λογισμοῦ μετασχεῖν ἥκιστα τότε δὴ δυνατός) and "cannot see or hear anything as he ought" (86c2–3: οὔθ' ὁρᾶν οὔτε ἀκούειν ὀρθὸν οὐδὲν δύναται).[143] Unable to scrutinize his/her version of reality, the madman becomes a threat to the civic body that ought to agree on the correct interpretation of sensory information. Plato returns to this idea in the *Laws*, where he distinguishes two types of irrationality: *mania* and *amathia* (ignorance),[144] the latter being associated with the dominance of the body over the soul.[145]

At this point, it is worth citing the work of Xenophon who contributes two key passages regarding Socrates' figurative use of madness in his teaching and how it came to be misconstrued in court. At *Memorabilia* 1.2.49, Xenophon explains that Socrates was accused of urging his young followers to be disrespectful toward their parents:

> "But" said his accuser, "Socrates was teaching sons to mistreat their fathers (τοὺς πατέρας προπηλακίζειν ἐδίδασκε): he persuaded them that he made his associates wiser than their fathers (πείθων μὲν τοὺς συνόντας αὐτῷ σοφωτέρους ποιεῖν τῶν πατέρων); he said that the law allowed a son to put his father in prison if convinced of insanity (κατὰ νόμον ἐξεῖναι παρανοίας); and using this as evidence, that it was lawful for the ignorant to be thrown to jail by the wiser (ὡς τὸν ἀμαθέστερον ὑπὸ τοῦ σοφωτέρου νόμιμον εἴη δεδέσθαι).

Taken literally, the metaphor implies that Socrates encouraged his followers to throw their fathers in jail on account of their conventional and rigid reasoning to the point of being irrational. However, Xenophon dispels the misunderstanding immediately (1.2.50): what Socrates argued was that an ignorant person *cannot* be treated as mad, because there is a difference between clinical madness and ignorance (τί διαφέρει μανίας ἀμαθία). Unlike the mad, who should be kept away for their own sake and that of their friends, the ignorant have a right to be educated (1.2.50: τοὺς δὲ μὴ ἐπισταμένους τὰ δέοντα δικαίως ἂν μανθάνειν παρὰ τῶν ἐπισταμένων).[146] Here, Socrates subtly but surely continues to refute the accusation that he is mad: by pointing out his enemies' simplistic conflation of the mad and the ignorant, similar to Theaetetus' conflation of perception with knowledge (see *Tht.* 151e3 on p. 46 above),[147] Socrates vindicates himself by showing that madness can be confused with other, symptomatically similar conditions. Despite his unconventional behavior, Socrates' sanity is shown by his ability to rework the concept of irrationality and to outwit his accusers.[148] Importantly, the medical tradition about the human intellect and wine's impact on it was also picked up by philosophers, especially Heraclitus, whom Plato (and Euripides) held in reverence.[149] Given the correspondence between Heraclitus and certain Hippocratic texts (including the *Regimen*),[150] in the next section I examine Heraclitus' fragments to trace an earlier, influential paradigm for the borrowing of metaphors across fields of knowledge—in this case, from medicine to philosophy.

Humoral Theories, Wine, and Intellect in Heraclitus

Plato's philosophical use of medical terms and imagery is not without precedent; in his blending of the themes of wine, heat, and intelligence, Plato follows in the footsteps of Heraclitus who frequently employed metaphors as a means of communicating his conception of the universe. For example, in fragment DK B65 he refers to fire, the eternal divine principle, as "craving and abundance" (= D88 in L526: χρησμοσύνην καὶ κόρον).[151] Plotinus reports that Heraclitus spoke about the soul through comparison, neglecting to clarify his argument (*Enn.* iv.8.1.17: **εἰκάζειν** ἔδωκεν, ἀμελήσας σαφῆ ἡμῖν ποιῆσαι τὸν λόγον),[152] while Diodotus spoke of Heraclitus' exposition of nature "by way of an example" (DL 9.1.15: τὸ δὲ περὶ φύσεως ἐν παραδείγματος εἴδει κεῖσθαι).[153] His esoteric approach to knowledge is evident in his surviving fragments:[154] in DK B123, Heraclitus refers to nature's tendency to hide its realities,[155] while in DK B93 (= D41) he is quoted as saying: "The lord whose oracle is at Delphi neither says nor hides but reveals by signs" (οὔτε λέγει οὔτε κρύπτει ἀλλὰ σημαίνει).[156] Thus, Plato refers to Heraclitus' maxims as "riddling buzzwords" (*Tht.* 180a4: ῥηματίσκια αἰνιγματώδη).[157]

Metaphorical representation had of course been well-established since the seventh century BCE in the Greek intellectual tradition of poetic interpretation.[158] Heraclitus, however, opposes such representations as incomplete and erroneous, aiming only to please the crowds,[159] who have little understanding of philosophical principles. Hence, in fragment DK B35 (=D40)[160] he claims that "the unintelligent (ἀξύνετοι) resemble the deaf, although they listen (ἀκούσαντες κωφοῖσιν ἐοίκασι); for them is the maxim 'They are absent despite being present' (φάτις αὐτοῖσιν μαρτυρεῖ παρεόντας ἀπεῖναι)."[161] Heraclitus takes aim at ritual performers—including the so-called Bacchoi—who promised their gullible followers a genuine ecstatic experience:[162] "For whom does Heraclitus of Ephesus deliver his warnings (τίσι δὴ μαντεύεται)? For those who wander at night, for the magi, the Bacchoi, the Mainads, the initiates (νυκτιπόλοις, μάγοις, βάκχοις, λήναις, μύσταις). It is them that he threatens with after death punishments, for them he predicts the fire; for, what people regard as mysteries are instructed impiously (τὰ γὰρ νομιζόμενα κατ' ἀνθρώπους μυστήρια ἀνιερωστὶ μυεῦνται)" (DK B14 = D18). Heraclitus expresses a similar preoccupation regarding people's grasp and performance of Bacchic rites in fragment DK B15 (= D16), where he is recorded as saying:[163] "For if it is not in honour of Dionysus that they make the procession and sing the hymn to the shameful parts, they would be acting most shamefully; but Hades and Dionysus are the same, in whose honour they rave and celebrate Bacchic rites (ὅτεῳ μαίνονται καὶ ληναΐζουσιν)." Clearly then, Heraclitus is unsatisfied[164] with both the poetic and ritual approach of his time to irrationality—a dissatisfaction that Plato escalates in the *Republic* to a threat to civic virtue and the young citizens' concept of justice.[165] In addition, in Heraclitus' DK B92 (= D42) we read:[166] "And the Sibyl, with frenzied mouth uttering (μαινομένῳ στόματι), according to Heraclitus, grim, unadorned, and unperfumed, reaches with her voice over a thousand years because of the god." The derivatives of the root *men–, where *mainomai* and *mania* come from, had probably already functioned as metaphors in the distant Indo-European past.[167] Although there is still skepticism about Heraclitus' knowledge of ancient Iranian and Indian ideas about the cosmic order,[168] scholarship has pointed out genuine parallels between Heraclitean thought and Sanskrit texts of spiritual teaching.[169] Importantly, despite recognizing wetness as a necessary condition for the creation of souls, Heraclitus insists that the human soul must be kept dry as a reflection of its virtuous conduct and its connection to the divine world essence, which is fire.[170] The concept is already familiar to us through the Hippocratic *Regimen*, which encourages humans to use the fiery essence in them to mimic the fiery mind of the gods.[171] In DK

B36 (= D100) he famously states that "[B]ecoming water is death for the souls, while becoming earth is death for water; but water comes from earth and soul from water" (ψυχῆσιν θάνατος ὕδωρ γενέσθαι, ὕδατι δὲ θάνατος γῆν γενέσθαι, ἐκ γῆς δὲ ὕδωρ γίνεται, ἐξ ὕδατος δὲ ψυχή).[172] Further, in fragment DK B117 (= D104) he claims that "[W]henever a man gets drunk (ὁκόταν μεθυσθῇ), he is led stumbling (σφαλλόμενος) by an unripe youngster, not knowing where he goes, because his soul is moist (οὐκ ἐπαΐων ὅκη βαίνει, ὑγρὴν τὴν ψυχὴν ἔχων)."[173] The inebriation, then, that *mania* refers to ought not to be confused with physical drunkenness; in this context, *mania*'s warming sensation involves the expansion of our perception, securing an unobstructed channel of communication with the divine fire-essence, enabling us to emulate the divine.[174] Thus, while engaging in playful speculation about the perceptible world of Becoming (*Ti.* 59d1–3: τοὺς γενέσεως (λόγους) . . . ἡδονὴν κτᾶται, μέτριον ἂν ἐν τῷ βίῳ παιδιὰν καὶ φρόνιμον ποιοῖτο), Plato, likely drawing on Heraclitean philosophy, discusses a certain fiery sap (a kind of water filtered through plants) called "wine," which warms both the body and the soul (60a6–7: τὸ μὲν τῆς ψυχῆς μετὰ τοῦ σώματος θερμαντικὸν οἶνος).[175]

Heraclitus' appreciation of fire as the cosmic creative power, aiming at the truth,[176] and his association of virtue with dryness offered Plato a(nother) sound paradigm for accommodating scientific lore in philosophical conceptions of virtue and the human constitution. Drawing on existing conceptions of the soul as hot matter, a notion extant in Euripides too,[177] Plato presents Socrates in the *Symposium* as impervious not only to wine but also to cold. Just after assuring the banqueters that no one has ever seen Socrates drunk, Alcibiades goes on to relate the time when he and Socrates served together during the Athenian military campaign at Potidaea (during which Socrates saved Alcibiades' life, *Symp.* 220e). The story is meant as another example of Socrates' ability to exercise self-control:

> But it was his endurance of winter (τὰς τοῦ χειμῶνος καρτε-ρήσεις)—in those parts winters are awful—that I remember among his other marvellous feats (θαυμάσια ἠργάζετο), and how once there came about a most awful frost; while we all would either not go out, or if anyone ventured out, we would dress up with great care, putting on our shoes and wrapping our feet with felt and small fleeces, he walked out in that weather wearing the same coat as he used to wear before, and barefoot

he made his way over the ice more easily than the rest of us in our shoes. The soldiers cast suspicious glances at him thinking that he despised them. (*Symp.* 220a8–b10)

Excited to recount Socrates' amazing abilities, Alcibiades barely catches his breath before adding another story, this time about Socrates' meditative habits:[178]

> Reflecting on some issue at dawn, he stood in the same spot thinking about it (συννοήσας γὰρ αὐτόθι ἕωθέν τι εἰστήκει σκοπῶν), and because he couldn't make progress in it, he did not let it go but stood there trying (καὶ ἐπειδὴ οὐ προυχώρει αὐτῷ, οὐκ ἀνίει ἀλλὰ εἰστήκει ζητῶν). It was already midday and the men started noting him, and said to one another in wonder that Socrates had stood there since dawn pondering on something. In the end, some of the Ionians, after having dinner in the evening—for it was summer then—brought out their mattresses and slept in the cool, at the same time keeping an eye on him, if he would stand there during the night too. He stood until the dawn came and the sun rose: then, he walked away after praying to the Sun. (*Symp.* 220c3–d5)

These descriptions seem to reference the theories that acknowledge the association of heat with rationality and imply that Socrates keeps both his body and his soul warm and dry by constantly engaging in philosophical enquiry. Perhaps due to the similar properties of wine, Socrates was also an eager oenophile, as Xenophon confirms: "Well, gentlemen," he said, "as far as drinking is concerned, you have my full approval; for wine does in fact 'moisten the soul' (ἄρδων τὰς ψυχὰς) and lulls our pains to sleep (κοιμίζει) just as mandragora lulls people, at the same time awakening (τὰς δὲ φιλοφροσύνας . . . ἐγείρει) kindly feelings just as oil does a flame" (*Symp.* 2.24). Xenophon reiterates that Socrates could consume copious amounts of wine without ever getting drunk, evoking Alcibiades' assertion in Plato's *Symposium* that "drinking up as much wine as one orders him, he [= Socrates] never gets drunk" (214a5–6: ὁπόσον γὰρ ἂν κελεύῃ τις, τοσοῦτον ἐκπιὼν οὐδὲν μᾶλλον μή ποτε μεθυσθῇ). Although aware of the medicinal properties of wine, Socrates nonetheless concedes that it can interfere with the balance of elements in our soul. Despite Alcibiades' colorful report, which demonstrates a young man's eagerness for gossip and a good story, Socrates maintains the balance of elements in his soul by paying attention to his eating and drinking habits. Socrates' symposiastic aptitude is also detailed in Xenophon's *Memorabilia*, completed after 371 BCE, where we read:[179]

> Whenever he accepted an invitation to dinner, he resisted without difficulty the common temptation to exceed the limit of satiety (τὸ ὑπὲρ τὸν κόρον ἐμπίμπλασθαι); and he advised those who could not do likewise to avoid appetizers that encouraged them to eat and drink what they did not want; for such trash was the ruin of stomach and brain and soul. "I believe," he said in jest, "it was by providing a feast of such things that Circe made swine; and it was partly by the prompting of Hermes, partly through his own self-restraint and avoidance of excessive indulgence in such things, that Odysseus was not turned into a pig." This was how he would talk on the subject, half joking, half in earnest (περὶ τούτων ἔπαιζεν ἅμα σπουδάζων). Of sensual passion he would say: "Avoid it resolutely: it is not easy to control yourself once you meddle with that sort of thing (ἰσχυρῶς ἀπέχεσθαι: οὐ γὰρ ἔφη ῥᾴδιον εἶναι τῶν τοιούτων ἁπτόμενον σωφρονεῖν)." (*Mem.* 1.3.6–8)

Since Socrates resorts to Homeric themes to support his argument, the quotation highlights the connection between drinking at symposia and the recitation of poetry[180] but also between drinking and one's erotic profile. Drinkers and lovers should exercise self-control or choose abstinence if unsure of their ability to manage themselves under the influence of wine or love.[181] Notably, the question that the participants of the *Symposium* are asked to respond to focused on the nature of love—a topic which, according to Phaedrus, the poets failed to address adequately.[182] Plato clearly perceived our attitudes to wine, love, and poetry as interrelated reflections of our ethical disposition.[183]

At *Laws* 645d7–646a5 the Athenian Stranger observes that although the drinking of wine intensifies our pleasure, pains, angers, and lusts (σφοδροτέρας τὰς ἡδονὰς καὶ λύπας καὶ θυμοὺς καὶ ἔρωτας ἡ τῶν οἴνων πόσις ἐπιτείνει), the drunk are completely deprived of perceptions, memories, opinions, and good sense (τὰς αἰσθήσεις καὶ μνήμας καὶ δόξας καὶ φρονήσεις . . . πάμπαν ἀπολείπει ταῦτα . . . ἂν κατακορής τις τῇ μέθῃ γίγνηται).[184] In fact, in an echo of Heraclitus DK B117, we are told that an intoxicated person experiences a reduction to his psychic state as a young child (*Leg.* 645e6–7: ἀφικνεῖται τὴν τῆς ψυχῆς ἕξιν τῇ τότε ὅτε νέος ἦν παῖς).[185] In this "second childhood," one is "least able to exercise self-control," running the risk of becoming "totally wicked" (645d6–646a2: ἥκιστα δὴ τότ' ἂν αὐτὸς αὑτοῦ γίγνοιτο ἐγκρατής . . . πονηρότατος). The soul's intoxicated state is akin to bodily weakness and ugliness (646b9–c1), and thus, the Stranger appreciates wine as a fear *pharmakon* (647e1: φόβου φάρμακον) that can cause terror in even the bravest persons (648a1–2). Wine has the same effect on people as numerous other passions, including "anger, love, arrogance, ignorance, avarice, cowardness, and even wealth, beauty, and power" (649d6–7: θυμός, ἔρως, ὕβρις, ἀμαθία, φιλοκέρδεια, δειλία, καὶ ἔτι τοιάδε, πλοῦτος, κάλλος, ἰσχύς), which can make a man "drunk with pleasure," inducing irrational behavior (649d8–9: πάνθ' ὅσα δι' ἡδονῆς αὖ μεθύσκοντα παράφρονας ποιεῖ). As I discuss in the next chapter, however, Plato is appreciative of the ability of wine to enhance our perception and suggests using it as a cheap and widely available test of a man's *ethos* (649d7–671d7). That Plato is creatively and metaphorically engaging with multiple discourses within his cultural horizon (medical, philosophical, and literary) is obvious in his comparison of the state to a mixing-bowl of wine at *Laws* 773c8–d4—where, despite insisting elsewhere that wine "moistens" the soul, here he praises "the sober deity of water" for balancing the madness of wine when stirred in it appropriately.[186]

Defending Socrates' Sobriety

Given his goal of defending the authenticity of Socrates' nonalcoholic inspiration, Plato's choice to stage the *Symposium* against the background of the Lenaia festival makes a comparison with Euripides' *Bacchae* most palpable. The suspicion of pseudo-ecstasy is a central theme of the play (*l.* 218: πλασταῖσι βακχείαισιν), produced at the Great Dionysia of 405 BCE, at least twenty years before Plato composed his *Symposium*.[187] The play revolves around king Pentheus' mistrust of Dionysus' divinity and, thus, the challenge of discerning between pseudo-believers and real Bacchants. Although the rationalist Pentheus suspects the female followers of Dionysus of drunkenness and wantonness (*Bacch.* 224, 260–262), the messenger tasked with reporting on their behavior denies that they showed any signs of drunkenness (686–687). Instead, he observed the women resting "soberly; they were not as you say, drunk with the wine bowl and the sound of the pipe" (*ll.* 687–689: σωφρόνως, οὐχ ὡς σὺ φῇς/ ᾠνωμένας κρατῆρι καὶ λωτοῦ ψόφῳ).[188] Importantly, the god does not enforce *sōphrosynē* through his rites but mainly allows his followers to exercise a feature inherent in their nature:[189] "Dionysus will not compel women to act modestly (σωφρονεῖν) where sex is concerned. Rather, modesty (τὸ σωφρονεῖν) lies in one's own nature . . . remember; even in ecstatic worship (ἐν βακχεύμασιν) a modest woman (ἥ γε σώφρων) will not be corrupted" (*Bacch.* 314–318). Euripides' Bacchants, then, are endorsed as genuine precisely because they are not drunk, like Socrates, who, as reiterated several times in the *Symposium*, is inebriated and inebriating without being intoxicated. The *Bacchae* highlights the civic framework of formal Dionysiac cult[190] and debates common beliefs about the use and abuse of wine that are highly relevant to the distinctions Plato guides us to adopt through the metaphor of Socratic inebriation.

Similarly, in the *Laws,* Plato defines *baccheia* as a type of inebriated dance in honor of Dionysus (ἀμφισβητουμένην ὄρχησιν):[191] "All dancing that is Bacchic (βακχεία . . . ἐστὶν) and pursued by those who *imitate in their drunken state* (**μιμοῦνται κατῳνωμένους**) the so-called Nymphs and Pans and Silenoi and Satyrs, as they say, while performing purifications and certain rites (καθαρμούς τε καὶ τελετάς τινας)" (*Leg.* 815c1–5). This kind of dance is the central motif of the *Bacchae*. While relating the items of his cultic costume in the *Bacchae* (175–180), Cadmus relies on Teiresias, characterized as wise (*l.* 186: σὺ γὰρ σοφός),[192] to teach him the Bacchic dance steps. Still, the twosome looks ridiculous to Pentheus, who comments on the seeming incompatibility of old age and Bacchic cult.[193] Being a god of opposites, Dionysus appears ridiculous, but in fact he bestows *sōphrosynē*; equally, he appears violent or as inciting violence, but his essence is categorically not violent. Thus, instead of causing *mania*, as suspected, he instills inner peace.[194] As Teiresias retorts, it is Pentheus' obstinate and unjustified rejection of Dionysus that points to his "diseased mind" (*l.* 311: ἡ δὲ δόξα σου νοσῇ); as a result, instead of embracing Bacchic peace, Pentheus is raging with madness: "You are mad with a most painful affliction (μαίνῃ γὰρ ὡς ἄλγιστα) neither can you be healed by drugs,/ but in fact, some drug has caused it (κοὔτε φαρμάκοις/ ἄκη λάβοις ἂν οὔτ' ἄνευ τούτων νοσεῖς)" (*Bacch.* 326–327). Accordingly, the cultic costume that Pentheus tries to ridicule—though he will be persuaded to don it later in the play—is an attempt to emulate the god;[195] the outer appearance is meant to mirror the inner constitution of the Bacchants and their god, but it is clearly not enough. Euripides describes the Bacchic constitution in the antistrophe of lines 416–431 where, addressed as *daimon*, Dionysus is said to "rejoice in banquets and peace" (*ll.* 417–420: χαίρει μὲν θαλίαισιν,/ φιλεῖ δ' ὀλβοδότειραν Εἰ-/ ρήναν).[196] Special mention is made of the god's gift of wine, which takes griefs away (423: οἴνου τέρψιν ἄλυπον; cf. *l.* 772: τὴν παυσίλυπον ἄμπελον δοῦναι βροτοῖς), and the god's "wise mind and perception," which he keeps hidden from presumptuous people (*ll.* 427–428: σοφὰν δ' ἀπέχειν πραπίδα φρένα τε/ περισσῶν παρὰ φωτῶν). Frustrated to be the only ones in the city to dance in honor of the god (195), Teiresias uses the verb πάσχειν (*l.* 18: "to suffer/undergo") to describe the Bacchic rejuvenation he and Cadmus experience even at an advanced age and asserts that they are the only ones "thinking rightly, the others think wrongly" (*l.* 196: μόνοι γὰρ εὖ φρονοῦμεν, οἱ δ' ἄλλοι κακῶς).[197]

This scene evokes Alcibiades' comparison of Socrates with the satyrs and Marsyas in the *Symposium* (as discussed in chapter 1) and makes the complexities of Plato's account of inebriation vivid. It is also reminiscent of the depiction of Socrates in Xenophon's *Symposium* (2.17–23), where he is eager to dance, inspired by the skill of the performers whom the host Callias had hired to sing and perform a *komos*[198]—a hymn notably associated with Dionysus.[199] However, Socrates' readiness is ridiculed by Philip the failed comedian who, as other Alcibiades, arrives uninvited (1.11–16) and himself causes laughter with his inordinate, over-the-top rendition of the dancing moves.[200] These actions display Philip's lack of the self-control and manly grace that Socrates strives to inspire in his fellow banqueters, an aspiration decidedly frustrated by the opulence on display (Xen. *Symp.* 2.2: θεάματα καὶ ἀκροάματα ἥδιστα παρέχεις):[201] spectacular performances, delicacies, and plenty of wine distract the participants from focusing on the ethical substance of their exchange with Socrates.[202] Thus, as soon as Philip completes his farcical dancing, he asks for more wine (2.23: "I'm thirsty: let the slave fill up for me the big cup [τὴν μεγάλην φιάλην])." The parasitic jester thus encapsulates the risk, inherent in the metaphor of *baccheia*, of slipping from Socratic inebriation into mere intoxication.

This risk cannot be avoided, however, because Socratic inebriation defies easy delimitation. In the *Symposium*, Alcibiades urges his fellow drinkers to admit that they "have all partaken in the philosopher's *mania* and *baccheia*" (218b3–4: πάντες γὰρ κεκοινωνήκατε τῆς φιλοσόφου μανίας τε καὶ βακχείας), which obviously does not refer to their shared drinking sessions. By qualifying this kind of madness as that "of the philosopher" and resorting to the metaphor of the *baccheia*, Alcibiades implicitly admits that he is at a loss for words when it comes to naming Socratic inebriation. Similarly, in the *Phaedrus* the difficulty of articulating philosophical inebriation is reflected in the beloved, who "is in love but does not know who with; and he does not understand his suffering, *nor can he express it*" (255d3–5: ἐρᾷ μὲν οὖν, ὅτου δὲ ἀπορεῖ· καὶ οὔθ᾽ ὅτι πέπονθεν οἶδεν οὐδ᾽ ἔχει φράσαι). The philosophical *modus vivendi*, Socrates argues, secures for its advocates the "greatest good, which neither human *sōphrosyne* nor divine *mania* can confer" (256b7–8: οὗ μεῖζον ἀγαθὸν οὔτε σωφροσύνη ἀνθρωπίνη οὔτε θεία μανία δυνατὴ πορίσαι)—a subtle but certain distancing of philosophical experience from the average human state of perception but also from forms of irrationality attributed to divine intervention.[203] Hence, although Socrates claims, rather jokingly, to have spoken in a manic way (265a8–9: μανικῶς),[204] he is not possessed by any of the gods who are responsible for other, socially recognized types of irrationality,[205] much in the way that in the *Symposium* he does not become intoxicated. He further describes *erōs* as "a *kind* of *mania*" (**μανίαν** γάρ **τινα**) before embarking on his second speech, guided by his *daimonion*.[206]

Those inspired to emulate Socrates are not irrational in the destructive manner of those who are drunk. That conclusion could only be reached by those who, like Pentheus, fail to approach the god with understanding. In this case, wine functions only as a medicinal or healing substance, preparing the audience for the illumination they are about to experience.[207] It seems then that the turmoil felt by Socrates' audiences is an expression or enactment of their own dissatisfaction with their former state of mind—their tears are a sign[208] of relief at having attained an alternative grasp of reality,[209] an act that symbolizes their breaking away from old ways and mentalities, occurring just before they reach the state of calmness exemplified by Socrates. As discussed in chapter 1, withdrawal from society or an urge for quiet contemplation, symptoms that evoke Socrates' meditational habits as described in the *Symposium* and in the *Phaedo* especially,[210] could also indicate Bacchic madness. The precise nature of the mental constitution of Pentheus' Bacchants or Socrates' followers is as indefinable as the "normality" that the Dionysiac cult was believed to challenge. While subjects must reflect on experiences of inebriation to recognize their meaning and realize their full impact, the metaphors they are forced to employ to describe these experiences to others can only convey a genus of experience, not its particulars. Although this mimetic representation of madness can be ineffective, as the *Bacchae* emphasizes (for example, when obsessing about procedural details), Plato's many witnesses attest to the sincerity of Socratic inebriation—Alcibiades, Socrates' utter opposite, foremost among them.

A link between the voice of the *daimonion* and an inward turn to self-reflection is forged when Socrates develops the theory of *anamnesis*; philosophically inclined souls, Socrates argues, "seek within themselves to find the nature of their god" (*Phdr.* 253a1–2: ἰχνεύοντες δὲ παρ' ἑαυτῶν ἀνευρίσκειν τὴν τοῦ σφετέρου θεοῦ φύσιν). Socrates never identifies philosophical inebriation with any other type of beneficial possession and is unwilling to associate philosophical inspiration with a specific divine patron;[211] rather, his comparison aims to establish the unequivocal superiority of philosophical inebriation (*Phdr.* 249e2–3: πασῶν τῶν ἐνθουσιάσεων ἀρίστη τε καὶ ἐξ ἀρίστων) as the only authentic form of ecstasy—which is only secondarily to do with imbibing wine.[212] Thus, in the *Timaeus* Plato claims that

> No man achieves true and inspired divination when in his rational mind (μαντικῆς ἐνθέου καὶ ἀληθοῦς), but only when the power of his intelligence is fettered (φρονήσεως πεδηθεὶς δύναμιν) in sleep or when it is distraught by disease or by reason of some divine inspiration (ἢ διά τινα ἐνθουσιασμὸν παραλλάξας). *But it belongs to a man when in his right mind to recollect and ponder* (ἀλλὰ συννοῆσαι μὲν ἔμφρονος τά τε ῥηθέντα ἀναμνησθέντα) both the things spoken in dream or waking vision by the divining and inspired nature (ὕπαρ ὑπὸ τῆς μαντικῆς τε καὶ ἐνθουσιαστικῆς φύσεως), and all the visionary forms that were seen, and *by means of reasoning* (πάντα λογισμῷ διελέσθαι) to discern about them all wherein they are significant and for whom they portend evil or good in the future, the past, or the present. But it is not the task of him who has been in a state of frenzy, and still continues therein, to judge the apparitions and voices seen or uttered by himself; for it was well said of old that to do and to know one's own and oneself belongs only to him who is sound of mind (λέγεται τὸ πράττειν καὶ γνῶναι τά τε αὐτοῦ καὶ ἑαυτὸν σώφρονι μόνῳ προσήκειν). Wherefore also it is customary to set the tribe of prophets to pass judgement upon these inspired divinations; *and they, indeed, themselves are named "diviners" by certain who are wholly ignorant of the truth that they are*

> *not diviners but interpreters of the mysterious voice and appa-*
> *rition, for whom the most fitting name would be "prophets of*
> *things divined"* (οὓς μάντεις αὐτοὺς ὀνομάζουσίν τινες, τὸ πᾶν
> ἠγνοηκότες ὅτι τῆς δι᾽ αἰνιγμῶν οὗτοι φήμης καὶ φαντάσεως
> ὑποκριταί, καὶ οὔτι μάντεις, προφῆται δὲ μαντευομένων δικαι-
> ότατα ὀνομάζοιντ᾽ ἄν). (*Ti.* 71e4–72b5)

Irrationality often accompanies ecstatic incidents; the experience per se is unreflective and must be followed by careful exercise of judgement before its value is realized.[213] Judgement distinguishes the philosopher from other subjects of intoxication because it represents sober intellectual synthesis after a cathartic and likely disturbing experience. Therefore, at *Phaedrus* 255a–256b, Socrates notes that the beloved has little clue about what is happening to him while he experiences the erotic appeal of the lover,[214] that is, while in the throes of madness. Nevertheless, happiness is still possible "if the better parts of his mind lead him" (256a9–b1: τὰ βελτίω τῆς διανοίας ἀγαγόντα). Socrates distinguishes *erōs*, our "innate desire for pleasures," from the acquired judgement that leads us to the best choices (237d8–10: ἡ μὲν ἔμφυτος οὖσα ἐπιθυμία ἡδονῶν, ἄλλη δὲ ἐπίκτητος δόξα, ἐφιεμένη τοῦ ἀρίστου).[215] In addition, the need to reflect on our encounters with states of altered consciousness to determine their significance does not undermine the reality we try to grasp or the images we must use as proxies of reality; on the contrary, reflection is necessary to render our experiences cognitively meaningful.[216] Judgement, therefore, requires systematic practice[217] and, in the case of the philosopher, inevitable withdrawal from everyday preoccupations and the crowds of people they usually involve.[218] Being in communion, through memory, with the things through which the god acquires his divinity (*Phdr.* 249c6–7: πρὸς οἷσπερ θεὸς ὢν θεῖός ἐστιν), the philosopher dedicates himself to the rites of virtue, as a kind of mental and moral purification.[219] Accordingly, he experiences ecstasy:[220] "Becoming detached (ἐξιστάμενος) from human concerns and veering toward the divine (πρὸς τῷ θείῳ), is chastised by the many as mad (ὡς παρακινῶν),[221] and although he is inspired (ἐνθουσιάζων), he eludes the many (λέληθεν τοὺς πολλούς)" (*Phdr.* 249d1–4). Plato also comments on the unjust prejudice against philosophers at *Republic* 488e1–501a7, where Adeimantus and Socrates agree that they ought to resort to extended metaphors to explain why and how the true philosopher is systematically excluded from public life in their society,[222] while the citizens side with sophists.[223] At *Symposium* 216d9–e6, Alcibiades uses the qualities that inspire this popular prejudice to praise Socrates' *sōphrosynē*: Socrates despises beauty, wealth, and honors, that is, the material possessions that most people value and crave, focusing solely on his pursuit of virtue. Socrates admits as much at *Apology* 29e7–30a2, where he rebukes his fellow citizens because they "attach little importance to the most important things and greater importance to inferior things" (ὀνειδιῶ ὅτι τὰ πλείστου ἄξια περὶ ἐλαχίστου ποιεῖται, τὰ δὲ φαυλότερα περὶ πλείονος).[224] He then outlines his mission of being a "gadfly" to the Athenians (*Apol.* 30e) and hints at the prejudice he has suffered at their hands, which had eventually culminated in the ruthless mobilization of the state against him during his trial.[225] Clearly, then, not only is there public misperception of the experiences that philosophers undergo, but metaphors seem to offer a fruitful way to try to communicate them.

This is reminiscent of the ancient anecdote about Democritus whom his fellow countrymen feared had lost his mind because he viewed *them* as miserable and mad on account of their fixation with attaining superficial goals such as wealth and social status. Democritus was famously exonerated by Hippocrates as an extremely wise man with exceptional perception (Δημόκριτον γὰρ εἶδον, ἄνδρα σοφώτατον, σωφρονίζειν ἀνθρώπους μοῦνον δυνατώτατον).[226] Notably, however, in Xenophon's *Memorabilia* it is other intellectuals whom Socrates accuses of madness! In line with his rejection of Anaxagoras' theories in the *Apology* and the *Phaedo*,[227] Socrates claims that those who study divine things are mad (*Mem.* 1.1.11: τοὺς φροντίζοντας τὰ τοιαῦτα *μωραίνοντας ἀπεδείκνυε*); by speculating about the divine,[228] such thinkers exemplify disregard for human affairs (ἢ τὰ μὲν ἀνθρώπινα παρέντες, τὰ δαιμόνια δὲ σκοποῦντες) and waste their time enveloped in hopeless disagreements with one another:

> As some madmen (τῶν τε γὰρ μαινομένων) have no fear of danger and others are afraid where there is nothing to be afraid of, as some will do or say anything in a crowd with no sense of shame, while others shrink even from going abroad among men, some respect neither temple nor altar nor any other sacred thing, others worship stones or pieces of wood or wild animals, so is it, he said, with those who worry about the nature of the universe. (Xen. *Mem.* 1.1.14)

Fixated on discrediting each other, such theorists resemble madmen (ἀλλὰ τοῖς μαινομένοις ὁμοίως διακεῖσθαι πρὸς ἀλλήλους),[229] unable to accept the limited abilities of the human intellect.[230] Socrates, therefore, is well-versed in the language of irrationality and its manifold paradigms, including those that might seem germane to his own.

In this light, Plato's explicit reversal of conventional depictions of Bacchic rituals is hard to miss. Plato does not object to these rituals, which he sees as a legitimate way of challenging our cognitive limits, but to the ways in which they are (in his opinion) misunderstood, misrepresented, and misapplied at the civic level. Plato sees hunger, thirst for wine, and the erotic desire epitomized by *baccheia* as arising in "the irrational and appetitive" part of the soul, which is "related to certain gratifications and pleasures" (*Resp.* 439d8–9: ἀλόγιστόν τε καὶ ἐπιθυμητικόν, πληρώσεών τινων καὶ ἡδονῶν ἑταῖρον).[231] While acknowledging the presence of desires that humans must satisfy, Plato insists that our response should not be impulsive, for fear of succumbing to irrational indulgence.[232] The Corybantic dances which Plato compares at *Laws* 790e2–4 to "the cures of the mad Bacchantes, that make use of this motion, together with dance and music" (αἱ τῶν ἐκφρόνων βακχειῶν ἰάσεις, ταύτῃ τῇ τῆς κινήσεως ἅμα χορείᾳ καὶ μούσῃ χρώμεναι) can, according to Belfiore,[233] allow their practitioners to restore order and harmony in their souls. Belfiore argues that the Corybantic *choreia* follows dithyrambic rhythm patterns, which regulate and calm down the manic state of souls in disorder.[234] Yet, Socrates also employs *choreia* in the *Laws* as a metaphor for misguided performances of civic ethos: hence, at *Laws* 815c1–5 cited above, Plato revisits the metaphor he employed in the *Symposium* to clarify that pseudo-Bacchic dancing, which involves drunken imitation of the so-called Nymphs and Pans and Silenoi and Satyrs, is not suitable for citizens (*Leg.* 815d2: οὐκ ἔστι/ πολιτικὸν τοῦτο τῆς ὀρχήσεως τὸ γένος). As he explains (667e–670b), if citizens lack the ability to judge the correct type of inebriation, they participate in this process without clear understanding of its goal and can be easily led astray. Furthermore, Socrates had earlier compared the Corybantic rites to the "confusing verbal gyrations" of the sophists Euthydemus and Dionysodorus[235] in the *Euthydemus*, written in 384 BCE—a metaphor partly derived from the impact that music and musical teaching had on ancient rhetorical theory.[236]

Wine, then, just like *baccheia*, does not *transform* consciousness but is a means of stimulating it and of revealing its state. Nevertheless, because of its heating properties, wine can cause older people "to acquire, temporarily, the fiery and mad disposition of the young,"[237] just as Cadmus and Teiresias are rendered "irrational" during their participation in the Bacchic rites. Thus, drinking provides a metaphor for one's ability to overcome distractions in our search for truth. Accordingly, in Xenophon's *Symposium*, Socrates is portrayed as saying: "Do not be surprized at my plain speaking (εἰ δὲ λαμυρώτερον λέγω, μὴ θαυμάζετε): the wine incites me (συνεπαίρει) and the love that ever dwells with me spurs me on (κεντρίζει) to say frankly (παρρησιάζεσθαι) what I think about its rival" (*Symp.* 8.24). Inebriation, therefore, despite being constantly subject to abuse, is a means of and a metaphor for retuning our sensibilities. Besides musing over the unpopularity of the philosophers, Plato's concern seems to be the correct way of understanding and achieving sublimity, a preoccupation that lies at the heart of his philosophy[238] and accords with his objections regarding pseudo-mysteries—a problem already noted by Heraclitus.[239] Hence, at *Symposium* 211b6–c1, Diotima specifies that "When someone . . . having climbed above these [fragmented images of the beautiful] begins to perceive the beautiful (τὸ καλὸν ἄρχηται καθορᾶν) by applying pederasty *correctly* (διὰ τὸ ὀρθῶς παιδεραστεῖν), he may almost get a feel of the final goal. For this is the *correct* way of going about (τὸ ὀρθῶς ἰέναι) or being induced by someone else to love-matters." As we saw in chapter 1, Plato returns to this preoccupation in the *Phaedo* (69c3–d2) where he characterizes those "who practice philosophy correctly" as Bacchoi but also in the *Laws* where he insists on the "correct" use of wine during the symposion.[240]

Concluding Remarks

The metaphor of Socratic inebriation draws on medical insights to highlight the exceptional ability of wine to enhance or destroy the balance of our bodily humors, which in turn affects our cognitive potential. This is a view foreshadowed by Heraclitus, who argued that "a dry gleam of light is the wisest and best soul" (DK B118 = D103: αυγὴ ξηρὴ ψυχὴ σοφωτάτη καὶ ἀρίστη),[241] and already explored artistically in Euripides' *Bacchae*. The concept of balance between elements that determines health in the Hippocratic tradition had a major impact on Socrates' concept of *sōphrosynē*. People of hot constitutions are intellectually acute and, importantly, able to generate better and more accurate representations of reality. Wine, then, can improve our natural constitution by heating our blood, allowing us to restore it to an ideal harmony;[242] in this state, our mind can achieve illumination and begin the process of recollection (ἀνάμνησις).[243] These discourses about irrationality, as an inextricable part of Plato's cultural milieu, are reflected in the *Symposium*, especially in Alcibiades' references to Socrates' imperviousness not just to wine but also to cold. Furthermore, as we saw in the *Laws* (see 649d6–9, cited above) drinking too much is listed as one of the excesses associated with lack of self-control and emotional indulgence.[244] In response, Plato recommends a "playful test of wine" (649d11–e1: τῆς ἐν οἴνῳ βασάνου καὶ παιδιᾶς),[245] a "cheap and harmless tool" (649d9–e1: εὐτελῆ τε καὶ ἀσινεστέραν . . . μηχανὴν)[246] by means of which—provided it is used carefully (649e2: μετ' εὐλαβείας)—we can "examine" and "exercise" (649d11: λαμβάνειν πεῖραν . . . μελετᾶν) the disposition of the soul (650a4–5: ἦθος ψυχῆς θεάσασθαι).

As well as distinguishing the symptomatology of inebriation in medical terms, Plato also attempts to graft the metaphor of Socratic inebriation to an established idea of the symposion as representative of civic ethics. Thus, in the following chapter I discuss the gradual and often agonistic association, from the archaic period to Plato, of wine with civic ethos. The closer reading of the relevant passages in the *Laws* that I undertake in that chapter can afford us a better understanding of the civic models displayed in the *Symposium*. Establishing the civic importance of wine drinking (and its attendant civic *theōria*) reveals the centrality of the symposion as the ideal space, both physical and mental, for individuals and groups to learn and perform their civic values. Plato is not satisfied with simply reiterating the need for moderate wine consumption and self-control; he relies on the didactic power of metaphors to illustrate Socrates' extraordinary perception and sense of virtue versus the qualities of those who epitomize intellectual "drunkenness" or "folly"—natural philosophers such as Anaxagoras, sophists such as Euthydemus, and politicians offended by Socrates' *elenchus*.[247] In the *Symposium*, Plato uses Alcibiades' drunkenness to illustrate the intoxicating effects of poets and sophists on promising young citizens, a theme systematically explored in the *Republic*.[248] By assuming the roles of the poet, prophet, lover, and (crucially) Bacchant, Socrates aims to distinguish between other, deceptive types of trance and Socratic enquiry, the only true and reliable way of enhancing human perception.[249] Thus, Plato establishes Socratic inebriation as the most authoritative way of debating the veracity of transcendental experiences.[250] From this perspective,[251] Socrates' historicity becomes less important, as Plato's reception in later periods will be firmly fixed on the persona of Socrates,[252] as a sage, a saint, and crucially a citizen.

Chapter 3

Drinking to Wisdom

The Civic Aspects of Platonic *Baccheia*

ἄοινος ἀεὶ μέθη καὶ σκυθρωπὴ ταῖς τῶν ἀπαιδεύτων ἐνοικεῖ ψυχαῖς

—Plutarch, *quaest. conv.* 716a4–5[1]

As argued so far, Plato employs inebriation as a new structural metaphor to express the suprahuman state of consciousness that philosophical enquiry can bestow—a state akin to ritual, erotic, poetic, and even
pathological madness, though distinct from all of them. Plato carefully
navigates contemporary views (medical, philosophical, literary) on human
cognition to defend the credibility of Socratic inebriation. It is necessary
to defend this kind of inebriation and set its parameters so it can be
accepted in a civic context. In an echo of Heraclitus' concerns about the
limited perception of the many, Plato must persuade[2] his audiences that
philosophical insight and Socratic inebriation fulfill valuable civic roles in
the ideal city;[3] thus, he must deal with the unjust marginalization of the
philosopher, whose eccentric insights about society attract ridicule from
those who, like comic playwrights, sophists, and corrupt politicians, thrive
on deceiving the average intellect.[4] The metaphor of wine drinking, then,
already a culturally accepted and encoded practice, offered Plato a unique
tool with which to embed profound experiences in a civic context and to
illustrate the mendacity of his opponents.

In this chapter, I discuss the cultural history of the symposion as a
locus of political debate, where the boundaries between different social

groups but also styles of discourse were negotiated; then, I examine how Plato utilizes the conventional tropes surrounding wine drinking in the *Symposium*,[5] the *Phaedrus*, and the *Laws*, to sketch a civic *ethos* in line with the Bacchic *sōphrosynē* exemplified by the followers of Dionysus in Euripides' *Bacchae*.[6] The larger metaphor at work in both the *Laws* and the *Symposium* is a comparison between a drinking party and the city,[7] a metaphor familiar from Euripides' seminal negotiation of the role of Dionysiac cult in the *polis*[8] as well as from Aristophanic comedy.[9] Since in the *Laws*, Plato systematically revisits "arguments and images from earlier dialogues,"[10] and since the ideal educational system envisaged there undeniably involves wine drinking, I examine the educational tenets of the *Laws* before "looking back" at the *Symposium* and, where relevant, the *Phaedrus*.[11] Especially in the *Symposium*, symposiastic performances aim to showcase philosophy, in contrast to poetic or political striving, as promoting the ideal civic ethos.[12] Thus, I revisit Aristophanes' representation in the *Symposium*, emphasizing his poetic "drunkenness," hinted by Socrates early in the dialogue when he states that Aristophanes' "whole occupation is concerned with Dionysus and Aphrodite, wine and sex" (*Symp.* 177e3–4: περὶ Διόνυσον καὶ Ἀφροδίτην πᾶσα ἡ διατριβή).[13] In my view, the comical depiction of Socrates in Aristophanes' *Clouds*[14] receives a powerful response in Plato's staging of a playful yet rhetorically insuperable Socrates in both the *Symposium* and the *Laws*;[15] accordingly, Aristophanic humor that might otherwise be seen as the kind of stylish banter perfectly suited to a drinking party is recharacterized as sophistic hyperbole. The uniqueness of Socrates' inebriation within his social order is further emphasized by Alcibiades' speech, which is placed last in the *Symposium* as an example of brazen alcohol misuse. This final speech encourages readers to appreciate all the earlier speeches as different styles or stages of flawed symposiastic discourse and hence as variant, inappropriate stages of "drunkenness." To support my argument, I draw additional insights from the *Protagoras* and the *Republic*, where Plato is also preoccupied with civic education and its distortion by sophists and poets. Finally, I return to the *Laws* to discuss Plato's attempt to accommodate the Bacchic insight of the philosophers in the ideal city of Magnesia.

The *Polis* and the Politics of Wine Drinking

Plato is not the first thinker to make the connection between drinking wine, composing music, or performing lines of poetry, and engaging in discourse.[16] Drinking wine had been a staple part of ancient Greek social life since at least the Bronze Age.[17] Its political context, however, was largely shaped during the archaic period, which had set an influential example of the symposion as a test of character reflected in one's ability to maintain witty yet decorous discourse without getting drunk. During the Archaic and early Classical periods there was a stage of "fermentation," when *poleis* sought to establish their internal networking systems and their distinctive civic ethos, bargained as much through factional alliances as through boisterous dissent. The verses of Alcaeus, blasting his opponents (frs. 72, 332, 348 Lobel-Page/L142) or lamenting his civic situation (frs. 70, 130), come immediately to mind. Private symposia, especially in the affluent societies of the Aegean islands, offered an increasingly important if informal forum for this process of discussion and dissent. Drinking wine acquired a prominently political character, especially as the emerging Greek polities started to engage more systematically with the cultural projections of the Homeric material, including its models of political leadership.[18] In the Homeric world, the prominence of wine in delivering hospitality (*xenia*) and firming up alliances among the upper classes—as in the embassy to Achilles in the *Iliad* (Hom. *Il.* 9.175–181, 202–204, 224, 484–495, 705–706) and the episode of the Phaeacians who host shipwrecked Odysseus (*Od.* 6.)—is instructive, as is the juxtaposition of this model with the uncouth drunkenness of the Cyclops in book 9 of the *Odyssey*.[19] Archilochus' iambics (fr. 124b West/L259) and several examples from the Theognidean corpus (31–34, 971–972, 981–982, etc.)[20] also reflect a sixth century BCE symposiastic culture revolving around local sociopolitical intrigues and the ethos of community leaders.[21] In this environment, wine drinking as an essential part of symposiastic etiquette provides an unexpected yet effective testing ground for the performance of one's ethos. Despite the strong urge to drink copiously, often reiterated in archaic poetry,[22] losing control because of intoxication was regarded as a sign of an ignoble, unsophisticated character.[23] According to Hipponax, "those who drink neat wine have few wits about them" (fr. 67 West; ὀλίγα φρονέουσιν οἱ χάλιν πεπωκότες). This sentiment is echoed by Theognis, who observes that "wine makes woozy the mind of the foolish and sensible man alike whenever he drinks beyond his limit" (497–498; ἄφρονος ἀνδρὸς ὁμῶς καὶ σώφρονος οἶνος, ὅταν δὴ πίνῃ ὑπὲρ μέτρον, κοῦφον ἔθηκε νόον).[24]

To avoid such embarrassment in front of one's fellow citizens, the poets prescribe moderation.[25] According to Theognis (line 478), the preferred condition for a drinker is to be "neither sober nor too drunk." The poem is worth citing in its entirety, as it perfectly encapsulates the ethical concerns that informed the drinking culture of the day:[26]

> I have reached the point where wine drinking is most pleasant (χαριέστατος) for a man, for I am neither sober nor too drunk (οὔτε τι γὰρ νήφων οὔτε λίην μεθύων). Whoever exceeds his limit of drink has no longer control of his tongue or his mind; he says reckless things which are disgraceful for the sober and is not ashamed of anything he does when drunk. Though he was sensible before, then he is a fool (τὸ πρὶν ἐὼν σώφρων, τότε νήπιος). Aware of this, don't drink wine to excess (ὑπερβολάδην), but either rise before you get drunk—don't let your belly overpower you as if you were a wretched hired help for the day[27]—or stay without drinking. But you say, 'Fill it up!' This is always your foolish chatter; that's why you get drunk. . . . That man is truly unbeatable (ἀνίκητος) who after drinking many cups will say nothing foolish (μάταιον). When you stay by the mixing bowl, make good conversation (εὖ μυθεῖσθε), long avoiding quarrels with one another and speaking openly to one and all alike. This is how a symposium turns out to be not half bad (χοὔτως συμπόσιον γίνεται οὐκ ἄχαρι). (Thgn. 477–496)

As Papakonstantinou notes,[28] "the moderate drinking habits of some upper-class sympotic drinkers and audiences were contrasted to the 'debased' excessive drinking practices of individuals from the lower social orders as well to the real or imaginary drinking attitudes of foreigners." Notwithstanding the issues with the scholarly assumption that archaic societies relied on a rigid class hierarchy, which appears to be a later development, the two models of drinking are clearly set out as being indicative of the moral substance of their advocates and point to a hierarchy of exclusion. In this context, "noble" men (defined on the basis of hereditary status, wealth, or military might) ought to be able to harness the dangerous aspects of wine drinking, employing them just enough to benefit from wine's liberating and inspiring effects[29] without risking social ridicule.

The archaic drinking etiquette with its Homeric overtones was especially entrenched in the minds of subsequent generations in Athens thanks to the maxims of Solon.[30] Solon defends the "Greek way" of drinking mixed (as opposed to unmixed) wine, a practice adopted at Athenian symposia as a marker by which to discern Greeks from barbarians.[31] Solon's advocation of moderation in drinking and its relation to the civic ethos is attested in Middle Comedy, where he is portrayed by Alexis as discussing symposiastic *topoi* (*PCG* 9). Although no explicit reference to drunkenness survives in Alexis' badly damaged text, the motif is also likely implied in the verses cited by Demosthenes in his *On the Embassy* (19.254–256). Here, the speaker cites Solon's elegiac verses referring to a city plagued by subservience to money and injustice; among the many symptoms that manifest the citizens' erroneous judgement and moral malaise is that "they do not know how to restrain excess or to conduct in an orderly and peaceful manner the festivities of the banquet that are at hand" (= poem 4, lines 9–10 in L258: οὐ . . . ἐπίστανται κατέχειν κόρον οὐδὲ παρούσας/ εὐφροσύνας κοσμεῖν δαιτὸς ἐν ἡσυχίῃ). The Solonian emphasis on "the orderly dinner/symposion" that functions "as a parallel to the order of relations between people in society"[32] explains why Plato in the fourth century BCE appreciates the symposion as the ideal setting for negotiating virtue.[33] Plato reiterates the Solonian focus on the virtue of the individual as a major prerequisite of political robustness, now realigned to tackle the challenge of sophists who seek to undermine the division between the noble by birth (*agathoi/esthloi*) and those who could afford excellence (*arētē*) through education.[34] Plato, despite his professed hostility to mimetic arts, was a thorough reader of Homer and archaic poetry[35] and incorporated the metaphor of drinking wine into his dialogues as an illustration of spiritual elevation and moral decline. The opening lines of Solon's fr. 26 offer an obvious example of this enduring motif in ancient Greek thought; interestingly, Plutarch introduces Solon's poem with a reference to *Laws* 839b,[36] where Plato claims that the law should be able to inspire virtue across all aspects of life:[37] "But now the works of the Cyprus-born [goddess] and of Dionysus and the Muses are dear to me; they bring men good cheer (τίθησ' . . . εὐφροσύνας), as though after the storm and stress of loving boys I placed my life in the calm of marriage and philosophy (ἔν τινι γαλήνῃ τῇ περὶ γάμον καὶ φιλοσοφίαν)" (Plut. *Amat.* 751e). Solon here anticipates Plato's analysis and comparison of erotic, divine, and poetic *mania* in the *Phaedrus*;[38] the speeches of the guests advocating for such forms of *mania* in the *Symposium* are part of the same storm that troubles Solon's civic sensibilities in the fragment cited above, since they all produce erroneous and irrational understandings of reality.[39] Only Socrates' continuous practice of self-control—a feature that also defines him as a speaker and as a drinker—allows him to approach the truth in a consistent manner.[40] Thus, Plato invites us to reflect on the drinking paradigms he presents and the versions of truth they produce, urging us to understand them as part of his broader metaphor.[41]

Metaphors of Civic Virtue in the *Laws*: The "Test of the Wine"

Socrates' habit of conducting his enquiries in a playful style[42] is consistent with the witty ambiance of the ideal symposium. In his *Memorabilia*, Xenophon provides a relevant example of this half-joking style, while relating how Socrates came to be accused of being defiant of the law.[43] Critias and Charicles, we are told, had passed an ad hoc law that "made it illegal to teach the art of words" (*Mem.* 1.2.31: ἐν τοῖς νόμοις ἔγραψε λόγων τέχνην μὴ διδάσκειν), which in effect forbade Socrates from conversing with young people; Socrates, then, seeks clarification from them about acceptable arguments in case he accidentally "contravenes the rules through ignorance" (*Mem.* 1.2.34: ὅπως δὲ μὴ δι᾽ ἄγνοιαν λάθω τι παρανομήσας): "Do you think that the art of words from which you bid me abstain is associated with sound or unsound reasoning (σὺν τοῖς ὀρθῶς λεγομένοις εἶναι νομίζοντες ἢ σὺν τοῖς μὴ ὀρθῶς)? For if with sound, then clearly I must abstain from sound reasoning; but if with unsound, clearly I must try to reason soundly (πειρατέον ὀρθῶς λέγειν)" (*Mem.* 1.2.34). Despite the gravity of the situation, the exchange that follows between Socrates and his prosecutors, both involved with the Sparta-sponsored Thirty Tyrants, which was led by Critias (Socrates' former student),[44] is full of disclaimers and second thoughts, more reminiscent of a comic script than a record of legal procedures—which, in my view, further confirms Critias and Charicles' confusion, a state of mind akin to that of the drunk and/or the mad. Despite Critias' firm advocation of the moderate Spartan style of drinking,[45] Xenophon insinuates that Critias was well-versed in *kottabos*, a popular drinking game probably originating in Sicily and associated with excess;[46] by showing how his words contradict his actions, Xenophon implies that Critias has little of the *sōphrosynē* that he advocates for others.[47] This kind of debauched behavior, as Plato argues in the *Republic*,[48] is a reflection of a tyrannical character.[49]

Humor is a weapon that requires dexterous handling. In the *Hellenica* (2.3.56), Xenophon relates how Critias condemns to death by hemlock another former associate Theramenes in a scenario that clearly evokes Socrates' situation. Upon drinking the hemlock, Theramenes, in a final act of scorn for his adversary, makes a toast, pretending to play *kottabos*, and adds: "may this be for beautiful Critias" (Κριτίᾳ τοῦτ᾽ ἔστω τῷ καλῷ).[50] Theramenes provides a remarkable parallel for Socrates not just in terms of his prosecution by the same tyrant but also in showing that ridicule is a powerful weapon against such attacks. Like Alcibiades, who is greeted as *kalos* in *Alcibiades* I (113b), and Callias, a great admirer of the sophists (*Apol.* 20a4–6) who is greeted as *kalos* in the *Protagoras* (362a), Critias, an accomplished poet and sophist, has twisted and compromised a fundamental civic ideal to serve his self-interest, despite his boisterous claims of virtue.[51] Thus, Theramenes' toast carefully modifies the civic ideal of *kalos kagathos* by leaving out its latter half, inviting comparison with Socrates who, across Xenophon's works, systematically teaches *kalokagathia*.[52] By exploiting preexisting cultural norms around the symposion as a place in which *kalokagathia* is demonstrated, Xenophon integrates the example of Socrates into the civic structure of the *polis* and criticizes Critias in the same breath. Critias' tendency to embrace the sophistic style and hide his penchant for drunken carousals is also evident in his critique of Archilochus for "speaking very ill of himself" (Aelian *VH* 10.13: ὅτι κάκιστα ἑαυτὸν εἶπεν . . .) by admitting terrible (yet true) details about himself.[53] Critias' attitude echoes the sophistic argument that because everyone has some knowledge of justice, anyone who publicly confesses to being unjust is mad—a view that Plato depicts Socrates as ridiculing in the *Protagoras*.[54]

Even more explicitly than Xenophon, Plato too uses symposiastic norms as a background to the discussion of civic ethos—most prominently in the *Symposium*, but throughout his other dialogues as well. Although at *Theaetetus* 173d4–6, the philosopher is explicitly said to not even dream about "the hassle and meetings of political clubs for offices, banquets and revels with singing girls" (σπουδαὶ δὲ ἑταιριῶν ἐπ᾽ ἀρχὰς καὶ σύνοδοι καὶ δεῖπνα καὶ σὺν αὐλητρίσι κῶμοι, οὐδὲ ὄναρ πράττειν προσίσταται αὐτοῖς), Plato is more lenient in the *Protagoras*. There, Socrates reproaches the "uneducated," whom he qualifies as those unable to hold a conversation over wine by relying on their own voice and arguments (*Prt.* 347c6–d2: διὰ τὸ μὴ δύνασθαι ἀλλήλοις δι᾽ ἑαυτῶν συνεῖναι ἐν τῷ πότῳ μηδὲ διὰ τῆς ἑαυτῶν φωνῆς καὶ τῶν λόγων τῶν ἑαυτῶν ὑπὸ ἀπαιδευσίας). Comparing discussions of poetry to "the drinking parties of the common people of the market" (347c4–6: τὸ περὶ ποιήσεως διαλέγεσθαι ὁμοιότατον εἶναι τοῖς συμποσίοις τοῖς τῶν φαύλων καὶ ἀγοραίων ἀνθρώπων), Socrates counter-proposes the polished conversational style of the gentry:

> But where the fellow-drinkers are noble and educated (καλοὶ κἀγαθοὶ συμπόται καὶ πεπαιδευμένοι) . . . they are able to converse with each other . . . through their own voice (διὰ τῆς αὐτῶν φωνῆς), by speaking and listening in turns and in an orderly manner, even if they drink a great deal of wine (κἂν πάνυ πολὺν οἶνον πίωσιν). . . . They *do not need another voice, not even that of poets* (**οὐδὲν δέονται ἀλλοτρίας φωνῆς οὐδὲ ποιητῶν**), who cannot be questioned (ἀδυνατοῦσι ἐξελέγξαι) on the meaning of what they say, and when people bring them into the discussion . . . they end up debating a matter that they cannot cross-examine. But the people who can converse with one another, taking turns to test each other *through their own speeches* (**ἐν τοῖς ἑαυτῶν λόγοις**), they avoid such gatherings. It seems to me that you and I should rather emulate these people, and leaving aside the poets, we should make our speeches to each other ourselves, putting to test the truth and our own selves (τῆς ἀληθείας καὶ ἡμῶν αὐτῶν πεῖραν λαμβάνοντας). (*Prt.* 347d4–348a6)

Furthermore, in the *Philebus* Plato illustrates our struggle for inner balance with the metaphor of the wine pourer: "We are like wine-pourers (οἰνοχόοις), and beside us are fountains—that of pleasure may be likened (ἀπεικάζοι) to a fount of honey,[55] and the sober, wineless fount of wisdom (τὴν δὲ τῆς φρονήσεως νηφαντικὴν καὶ ἄοινον) to one of pure, health-giving water—of which we must do our best to mix as well as possible" (*Phil.* 61c5–8). Similarly, in the *Republic* Plato stipulates that symposia ought to be harnessed by law lest citizens embrace tyrannical ways,[56] especially since only few individuals can suppress their urge to drink by the power of reason (ἐκ λογισμοῦ) so to overcome the afflictions and illnesses that threaten the soul.[57]

Plato returns to the theme of balancing pleasure, pain, and wine in the *Laws*, where Socratic virtue is projected as "this *symphônia* of appropriate education, rational account, and metacognitive endorsement of the soul's disposition."[58] Adopting a series of metaphors, for example that of the soul as a city,[59] Plato advocates a similar understanding of virtue in the *Laws* as the attempt to find equilibrium between the experiences of pleasure and pain. The Bacchic context of Plato's discussion of virtue in the *Laws* is emphasized through the metaphor of the human soul as divine puppet (*Leg.* 644d7–8 θαῦμα . . . θεῖον),[60] "whether a plaything in the hands of the gods or some serious experiment of theirs" (. . . ὡς παίγνιον ἐκείνων εἴτε ὡς σπουδῇ τινι συνεστηκός). Susceptible to passions, the soul is tugged in every direction over a line that divides goodness and badness (644b1–5: τὰ πάθη ἐν ἡμῖν . . . ἀλλήλαις ἀνθέλκουσιν ἐναντίαι οὖσαι ἐπ' ἐναντίας πράξεις, οὗ δὴ διωρισμένη ἀρετὴ καὶ κακία κεῖται). To illustrate how passions render the soul "drunk" and/or "mad," Plato further proposes getting the puppet of his tale drunk (645d1–2: προσφέροντες τῷ θαύματι τούτῳ τὴν μέθην).[61] The puppets, called θαύματα, seem to share their essence with Dionysus, whose wondrous effect on his followers is typically described as θαῦμα, as Euripides repeatedly reminds us in the *Bacchae*.[62] Thus, Plato urges the Magnesians to establish laws that promote living in accordance with a sense of inner harmony (645b) and *sōphrosynē*, that is essentially Bacchic.[63] Plato also refers to humans as playthings of the gods at *Laws* 803c6–7 (ὅπερ εἴπομεν ἔμπροσθεν, θεοῦ τι παίγνιον εἶναι μεμηχανημένον) and at 804b3 (θαύματα ὄντες), where he advises the Magnesians to "live their lives playing at certain pastimes—sacrificing, singing and dancing, so as to be able to win Heaven's favour and to repel our foes and vanquish them in fight" (803d10–e4: παίζοντά ἐστιν διαβιωτέον τινὰς δὴ παιδιάς, θύοντα καὶ ᾄδοντα καὶ ὀρχούμενον, ὥστε τοὺς μὲν θεοὺς ἵλεως αὑτῷ παρασκευάζειν δυνατὸν εἶναι, τοὺς δ' ἐχθροὺς ἀμύνεσθαι καὶ νικᾶν μαχόμενον).[64]

Plato imagines entering a poetic competition with his puppet show against remarkable rivals such as Homer but also tragic and comic playwrights; his show, which represents "the truest tragedy" (817b5–6: τραγῳδίαν τὴν ἀληθεστάτην), is designed to equip the city for the ultimate challenge of life (cf. 831a2–3: τὴν πόλιν ὅλην εἰς τὸν ἀληθινὸν ἀγῶνα διὰ βίου παρασκευάζῃ χρησίμην); being optimistic, Plato reckons he has good hope of winning the competition (658b10–c1: θαύματα ἐπιδεικνὺς μάλιστ' ἂν νικᾶν ἡγοῖτο). In the *Laws*, therefore, Plato allows himself to be inspired by Dionysus, the divine leader of the most senior Chorus in Magnesia, in a way that differs from current-day dithyrambs composed in the name of the god (700b5).[65] Plato espouses the Dionysus of nursing mothers who lull their children to sleep with a kind of Corybantic charm, rocking them in their arms and soothing them with a crooning song (790d5–e4). Concerned about the poor condition of our souls,[66] he hopes that, like the shaking puppets, we can be lulled "into a sound state of mind" (791b2: ἀντὶ μανικῶν ἡμῖν διαθέσεων ἕξεις ἔμφρονας ἔχειν) "by employing a combination of dance and song, like the cures of the ecstatic Bacchants" (790e2–4: καθάπερ ἡ τῶν ἐκφρόνων βακχειῶν ἰάσεις, ταύτῃ τῇ τῆς κινήσεως ἅμα χορείᾳ καὶ μούσῃ χρώμεναι).

The analogy of the drunken puppet also provides the framework for Plato's discussion in the *Laws* of the "correct use of wine-drinking sessions" (652a5: ἐν τῇ κατ᾽ ὀρθὸν χρείᾳ τῆς ἐν οἴνῳ συνουσίας), a matter that "fully merits prolonged discussion" (645c4–8: τὸ περὶ τῆς ἐν τοῖς οἴνοις διατριβῆς . . . τοῦ μήκους . . . οὐκ ἀπάξιον). As part of Magnesia's educational program, Plato insists that the observance of the laws ought to be entrusted to guardians (νομοφύλακες) who would act as "calm and sober commanders over the un-sober (671d6–10: τοὺς ἀθορύβους καὶ νήφοντας τῶν μὴ νηφόντων στρατηγούς), for to fight drunkenness without these would be more daunting than to fight enemies without calm leaders" (χωρὶς μέθῃ διαμάχεσθαι δεινότερον ἢ πολεμίοις εἶναι μὴ μετὰ ἀρχόντων ἀθορύβων).[67] Drinking sessions, as the speakers in the *Laws* know from their own experience of present-day symposia, tend to become boisterous (671a6–7: **θορυβώδης** μέν που ὁ σύλλογος ὁ τοιοῦτος ἐξ ἀνάγκης προϊ-ούσης τῆς πόσεως; 640c1–2: ἔστιν δέ γε ἡ τοιαύτη συνουσία, εἴπερ ἔσται μετὰ μέθης, **οὐκ ἀθόρυβος**).[68] Accordingly, revisiting an(other) image he had already introduced in the *Republic*,[69] Plato includes a proviso for a sober symposiarch at drinking bouts:[70] "Then should the commander we set over drunken men be sober and wise (νήφοντά τε καὶ σοφὸν ἄρχοντα μεθυόντων δεῖ καθιστάναι), rather than the opposite? For a commander of drunkards who was himself drunken, young, and foolish would be very lucky if he escaped doing some serious mischief" (*Leg.* 640d4–7). Plato then subsumes symposia under the rubric of "right education" (653a1–2: ὀρθὴν παιδείαν) and its salvific role in the ideal city.[71] We have our first taste of education, he claims, when we learn as children to distinguish pleasure from pain (653a6–7); but we ought to cultivate this initial sense of judgement as we grow up and can only hope to acquire wisdom and true opinions by the time that we reach old age (653a9–11: φρόνησιν δὲ καὶ ἀληθεῖς δόξας . . . καὶ πρὸς τὸ γῆρας παρεγένετο). At *Laws* 653b1–c4 we read:[72]

"Education" (παιδείαν), then, I define as the virtue that first comes to children: for when pleasure and love, and pain and hatred are bred rightly in the souls of those who are yet unable to grasp things by reason, after acquiring reason, they consent in accordance with it that they have been rightly trained in appropriate habits;[73] this consent, considered in its entirety, is virtue (ἡ συμφωνία σύμπασα μὲν ἀρετή),[74] while the part of it that is rightly nourished in respect of pleasures and pains . . . if you were to mark this part off in your definition and call it "education," you would be giving it, in my opinion, its right name (ὀρθῶς ἂν προσαγορεύοις).

Virtue, Plato goes on to argue, requires the ability to anticipate pain (in the form of shame) and its opposite (daring).[75] Bouts of drinking are thus a useful educational tool, as they expose the drinker to a situation in which he is strongly tempted to act in a shameful manner. Because wine acts as a "potion" that artificially lowers one's sense of shame, it allows the educator to test a student's natural capacity for self-control and the student to practice restraint in the face of temptation. This process, as Belfiore has argued, follows the principles of allopathic medicine and attempts to produce moderation through excess by teaching citizens to manage their drinking so to avoid public humiliation. Plato referred to this kind of civic training as the "Inspection of Dionysus" (650a1: τῆς τοῦ Διονύσου θεωρίας), thus introducing *baccheia* as a prerequisite of contemplation/examination that in Magnesia is no longer the prerogative of philosophers but ought to be practiced by all citizens. In what follows, I will refer to it as the "Test of the Wine."

Plato reiterates his concerns around moderation at *Laws* 667c6–7, where he is preoccupied with "the correctness and utility, and goodness and nobleness" [produced by the truth of learning] (τὴν δὲ ὀρθότητα καὶ τὴν ὠφελίαν καὶ τὸ εὖ καὶ τὸ καλῶς).[76] Taking his start from our innate ability for "the pleasurable perception of rhythm and harmony" (653e8–9: τὴν ἔνρυθμόν τε καὶ ἐναρμόνιον αἴσθησιν μεθ᾽ ἡδονῆς), Socrates argues that choric performances are "representations of character" (655d5: μιμήματα τρόπων)[77] and that citizens ought to be instructed early on in life how to achieve this harmony for the benefit of the city.[78] To uphold the standards for the criterion of music—which is pleasure (658e8: δεῖν τὴν μουσικὴν ἡδονῇ κρίνεσθαι)[79]—cities ought to appoint their best citizens as judges of it: "But I would regard as nearly the noblest the music which pleases the best and adequately educated men (τοὺς βελτίστους καὶ ἱκανῶς πεπαιδευμένους), and as especially noblest the music that pleases the one man who excels in virtue and education; and we say that the judges of these matters need virtue because they also need to possess, apart from judiciousness, above all courage" (*Leg.* 658e9–659a5). Thus, the type of music that possesses a "natural correctness" lies at the heart of a stateman's agenda and must be strictly legislated (657a7–10: περὶ μουσικὴν . . . δυνατὸν ἄρ᾽ ἦν . . . νομοθετεῖσθαι βεβαίως θαρροῦντα μέλη τὰ τὴν ὀρθότητα φύσει παρεχόμενα), if we are to become "the fellow-dancers of the gods" (665a5: τοὺς θεοὺς συγχορευτὰς), that is, of Apollo, the Muses, and above all, Dionysus (cf. 653a7–654a5). Later, at *Laws* 775c4–d3, Plato refers to a drunken man who "is moved and moves everywhere, raging both in body and soul" (ὁ δὲ διῳνωμένος αὐτός τε φέρεται πάντη καὶ φέρει, λυττῶν κατά τε σῶμα καὶ ψυχήν);[80] this type of wine-fueled dancing, which evokes the dancing of Philip the farceur in Xenophon's *Symposium*, is pseudo-Bacchic and thus unsuitable for citizens (815d2: οὐκ . . . πολιτικὸν),[81] who ought to aspire to the moderation advocated by Euripides and his sober Bacchants (as discussed in the previous chapter) but also by the example of Solon the lawgiver.

Plato's metaphors about Socrates' unparalleled intellectual agility, notably evident in his superior drinking ability, aim to accommodate his philosophical ethos to civic life in the *polis*. He postulates that *sōphrosynē* can be achieved as a result of a civic regime that uses wine as a training substance (646d11: σωμασκίαν),[82] insofar as the "Test of the Wine" allows the examination of the disposition of a soul and its proclivity toward irrational behavior.[83] Although the "Test of the Wine" is explicitly set out as a practical, educational application of wine drinking that demonstrates one's civic ethos in the *Laws*, it can also be seen at work in *Symposium*, implicitly assigning praise and blame within the dramatic context. Having seen the important role symposiastic conduct plays in Plato's educational program in the *Laws* in inspiring and regulating the optimum civic ethos, I am encouraged to use the "Test of the Wine" in reading the speeches in the *Symposium* to examine the ways in which the ability to deliver a speech, to recite poetry, and to handle wine are used there to convey civic character. However, firstly, I must examine the role of poetry in symposiastic discourse.

Norms of Symposiastic Discourse: Poetry and Conversation

As Capra has pointed out, Socrates always seeks to differentiate his speech, dedicated to revealing the truth, from the embellished, deceptive speech of the sophists with whom he is assimilated by his critics.[84] Thus, in the same way that he sought to reinterpret *mania*, calling mad those who study divine things,[85] Socrates actively reworks the concept of eloquence (*Symp.* 198c5–6: δεινότης ἐν τῷ λόγῳ) by associating it squarely with the sophists and denying that he has any skill in speaking other than telling the truth (*Symp.* 198d–199b).[86] As shown above, strong cultural norms governed the kinds of speech appropriate to symposia; citizens were expected to display their ethos through skillful conversation in accordance with these norms. To cement the place of Socratic inebriation within the civic structure of the *polis*, Plato was thus obliged to demonstrate that philosophical conversation is as appropriate to the symposion as traditional kinds of discourse—and indeed, can improve them, by introducing sober reason to the inspired, poetic speech previously common to conventional depictions of symposia. The weakness of traditional symposiastic speech in the absence of philosophical rigor is therefore hinted at throughout the *Symposium*.

Plato's negotiations with the poetic speech traditionally associated with symposia were clear to later audiences. In Plutarch's dialogue *The Oracles in Delphi No Longer Given in Verse*, Theon argues that in the past men had "an easy fluency and a bent towards composing poetry" (405e5–6: κράσεις καὶ φύσεις . . . εὔρουν τι καὶ φορὸν ἐχούσας πρὸς ποίησιν) as well as a "psychic alertness" (405e7: ψυχῆς ἑτοιμότητα), especially evident in astronomers and philosophers. Even simpler men, Theon posits, when influenced by "much wine or emotion" (405e10: ἐν οἴνῳ τε πολλῷ καὶ πάθει γιγνομένων) could in the past readily compose poetry. Thus, "their banquets and books were full of amatory verses" (405f2–3: γῆρυν' ἐρωτικῶν τε κατεπίμπλαντο μέτρων καὶ ᾀσμάτων τὰ συμπόσια καὶ τὰ βιβλία γραμμάτων). Theon then turns his attention to those who claimed that the gatherings of Socrates and Plato were loveless because they did not compose any poems (406b); while strongly rejecting this view, especially since their amatory discourses can easily prove the opposite, Plutarch reports him as quoting Chaeremon on the ability of wine to enhance the natural qualities of the drinkers: "Wine mixes, as Chaeremon said, with the manners of each drinker (τοῖς τρόποις κεράννυται τῶν πινόντων), while prophetic inspiration (ἐνθουσιασμός), just like erotic enthusiasm, makes use of the stimulus at hand (χρῆται τῇ ὑποκειμένῃ δυνάμει) and moves each of the recipients according to their individual nature (ἕκαστον καθ' ὃ πέφυκεν)" (*De Pyth. or.* 406b2–6). Hence, later intellectual circles recognized the competition between poetic, amorous, and philosophical styles of discourse, which Plato displays in the *Symposium* and the role of wine in achieving a state of consciousness conducive to them. Eryximachus' suggestion in Plato's *Symposium* that the guests avoid excessive drinking was thus seen as aiming at achieving a sublime state, in which each guest can reveal his personal qualities through elevated philosophical discourse, without lapsing into unphilosophical rhapsody.[87]

Socrates, in the *Protagoras*, resolves to give his audience an example of how one can get lost in a poetic analysis of the kind he ascribes to second-rate banqueteers. Employing his usual technique of playing devil's advocate and even assuming the role of his interlocutors so he can provide answers on their behalf,[88] Socrates impersonates the sophist Protagoras as he attempts to interpret a difficult poem of Simonides. While Protagoras criticizes the poet for contradicting himself in the Scopas lyric, which debates the character of the perfectly virtuous man, Socrates proposes a novel interpretation of the poem by arguing that Simonides' verses can be reconciled if we accept a distinction between "being" and "becoming" virtuous.[89] Nevertheless, Socrates' argument, brilliant and plausible as it may appear, is totally arbitrary and finds no support in the actual verses of this or any other poem by Simonides. Socrates thus imitates the sophistic arguments of Protagoras to parody the sophists and their extravagant interpretations of poetry—an implicit rebuff to the prevalence of such discourse at the symposia of contemporary Athens.[90]

He assumes a similar role in the *Phaedrus*, where he eagerly accepts the challenge of delivering an equally great speech on a matter already exhausted by Lysias (235c3–d4); on this occasion, Socrates defends his confidence that he is able to deliver such a speech by employing another drinking metaphor: he is, he argues, "filled through the ears like a pitcher with the draughts of others" (235d1–2: ἐξ ἀλλοτρίων . . . ναμάτων διὰ τῆς ἀκοῆς πεπληρῶσθαί με δίκην ἀγγείου). His audience can readily appreciate the double-meaning of *nama* (draught), which typically refers to streams and thus metaphorically to the fountains of poetic inspiration[91] but is also associated with strong wine. Hesiod concurs in this association of streams with alcohol, advising his audience to spend the dog days of summer under a thick shade tree, next to a gurgling spring whose water should be mixed into the flowing wine.[92] In the *Bacchae*, Euripides reminds us that people forget their sorrows when filled with vine (*l.* 281), Dionysus' "liquid drink of the grape" (*l.* 279: βότρυος ὑγρὸν πῶμ')—a claim reflected in Plato's approval of the restorative qualities of wine in the *Laws*. This ambiguity is stressed by Plato, who presents Socrates as invoking the Muse in a typically poetic manner (*Phdr.* 237a8–10) and yet in the pangs of poetic frenzy (238d2: νυμφόληπτος . . . γένωμαι).[93] In fact, we are told, Socrates is on the verge of breaking into dithyrambs (238d3–4: οὐκέτι πόρρω διθυράμβων φθέγγομαι), a phrase evocative of Archilochus' dithyrambs in honor of Dionysus (quoted in chapter 1, p. 25). In this state of poetic *mania*, Socrates becomes carried away and ends up praising the non-lover over the lover (241e1–242a2), clearly contradicting himself.

Upon realizing that his speech has been "foolish and somewhat impious" (*Phdr.* 242d7: εὐήθη καὶ ὑπό τι ἀσεβῆ),[94] Socrates delivers a recantation, a type of purification closely associated with Stesichorus (*Phdr.* 243a3: ἐμοὶ . . . καθήρασθαι ἀνάγκη).[95] Socrates' palinode is a second speech, this time in honor of the god Erōs—thus similar to the speech he delivers in the *Symposium*, aimed at the truth of the matter.[96] Again, although Phaedrus recognizes the teasing style of Socrates (264e3–4: σκώπτεις τὸν λόγον ἡμῶν, ὦ Σώκρατες), the latter enthusiastically points out that his speeches end up taking two contradictory positions on the phenomenon of *erōs*:[97] in seeking to understand this, Socrates defends dialectic as the only way to avoid the frills of poetry and rhetoric.[98] In line with his preoccupation with the truth in the *Symposium*, Socrates counterproposes that poets and rhetoricians ought to dedicate their undivided attention to the truth of the matter under examination, which they otherwise typically neglect.[99] Truth is the only acceptable goal for those who aim to persuade (271a2: πειθὼ γὰρ ἐν τούτῳ ποιεῖν ἐπιχειρεῖ) and to lead the souls of their audiences with their arguments (271c12–d1: . . . λόγου δύναμις τυγχάνει ψυχαγωγία οὖσα). Having thus totally recovered from his manic enthusiasm (263d3–4: διὰ τὸ ἐνθουσιαστικὸν οὐ πάνυ μέμνημαι), Socrates leaves aside his usual playfulness[100] and pledges his allegiance to a different stream of inspiration—one in which truth, not eloquence, is privileged. Socrates then instructs Phaedrus in this alternative form of creativity: "Tell Lysias that the two of us came down to the fountain and sacred place of the nymphs, and heard words which they told us to repeat to Lysias and anyone else who composed speeches. . . . If he has composed his writings with knowledge of the truth (εἰδὼς . . . τὸ ἀληθές), and is able to support them by cross-examination (εἰς ἔλεγχον ἰὼν) of that which he has written, and has the power *to show by his own speech* (καὶ **λέγων αὐτὸς δυνατὸς**) that the written words are of little worth, such a man ought not to derive his title from such writings, but from the serious pursuit which underlies them" (*Phdr.* 278b10–d1). Socrates marks here the distinction between a *logographos*[101] and a *philosophos*.[102]

This sublime state of mind in which one achieves "a divine release from habitual norms" (265a13–14: τὴν δὲ ὑπὸ θείας ἐξαλλαγῆς τῶν εἰωθότων νομίμων γιγνομένην) and which Phaedrus finds very pleasant to listen to (265c5: καὶ μάλα ἔμοιγε οὐκ ἀηδῶς ἀκοῦσαι) seems to correspond to the daemonic or intermediate—that is, neither divine nor human—nature of Erōs in the *Symposium*[103] but differs notably from philosophical inspiration, which rejects ornament and focuses exclusively on the truth.

The prominence of the poets and their civic role is also stressed at *Laws* 662b5–6, where the Athenian Stranger insists that, as a legislator, he would aspire to compel poets and citizens alike to speak out in favor of justice.[104] Instead of the then contemporary practice in Greece and Sicily of entrusting the judgement of poetry to the attendant crowds, which inadvertently fosters corruption of poetic standards (659b7–c4),[105] leading to what Plato describes as "wicked theatrocracy" (701a3: πονηρὰ θεατροκρατία), a topic he debated at length in the *Republic*,[106] legislators should approach poetic education as doctors responsible for providing a correct regime of nutrition to their patients (659e6–660a4).[107] Thus, legislators ought to instill an adequate civic ethos in poets: "Similarly, a proper legislator (ὁ ὀρθὸς νομοθέτης) will persuade the poet by noble and praiseworthy words (ἐν τοῖς καλοῖς ῥήμασι καὶ ἐπαινετοῖς πείσει)—and, failing persuasion, he will compel him (ἀναγκάσει μὴ πείθων)—to portray by his rhythms the gestures, and by his harmonies the tunes, (the actions) of men who are temperate, courageous, and good in all respects (τῶν σωφρόνων τε καὶ ἀνδρείων καὶ πάντως ἀγαθῶν), and to compose poems correctly" (μέλη . . . ὀρθῶς ποιεῖν; *Leg.* 660a4–9).[108] He further argues that civic education should be guided by a chorus of Dionysus, comprising dancers of advanced age[109] tasked with producing finer tunes, since they "know of a music better than that of choruses and public theatres" (667a10–b1: εἰ γὰρ ἔχομεν μοῦσαν τῆς τῶν χορῶν καλλίω καὶ τῆς ἐν τοῖς κοινοῖς θεάτροις).[110] The chorus would be responsible for judging which musical work is the "noblest or most dignified" (671a1: τῆς ἐκλογῆς ἕνεκα τοῦ καλλίστου)[111] according to the three aspects of any copy (669a8: ἑκάστην εἰκόνα): with regard to the nature of the original, the correct execution of the copy, and the excellence of the copy. Plato later recapitulates his argument in favor of the role of the Dionysiac Chorus[112] in the context of inebriation, arguing that a good legislator should teach banqueters "the proper limits of silence and speech, of drinking, and of music" (671b8–9: καὶ τὸ κατὰ μέρος σιγῆς καὶ λόγου καὶ πόσεως καὶ μούσης).[113] Thus, he recommends the passing of a law according to which[114]

No children under eighteen may touch wine at all, *teaching that it is wrong to pour fire upon fire either in body or in soul* (**διδάσκοντες ὡς οὐ χρὴ πῦρ ἐπὶ πῦρ ὀχετεύειν εἴς τε τὸ σῶμα καὶ τὴν ψυχήν**),[115] before they set about tackling their real work, and thus guarding against the excitable disposition of the young. And next, we shall rule that *the young man under thirty may take wine in moderation, but that he must entirely abstain from intoxication and heavy drinking* (**μετὰ δὲ τοῦτο οἴνου μὲν δὴ γεύεσθαι τοῦ μετρίου μέχρι τριάκοντα ἐτῶν, μέθης δὲ καὶ πολυοινίας τὸ παράπαν τὸν νέον ἀπέχεσθαι**). (*Leg.* 666a1–b2)

Unlike barbaric peoples, including the Thracians, the Scythians, and the Persians who, as Plato notes, had a reputation for disorderly drunkenness (647e2–6: . . . Σκύθαι δὲ καὶ Θρᾷκες ἀκράτῳ παντάπασι χρώμενοι . . . Πέρσαι δὲ σφόδρα μὲν χρῶνται), the Magnesians ought to reject such practices in favor of the Spartan way which insists on abstaining from heavy drinking (τὸ παράπαν ἀπέχεσθε).

Drinking and Performing Civic Ethos in the *Symposium*

The question of how to drink best is raised early in the *Symposium* by Pausanias (176a7–8: τίνα τρόπον ῥᾷστα πιόμεθα; repeated at 176b1), who admits that he feels exhausted after an extreme drinking session the night before and he rather needs a break (176a9: τῷ ὄντι πάνυ χαλεπῶς ἔχω ὑπὸ τοῦ χθὲς πότου καὶ δέομαι ἀναψυχῆς τινος).[116] In his speech about the nature of love, Pausanias takes drinking wine as an example. No action, he argues, can be deemed right or wrong per se without examining how it is carried out:[117]

> . . . for every action is as follows: performing an action is in itself neither good nor shameful (αὐτὴ ἐφ᾽ ἑαυτῆς πραττομένη οὔτε καλὴ οὔτε αἰσχρά). Take, for example, what we are doing now, whether drinking or singing or having a conversation. None of these [actions] is good in itself, but its quality is determined during its performance, [depending on] how it may be performed: for if something is done correctly and accurately (καλῶς μὲν γὰρ πραττόμενον καὶ ὀρθῶς) it turns

out to be good; if inaccurately, then it turns out to be shameful. Exactly so is [the action of] being in love: Not every kind of *erōs* is good or praiseworthy, but the *erōs* that urges us to love correctly (καλῶς προτρέπων ἐρᾶν). (*Symp.* 180e4–181a6)

His sentiment finds wide acceptance, and thus, "upon hearing these words, they all consented not to direct the present gathering to getting drunk but to drinking in a manner geared to pleasure" (176e1–2: ταῦτα δὴ ἀκούσαντας συγχωρεῖν πάντας μὴ διὰ μέθης ποιήσασθαι τὴν ἐν τῷ παρόντι συνουσίαν, ἀλλ᾽ οὕτω πίνοντας πρὸς ἡδονήν). In my view, the discussion evokes the definition of virtue in the *Laws* as the distinction between pleasure and pain, further stressing the parallels between the two dialogues. Urged by Pausanias to think about their drinking mode, the guests at Agathon's symposion agree to avoid intoxication, especially since Eryximachus advises them to do so based on his medical knowledge.[118] Aware that they missed the mark in their drinking the night before, the symposiasts desire to avoid the unpleasant consequences of excess. Thus, they will instead seek entertainment in praising Love (177d2–4: δοκεῖ . . . ἕκαστον ἡμῶν λόγον εἰπεῖν ἔπαινον Ἔρωτος)—a topic totally neglected, as Phaedrus alleges, by the poets (177c3: ἀλλ᾽ οὕτως ἠμέληται τοσοῦτος θεός).[119] Once more, wine, poetry, and discourse are compared as intellectual pursuits;[120] Plato seems to disapprove of excessive reliance on poetry in the same way that he rejects drunkenness. The profile of each guest as a drinker corresponds to their tendency to intersperse their speeches in praise of Love with poetic verses, with Socrates citing poets the least.[121] The guests' ability to handle wine and poetry becomes thus a marker of their intellectual (and ultimately civic) competence.

Despite his ability to cite poetry,[122] Phaedrus comes across as an overconfident young student, totally oblivious of his boldness when he claims that poets have failed to praise E/erōs adequately;[123] there is, for example, no mention of archaic lyric in his swaggering claims.[124] Accordingly, he meanders through the details of the myths he cites, making precipitous and unsubstantiated connections that undermine his argument that the gods prefer *paidika*.[125] Phaedrus' poor ability to use poetry in a manner that meaningfully advances the argument at hand reflects his profile as a weak drinker, already pointed out by Eryximachus at 176c1–4:[126] "It would be a boon, it seems . . . for me, for Aristodemus, for Phaedrus, and the other people here—if you the stoutest drinkers are already exhausted: for we are always the weak ones!" (εἰ ὑμεῖς οἱ δυνατώτατοι πίνειν νῦν ἀπειρήκατε:

ἡμεῖς μὲν γὰρ **ἀεὶ ἀδύνατοι**). Agathon, however, being an acclaimed play-wright, has a deeper grasp of poetry;[127] he quotes freely from past poets and, perhaps inspired by wine in the manner of Archilochus, improvises a few verses (197c3–4: ἐπέρχεται δέ μοί τι καὶ ἔμμετρον εἰπεῖν). Yet, as Socrates observes, Agathon's beautiful speech is rife with Gorgias' sophistic rhetorical devices;[128] therefore, while it can certainly impress the crowd[129] with its "beauty of words and phrases" (198b8–9: τοῦ κάλλους τῶν ὀνο-μάτων καὶ ῥημάτων τίς οὐκ ἂν ἐξεπλάγη ἀκούων),[130] it can hardly achieve any breakthrough in the matter under investigation. Despite compelling everyone to sing to his tune, "bewitching the mind of all gods and men" (197e5–7: θέλγων πάντων θεῶν τε καὶ ἀνθρώπων νόημα),[131] Agathon fails to make the basic distinction between *erōs* and its object. As soon as the applause has died out, Socrates makes him agree that while the beloved is both good and beautiful, *erōs* itself lacks both qualities (199c–201c).[132]

Between the speeches of Phaedrus and Agathon, Pausanias the sophist, Eryximachus, and Aristophanes offer their own defective attempts to praise Erōs. As Dorter has pointed out,[133] Pausanias claims that the actions of the lover and the beloved are judged in accordance with an unwritten law[134] that, in his view, noble men apply in their pursuit of male lovers, which privileges the personal goals of the individuals involved in the relation-ship: for the lover, attaining the beloved at all cost,[135] and for the beloved, having the lover teach him virtue.[136] Pausanias employs this unwritten rule to evaluate the legal standing of *paidika* in various places throughout Greece, including Elis, Boeotia, Ionia, and finally Athens (182a–d). His sophistic equation of the law with the morally good is absurd and, to quote Dorter, "a sign of philosophical failure."[137] Interestingly, Pausanias states that the law ought to function as a test for determining who, in a pederastic context, is to be favored or avoided (184a2–3: ὁ ἡμέτερος νόμος εὖ καὶ καλῶς βασανίζειν, καὶ τοῖς μὲν χαρίσασθαι, τοὺς δὲ διαφεύγειν); the use of βασανίζειν here is reminiscent of the "Test of the Wine" in the *Laws* (βάσανος in 649d11, 650a2 and b4),[138] where Socrates posits that, compared to his light-hearted use of wine as a means of testing moral disposition, a test focused on men's ability to control their sexual urges would entail real danger.[139] Predictably, Pausanias, who was quick at the start of the *Symposium* to advocate moderate drinking, makes very selective use of literary sources, which he, totally focused on promoting his shaky argument, does not even acknowledge.[140]

Eryximachus' attempt to appreciate the double nature of *erōs* from a medical viewpoint in terms of health and sickness is similarly narrow;[141]

thus, at *Symp.* 186b4–10, Eryximachus insists that "the desire felt by a sound body is quite other than that of a sickly one" (ἄλλος μὲν οὖν ὁ ἐπὶ τῷ ὑγιεινῷ ἔρως, ἄλλος δὲ ὁ ἐπὶ τῷ νοσώδει). Plato contributes to the tension that undeniably existed at the time between medicine, focused on curing symptoms, and philosophy, focused on causes and principles, by ridiculing Eryximachus, who entrusts the distinction between the two types of *erōs* to divination:[142] "To divination is appointed the task of supervising and medicating those in love (ἐπισκοπεῖν τοὺς ἐρῶντας καὶ ἰατρεύειν); and again divination is the purveyor of friendship between gods and men by knowing which human love affairs will lead to justice and piety (ὅσα τείνει πρὸς θέμιν καὶ εὐσέβειαν)" (*Symp.* 188c8–d3). As a doctor, Eryximachus recognizes the symptoms and effects of the two types of love and knows how to harmonize the opposed forces at work in our bodies (186d); however, his observations remain superficial and cannot offer a secure criterion for guiding our love toward the morally good.[143] Eryximachus' apparent misquotation[144] and thus misinterpretation of Heraclitus reveals his lack of theoretical astuteness, a point also stressed by his use of the Heraclitean notion of cosmic harmony to discuss musical harmony.[145] In trying to second-guess the meaning of Heraclitus' words (*Symp.* 187a3–4, 9: ὥσπερ ἴσως καὶ Ἡράκλειτος βούλεται λέγειν, ἐπεὶ τοῖς γε ῥήμασιν οὐ καλῶς λέγει . . . ἀλλὰ ἴσως τόδε ἐβούλετο λέγειν), Eryximachus mirrors Phaedrus' attitude toward Aeschylus and his portrayal of Achilles. As the mature *erastēs* in his relationship with Phaedrus,[146] he is responsible for having passed on to his young *erōmenos* this tendency to distort ideas. Their inability and reluctance to exert themselves intellectually corresponds to their inability to handle wine: Phaedrus and Eryximachus are among the first to depart from the banquet when the original agreement on moderate drinking comes under threat (*Symp.* 223b7–8: τὸν . . . Ἐρυξίμαχον καὶ τὸν Φαῖδρον καὶ ἄλλους τινὰς . . . οἴχεσθαι ἀπιόντας).

Aristophanes, having recovered from his incessant hiccups thanks to Eryximachus' tips, delivers his speech next. I will return to it later in this chapter, but for the moment it is important to note that, although Aristophanes describes himself as a comic playwright dedicated to his Muse, he is nonetheless conscious of having to rise to the occasion. Accordingly, when Eryximachus accuses him of buffoonery (189a9: γελωτοποιεῖς), Aristophanes responds thus: "With regard to what is going to be said, I'm not afraid I may say something humorous (οὔ τι μὴ γελοῖα εἴπω)—for this would be an advantage and characteristic of my Muse—but rather something ludicrous (καταγέλαστα)"[147] (*Symp.* 189b6–9).

Aristophanes' story is a substantial, original composition (or rather adaptation),[148] witty in the manner of much traditional symposiastic discourse.[149] He is quick to forbid Eryximachus from making fun of his speech (193d10: μὴ κωμῳδήσῃς αὐτόν [= τὸν λόγον]); it is humorous but delivered with enough skill and gusto as to avoid seeming ridiculous. Yet Aristophanes, despite being a competent drinker, refuses to engage seriously with the topic, satisfied with meeting the traditional requirements of the task handed to him. His narrative, in which Zeus cuts the hermaphroditic ancestors of humankind in half (190c9–12) as a divine punishment for impiety, offers a plausible *aition* (cause) for differences of sex and sexual orientation, but no insight on how we are meant to restore piety,[150] or how this would impact the human search for happiness. Aristophanes leaves the piety he prescribes undefined; furthermore, he does not explain how people, once reunited, might avoid their past arrogance,[151] nor does he elaborate on the role of *erōs* in people's lives before suffering Zeus' punishment or after a potential restoration.

Norms of Symposiastic Discourse:
Pouring out Wine and Jokes

Comedy has a prominent civic character in classical Athens;[152] equally, the ancient banquet is associated with laughter and stylish wit. Thus, the ability to control the flow of wine is commonly associated with one's sense of humor. For Plutarch, symposiastic laughter is[153]

> where the poet shows . . . the difference between exhilaration and drunkenness (οἰνώσεως . . . καὶ μέθης . . . διαφοράν). For song, laughter, and dancing are characteristic of men who drink wine in moderation (οἰνωμένοις μετρίως), but babbling and talking about what is better left in silence is at once the work of actual intoxication and drunkenness (παροινίας . . . καὶ μέθης ἔργον). Hence Plato holds that most men show their real natures most clearly when they drink (ἐν οἴνῳ μάλιστα καθορᾶσθαι τὰ ἤθη), and Homer too . . . (*quaest. conv.* 645a4–9 on. *Od.* 14.464)

In fact, Plato is able to stage a competition between Socrates and Aristophanes in the matter of civic ethics,[154] a competition that continues to inform Plato's views about the civic role of comic performances in the *Laws*. While representations of symposia provide a framework for much of Aristophanes' comedic critique of contemporary politicians and their unscrupulous civic behavior,[155] Plato stipulates that comedy, like wine drinking and Dionysiac merriment, ought to be regulated by law (816e12–817a1: ὅσα μὲν οὖν περὶ γέλωτά ἐστιν παίγνια, ἃ δὴ κωμῳδίαν πάντες λέγομεν, οὕτως τῷ νόμῳ καὶ λόγῳ κείσθω); Plato reworks here his criticism of comedy in the *Republic* where Socrates warns his interlocutors that imitation of distasteful comic representations is a dangerous way to absorb, perhaps even "imbibe," reality (395c7: ἐκ τῆς μιμήσεως τοῦ εἶναι ἀπολαύσωσιν), which free citizens ought to avoid.[156] The Socratic style of symposiastic discourse corresponds to Plato's vision for the role of wine in the ideal city:[157] one "pours" jokes in a measured, probative way. Thus, besides nodding off to sleep by the end of the banquet (likely a hint to his drunkenness; cf. n243 below), Aristophanes is depicted as forfeiting his turn to deliver a eulogy of Erōs because of his incessant hiccups—given that hiccups remain a common unpleasant side effect of drunkenness, Socrates seems be alluding to Aristophanes' excessive wine consumption.[158]

In addition, Aristophanes cures his hiccups through sneezing: "It [the hiccupping] has stopped, though not before sneezing was applied to it, so that I marvel that bodily decorum requires such noises and titillations, like sneezing;[159] for it stopped straightaway when I applied sneezing to it" (*Symp.* 189a2–7). There is a long tradition in Greek literature and folklore associating sneezing with omens, starting with Homer[160] and continuing palpably in the writings of Xenophon;[161] Plutarch, too, in his *De genio Socratis*, famously entertains a theory that Socrates' *daimonion* was ordinary divination, like sneezing before refuting an argument.[162] As noted above, Eryximachus mistakes Aristophanes' opening remarks for the beginning of one of his jokes to which Aristophanes responds that he fears what he is about to say will not be just funny but rather "utterly ridiculous" (189a8–b3: γελωτοποιεῖς μέλλων λέγειν)—that is, it will be incoherent or incompetent, which in Socratic terms means failing the elenctic process.[163] Since this fear strikes Aristophanes while he is trying to cure his hiccups, Plato implies that the sneezing, far from a sign of divine inspiration, is a clear omen of the ridiculous, wine-affected praise of Erōs that Aristophanes is about to deliver.

The conflict between Socrates and Aristophanes revolves around their antithetical versions of the truth, with Aristophanes having the advantage of being able to address large audiences during his performances, often through the chorus leader.[164] Aristophanes is especially threatening to Socrates because of his self-projection as an idiosyncratic poetic genius, who, despite his resolve to fight for civic reforms in the manner of Solon, is often misunderstood by his audiences.[165] As an unappreciated public benefactor, tirelessly committed "to justice (*to dikaion*) and to the interests of the *polis*,"[166] Aristophanes adopts in the *Frogs* the Socratic *elenchus* to defend the social role of poetry. Claiming that poetry makes people "better members of their communities" (*Ran.* 1009–1010: βελτίους τε ποιοῦμεν/ τοὺς ἀνθρώπους ἐν ταῖς πόλεσιν),[167] Aristophanes, like Socrates in the *Euthyphro*, adopts the persona of the lonesome philosopher whose counsel the citizens fail to heed.[168] Furthermore, he claims to have understood what kind of poetry the Athenians prefer, comparing it to their taste in wine:[169] "Pramnian wine . . . is neither sweet nor full-bodied (οὔτε γλυκὺς οὔτε παχύς) but dry, hard, and exceptionally strong (ἀλλ' αὐστηρὸς καὶ σκληρὸς καὶ δύναμιν ἔχων διαφέρουσαν). Aristophanes says that the Athenians do not like it when he writes that the Athenian people enjoy neither poets who are hard and dry nor Pramnian wines that contract the brows and the bowels but prefer a rich bouquet and a taste of nectar (ἀλλ' <ἀνθ>οσμίᾳ καὶ πέπονι νεκταροσταγεῖ)" (fr. 688 ap. Ath. *Epit.* 1.30b–c). Moreover, Aristophanes relies on his own voice, issuing bold statements against his dramatic rivals; in the first parabasis of the *Clouds*, he addresses the audience through the chorus, and after flattering them for their sophisticated taste, he vouches "in the name of Dionysus, who has nurtured him, to candidly tell them the truth about his art" (519–520: ὦ θεώμενοι κατερῶ πρὸς ὑμᾶς ἐλευθέρως/ τἀληθῆ νὴ τὸν Διόνυσον τὸν ἐκθρέψαντά με). While explaining his artistic decisions in a lengthy monologue likely designed to avert a second failure of the play, which ranked third when originally produced at the City Dionysia of 423 BCE,[170] Aristophanes presents to the audience his Comedy personified, stating that "she has come relying on herself and her words" (544: ἀλλ' αὑτῇ καὶ τοῖς ἔπεσιν πιστεύουσ' ἐλήλυθεν), before adding: "Rather I have the skill to present ever new forms of comedy (καινὰς ἰδέας . . . σοφί-ζομαι), none of them like the others and all of them ingenious" (*Nub.* 547–548). Aristophanes adds that his comedy is "modest by nature" (537: ὡς δὲ σώφρων ἐστὶ φύσει),[171] a boast that is likely to further antagonize Socrates, whose quintessential quality, as identified by Alcibiades in the *Symposium* (216d6–9; cf. 219d5), is *sōphrosynē*.

Drunken symposia offer a dramatic scenario guaranteed to generate uncritical laughter, threatening the orderly, discussion-focused version of the symposium that Socrates advocates. In addition, comic poets, including Aristophanes, often tried to discredit their rivals as drunkards,[172] a theme that in the context of an important fifth century debate about the nature of poetic inspiration acquires new connotations.[173] As Bakola has argued,[174] the moral substance of poetry had been greatly undermined by mid-fifth century, due partly to the sophistic movement and its emphasis on speaking techniques. In her words:[175]

> Common sophistic doctrine was that poetry was essentially deceptive and its aim was to produce pleasure (cf. Gorgias fr. B23 DK, *Dissoi logoi* 3.17 DK, Pl. *Grg.* 502b–c). Skill, sophistication, and learning were the qualities which offered this kind of pleasure. Sophistic education often used poetry for the exhibition of virtuosity in the form of citing from a variety of poets and thereby displaying sophistication (cf. e.g., Hippias B6 DK; Pl. *Leg.* 810e–11a). The terms *dexiotes* and *kainotes* were closely associated with such exhibitions of learnedness (Ar. *Ran.* 1113–1114; *Vesp.* 1052–9; Hippias B6 DK).

In this debate, despite admitting his polished style (cf. n183), Aristophanes sides with traditional values.[176] Thus, in his long-standing rivalry with his older contemporary Cratinus, the latter assumes in his plays the persona of the "Dionysiac poet" and is associated with Archilochus, known for composing in a drunken delirium, as advocated in fr. 120.[177] Constant allusions to Archilochean poetry can be also found in Cratinus' *Archilochoi*, a play involving a poetic competition between iambic and epic poets (where iambic poets claim victory).[178] In an echo of Socrates' condemnation of pseudo-Corybantic dancing in the *Laws*, Aristophanes presents the chorus of the *Frogs* as bidding those "who have not been initiated in the Bacchic rites of bull-eating Cratinus' language" (355–357: ὅστις . . . μηδὲ Κρατίνου τοῦ ταυροφάγου γλώττης Βακχεῖ' ἐτελέσθη) to abstain from Bacchic dances.[179] Amid this debate on inspiration and its civic mission, it is easy to perceive how Socrates could, with his odd philosophical trances, be mistaken for a boozy bard like Cratinus or Archilochus.

As Rosen has noted,[180] there is a long tradition of associating "performers who mock, satirize, or otherwise engage in comic blaming" with trickster figures, which in my view encourages a comparison between the self-righteous, glory-seeking Odysseus of the post-Homeric comic tradition and Aristophanes in his guise as the self-proclaimed champion of public morality. Incapacitated morally and intellectually by comedy's deceiving wine, like the Homeric Cyclops, the Athenians need unwavering Socratic guidance in the face of a wily Odysseus like Aristophanes. Odysseus, like Aristophanes, is allowed the privilege of relaying his adventures in his own voice[181]—or at least this is the illusion Homer affords us—and the comparison is further supported by Odysseus' profile as a model of sophistic education.[182] In the *Symposium*, Plato is thus tasked with revealing that Aristophanes' persona is a self-serving construction, concocted in the context of trivial rivalries between playwrights and that his jokes are factually false, employing sophistic exaggeration to betwitch the audience into laughter.[183] In other words, Plato sets out to discredit Aristophanes and his version of truth.[184] Thus, he revises Aristophanes' portrayal of Socrates as an eccentric sophist, revealing the former as the one who in fact resorts to sophistic devices.[185] This was not a unique criticism. Cratinus, during his rivalry with Aristophanes, famously coined the word εὐριπιδαριστοφανίζων ("euripidaristophaniser") in a dig at the quasi-intellectual pretesions Aristophanes shared with Euripides.[186] The claim that Aristophanes emulated Euripides' eloquent, sophistic style carries the added charge of hypocrisy,[187] as Aristophanes elsewhere criticizes Euripides: in the *Frogs*, Aristophanes turns the poetic competition between Euripides and Aeschylus into an "*agōn* of wisdom" (884: ἀγὼν σοφίας)[188] where Euripides is attacked for his novel style and from which Aeschylus emerges victorious.

Plato was likely inspired by Aristophanes' *Frogs* in his portrayal of Aeschylus as a poet of Bacchic inspiration,[189] on whom he modeled his analogy between poets in trance and the Dionysiac Bacchants in the *Ion* (534a). His discussion also reflects the association between comedy and Corybants.[190] The Corybants were believed both to cause and heal madness, a view entertained by Aristophanes in the *Wasps*.[191] Corybantic frenzy, preoccupied with reforming the earthly lives of its adherents,[192] was collective and easily transmitted from one person to another.[193] Plato notably relates the main Corybantic ceremony, called *thronôsis*, when debating the nature of knowledge in the *Euthydemus*.[194] The text reads:

> They are doing the same thing as the participants of the Corybantic rites (οἱ ἐν τῇ τελετῇ τῶν Κορυβάντων), when they

perform the enthronement of the person whom they are about to initiate. For there, if perhaps you have been through it, there is dancing and cheerfulness (χορεία τίς ἐστι καὶ παιδιά): so now these two are merely dancing about you and performing their playful frolics (χορεύετον περὶ σὲ καὶ οἷον ὀρχεῖσθον παίζοντε) with a view to your subsequent initiation. Therefore, you must now think that you are listening to the first part of their sophistic mysteries (τὰ πρῶτα τῶν ἱερῶν ἀκούειν τῶν σοφιστικῶν). (*Euthyd.* 277d5–e3)

The argument that follows (*Euthyd.* 278a4–5), based on the difference between learning and understanding, is Socrates' attempt to warn his young interlocutor about the futility of sophistic claims. Given Aristophanes' attempt in the *Frogs* to envelop "the concept of spiritual renewal" with initiatory patterns derived from the Eleusinian mysteries,[195] Plato's investment of Socratic philosophy with mystic references is best explained in the context of his conflict with contemporary poets, particularly Aristophanes, and their implicit promise to "initiate" spectators into the correct civic ethos.[196] Despite his promises to save the *polis*[197] by reviving the traditional values of Aeschylean poetry,[198] Aristophanes reveals his inability to rise to the occasion by falling asleep in the final scene of the *Symposium* while debating with Socrates and Agathon in a setting reminiscent of the *Frogs* and its poetic competition between Euripides and Aeschylus.[199] In this light, Socrates' "sober inebriation" reconfigures the conflict between poetry and philosophy in favor of the philosopher.

Let us assume that in the *Symposium* Plato plays a joke on Aristophanes, turning the tables on him and targeting his ineffective, pretentious inspiration. Plato certainly seems to distinguish Socrates from those who are ridiculous as they are defined in the *Philebus*:[200] firstly, although ridiculous people are typically unaware of their circumstances, Socrates has a sound appreciation of his situation, including his odd, Satyr-like appearance (*Symp.* 215b6–8; cf. *Phil.* 48d8–e10); he is also the first one to admit his ignorance,[201] in contrast with Aristophanes' sophistic dislike for admitting ignorance and his presumptuous attempt to explain human nature.[202] Secondly, unlike the truly laughable person who cannot respond to his mockers (*Phil.* 49b6–8: ἀδύνατοι καταγελώμενοι τιμωρεῖσθαι . . . γελοίους τούτους φάσκων εἶναι τἀληθῆ φθέγξει), Socrates delivers a powerful criticism of Aristophanes' speech in the voice of Diotima, refuting the claim that all those who seek their other half are in love,[203] while Aristophanes is not given a chance to respond due to Alcibiades' noisy entrance.[204] Thirdly, those who laugh at the misfortunes of their friends are ridiculous (*Phil.* 49d1–8, 50a5–9). Although readers can appreciate how this statement might apply to Socrates,[205] it seems to me to apply equally to all the symposiasts who are "mocked" by Aristophanes' ridiculous story.[206] Socrates thus seeks to regulate the flow of jokes just as he encourages the regulation of wine, stoppering Aristophanes' tendency to deride him—interweaving metaphors and themes he revisits in the *Laws*, with Aristophanes, always the jester, being framed as an obvious example of inappropriate civic humor.[207] Socrates' predilection for speaking in his own words is, in the symposiastic context, joined to his superior sense of humor to demonstrate his excellence as a model of civic education.

Socrates and Alcibiades: Staging Truth and Drunkenness

The early speeches in the *Symposium* are followed by a speech from Socrates. In his sharp criticism of the previous speakers, Socrates targets (what he perceives as) their disinterest in engaging in a profound and truthful praise of Erōs (198d–e). Initially confident in his ability to deliver a eulogy of the god, since he knew the truth about the task at hand (198d7–8: ὡς εἰδὼς τὴν ἀλήθειαν τοῦ ἐπαινεῖν ὁτιοῦν), Socrates is disheartened to learn that truth has little to do with "a good speech of praise":[208] "But now, it seems, this was not what a good speech of praise is about, but [it is about] the ascription of the greatest and fairest qualities (ὡς μέγιστα ἀνατιθέναι τῷ πράγματι καὶ ὡς κάλλιστα), whether this is the case or not. It is really no issue if they are false (ψευδῆ). For, apparently, we agreed earlier that each of us should appear to praise Love (ἐγκωμιάζειν δόξει), not actually do it" (*Symp.* 198d9–e5). Such superficial style can perhaps impress the ignorant (199a1–3: φαίνηται ὡς κάλλιστος καὶ ἄριστος, δῆλον ὅτι τοῖς μὴ γιγνώσκουσιν) but certainly not Socrates, who refuses to follow the example of others and seeks permission to praise Love in his own way (199b2: ἐθέλω εἰπεῖν κατ' ἐμαυτόν).[209] According to Socrates, by rejecting the literary overflow that characterized the previous eulogies and relying on his own words, he is able to get to the truth of the matter (199b4–5: περὶ Ἔρωτος τἀληθῆ λεγόμενα ἀκούειν).[210]

Given that his speech relies on an exchange he had with Diotima, a prophetess from Mantineia (even if we as readers are meant to appreciate Diotima as a doppelgänger of Socrates who allows him to enlist his favorite dialectic method), his claim that he relies on his own words sounds paradoxical.[211] However, it is important to appreciate that by adopting the dialectic method (a method he allegedly picked up from Diotima; 201e3–4: ὥς ποτέ με ἡ ξένη ἀνακρίνουσα διῄει), Socrates offers a sound example of his famous *elenchus* (201e7: ἤλεγχε δή με τούτοις τοῖς λόγοις οἷσπερ ἐγὼ τοῦτον).[212] During his cross-examination by Diotima, Socrates becomes convinced by her arguments and is able to defend them in his own words rather than simply regurgitate them.[213] Thus, he states: "These are the opinions, Phaedrus and the rest of you, that Diotima claimed—and *I was persuaded* (πέπεισμαι δ᾽ ἐγώ) and *having been persuaded I try to persuade* others too (πεπεισμένος δὲ πειρῶμαι καὶ τοὺς ἄλλους **πείθειν**)" (*Symp.* 212b1–3). Nonetheless, Socrates' long speech at the *Symposium*, rife with his own assertions about the nature of *erōs* and his sharp criticism of the other speakers, feels rather one-sided and in need of additional endorsement. Although we have been assured of Socrates' superior drinking abilities at the start of the dialogue, it is important to observe two things. Firstly, Plato associates correct symposiastic practice (dependent on the ability to withstand the negative effects of wine drinking) with the ability to rely on one's own voice.[214] The weak drinkers at Agathon's dinner party cannot think clearly, and therefore their praise of Erōs relies on poetry and opinions, which they typically misquote and misinterpret, in a fashion reminiscent of Socrates's condemnation of vulgar discussions of poetry in the *Protagoras*. Secondly, while the inability of the other symposiasts to handle wine drinking reflects their intellectual weakness(es) and their relative distance from correct judgement, Alcibiades, who barges into the banquet already drunk, represents the polar opposite of Socratic inebriation. Thus, Plato uses the cultural dynamics of the symposion to stage a face-off between Socrates, whose quasi-drunkenness serves the truth and the state, and Alcibiades' wine-fueled, self-serving *parrhēsia*.

Alcibiades arrives at Agathon's house in a manner that exemplifies his arrogance. He is hardly a master of himself, utterly drunk, barely able to drag his feet;[215] he enters banging at the door with his companions (212c8–9: τὴν αὔλειον θύραν κρουομένην πολὺν ψόφον), shouting (212d5–6: μέγα βοῶντος, ἐρωτῶντος . . . κελεύοντος), supported by a flute girl and his entourage (212d7–9: ἄγειν οὖν αὐτὸν παρὰ σφᾶς τήν τε αὐλητρίδα ὑπολαβοῦσαν καὶ ἄλλους τινὰς τῶν ἀκολούθων), shamelessly aware of his intoxication (213a1: μου . . . μεθύοντος, 212e3–4 and 214c7: μεθύοντα . . . ἄνδρα, 212d5: σφόδρα μεθύοντος). Although he accepts Eryximachus' invitation to infuse the drinking with poetry and discourse, lest he appear drunk,²¹⁶ Alcibiades appoints himself symposiarch and asks for the largest possible wineglass (213e12: εἴ τι ἔστιν ἔκπωμα μέγα), before settling for a wine cooler (!) instead (213e13: τὸν ψυκτῆρα ἐκεῖνον). This he fills to the brim and drinks, asking for more to be served for Socrates (214a2–3: τοῦτον ἐμπλησάμενον . . . τῷ Σωκράτει κελεύειν ἐγχεῖν), while acknowledging that, given the latter's remarkable ability to withstand the effects of wine, his ploy will be to no avail (214a4: τὸ σόφισμά μοι οὐδέν). Alcibiades' drunken entrance and his audacious self-proclamation as symposiarch intent on imposing excessive drinking on the banqueters (213e9–10: ἄρχοντα οὖν αἱροῦμαι τῆς πόσεως, ἕως ἂν ὑμεῖς ἱκανῶς πίητε, ἐμαυτόν) invite comparison with Plato's discussion of the sober symposiarch in the *Laws*. The obvious implication of the comparison is that Alcibiades—young, impetuous, and determined to make his mark in Athenian politics—lacks moderation²¹⁷ and is therefore unable to pursue pleasure moderately.

Alcibiades refuses to praise Erōs, offering instead a striking description of Socrates (*Symp.* 215a1: Σωκράτη δ᾽ ἐγὼ ἐπαινεῖν) as a drinker and speaker.²¹⁸ He then proceeds to admit to everyone's amusement that he still has feelings for Socrates even though the latter has rejected his sexual advances,²¹⁹ counter-proposing that the two should have long discussions on virtue (*Symp.* 218c1–221d8).²²⁰ This unfettered, drunken style of honesty invites comparison with Socrates against the background of symposiastic norms. That Alcibiades is sincere, as he insists (*Symp.* 214e3–215a2 and 8–9: **τἀληθῆ ἐρῶ** . . . τά γε **ἀληθῆ** παρίημι καὶ κελεύω λέγειν . . . ἐάν τι μὴ **ἀληθὲς** λέγω . . . ἔσται δ᾽ ἡ εἰκὼν **τοῦ ἀληθοῦς ἕνεκα**), is also indicated by the fact that a considerable part of his speech is unflattering for him.²²¹ Further, given his explicit use of the common proverb "there is truth in wine,"²²² Alcibiades' sincerity functions as a marker of his defective civic ethos, which he (mis-)characterizes as a display of *parrhēsia*.²²³ Alcibiades' version of free speech, in contrast to the kind of genteel, witty banter demanded of a symposiast, is reminiscent of a banquet getting out of hand, as described by the Athenian Stranger: "Everyone is uplifted above his normal self (κουφότερος αἴρεται), and is merry (γέγηθέν) and is full with loquacious audacity (παρρησίας ἐμπίμπλαται), while turning a deaf ear to his neighbours, and regards himself as competent to rule both himself and everyone else (ἄρχων δ᾽ ἱκανὸς ἀξιοῖ ἑαυτοῦ τε καὶ τῶν ἄλλων γεγονέναι)" (*Leg.* 671b3–6). As Plato explains in the *Laws*, *parrhēsia* is a civic privilege²²⁴ that the Persian king Cyrus first bestowed on his subjects as a means of enhancing his soldiers' sense of duty in times of danger (*Leg.*

694a8–b1: μᾶλλον φίλοι τε ἦσαν στρατιῶται στρατηγοῖς καὶ προθύμους αὑτοὺς ἐν τοῖς κινδύνοις παρείχοντο).[225] In this setting, provided that the king was not jealous of wise men, the latter were able to contribute their intellectual acumen for the benefit of their community:

> And if there was any wise man amongst them, able to give counsel, since the king was not jealous but allowed free speech (διδόντος δὲ παρρησίαν) and respected those who could help at all by their counsel (τιμῶντος τοὺς εἴς τι δυναμένους συμβουλεύειν), such a man had the opportunity of contributing to the common stock the fruit of his wisdom. Consequently, at that time all their affairs made progress, owing to their freedom, friendliness, and mutual interchange of reason (δι' ἐλευθερίαν τε καὶ φιλίαν καὶ νοῦ κοινωνίαν). (*Leg.* 694b2–8)

However, Cyrus did not confer his model of governance on posterity; despite being "a good and patriotic commander" (694c6–7: στρατηγόν τε ἀγαθὸν εἶναι καὶ φιλόπολιν), he lacked proper education (694c7: παιδείας δὲ ὀρθῆς οὐχ ἧφθαι) and failed to anticipate that his sons, "overpampered and undisciplined" (695b3–4: οἱ παῖδες . . . Κύρου τρυφῆς μεστοὶ καὶ ἀνεπιπληξίας), would be unable to rule.[226] "Mad with drunkenness and boorishness" (695b6: μαινόμενος ὑπὸ μέθης τε καὶ ἀπαιδευσίας), one of his sons murdered his brother in a desperate attempt to secure absolute power, before yielding to the Medes and bringing his dynasty to an inglorious end. Given Alcibiades' Persian sympathies[227] and Socrates' profile as a model of philosophical *parrhēsia*, which entails telling the truth to oneself and one's fellow citizens,[228] the civic connotations of drunkenness in the *Laws* and the *Symposium* become more palpable.[229] In contrast to the sober and *sōphrōn* Socrates, Alcibiades equates freedom of speech with drunken license that threatens the order of the group.[230]

Alcibiades introduces numerous Dionysiac images, including that of the satyr Marsyas, to describe Socrates—so much so that Socrates, drawing attention to the comical aspects of his performance,[231] refers to Alcibiades' speech as his satiric or Silenic drama (222d4–5: τὸ σατυρικόν σου δρᾶμα τοῦτο καὶ σιληνικὸν). Unlike Marsyas, however, who mythically challenged Apollo to a musical contest,[232] Socrates does not use musical instruments; his words, however, have the same effect on his listeners (215c9–10: ἄνευ ὀργάνων ψιλοῖς λόγοις ταὐτὸν τοῦτο ποιεῖς), enthralling them and urging them to reconnect with the divine. "[Marsyas' tunes] uniquely make one possessed (μόνα κατέχεσθαι ποιεῖ) and, because they are divine (διὰ τὸ θεῖα εἶναι), they reveal those who need the gods and their rites (δηλοῖ τοὺς τῶν θεῶν τε καὶ τελετῶν δεομένους)" (*Symp.* 215c6–8). As he admitted, Alcibiades suffered a complete Dionysiac experience mesmerized by the philosopher's speeches:[233] "As for myself, gentlemen . . . I would have sworn about the effects I have suffered myself (οἷα δὴ πέπονθα αὐτὸς) from his words and still do even at this very moment (καὶ πάσχω ἔτι καὶ νυνί)" (*Symp.* 215d6–e4). In effecting such wild reactions in his audiences, Socrates resembles the dangerous Sirens (216a7–9: **ὥσπερ** ἀπὸ τῶν Σειρήνων . . . φεύγων), a common metonymy for the seductive stylishness of poetry, which Plato, preoccupied with its dangers, also employed in the *Phaedrus*.[234] Perhaps drawing on Marsyas' association with wisdom,[235] Alcibiades differentiates Socrates from the poets by stressing his extraordinary talent for self-control.[236] To enthuse his audiences, Marsyas performs his music with mastery, absorbed in the execution of his art; equally, Socrates' obsession with self-control, reiterated and enacted in his speeches, encourages his audiences to reassess their priorities and rise above their everyday cares to appreciate the more profound questions.

Plato actively reworks common perceptions of *mania*, familiar to us from the frantic scenes of drunken revelry celebrated on Attic vases as well as the representations in Athenian dramas of the Dionysiac rites celebrated throughout ancient Greece,[237] by introducing an element of sublimity and inner calm achieved by maintaining focus and clarity of thought in an otherwise busy and distracting environment. Being manic in this sense of being completely focused on his intellectual pursuits causes Socrates to appear detached and odd. Despite the typical association of wine consumption with violence (sexual violence but also violence as represented in the Dionysiac *sparagmos*),[238] the Socratic *baccheia* (*Symp.* 218b3–4)[239] does not incite violence, nor is Socratic introspection to be mistaken for melancholy.[240] Alcibiades insists on Socrates' ability to maintain his self-control, despite warning Agathon about Socrates' erotic effect on people (222b) and redeploying the Dionysiac imagery he started with (221d9–e1). While *baccheia* is often linked with Dionysian *sparagmos*, "a feeling of being pulled to pieces,"[241] Plato more closely echoes the description of Teiresias and Cadmus in the *Bacchae*, who embrace the Dionysiac cult even though it appears at odds with their old age. Like Teiresias and Cadmus, Plato is worried about Socrates being misinterpreted and misrepresented[242] and is at pains to show Socratic *baccheia* as contingent on inner peace.

Soon after Alcibiades concludes his speech, a large drunk group arrives and a new drinking regime prevails, as "suddenly a great crowd of revellers arrived at the door . . . the whole place was in an uproar and, losing all order, they were forced to drink a vast amount of wine" (223b2–3 and 5–6: ἐξαίφνης δὲ κωμαστὰς ἥκειν παμπόλλους ἐπὶ τὰς θύρας . . . καὶ θορύβου μεστὰ πάντα εἶναι, καὶ οὐκέτι ἐν κόσμῳ οὐδενὶ ἀναγκάζεσθαι πίνειν πάμπολυν οἶνον). The only ones who manage to maintain their drinking pace are Socrates, Agathon, and Aristophanes, who continue drinking *and* conversing till dawn. The scene is perhaps designed to remind us of Agathon's prediction at 175e7–9 that Dionysus would judge between him and Socrates on their respective claims to wisdom; but while Agathon and Aristophanes fall asleep under the influence of wine—another comical jibe at their inability to handle it[243]—Socrates collects himself and heads to the agora to continue his philosophical examination (cf. *Symp.* 220c–d).[244]

By portraying Alcibiades, as wine-soaked and unable to lie, keen to relate his personal experiences of Socrates, including the time when they served together at Potidaea, Plato stages the ultimate defense of the philosopher. Socrates responds to Alcibiades' praise of him in jest, by noting: "You seem to me sober (νήφειν μοι δοκεῖς), Alcibiades. For otherwise you would never have wrapped yourself up so charmingly all around trying to hide from sight why you have said all these things" (*Symp.* 222c3–6). Socrates' caustic response emphasizes Alcibiades' drunken state to the point of being painfully transparent. Furthermore, Socrates' dedication to philosophical examination illustrates once more his aversion to drunkenness in tandem with his aversion to politics—at least contemporary politics.[245] By contrast, despite having witnessed Socrates' "divine and gold, and all-beautiful and marvellous" *agalmata* (images/ representations),[246] Alcibiades remains irredeemably corrupt and unable to live up to the ideal of Socratic inebriation—leading to the shameful incident of 415 BCE, when, utterly drunk, he desecrated the *hermae*, the Athenian emblem of civic order.[247] Political ambition, as manifested in Alcibiades' case, goes hand-in-hand with unruly symposiastic behavior and a rejection of Socrates' exemplary civic ethos.[248] In a passage that, in my view, is evocative of *Symposium* 223d9–14, Plutarch four centuries later reaffirms Socrates' sense of symposiastic decorum by reminding us of the difference between drinking and getting drunk:[249]

> Surely it is not the same thing to be drinking and to be drunk
> (τὸ πίνειν τοῦ μεθύειν). When men have drunk till they ram-
> ble (ὥστε ληρεῖν), it is time, we assume, for them to go off
> to bed; but with men who can take a good deal of wine and
> go on drinking, who are, apart from that, men of sense (νοῦν
> ἔχοντας ἄνδρας), there is no reason to fear that they will
> miss the mark in reasoning (μὴ σφαλῶσι τῷ λογισμῷ), or be
> divested of their practised touch (τὴν ἐμπειρίαν ἀποβάλωσιν).
> (*quaest. conv.* 715d1–5)

While the *Symposium* debates the distinction between physical and philosophical drunkenness, one wonders how Plato sought to accommodate the
genuinely Bacchic insight of philosophers in the ideal city he describes in
the *Laws*. For, although Plato urges the Magnesians to practice wine-induced
sōphrosynē, he does not discuss the civic role of the philosopher explicitly.
Nevertheless, a special place for philosophical inspiration in Magnesia is
reserved by expanding on Solon's concept of *theōria* and its civic benefits.

Civic *Theōria* and Bacchic *Sōphrosynē*: Accommodating Philosophy in the City

Sōphrosynē is defined in the *Symposium* as "exercising control over pleasures and desires" (196c4–5: τὸ κρατεῖν ἡδονῶν καὶ ἐπιθυμιῶν),[250] but at
its heart Socratic *sōphrosynē* relies on the juxtaposition of Socrates' inner
restraint, which reflects his superior, divinely inspired perception and his
deceptively carefree external demeanor, which enables his comparison
to Dionysiac figures such as Marsyas, the Silenoi, and the Bacchants.
In the *Phaedo*, philosophers are praised for exercising virtues, including
sōphrosynē, in exchange for wisdom (69b1: φρόνησις)[251] but are also
famously characterized as the only true Bacchoi.[252] Socratic *sōphrosynē*
has therefore an essentially Bacchic dimension and is characterized
as a kind of intoxication-free dedication to Dionysus and his rites. In
defending *sōphrosynē* as the prerogative of the philosopher, Plato writes:
"Therefore *sōphrosynē*—what the many also refer to as *sōphrosynē*, that is:
not being excited by the passions (περὶ τὰς ἐπιθυμίας μὴ ἐπτοῆσθαι) but
being indifferent to them and behaving in a seemly manner (ὀλιγώρως
ἔχειν καὶ κοσμίως)—does it not suit uniquely those who despise the body
above all and pass their lives in philosophy (τοῖς μάλιστα τοῦ σώματος

ὀλιγωροῦσίν τε καὶ ἐν φιλοσοφίᾳ ζῶσιν)?" (*Phd.* 68c6–d1). As the genuine *Bacchoi*, having achieved purity from the senses so to witness reality with the eyes of their soul,[253] philosophers are uniquely positioned to advise their fellow citizens on the nature of *sōphrosynē*[254] and how it enables fostering alternative perspectives in the city.

Sōphrosynē is Socrates' core quality. Since *sōphrosynē* is also, as Plato argues in the *Laws*, the greatest civic virtue,[255] Socrates is the ideal citizen.[256] Accordingly, the insight that Plato claims for philosophers, although more often associated with solitary meditation than social interaction, lies at the heart of the Greek *polis*. This is the kind of civic consciousness that the "Test of the Wine" aims at in the *Laws*, which the Dionysiac Choir aspires to in instructing the citizens how to discern the right kind of *choreia* from pseudo-Bacchic dances;[257] equally, as Kleinias admits at 648e6–7, when citizens leave banquets for fear of becoming too drunk and suffering public ridicule, they are precisely displaying *sōphrosynē* (ναί· σωφρονοῖ γὰρ ‹ἄν›, ὦ ξένε, καὶ ὁ τοιοῦτος οὕτω πράττων).[258] The point is reiterated at *Laws* 673e3–6 where Plato concedes that the purpose of the Test, provided it is applied in "a lawful and orderly manner" (μετὰ νόμων καὶ τάξεως), is to achieve *sōphrosynē* (ὡς τοῦ σωφρονεῖν ἕνεκα).[259] In my view, the need to accommodate philosophical/true *baccheia* in the *polis*, as exemplified by these negotiations between Socratic intoxication and mere drunkenness, is paralleled by the need to accommodate Dionysus and his rites in Euripides' *Bacchae*—after all, the dramatic performances staged in the context of the Great Dionysia offered the Athenians the paramount forum for debating civic virtue.[260] As Dionysus declares in the *Bacchae*, "the city must learn . . . my Bacchic revels" (*ll.* 39–40: δεῖ γὰρ πόλιν τήνδ᾽ ἐκμαθεῖν . . . τῶν ἐμῶν βακχευμάτων).

Furthermore, as discussed in chapter 2, in the *Bacchae*, Euripides defends the sound-mindedness of the Bacchants but portrays Pentheus as "drunk" with the license of his newly acquired kingship—a "drunkenness" that the guests in the *Symposium*, especially Alcibiades but also Aristophanes, exemplify with their flawed performances of civic virtue.[261] The civic importance of the contrast between the literal-minded yet delusional king and the *polis*-minded though strange-looking followers of Dionysus becomes more palpable when Teiresias accuses Pentheus of doing disservice to the city by refusing to acknowledge Dionysus' divinity: "A bold and powerful man, one capable of speaking well, becomes a *bad citizen* if he lacks *sense* (κακὸς πολίτης γίγνεται νοῦν οὐκ ἔχων)" (*Bacch.* 270–271). Indeed, although initiating the Thebans into the rites of the God is a mission for the few, as Teiresias and Cadmus know too well (*l.* 196 cited in chapter 2, p. 63), and despite the citizens' original unwillingness (*l.* 39: κεἰ μὴ θέλει), Bacchic consciousness eventually prevails over Thebes (*l.* 1295: ἐμάνητε, πᾶσά τ᾽ ἐξεβακχεύθη πόλις). Thus, in Euripides, Teiresias and Cadmus act as the true Bacchoi urging the city to embrace Bacchic *sōphrosynē*. Although the civic profile of the Socratic philosopher, wholly preoccupied with saving his soul, is not explicit in the *Phaedo*, Plato seems to make a concerted effort to accommodate philosophical insight into the constitution of Magnesia in the *Laws*.

Lawgivers, we are told in the *Laws*, should aim at delivering to the citizens "all things that are good, both human and divine" (631b6–8: πάντα γὰρ τἀγαθὰ πορίζουσιν . . . τὰ μὲν ἀνθρώπινα, τὰ δὲ θεῖα·), aiming to secure their happiness (εὐδαίμονας ἀποτελοῦντες). As Plato reiterates in *Alcibiades I*, happiness is the result of being *sōphrōn* and good (134a12–13: οὐκ . . . ἐὰν μή τις σώφρων καὶ ἀγαθὸς ᾖ, εὐδαίμονα εἶναι), conditions that are fulfilled only when citizens are instructed in virtue:[262] "If you intend to manage the affairs of the city correctly and finely (ὀρθῶς καὶ καλῶς), you must impart virtue to the citizens (ἀρετῆς σοι μεταδοτέον τοῖς πολίταις)" (*Alc.* I 134b12–13). To achieve this goal, lawgivers (already identified with symposiarchs; see n70 above) are tasked with introducing the civic body to the divine hierarchy of virtues, featuring both *phronēsis* (understood as perception/awareness/insight) and *sōphrosynē*, as well as the principles of divine order to which the city ought to attune itself:[263]

That, then, which has first place among the divine goods, is wisdom (φρόνησις), and second is the judicious disposition of the soul applied with reason (μετὰ νοῦ σώφρων ψυχῆς ἕξις), and from them when combined with courage, justice is issued as the third and manliness as the fourth. All these are ranked by nature before the human goods and indeed the lawgiver must also rank them so. Then it must be declared to the citizens that all other rulings have these in view, and that the human goods look up to the divine and that all divine things look up to reason as their chief (τὰ δὲ θεῖα εἰς τὸν ἡγεμόνα νοῦν σύμπαντα βλέπειν). (*Leg.* 631c5–d7)

As Pfefferkorn has argued,[264] the sensible man ought to be preoccupied with deeds that are "dear and compliant with God" (716c1: πρᾶξις φίλη καὶ ἀκόλουθος θεῷ) since, according to the Athenian Stranger, "God may be the measure of all things in the highest degree" (716c4–5: ὁ δὴ θεὸς ἡμῖν πάντων χρημάτων μέτρον ἂν εἴη μάλιστα)—not man, as Protagoras argued (πολὺ μᾶλλον ἤ πού τις, ὥς φασιν, ἄνθρωπος).[265] Thus, "the moderate man is dear to God for he is similar to him" (ὁ μὲν σώφρων ἡμῶν θεῷ φίλος, ὅμοιος γάρ). Later in the dialogue, evoking Agave's creed in the *Bacchae* that "the best thing is to act in accordance with *sōphrosynē* and worship the gods" (*Bacch.* 1150–1151: τὸ σωφρονεῖν δὲ καὶ σέβειν τὰ τῶν θεῶν κάλλιστον), the Athenian Stranger claims that *sōphronein* is an essential part of virtue that belongs to the gods,[266] although traces of it remain in humans:[267]

> Since we have agreed among us that heaven is full of many good things but also of their opposites (πολλῶν μεστὸν ἀγα- θῶν, εἶναι δὲ καὶ τῶν ἐναντίων), and that the not-good things are more numerous, we say that such a battle is immortal (μάχη . . . ἀθάνατός), and needs incredible alertness (φυλακῆς θαυμαστῆς δεομένη); for the gods and daemons are our allies (σύμμαχοι δὲ ἡμῖν θεοί τε ἅμα καὶ δαίμονες), and we the pos- session of the gods and daemons (ἡμεῖς δ᾽ αὖ κτῆμα θεῶν καὶ δαιμόνων); and injustice and hubris combined with folly (μετὰ ἀφροσύνης) destroys us, but justice and *sōphrosynē* combined with wisdom saves us (σωφροσύνη μετὰ φρονήσεως), residing in the animate powers of the gods (ἐμψύχοις . . . δυνάμεσιν), while some small trace of them may be clearly seen here as also residing in us (βραχὺ δέ τι καὶ τῇδε ἄν τις τῶν τοιούτων ἐνοικοῦν ἡμῖν σαφὲς ἴδοι). (*Leg.* 906a3–b4)

In this context, the guardians of the laws ought to emulate the gods, who are "the greatest of all guardians and regarding the greatest things" (907a1–2: ἀλλ᾽ οὐ πάντων φυλάκων εἰσὶ μέγιστοι καὶ περὶ τὰ μέγιστα ἡμῖν οἱ πάντες θεοί).[268]

Plato also admits the need for a group of inspectors responsible for scrutinizing the conduct of the magistrates, while in the final book of the *Laws* we hear about the so-called Nocturnal Council (νυκτερινὸς σύλλογος, 909a3–4, 968a7; ὄρθριος σύλλογος, 961b6), dedicated to the salvation of the city. As Bartels has argued,[269] the Nocturnal Council combines/"mixes," "the most beautiful αἰσθήσεις and νοῦς, the two faculties upon which the σωτηρία of the polis as a whole depends. Νοῦς is informed by the senses: ὄψις, embodied probably by the θεωροί, and the ὄψις and ἀκοή of the younger members." Plato's concept of these special *theōroi* harkens back to the institution of religious *theōria*, which involved sending state delegates to perform religious functions abroad, and often comprised choric performances,[270] but also to the *theōria* ascribed to Solon, the celebrated lawgiver of Athens.[271] Solon's decision to leave Athens after he had imparted his laws and travel far and wide so to observe the constitutions of other cities and peoples is referred to as *theōria* (observation/spectation) in Herodotus (1.29–30) and the pseudo-Aristotelian *Constitution of the Athenians* (11.1). Similarly, Plato's *theōroi* are men of exceptional standing, entrusted with the task of visiting other cities,[272] who may on occasion be invited to join the Nocturnal Council upon their return to the city.[273] But unlike religious delegates, Plato's *theōroi* must seek intellectual exchange with the few divinely inspired men that exist across good or bad cities to benefit from their insights.[274] Plato's *theōroi* in the *Laws* combine Solon's literal traveling in search of different constitutions in distant cities with the metaphorical *theōria* of certain inspired individuals, established as the result of their inner philosophical efforts.[275] Furthermore, like Platonic *theōria* is used in the *Symposium* and the *Phaedrus* with reference to mystic visions,[276] the Nocturnal Council is also responsible for debating theological matters, especially the existence of gods and our ability to grasp their powers,[277] moving on to the issue of the divine origin of the soul (966d10–e1: ἐν μὲν ὃ περὶ τὴν ψυχὴν ἐλέγομεν, ὡς πρεσβύτατόν τε καὶ θειότατόν ἐστιν πάντων) and the rational principle that brought about the order of the universe (966e2–4: ἓν δὲ τὸ περὶ τὴν φοράν, ὡς ἔχει τάξεως, ἄστρων τε καὶ ὅσων ἄλλων ἐγκρατὴς νοῦς ἐστιν τὸ πᾶν διακεκοσμηκώς).[278] Without this kind of inspection and enquiry, Plato insists, a state will not remain perfect forever (951c3–5: ἄνευ γὰρ ταύτης τῆς θεωρίας καὶ ζητήσεως οὐ μένει ποτὲ τελέως πόλις).[279]

This is not, however, the mere abstract contemplation of the kind that Socrates denigrates in the *Phaedo*.[280] Because in the *Laws* Plato identifies *sōphrosynē* and its essentially Bacchic nature[281] as the goal of lawgiving and the citizens' attempt to develop their self-awareness, this raises the question about the role of the philosopher in the city.[282] In the *Laws*, Plato expounds a metaphor of the lawgiver as a musician, probably involving a pun on *nomos*, which can mean both law and (musical) genre.[283] From this perspective, the philosopher, who is both skilled in "the greatest form of music" (*Phd.* 61a4–5: ὡς φιλοσοφίας μὲν οὔσης μεγίστης μουσικῆς)[284] and has witnessed the eternal form of *sōphrosynē* and the other virtues,[285] is preoccupied with the practical application of his insights so that the city can be attuned correctly to them. Plato presents Bacchic *mania* as the first stage of our engagement with philosophy; provided that one exercises the *sōphrosynē* that befits a true Bacchant, one moves to the next stage where one experiences a mystic *epopteia* or *theōria* of divine truth.[286] Despite Plato's occasional arguments that the philosopher is disinclined to participate in politics,[287] Bacchically inspired philosophers, determined to convince the citizens that the most pleasant life is also the best according to the gods (*Leg.* 664b8–9: τὸν αὐτὸν ἥδιστόν τε καὶ ἄριστον ὑπὸ θεῶν βίον λέγεσθαι),[288] have an affinity with the philosophically trained magistrates of *Laws*. The philosopher represents the ideal instructor for Magnesia's Dionysiac Choir and its Nocturnal Council (while in this respect Magnesia resembles the heavenly city of the *Republic*, the only city in whose affairs the philosopher would be inclined to participate): "Perhaps there is a model (παράδειγμα) (of a city) in heaven for him who wishes to contemplate it and by contemplating it to become its citizen (τῷ βουλο-μένῳ ὁρᾶν καὶ ὁρῶντι ἑαυτὸν κατοικίζειν). It does not matter whether it exists or it will ever exist. The affairs of this city alone he would manage and of no other (τὰ γὰρ ταύτης μόνης ἂν πράξειεν, ἄλλης δὲ οὐδεμιᾶς)" (*Resp.* 592b1–5). The philosophical engagement of the Nocturnal Council is also shown insofar as Plato stipulates that its members are expected to examine the ethical principles of law, studying the nature of virtue and its various manifestations.[289] In Magnesia, the Nocturnal Council ensures good governance with the aid of inspiration provided by the *theōroi*;[290] Plato thus illustrates in the *Laws* how philosophical principles are to be debated and communicated across the city with *theōria* reserved for the truly inspired few but *baccheia* available to all citizens. In doing so, he reiterates the importance of *theōria*/contemplation as the key educational principle of the ideal city, but unlike his focus on the negative effects of drunkenness in the *Republic*,[291] in the *Laws* Plato elaborates his political vision with positive images of inebriation, which aid the cognitive and moral development of the citizens. As we shall see in chapter 4, Philo turns "sober inebriation" of the sage philosopher into the only guiding principle that can secure direct communication with the divine.

Concluding Remarks

A closer examination of Plato's metaphorical use of drunkenness points to a nexus of ideas shaped in the poetry of the archaic period, when the various *poleis* negotiated their individual norms and character. As these ideas were reworked in the shadow of Solon's influential paradigm in Plato's time, drinking wine came to be employed as a locus for discussing the ethical soundness of the citizens, as highlighting one's ability to construct an argument, recite or compose poetry, and, notably, crack jokes. Plato's appreciation of philosophy in Bacchic terms allows him the possibility to restore its value in the civic context, as indicated by the philosophical concerns of the Nocturnal Council and their commitment to the practice of *theōria*—whereby Plato reworks a Solonian practice to suggest that civic *theōria* should be primarily dedicated to philosophical debates at the highest level. While the citizens are encouraged to use actual wine to train in the highest civic virtue of *sōphrosynē*, Bacchically inspired philosophers are tasked with producing sober, reasoned reflections on how the city can best overcome the obstacles of the senses and emulate divine virtue.[292]

While in the *Laws* these topics are theorized in a more systematic way, the *Symposium* offers a vivid illustration of the forces that the philosopher is tasked to confront: the amoral, self-centered educator, preoccupied with securing accolades at all costs (Aristophanes), and the power-thirsty, ruthless politician, who despite his noble background[293] has anything but noble motives (Alcibiades). The association between Alcibiades and Aristophanes had been etched in the minds of the Athenians since at least the *Frogs*, where the chorus leader defends his right to "educate" the citizens (*ll.* 686–687: τὸν ἱερὸν χορὸν δίκαιόν ἐστι χρηστὰ τῇ πόλει ξυμπαραινεῖν καὶ διδάσκειν), enthralling the audience and claiming the first prize for the play (and even a second performance).[294] The first question that Dionysus poses there to the competing poets is about Alcibiades (*l.* 1424: πρῶτον μὲν οὖν περὶ Ἀλκιβιάδου τίν' ἔχετον/ γνώμην ἑκάτερος). The fact that Aeschylus, the poet who will end up victorious in the *Frogs*, recommends rehabilitating Alcibiades into the city (*ll.* 1431a–b),[295] recalls the Bacchic argument between the playwright and the philosopher, and foreshadows the conflict between the models of civic education supported by Aristophanes and Socrates.

In addition, the obvious drunkenness of Alcibiades creates a parallel to the manic inspiration of Socrates, as both are similar to the creative delirium claimed by poets and frantically debated in contemporary comedy. As Scott argues,[296] "the ways in which metaphorical language can slip into the funny and absurd are not only sources of humour, they are arguably also another manifestation of comedy's impulse towards exposure and revelation." Thus, the matter at the heart of the Platonic debate is whether philosophy is the only legitimate method of encouraging and guiding intellectual development and therefore the only force to shape civic ethos in the ideal city; his challenge arises from his reliance on symbols that are constantly (re)claimed by the arts[297] as well as religion,[298] and the practical solutions that he suggests in the *Laws* are unavoidably (and dangerously) deterministic. Aware of the similarities between poetry and philosophy stemming from their common need to find a persuasive style,[299] Plato wishes to stage a competition between true and sophistic persuasion.[300] After all, poetry and philosophy are styles of discourse that compete for the same audiences, appealing to their love for learning:

> For all the spectacle-lovers (οἵ . . . φιλοθεάμονες) seem to me to be such because they delight in learning things, and those who love listening to things (οἵ τε φιλήκοοι) would be most out of place (ἀτοπώτατοί) if included among the philosophers. They would not want of their own accord (ἑκόντες) to attend debates and that type of activity, but as if they have hired out their ears to listen to every chorus, they run around to the Dionysiac festivals, never missing one, either in the towns or in the villages. So, are we to call all these and other easily taught people, like these and the practitioners of the minor arts, philosophers?"
>
> "Not at all," I said; "but only those who are like philosophers (οὐδαμῶς, εἶπον, ἀλλ᾽ ὁμοίους μὲν φιλοσόφοις).
>
> "Who, then," he said, "do you mean the real ones?"
>
> "Those who love seeing the truth," I said (τοὺς τῆς ἀλη-θείας . . . φιλοθεάμονας). (*Resp.* 475d2–e5)

Furthermore, at the end of the *Symposium* Socrates is portrayed alongside Agathon and Aristophanes, the only ones still awake and drinking from the same cup (223c7: Ἀγάθωνα δὲ καὶ Ἀριστοφάνη καὶ Σωκράτη ἔτι μόνους ἐγρηγορέναι καὶ πίνειν ἐκ φιάλης μεγάλης). Unfazed by wine and fatigue, Socrates continues to hold sensible conversation, compelling his interlocutors to agree that a skilled poet ought to compose both tragedies and comedies (223d3–6: προσαναγκάζειν τὸν Σωκράτη ὁμολογεῖν αὐτοὺς τοῦ αὐτοῦ ἀνδρὸς εἶναι κωμῳδίαν καὶ τραγῳδίαν ἐπίστασθαι ποιεῖν, καὶ τὸν τέχνῃ τραγῳδοποιὸν ὄντα <καὶ> κωμῳδοποιὸν εἶναι). The scene, long discussed in scholarship,[301] points to the similarities between the two styles, which share Dionysus' patronage, performance spaces, and occasions of performance. However, tragedy and comedy are equally deceptive in their use of rhetoric and the way they develop citizens' civic ethos—or to put it more boldly, tragedy and comedy encourage tyranny, both in terms of their aesthetics and of the civic ethos they promote.[302] Tyranny is intoxicating,[303] like beautiful, meaningless verses; Pythagoras, we are told, appreciated drunkenness as a training course in madness[304] and urged alcoholics to constantly observe their conduct as the most effective means of shaking off their habit.[305] In many ways, this is precisely what Plato tries to achieve at the *Symposium*, where the drinking ethos and the arguments of the symposiasts reflect their level of ignorance. Like those in the *Republic* who watch beautiful spectacles but are unable to perceive true beauty,[306] the symposiasts have opinions but no knowledge. Although Socrates claims that being unable to control one's thirst or desire for wine is a clear symptom of uncritically giving in to bodily urges, he does not discount wine's ability to instill a sublime state of mind and suggests that, like humorous[307] and poetic styles of speaking, wine should be poured out carefully to bolster citizens' ethical training. Importantly, through his use of wine imagery in the *Symposium* and the *Laws* Plato offers practical examples of how to cope with metaphor itself; aware of the danger of getting carried away when applying allegorical interpretation, especially for the young (often the target of the sophists), Plato resolves that its use remains valuable as long as it serves civic values.[308] His dream, however, of the ideal city where education would be strictly regulated remained unattainable not only because of its unpopular reliance on philosophy but mainly because the *polis* became a thing of the past in the next historical period, the period of Alexander the Great and of the Hellenistic kingdoms.

Still, Plato's texts and the core metaphors they employ had a huge impact on later thinkers, who, fascinated with classical antiquity and full of nostalgia for a democratic distant past, continued to quote, paraphrase, and adapt Plato's ideas and his style of expression. Socrates' penchant for irony[309] and his habitual engagement with comic styles coincides with the widespread use of metaphors across classical literature as a common way of prompting self-reflection;[310] in this framework, Plato's confidence in the Bacchic nature of inspiration makes a lasting, though ever-controversial, impression.

Chapter 4

Platonic Inebriation after Plato

Rome and Alexandria

nihil aliud esse ebrietatem quam voluntariam insaniam

—Seneca, *Ep.* 83.18[1]

As I have shown, the metaphor of inebriation developed by Plato relied heavily on preexisting literary tropes and the structuring constraints of classical *polis* social norms. As society underwent profound changes during the fourth and later the third century BCE, the delicate structure of this Platonic metaphor began to fray. In the Hellenistic period, when Homeric ideas about benevolent kingship were rehashed by the Macedonian royal household and its opponents,[2] the use of inebriation as a cultural paradigm intensified. Separated from its city-state framework, inebriation became a means of expressing the ambiguities of a person's identity, especially the subtleties of belonging and exclusion—now experienced in a pronounced manner. Like the figure of Dionysus in the *Bacchae*, drinking became foreign and familiar at the same time.[3] In this bazaar of competing cultural visions, of being torn between own and other traditions, the adoption or rejection of cultural institutions such as the symposion became a statement about what people were prepared to defend. In the context of the kingdoms of Alexander's successors, inebriation was employed as a political tool to highlight the grandeur of rulers or their tyrannical decadence, but also as a literary reference signifying creative compulsion.[4] In this time of upheaval and intense political reorganization in the eastern Mediterranean, inebriation often remained associated with Bacchic frenzy and its theatrical cum religious performance; theatre, a major mode of imperial self-representation,[5] offered the subjects of the Hellenistic kingdoms a fruitful platform to debate the distinctiveness of their identity within a new multicultural political framework. Dionysus and his liquid came to stand for a keenly desired release (*lusis*),[6] from quandaries, whether religious, political, personal, or collective. While watching the god on stage as he alters the Bacchants' emotions, behavior, and perception of the world and their place in it, audiences underwent a merging of self into the Other and were urged to enact a transformation of their own consciousness.[7] From this perspective, the play, which represents the pinnacle of the respect that Euripides commanded across the Greek-speaking world in the post-classical period,[8] afforded its audiences an extraordinary experience of *theōria*, a concept that, as discussed in chapter 3, carried crucial civic but also religious and mystical associations eagerly exploited by Plato.

However, in the wake of the ferment of the Hellenistic period philosophers contributed to an ever-stronger wave of anti-intellectualism: the Socratic metaphor of inebriation was not only divorced from the social and political realities that informed it but was increasingly associated with the vanity of ambitious intellectuals. Images of drunkenness, characteristically deployed in the fierce debate between the Academicians and the Stoics on the metaphorical infrastructure of the new epistemological doctrine of *kataleptike phantasia*,[9] illustrate the factional preoccupation of intellectuals with monopolizing truth early on. This "unbrotherly aristocracy," to use Weber's characterization of intellectuals,[10] bequeathed to the writers of the Roman empire, a tainted metaphorical expression for debating our journey to wisdom:[11] now deracinated from its origins in the *polis*, inebriation continued to be employed by the various post-classical intelligentsias who sought to appropriate Plato's authority to castigate the erring views of their "drunken" opponents. In their effort to reinterpret Socratic inebriation, writers of the early imperial period often dismembered and only partially reappropriated Plato's complex metaphor. Hence, eliding the distinction between the Platonic metaphor and mere drunkenness, Lucian recapitulates it in the sharp idiom of a comic critic, ridiculing Plato's bombastic use of metaphor and the heady philosophical enthusiasm it signifies. Later Stoic thinkers such as Seneca often combined Socratic *sōphrosynē* with a stern proscription of excessive wine consumption.[12] Still, the Stoic physicalism about the soul allowed the probative and medicinal use of wine to be regrounded in physiological theory; because the soul is physical, physical remedies, such as wine, can assist in its development. Thus, Seneca's advice in the *De tranquillitate animi* to "drink generously" can be seen as representing a surprising continuation of Plato's use of inebriation—one that includes a more literal and more practical register closer to the "Test of the Wine" that Plato prescribed in the *Laws*. During this period, authors like Plutarch adopted the symposium as a literary genre that allowed contemporary intellectuals to indulge in the cultural ideals of the classical period, especially its philosophical tenets. The symposium presented Plutarch with a device to demonstrate his connection with Socrates, Plato, and other figures of the golden age of Greek philosophy; the wine-stained atmosphere that dominated the Platonic dialogues, however, is bleached by Plutarch's emphasis on sobriety. In line with the figure of the *homo intellectualis*, which emerges during the Second Sophistic, when "the study of Plato was vigorously promoted,"[13] Plutarch focuses on wine as a rhetorical tool for instigating a congenial exchange of ideas.[14] Drawing on Euripides' *Bacchae*, Plutarch is keen to redefine the Bacchic state of mind as follows:[15]

On the contrary, the ancients called the god Eleuthereus [Liberator] and Lusios [Releaser], and they thought that he had a great part in divination *not because* of the "Bacchic and mad" element (οὐ διὰ ‛τὸ βακχεύσιμον καὶ μανιῶδες᾽), as Euripides said (i.e., *Bacch.* 295), but because by removing from the soul its slavish and timorous and suspicious nature and freeing it from these, he grants us the benefit of treating each other with truthfulness and frankness (ἀπολύων τῆς ψυχῆς ἀληθείᾳ καὶ παρρησίᾳ χρῆσθαι πρὸς ἀλλήλους δίδωσιν). (*quaest. Conv.* 716b6–c2)

An alternative literary appropriation of Plato emerges with the tendency to resort to allegory, a form of speech previously known as *huponoia*,[16] which allowed Socratic inebriation to be renewed in later times as the main exegetical paradigm for profound truths. Nowhere was this cross-fertilization of intellectual traditions more productive than Ptolemaic Alexandria, a city that "occupies a special place in the history of Platonism."[17] Alexandria hosted important representatives of Middle Platonism such as Eudorus,[18] Numenius,[19] and Ammonius Saccas,[20] all of whom championed Plato's penchant for allegories and his apophatic thinking. Plotinus, the so-called founder of Neoplatonism,[21] spent eleven years in the city before traveling to Persia and eventually Rome. The Septuagint translation of the Hebrew Bible into Greek, commissioned by Ptolemy II Philadelphus, was also likely produced at Alexandria.[22] More than two centuries later, Philo, an Alexandrian Jew who was thoroughly familiar with Plato,[23] wrote philosophical treatises, allegorical commentaries, interpretations of Biblical law, and six exegetical books on Genesis and Exodus in Greek. Although often considered as unoriginal, Philo reiterates Plato's metaphor of philosophical rapture as drunkenness (although without adopting the symposiastic form) in his *De ebrietate*, an offshoot of his commentary on Noah's drunkenness (Gen 9:20–29). Philo accepts that wine can be consumed either decadently or wisely. Thus, he interprets Noah's drunkenness allegorically and includes him in the second group of insightful sages (*On Gen.* 2.68, commenting on Gen 9:21). Philo recasts the metaphor of inebriation as a biblical allegory in which inebriation no longer captures the phenomenological reality of philosophy, even loosely, but instead corresponds to an esoteric meaning of the scriptural text. Let us, however, begin to trace the post-classical reception of Plato's metaphor of inebriation by documenting its use in the intellectual crisis that broke out among his heirs at the Academy around the impact of the Forms on human perception.

The Symposion after Plato:
Debates on Perception and Drunkenness in the Academy

In the philosophical circles of the Hellenistic period, a debate on whether we can trust our perceptions (at least while embodied) had been brewing for some time. As part of this debate, the Stoics formulated the notion of *kataleptike phantasia* (conclusive or positive perception).[24] This notion of the "cognitive impression" (*kataleptike phantasia*), an impression that by itself guarantees the truth of a belief based on it, was (and remains) divisive. Defended by Stoics as a vital element of their epistemology, it was attacked by Academicians like Arcesilaus on the grounds that there could be no way to distinguish consistently ordinary, error-prone impressions from unimpeachable cognitive ones. In response, Carneades developed the theory of *pithanon*,[25] which as Cicero notes, is "something . . . 'probable,' or as it were resembling the truth," which provides us "with a canon of judgement both in the conduct of life and in philosophical investigation and discussion" (*Acad.* 2.10.32: *volunt enim . . . probabile aliquid esse et quasi veri simile, eaque se uti regula et in agenda vita et in quaerendo ac disserendo*).[26] Eventually, an eclectic approach gained pace that saw benefit in combining Platonic and Stoic views, leading to the so-called Middle Platonism of Eudorus and Philo.[27]

In the war of words that erupted around the concept of *kataleptike phantasia*, drunkenness provided a wealth of tropes to both sides of the debate. One of the central Academic counterexamples to the uniqueness of cognitive impressions involved "abnormal states of mind, such as dreams, illusions, drunkenness, and fits of madness. . . . In any of these states . . . we can have false impressions with the same representational detail and causal effects on us as waking impressions under normal conditions. So, in either case, the Academics argued, whether the nature of the objects or of our minds was at fault, it was always possible to have a false impression with exactly the same phenomenal content as a true impression."[28] Cicero, by contrast, relates the Stoic defense of the *kataleptike phantasia* against these objections. Despite the blurring of reality that occurs when sleep, wine, or mental disturbance affect us, as soon as we wake up, Cicero argues, we are still able to distinguish the two:

> Consequently, there is only one way of routing the problem of unreal presentations (*inanium visorum*), whether depicted by the imagination, which we admit frequently to take place, or in slumber or under the influence of wine or insanity (*siue in quiete siue per vinum sive per insaniam*): we shall declare that all presentations of this nature are devoid of perspicuity (*perspicuitatem . . . abesse*), to which we are bound to cling tooth and nail. For who, when he fashions something in his mind and paints it in his imagination (*sibi fingit aliquid et cogitatione depingit*), does he not, as soon as he has bestirred and recalled himself to sense (*se ipse commovit atque ad se revocauit*), immediately perceive the difference between perspicuous presentations and unreal ones (*perspicua et inania*)? The same logic applies to dreams. (*Acad.* 2.51)

In other words, despite being in a subconscious mental state, people can still be aware, and even intentional, about indulging its projections. A couple of paragraphs later, Cicero revisits the issue as follows:

> We are looking for a criterion of dignity, consistency, firmness and wisdom (*gravitatis, constantiae, firmitatis, sapientiae*); yet we find examples of dreamers, lunatics, and drunkards (*utimur exemplis somniantium, furiosorum, ebriosorum*). Do we notice in all this genre how inconsistent that talk is? If we did, we should not bring forward people who are tipsy or fast asleep or out of their minds (*vino aut somno oppressos aut mente*) in such a ridiculous fashion as at one moment to say that there is a difference between the presentations of the waking and sober and sane and of those in other conditions, and at another moment to say that there is no difference. (*Acad.* 2.53)

However, despite Cicero's general preference for reconciling Academic Scepticism and Stoicism,[29] his use of the trope of drunkenness betrays his impatience at Arcesilaus' stubborn assertion that nothing can be known.[30]

Like Cicero, Numenius polemicizes against Arcesilaus using the Corybantic nature of philosophical delirium. Although he does not explicitly use the intoxication paradigm against the Academicians, Numenius employs the language of *mania* to castigate their allegedly excessive and nonsensical attack on the Stoics. In this, he was probably inspired by Arcesilaus' reputation for his fondness of wine and excessive drinking habits—Diogenes Laertius characterizes him as "another Aristippus" (4.6.40: ἔτερος Ἀρίστιππος—ἐπὶ τὰ δεῖπνα πρὸς τοὺς ὁμοιοτρόπους), the most dissolute student of Socrates and a proponent of Cyrenaic hedonism (which, in direct opposition to Socratic teaching, defended bodily pleasures).[31] Diogenes also reports Hermippus' claim that Arcesilaus died after being rendered mad by intoxication (DL 4.6.44: Ἐτελεύτησε δέ . . . ἄκρατον ἐμφορηθεὶς πολὺν καὶ παρακόψας),[32] which corroborates Numenius' portrayal of him as a hypocritical, unworthy heir of the Platonic tradition who excelled in nothing more than wine-soaked blather. Numenius describes Arcesilaus' bursting, raging surge of words against the Stoics as follows: "The Stoics listened in amazement (ἐκπεπληγμένοι). For their Muse was not even then learned nor productive of such graces as those by which Arcesilaus talked them down, knocking off this argument, cutting away that, and tripping up others, and so succeeded in persuading them. When therefore those against whom he argued were worsted, and those in whose midst he was speaking were astounded (καταπεπληγμένων) . . ." (Num. fr. 25, des Places 1973, 71, *ll.* 150–156, trans. Gifford 1903). The fact that Numenius uses vocabulary familiar to us from Plato's description of Socrates' *baccheia* in the *Symposium* (note the use of the participle ἐκπεπληγμένοι; cf. καταπε-πληγμένων in the excerpt cited above) indicates how entrenched was by now the analogy between astounding one's audience with rapid, bombastic arguments and the effects of unregulated drinking. This essentially over-turns Plutarch's image of many speakers seeking in wine the confidence to overcome their inhibition (*quaest. conv.* 715d9–e4: πολλοῖς δ᾽ ἰταμότητα θάρσους συνεργὸν ὁ ἄκρατος);[33] for, while Plutarch specifies that this confidence ought to be graceful and persuasive (εὔχαριν καὶ πιθανήν)[34] and certainly not offensive or over the top (οὐ βδελυρὰν οὐδ᾽ ἄκρατον), Arcesilaus' flow of arguments was just that.[35] Notably, Numenius presents the feud between Arcesilaus and Zeno in terms of a brutal Homeric battle, possibly alluding to Arcesilaus' reputation as a poet,[36] and insisting that his attacks, while successful in wearing out his fellow dialectician, were basically unconvincing.[37]

Furthermore, Numenius carries this rhetoric over into his critique of Carneades, whose equally wondrous eloquence confuses his listeners into accepting drivel. Numenius writes: "for while he used to convince with his charm (**τῇ φαρμάξει**) his companions in frenzy (**τοὺς συγκορυβαντιῶ-ντας**), he was unaware of having first misled himself in not confirming the truth of his argument through perception but through persuasion by refusing all things at once" (fr. 27, des Places 1973, 76, *ll.* 15–19). Despite appearing convincing to some (τοῦ φαινομένου τοῖς πολλοῖς πιθανοῦ), Carneades' belligerent rhetoric (ἐριστικῶς), which is compared to a noisy, violent river current just a few lines above the text cited here,[38] had nothing to do with the truth (οὐ τῆς ἀληθείας στοχαζόμενος, fr. 26, des Places 1973, 75, *ll.* 112–114).

In undermining the reasoning faculty of Arcesilaus and Carneades, Numenius sides with the Stoics who claim that it is against reason (ἄλογον) to succumb to desires and excess, including drunkenness.[39] In his *Epitome of Stoic Ethics*, which became very popular among Christian writers,[40] Arius Didymus denies that the worthwhile man may use sarcasm and irony[41]—a trope that Plato's successors including Arcesilaus,[42] Lacydes,[43] and Car-neades[44] excelled at—or that he may speak to ingratiate himself,[45] which is in clear contrast with Arcesilaus' reputation for being a "friend of the mob" (DL 4.6.42: φίλοχλον). Arius' *Epitome* had encouraged the growth of Stoicism in Rome, further upheld by the fact that Stoicism complemented theoretical enquiry with practical participation in public life as a means of promoting virtue and limiting vice[46]—indeed, Arius himself had left Alexandria after 44 BCE to become the teacher and eventually friend of young Gaius Octavius (later emperor Augustus). Regarding drunkenness and the wise man, Arius echoes the views of Zeno and especially of Epictetus:[47] "It is not possible for a person with intelligence (τὸν νοῦν ἔχοντα) to get drunk. For drunkenness encompasses the wrongful (ἁμαρτητικὸν), since it is raving caused by wine (λήρησιν . . . παρὰ τὸν οἶνον), and the worthwhile man (τὸν σπουδαῖον) does wrong in nothing. Hence, he does everything in accord with virtue and the correct reasoning derived from it (κατ' ἀρετὴν ποιεῖν καὶ τὸν ἀπὸ ταύτης ὀρθὸν λόγον)" (*Epit.* 11m35–30, Pomeroy 1999, 88–89). In other words, in his criticisms of Plato's heirs Numenius eagerly employed Stoic theses, as crystalized in the writings of Arius, which had become the accepted view of Stoicism in Rome.

Yet Plato never ceased to fascinate the Roman literati. According to Epictetus[48] (who adds an air of scandal to his report), Plato was widely read in Rome, and his readership included women, who were especially attracted to the *Republic*. Furthermore, Plato's dialogues were performed at dinner parties during the Roman imperial period,[49] and under the Flavians, interest in Plato was notably renewed.[50] Perhaps because of this revival of interest, the genre of symposiastic writing was revitalized, most notably by Plutarch's *Quaestiones convivales*. However, although the symposium was retained as a literary form, in Plutarch's hands its Bacchic aspects drop away. Plutarch's drinking party is a curiously sober affair. In his work *On Garrulity*, echoing the Peripatetic tradition as distilled in the *Problems*,[51] Plutarch writes:[52]

Again, every self-respecting and orderly man would, I think, avoid drunkenness. For while, according to some, anger lives next door to madness (μανία . . . ὁμότοιχος), drunkenness lives in the same house with it (σύνοικος); or rather, drunkenness is madness, shorter in duration, but more culpable, because the will (τὸ αὐθαίρετον) also is involved in it. And there is no fault so generally ascribed to drunkenness as that of intemperate and unlimited speech (ὡς τὸ περὶ τοὺς λόγους ἀκρατὲς καὶ ἀόριστον). "For wine," says the Poet,

"urges a man to sing, though he be wise,
And stirs to merry laughter and the dance."[53]

And what is here so very dreadful? Singing and laughing and dancing? Nothing so far. But it lets slip some word better unsaid: this is where the dreadful and dangerous part now comes in. And perhaps the Poet has here resolved the question debated by the philosophers, the difference between being under the influence of wine and being drunk (οἰνώσεως καὶ μέθης διαφορὰν), when he speaks of the former as relaxation, but drunkenness as sheer folly (οἰνώσεως μὲν ἄνεσιν μέθης δὲ φλυαρίαν).[54] For what is in a man's heart when he is sober is on his tongue when he is drunk, as those who are given to proverbs say. . . . And the philosophers even in their very definition of drunkenness say that it is intoxicated and foolish talking (τὴν μέθην λέγουσιν εἶναι λήρησιν πάροινον); thus drinking is not blamed if silence attends the drinking, but it is foolish talk (μωρολογία) which converts the influence of wine into drunkenness. While it is true that the drunken man talks foolishness in his cups (ληρεῖ παρ' οἶνον), the chatterer talks foolishness on all occasions (ὁ δ' ἀδόλεσχος πανταχοῦ ληρεῖ),[55] in the marketplace, in the theatre, out walking, drunk or sober, by day, by night. (*garr.* 503D)

By understanding philosophical self-discipline[56] as requiring the rejection of physical drunkenness,[57] Plutarch amplifies Plato's ideal of moderation at the expense of his exploration of altered states of consciousness. Plutarch's "Socratic" banquet[58] represents a literary space, shaped by cultural memory[59] in which bonds of friendship and allegiance are fostered among the guests,[60] who are invited alongside the reader to see themselves as part of an intellectual continuum with classical thinkers, above all Plato and Socrates.[61] His contemporary Dio Chrysostom also adopted a moralistic approach to the symposion, typically relating images of drunken behavior to substantiate accusations of corruption against city governors,[62] while in *Discourse* 27 he echoed closely Plutarch's views about the symposion of the gentry.[63] Plutarch's sober, erudite banquet became a powerful model, as shown by Athenaeus' *Deipnosophistae* and Macrobius' *Saturnalia*.[64] His influence on Gellius and Apuleius is equally palpable.[65]

Undoubtedly, philosophical enquiry or *zētēsis*[66] after Plato, despite differences in style, audiences, and authorial purposes,[67] can still be mediated by wine. "Just as the wine must be common to all," Plutarch writes, "so too the conversation must be one in which all will share" (*quaest. conv.* 614e: δεῖ γὰρ ὡς τὸν οἶνον κοινὸν εἶναι καὶ τὸν λόγον, οὗ πάντες μεθέξουσιν).[68] However, Plutarch's efforts to construe the symposiastic framework of intellectual exchange emphasize congeniality and moderation, as reflected in his emphasis on restraint in both drinking and speech, including the jokes that banqueteers ought to demonstrate. Nonetheless, his works can still be read as a defense of Plato and his influential portrayal of Socrates in the context of a wider debate on intellectual advancement and our means of ascertaining it. At the start of his *Quaestiones convivales*,[69] Plutarch explains the nature of the philosophical banquet as follows:[70] "To consign to utter oblivion (ὅλως ἀμνημονεῖν) all that occurs at a drinking-party is not only opposed to what we call the friend-making character (τῷ φιλοποιῷ λεγομένῳ) of the dining-table but also has the most famous of the philosophers to bear witness against it: Plato, Xenophon, Aristotle. . . ." (*quaest. conv.* 612d). Although the figure of Socrates remains at the center of the banquet, the Bacchic Socrates of the *Symposium* and the *Phaedrus* gives way to a didactic Socrates;[71] accordingly, Plutarch defines the banquet as "A passing of time over wine which, guided by gracious behaviour, ends in friendship" (*quaest. conv.* 621c: διαγωγὴ γάρ ἐστιν ἐν οἴνῳ τὸ συμπόσιον εἰς φιλίαν ὑπὸ χάριτος τελευτῶσα).[72]

Reworking the image of the aloof and misunderstood philosopher, exemplified by Socrates in the Platonic dialogues,[73] Plutarch compares true philosophers to the Maenads. His comparison, however, does not rely, as one might expect, on their similar consumption of wine, nor their common ecstatic experiences; rather, Plutarch compares the ritual wands of the Maenads to the jokes of the philosophers, explaining the effect of the philosophers on their audiences as follows:[74]

> For he knows that, while men practise oratory only when they talk (ῥητορεύουσι . . . διὰ λόγου), they practise philosophy when they are silent, when they jest (φιλοσοφοῦσι δὲ καὶ σιωπῶντες καὶ παίζοντες), even, by Zeus, when they are the butt of jokes and when they make fun of others (καὶ . . . σκωπτόμενοι καὶ σκώπτοντες). Indeed, not only is it true that "the worst injustice is to seem just when one is not," as Plato says, but also the height of sagacity (συνέσεως ἄκρας) is to talk philosophy without seeming to do so (φιλοσοφοῦντα μὴ δοκεῖν φιλοσοφεῖν), and in jesting (καὶ παίζοντα) to accomplish all that those in earnest could. Just as the Maenads in Euripides, without shield and without sword, strike their attackers and wound them with their little *thyrsoi*, so the jokes and laughter of true philosophers (τῶν ἀληθινῶν φιλοσόφων) somehow arouse men who are not altogether invulnerable and make them attentive. (*quaest. conv.* 613f4–614a8)

In line with Plato's description of wine as a βάσανος ("test") of our ethical disposition in the *Laws*,[75] Plutarch subscribes to the view that wine does not affect one's moral substance but simply brings it to the surface.[76] Drunkenness, we are told, is used metaphorically by philosophers to connote "intoxicated and foolish talking"; although speech abnormalities, such as garrulity, reveal an impaired mental and ethical state, drinking per se is not blameworthy, a view reiterated by Dio Chrysostom.[77] Plutarch returns to the topic of silence and irregular speech patterns in his *Quaestiones convivales*, attempting to differentiate between garrulous orators (and their shaky moral basis) and real philosophers who thrive in silent contemplation.

In the nostalgia that characterizes the Second Sophistic, appearances took precedence over substance; in this context, symposiastic etiquette, crystallized in quotations from bygone poets and thinkers, stood for one's moral values in a more literal manner than Plato had ever envisaged. It was not merely suggestive of one's character but almost proof of one's moral and intellectual pedigree: to practice philosophy, one had to act the part. As Dio Chrysostom suspected, being familiar with the symposiastic etiquette and its attendant intimations about one's character and abilities made it easy to pretend to be a true lover of wisdom:

> But if one is devoted to philosophy and partakes of this study, one could never desert the highest things, nor, neglecting these things, could one prefer to engage in anything which is shameful and low (αἰσχρόν τι καὶ φαῦλον), or to be lazy and gluttonous and drunken. For to refuse to admire these things and to banish the desire for them from the soul and on the other hand, to lead the soul to hate and condemn them, is the essence of philosophy (προάγειν φιλοσοφία ἐστίν). However, possibly there is nothing to prevent one's claiming to be a philosopher and at the same time playing the impostor (ἀλαζονεύεσθαι) and deceiving (ἐξαπατῆσαι) oneself and everybody else. (*Disc.* 70.10)

Such impostors, preying on impressionable philosophy students, anxious to improve their lives through education, mushroomed in the post-classical era, and as we shall see in the next section, contributed considerably to the ever-popular suspicion against philosophers, mainly Platonic philosophers, who were relentlessly parodied in the prose dialogues of Lucian of Samosata.

Targeting Platonic Inebriation in Lucian's Comic Dialogues

The difficulties inherent in the metaphor of Socratic inebriation, explored in detail in chapter 1, mean that it represents an ideal target for criticism; a metaphor about wine drinking and higher levels of consciousness is always at risk of being collapsed into ordinary drunkenness. As Millett pointed out,[78] Socrates was already a controversial figure in his own time, and shortly after his death a plethora of Socratic literature came into circulation, including "the so-called Sokratikoi Logoi or 'Conversations with Socrates,' which was possibly as much hostile to Socrates as in his favour." Against the background of this variety of approaches to Socrates, Plato's metaphorical attempts to articulate Socratic wisdom were criticized. In the fourth century BCE, for instance, Dicaearchus shows little sympathy for Socrates' discursive tropes and accuses Plato of encouraging people to engage with philosophy at a superficial level:[79]

> . . . Plato renewed yet again (ἐπανεκαίνιϲ[ε]) the entire art and, in doing so, he added good rhythm (εὐρυθμίαν) to his dialogues.[80] However, he introduced many things of his own (ἴδια). [Through] these—if (I may) speak . . . frankly—he promoted and destroyed philosophy more than anyone else (εὔξηϲε[ν φ]ιλοϲοφίαν καὶ κατέλυϲ[ε]ν). For he urged everyone, so to speak, to practice it by writing down his dialogues. However, he also caused some people to philosophize in a superficial manner (ἐπιπολᾳίωϲ), leading them astray to an obvious pastime (ἐκτρέ[πων] εἰ[ϲ] τριβῄ[ν]). And he (sc. Dicaearchus) says that . . . [he] gave an impulse for practicing philosophy . . . so that those who did not learn. . . . (Phld. *Hist. Acad.*, *PHerc.* 1021, col. 1.1–22, trans. based on Fleisher 2023, 166)

This mode of criticism was still operative in the first century CE. Hence, Demetrius, the author of *On Style*,[81] offers aspiring writers the following advice about the use of metaphors in speeches:[82] "When a metaphor seems bold (κινδυνώδης ἡ μεταφορὰ), convert it into a simile (εἰς εἰκασίαν) for greater safety. A simile is an expanded metaphor (εἰκασία δ ἐστὶ μεταφορὰ πλεονάζουσα) . . . the result is a simile and a less risky form of expression, while the former was a metaphor and more dangerous. This is why Plato's use of metaphor in preference to simile is thought risky. Xenophon by contrast prefers the simile" (*Eloc.* 80). Socrates' superior state of mental agility and the process of acquiring it cannot be communicated and experienced precisely, which, as Halliwell pointed out, undermines the truth that ecstasy is alleged to lead to.[83] Thus, the boundaries between metaphor, experience, diction, and reality in the metaphor of Socratic inebriation increasingly become a locus for satire in the Hellenistic and early Imperial periods.[84]

This wariness around philosophical discourse[85] reflects a heated debate in the centuries after Plato,[86] a debate that does not always differentiate between Plato, Socrates, and their followers. Pseudo-Longinus names Caecilius Calactinus, who wrote at the time of Augustus,[87] as one of many later readers who criticized Plato's metaphor of inebriation:[88]

> However, it is obvious without my stating it, that the use of metaphor (ἡ χρῆσις τῶν τρόπων), like all the other beauties of style, always tempts writers to excess (πρὸς τὸ ἄμετρον). Indeed, it is for these passages in particular that critics pull Plato to pieces, on the ground that he is often carried away by a sort of Bacchic possession (ὥσπερ ὑπὸ βακχείας) in his writing into harsh and intemperate metaphors (εἰς ἀκράτους καὶ ἀπηνεῖς μεταφορὰς) and allegorical bombast (ἀλληγορικὸν στόμφον). "It is by no means easy to see," he says, "that a city needs mixing like a wine bowl, where the mad wine seethes (μαινόμενος . . . οἶνος . . . ζεῖ) as it is poured in, but is chastened by another and a sober god (νήφοντος . . . θεοῦ) and finding good company makes an excellent and temperate drink." To call water "a sober god" and mixing "chastisement," say the critics, is the language of a poet who is far from sober (ποιητοῦ . . . οὐχὶ νήφοντός ἐστι). (*Subl.* 32.7 = Caec. Cal. fr. 150, Ofenloch 1967, 129)

Although pseudo-Longinus defends Plato using vocabulary that evokes the *Symposium*,[89] Plato evidently did not escape being misunderstood. His critics were particularly challenged by Plato's mischievous awareness of the paradox of a philosophical mind overcome by frenzy but also able to secure a glimpse of transcendental truth(s).[90] Although both comedy's self-reflective properties and the Stoic emphasis on the usefulness of poetry might have been deployed to defend the Socratic style,[91] it was nonetheless the target of ridicule.

Lucian, who was thoroughly familiar with the Platonic dialogues, epitomizes this satirical mode of receiving both symposiastic laughter and the metaphor of Socratic inebriation[92] as an expression and articulation of philosophical consciousness.[93] In Lucian's *Lexiphanes*, the eponymous character (whose name etymologically connotes bombast), claims to have composed a *Symposium* to compete with Plato's famous dialogue:[94]

> ". . . I am counter-banqueting (ἀντισυμποσιάζω[95]) the son of Aristo in it."
>
> "There are many 'Aristos,' but to judge from your 'banquet' I suppose you mean Plato."
>
> "You read me right." (*Lex.* 1)

When invited by Lycinus, Lucian's alter ego,[96] to recite part of his new work (an invitation expressed in notably symposiastic terms),[97] Lexiphanes embarks on an incoherent exhibition of utter verbalism, replete with Atticisms,[98] to which Lycinus replies:

> Enough, Lexiphanes, both of the drinking-party and of the reading (καὶ ποτοῦ καὶ ἀναγνώσεως). I am already drunk and nauseous (μεθύω σοι καὶ ναυτιῶ), and if I do not very soon vomit all this gallimaufry of yours, know it well, I expect to go raving mad with the roaring in my ears (κορυβαντιά-σειν . . . περιβομβούμενος) from the words with which you have showered me. At first I was inclined to laugh at it all, but when it turned out to be such a quantity and all of a sort, I pitied you for your hard luck (τῆς κακοδαιμονίας), seeing that you had fallen into an inescapable labyrinth and were afflicted with the most serious of all illnesses—likely melancholy (μᾶλλον δὲ μελαγχολῶντα). (*Lex.* 16)

For Lucian, Plato's refutation of rhetoric is but another form of it, capable of obscuring the purpose of philosophical enlightenment when entrusted to the wrong people.[99] In adopting this approach, Lucian responds to the contemporary belief that few people can grasp complex philosophical arguments or the stamina to change their life in a way that accords with them. This image, however, is in clear contrast to the hordes of young men who in Lucian's time flocked to philosophers and oratory schools to improve themselves. The impetus for self-improvement, fueled by aspirations of social advancement, led to a systematic misreading or misapplication of Plato's dialogues.

Lycinus' informal diagnosis of Lexiphanes' insanity is confirmed a couple of paragraphs later by Sopolis,[100] a doctor who happens to approach the pair:

> But what luck! Here I see Sopolis the physician drawing near. Come now, suppose we put you in his hands, have a consultation with him about your complaint, and find some cure for you (ὑπὲρ τῆς νόσου ἴασίν τινά σοι εὑρώμεθα). The man is clever (συνετὸς), and often before now, taking charge of people like yourself, half crazed and full of drivel (ὥσπερ σὲ ἡμιμανεῖς καὶ κορυζῶντας), he has relieved them with his doses of medicine (ἀπήλλαξεν ἐγχέας φάρμακον). "Good-day to you, Sopolis. Do take charge of Lexiphanes here, who is my friend, as you know, and at present has on him a nonsensical, outlandish distemper affecting his speech (λήρῳ δὲ νῦν καὶ ξένῃ περὶ τὴν φωνὴν νόσῳ ξυνόντα) which is likely to be the death of him outright. Do save him in one way or another." (*Lex.* 18)

Thus, pretentious, exaggerated speech is firmly identified as a symptom, like Corybantic frenzy or drunkenness, of a disorder bordering on madness. Importantly, this condition is not to be confused with the insights of a true philosopher—with all his eloquence Lexiphanes is but a deluded impostor. By extension, Lucian also criticizes Plato, Lexiphanes' confessed model, for his florid metaphorical language.

Lucian returns to the theme of the exaggerated and haphazard metaphors employed by philosophers in *Hermotimus* 59, where Lycinus attempts to dissuade his friend Hermotimus from his eager desire to be tutored in philosophy. After comparing philosophers to wine merchants, always keen to deceive their customers,[101] Lycinus asks Hermotimus:

> Then how could you have known everything from just the first taste? There were not the same, but always new things being said on new subjects (ἀλλὰ ἀεὶ ἕτερα καινὰ ἐπὶ καινοῖς ἐλέγετο), unlike wine, which is always the same. So, my friend, unless you drink the whole butt, your tipsiness has been to no purpose; god seems to me to have hidden the good of philosophy right down at the bottom beneath the very lees (ὑπὸ τὴν τρύγα αὐτήν). You will have to drain it all to the end or you will never find that nectarous drink (τὸ νεκτάρεον ἐκεῖνο πόμα)

for which I think you have long thirsted. But you imagine it
to be such that, if you were but to taste and draw just a drop,
you would at once become all-wise, as, they say, the prophetess
at Delphi becomes inspired (ἔνθεον . . . γίγνεσθαι) as soon
as she drinks of the sacred spring and gives her answers to
those who consult the oracle. But it seems it is not so: you
had drunk over half the butt, and you said that you were still
at the beginning. (*Herm.* 60)

The condemnation of the intoxicating effect of philosophical rhetoric in
this dialogue is, however, marked by ambiguity. Hermotimus starts the
dialogue anxious to become a distinguished philosopher,[102] but when he
comes to his senses, as if recovering from a previous drunkenness (*Herm.*
83: ὥσπερ ἐκ μέθης ἀνανήφων), he pledges to drop his study of philosophy in tandem with its accompanying apparel (*Herm.* 86): he will cut his
long beard, refrain from his punitive lifestyle, maybe even wear purple.[103]
Notably, Lycinus introduces his attempt to sober up Hermotimus with a
reference to *Symposium* 215e1–2: "Take no notice of my Corybantic frenzy
but let me speak nonsense" (*Herm.* 63: ἐμοὶ μὲν ὥσπερ κορυβαντιῶντι
μὴ πρόσεχε τὸν νοῦν, ἀλλ᾽ ἔα ληρεῖν). For Hermotimus to be swayed by
Lycinus' counterarguments, he must have experienced another kind of
intellectual illumination, similar in its description at least to the mesmerizing effect his teacher's words used to have on him.[104] Lycinus is a deft
speaker, as Hermotimus protests repeatedly.[105]

In his *Wisdom of Nigrinus*,[106] which contains striking allusions to
Plato's *Symposium*,[107] Lucian moves from attacking conceited eloquence to
targeting Socratic inebriation directly. In the *Symposium* Plato is constantly
aware of the ineptness of the metaphors at his disposal to describe the
Socratic effect; therefore, Alcibiades' comic descriptions of the experience
of philosophy do not undermine Socrates' moderation, self-evident in
his sobriety while in the company of tipsy fellow symposiasts. Socratic
inebriation is cast as a genuine phenomenon, not a desperate attempt to
recreate it.[108] In *Nigrinus* 38, however, a description of Socratic inebriation,
based on both the *Symposium* and the *Phaedrus*, represents only heady
enthusiasm:

What a grand, wonderful, and indeed divine tale you have told
(σεμνὰ καὶ **θαυμάσια**[109] καὶ θεῖά . . . **διελήλυθας**[110]), my friend;
I did not realize (ἐλελήθεις . . . με) but you have been truly

chock-full of ambrosia and lotus! So that while you spoke, I felt something in my soul (ἔπασχόν), and now you have stopped I am vexed (ἄχθομαι):[111] to speak in your style, I am wounded (τέτρωμαι).[112] And no wonder (μὴ θαυμάσῃς)! For you know that people bitten (δηχθέντες) by rabid dogs not only go mad themselves, but if in their fury (ἐν τῇ **μανίᾳ**) they give the same thing to others, they too go out of their minds (**ἔκφρονες**[113]). Something of the affection is transmitted with the bite (τῷ δήγματι);[114] the disease multiplies, and there is a great run of madness (πολλὴ . . . τῆς **μανίας** διαδοχή). (*Nigr.* 38)

The character Nigrinus, described as a Platonic philosopher (par. 2), praises philosophy and the freedom it bestows, while criticizing in a distinctly Socratic manner people's preoccupation with wealth, money, and reputation (*Nigr.* 4: αὐτήν τε φιλοσοφίαν ἐπαινέσαι καὶ τὴν ἀπὸ ταύτης ἐλευθερίαν . . . πλούτου τε καὶ ἀργυρίου καὶ δόξης).[115] His words allegedly restore the "soul sight" of the zealous student who relates the story (*Nigr.* 5: τὴν δὲ ψυχὴν ὀξυδερκέστερος κατὰ μικρὸν ἐγιγνόμην)[116] and inspire him to offer an accurate (if ironic) interpretation of Plato's Socrates in the *Symposium* couched in the language of medicine, like that of the Hippocratic *Regimen*:[117]

> What he said has made me proud and exalted (γαῦρός[118] τε . . . καὶ μετέωρός[119]), and in short, I am no longer concerned with trifles. I suppose I have had a similar experience with philosophy that the Hindus are said to have had with wine when they first tasted it. As they are by nature warmer than we (θερμότεροι . . . ὄντες φύσει), on taking such strong drink *they went into frenzy* at once (αὐτίκα μάλα **ἐξεβακχεύθη-σαν**) and *became manic* by the unmixed drink twice as much (διπλασίως ὑπὸ τοῦ ἀκράτου **ἐξεμάνησαν**). There you have it! I am going about enraptured twice (ἔνθεος . . . διπλασίως) as much by his words. (*Nigr.* 2)

Although the interlocutor of Lucian's character protests that "this is not drunkenness but sobriety and temperance" (*Nigr.* 6: καὶ μὴν τοῦτό γε οὐ μεθύειν, ἀλλὰ νήφειν τε καὶ σωφρονεῖν ἐστιν), Nigrinus' student, like Hermotimus above, clings to the bombastic descriptions of his transformation and revels in the license philosophy provides to use this kind of language; Nigrinus himself, trapped in his image, watches on in guilty awareness and is unable to react.

Peterson, in her 2010 thesis, argues that Lucian is critical not only of the intoxicated student in *Nigrinus*[120] but also of the Platonic philosopher himself. Although Lucian insists, in the *Letter to Nigrinus* that prefaces the dialogue, that the work was meant as a compliment to Nigrinus,[121] Peterson claims, drawing on Plato, Aristophanes, and Thucydides, that Lucian is critical of Nigrinus' love for *logoi*[122] and of his inability to protect the student from his enthusiastic yet shallow appreciation of philosophy. Despite his complicity in the misapprehensions of his student, Nigrinus shows some degree of awareness of his contribution to contemporary Roman culture, which Lucian castigates as preoccupied with spectacles and superficial impressions; in *Nigrinus* 19, the philosopher compares himself to Odysseus in trying to deal with the Siren-like temptations of Rome.[123] As Peterson points out, Lucian also uses a pejorative comparison in *Hermotimus* 86,[124] where he writes that he would run away from a philosopher as if from a mad dog (ὥσπερ τοὺς λυττῶντας τῶν κυνῶν).[125] Although this seems to imply criticism of Platonism generally, it is worth noting that such metaphors are themselves embedded within Platonism; in the *Symposium*, for example, as we saw, Alcibiades compares Socrates to the Sirens (216a7–9) and his speeches to the bite of a snake (*Symp.* 217e, 218a with n114). Could we not, then, appreciate the self-critical metaphor that Lucian puts in the mouth of the Platonic Nigrinus as a comic exaggeration that originates within and expands the banter between the guests in Plato's *Symposium*? While I agree with Peterson that both Nigrinus and his student are subjects of Lucian's satire, in my view, the real target of the *Nigrinus* is the conversion to philosophy and its articulation in general, more than any specific character.[126]

In Lucian's *Bis Accusatus*, Academy is portrayed as claiming victory at court over Drunkenness because she has been able to change the drunken ways of the bad-boy-turned-philosopher Polemon,[127] whose description readily evokes Alcibiades in the *Symposium*.[128] Polemon's physical drunkenness corresponds to his "inspirational" way of teaching,[129] yet when Drunkenness is too intoxicated to defend her case, Academy offers to speak for her, alluding to the disconcerting Socratic practice of delivering arguments on behalf of his rhetorical opponents—appreciated as a key feature of Socratic irony by Cicero, who describes it as *severe ludas* at *De Or.* 2.269–270.[130] As Lane has pointed out,[131] Socrates employed his ironic, playful style both in the Aristophanic way, where it means "concealing by feigning," and in the Aristotelian way, where the emphasis is put on self-deprecation. This style has confused ancient as well as modern readers[132]—hence, in *Bis Accusatus* Academy uses the opportunity to discredit further the arguments of Drunkenness instead of delivering a fair defense on her behalf.[133] As an author of satiric dialogues, Lucian engages with Old Comedy,[134] recognizing its affinity with philosophy and its equal claim to *parrhēsia*.[135] In this guise, he recalls the evaluation of the flow of wine and jokes[136] in the post-Platonic era.

Lucian's characters, keen to make progress in philosophy but wary of the risk of misguided enthusiasm, embody a cultural anxiety seen also in Horace's semi-autobiographical writings. Philosophical *mania* and its symptoms presented a major challenge for the Romans authors; to start with, Bacchic religion was shocking in its "transgression of distinctions of gender, age, and class."[137] Equally troubling was the aloofness of Socratically inebriated philosophers and their indifference to everyday problems, as Horace reminds us. In his first *Epistle*, Horace pretends to complain about Maecenas' continual demands that he should write poetry[138] and informs us of his recent decision to return to philosophical study,[139] a long-forgone pursuit of his youth.[140] He cannot disguise his trepidation, although his age makes the choice appealing, and he confidently states that he is "totally absorbed" in his enquiry. Horace is very aware that meddling with philosophy may not get him all that far.[141]

Horace clearly outlines not only his mistrust of philosophical gurus but also the traps that intellectually inclined individuals should be aware of in contemporary Rome, where "wise men" were always looking to secure financially stable students. His verses evoke Plato's warning about charlatans performing rites in the names of Musaeus and Orpheus[142] and anticipate the enticing mantras of philosophy teachers in Lucian's time. How can he possibly be "royally right,"[143] and maintain his sanity, given the self-serving nature of people,[144] who are often fixated on appearances more than the essence of things? "What, when my judgement (*mea . . . sententia*) is at strife with itself, scorns what it craved, asks again for what it lately cast aside; when it rages (*aestuat*), and in the whole system of life is out of joint, pulling down, building up, and changing square to round? You think my madness is the usual thing (*insanire putas sollemnia me*) . . ." (*Ep.* 1.1.97–101). Horace stages a dramatic depiction of prospective students attacked on all sides, including from the money-savvy bankers who operated in the arcade of Janus[145] and urged prioritizing money over virtue. The students' choice is not a straightforward one: resorting to fables and mythical narratives such as Heracles' adventure against the monster Cacus (1.1.74–75), Horace decides to take a stand against the dissenting voices that seek to lure him in; in doing so, however, he continues to employ the metaphorical language that teachers of philosophy habitually used.

Horace's turn to Stoic theories and his resultant involvement in politics[146] is rather shaky; hence, as he prepares "to guide and solace himself" with the little doctrinal knowledge he can recall (1.1.27: *his ego me ipse regam solerque elementis*), he feels tormented like a sailor at sea, torn between the theories of the various schools (*Ep.* 1.1.15: *quo me cumque rapit tempestas, deferor hospes*). Nevertheless, he tries to muster courage by reminding himself (and his readers) of the great lengths to which people go for profit rather than virtue:

> To flee vice is the beginning of virtue (*vitium fugere*), and to have got rid of folly (*stultitia caruisse*) is the beginning of wisdom (*Virtus est . . . et sapientia prima*). You see with what anxious thought and peril of life you strive to avoid those ills you deem the greatest, a slender fortune and the shame of failure at the polls. Ardent trader that you are, you rush to the furthest Indies, fleeing poverty through sea, through rocks, through flame: but that you may cease to care for the things which you foolishly admire and crave, will you not learn and listen and trust one wiser than yourself? What wrestler in the village games and at the crossways would scorn being crowned at the great Olympic games, who had the hope,[147] who had the surety of victory's palm without the dust? Of less worth than gold is silver, than virtue gold (*Vilius argentum est auro, virtutibus aurum*). (*Ep.* 1.1.41–52)

In his mocking approach, he assumes the role of a "doctor of the soul"[148] and gives a detailed account of the bogus remedies often prescribed for the malady of vice, ranging from certain spells and magical incantations (1.1.34: *sunt verba et voces*), to rites (1.1.36: *certa piacula*), to readings that can bring about purification (1.1.37: *ter . . . lecto . . . libello*).[149] Horace's preoccupation with money here is probably informed by the Epicurean emphasis on social criticism[150] and meant as a taunt against the Stoics and their contentious relationship with wealth.[151] Finally, Horace appears to put an end to his professed turn to philosophy by revoking his involvement in public affairs and satirizing the Stoic sage: "In sum: the sage is less than Jove alone; he is rich, free, honourable, beautiful, indeed, king of kings and above all of sound mind (*praecipue sanus*), except when he has a troublesome cough" (*Ep.* 1.1.106–108). Given the intertextual affinities between Horace and Seneca,[152] I think that Seneca picks up several of the themes of *Epistle 1* in *De tranquillitate animi*, a treatise written to console his young mentee, Annaeus Serenus, who, impatient and insecure about his philosophical competence, evokes Horace's inner turmoil and anticipates Lucian's confused students of philosophy. When he turns to Seneca for advice, he receives a controversial response: drink liberally!

Platonic Inebriation in Seneca and the Stoic Emotion of Elation

Written between 49 and 62 CE, *De tranquillitate animi* was addressed to a young Serenus, who, although his name connotes tranquility,[153] found himself, like Horace (1.1.15 cited above), feeling "like a boat tossed about by the rolling of the ship" (1.18),[154] worn out with worry about his ability to distinguish himself philosophically. Energetic and ambitious to enter public life,[155] Serenus readily evokes Plato's Alcibiades,[156] and, like Socrates in *Alcibiades I*, Seneca tries to reassure him (3.3–4) by encouraging him to seek self-knowledge[157] and offering practical guidance for regaining his equilibrium.[158] Alongside other remedies such as getting enough sleep (17.6), taking walks to get fresh air, going on a trip, and engaging in social interaction (17.8–9), Seneca recommends *liberalior potio* ("generous drinking"). Echoing Plato, Seneca cautions his reader that drinking should be ruled by the principle of "healthy moderation" to avoid the risk of becoming addicted. The most controversial part of the text reads as follows:[159]

> We must be indulgent to the mind, and from time to time must grant it the leisure that serves as its food and strength. And, too, we ought to take walks out-of-doors in order that the mind may be strengthened and refreshed (*augeat attollatque se animus*) by the open air and much breathing; sometimes it will get new vigour from a journey by carriage and a change of place[160] and festive company and generous drinking (*liberalior potio*). At times we ought to reach the point even of intoxication, not drowning ourselves in drink, yet succumbing to it (*non numquam et usque ad ebrietatem veniendum, non ut*

> *mergat nos, sed ut deprimat*); for it washes away troubles, and stirs the mind from its very depths (*ab imo animum movet*) and heals (*medetur*) its sorrow just as it does certain ills of the body; and the inventor of wine is not called the Releaser on account of the license it gives to the tongue (*Liberque non ob licentiam linguae dictus*), but because it frees the mind from bondage to cares (*liberat servitio curarum animum*) and emancipates it and gives it new life and makes it bolder in all that it attempts. *But, as in freedom,*[161] *so in wine there is a wholesome moderation* (**Sed ut libertatis ita vini salubris moderatio est**). (*Tranq.* 17.8–9)

Described as "the *locus classicus* for the Senecan theory of the enthused poet,"[162] these lines appear to oppose the Stoic rejection of drunkenness[163] to which Seneca subscribes in one of his *Letters*.[164] Yet despite the appearance of contradiction,[165] Seneca's valorization of wine as conducive to philosophical inspiration has precedents within Stoicism.[166]

As Tieleman has argued,[167] Zeno and Chrysippus accepted that psychological conditions could sometimes be treated through physical means such as diet or exercise. Several sources even report that Zeno treated his own melancholic disposition by drinking and that he quipped that the reason why an austere man such as himself drank so freely at social gatherings is that "lupini beans too are bitter but become sweet when soaked."[168] In Tieleman's opinion,[169] this is an application of the principle that food and drink "may serve to reduce certain excesses and deficiencies inherent in one's physique," which explains why "Zeno's too dry and cold soul is brought into balance by means of wine (which was generally considered as a hot liquid)." Zeno seems to be borrowing here from the same medical and philosophical traditions that Plato employed in the *Laws* and the *Symposium*. Indeed, as we saw in chapter 2, works like the Hippocratic *Regimen*[170] assume a balance between body and soul achieved by "a correct mixture of hot, cold, moist and dry."[171] When the consistency of this mixture suffers an imbalance, due to age or other reasons, a doctor can intervene by prescribing a specific restorative diet, which may include wine. Wine was also believed to induce heat in the body.[172] Just as Plato, under the influence of Heraclitus and Hippocrates,[173] presented Socrates in the *Symposium* as keeping his soul warm and impervious to both wine and cold with constant philosophical cogitation, Seneca cites the examples of Solon, Arcesilaus, and Cato, all virtuous men with a reputation for indulging occasionally in heavy drinking.[174]

The question nonetheless remains as to how Seneca could justify the need for an excited mind (*mota mens*) from a Stoic point of view.[175] Before demonstrating that the *mota mens* Seneca praises in the passage above is not, in fact, an irrational state, it is worth pointing out that recent scholarship has turned away from the belief that *apatheia* was at all times a "fundamental rule"—as Mazzoli puts it[176]—to which aspiring Stoics were beholden.[177] Stoics of the Imperial period, such as Seneca and Epictetus, explicitly discussed the possibility that Stoic *proficientes* could feel what Graver calls "progressor emotions" and Brennan calls "veridical emotions," which are based on a correct valuation of good and evil and inform Seneca's prescription of regular moral self-assessment.[178] The excited mind praised by Seneca in *De tranquillitate* can be interpreted as undergoing such a "progressor emotion," a feeling of self-transcendence achieved when the mind is temporarily freed from mundane worries, giving the Stoic sage a foretaste of the sublime joy to which he aspires. In its use of this kind of altered state of consciousness and the emotions that accompany it, Stoicism seems indeed to anticipate recent developments in cognitive phenomenology.[179]

Although the Romans were long familiar with wine drinking,[180] and appreciated both its positive, therapeutic properties[181] as well as the problems of alcoholic addiction,[182] our sources insist on its moral (rather than social) dimensions. As Foucault has noted, this typically (albeit not exclusively) Platonic[183] theme of ecstatic transcendence often involves an element of self-examination:[184] "The movement by which the soul turns to itself is a movement in which one's gaze is drawn 'aloft'—towards the divine element, towards essences and the supra-celestial world in which they are visible." Foucault explained Seneca's practice of self-reflection as "a turning round on the spot," aimed at establishing "certain relations with oneself"[185] alone. Emotions, however, play an important role in this process for Seneca, and as such, alcohol and other worldly means of mood alteration can be employed to help bring it about. Importantly, Seneca appreciates the medium of the senses in achieving spiritual elevation, and the wine drinking he prescribes to Serenus serves exactly this purpose—to release him from everyday anxiety and prepare him for serious philosophical progress. Thus, in my view Seneca engages with Platonic *mania* as a way of discussing the nature of personal progress in philosophy. In *De vita beata* 8.4 (which concludes with explicit references to Plato's *Phaedrus* and *Alcibiades* I)[186] Seneca writes:

> Let reason (*ratio*) search into external things at the instigation of the senses (*sensibus irritata*), and, while it derives from them its first knowledge (*principia*)—for it has no other base from which it may operate, or begin its assault upon truth (*ad verum impetum capiat*)—yet let it fall back upon itself (*in se revertatur*). For God also, the all-embracing world and the ruler of the universe (*rectorque universi*), reaches forth into outward things (*in exteriora quidem tendit*), yet, withdrawing from all sides, returns into himself (*introrsum undique in se redit*).[187] And our mind (*nostra mens*) should do the same; when, having followed the senses (*secuta sensus*) that serve it, it has through them reached to things without (*ad extema porrexerit*), let it be the master both of them and of itself (*illorum et sui potens sit*).

Seneca recognizes that progress toward tranquility is not uniform, and that interventions, like those facilitated by wine, are needed along the way; thus, in his *De Otio* he recommends the constant monitoring of one's progress in virtue, albeit with no precise reference to drunkenness.[188] In my view, by advising Serenus to drink liberally in *De tranquillitate*, Seneca tries to pace Serenus' intellectual progress. Monitoring our progress in philosophy is akin to the Socratic *elenchus*, about which Plutarch, Seneca's much younger contemporary, notes:[189] "So too in philosophy one may take as a proof to himself of making progress the consistency and continuity of his course (τὸ ἐνδελεχὲς καὶ τὸ συνεχὲς τῆς πορείας), without making many stops on the way (ἐπιστάσεις), followed by leaps and bounds (ὁρμὰς καὶ ἐπιπηδήσεις), but smoothly and firmly ever forging ahead and without stumbling (ἀπταίστως) going through philosophic reasoning (τεκμήριον . . . ποιήσαιτο προκοπῆς)" (*De profect. in virt.* 86c). Plutarch recognizes that interruptions may happen and urges sufferers to expel their sluggishness through diligence and practice (*De profect. in virt.* 76f: ἐκθλιβομένης πόνῳ καὶ ἀσκήσει τῆς ῥαθυμίας). Citing the example of Diogenes, who experienced a moment of weakness, he concludes: "Now when such fits of dejection (κατασπασμοὶ γέ) become infrequent, and the objections and protests made by the mind (αἴ . . . ἐξαιρέσεις καὶ ἀνακρούσεις τοῦ φρονήματος) against them arrive quickly, just as after taking a turn, and they dispel easily our depression and dismay (ῥᾳδίως τὸν ἄλυν καὶ τὴν ἀδημονίαν), we may well believe that our progress rests on a firm foundation (ἔν τινι βεβαίῳ τὴν προκοπὴν εἶναι δεῖ νομίζειν)" (*De profect. in virt.* 78a).

Despite Plutarch's allegations, that the Stoics do not always admit to enlisting passion for educative purposes,[190] using wine to alleviate "fits of dejection" is a soundly Stoic attitude. For the Stoics, as Seneca argues at *De vita beata* 3.3 and 6.1–2, the harmony of the soul with its own nature and its circumstances is the greatest virtue. Because the human soul is perceived as unified with the body, it can react to certain food and drinks.[191] Seneca, who perceived virtue as the health of the soul and himself as its doctor,[192] discusses the role of physical remedies at his *De ira* 2.19–20. There he distinguishes between minds dominated by the element of fire, which are disposed to anger, and minds dominated by the cold element, which are timid, gloomy, and suspicious.[193] Those with fiery temperaments should engage in games or physical exercise but avoid drinking, because alcohol increases heat and kindles anger;[194] whereas those with cold temperaments "ought to be encouraged and indulged and summoned to happiness" (2.20.4: *extollenda itaque fovendaque . . . et in laetitiam evocanda sunt*) even by means of drunkenness (*ebrietas*).[195] Seneca writes: "In this manner drunkenness too [is beneficial] (*ebrietas [utilis est]*);[196] for it makes men forward and bold (*protervos et audaces*), and many have been better at the sword (*meliores ad ferrum*) because they were the worse for drink. In this manner you can also say that lunacy and madness are essential to strength (*phrenesin atque insaniam viribus necessariam*), since frenzy often makes men stronger (*validiores furor reddit*)"[197] (*De Ira* 1.13.3). Based on Serenus' own description of his weakness of will and Seneca's diagnosis of his condition as a form of inertia and self-doubt (*bonae mentis infirmitas*),[198] Serenus is a perfect illustration of such a cold, sluggish temperament. Accordingly, Seneca's suggestions that Serenus should drink, go out, and seek company are meant as physical remedies to counter his nervous disposition and help him regain his mental equilibrium[199] and indeed a sense of his progress in philosophy.

In the *De ira*, Seneca explicitly dismisses the belief that emotions themselves can ever bring about moral greatness. An enraged person, he argues, may think that he "breathes forth something lofty and sublime" (1.20.2: *altum quiddam et sublime spirare se*), but his condition is merely a "swelling" of the soul (*tumor*), without any solid foundation (*nil solidi subest*).[200] The philosopher, Seneca notes in one of his *Letters* to Lucilius, will only have reason to rejoice when he manages to complete his intellectual illumination:[201]

> Then our mind (*animus noster*) will have reason to rejoice in itself (*gratuletur sibi*) when, freed from this darkness in which it roams, not only will it glimpse the light with weak vision (*tenui visu*), but it will absorb the full light of day and will be restored (*redditus*) to its place in the sky, when it will regain the place (*receperit locum*) that it occupied as its allotment at birth. Its own foundations call it back upward (*sursum illum vocant initia sua*). And it will reach that goal even before it is released from its prison below (*antequam hac custodia exsolvatur*), as soon as it has cast off its vices, and, in purity and lightness, has leaped up into divine thoughts (*purusque ac levis in cogitationes divinas emicuerit*). (Sen. *Ep.* 79.12)

Elsewhere, however, Seneca explicitly contrasts a rational form of enthusiasm that strengthens the mind with an irrational counterpart that leads to emotional turmoil.[202] In *Letter* 76.17, for example, he writes:

> If every good is in the soul, then whatever strengthens, uplifts, and enlarges (*confirmat, extolit, amplificat*) the soul, is a good; virtue, however, does make the soul stronger, loftier, and larger (*validiorem . . . et excelsiorem et ampliorem*). For all other things, which arouse our desires, depress the soul and weaken it (*inritant deprimunt quoque . . . labefaciunt*), and while they seem to uplift it (*cum videntur attollere*), they are merely puffing it up and deceiving it with much vanity (*inflant ac multa vanitate deludunt*).

In a similar vein, Seneca argues that good things "do not corrupt the spirit, and they do not tempt us. They do, indeed, uplift and broaden the spirit, but without puffing it up" (*Ep.* 87.32: *non corrumpunt animos, non sollicitant; extollunt quidem et dilatant, sed sine tumore*). Seneca's notion of philosophical enthusiasm, then, is not a form of irrational ecstasy, but a fundamentally rational feeling of moral elevation, which can be assisted by ordinary sensual experience, including, crucially, inebriation. By appropriating the vocabulary of sublimity to sketch an inspiring portrait of ordinary inebriation, Seneca offers a revision of Platonic inebriation, here used to demonstrate to Serenus that the pursuit of Stoic tranquility need not be a glum, uninspired affair. As Graver has pointed out, Seneca accepts that Stoics experience joy not only as a permanent state resulting from practicing virtue and attaining wisdom[203] but also "as a response to circumstances that accord with nature."[204]

Despite the criticism that *De tranquillitate* oscillates between reiterating common philosophical *topoi* and responding to Serenus' troubles,[205] it is worth noting that at the end of the work Seneca responds to precisely the condition that Serenus self-diagnoses at *Tranq.* 13–14.[206] There, Serenus describes how, even as he attempts to cultivate the simple, unpretentious writing style that seems appropriate for a practicing Stoic, he occasionally gets carried away by his inspiration. Serenus deplores this tendency in himself and chastises himself in strong terms because "forgetting then the rule and a more disciplined judgment, I am swept to loftier heights by an utterance that is no longer my own" (1.14: *oblitus tum legis pressiorisque iudicii sublimius feror et ore iam non meo*).[207] Seneca unmistakably echoes this expression when he returns to the topic of sublimity in *Tranq.* 17.11 and describes how the mind when inspired "chants a strain too lofty for mortal lips" (*cecinit grandius ore mortali*).[208] In addition, Seneca's exhortation that the mind "must forsake the common track and be driven to frenzy . . . and rush to a height that it would have feared to climb by itself" (*desciscat oportet a solito et efferatur . . . rapiat suum eoque ferat, quo per se timuisset escendere*) can be read as an attempt to rework Serenus' anxiety[209] by reassuring him that it is not symptomatic of a real crisis.

De tranquillitate animi concludes with references to Plato's *Phaedrus* and his acknowledgment of the benefits of poetic *mania*: *frustra poeticas fores compos sui pepulit* (*Tranq.* 17.10: "The sane mind knocks in vain at the door of poetry"; cf. *Phdr.* 245a). Seneca further cites Aristotle and his conviction that "no great genius has ever existed without some touch of madness" (*nullum magnum ingenium sine mixtura dementiae fuit*; cf. *Pr.* 30.1 in n169 above). In the next paragraph, Seneca sinks further into the Platonic metaphor by adapting the image of the charioteer struggling to stir the horses of the soul[210] to extol the moral elevation achieved when one's mind is freed from cares:[211]

So long as it (i.e., the mind) is left to itself (*quam diu apud se est*), it is impossible for it to reach any sublime and difficult height (*non potest sublime quicquam et in arduo positum contingere*); it must forsake the common track (*desciscat oportet*

> *a solito*) and be driven to frenzy (*efferatur*) and champ the bit and run away with its rider (*mordeat frenos et rectorem rapiat suum*) and rush to a height that it would have feared to climb by itself (*eoque ferat, quo per se timuisset escendere*). (*Tranq.* 17.11)

Citing or adapting Plato does not necessarily mean that Seneca confuses or equates poetic with philosophical or Bacchic *mania*, any more than Plato embraces physical drunkenness;[212] equally, it does not mean that Seneca is here attempting to formulate a poetic theory.[213] In this context, Seneca's endorsement of the enthusiasm Serenus earlier harshly condemned can be understood as a rebuff to the belief that such feelings, and the kind of writing inspired by them, are universally un-Stoic.[214] Indeed, when we look at Serenus' self-criticism through the lens of Seneca's own arguments about philosophical style, there seems to be nothing whatsoever to find fault with. After all, Serenus clearly indicates that when he gets carried away by his literary imagination, he does so not out of vainglorious ambition but to match the dignity of his subject matter. His expression *ad dignitatem rerum exit oratio* ["speech comes out (fit) to the dignity of the topics"] not only is reminiscent of Cleanthes' argument that poetic speech alone can adequately express divine greatness but also echoes Seneca's argument that philosophical writing does not have to be "meagre and dry," since "even philosophy does not reject ingenuity," but can be eloquent as long as it is uncontrived.[215]

> Our words should aim not to please, but to help (*non delectent . . . sed prosint*). If, however, you can attain eloquence without overexcitement (*eloquentia non sollicito*), and if it comes to you easily or with little effort (*parata est aut parvo constat*), make the most of it and apply it to the noblest things. But let it be such that it displays facts rather than itself (*res potius quam se ostendat*). It (i.e., eloquence) and the other arts are wholly concerned with ingenuity; but our business here is the soul. (*Ep.* 75.5)

Serenus, in other words, imposes rules of literary restraint on himself that go well beyond what his commitment to Stoicism requires. When Seneca concludes his response with an unexpected injunction to occasionally drink liberally and to yield to feelings of enthusiasm, what he is offering is a corrective to his friend's excessive uptightness.

The Platonic imagery that Seneca relies on in in *De tranquillitate animi* is common throughout his writing; in *De otio*, for instance, Seneca describes achieving knowledge about the state of the universe (*quis fuerit universi status*) in these terms: "Our thought bursts through the ramparts of the sky and is not content to know that which is revealed."[216] In arguing that contemplation of the heavenly realm is crucial in our search for "what lies beyond the world" (*scrutor, quad ultra mundum iacet*), Seneca appears to be very consciously echoing Plato. Although Seneca is aware of the imprecise nature of Platonic metaphors,[217] he clearly appreciates the benefit of using metaphors and similes to "render the subject matter visible"[218] and his arguments persuasive.[219] Although Seneca probably clashed with Cornutus over the latter's penchant for allegorico-etymological interpretations[220] and so "was a Stoic but no allegorist,"[221] he nonetheless employs metaphor to articulate the moment that the mind perceives the divine principle of the world. At any rate, as Ramelli notes,[222] "The inclusion of allegoresis in philosophy, a typical feature in Stoicism, returns in Middle and Neoplatonism—which incorporated significant Stoic elements—both on the 'pagan' and on the Christian side." While, however, the reception of Platonic allegory and more so, of Platonic *baccheia*, among Christian writers will be the focus of another volume, we simply cannot ignore Philo's influential contribution to transforming Platonic imagery into the intellectual *lingua franca* of the eastern Mediterranean. Philo reinvests Platonic inebriation, which had been by this point reduced to a debatable figure of speech, with the aesthetics of the profound, as he seeks to antagonize the philosophical tradition of the Greeks with the wisdom of the Jewish God.

The Reception of Plato at Alexandria:
Philo and the Rites of Allegory

The Greco-Roman culture was not the only belief system in the ancient Mediterranean that coupled wine and philosophical contemplation, nor the only one that emphasized esotericism. Judaism also retained a set of cultural tropes around drinking and inebriation: wine is celebrated as a substance that "gladdens the hearts of man" at Psalms 104:15 (cf. Eccl. 10:19),[223] while in the Proverbs Solomon councils (in an almost Senecan fashion): "give strong drink to one who is perishing, and wine to the bitter in soul."[224] Equally, the destructive effects of intoxication are recognized;

hence, in Deuteronomy wine is compared to the poison of the serpents (32:33), a phrase that evokes Alcibiades' comparison of Socrates' discourse with a snake bite.[225] Furthermore, the Jewish tradition recognizes the dangerous association of wine with "heat" (Hebrew *hemah*), which was prevalent, as we saw, in the Greek cultural register; therefore, at Hosea 7:5, the "heat of wine" is said to have made the princes sick during the king's coronation or birthday.

Writing in the first century, Philo, a Jewish thinker with thorough knowledge of Greek literature and a passion for Plato,[226] approached Jewish sacred literature as a repository of allegories in need of interpretation.[227] Despite the Platonic references in his work, Philo who also subscribes to Stoic and Pythagorean theses,[228] "criticises literary depictions of symposia," including those of Plato and Xenophon.[229] In Philo's view, Xenophon's *Symposium* is rather mundane, while Plato's is consumed by tedious and dangerous discussions of common vulgar love.[230] Although he admits that these literary symposia are famous and "serve posterity as models of the happily conducted banquet" (*Contempl.* 7.57: χρήσεσθαι παραδείγμασι τοὺς ἔπειτα τῆς ἐν συμποσίοις ἐμμελοῦς διαγωγῆς),[231] ". . . even these, if compared with those of our people who embrace the contemplative life, will appear as matters for derision" (*Contempl.* 7.60: τὸ γὰρ πλεῖστον αὐτοῦ μέρος ὁ κοινὸς καὶ πάνδημος ἔρως διείληφεν). Nevertheless, unequivocally committed to Judaism and its superior claim to wisdom,[232] Philo makes extensive use of the metaphor of Socratic inebriation, which he transforms into "mentalizing" our relationship with God.[233] Crucially, in Plato's steps, Philo has a thorough appreciation of the way mental experiences are mediated through the senses and, thus, of how metaphors anchored in the sensible world can offer us valuable tools for recognizing the patterns of constructing and deconstructing selfhood in search of advanced modes of cognition. His approach is fundamentally phenomenological,[234] yet he still feels the need to explain that he refers to "sober inebriation." Thus, Philo describes the attempt of the human mind, "the sovereign element of the soul" (κατὰ τὸν τῆς ψυχῆς ἡγεμόνα νοῦν),[235] to engage in contemplation in pursuit of wisdom, as follows:

> Again, when on soaring wing it has contemplated (κατασκεψά-μενος) the atmosphere and all its phases, it is borne yet higher (ἀνωτέρω φέρεται) to the ether and the circuit of heaven, and is whirled round with the dances of planets and fixed stars, in accordance with the laws of perfect music (κατὰ τοὺς μουσικῆς

τελείας νόμους), following that love of wisdom which guides its steps. And so, carrying its gaze beyond the confines of all substance discernible by sense (πᾶσαν τὴν αἰσθητὴν οὐσίαν ὑπερκύψας), it comes to a point at which it reaches out after the intelligible world (ἐνταῦθα ἐφίεται τῆς νοητῆς), and on descrying in that world sights of surpassing loveliness, even the patterns and the originals of the things of sense which it saw here (καὶ τὰς ἰδέας **θεασάμενος**), it is seized by a sober intoxication, like those filled with Corybantic frenzy, and is inspired, possessed by a longing other than theirs and a nobler desire (μέθῃ νηφαλίῳ κατασχεθεὶς ὥσπερ οἱ κορυβαντιῶντες ἐνθουσιᾷ, ἑτέρου γεμισθεὶς ἱμέρου καὶ πόθου βελτίονος). (*Opificio Mundi* 70–71)

It is evident that, like Plato, Philo regards drunklike frenzy as a necessary symptom of contemplative meditation that entails an enhancement of our mental/psychic sight,[236] enabling us to acquire insight (φρόνησις).[237] In his *Therapeutae* or *De vita contemplativa*, Philo details the way of life of an ascetic Jewish sect.[238] They practice, he tells us (*Contempl.* 1.2), a superior art of healing (ἰατρικὴν) that does not cure only the bodies but also souls "overwhelmed by diseases grievous and hard to heal (χαλεπαῖς τε καὶ δυσιάτοις), inflicted by pleasures and desires and griefs and fears, acts of greed and folly and injustice and many of the other passions and vices" (ἡδοναὶ καὶ ἐπιθυμίαι καὶ λῦπαι καὶ φόβοι πλεονεξίαι τε καὶ ἀφροσύναι καὶ ἀδικίαι καὶ τὸ τῶν ἄλλων παθῶν καὶ κακιῶν ἀνήνυτον πλῆθος). Philo's language echoes Plato's description of the transgressions, which lawgivers ought to punish in the *Laws*.[239] In addition, Philo's community of healers, residing on the shores of Lake Mareotis outside the city of Alexandria, undergo philosophical trances in strikingly Platonic terms: having trained their soul sight to "desire the vision of the existent" (*Contempl.* 11: ὁ δὲ θεραπευτικὸν γένος **βλέπειν** ἀεὶ προδιδασκόμενον τῆς τοῦ ὄντος **θέας** ἐφιέσθω) and rise above "the sun of our senses" (καὶ τὸν αἰσθητὸν ἥλιον ὑπερβαινέτω), they are led to "perfect happiness" (*Contempl.* 11: πρὸς τελείαν ἄγουσαν εὐδαιμονίαν).[240] And he continues: "Those who set themselves to this service, not just following custom nor on the advice and admonition of others but carried away by a heaven-sent passion of love (ὑπ᾽ ἔρωτος ἁρπασθέντες οὐρανίου), remain rapt and possessed *like* Bacchanals or Corybants until they see the object of their yearning (**καθάπερ** οἱ βακχευόμενοι καὶ κορυβαντιῶντες, ἐνθουσιάζουσι μέχρις ἂν τὸ ποθούμενον ἴδωσιν)" (*Contempl.* 12–13). Euripidian as well as Platonic influences are evident in Philo's description of the two choirs of healers, a choir of men and a choir of women, described as celebrating a feast by singing in turns, "having drunk as in the Bacchic rites of the strong wine of God's love" (11.85: καθάπερ ἐν ταῖς βακχείαις ἀκράτου σπάσαντες τοῦ θεοφιλοῦς) before joining their voices in a single choir.[241] Philo's conception of these exceptional healers in terms of two choirs, clearly evoking the Dionysiac Choir of the *Laws*, confirms the fundamental role of their Bacchic insight in Plato's Magnesia, an insight vital for any self-reflective society. Like Plato's Socrates, Philo's healers "continue until dawn, drunk with this fine drunkenness (*Contempl.* 89: τὴν καλὴν ταύτην μέθην), without heavy heads or drowsy eyes (οὐ καρηβαροῦντες ἢ καταμύοντες) but more alert and wakeful than when they came to the banquet" (ἀλλὰ διεγηγερμένοι μᾶλλον ἢ ὅτε παρεγένοντο εἰς τὸ συμπόσιον). Having prayed for "clear-sightedness of reasoning" (ὀξυωπίαν λογισμοῦ), the healers are aware that their wisdom is the result of hard toiling,[242] and therefore it is rewarded with God-like virtue.[243]

Philo is aware that the same repository of images and analogies allows him to dramatize instances of pseudo-ecstasy and folly. Thus, drawing on Deut. 21:18–21, which relates the example of a rebellious son accused by his parents of four moral failings, the most severe of which is drunkenness (*Ebr.* 15), Philo adapts Plato's image of the chariot of the soul to detail the downward spiral of the son's soul, as it "begins to cast off the reins (ἀφηνιάζειν) and taking its course through strife and dissention it reaches the final limit, drunkenness, the cause of frenzy and madness (ἔρχεται, μέθην, τὴν ἐκστάσεως καὶ παραφροσύνης αἰτίαν)." His imagery becomes bolder in *Ebr.* 27–28, enriched with references to the fire of wine that consumes the soul, again alluding to motifs about the ways wine influences our mental faculties: "For the phrase here used, "fired with wine" (οἰνοφλυγεῖν) is as much as to say that the poison which causes folly, that is lack of discipline (ἀφροσύνης φάρμακον, ἀπαιδευσίαν), burns slowly within the man, then bursts into fire and flame impossible to quench (ἐντύφεσθαι καὶ ἀνακαίεσθαι καὶ ἀναφλέγεσθαι μηδέποτε σβεσθῆναι δυναμένην), consuming with blaze and setting alight the whole soul throughout (ὅλην δι᾽ ὅλων αἰεὶ τὴν ψυχὴν ἐμπιπρᾶσάν τε καὶ πυρπολοῦσαν)" (*Ebr.* 27–28). Calling for the purification of a mind that has suffered in the flames of folly, Philo describes reason as the father of the soul and school education as its mother and urges the soul to abide by their admonitions (*Ebr.* 33–34). He then describes types of souls on the basis of their relationship with their "father" and "mother," and those too attached to their mother he classifies as demagogic (*Ebr.* 37). Yet even this type of soul, Philo argues, is pitied by Moses, who "thinks that he should retrain it (μεταδιδάσκειν) and persuade it (ἀναπείθειν) to depart from its empty opinions (ἀποστῆναι μὲν τῶν κενῶν δοξῶν) and follow truth steadfastly (ἀκολουθῆσαι δὲ παγίως τῷ ἀληθεῖ)" (*Ebr.* 38–39).

Philo, like Plato, makes a powerful contribution to the motif of the enamored soul that is "poured out" in love. Of course, starting with Homeric poetry, Greek literature offers numerous examples of love's ability to waste away its victims and liquify them;[244] as we saw in chapter 1, Plato picks up the metaphor, employing the verb ἀρύ(τ)ω ("to draw water") at *Phaedrus* 253a8–9 to refer to lovers who "draw their inspiration from Zeus, like the Bacchants" (ἐκ Διὸς ἀρύτωσιν, ὥσπερ αἱ βάκχαι)[245] and are able "to pour it out on the soul of the beloved and make him, as far as possible, similar to their god" (ἐπὶ τὴν τοῦ ἐρωμένου ψυχὴν ἐπαντλοῦντες ποιοῦσιν ὡς δυνατὸν ὁμοιότατον τῷ σφετέρῳ θεῷ). The image of pouring out and drinking the soul of the enamored accords with the symposiastic character of archaic amatory verse—in literature lovers typically poured out their soul before the beloved in anticipation of erotic reciprocity and pleasure—however, Plato is clear that, despite the prompting of the unruly horse of the soul,[246] the "inspired lover" (255a8: ἔνθεος φίλος) ought to guide the beloved away from the physical consummation of their friendship until they are able to achieve "a life of happiness and harmony here on earth, being self-controlled and demure" (256b1: μακάριον μὲν καὶ ὁμονοητικὸν τὸν ἐνθάδε βίον διάγουσιν, ἐγκρατεῖς αὑτῶν καὶ κόσμιοι ὄντες).[247]

That this idea remained firmly embedded in Hellenistic love poetry is shown by epigram 5.78 (attributed to Plato)[248] and 5.171 (by Meleager) of the *Greek Anthology*. Furthermore, in Apollonius Rhodius' *Argonautica*, young Medea is so affected by love that, ". . . then she would even have drawn out her whole soul (ἀρύσασα/ ψυχὴν) from her breast and put it in the palm of his hand, gloating in his need for her (ἀγαιομένη χατέοντι)" (*Arg.* 3.1015–1016). As an ancient scholiast notes,[249] Apollonius, like Plato, uses the verb ἀρύ(τ)ω. Philo, too, employs the motif, investing it with language that also evokes the experience of the soul's ability to break away from its bodily bonds in Plato's *Phaedo*. Philo imagines the mind that has drunk from unaffected abstinence as a libation that can be poured to God:[250]

> Secondly, she declares that she has not partaken of wine or strong liquor (οἶνον καὶ μέθυσμα), boasting that her whole life has been one of unbroken sobriety (παρὰ πάντα τὸν βίον νήφειν). And rightly, for indeed it was a great and wonderful feat (μέγα καὶ θαυμαστὸν . . . ἔργον) to follow the free and pure reason, that is not intoxicated by any passion (ἐλευθεριάζοντι καὶ καθαρῷ χρῆσθαι λογισμῷ πρὸς μηδενὸς πάθους παροινουμένῳ). And the result of this is that the mind, which has drunk deep of sobriety unmixed (νήψεως ἀκράτου), becomes a libation in its whole being and is poured out to God (σπένδεσθαι θεῷ). What else was meant by the words, "I will pour out my soul before the Lord" but "I will consecrate it all to him, loosening all the chains that previously bound it tight, which the empty aims and desires of mortal life had fastened upon it; I will send it abroad, extend and diffuse it to that extent that it shall touch the bounds of the All (ὡς καὶ τῶν τοῦ παντὸς ἅψασθαι περάτων), and hasten to that all-good and famous Vision of the Uncreated (καὶ πρὸς τὴν τοῦ ἀγενήτου παγκάλην καὶ ἀοίδιμον θέαν ἐπειχθῆναι). (*Ebr.* 151–152)

Thus, Philo imagines pouring out his soul in front of God as proof that he is no longer in the grip of bodily desires. For Philo, in agreement with Plato's understanding of desire in the *Laws*,[251] our bodily substance gives rise to ignorance, for which process physical drunkenness is a metonymy.[252]

Thus, Philo recapitulates the imagery Plato used to describe Socratic inebriation and furthermore sets out a theory of this imagery as not merely metaphorical, but allegorical. This allegorical approach to Plato's new structural metaphor can be seen clearly in Philo's interpretation of Noah's drunkenness. In his *Questions and Answers on Genesis*, Philo focuses on Gen 9:21 and the meaning of the words "He [Noah] drank the wine and became drunken" (καὶ ἔπιεν ἐκ τοῦ οἴνου καὶ ἐμεθύσθη). Elsewhere, Philo signals that he is conscious that "many philosophers have given no slight attention to the question" whether "the wise man will get drunk" (*Plant.* 142: εἰ μεθυσθήσεται ὁ σοφός),[253] echoing Seneca's *Letter* 83.27,[254] and argues that "a man of moral worth will get drunk as well as other people without losing any of his virtue" (*Plant.* 172: μεθυσθήσεται τοιγάρτοι καὶ ὁ ἀστεῖος μηδὲν τῆς ἀρετῆς ἀποβαλών) and that "there would be nothing amiss in a wise man quaffing wine freely on occasion" (*Plant.* 174: οἴνου δὲ σπάσαι πλείονος οὐκ ἂν εἴη χεῖρον ἐν καιρῷ σοφόν).[255] Nonetheless,

Philo feels compelled to defend Noah's reputation against the implications of intoxication. He writes:

> Based on the aforesaid, one could argue that he did not drink all the wine but a portion of it because of his self-control (δι' ἐγκράτειαν) through which he determined his use of it. For the unrestrained man (τοῦ ἀκρατοῦς) does not leave from drinking-bouts before drinking up all the unmixed wine. And therefore, the scripture uses in this occasion the expression "becoming drunken" in the sense of "making use of wine." For becoming drunken has two meanings: one is to drink wine to excess (ἐν μὲν τὸ ληρεῖν παρ' οἶνον) which is a sin characteristic of the wicked man (ἁμάρτημα καὶ φαύλου ἴδιον); the other is to partake of wine, which happens to the wise man (ἕτερον δὲ τὸ οἰνοῦσθαι, ὅπερ καὶ εἰς σοφὸν πίπτει). (Greek text from Petit 1978, frs 68a and b)

Accordingly, it is in the second signification that the virtuous and wise man "is said to be drunken, not by drinking wine to excess, but merely by partaking of wine."[256]

In the second book of his *De ebrietate*, Philo insists not only that Noah was not drunk in a conventional sense but also that Mosaic drunkenness is polyvalent and allegorical:[257] "Moses uses strong liquor as a symbol (σύμβολον τὸν ἄκρατον) for more than one, in fact for several, things: for foolish talking and raving (τοῦ ληρεῖν καὶ παραπαίειν), for complete insensibility (ἀναισθησίας παντελοῦς), for insatiable and ever-discontented greediness (ἀπληστίας ἀκορέστου καὶ δυσαρέστου), for cheerfulness and gladness (εὐθυμίας καὶ εὐφροσύνης), for the nakedness which embraces the rest and manifests itself in all the qualities just mentioned, in which condition Noah was, we read, when intoxicated" (*Ebr.* 4). Since the sober also experience such emotions (*Ebr.* 5), Philo claims that shameful "intoxication" results from unwillingness to submit to discipline,[258] not mere lack of formal education (*Ebr.* 6: λέγω δ' οὐ τὴν παιδείας ἀνεπιστημοσύνην, ἀλλὰ τὴν πρὸς αὐτὴν ἀλλοτρίωσιν), contributing to the long-established metaphor of corresponding somatic and psychic ailments. The "insensibility" into which Noah slips is also qualified allegorically:

> Insensibility is caused by treacherous and blind ignorance (τοῦ δ' ἀναισθητεῖν ἡ ἐπίβουλος καὶ πηρὸς ἄγνοια); greediness

because of that most painful of the soul's passions, lust; while joy arises both from the possession and the practice of virtue (εὐφροσύνης δὲ κτῆσις ὁμοῦ καὶ χρῆσις ἀρετῆς). Nakedness has many causes: ignorance of opposites (ἄγνοια τῶν ἐναντίων), innocence (ἀκακία) and simplicity of manners (ἀφέλεια ἠθῶν), truth, that is, the power which unveils what is wrapped in obscurity (ἀλήθεια ἡ τὰ τῶν συνεσκιασμένων πραγμάτων ἀνακαλυπτήρια ἄγουσα δύναμις). (*Ebr.* 6–7)[259]

Philo thus repurposes the structural metaphor of Socratic inebriation into an allegorical key to the meaning of scripture; whereas Plato employed the metaphor outline of the real experience of philosophy, Philo understands inebriation as pure allegory, defusing the difficulties presented by a literal reading of scripture.

Later in his treatise on inebriation, Philo returns to the image of the soul drunken and inflamed by folly, declaring it deserves to be stoned (*Ebr.* 95); this soul, he contends, is disobedient to its "parents" and has chosen the body as its god, worshiping it like the Egyptians worship Apis, which Philo conveniently identifies with the golden calf of Exodus:[260]

Around it the frantic celebrants (φρενοβλαβεῖς) make their dances and sing and join in the song, not that most sweet song of drinking and merrymaking as in feasts and banquets (οὐ παροίνιον καὶ κωμαστικὸν οἷα ἐν ἑορταῖς καὶ θαλίαις ἥδιστον μέλος) but the true dirge (ἀληθῆ θρῆνον) as if of their own funeral, like men driven mad by wine, who have loosened and destroyed the tone of their souls (ὥσπερ ἔξοινοι καὶ τῆς ψυχῆς τὸν τόνον ὑπεκλύσαντές τε καὶ φθείραντες). (*Ebr.* 95)

The moral weaknesses of which drunkenness is symbolic are therefore dangerous and must be avoided. God, furthermore, is said to refuse sacrifices that are not sober.[261] Importantly, Philo identifies prayer as the way to avoid the pitfalls of inebriation (*Ebr.* 125).[262] Only the philosopher can maintain his psychic sobriety when challenged by the first three types of Mosaic inebriation, which cause raving, loss of sensibility, and greediness as specified in *De ebrietate* 4 above,[263] but Philo also warns against being overconfident in one's intellectual ability, citing the example of Lot, who became intoxicated by his own daughters despite thinking that he could be impervious to wine.[264] The remaining two types of inebriation (cheerfulness and gladness), although equally comparable to physical drunkenness, do not involve imbibing wine.

In a very Platonic fashion, inebriation according to Philo can stand not merely for weakness but also for contact with the divine. At *Ebr.* 145, Samuel is said to have been always cheerful on account of his admission to the company of God.[265] In the next paragraphs, perhaps drawing on Plato's concerns about the wise man being misunderstood as drunk, the joy of the virtuous is explained thus:

> Now when soul is filled by grace (χάριτος δ' ἥτις ἂν πλη-ρωθῇ ψυχή), it immediately rejoices and smiles and dances (γέγηθεν εὐθὺς καὶ μειδιᾷ καὶ ἀνορχεῖται), for it is possessed and inspired, so that to many of the uninitiated it may seem to be drunken, crazy, and beside itself (βεβάκχευται γάρ, ὡς πολλοῖς τῶν ἀνοργιάστων μεθύειν καὶ παρακινεῖν καὶ ἐξεστά-ναι ἂν δόξαι . . . [266]). . . . For with the God-possessed (τοῖς θεοφορήτοις) not only is the soul stirred and goaded as it were into ecstasy (οὐχ ἡ ψυχὴ μόνον ἐγείρεσθαι καὶ ὥσπερ ἐξοιστρᾶν) but the body also is flushed and ablaze (ἐνερευθὲς εἶναι καὶ πεπυρωμένον), because of the overflowing and warm-ing joy within which passes on the sensation to the outside (τῆς ἔνδον ἀναχεούσης καὶ χλιαινούσης χαρᾶς τὸ πάθος εἰς τὸ ἔξω διαδιδούσης). Thus, many of the foolish are deceived and suppose that the sober are drunk (πολλοὶ τῶν ἀφρόνων ἀπατηθέντες τοὺς νήφοντας μεθύειν ὑπετόπασαν). Though, indeed, it is true that these sober ones are drunk in some way (μὲν τρόπον τινὰ μεθύουσιν οἱ νήφοντες), having drunk all good things and having received the toasts of perfect virtue (τὰ ἀγαθὰ ἀθρόα ἠκρατισμένοι καὶ τὰς προπόσεις παρὰ τελείας ἀρετῆς δεξάμενοι). (*Ebr.* 146–149)

Philo therefore employs the metaphor of drunkenness to discuss both spiritual elevation and deviation from God (in the form of ignorance and submission to bodily desires). Like Plato, Philo clarifies that the state of inebriation associated with spiritual elevation, although it seems similar to physical drunkenness, does not involve consumption of wine.

Intoxication becomes an allegory both of our profound experience of God and of the dangers of sin in Philo. Under his influence, later Platonists and early Christians will embrace an allegorical appreciation of truth as a well-kept secret intended for those willing and able to perceive it.[267] Philo's use of philosophical concepts to discuss theological matters marks a new chapter in intellectual history, albeit one totally predicated on metaphorical thinking.

Concluding Remarks

Plato's reception in the Hellenistic and Roman periods is marked by a deeply entrenched debate about the meaning and truth of philosophical engagement. As philosophy becomes increasingly identified with rhetoric and the more communicable skill of persuasion, the metaphor of inebriation is reduced to a rhetorical ruse that aims to pass common drunkenness as philosophical inspiration. In this later interpretive framework, characterizing symposiastic *euphrosyne* in Socratic terms as "the motion of the soul in harmony with the universe" (*Cra.* 419d: τοῦ εὖ τοῖς πράγμασι τὴν ψυχὴν ξυμφέρεσθαι) appears as imagistic and odd as the language of the sophists. If ancient audiences were already suspicious of Socrates and his bacchic trances, the doctrinal conflicts that overwhelmed the Academy after Plato's death further congeal this view of philosophers as standoffish hypocrites, interested merely in their own reputation and material gain; for example, Numenius' use of inebriation to undermine other philosophers enhances the profile of philosophers as a dissolute and self-serving guild.

Gradually, in tune with the use of symposia by Hellenistic kings to showcase their good fortune and invest it with past notions of aristocratic grandeur, Roman banquets are transformed by the Second Sophistic into occasions for staging one's fine-tuned aesthetic sense and education. Furthermore, as *homines novi* such as Cicero and Sallust seek to infiltrate the echelons of traditional Roman aristocracy, the example of Socratic virtue as filtered through Stoic theory, with its emphasis on attainable virtues such as self-control and a sense of civic duty, informs Roman education and political life.[268] The metaphor of inebriation is now reduced to moralistic examples of prominent men of the past who fell from grace or revealed their tyrannical tendencies by failing to exercise moderation.[269] At the same time, drinking decorum becomes a way of performing sophistication and claiming the moral high ground. As a result, on the one hand, pretentious teachers of philosophy are fiercely satirized in Lucian's dialogues for trying to hide their moral shortcomings and penchant for excessive wine drinking behind the metaphor of inebriation; on the other hand, even while appreciating the metaphorical nature of Socratic inebriation, Seneca urges young Serenus not to be excessive in his moderation and to occasionally indulge in wine drinking as a practical way of prompting moments of philosophical inspiration.

This highly stylized and rather superficial use of Platonic inebriation, the direct result of the metaphor's transferal from its original context in the Greek *polis* into that of the Hellenistic kingdoms and eventually the Roman Empire, is drastically revised in the work of Philo. Philo reads Plato in tandem with Euripides' discussion of Bacchic inspiration and anticipates the Neoplatonic and Christian exegetical tradition(s) by employing inebriation as a profound allegory of man's encounter with God. Jewish mysticism finds new, bold forms of expression in the imagery of inebriation in the thought of Plato and Euripides; as the focus of cultural innovation shifts firmly toward Alexandria, the Greco-Roman world is gripped by the "drama of Jesus" and the staging of his divine banquet, where the disciples feast not on bread and wine but on his body and blood.

Conclusion

Using Bad Metaphors and Using Metaphors Badly

εὖ ἂν ἔχοι, φάναι, ὦ Ἀγάθων, εἰ τοιοῦτον εἴη ἡ σοφία ὥστ᾽ ἐκ τοῦ
πληρεστέρου εἰς τὸ κενώτερον ῥεῖν ἡμῶν, ἐὰν ἀπτώμεθα ἀλλήλων. . . .

—Symp. 175d4–9[1]

A Kind of Trade: Words and Wine

In this book I set out to examine Platonic or Socratic inebriation as a
metaphor for philosophical creativity that challenges the mainstream
association of drunkenness with loss of reason and self-control. My key
premise has been that Plato appreciated metaphors as a mainstream
intellectual currency and therefore, the most effective means of communicating the value of Socratic philosophy and its therapeutic properties.
In this context, comparing the words of Socrates to the *pharmakon* of
Dionysus is an astute analogy, as Aristotle would no doubt agree. This
basic comparison allows for numerous additional associations, notably
the comparison of Socrates with Dionysus' followers, developed in the
Symposium, but also the comparison of Socrates with poets on which
Plato expands in the *Phaedrus*, where he further revises the traditional
associations of godsent inspiration with poetry, prophecy, ritual, and
erōs—the latter transformed from carnal to intellectual desire.[2] Another
important comparison, established in Plato's cultural register since the
archaic period, is that of the city with a banquet, which he utilized in the
Protagoras and the *Republic* but developed more emphatically in the *Laws*.
Nevertheless, while poets, like Aristophanes and Agathon, and poetically
gifted politicians, like Dionysius I,[3] typically aspired to perform at public

153

festivals, the real stage on which philosophers and their rivals compete is the cognitive showground of their audiences.[4]

Indeed, we may imagine that words can be "poured" into people like wine, as Socrates claims in the *Symposium* (175d–9 cited above), filling them up with content. Each draught causes us to embody the experiences and identities contained in the words we imbibe. Drinking and discoursing, discoursing and drinking, we are swayed to enact the identities our senses absorb. However, the double nature of Dionysus—a god foreign and yet native, effeminate and yet masculine, drunk and yet sober, aptly reflected in the double meaning of *pharmakon* as both medicine and poison[5]—makes it clear that the identities our senses "touch upon" (but also "see," "hear," "smell," and/or "taste") do not ensure a successful transformation for individuals and their cities. Since the cognitive reality produced by the senses is fraught with deception, it requires metacognitive skills before endorsing it; furthermore, the sensory stimuli broadcasted in a city must be carefully chosen since they project not only what a city stands for in the present moment but crucially what it aspires to become.[6] As discussed in chapter 1, Plato's confidence in the power of the senses to enhance cognition and produce new states of consciousness verily places him as a precursor of perceptual phenomenology and its role in cognition.[7]

The main problem, however, that Plato encountered is that cognitive phenomena can be readily conflated with (the traits of) their representations, leading to erroneous conclusions about their true nature. Plato raises this difficulty in the *Theaetetus* where he presents Protagoras as conflating perception with knowledge.[8] In chapter 2, then, I explained Plato's preoccupation with delimiting the nature of Socratic ecstasy as a result of the phenomenal similarities it shares with clinical madness and intoxication, similarities also evident in the use of the same vocabulary to describe the causes and symptoms of all three experiences. Plato resolved to employ the analogy between words and wine to defend Socratic *baccheia* as genius-associated eccentricity, a type of ecstasy deceptively similar to drunken absurdity yet far superior to it. Socrates' unusual sobriety, despite appearances, also finds support in the ancient medical *and* philosophical lore, notably in Heraclitus: our sources associate heat, including the warm sensation often induced by wine drinking, with superior levels of cognition. In this context, Socrates' sobriety is a sign of his extraordinary intelligence, which others can only try to approximate by drinking wine: but Socrates, cognitively "warm" at all times[9] and therefore unaffected by wine, demonstrates both symposiastic decorum and sharp wit, claiming dialectical and moral victory over his fellow banqueters as he counters both Aristophanes' drunken blabbery and Alcibiades' shameless intoxication.

The importance of Socratic inebriation as a model that defuses the stimuli threatening the citizens' confidence in their assessment of real virtue is exemplified in the *Laws*. Here, Plato fully embraces the sensory basis of his metaphor, acknowledging the ways in which experience informs cognition; thus, he claims, cities ought to promote morally robust storylines to trigger the imagination of their citizens alongside expedient, *sōphrosynē*-inducing practices, like the Test of the Wine.[10] Only then, as discussed in chapter 3, will wine, discussion, music, and jokes alike be flowing sociably to refresh the souls of the Magnesians and renew their civic coherence, since everyone will be guided to "drink from the same cup." Just like wine takes grief away, according to Euripides and Plato, so does speech, according to Gorgias:[11] "speech (λόγος) . . . is able to stop fear and remove sorrow (δύναται γὰρ καὶ φόβον παῦσαι καὶ λύπην ἀφελεῖν) and to create joy and to augment pity (καὶ χαρὰν ἐνεργάσασθαι καὶ ἔλεον ἐπαυξῆσαι)" (*Hel.* 8; trans. MacDowell 1982, 25). Thus, discourse and wine can disrupt the relentless influence of emotion over humans, securing them a mental space for reflection.[12] In the civic context, discourse must be characterized by freedom (*parrhēsia*), yet like wine (and like music and humor), it must be protected from corrupting excess, if a city is to preserve its identity and its values in the way the Athenians famously ensured the salvation of themselves and of Hellas when faced with the Persian threat. At that time, as Plato reminds us in the *Laws*, the Athenian polity was ruled by *aidōs* (698b5: δεσπότις ἐνῆν τις αἰδώς) and its citizens obeyed the laws voluntarily (699c4–5: δουλεύοντες τοῖς τότε νόμοις ζῆν ἠθέλομεν; cf. 700a5: ὁ δῆμός . . . ἑκὼν ἐδούλευε τοῖς νόμοις).[13]

The praise of Socrates' wine drinking aptitude in the *Symposium*, alongside the central role of the Dionysiac Choir in the educational system of Magnesia, leaves no doubt about Plato's appreciation of wine as a substance suitable for fostering philosophically inclined mindsets but also for debating the parameters of his proposed enterprise—at which point his metaphorical use of wine becomes plainly obvious. For, not only is Socratic inebriation unrelated to wine consumption per se but the Test of the Wine, despite involving actual wine drinking, is a token for all the excesses, material and emotional, that threaten to cloud the judgement of the Magnesians with "drunkenness." Thus, Socratic *baccheia* is a bold metaphor inspired by the ubiquitous presence of drunkenness, literal and not, in Plato's contemporary popular culture.

Indeed, even a cursory glance at pottery iconography is sufficient to reveal the obsession of the Athenians during Plato's time with Dionysus and his gift. It seems that in the aftermath of the Persian Wars, "drunk" with their newly found political power and the privileges it afforded them, the Athenians acquired a taste for fine things,[14] like strong wine from Thasos.[15] Thasos and its rich natural resources played an important role in imperial Athenian politics, offering ambitious politicians like Alcibiades who owned large estates on the island,[16] "both an alternative to the stifling environment of egalitarian Athens and a means to win over the demos and overcome rival claimants to influence." For Plato, however, contemporary Athens was anything but egalitarian;[17] wary of the enthusiasm with which his fellow citizens sought to reinvent their place in the world, Plato criticized the influx of new images[18] that inundated the Athenian public space, corrupting the cognitive lens of the citizens. For example, alongside its wine, Thasos was renowned for its cult of Dionysus, reflected on its enduring coin iconography that dates as early as the last quarter of the sixth century BCE.[19] Thasian coins typically portrayed Satyrs carrying off nymphs and sometimes, as in the cover of this book, a Satyr holding a cantharus, indulging in wine drinking.[20] In my view, it is the popularity of such images that Plato tries to counter with his portrayal of Socrates as a Satyr or Silen, actively engaging in an exercise of intellectual currency exchange.[21] For Plato, a city ought to be responsible for its coinage (*nomisma*) in the same way that it ought to regulate its laws and its music (*nomoi*), all understood as testaments of its core values and of the "wine" its citizens like better. By defending the philosophical premises of the law, Plato insists that lawgivers act as symposiarchs who oversee the version(s) of reality the city chooses to imbibe.[22] Thus, Socratic inebriation, now disseminated through education to be sampled by all, becomes the key argument for the rehabilitation of philosophical enquiry into society.[23]

The Theatrics of Philosophical Medit/cation

Besides the increased presence of Dionysus and his entourage in fifth century Athens, "the appearance of the god on the stage must have been equally effective—perhaps even more so."[24] Thus, in choosing to present Socrates as a bold, eloquent Bacchos who did not hold back in his criticism of the city, Plato likely antagonizes contemporary playwrights (cf. Eur. *Bacch.* 491: . . . θρασὺς ὁ βάκχος κοὐκ ἀγύμναστος λόγων). Socrates reproves the Athenians for their ignorance (ἀμάθια)—repeatedly associated in the *Republic* with injustice and excess,[25] like Euripides' Dionysus charged Pentheus with "ignorance and impiety towards the god" (*l.* 490: ἀμαθίας γε κἀσεβοῦντ᾽ ἐς τὸν θεόν) in an *agōn sophias* (a debate about wisdom).[26] The narratives and images that the poets relay in the minds and souls of the citizens depend on whether the city has used words as a medicine or as a poison and ultimately on whether they have represented the true nature of Dionysus. Accordingly, in the *Republic* Socrates is critical of deceptive theatrical representations because they "cast a spell upon the mind" of the spectators (413c4: γοητεύειν πάντα ὅσα ἀπατᾷ),[27] getting them "drunk" and "mad" with the tyranny of desire (573b10–c9),[28] urging them to imagine themselves as getting drunk all day long, both here and in the afterlife,[29] and prepping them to put up with weak leaders—aptly compared to bad wine stewards (562d1–2). In other words, contemporary poetry normalizes the wrong kinds of atypical mental states[30] and, therefore, undermines the genuine transformation of consciousness that the education of the guardians is designed to achieve in the *Republic*.[31] Equally, under the watchful eye of the Dionysian Choir in the *Laws*, the citizens of Magnesia are introduced to the correct way of enjoying wine and thus to the true nature of Dionysus, which, as in the case of Euripides' Bacchants, is characterized by *sōphrosynē* and has nothing to do with drunken excess. This argument further explains Plato's choice to depict Socratic *baccheia* as an alternative form of inspiration that ought to replace the pseudo-Bacchic forms of rapture that contemporary playwrights systematically favored,[32] turning "good, upstanding people into obvious scoundrels" (Ar. *Ran.* 1010: ἀλλ᾽ ἐκ χρηστῶν καὶ γενναίων μοχθηροτέρους ἀπέδειξας . . .). By giving stage priority to "praising and pitying (ἐπαινεῖν καὶ ἐλεεῖν) of characters who claim to be good (ἀγαθὸς φάσκων εἶναι) yet give in to "excessive mourning" (ἀκαίρως πενθεῖ; *Resp.* 606b3–4)—a phrase that takes aim at the definition of tragic heroes as echoed in Aristotle's *Poetics*[33]—the poets weaken that part in us that is "best by nature" (606a7–8: φύσει βέλτιστον), prompting us to contravene "reason and law" (604a10–11: λόγος καὶ νόμος), especially when the soul "has not been sufficiently educated by reason and habit" (606a8–b1: οὐχ ἱκανῶς πεπαιδευμένον λόγῳ οὐδὲ ἔθει). This indoctrination to cowardice, lamentation, and uncritical surrender to desires, forced upon the Athenians in the name of Dionysus, is the exact opposite of philosophy and reason (587a8–9: πλεῖστον φιλοσοφίας τε καὶ λόγου ἀφέστηκεν). Like Cadmus and Teiresias in the *Bacchae*, dressed up in Bacchic attire and clumsily attempting to learn the steps of the god's rites, the whimsical sight of Socrates mesmerizing his audiences with his melodious arguments—every bit a Marsyas fighting the cacophony of contemporary musical trends (*Resp.* 700d–e)—is a dramatic staging designed to invite Plato's audiences to mimic the *sōphrosynē* and manliness of his master.[34] Like Aeschylus taught his audiences to "always defeat the enemy" (1025: νικᾶν ἀεὶ τοὺς ἀντιπάλους) so Plato aims to teach the Athenians to be brave and sober in their lives rather than "drunk with fear" (*Leg.* 639b8: ὑπὸ μέθης τοῦ φόβου ναυτιᾷ). Plato, therefore, stages his own prose plays, his puppet show in the *Laws* but also Socrates' *agōn* against his interlocutors in the *Symposium*—where Dionysus is invoked to be the judge,[35] as a "countercharm" (*Resp.* 608a5–6: ἐπᾴδοντες ἡμῖν αὐτοῖς τοῦτον τὸν λόγον, ὃν λέγομεν, καὶ ταύτην τὴν ἐπῳδήν) to the cultural trends that, in his view, threaten the mental and moral integrity of contemporary Athenians.[36]

Accordingly, in the *Symposium* Plato uses the word ἔκπληξις—an important component of every tragic play[37]—to describe the effect of Socrates' inebriation on his audiences: Socrates "astounds" (the perceptual horizon of) his listeners with his own performance of "drunkenness," charming them out of other forms of intemperance, moral and physical. Equally, in the *Laws*, the Athenian Stranger insists that true judges of music are those who can withstand the dictations of the audience and resist becoming "astounded" by the "noise of the many"—which alludes to the noisy mood of second-rate banquets and their own lack of education (*Leg.* 659a7–8: οὔτε γὰρ παρὰ θεάτρου δεῖ τόν γε ἀληθῆ κριτὴν κρίνειν μανθάνοντα, καὶ ἐκπληττόμενον ὑπὸ θορύβου τῶν πολλῶν καὶ τῆς αὑτοῦ ἀπαιδευσίας).[38] Socratic ἔκπληξις relies on virtue (cf. *Leg.* 659a3), not excess, in the same way that Socratic inebriation is not the result of intoxication but of imbibing self-discipline. By impersonating a true follower of Dionysus, a true Bacchos, Socrates exemplifies the positive effects of "wine," as advocated by Euripides, championing the spectacle of truth.[39] "Wine," then, is a symbol not only of civic morality but also of the proactive regime we ought to establish to harmonize our investment in reason with our emotions (a harmony that should also be reflected in the material well-being and safety of the city). "Wine" is the correct way of rousing the senses so to minimize the distance between perception and cognition; it is this | mental shortcut, the reassuring immediacy of achieving cognition that causes Socrates' audiences to be amazed, giving rise to a new set of feelings of fulfillment and belonging.[40] Furthermore, Socratic *baccheia*, as dramatized in Plato's dialogues, is an open invitation to each member of the audience to take on the lead role in the theatre of their mind. The physical symptoms—crying, sweating, shaking—that are often experienced by Socrates' audiences in the *Symposium* and the philosophically inclined lovers in the *Phaedrus* are a response to the shaking that Plato's puppets experience in the *Laws* when in the grip of various passions;[41] wine, a physical means of "shaking" the mind or the soul out of its conventional patterns and the danger of being rendered insensitive, is still a token of our need to prompt the mind to take responsibility for its cognitive and emotional reframing by engaging in discursive reasoning.[42]

Plato's appreciation of the cognitive aspects of sensory emotions, which play a key role in his theory of recollection,[43] agrees with his systematic use of images to "educate" the human soul in handling fear and the other emotions that threaten to overwhelm its rational part,[44] notwithstanding his mistrust for the deception lurking in artistic representations, particularly Homeric poetry.[45] Likewise, although Plato despairs over the power that poetry and sophistic arguments have over the masses,[46] notably their misleading representation of the afterlife (*Resp.* 388b4–6),[47] he believes in the power of well-intentioned rhetoric to counter their typical fearmongering and flattery.[48] That Socrates failed to convince his judges during his 399 BCE trial,[49] in the performance of his life, as it were, further urges Plato to rehash in his dialogues the performative aspects of Socratic discourse, whether against award-winning poets, like Agathon and Aristophanes, or sophists, like Protagoras, with a view to exonerate it from malicious ridicule and defend it as the safest way for curing the Athenians from their insecurities by means of embracing an alternative way of assessing reality.

However, as the experience of Socratic inebriation is recorded time after time, it becomes ingrained in the cultural semantics of ancient societies and eventually "objectified." As discussed in chapter 4, the apparatus and meaning(s) of Socratic inebriation had to be renegotiated in the aftermath of the Classical period by which time it had been reduced to perfunctory displays of intellectual abstraction. Nevertheless, while Horace and Lucian are keen to point out the farcical aspects of philosophical pretense, already recorded in the circles of the Academicians soon after Plato's death, early Stoics defend the ability of sensory images to guide reason in becoming cognitively fluent and successful in its evaluation(s) of truth. In this context, inebriation is once more employed to highlight the need to interrupt normal cognitive patterns to achieve philosophical insight while Seneca, well versed in Plato's *Laws,* does not hesitate to subscribe actual wine drinking as a practical way of suppressing ordinary reasoning in the hope of inducing philosophical inspiration. Furthermore, although later literary symposia such as those we come across in Plutarch and Athenaeus appear contrived, Plutarch, who firmly supports philosophy's contribution to public life,[50] insists that virtue is not the result of rejecting sensory emotions but of "moderating" them with the help of reason:[51] "The impulse of passion springs from moral virtue (τὴν δ' ὁρμὴν τῷ πάθει ποιεῖ τὸ ἦθος); but it needs reason to moderate it (λόγου δεομένην ὁρίζοντος ὅπως μετρία παρῇ) so it does not exceed nor forsake an opportune occasion (καὶ μήθ' ὑπερβάλλῃ μήτ' ἐγκαταλείπῃ τὸν καιρόν)" (Plut. *virt. mor.* 444b1–4). By expanding on Plato's *Laws*, Plutarch claims that just as those who are afraid of getting drunk do not pour their wine on the ground but dilute it with water (*virt. mor.* 451c12–d2: οὔτε γὰρ οἶνον οἱ φοβούμενοι τὸ μεθύειν ἐκχέουσιν), so those who fear the commotion of passion do not destroy it but temper it (οὔτε πάθος οἱ δεδιότες τὸ ταρακτικὸν ἀναιροῦσιν ἀλλὰ κεραννύουσι). Notably, as the stages and performers of Socratic inebriation become more cosmopolitan, Philo powerfully renews the Platonic metaphor with his version of the wise leader, blessed with drunklike reverie.

Reasonable Unreason

Since emotion can influence cognition, as Plato argues both in the *Republic* and more explicitly in the *Laws*, cities must strive to nourish the correct type of emotions among their citizens. This, however, necessarily means actively engaging with nonrational experiences to test and defend our rational account of things, which in turn implies that the key filter for reality is not reason *but* unreason. In this context, drunkenness operates as the nonrational filter we must employ to instigate the emotional responses that will nourish reason and guide it correctly in its evaluations. Thus, Plato proposes the Test of the Wine[52] as a means of temporarily disabling reason while arousing the passions in us to the point of being reduced to a "second childhood," when we first learn what is pleasant and what not, informed by our senses albeit in a direct, guileless manner. As Plato notes a few pages later, this ability to reframe our mindset by delving into the time when our senses registered our experiences more accurately, given that our reason was still undeveloped, was bestowed upon us by Dionysus. Having been "robbed of his soul's judgement" by Hera (*Leg.* 672b4–5: ὡς

ὁ θεὸς οὗτος ὑπὸ τῆς μητρυᾶς Ἥρας διεφορήθη τῆς ψυχῆς τὴν γνώμην),
Dionysus is said to have introduced "Bacchic rites and all the frenzied
choristry" (672b5–6: διὸ τάς τε βακχείας καὶ πᾶσαν τὴν μανικὴν ἐμβάλλει
χορείαν) to punish people (672b6–7: τιμωρούμενος) and render them mad
(672d6: ἵνα μανῶμεν, φησὶν ἐπὶ τιμωρίᾳ τῇ τῶν ἀνθρώπων δεδόσθαι).[53]
Plato, however, objects to the conventional interpretation of this tale,
claiming instead that

> no creature is ever born with that reason or that much rea-
> son as it befits it when fully developed (πᾶν ζῷον, ὅσον αὐτῷ
> προσήκει νοῦν ἔχειν τελεωθέντι, τοῦτον καὶ τοσοῦτον οὐδὲν
> ἔχον ποτὲ φύεται). During the time when it is still lacking
> in its proper intelligence (ἐν τούτῳ δὴ τῷ χρόνῳ ἐν ᾧ μήπω
> κέκτηται τὴν οἰκείαν φρόνησιν), it continues all in a frenzy,
> crying out wildly (πᾶν μαίνεταί τε καὶ βοᾷ ἀτάκτως), and as
> soon as it gets on its feet is leaps wildly (καὶ ὅταν ἀκταινώσῃ
> ἑαυτὸ τάχιστα, ἀτάκτως αὖ πηδᾷ). (*Leg.* 672b10–c6)

The description of the wild creatures here evokes Euripides' Bacchants as
well as the philosophically inclined lovers in the *Phaedrus*.[54] The Bacchic
state, then, is a manifestation, a premonition even, of our innate desire to
acquire, restore, and transform (and importantly, to describe and debate)
our connection with reason—aptly identified with the golden cord of
Plato's puppets in the *Laws* (645a1: τὴν τοῦ λογισμοῦ ἀγωγὴν χρυσῆν καὶ
ἱεράν, τῆς πόλεως κοινὸν νόμον ἐπικαλουμένην), which is called "law"
when it has become the public decree of the state.[55] Since the puppets
are described as the gods' playthings, reason is also what connects us to
the divine; the notion agrees with Plato's assertion that humans, being the
possession of the gods and daemons, can still access the divine *sōphrosynē*
of the gods and the ἐγκρατὴς νοῦς, the rational principle that rules the
cosmos.[56] Virtue, then, equated with Bacchic virtue (when the god or his
wine makes us *entheoi*), can achieve a verifiable grasp of reality; although
entering a Bacchic state can be a rational choice, it presupposes the
absence of reason.

In phenomenological terms, although the reality of the world is
rationally confirmed through our experiences,[57] the world, being the result
of relative things that can be rendered only through appearances and cultural constructs, is contingent on certain syntheses in our consciousness;[58]
thus, the world is irrational.[59] As Cimino notes,[60] the "rationality of the

world's fixed style and constantly fulfilling harmony is, in itself, irrational." Furthermore, the world can turn out to be "other" than previously apprehended.[61] Thus, Plato's suggestion to employ the Bacchic lens for verifying our reality is ideal because its unreason (reducing us to a child-like, pre-reasoning state) mimics the irrationality of the world and allows for sensory experiences to be as close to reality as possible. Furthermore, the symposiastic setting ensures that *baccheia* and its attendant *theōria* are experienced at the collective level and therefore individuals are assured of support in their groups should reality turn out to be different.

Plato's appreciation of the reason that rules the cosmos, in a seemingly unreasonable yet perfectly harmonious whole,[62] also encourages a less hierarchical understanding of his tripartite model of the soul,[63] mainly expounded in the *Republic* (436a–444e6), the *Phaedrus* (246a3–249d3) and the *Timaeus* (41a5–45b2, 69a6–71a3) and evoked by Plato's puppets, controlled by three cords, in the *Laws*. Although Plato often describes the role of reason in the soul in terms of a civil strife, a *stasis* that must be resolved by suppressing and carefully monitoring the desirous part of the soul,[64] this does not mean that sensation and emotion do not have discriminating powers, even if they form their beliefs based on imagistic, uncertain input.[65] Furthermore, although philosophers in the *Phaedo* are portrayed as able to excise emotion and sensory input from their lives,[66] which corresponds to Socrates' imperviousness to wine, other members of society rely on actual wine drinking to train their senses so they learn to trust the right emotions. Thus, while reworking Platonic premises to attack Stoic *apatheia*, Plutarch claims that the wise man will try to harmonize the parts of his soul and attain *sōphrosynē* (νῦν δὲ σωφροσύνη μέν ἐστιν), which arises[67] "where reason guides and controls the passionate part (οὗ τὸ παθητικὸν . . . ὁ λογισμὸς ἡνιοχεῖ καὶ μεταχειρίζεται), making it compliant to its desires (περὶ τὰς ἐπιθυμίας χρώμενος ὑπείκοντι) and willingly receptive of what is moderate and appropriate (δεχομένῳ τὸ μέτριον καὶ τὸ εὔσχημον ἑκουσίῳ)" (Plut. *mor. virt.* 445b6–10). The moderate person, Plutarch continues, achieves serenity and freedom from passion "by which the irrational is harmonized and blended with reason, when equipped with great persuasion and a wonderful gentleness" (*mor. virt.* 446d1–5: τῆς δὲ σώφρονος ψυχῆς τὸ πανταχόθεν ὁμαλὲς καὶ ἄσφυκτον καὶ ὑγιαῖνον ᾧ συνήρμοσται καὶ συγκέκραται τὸ ἄλογον πρὸς τὸν λογισμὸν εὐπειθείᾳ καὶ πραότητι θαυμαστῇ κεκοσμημένον). Unlike the Stoics who believe that "passion is not essentially different from reason" (*mor. virt.* 446f1–2: ἔνιοι δέ φασιν οὐχ ἕτερον εἶναι τοῦ λόγου τὸ πάθος) but a conversion of the same reason to one of its two aspects (447a1: ἑνὸς λόγου τροπὴν ἐπ᾽ ἀμφότερα), Plutarch advocates Plato's tripartite model of the soul[68] but highlights more emphatically the role of reason in coaxing the nonrational parts of the soul.[69] Thus, while being nonrational, passions guide reason to its judgements. As Plutarch writes, a human being[70]

> also participates in the nonrational (μέτεστιν οὖν αὐτῷ καὶ τοῦ ἀλόγου) and has inborn the source of passion (σύμφυτον ἔχει τὴν τοῦ πάθους ἀρχήν) not as an addition but because it is necessary (οὐκ ἐπεισόδιον ἀλλ᾽ ἀναγκαίαν οὖσαν); nor should it be removed altogether but it needs treatment and education (οὐδ᾽ ἀναιρετέαν παντάπασιν ἀλλὰ θεραπείας καὶ παιδαγωγίας δεομένην) (Plut. *virt. mor.* 451c2–5).

The only virtue that is not dependent on the nonrational parts of the soul and is completely free from passion is wisdom, defined as "a kind of self-sufficient superiority and power of reason through which the most divine and blessed knowledge results" (*virt. mor.* 444c10–d3: σοφία . . . αὐτοτελής τίς ἐστιν ἀκρότης τοῦ λόγου καὶ δύναμις, ᾗ τὸ θειότατον ἐγγίνεται τῆς ἐπιστήμης καὶ μακαριώτατον). While there is no doubt that only the philosophers can acquire wisdom through uninterrupted dedication to theoretical contemplation, the question that arises for the average person is how to ensure that reason achieves "order and regulation of the non-rational parts of the soul" (*virt. mor.* 444d6–7: τοῦ ἀλόγου τῆς ψυχῆς . . . τάξις καὶ διακόσμησις), how to choose, in other words, which "wine" is optimal.

As far as Plato is concerned, an answer is glimpsed in *Theaetetus* where Socrates defines perception (αἴσθησιν) in relation to sensation as "that which includes seeing, hearing, smelling, being cold, and being hot" (186d10–187a9: τῷ ὁρᾶν ἀκούειν ὀσφραίνεσθαι ψύχεσθαι θερμαίνεσθαι); although sensation can never be equated to knowledge,[71] yet sensation can guide us to grasp knowledge as "true opinion" (187b6–7: ἀληθὴς δόξα ἐπιστήμη εἶναι).[72] Although Plato admits the absurdity of choosing to have opinions, aware that may be wrong (196c7–9),[73] the exercise is most worthwhile, for by being proactive either "we find what we are after or we are less inclined to claim that we know what we do not" (187b9–c2: ἐὰν γὰρ οὕτω δρῶμεν, δυοῖν θάτερα, ἢ εὑρήσομεν ἐφ᾽ ὃ ἐρχόμεθα, ἢ ἧττον οἰησόμεθα εἰδέναι ὃ μηδαμῇ ἴσμεν).[74] Furthermore, in *Statesman* 277d1–278e10, Plato advocates the use of examples to describe our experience of knowledge (τὸ περὶ τῆς ἐπιστήμης πάθος ἐν ἡμῖν), once more a phenomenon best observed in the learning practices of young children, who rely on recognizing similarities in things through comparison (καὶ παραβάλλοντας ἐνδεικνύναι τὴν αὐτὴν ὁμοιότητα καὶ φύσιν). Thus, the only way to navigate the confusing or irrational aspects of truth and the world that our soul is unable to discern is by giving examples of our experiences and rationally trying to figure out small pieces of the bigger puzzle which escapes us. Wine tasting is such an example: firmly rooted in everyday practice and the senses, it offers a reasonable representation of virtue, which is nothing more than a sober grasp of our limits.

Platonic Inebriation after Plato

In early Christianity, while drunkenness is rejected as pagan folly typically exemplified in impious Dionysian rituals, Socratic inebriation is reworked to refer to partaking in the wisdom of Christ and his Heavenly City;[75] the profound importance of the metaphor in Christianity is evident in the symposiastic character of the mystery of the Eucharist,[76] the pinnacle of Christian spirituality and an invitation to the mind-altering experience of Christ. Inebriation is also revised in Quattrocento Florence to defend the civic benefits derived from ecstasy, now in the service of a god-inspired ruler and his intellectual circle.[77]

The more we study the transmission paths through which Platonic thought was disseminated in the East, especially once Alexandria replaced Athens as the center of Platonic studies, the clearer it becomes that later thinkers never ceased to engage with the work of Plato and/or that of his commentators.[78] Plato's thought appealed to intellectuals of all religious persuasions, prompting robust intellectual exchanges among pagans, Jews, and Christians.[79] The work of Philo, discussed in chapter 4, set the pace for the interpretation of Platonic *baccheia* in the context of the Jewish exegetical tradition; at the same time, thinkers such as Numenius and Ammonius infused Platonism with notable Pythagorean elements, claiming that Socrates was also a Pythagorean who taught his audiences the doctrine of the three gods (that is, the One, Intellect, and the creator-demiurge). The doctrine was teased out by Numenius in his treatise *On the Good*, inspired by Plato's *Timaeus*.[80] The dialogue was also influential for Plutarch who believed that the tale of the Demiurge and his "creation" of the world ought to be taken literally.[81] These ideas appealed greatly to early Christian thinkers who often frequented the same intellectual circles, alongside the Middle Platonic notion of the Forms as thoughts of God,[82] which humans ought to approximate by following a contemplative life so to achieve "likeness to God"—a concept famously expounded by Plato in the *Theaetetus* (176b1: ὁμοίωσις θεῷ).[83] Hence, Clement of Alexandria, an avid reader of Plato, whom he mentions by name 134 times in the *Stromata* alone,[84] reads Genesis 1:26–27, where God is portrayed as creating humans in his image and likeness (κατ᾽ εἰκόνα and καθ᾽ ὁμοίωσιν), by systematically referring to Plato.[85] Following Philo's allegorical reading of Plato,[86] Clement appreciates the language of heathen poets as a παραπέτασμα (= veil)[87] of profound truths that ought to be protected from the uneducated. Thus, Clement anticipates Porphyry's collapse of the distinction between poetry and philosophy[88] and Proclus' systematic use of the word παραπέτασμα to signify Plato's allegorical moments.[89] In this context, while the Jewish traditions about wine, which were absorbed in the New Testament,[90] coincide with the Stoic rejection of wine as a means of achieving spiritual growth, Clement adapted the metaphor of Platonic inebriation to discuss Christian spiritual progress.[91] In his preoccupation to define the "true gnostic,"[92] Clement engages both with Euripides' *Bacchae*—which reflects the play's popularity in post-classical Alexandria,[93] and Plato's references to wine-fueled ecstasy. Clement transforms Plato's philosophical *baccheia* into a process of spiritual illumination that leads its most adept adherents to contemplation (*theōria*) and eventually faith, allowing them to gain citizenship in God's heavenly kingdom.[94]

Borrowing directly from Plato, Origen of Alexandria, Clement's student, employed wine in his *Commentary on the Song of Songs*,[95] to refer allegorically to "drinking" the teachings of Christ in accordance with Paul's appeal to the Ephesians to "not get drunk with wine, in which is excess, but be filled with the Spirit" (Eph 5:18: καὶ μὴ μεθύσκεσθε οἴνῳ ἐν ᾧ ἐστιν ἀσωτία ἀλλὰ πληροῦσθε ἐν πνεύματι).[96] Origen imagines Wisdom as addressing the Christians thus: "Come drink the wine I have offered you; for it symbolizes the divine spirit" (PG 17.281B8–9: δεῦτε, πίετε οἶνον ὃν κεκέρακα ὑμῖν· καὶ δηλοῖ τὸ πνευματικὸν πνεῦμα), a theme further developed in his commentary on *Psalm* 35.9, where we read: "They will become intoxicated with the richness of your home . . . This drunkenness is virtuous, for 'your cup inebriates like the best' (Ps. 23:5)" (PG 12.1316A11–13: μεθυσθήσονται ἀπὸ πιότητος οἴκου σου . . . ἀγαθὴ αὕτη μέθη, 'καὶ τὸ ποτήριόν σου μεθύσκον ὡσεὶ κράτιστον').[97] Under Origen's influence, Plato-inspired "sober intoxication"[98] becomes ubiquitous in fourth century Christian authors, like Gregory of Nyssa,[99] and the proto-hesychasts, including pseudo-Macarius.[100] While Platonic inebriation was adapted to articulate profound Christian experiences, including the mystery of the Eucharist,[101] metaphors of transcendence were increasingly invested with theurgic elements in the Neoplatonic exegetical tradition.[102] Origen's recon-figuration of Platonic ecstasy runs in parallel with Plotinus' Neoplatonic image of the intellect as being "drunk with nectar,"[103] leading to Proclus' preoccupation with *hēnōsis* and the theurgical properties of allegorical reasoning.[104] In this context, the mystery of the Eucharist, explicated by pseudo-Dionysius as a mystic union with God, can be understood as a Christian variant of Neoplatonic theurgy.[105] Invested with the sacramental capacity to become Christ's blood,[106] wine continues to provide a physical token of our spiritual union with god.[107]

In the Latin-speaking Western part of the Roman empire, the educational system that emerged out of its Roman forebear encouraged the continuous interaction of learners with pagan textual traditions.[108] Still, while the influence of Aristotle and Stoic moralists like Pliny on late antiquity and medieval virtue ethics is widely recognized,[109] it took a long time for scholars to recognize the role of Platonic and Neoplatonic ideas in shaping western Christian thought;[110] thus, Origen's role in the transmission of Platonic ideas is only gradually receiving the attention it deserves,[111] vindicating Hooker's view that "Platonism never really faded out of the Western tradition."[112] Origen, translated in Latin by Rufinus, had phenomenal influence on medieval theologians, especially on Bernard of Clairvaux who urged Christians to drink "sweet draughts of secret, holy teachings."[113] Even, Augustine, arguably the most influential Christian Father, who had read the works of some Platonist authors,[114] endorsed "the sober intoxication of the spirit,"[115] making a distinction between physical and spiritual drunkenness. Furthermore, the work of Dionysius Areopagite, thoroughly imbued by the ideas of Plotinus and Proclus,[116] became increasingly available in the West in the ninth century. Diony-sius' confident translation of Neoplatonic tropes in Christian theological thought and practice had palpable impact on Eriugena, who was tasked with improving Hilduin's 838 translation of the Dionysian corpus, but also on later thinkers such as Aquinas and Nicholas of Cusa.[117] Later, Dante's distinction between poetic and theological allegory[118] renews the rivalry between poetry and philosophy and paves the way for the reworking of the metaphor in the Medicean court.[119] In quattrocento Florence, Plato's *Sym-posium*, hardly popular among the ancient commentators, is rediscovered by Landino and Ficino, who read it equipped with their knowledge of pseudo-Dionysius and Hermias' *Commentary on the Phaedrus*.[120] In their hands, Plato's and Plotinus' nectar (wine's ancient alternative) becomes the symbol of divine inspiration,[121] which is once more situated at the heart of a debate about truth, poetry, and civic duty, identified as contemplation of God.[122] While the Christian reception of Platonic inebriation, broadly sketched here, will be the focus of another volume,[123] it is clear that thanks to Plato, inebriation, far from being a "lost object" of social and cultural history,[124] lies at the heart of modernity and its complicated relationship with reason.

Notes

Introduction

1. https://dataportal.arc.gov.au/NCGP/Web/Grant/Grant/FT160100453

2. https://www.grants.gov.au/Ga/Show/9d31a476-d87e-4c6c-b43f-909c087a6
d5d

3. "It is a bad thing to drink a lot of wine, but if one drinks it with understanding, it is not bad but good."

4. I return to Philo's role in disseminating Platonic/Socratic inebriation among the Christian Fathers in my next volume, *Drunk with the Spirit*.

5. Rix 1989 adds a distinction between intoxication, referring to the clinically proven presence of alcohol in one's bloodstream, and drunkenness, defined as the behavior of those who have consumed alcohol, believe themselves to have done so, or want to give that impression. Throughout the book, I use "drunkenness/ intoxication" to refer to the state of being drunk and the negative effects of wine drinking; for its positive effects I use only "inebriation."

6. Murray 2018/2016, 84–88, with Dentzer 1982, 51–69; Murray summarizes the connections of the Greek symposion with the Near Eastern group drinking practice known as *marzēaḥ* (which had a prominent upper-class character and was associated with heavy drinking; McLaughlin 2001, 55–66 and 189–200; McGovern 2009, 179) and the practice of drinking beer from a communal vessel with straws. For a review of the evidence, see Wecowski 2014, 151–158; cf. McGovern 2009, 69–71, 97–100; Bowie 2003.

7. Hsch. s.v. Βακχεῖα (Ar. *Ran.* 357)·ἑορτὴ Διονύσου ("*baccheia*: celebration [in honour] of Dionysus") and s.v. βακχεύει (Aesch. fr. 57)·μαίνεται. τραγῳδεῖ ("to act the Bacchus: to be manic. To represent in a tragedy"; Schmidt 1867, 287.9–10); cf. Hsch. s.v. ὀρχεῖται· διασείεται. βακχεύει (to dance: to shake to and fro, to act the Bacchus"; Schmidt 1867, 1148.76) and s.v. χορεύει (Phryn. p. 583; Eubul. p. 242)· μελωιδεῖ. βακχεύει. ὀρχεῖται ("to dance: to sing, to act the Bacchus, to dance"; Schmidt 1867, 1561.3–4). Cf. Suda s.v. βακχευούσας σὺν τῶι μέλει

τῶι βακχείωι τε καὶ ἐνθέωι ("Maidens celebrating with Bacchic and god-inspired singing"; Adler 1967, B53 in 1.449).

8. In Eur. *Bacch.* 120–134, the Corybants are named, along with the Curetes, as the inventors of the *tympanon* for Rhea, who later gifted the instrument to the mad satyrs. Graf and Johnston 2007, 210–211 with nn52 and 58. Pausanias (8.37.6) reports that the Corybants danced around baby Zeus, but in Orphic traditions the Corybants were said to guard infant Dionysus; Strabo 10.3.7 and 10.3.11; Diod. Sic. 5.49; cf. Edmonds 2006, 353–358. On the assimilation of the Corybants and the Curetes under Anatolian influence, see Unwin 2017, 84–86.

9. *Leg.* 649d7: δι᾽ ἡδονῆς αὖ μεθύσκοντα; cf. Vogt 2017 on Plato's discussion of thirst and hunger in *Resp.* 437d–439a as examples of human desire and the need to qualify them before determining that humans have an innate desire for good, just as we should qualify our desire for wisdom. The nature of human desires is also discussed by Moss 2022, and in the same volume, Evans 2022; McCabe 2022; and Price 2022, esp. 107–108 with Carone 2001.

10. Rinella 2010, 28, 38, 52 and 58; chapter 3, pp. 76 and 78 with nn48–49, 56, and 217.

11. The harmful effects of excessive or prolonged wine drinking were widely observed among the Greeks and later the Romans. O'Brien and Rickenbacker 1999, with Austin 1985; Murray 1990b; and D'Arms 1995; cf. Rolleston 1927; Leibowitz 1967; Mortensen 2002.

12. McCabe 2022, 99.

13. McCabe 2022, 104; cf. Price 2022, 110–113, with Harte 2004 on pleasure in the *Philebus*, esp. 39a1–c1. Price discusses the role of perception and memory in establishing what pleasure is and our responses to desire. The latter, defined as "emptying" of the usual state of body or the soul, is "replenished" based on our memory of a state of fulfillment. Cf. Warren 2014, 33. According to Price (p. 112), Plato's comments in the *Philebus* correspond to *Resp.* 585d11 (εἰ ἄρα τὸ πληροῦσθαι τῶν φύσει προσηκόντων ἡδύ ἐστι) where he "anticipates a conception of pleasures as replenishings." Also, see Warren 2022, 147–150; cf. Harte 2014.

14. See Warren 2014, 146–147, on *Phil.* 40b–c and the importance of aligning human with divine reason.

15. On Aristotle and the Stoics, see, for example, Arist. *Eth. Nic.* 1147a15–1; *Pol.* 1314b29–36; *SVF* 2.479–480 ("A drop of wine stains the sea"); Pliny *NH* 14.[28].137–148; Philo, *VC* 48–9.

16. See Brown 2017 with extensive bibliography.

17. Trans. based on Beresford 2020, 38; cf. *Eth. Nic.* 1106b25–27: ἡ δ᾽ ἀρετὴ περὶ πάθη καὶ πράξεις ἐστίν, ἐν οἷς ἡ μὲν ὑπερβολὴ ἁμαρτάνεται καὶ ἡ ἔλλειψις [ψέγεται], τὸ δὲ μέσον ἐπαινεῖται καὶ κατορθοῦται; *Eth. Nic.* 1109a20–24: Ὅτι μὲν οὖν ἐστιν ἡ ἀρετὴ ἡ ἠθικὴ μεσότης, καὶ πῶς, καὶ ὅτι μεσότης δύο κακιῶντῆς μὲν καθ᾽ ὑπερβολὴν τῆς δὲ κατ᾽ ἔλλειψιν, καὶ ὅτι τοιαύτη ἐστὶ διὰ τὸ στοχαστικὴ τοῦ μέσου εἶναι τοῦ ἐν τοῖς πάθεσι καὶ ταῖς πράξεσιν, ἱκανῶς εἴρηται. Aristotle

reiterates his view in *Eth. Eud.* 1220b35–36 (ἀνάγκη τὴν ἠθικὴν ἀρετὴν περὶ μέσ᾿ ἄττα εἶναι καὶ μεσότητά τινα); see Maso 2020, 84 with n3. On the meaning of *hexis* in Aristotle, see Hutchinson 1986, 8–14 and 108–122; cf. Lu 2014 and Rodrigo 2011.

18. Candiotto and Renaut 2020, 3–4, with Fortenbaugh 1975/2002; Konstan 2006, 32–40; Lorenz 2006, 47; Wolfsdorf 2012, 184–185.

19. On Aristotle's appreciation of virtue as nonrational, which prompts him to hold that happiness must be determined by each person based on "the non-rational habituation of the non-rational part of the soul," see Moss 2012a, 163–179; in her view (p. xv), Aristotle agrees with Plato "that the non-rational part of the soul is the seat of perception and appearance-perception, and that it is subject to evaluative appearances which explain its passions and desires"; cf. Moss 2006, 2008, and 2012b. On the role of *phronēsis* in Aristotle, see Moss 2012a, 192–198. See Cagnoli Fiecconi 2024, esp. 129–143 on Aristotle's argument that *phantasiai* take over our cognitive processes "when thought is obscured by bodily affections like sleep, emotions, or illnesses (p. 143)"; Lorenz 2006, 189 and 197n27; also, Theodoropoulou 2023, 44–46, with Arist. *On the Soul* 431a17 (οὐδέποτε νοεῖ ἄνευ φαντάσματος ἡ ψυχή). On the role of persuasion in Plato's *Laws*, see Pfefferkorn 2022, 139–140, with relevant bibliography including Bobonich 1991; Stalley 1994; Lane 2010a; and Baima 2016.

20. Cf. *Euthyd.* 277b8 where Socrates distinguishes between learning and understanding, anticipating Aristotle's differentiation between intellectual and moral knowledge, as articulated in *Eth. Nic.* 1035a14–20.

21. See *Eth. Nic.* 1145b22–27 with Pl. *Prt.* 352d6–7, 352c9; cf. *Rhet.* 1378a, esp. 20–21, where he defines τὰ πάθη, as "those affections which cause men to change their views regarding their judgements" (δι᾿ ὅσα μεταβάλλοντες διαφέρουσι πρὸς τὰς κρίσεις). Striker 1996, esp. 286–288; also, Moss 2012a, 80–84 and 2012b; Dow 2015, 183–222, esp. 213ff. Aristotle further believes that reason has its own desire (*boulēsis*), which we can shape through experience; *Eth. Nic.* 1113a23–24 and 1136b7–8. On rational *boulēsis* in Aristotle, see Pearson 2012, 183–198.

22. See, for example, Ar. Didymus, *Epit.* 10.1–5 and 10a.23–30; DL 7.110–111; Galen, *PHP* 4.1.15.9–10 (on Chrysippus' definitions of passions), 4.2.6.5–8, 4.2.8.11–16, 4.2.10–12, and 14–18; 4.3.2.1–3; Plut. *virt. mor.* 441c; Cic. *Tusc. disp.* 3.23–25 and 4.11.2–5. For the Stoics, acting against reason was synonymous with acting against nature; see, for example, DL 7.85–89; Cic. *Fin.* 3.7.26, 4.10.26; *Tusc. disp.* 5.28.82; also, Sen. *Ep.* 4.10–11 and 121.6–21; *Ot.* 5.1 and 8; *Vit. beat.* 8.2. Cf. Wolfsdorf 2012, 195; also, Cooper 1999, 461–474, and 1998, 81–90.

23. Ath. *Deipn.* 1.34b and 5.186e (on Aristotle's advice about appropriate symposiastic conduct) and esp. 15.674f, with Hobden 2013, 230, who suggested that Aristotle's treatise may have been entitled *Symposium*; cf. Jaworska-Wołoszyn 2016 and Petrova 2020. On drunkenness in the Aristotelian corpus, see Bonitz 1870, 449b3–11 (s.v. μέθη), 450a40–58 (svv. μέθυ, μεθύειν, μεθύσκειν), and

501a42–b15 (s.v. οἶνος); cf. 501b19–20 (s.v. οἰνοφλυγία) and 501b29–33 (s.v. οἰνωμένος). Also see L316: 96n1.

24. Fortenbaugh (with Gutas) 2011, 222–224 s.v. *On Drunkenness* (= no.31).

25. Cagnoli Fiecconi 2024, 195–198; Moss 2012a, 202, with *Eth. Nic.* 1104b8–13, where Aristotle agrees with Plato's definition of correct education so that one learns from childhood to be pleased and pained by the things s/he ought to; cf. Dow 2015, 185–186 and 221–222; also see Plut. *virt. mor.* 452d3–8.

26. Moss 2012a, 183–187, with n19 above; however, as Moss notes (2012a, 211n22), Aristotle does agree with Plato that it is the state's responsibility to inspire its citizens to (collectively appreciated notions of) virtue and happiness through musical education.

27. Lynch 2007; Murray 1990a; Slater 1991; Murray and Tecuşan 1995; Orfanos and Carrière 2003; Corner 2005 and 2010; Lissarrague 2016. On ancient Greek wine production techniques, see McGovern 2003 and 2009; cf. McGovern et al. 1995; Dodd 2020; Kourakou-Dragona 2015; Pratt 2021; Komar 2021; Slingerland 2021.

28. McGovern 2003, 29–39; cf. McGovern et al. 2017.

29. McGovern 2003, 305–306, 308–312, and 2020; Rinella 2010, 3–10. Cf. Carrigan 2020, 41 noting: "Humans' predilection for ethanol is . . . surprising, given the adverse consequences that follow from overuse. However, the palae-ogenetic evidence . . . in conjunction with palaeoclimate, palaeontological, and animal behaviour studies, provides strong support for the suggestion that this predilection for ethanol consumption is related to evolution of ethanol metabolism that enabled our ancestors to exploit fermented sugars as a source of energy."

30. McGovern 2003, 239–278; cf. Valamoti et al. 2007, who relied on residue analysis of charred wine presses from the Neolithic site of Dikili Tash in northern Greece to suggest that wine was introduced to Greece at least 6,500 years ago, at a time when McGovern et al. (2017) argue that wine was produced in ancient Georgia in the Caucasus region; also see Garnier and Valamoti 2016; cf. *Phdr.* 244b8–9 referring to "the people of old" (τῶν παλαιῶν) who acknowledged the benefits of religious ecstasy (also cited in chapter 1 n5).

31. Chapter 1, pp. 14–15, with nn10–12.

32. Roochnik 2020, 86–90, introduces the metaphorical nature of Socratic inebriation; cf. Slingerland 2021, 103–106 and 204–223, on our need to suppress our perifrontal cortex, the seat of abstract reasoning, from time to time. For Slingerland, the perifrontal cortex is the seat of Apollo, which must be occasionally subjected to Dionysus to balance between orderly restraint and creativity; cf. Huxley 1954/2009, 77, also cited by Slingerland.

33. The trope is common across the ancient sources; see, for example, Hdt. 3.80.5; Eur. *Supp.* 452–454; Ath. *Deipn.* 10.434a–438e; Cic. *Verr.* 2.5. 28–32, 62–75, and *Phil.* 2.63 with Quint. *Inst. Or.* 8.4.8–9. Also, see Dunkle 1971; Jellinek 1976; Graf 1980; Goddard 1994, 67–82; Coarelli 1995; D'Arms 1995; Bettini 1995;

Leigh 1996, 171–197; Mortensen 2002, 73; Arena 2007; Papakonstantinou 2012; Henderson 1999; Hobden 2013; Guerra Doce 2014 and 2020; and Anagnostou-Laoutides 2020a.

34. See Bartels 2017, 90–103; Belfiore 1986; Hunter 2004, 5–22, 42, 52; Berg 2010; Rinella 2010; Hobden 2013, 195–246; Roochnik 2020; Anagnostou-Laoutides and Van Wassenhove 2020; Palumbo and Motta 2020; in the same volume, see the contributions of Bartels 2020 and also Pfefferkorn 2020, 257–258 (reiterated in her 2022 book, pp. 149–157, 194–198, 294); cf. Pfefferkorn 2021a; and Anagnostou-Laoutides and Payne 2021.

35. Rinella 2010, xv–xvi, 235–240, and 258–259; also see Rinella 2007.

36. See Rinella 2000 and 2010, 127–138, on ecstasy in Plato's *Phaedrus*.

37. Rinella 2007, esp. 136–146, and 2010, 233–248. The evidence on recreational use of drugs in ancient Greece is contested; see Ustinova 2017, 61, on the hypothesis that the Pythia prophesized after inhaling ethylene, with Lehoux 2007; Foster and Lehoux 2007; also, Spiller et al. 2002. Thus, I do not use the term drugs as contrasted to alcohol in the modern sense; I refer to alcohol as a *pharmakon* (medicine/remedy but also poison/drug) based on the psychoactive effects of both (see Dietler 2020, 115, cited by Slingerland 2021, 17n1) and to the *pharmakon* of philosophy given that it is described as having the same psychosomatic effects as alcohol (see chapter 2). Cf. Ustinova 2017, 276, who observes that Homer uses the same verb *thelgein* ("to bewitch") to refer to the effects of music and drugs on humans (*Od.* 10.213, 29, 318, 12.40, 44, and 17.517–521).

38. *Resp.* 414b–c with Schofield 2007. In my view, however, the "noble lie" of philosophy is not "a drug of deceit that supplements the partially or fully deceitful drugs of philosophy's many competitors," as Rinella argues (2010, 247), but rather is the *right* kind of "drug" that affects the mind in a way amenable to the common good. On Plato's use of the "noble lie" in the *Laws*, see Williams 2013; also, Balot 2024, 54–55.

39. See, for example, Rinella 2010, 30–40 (on the ethical and political aspects of the ancient symposion), 49–63 (on Plato's use of sympotic etiquette in the *Symposium* and the *Laws*), 149–165 (on the medical discourse underpinning ecstatic intoxication), and 184–195 (on Plato's association of physical and noetic health).

40. See *Resp.* 473c11–e5 and 484a–487a.

41. Pfefferkorn 2022, 155–158, 165–166, 179, 187, 189–190, 194–198, 308; cf. Pfefferkorn 2021a, 353–361, and 2021b, 342; cf. Bartels 2017, esp. 92–99 (on the symposion as a form of training in αἰδώς/shame).

42. Slingerland 2021, 96.

43. Cf. Slingerland 2021, 141, arguing that "extreme levels of intoxication—especially when combined with music and dance—can be a tool for effectively erasing the distinctions between self and other." Thus, drinking together or, to be more precise, learning how to drink together becomes a major factor of social coherence. On the educative role of wine drinking in the *Laws*, see chapter 3.

44. Pfefferkorn 2022, 157, with Tecuşan 1990 and Kidd 2019, 14–19, 29–36, 56–69; cf. n59 below.

45. On *sōphrosynē*, see chapter 2, pp. 37, 62, 64, 67 and chapter 3, pp. 103–109.

46. Hobden 2013, 7; cf. Rinella 2010, 10–16.

47. König 2012, 60–89 (Plutarch) and 89–120 (Athenaeus); cf. Lukinovich 1990; and Paul 1991.

48. Here, I quote from the book's blurb.

49. Anagnostou-Laoutides 2020b, 95–99; also discussed in Anagnostou-Laoutides 2021a, 4, 24, and 2025, 57. The Eucharist as a Christian form of theurgy, developed through continuous engagement with Neoplatonic authors, is discussed in the second volume from this project, *Drunk with the Spirit.* Indicatively, see Struck 2001; Shaw 1999; and Pavlos 2019, esp. 164.

50. Roth 2005, esp. 103, 144, 148–149.

51. Roochnik 2020, 45–74, 79–94; cf. Roskam 2010; also, Slingerland 2021, 204–210, citing Nietzsche 1872/1967, 37 and Luyster 2001.

52. Ustinova 2017, 170–216.

53. Ustinova 2017, 2–3.

54. For *mania* as a disease, see Hdt. 6.75.1: αὐτὸν αὐτίκα ὑπέλαβε μανίη νοῦσος (on Cleomenes of Sparta), cited by Thumiger 2017, 18n7; cf. chapter 2, n61.

55. Thumiger 2017, 220–228; cf. Gourevitch and Demigneux 2013 (on alcoholism as disability) and van der Eijk 2005, 108–109, 148, and 157–159.

56. Thumiger 2017, 50–51; cf. Thumiger 2013 and 2015. Also see Perdicoyianni-Paléologou 2009a and 2009b.

57. The earliest evidence for wine production has been found in Georgia and dates from the early Neolithic period; see McGovern et al. 2017.

58. Jouanna 2012a; Bartoš 2015, 230–291, and 2020; cf. Camden 2023, 214, 252–255.

59. For example, see the contributions of Schmitt-Pantel; Slater; and Murray in the same 1990 volume. Papakonstantinou 2012 and 2009, esp. 19–20, notes that Homeric societies, while aware of the harmful aspects of intoxication, adopted an "integrated drinking culture," which stressed the overall positive effects of wine drinking. He also defines archaic symposia as spaces where "a valorous political and military leader" sought reaffirmation by his peers and the people.

60. Pfefferkorn 2022, 247, with Griffith 2009, 88.

61. Szaif 2019, 103. For Tecuşan 1990, 260, Plato's approval of wine drinking in the *Laws* reflects a changed stance toward the irrational; cf. Bartels 2017, 102n113; Belfiore 1986. In my view, Plato revisits the challenge of incorporating the irrational in the ideal city in the *Laws,* but his approach remains consistent across his dialogues.

62. Anagnostou-Laoutides 2021a, 11–21, with bibliography.

63. Hobden 2013, 198–212; cf. Rinella 2010, 207–210, and Pellizer 1990.

64. McCloskey 2017, 239, 243.

65. For the importance of symposia in Athenian comedy, see Wilkins 2003; in the same volume, see Carriére 2003, 176–179 (on Aristophanic "utopian banquets") and 187ff. (on banquets involving the *dēmos*), and Orfanos 2003, 208–213, on the political importance of banquets as negotiated in Euripides' *Cyclops*. For comedic discourse as a kind of spell in *Republic* 10, see Rinella 2010, 208; cf. chapter 3, n148.

66. Cf. Dietrich and Dietrich 2020, 99, 109–112, discussing communal feasting that included mind-altering beverages in the early community of Göbekli Tepe (more than 11,000 years old) as evidence of how identities and social cohesion are produced rather than expressed; regarding the same community, Slingerland 2021, 150–155, notes: "The political function of alcohol is practical as well as symbolic."

67. DL 4.28 and 4.59; cf. Cic. *Acad.* prior. 2.1–16; also, chapter 4, n30.

68. DL 7.65; S.E. *M.* 7.151 and 8.397. Nawar 2014 with Sedley 2002; Moss 2012a, 89, 92–98; cf. Sandbach 1971.

69. Niehoff 2010, 35 with n2, citing DL 3.61–62; Chroust 1965; Bonazzi and Helmig 2007; Dillon 1996, 114–135; on Philo, see Runia 1993a and Dillon 1996, 139–183.

70. Cf. the statue of the drunken old woman (first century CE Roman copy of a Greek original, third/second century BCE), now in the Glyptothek, Munich (Inv. 437).

71. See, for example, *Anth. Gr.* 5.134–137, 5.167, 5.169, 5.171, 5.190, 5.199, 6.44, 9.331, and 12.50; cf. Theoc. *Id.* 7.154; Call. fr. 544 Pfeiffer (in L421); and Ath. *Deipn.* 11.473a. The hedonistic surrender celebrated here survived down to the sixth century CE; see Paulus Silentiarius (*Anth. Gr.* 5.226, 5.266, 6.71) and Agathias Scholasticus (5.261 and 5.296); cf. chapter 4, n4. Following their Hellenistic models, Roman neoteric poets employed intoxication to challenge traditional Roman literary and social hierarchies; see Sandilands 1966; also, Yardley 1991.

72. Epigrams often recorded alcoholism as a cause of death (as in *Anth. Gr.* 7.104, 7.329, 7.422, 7.703, and 7.725), including that of women (7.233), particularly of older women (7.353 and 7.455–457), but also of philosophers (though clearly in a mocking tone, as in *Anth. Gr.* 7.106 on Epicurus and 7.706 on Zeno).

73. Long 2006, 10 (1993, 152).

74. The term is coined by Lynch 2018a, 233; in the same volume, cf. Strootman 2018 on Hellenistic kings and civic feasting; also see Murray 2018/1996.

75. Anagnostou-Laoutides 2020a, 130–138.

76. For example, see Sen. *Ep.* 83.18–25 and Lucan, *BC.*10.20–52, with Spencer 2002, 93–94; cf. Hobden 2013, 242–246; also, chapter 4, p. 113 with nn2 and 4.

77. On Marc Antony's drunkenness, see Cic. *Phil.* 2.13.25–28, 2.42, 2.63, 2.7, 2.104–105, 6.4, 13.31; Sen. *Ep.* 83.25; Dio Cass. 48.27.1–2; also, Marasco 1992; cf. Scott 1929. On Verres' drunkenness, see Cic. *Verr.* 2.1.66, 2.3.23, 2.3.31, 2.5.28–32, and 62–75.

78. Verg. *Aen.* 3.618–627; cf. Ov. *Met.* 13.768–769; *Anth. Gr.* 9.519.

79. On ambitious generals drinking blood (instead of wine) in the works of Lucan and Statius and Plato's contribution to the development of the motif in the Roman imperial period, see Anagnostou-Laoutides 2017. For Cicero's use of the theme, see Köster 2014.

80. See the contributions of Wilkins, Pociña, and Aygon in the same 2003 special issue. Also, Papakonstantinou 2009, 1 (on Polyphemus' drunkenness, Homer, *Od.* 9.362, 454, 516 and on the Centaurs' drunkenness, 5–6); cf. Orfanos 2003 in n65 above.

81. Schiesaro 2003, 21; cf. Ustinova 2017, 272.

82. Arist. *Eth. Nic.* 1145a153–30; Vander Waerdt 1985; Roochnik 2009.

83. Strabo, *G.* 15.1.64; Plut. *Alex. fort.* 332e–333f; Desmond 2011, 51.

84. Bringmann 1965; Ehrenberg 1969, 277–8; Konstan 2004.

85. Atack 2018a and 2018b, and 2019.

86. DL 7.121; Cic. *fin.* 3.20.68; cf. Colish 1985, 89–109; Schofield 2015 and 2021, 71–78.

87. Roskam 2020, 131.

88. DL 7.118; Stob. 2.7.11m (Wachsmuth and Hense 1884, 109.5–9) with Ahonen 2014, 121; also, Ahonen 2018b.

89. Bartsch 2007, 89 with Epict. *Disc.* 3.1–2.

90. As Hobden (2013, 229) notes: "[I]n contrast to fourth century Symposia, later representations were not primarily creative engagements with an existing convivial form, but rather meta-Sympotic responses to the literary tradition in which they operated"; cf. König 2012, 11.

91. As discussed by Plato in *Resp.* 596a–b; cf. *Phd.* 100c–d.

92. Novak 2019, 107–139.

93. Runia 1986, 113, 159, 165 and 490; also, Dillon 2011, par. 19–20, and 1996, 139–183; cf. Jer. *vir. ill.* 11 on the Greek saying: "either Plato philonized (φιλωνίζει) or Philo platonized (πλατωνίζει)," inspired by the "great similarity of their ideas and language (*tanta . . . similitudo sensuum et eloquii*)"; for the text, see Richardson 1896, 15.12–15); cf. Photius, *Bibl.* 105 (PG 103.3, 373B15–16); also, Suda s.v. Ἀβραάμ (Adler 1967, A69 in 1.10.15–16).

94. On Philo's allegorical reading of Noah's drunkenness in Gen 9:20–29, see Cohen 1974, 6–8 (who explained Noah's nakedness, resulting from his drunkenness, as reference to wine's ability to enhance his procreative powers). On Moses as the ideal sage-king, inspired by Plato's philosopher king, see Borgen 1996; cf. Litwa 2014 and 2021, 74–93.

95. See, for example, ps.-Long. *Subl.* 32.7 = Caec. Cal. fr. 150 (Ofenloch 1967, 129); cf. Phld. *Hist. Acad.* (*PHerc.* 1021 et 164) col. 13.1–27 (Fleischer 2023, 190–191).

96. Anagnostou-Laoutides and Van Wassenhove 2020, 16 with n8. Chrysippus believes that virtue could be lost through drunkenness (DL 7.127 = SVF 3.237), while Zeno crafted a syllogism to establish that a good man will not get

drunk, which Seneca quotes in his letter against drunkenness (Sen. *Ep.* 83.9 = SVF 1.229); Szaif 2019, 97.

97. Anagnostou-Laoutides and Van Wassenhove 2020, esp. 16–18 and 21.

98. Philo, *Gig.* 49; *Sacr.* 78; *Somn.* 1.71; *Opif.* 70–71, with Wyss 2023, 176–177.

99. Philo, *all.* 3.1: ὁ . . . σοφίας μεστὸς ᾿Ιακὼβ καὶ πολίτης ἐστὶ καὶ οἰκίαν τὴν ἀρετὴν κατοικεῖ; cf. *all.* 1.64–5 and 78.

100. Anagnostou-Laoutides 2025, 44 and 56–57; the concept is discussed in detail in the second volume of this project.

101. To paraphrase (the title of) Foucault 1972. This is my major difference with Slingerland 2021, esp. 61–158, who offers excellent insights to our historical relationship with drinking wine before focusing on the consumption of alcohol in the modern world. Slingerland 2021, 71ff., appreciates the role of wine in helping us to respond to the challenges of the three Cs (that is, being creative, cultural, and communal) but hardly discusses the role of Plato in shaping the way we articulate our experiences. His work, interspersed with numerous examples of wine consumption and related attitudes from traditional Chinese cultures and thought, adopts a more universal approach to the human consumption of mind-altering intoxicants.

102. *Symp.* 218b3–4; *Phdr.* 244a–245a; Ustinova 2017, 315–328; cf. Philo, *Vit. compl.* 1.2 and 2.11–13; *Ebr.* 145–149.

103. See Tietjen 2021, 12, with Ricoeur 1986, 87–89 and 131, on the importance of feeling in binding us together and the role of metaphors in achieving it; cf. Bougher 2014.

Chapter 1

1. See introduction, p. 3.

2. See Geertz 2014, 38, on our brain's constant assessment of our expectations against the sensory input we receive. The human tendency to rely on divine authority and its human conduits (priests, prophets, wise men, etc.) is a way of coping, especially at the collective level, with issues of epistemic trust. Cf. Geertz 1993, 109–110. On the issue of epistemic vigilance and religious authority, see Sperger et al. 2010; cf. Talmont-Kaminski 2020.

3. Druckman and Bjork 1994, 207. On the ancient debate on whether the brain or the heart is the seat of human cognition, see Mansfeld 1990, 3105–3107; Walshe 2016, 107–135; cf. Tracy 1976, 46–47. On Socrates' appreciation of the soul as "the ground of our rational and moral as well as our biological self," see Robinson 2000, 38 with n6, citing *Euthyd.* 295e4–5; *Charm.* 157a1–b1; and *Crito* 47d3–4. Geertz 2014, 32–33, discussed the process of acquiring awareness of ourselves and others as "mentalizing," which Bateman and Fonagy 2004, xxi, defined

as a "mental process by which an individual implicitly and explicitly interprets the actions of himself and others as meaningful on the basis of intentional mental states such as personal desires, needs, feelings, beliefs and reasons."

4. Druckman and Bjork 1994, 207–208, draw on Kihlstrom 1984, 207, to identify the four features whose unique combination can result in an altered state of consciousness: (1) operationally, as the product of a particular induction technique; (2) phenomenologically, as an individual's subjective report of altered awareness or voluntary control; (3) observationally, as changes in overt behavior corresponding to a person's self-report; and (4) physiologically, as a particular pattern of changes in somatic functioning. Geertz 2014, 43; Ustinova 2017, 20.

5. Nissinen 2017, 172–173, with Siikala 1992, 26–34; on the differences between trance and ecstasy, see Rouget 1990 with Ustinova 2017, 20–21. Cf. *Phdr.* 244b8–9, on the positive aspects of *mania* as recognized by "the people of old."

6. On the physical symptoms of *mania*, see Ustinova 2017, 219 (battle frenzy), 279 (poetic inspiration), 315 (*baccheia*), and 315–328 (Socratic *mania* and Plato's experiences of philosophical rapture); cf. DeBevoise Corcoran 2016, 44–45.

7. See Geertz 2014, 18 and 23, citing Donald 2001, 285–287, on the contribution of culture in developing "metacognitive awareness"; also, Lieberoth 2014 and nn87 and 119 below.

8. See, for example, Lössl 2007 with Nagy 1990.

9. Cf. Dodds 1960, xx, on Eur. *Bacch.* 75 and Bacchic ecstasy as merging individual and community consciousness.

10. Ustinova 2017, 265–293; cf. Nissinen 2017, 16, 34, 135, 193–195.

11. Ustinova 2017, 83, 117–129, 130, 134–136, 174–179, 182, 186, 193–195, 332; Hamilton 2008, 41–46; cf. Nissinen 2017, 178, 187, 190, 205 with n18, 247.

12. Papakonstantinou 2012; Henderson 1999; Hobden 2013, 66ff.

13. On Plato's engagement with poetry, see the chapters by Belfiore (2011), Pender (2011), and Halliwell (2011a) in the same volume. Cf. Hunter 2012, 38–108 (on Plato and Homer); Capra (2014) claims that in the *Phaedrus* Plato relies on important poetic models to produce philosophical poetry; cf. Planinc 2003, 22. Roth 2005, 48, refers to the *Symposium* as Plato's "unique contribution . . . to the domain of Literature"; cf. Holowchak 2003 on Plato's use of literary devices in the *Symposium*.

14. Cf. *Phdr.* 230c8 for Socrates' description as ἀτοπώτατος ("most odd/ strange"); cf. nn181–182 and 196 below. Cf. Holowchak 2003, 416, arguing that Plato draws on "Socrates the man" in the *Symposium*.

15. On the way images inform metaphors, see Ricoeur 1975, 238–272, and 1977, 222–254); also, see n29 below.

16. See Skinner 1969 with Finkelberg 2017, 9–10; also see Skinner 1975, 227–228, who claims, rather alarmingly, that literary historians inevitably interpret authorial purpose by drawing on their personal experiences and sensibility.

17. Derrida 1981, 77–84, was wary of images because they could be miscon-strued, yet he appreciates our need to turn to words or images since we simply cannot speak of the Good in a direct manner. For the similarities and differences between Plato's *agathon* and Derrida's Good, see White 2017, 284. Cf. Rinella 2007, 139–140, and 2010, 237–238.

18. See Stoller 2009, 707–719, for a summary of the arguments.

19. For a criticism of structuralism's understanding of metaphor, see Ricoeur 1975, 129–219, and 1977, 117–203, that is, studies 4 and 5), and Garver 1986, 75–77.

20. Morris 2000, 226–227 and 240–244; Derrida 1982, 224–220; cf. Kennedy 2010 and Driscoll 2020, 124–125.

21. Burden 1998, 92–93. In my view, Lacan's definition of metaphor (as condensation) and metonymy (as displacement) is flawed, certainly regarding the function of metaphors in ancient texts. Cf. Silk 2003, 135, criticizing Jakobson, who developed Saussurean linguistics into a literary theory but associated met-aphor only with verse and metonymy with prose. Ricoeur 1975, 170, and 1977, 155, argues that "Metaphor prevails over metonymy . . . because metaphorical equivalences set predicative operations in motion that metonymy ignores." Cf. Thompson 1981, xvii–xxi, on Ricoeur's critical approach to structuralism and his disagreement with Lacan's attempt "to interpret condensation as metaphor and displacement as metonymy" (p. xviii). For an attempt to reconcile Lacanian psychoanalysis with cognitive neuroscience, see Pizzato 2006, 97–113, on how the human brain operates as a stage on which we enact ourselves, thus developing consciousness; also, Pizzato 2011, 120–122, on synesthesia as the key human ability from which metaphors evolved in our prehistory, although his concept of a "Western cultural unconscious" (p. 82) is disconcerting.

22. Calame 1995, 3–26.

23. Honorato 2017, 444–448; Calame 2003, 14, argues that, by choosing myths as "instruments of philosophical demonstration," Plato uses *mythos* as *logos*; cf. Trabattoni 2012, 309–311, 319–21, on philosophical myth as a way of communicating effectively metaphysical realities; Hartmann 2017, 430–433; Tarrant 2012 and 1990.

24. Cf. Pender 2003, 61, claiming that Plato uses metaphors as a preliminary or second-best way of undertaking an enquiry.

25. See Ricoeur 1975, 25, reiterated on p. 364, and 1977, 19 and 339, respectively; cf. Johnson 2008, esp. 48.

26. Merleau-Ponty 1962, 151; cf. Crowther 2003, 88, on metaphor as the "articulation of perception."

27. Merleau-Ponty 1962, 28.

28. Ricoeur 1975, 272, and 1977, 254, citing Bachelard 1960, 16. Cf. Calin 2014, 271–272, on Ricoeur's attempt to develop a nonlinguistic semiotics of image that explain the role of imagination in renewing figurative language.

29. See Ricoeur 1975, 272, and 1977, 254, citing Bachelard 1957, 8, on the role of poetic images in creating realities: "The poetic image 'becomes a new being in our language, expressing us by making us what it expresses; in other words, it is at once a becoming of expression, and a becoming of our being. Here expression creates being.'"

30. Andén 2019, 209–211. Cf. Apostolopoulos 2019, 262, on Merleau-Ponty's appreciation of the aesthetics of metaphor.

31. Merleau-Ponty 1962, 343: ". . . in our knowledge of ourselves, appearance is reality."

32. For example, Burke 1757/2008, 75–103, appreciates the sublime as an irrational, irresistible force; cf. Kant 1764/2011, esp. 2:217, who (despite his flawed comments on the beautiful and the sublime as reflected in different measures in the two genders and people of different races, 2:228 and 2:243) notes that the sublime presupposes the excitability of the soul. Cf. Schönfeld 2000, 230. For Kant, the sublime is rational and serves as a reminder of a "higher" morality.

33. Hence, ps.-Longinus, discussing sublimity in literature (*Subl.* 1.4), argues that it "does not aim to persuade the audience but lead them to ecstasy" (οὐ γὰρ εἰς πειθὼ . . . ἀλλ εἰς ἔκστασιν). Halliwell 2011b, 342.

34. Edmonds 2017, 203. See Trabattoni 1998, 330–331, on the existence of Platonic doctrine at two levels, an esoteric and an exoteric level; also, Trabattoni 2007, 113, on Plato's appreciation of writing as "[A]n imperfect tool for describing that which really matters." Trabattoni has long argued that Plato favors oral over written discourse; for example, see Trabattoni 2007, 117–126, and 2020, 345–350; cf. Ford 2002, 241–249; also, Reames and Sloey 2021 challenging the alleged objectivity of written discourse as problematized in the *Phaedrus*. Cf. Szlezák 1999, 31–32, who speaks of two types of esotericism, an "interpretative" and a "historical" esotericism.

35. Ustinova 2017, 267; cf. Lier 2019, 116–118. Jensen 2014, 252, refers to the human ability to express "complicated and abstract collective experiences" through existing systems of signs. Cf. Jessen 2014, 328–329, on the two main theories of relational cognition: "blending theory," based on the premise that mental space is organized in blocks, and "metaphor theory," focusing on conceptual mappings, informed by bodily experiences. For the main advocates of these theories, see Fauconnier and Turner 2002; also, Lakoff and Johnson 1980, 262–270.

36. Kirby 1997, 528–531, with McCall 1969, 11–18; cf. Pender 2003, esp. 71–72. For early studies of metaphors in Plato, see Berg 1903 and Louis 1945.

37. Geldard 2000, 23; Morgan 2000, 27–30, 68; Nikolitseas 2014, 93–116; cf. Carabine 1995, 13–190, and Franke 2007, 9–26.

38. Cf. Arist. *Poet.* 1459a5: "the most important by far is the use of metaphors" (πολὺ δὲ μέγιστον τὸ μεταφορικὸν εἶναι).

39. Cf. Arist. *Rhet.* 1405a8–9: καὶ τὸ σαφὲς καὶ τὸ ἡδὺ καὶ τὸ ξενικὸν ἔχει μάλιστα ἡ μεταφορά. καὶ λαβεῖν οὐκ ἔστιν αὐτὴν παρ᾽ ἄλλου. δεῖ δὲ καὶ τὰ ἐπίθετα

καὶ τὰς μεταφορὰς ἁρμοττούσας λέγειν. **τοῦτο δ᾽ ἔσται ἐκ τοῦ ἀνάλογον** ("Most of all metaphor gives clarity, pleasure, and an air of strangeness, and it cannot be learned from anyone else. Also, we must choose epithets and metaphors that fit together. This will come from analogy"). Also, Silk 2003, 127–128 and n44 below.

40. Kotarcic 2021, 167–169, quotation from p. 169.

41. See Ricoeur 1975, 13–34, and 1977, 8–26, on Aristotelian epiphora and 1975, 34–40, and 1977, 26–30, on Aristotle's subordination of simile to metaphor. Also see O'Rourke 2006, 156–157, and Patsioti-Tsacpounidi 2006, esp. 180, drawing attention to Ricoeur 1996.

42. At *Poet.* 1458a21–23, Aristotle identifies metaphor as a technique of replacing ordinary words with unfamiliar/exotic ones; he writes: ξενικὸν δὲ λέγω γλῶτταν **καὶ μεταφορὰν** καὶ ἐπέκτασιν ("by unfamiliar/exotic I mean loan words, metaphors, lengthenings, . . ."). Also see Kotarcic 2021, 82–83; cf. n39 above and Ricoeur 1978, 146–148; cf. Silk 2003, 122.

43. Kotarcic 2021, 90. Her observations agree with Pfefferkorn 2022, 155–158 (cf. Introduction, n39), who explains the use of wine by the leaders of the Dionysiac Choir as a *pharmakon* that will enable them to overcome their reluctance for choric performances and communicate better with their younger students.

44. On metaphor as compressed simile, see Henle 1981, 86–91. On metaphor and analogy, Johnson 1981, 25, notes: "In metaphor there is an underlying analogy in which one component (the iconic) is used to present the other"; cf. Henle 1958, 178; Black 1981, 68–71. Also, see Turner 1987, 69, on similes as extended conceptual metaphors.

45. Kirby 1997, 542, 547. Also, Kotarcic 2021, 166, with Ricoeur 1975, 19.

46. Kotarcic 2021, 100 and 110 with n28.

47. Ricoeur 1975, 245–254, esp. 252, and 1977, 222–237, esp. 234.

48. O'Rourke 2006, 171, with n72 citing Arist. *Poet.* 1457b2, 1458a33, and 1459a12–14, differentiating between "ordinary word, metaphor, and ornament" (τὸ κύριον καὶ μεταφορὰ καὶ κόσμος).

49. Arist. *Rhet.* 1405b3–5 on "good metaphors" with Ricoeur 1977, 37, with n60 further citing *Rhet.* 1405b17–18, where Aristotle specifies that apart from clarity, as discussed on p. 18, τὰς δὲ μεταφορὰς ἐντεῦθεν οἰστέον, ἀπὸ καλῶν ἢ τῇ φωνῇ ἢ τῇ δυνάμει ἢ τῇ ὄψει ἢ ἄλλῃ τινὶ αἰσθήσει ("Metaphors, then, should be derived from what is beautiful, either in sound, or in signification, or to sight, or to some other sense").

50. Kotarcic 2021, 171; cf. n55 below.

51. Trans. Kennedy 2007, 223; O'Rourke 2006, 158 with n17. Kotarcic 2021, 172 with n34.

52. Trans. from Kennedy 2007, 163, and L193: 274; also, Kennedy ²2007, 223n124, and Lefkowitz 2022, 57.

53. Aristotle has been understood to object to the use of metaphors in philosophical discourse because of their vague meanings; see Vogiatzi 2019,

239–242; cf. Innes 2003, 12–13. Also, Morgan 2000, 179–184, on the limitations of articulating philosophical concepts through myths.

54. Lakoff and Johnson 1980, 295; cf. 260–264 for what they refer to as "the objectivist account of conventional metaphor"; also, Johnson 1981, 35–42.

55. Kotarcic 2021, 102–109 and 163–169 criticizes Derrida (1972, 274–307), Ricoeur (1975, 13–62), and Newman (2005) for understanding Aristotle's concept of *lexis* merely as "style," which led them erroneously "to integrate *mimēsis* into the metaphoric process" (p. 164). On Plato's discussion of *lexis* and its unclear relationship with the concepts of *diēgēsis* (narration) and *mimēsis* in *Republic* 3, see Kotarcic 2021, 16–23, with Halliwell 2009.

56. Lakoff and Johnson 1980, 234; cf. Johnson 1981, 7–8. Notably, according to Ricoeur (1975, 43–51, and 1977, 33–39), despite failing to situate metaphor in discourse (in the sense that he chose to treat the meaning of single words instead), Aristotle did stress its cognitive value. See Silk 2003, 141–146.

57. Pender 2003, 63–72; cf. Lorenz 2006, 99–110, on reason influencing the appetitive part of the soul through "images and appearances," as detailed in *Timaeus* and the *Philebus*; cf. Moss 2006; 2008; 2012a, 85–87; 2012b.

58. Lakoff and Johnson 1980, 190, citing Arist. *Rhet.* 1410b12–13 where metaphor's ability to give meaning to something new is praised (αἱ μὲν οὖν γλῶτται ἀγνῶτες, τὰ δὲ κύρια ἴσμεν. ἡ δὲ μεταφορὰ ποιεῖ τοῦτο μάλιστα).

59. Wilson-Nightingale 2021, 40.

60. Ricoeur 1977, 36–39 (also see n49 above), 46, 68–69, 81–82, 112–113, 230, 278, 284–285, 352–354. However, higher familiarity does not ensure that the metaphor will be interpreted as the speaker wishes. On the concepts of metaphor familiarity and aptness, see Rákosi 2020; Whiteford-Damerall and Kellogg 2016.

61. Rendered in capitals to distinguish them from individual instances of metaphorical language.

62. Lakoff and Johnson 1980, 14–15, discuss structural metaphors versus orientation metaphors, where a whole system of concepts is organized "with respect to one another" (such metaphors focus on giving a concept special orientation as, for example, HAPPY IS UP); cf. Turner 1987, 18–22, 161–165, claiming that such metaphors do not fit Aristotle's definition, which (in his view) relies merely on recognizing "objectively preexisting similarities" or shared properties between two concepts.

63. Lakoff and Johnson 1980, 327: "Abstract concepts are not complete without metaphors. For example, love is not love without metaphors of magic, attraction, madness, union, nurturance, and so on."

64. Lakoff and Johnson 1980, 4; on Plato's use of metaphor in his theory of the tripartite division of the soul, see Cairns 2017 and more recently 2021 drawing on Lakoff and Johnson.

65. Lakoff and Johnson 1980, 139.

66. Lakoff and Johnson 1980, 145, reiterated on pp. 196, 211, 228, 235–236; cf. Apostolopoulos 2019, 78–79, 99, and esp. 253–254, on Merleau-Ponty's views on transcendental reflection and the use of metaphors in relating our experiences of the invisible; judging symbolic or metaphorical readings as "abstract and insufficient," Merleau-Ponty opts for "creative expressions or descriptions"; Merleau-Ponty 1962, 167–177 and 1964, 110, 117; also, Baldwin 2007, 100. On Merleau-Ponty as indirect source for Lakoff and Johnson, see Sambre 2009, 191; Zlatev 2010, 418.

67. Kirby 1997, 529; Hunter 2004, 101–102.

68. On the torpedo fish, see Arist. *Hist. an.* 620b28; Aelian, *Nat. an.* 1.36.1 and 9.14.1. Cf. Ar. *Vesp.* 713, comparing Bdelycleon to a torpedo fish because his words have a paralyzing effect on his father; Hartmann 2017, 283–288.

69. Hartmann 2017, 228. Still, Plato refers often in his dialogues to the playful style of Socrates; chapter 3, n15.

70. *Phdr.* 268b3–5; cf. *Prt.* 319c–d; *Meno* 90b–e; *Grg.* 453d–454a, 465a.

71. *Grg.* 453a1–2: πειθοῦς δημιουργός . . . ἡ ῥητορική; cf. 452e1. For Szlezák 1999, 4, Plato "appears to need his own specific system of hermeneutics for being understood"; cf. his p. 112 arguing that Plato "did not consider his thinking on the principles as secret (ἀπόρρητα), but as not prematurely communicable (ἀπρόρρητα)."

72. Roth 2005, 51.

73. On the suggestion that Agathon's *epinikia* (the celebration of his dramatic victory) in the *Symposium* is structured as a miniature City Dionysia, see Biles 2007, 23–27, with Sider 1980. On Dionysus' connection to wine production and the role of women at the Lenaia festival at Athens, see Valdés Guía 2013, 103–109; cf. Peirce 1998, 83–84, on maenadic and nonmaenadic types of Bacchic ecstasy.

74. For the ancient definitions of *baccheia*, see introduction, nn5 and 6.

75. On Dionysus' connection to wine and drunkenness, see Seaford 2006, 15–22; cf. *Bacch.* 704–7, where Dionysus strikes a spring with his thyrsus to make it flow with wine. On Drunkenness (μέθη) considered as an offspring of Dionysus, see *Anacreontea* fr. 38.7. On Dionysus and Silenoi portrayed as drunken in ancient art, see van de Grift 1984; also, Shaw 2014, 34–37, discussing the popular myth of Hephaestus' return to Olympus, after he was made drunk. For Dionysus as *mainomenos*, see Hom. *Il.* 6.132 with ancient scholia crediting Eumelus for this representation of the god; cf. Ustinova 2017, 169 with n1. For Dionysus as *mainomenos* in art, esp. in the story of the Thracian king Lycurgus, see Carpenter 1997, 36–38; Ustinova 2017, 170–171 and 175–176. Porres Caballero 2013 argues that Euripides' *Bacchae* influenced ancient perceptions of maenadism and the worship of Dionysus, especially from the Hellenistic period onward. Cf. Cole 2007 on the ambiguity of Dionysus as represented in myth and cult.

76. Halperin 1990, 121, explains Diotima of Mantineia in etymological terms as "Zeus-honor from Prophetville"; cf. Nussbaum 1986, 177. For Diotima

as Socrates' alter ego, see Sheffield 2006a, 68. In *Phdr.* 252c6–253a10 and 255c, the philosophically inclined lovers are said to be inspired by Zeus, like the Bacchants (253a9: ὥσπερ αἱ βάκχαι). The familial connection of Zeus and Dionysus is stressed repeatedly by Euripides in the *Bacchae* where Dionysus is described as "the son of Zeus" no fewer than five times; see *ll.* 366, 418 (ὁ δαίμων ὁ Διὸς παῖς), 550, 725, 859–860.

77. Yet, for White 1989, 157, Diotima does not identify the beautiful with the good; rather, she regards both "the beautiful and Beauty as subservient to the good"; cf. *Phdr.* 250d4–e2 where Socrates claims that visible beauty is likely to prompt our memory of the spiritual world (also see conclusion, n43); cf. Shelton 2024 on the theory of the anamnesis in the *Phaedrus* as a way for becoming godlike.

78. Roth 2005, 51.

79. Cf. Porph. *De ant. nymph.* 16 (Nauck 1963, 68.6–7) who equates nectar with honey and wine and focuses on its deceptive effects. Hence, for Porphyry nectar and honey signify that "divine beings are ensnared by pleasure and drawn down into γενέσις" (δι᾽ ἡδονῆς δεσμεῖσθαι καὶ κατάγεσθαι τὰ θεῖα εἰς γένεσιν; trans. Lamberton 1983, 31); Scheinberg 1979, 18 with n73; cf. *Sent.* 37 (Lamberz 1975, 45.5–9).

80. See Lakoff and Johnson 1980, esp. 245–260, on Conceptual Metaphor Theory (CMT) *but* with Zlatev's criticisms (2010 and 2016) about the theory's lack of sociocultural perspective; cf. Yoos 1971, 83, stressing the need to ask, "why the speaker has put two ideas together," in other words to tease out the intention of the speaker. Still, as Zlatev argues, although phenomenology and cognitive linguistics are rife with internal controversies, language remains the only available medium for describing lived experiences (cf. Zlatev 2007 and 2008) and even of reflecting on its limitations. To this direction, Geertz's work on the cultural framing of language and experience (2010, 2014) offers an important way forward; cf. Gibbs 1999, 10, 15, and 17 (on the constraints of theories) and 2011 (defending CMT).

81. Rinella 2010, 210, 213–216, 241; cf. Horky 2006, 376–378; also, Hartmann 2017, 157, with Murray 1998a.

82. Trabattoni 1993, 245–246; cf. Morgan 2000, 69–70, on Parmenides, fr. 2.3–6 (Gallop 1984, 54–55).

83. Hartmann 2017, 81–83, with Noël 1994. See Kotarcic 2021, 19, noting the moral importance Plato appends to representations (or "impersonations"), further evident when he asks "whether we should allow poets to narrate as impersonators or in part as impersonators and in part not, and what sort of things in each case, or not allow them to impersonate at all" (*Resp.* 394d2–4: πότερον ἐάσομεν τοὺς ποιητὰς μιμουμένους ἡμῖν τὰς διηγήσεις ποιεῖσθαι ἢ τὰ μὲν μιμουμένους, τὰ δὲ μή, καὶ ὁποῖα ἑκάτερα, ἢ οὐδὲ μιμεῖσθαι); cf. n55 above.

84. Merleau-Ponty 1962, 249–250. Sambre 2009, esp. 198–212; cf. Apostolopoulos 2019, 227–229, on Merleau-Ponty's appreciation of the role of language

in shaping experience; overall, Merleau-Ponty "seems hesitant to take a strong position on the extent to which expression invents, transforms or preserves perceptual meaning."

85. Merleau-Ponty 1962, 467.

86. Wittgenstein, *RC* 53 (in Anscombe 1977, 9); cf. Szlezák 1999, 28–32 and 109–111, discussing Wittgenstein's reference to Plato's use of "expressive metaphor."

87. Geertz 2010, 311–312, citing Donald 2001, 254, where he states that "[E]nculturation dominates human cognitive development" and 1999 where he discusses the four stages of human evolution: the final stage, defined as the theoretic, coincides with our use of symbols and material artefacts, including writing, as "external memory and data banks."

88. Khachouf et al. 2013. Cf. Turner 1996, 159–160, on the influence of language on the brain; also, Jensen 2014, 252. Husserl 1913/1981, par. 27–33, appreciated phenomenology as "the science of the essence of consciousness" (in Smith 2016a, 113); see, for example, Smith and Smith 1995, esp. 33–34, on Husserl's preoccupation with "grades of evidence in our knowledge of the world around us and of our own consciousness." On the relationship between truth and intentionality in Husserl, see Smith 2016a, esp. 121–122 (on perception as "intuition") and 126 (on language as a freely reinterpretable calculus rather than a universal medium; with Kusch 1989, 133, in whose opinion "Husserl argues for the possibility of a transcendental language as a true metalanguage with respect to natural ordinary language"); cf. Smith 2016b, 146–147, 152–155 and esp. 158–160 (on meta-cognition in Husserl). Also see Belt 2020 for a defense of Husserlian phenomenology against the criticism that it is unreliable and subjective.

89. See Maturana and Varela 1984, 154; on p. 155 they continue thus: ". . . We realize ourselves in a mutual linguistic coupling, not because language allows us to say who we are, but because we are in language, in a continuous being in the linguistic and semantic worlds that we bring to bear with others." Cf. Maturana 1990, 16–18 and 67, on the emotional basis of rational systems (which necessarily undermines our concept of objectivity); and Maturana 1997, 127–129, on analogical reasoning, which relies on symbols to transfer analogies in different contexts.

90. Hunter 2004, 103–104; also, Nichols 2007; Wilburn 2015, 20–24; and McBrayer 2017.

91. Adams 2007, 3. Cf. Ricoeur 1981 who develops the concept of *distanciation*, according to which we should approach texts as: (1) speech committed to writing; (2) pieces that have their own structure; (3) projections of a world; and (4) mediums of self-understanding. In my view, the Platonic dialogues operate at all these levels to some extent.

92. On the history of theories of transcendence from Aristotle to the Middle Ages, see Goris and Aertsen 2019; cf. Hughes 2003, 8–13, 29–37, 65–83, 102–105, on transcendental truth and Voegelin who, especially in *The Ecumenic Age*, is

preoccupied with the limits of history on truth. According to Hughes, Voegelin understood history "as a continual crossroads of eternity and time in the unfolding story of divine movement and human response" (p. 70), which corresponds "to the ontological status of human consciousness as a reality 'in-between' immanence and transcendence" (p. 104); Voegelin borrows the Platonic term *metaxy* ("between"), widely used in the *Symposium* and the *Philebus*; Hughes 2003, 69 with n10. Also see Heys 2014, 54–55, on Bloom and Derrida's reception of Platonic truth. Cf. Pl. *Meno* 80d, where Socrates develops the theory of *anamnesis* as the only credible way to pursue new knowledge given that we have no grasp of its nature; Allen 1959, 167.

93. Peltonen 2019, 235, with Hadot 1995 and Nussbaum 1998; cf. Aertsen 1992.

94. Neuroscientists disagree on whether mystical experiences should be understood as instances of brain malfunction (for example, Persinger 1987, esp. 111–135, and 2001; Alper 2001) or whether they point to a transcendent reality (for example, Newberg et al. 2002, 98–127, 133, 140–141, 159–162, 168–172; Hood 2002; and Newberg 2018, 72–74, 98–99, 184–193; cf. Yaden et al. 2017 on the positive outcomes of religious, spiritual, or mystical experiences induced with psychedelic substances). See Austin 1998 and 2000, esp. 228, on meditation practices as a method of minimizing emphasis on the self, thus opening our mind to the world "as *it* really is." For Voegelin, again, as Hughes (2003, 154) notes, "[T]he conventional misunderstanding of the language of transcendence and immanence . . . derives from a lack of familiarity with the experiential basis of that language."

95. Jensen 2014, 250–251; also, see Wilson-Nightingale 2004, 127, on the philosopher occupying an "outside position"; cf. Wilson-Nightingale 2021, 202–203.

96. On Heraclitus' famous distrust of the average person's intellectual ability, see B5 DK (= D15), B15 (= D16), B17 (= D3), B19 (= D5), B34 (= D4), B70 (= D6); cf. B1–2 DK (= D1–2) and B104 (= D10). Democritus also expressed similar sentiments: Arist. *Met.* 1009b11–12; DL 9.11.72; cf. Theophr. *De sens.* 71 (Stratton 1917, 128); Sext. Emp. *Against the Logicians* 1.135–139; and Cic. *Acad.* 2.73 (on Democritus' admirer, Metrodorus of Chios).

97. Carabine 1995, 18–34. See Pl. *Ti.* 28c3–5 (on the unknowability of God), echoing Parmenides (D6 and D8) and 52a3–4 (on the Idea being invisible (ἀόρατον) and imperceptible (ἀναίσθητον); *Resp.* 509b8–10 (on the Good existing beyond Being: ἐπέκεινα τῆς οὐσίας); cf. *Resp.* 527b. Cf. Ustinova 2017, 322–323, on apophaticism in Plato's *Seventh Letter* as a way of protecting philosophers from slander and mockery; also see Morgan 2000, 181–182, and Trabattoni 2007, 120. The ascription of the letter to Plato is still debated; on this, see Burnyeat and Frede 2015, with Kahn 2015.

98. According to Block 1970, 2, moderate alcohol consumption "relieves self-consciousness, loosens the tongue, encourages congeniality, and raises our level

of tolerance for the inadequacies we encounter both in others and in ourselves." Cf. Schwartz 2019 on the measurable physical changes and aesthetic reactions caused by wine when subjected to intentioned awareness by meditators.

99. Pender 2003, 60, with *Cra.* 432d1–4, on the difference between images and the actual things they represent; cf. Tallis 1988, 125–126. Socrates' critique of etymological approaches in this dialogue (see Baxter 1992) and Cratylus' withdrawal from language point to his awareness of the arbitrary association of symbols and meaning in language (Trabattoni 2020, 115–120, 153–157). Sedley 2006a, 36, appreciates Plato's endeavor here as more akin to modern literary criticism than etymology.

100. Ricoeur 1975, 376, and 1977, 349–350; cf. Farber 1967, 248–250, on Husserl's objections to metaphorical representations, esp. 251: ". . . a theory of abstraction also misses its goal if it confuses phenomenological and objective analysis, i.e., if that which the acts of meaning merely ascribe to the objects is regarded as a real constituent of the acts themselves"; cf. n88 above.

101. Ricoeur 1975, 318, and 1977, 299: "In brief, critical consciousness of the distinction between use and abuse leads not to disuse but to re-use of metaphors, . . ."

102. Hom. *Od.* 5.93, *h. Dem.* 49, *h. Ap.*10; Hes. *Th.* 640, 795; cf. Baratz 2015, 152–158, with Arist. *Met.* 1000a9–15, criticizing the poetic approach of Hesiod and πάντες ὅσοι θεολόγοι ("all those who speak about god"); in his view, while nectar and ambrosia can make humans immortal, the gods' immortality does not depend on their consumption. Nectar was at times imagined as solid; see Anaxandrides (fr. 58) and Alcman (fr. 42) cited in Ath. *Deipn.* 2.39a. Witzel 2012, 158, argues that nectar is derived from the IE root *nec- (to die), supplemented by the suffix -ter that signifies the means of achieving something, so nectar was probably seen as a means of achieving immortality; cf. Roscher 1883, 51–66. Ambrosia, which typically appears with nectar as the other type of divine sustenance (as in Pind. *Ol.* 1.62, *Pyth.* 9.63, and Ar. *Eq.* 1095), means immortality, negating (ἀ-) the essence of being βρωτός (perishable); cf. West 2007, 157, on the Vedic adjective amṛtāḥ ("immortal"), which is etymologically equivalent to ambrosia.

103. Sappho fr. 2.13–16: ἔλοισα Κύπρι/ χρυσίαισιν ἐν κυλίκεσσιν ἄβρως/ ὀμμεμείχμενον θαλίαισι νέκταρ/ οἰνοχόαισον. Cf. Eur. *Bacch.* 403–416 for Dionysus invoked with Aphrodite and Erōs.

104. Philoxenus of Leucas (fr. 836d = Ath. *Deipn.* 11.476d–e) describes the kings of Paeonia as drinking nectar from golden goblets; cf. Hom. *Od.* 9.359 and *Il.* 19.347. In Arch. fr. 2 (= Ath. *Deipn.* 1.30f.) Naxian wine is compared to nectar. For descriptions of strong wine as honey-sweet, see Alcaeus frs. 338 and 369: μέλιχρον; 398: μελιάδεος (= Ath. *Deipn.* 2.38e, 10.430a–b, and 11.462c); also, Xenoph. fr. 1.5–6: οἶνος . . . μείλιχος; Pind. fr. 166.2: ῥιπὰν μελιαδέος οἴνου.

105. For the conflation of nectar and honey, see Roscher 1883, 17–33, and n79 above. Ath. *Deipn.* 2.38f–39a quotes Ariston of Chios about people near

Mount Olympus in Lydia who "prepare what they refer to as *nectar* by mixing wine and honeycomb together with sweet-smelling flowers" (= fr. 23, Wehrli 1952). On honey from poisonous flowers, known as "maddening honey" (μέλι μαινόμενον), see Strab. *G.* 12.3.18; Pliny, *HN* 21.45.77; Xen. *Anab.* 4.8.20; Diod. Sic. 14.30.1–2; ps.-Arist. *Mir. ausc.* 831b24–26; cf. Ael. *NA.* 5.42 with Kelhoffer 2005, 89–94. On Dionysus *mainomenos*, see n75 above.

106. See Porph. *Abs.* 2.20 (Nauck 1963, 155) quoting Theophr. *piet.*12 (Pötscher 1964, 164, 166).

107. Honey was used in funerary practices, probably because bees were believed to embody the soul; see Cook 1895, 19 and 23; also, Hom. *Il.* 23.170 and *Od.* 24.68; Aesch. *Pers.* 204; Soph. *Oed. Col.* 468; Eur. *Orest.* 114; cf. Soph. fr. 879 comparing the dead to a buzzing swarm (βομβεῖ δὲ νεκρῶν σμῆνος); Porphyry, who preserved Sophocles' fragment, used bees as a symbol of just souls after death; *De ant. nymph.* 18 and 19 (Nauck 1963, 69); cf. Verg. *Aen.* 6.707–709.

108. For bees and sweetness from honey as symbols of the inspired poet and/or prophet in Greek literature, see Crane 1987, esp. 402. Cf. Hom. *h. Herm.* 550–567, describing the nymphs of Mt Parnassus as flying in search of honey; after eating honeycomb, they are filled with prophetic enthusiasm and start telling the truth. Scheinberg 1979, 17, with n66, citing Eur. *Bacch.* 298–301; Herren 2008, 50–52. Cf. *scholia* fr. 887, 2 (L144: 280–281), where the nymphs are called *bromiai* (i.e., of Bromius, an epithet of Dionysus repeatedly found in the *Bacchae*; *ll.* 66, 83, 88, 115, 140, 329, 375, 412, 446, 536, 546, 584, 592, 629, 726, 790, 976, 1031, 1250). For the connection of bees with prophecy and poetry, see Pind. *Ol.* 6.45–62; Paus. 9.40.1. For bees in omens, see Ransome 1939, 109–110. Cf. Liebert 2010 on Socrates reworking the image of the inspired bee-poet in the *Republic* to fashion the figure of the dronelike citizen who is harmful to the state. According to Rinella (2010, 38, 162–163, 217, 224, 236–237, and 246), Plato compares the drones, described at *Resp.* 572e5 as δεινοὶ μάγοι τε καὶ τυραννοποιοὶ ("terrible magicians and tyrant-makers"), with Homer's Lotus-eaters (*Od.* 9.82–104), a comparison Derrida failed to note.

109. Ustinova 2017, 267; cf. *Anth. Gr.* 11.20 with Knox 1985, 108–109, with n8.

110. Kelhoffer 2005, 95; cf. n76 above.

111. Sapph. fr. 130. Cf. Sapph. frs 146: μήτε μοι μέλι μήτε μέλισσα ("I want neither honey nor bee"), a proverbial phrase spoken by a bride; and 112.3–4 (referring to the honey-sweet eyes of the groom). Also, see Semonides of Amorgos, who praises the bee-woman as the best possible type of wife (7.83–93), and Hesiod (*Th.* 594–602) who is preoccupied with the threat dronelike women pose to their households. Pindar (fr. 165+252, Maehler 2001, 131) likely speaks of bees attacking impure or adulterous lovers, a theme also employed by Theocritus (*Id.* 1.105–107), according to Plutarch (*quaest. nat.* 36); see L426: 220–221 with

footnotes a/b; also, Pomeroy 1994, 279, who traces a different version of the motif in Charon of Lampsacus (FGrH 262F12).

112. Pritchard 1975, 203; Leick 1994, 116–117, 121, 123, 164. The imagery of the poem (a metaphor for the favor the goddess showed to her chosen kings) remained popular down to the first millennium, as Leick 1994, 183, 194, notes. On the drunkenness of the gods in ANE mythology, a motif especially linked with the trickster god Enki, who employs drunkenness "to bring about new circumstances" and effect an "unnatural manipulation of the world," see Annus 2013.

113. The connection, long established in classical literature (see, for example, Hdt. 1.105), was renewed during the Hellenistic period; thus, Theocritus and Bion famously describe the love affair of Aphrodite and Adonis in terms that evoke the relationship of Inanna/Ishtar with Dumuzi/Tammuz in Near Eastern traditions; for example, Bion refers to Adonis as Aphrodite's "Assyrian husband" (*Lament for Adonis* 24: Ἀσσύριον . . . πόσιν); see Anagnostou-Laoutides 2005, 33 and 134–154, esp. 151; also, Anagnostou-Laoutides and Konstan 2008.

114. Ps.-Theocritus *Id.* 19 shares similarities with *Anacreontea* 35; cf. *Anacreontea* 28.5–6, where the goddess is said to dip the points of her arrows in honey.

115. See Forbes 1955, vol. 3, p. 60, noting: "nectar and ambrosia were probably mead-like concoctions"; further, see McGovern 2003, 266–268, 287, on the so-called Homeric *kykeon* ((*Il.* 11.628–643), apparently a mixture of mead, Pramnian wine, and beer. On the Phrygian "grog," also containing mead, see McGovern 2003, 279–292, and 2009, 134–135; also, Guerra Doce 2014 who discusses the earliest archaeological evidence regarding the production of mead.

116. Scheinberg 1979, 23–24; cf. Roscher 1883, 69–75; Cook 1895, 2; Ransome 1939, 119, 123. On Greek sources relating the early use of mead, see Scheinberg 1979, 17–18; cf. Nissinen 2017, 194–195.

117. Scheinberg 1979, 19; cf. Witzel 2012, 158–159, on the Indian Vedas where another drink, *soma* (Old Iranian *haoma*), is also characterized as *madhu* and was believed to inspire poets; on Heraclitus' familiarity with the Vedas, see chapter 2, n167.

118. The Suda s.v. μέθυ: οἶνος (Adler 1967, M437 in 3.349) cites Antipater of Sidon, *Anth. Gr.* 7.23,4: εὐῶδες δ' ἀπὸ γῆς ἡδὺ χέοιτο μέθυ . . . ("May fragrant, sweet wine pour forth from the earth . . ."); cf. Homer, *Il.* 7.471.

119. See Geertz 2014, 39–40, and 2010, esp. 304: "cognition is embrained, embodied, encultured and distributed."

120. For example, see *Bacch.* fr. 20b, 6–10; Ion of Chios, fr. 744 (= Ath. *Deipn.* 2.35d–e); Anacr. fr. 12 (*Anth. Gr.* 7.27,7–8) is Antipater of Sidon's epitaph for Anacreon, stating that the poet would spend his days ἡδὺ μέθυ βλύζων, ἀμφίβροχος εἵματα Βάκχῳ, / ἄκρητον θλίβων νέκταρ ἀπὸ στολίδων ("Drenched with Bacchus, wringing unmixed nectar from its folds"), devoted to the Muses, Dionysus, and Erōs (9–10); cf. Anacr. fr. 357, 10–11; *Anacreontea* 4; and Solon,

fr. 26 (in Plut. *Amat.* 5.751e). Breitenberger 2013, 181–185, discusses the motif of poets addressing slave-boys (whom they pursue erotically) to pour wine. The theme becomes prominent in the *Greek Anthology*: see, for example, 5.167 and 12.135 by Asclepiades and numerous epigrams by Meleager, including 5.136 and 137, 5.171, 5.190, 12.49, 12.74, 12.85, 12.117, 12.133 (where a kiss is compared to nectar and the honey of the soul), and 12.164. For Erōs *mainomenos*, like Dionysus, see Eur. *Hipp.* 1274–1275; cf. *Med.* 432–433 and Pind. *Pyth.* 2.26–27; also, Ustinova 2017, 298–305.

121. Wilson-Nightingale 2021, 40: "The love-mad philosopher achieves an enhanced state of mind, "manic reason." For a thorough examination of the metaphor of falling in love and pursuing philosophy across the *Symposium*, the *Phaedrus*, the *Phaedo*, and the *Timaeus*, see Wilson-Nightingale 2021, esp. 76–88, 102–104, 183, 190, 200, 208–212. Trawny 2012, 24, with Levinas 1961, 243. I use "symbol" here as per Kotarcic 2021, 171, cited in n50 above.

122. Alcibiades refers to Socrates as a "truly divine and remarkable creature" (*Symp.* 219c1–2: δαιμονίῳ ὡς ἀληθῶς καὶ θαυμαστῷ) on account of his sobriety (σωφροσύνην), manliness, wisdom (φρόνησιν), and steadfastness (καρτερίαν; *Symp.* 219d4–8). Cf. Freidenberg 1997, 73–74, who argues that Plato structures the dialogue through Saussurean opposites, especially the central theme of "truth-phantom." Also, Segal 1986, 56, on applying the semiotic approach to Greek myths, especially in tragedy; while Plato does engage here with Saussurean opposites (for example, sober Socrates/drunk Alcibiades), the value of the approach is curbed by its inability to accommodate metaphorical cognitive patterns.

123. *Symp.* 176c–e1, 203b6, 212d5 and e3–4, 213a1, 214a6 and c7, 215d7.

124. *Symp.* 256b10–c1: τάχ᾽ ἄν που ἐν μέθαις.

125. *Phdr.* 238b4–6. Cf. *Phdr.* 240e4–8 on the lover indulging in temporary pleasure by getting drunk (εἰς δὲ μέθην ἰόντος), as evident in his "wearisome and unrestrained freedom of speech" (παρρησίᾳ κατακορεῖ καὶ ἀναπεπταμένη χρωμέ-νου); *Leg.* 649d4–8 on excesses "intoxicating people with pleasure, rendering them out of their minds" (παράφρονας ποιεῖ); *Phd.* 79c7 cited on p. 33 and 81e6–9 on the souls of those who have indulged in gluttony, violence, or drunkenness likely passing into the bodies of asses and other such beasts; cf. *Resp.* 488c6; also, see chapter 2, pp. 44–45 and 48–49.

126. Ustinova 2017, 294–343.

127. Wilson-Nightingale 2021, 21–22, with *Resp.* 475e5, where philosophers are described as "lovers of the sight of truth" (τοὺς τῆς ἀληθείας . . . φιλοθεάμο-νας), further discussed on p. 110; cf. *Resp.* 490b6 cited on p. 20.

128. Goodenough 1928; cf. Athanassiadi 2018.

129. Chesnut 1978.

130. Rice 1983, 66–67, 84–85.

131. See Annas 2017, 190, on Philo's use of Plato's *Laws* to emphasize "the superiority, as well as the antiquity, of the Jewish tradition."

132. More recently, see Wilson-Nightingale 2021, esp. 148–155; cf. Vogt 2013, 181–186.

133. Cf. Spiegelberg 1940, 86–96.

134. Cf. Wilson-Nightingale 2021, 52, 172, and 188–189, on Plato's widespread use of the metaphor of nourishment in the *Phaedrus*, citing 246e1–4, where the soul is "nourished" by the divine, described as beautiful, wise and good, and thus grows its wings (τούτοις δὴ τρέφεταί τε καὶ αὔξεται μάλιστά γε τὸ τῆς ψυχῆς πτέρωμα); also, see 248b9–c2 referring to the realm of the Forms as a fitting pasture for the best part of the soul, which, again, it turn nourishes its wings (. . . ἥ τε δὴ προσήκουσα ψυχῆς τῷ ἀρίστῳ νομὴ ἐκ τοῦ ἐκεῖ λειμῶνος τυγχάνει οὖσα, ἥ τε τοῦ πτεροῦ φύσις, ᾧ ψυχὴ κουφίζεται, τούτῳ τρέφεται), and 247a10 where the divine souls drive their chariots to the edge of the celestial dome to get a glimpse of hypercosmic reality (i.e., the Forms), described as attending a feast and a banquet (πρὸς δαῖτα καὶ ἐπὶ θοίνην ἴωσιν). This deeper metaphor is powerfully at play in the *Symposium*.

135. *Symp.* 175a1–b4 and 220c3–d5.

136. At *Tht.* 189e4–190a2 Socrates defines thought as the soul's discussion with itself (τὸ δὲ διανοεῖσθαι . . . Λόγον ὃν αὐτὴ πρὸς αὑτὴν ἡ ψυχὴ διεξέρχεται περὶ ὧν ἂν σκοπῇ; cf. *Soph.* 264b1: διάνοια μὲν αὐτῆς πρὸς ἑαυτὴν ψυχῆς διάλογος and n192 below; at *Tht.* 173e–174a he claims that while the philosopher's body lives in the city, his mind is carried away to loftier concerns (ἡ δὲ διάνοια . . . πανταχῇ φέρεται); cf. *Phdr.* 249d1–4 (chapter 2, p. 66) and n95 above; Frede 1989, 28–31; Pelosi 2010, 91.

137. Socrates detailed these visitations during his trial, as both Plato and Xenophon report: Pl. *Apol.* 31c–d, 40a–c, 41c–d; *Phdr.* 242b–d; *Resp.* 496c; *Tht.* 150e–151a; *Euthphr.* 3b; *Alc.* I 105e–106a; *Euthyd.* 272e–273a; *Theag.* 128d–129e; and Xen. *Mem.* 1.1.1–5 and *Apol.* 12–13; cf. *Resp.* 496c5. Ustinova 2017, 318–321; cf. Destrée 2005.

138. By the fifth century BCE, several stage conventions were used to identify a theatrical character as an intellectual; the most popular technique, frequently used by Aristophanes, was to present actors in bizarre poses (for example, *Clouds* 188–199); Whitehorn 2002, 33–34. Cf. *Tht.* 155e5–8 where Socrates defines anti-intellectuals (referred to as uninitiated, ἀμύητοι) as "those who do not accept that actions and generations and everything that is invisible participates in nature" (πράξεις δὲ καὶ γενέσεις καὶ πᾶν τὸ ἀόρατον οὐκ ἀποδεχόμενοι ὡς ἐν οὐσίας μέρει); Green 1979, 15–16; cf. Bromberg 2017, 32–35.

139. *Symp.* 214a5–6; cf. 176c4–6.

140. *Symp.* 215a1–216a2, 216d6–7, and 221d6–8.

141. In myth, Marsyas interacts with Apollo (Hdt 7.26.3; *Euthyd.* 285c; Xen. *Anab.* 1.2.8); nevertheless, he is typically described as a satyr from Phrygia, where Dionysus' cult supposedly originated (Eur. *Bacch.* 14). Cf. Paus. 1.24.1 on Marsyas the silenos. Drawing on the theory of the symbol, Hamilton 2008, 40–41, argues

that Apollo's punishment of Marsyas by flailing exemplifies the concept of being extracted from oneself (by means of music).

142. Hedreen 1992, 161–165. On the association of the *silenoi* (or their leader, Silenos; Carpenter 1986, 76) with drunkenness, see Eur. *Cycl.* 139–161; on Drunkenness (Μέθη) represented with Silenos at his temple at Elis, Paus. 6.24.8. Silenos was held to have nursed Dionysus: Diod. Sic. 4.4.3; OF 54. Roth 2005, 54.

143. Cf. Eur. *Bacch.* 1122–1124: ἣ δ᾽ ἀφρὸν ἐξιεῖσα καὶ διαστρόφους/ κόρας ἑλίσσουσ᾽, οὐ φρονοῦσ᾽ ἃ χρὴ φρονεῖν,/ ἐκ Βακχίου κατείχετ᾽ ("She was foaming at the mouth and rolled her distorted eyes / without thinking as she should think, possessed by Bacchus . . ."); Roth 2005, 39. As mentioned on p. 28, persuasion is also able to drive people "out of their minds"; on this, see Gorgias, *Hel.* 12: τὸ γὰρ τῆς πειθοῦς ἐξῆν ὁ δὲ νοῦς ("persuasion expelled sense").

144. Eur. *Bacch.* 32–33: "I stung them with madness (ᾤστρησ᾽ ἐγὼ/ μανίαις) from their homes, and they inhabit the mountain, driven out of their minds (παράκοποι φρενῶν)."

145. Discussed in chapter 3, p. 98.

146. Kirby 1997, 521. Quintilian's definition of allegory is very similar (*Inst. Or.* 8.6.44): "Allegory, which people translate as *inversio*, reveals one thing by words and another by its sense or even something totally opposite. The first type is generally produced by a sequence of metaphors (*prius . . . genus . . . continuat . . . tralationibus*)." Henle 1981, 91; Copeland and Struck 2010, 2–3, with n2; Struck 2004, 23; Obbink 2010, 16. Also, Plut. *De aud. poet.* 19e–19f and chapter 4, n221, on the difference between allegory and allegoresis.

147. On the modern debate on understanding metaphors through comparison, see for example, the Pragglejaz Group 2007, 31–32, with more bibliography; also, Glucksberg 2008, 76–80, and Gokcesu 2009, 567–568, for an analysis of modern theories of metaphor that examine it either as a form of comparison or of categorization. Here I chose to be guided by the grammatical features of the text (that is, Plato's use of comparisons) in accordance with Gokcesu 2009, who stressed the role of grammatical forms in understanding metaphors.

148. Fehr 2008, 140–143; cf. n141 above.

149. *Symp.* 215b8: ὡς δὲ καὶ τἄλλα **ἔοικας** ("You *are like* them in all other aspects").

150. *Symp.* 216c8–10: ἀκούσατε ὡς **ὅμοιός** τ᾽ ἐστὶν οἷς ἐγὼ **ἤκασα** αὐτὸν ("listen how *similar* he is to the figures I *compared* him with"). On the vocabulary of imitation in the *Phaedrus*, see Morgan 2010, 62 and n172 below.

151. *Symp.* 216d5–6: τοῦτο [i.e., τὸ σχῆμα αὐτοῦ] οὐ **σιληνῶδες**; ("Isn't his figure *Silenus-like*?") and 216d7: **ὥσπερ** ὁ γεγλυμμένος σιληνός ("*Like* the sculptured Silenus"). The adverb ὥσπερ introduces a comparison, while the adjective σιληνώδης means "resembling a Silenos." Cf. Xen. *Symp.* 5.7, where Socrates jokingly admits his resemblance to the Silenoi ("even the Naids who are goddesses give birth to Silenoi who are resembling me more than you (τοὺς

Σειληνοὺς ἐμοὶ ὁμοιοτέρους)"; on Socrates' representation as a satyr, see Catoni and Giuliani 2019, 696–713; Zanker 1995, 34, and Richter 1965, 109–19, with Belfiore 2006, 200n46.

152. Anderson 1950, 113–118 (on Grenet 1948, 234 and Gardeil 1935, 11) views Plato's use of metaphorical proportionality and analogy as "likeness mingled with unlikeness."

153. Definition drawn from the *Cambridge Greek Lexicon*. Pender 2003, 56 and 58, with *Leg.* 655a4–8 on the use of ἀπεικάζω in the then common metaphor of musical harmony as "shapely" or "nicely hued"; for the use εἰκάζω in metaphors in the *Republic*, see on pp. 29, 34.

154. Lakoff and Johnson 1980, 142–147; cf. Mac Cormac 1985, esp. 34–36 (on metaphor and simile) and 149 and 185 (on the role of culture in making metaphors meaningful). On cognitive theories and metaphor, see Shen 1992; Steen 2002; Camp 2006; Wentura 2019; cf. Geertz 2014 and Jessen 2014 cited in n35 above. For a discussion of analogy as a way of "surpassing the limits of experience," see Grenet 1948, 39–68 with Anderson 1950, 125.

155. For example, Madsen 2016 criticized the tendency to assume an underlying conceptual structure in cognitive metaphor theory, because "not everyone has the same sense of immediate experience"; cf. nn 88 and 100 above.

156. *Symp.* 215b4–5 reads: ". . . which when cut open in half are seen to contain images of gods (ἀγάλματα ἔχοντες θεῶν)"; also, see 216d8–9: ". . . but if opened, you cannot imagine, fellow drinkers, how much he is full of moderation inside (γέμει . . . σωφροσύνης)."

157. Alcibiades repeatedly expresses his admiration for Socrates using the verb θαυμάζω and its compounds: at *Symp.* 215c1, where he compares Marsyas as a musician to Socrates (πολύ γε θαυμασιώτερος ἐκείνου); at 220c7, where people are reported to admire Socrates for his meditating skills (θαυμάζοντες); and at 221c3–4: "Surely, one could praise Socrates for many other wonderful things" (πολλὰ . . . καὶ ἄλλα ἔχοι Σωκράτη ἐπαινέσαι καὶ θαυμάσια); also, 221c6–8 on p. 15 and 219c1–2 in n122 above. As Candiotto and Politis 2020, 21ff., argue, θαυμάζειν ("wonder") denotes the philosopher's disposition to knowledge and is closely associated with philosophical *aporia*. For wonder (and *aporia*) in Aristotle, see Berti 2007, v–vii, 237, with Candiotto and Politis 2020, 26n22. For the association of θαῦμα with Dionysiac rites as discussed in Euripides' *Bacchae* and the puppet allegory in the *Laws*, see chapter 3, p. 79.

158. Cf. Gorgias, *Hel.* 8 cited on p. 22.

159. As Griswold 1986, 226–229, observed, Plato also utilizes this inside-outside juxtaposition in the *Phaedrus* (245e; 275a). Furthermore, at 279b9–10, Socrates prays to Pan, who was increasingly associated with Dionysus after 490 BCE (Porres Caballero 2012, esp. 70–72), to grant him "beauty inside" (δοίητέ μοι καλῷ γενέσθαι τἄνδοθεν) and to ensure his external appearance is in harmony with the qualities of his soul (ἔξωθεν δὲ ὅσα ἔχω, τοῖς ἐντὸς εἶναί μοι φίλια).

The internal beauty of Pan corresponds to the inside beauty of the physically unattractive yet wise Satyrs and Socrates, their lookalike, in the *Symposium*. Pan also features at *Phdr.* 263d7, where he is mentioned as the son of Hermes (Πᾶνα τὸν Ἑρμοῦ), the inventor of *logos*; Hermes and Pan are also discussed in *Cratylus* where Pan, addressed as the "double-natured son of Hermes" (408d1: διφυὴς Ἑρμοῦ υἱός) is identified with logos (408d2–3: ἔστιν ἤτοι λόγος ἢ λόγου ἀδελφὸς ὁ Πάν). As such, the god, like speech, is both true and false (ὁ λόγος . . . ἔστι διπλοῦς, ἀληθής τε καὶ ψευδής). Also, see Trusso 2015, 151–154, who further notes that the *Homeric hymn to Pan* (19.14–20) celebrates the god's repute for music; thus, when Socrates prays to Pan and the Nymphs in the *Phaedrus*, he wishes them to infuse his speech with rhetorical skill; in my view, Pan is comparable to the figure of Marsyas, another exceptional musician (see n157 above), in the *Symposium*. The two examples highlight the comparison of speeches to music and their educative role (provided this is entrusted to the philosophers); cf. Moss 2013, 2–6.

160. Jiménez San Cristóbal 2009, 46–47. On the use of wine in *baccheia*, Jiménez San Cristóbal (p. 55 with n22) cites schol. Ar. *Nub.* 606 (Dübner 1841, 110b.37–38), s.v. κωμαστὴς • ὅτι καὶ μεθύοντες βακχεύονται καὶ ὥσπερ ἐκμαίνονται ("Who participates in a festival: because those who are drunk experience deliria as if they were beside themselves") and Hsch. s.v. ληνεύουσι· βακχεύουσιν (Schmidt 1867, 981); cf. Bernabé and Jiménez San Cristóbal 2008, 143, and Valdés Guía 2013 cited in chapter 2, n187. On the connection of enthusiasm with maenadism and drunkenness, see Suda s.v. Ἐνθουσιώσας· Πισίδης· καὶ τὰς ἀθέσμους ἡδονὰς τοῦ Σαρβάρου ἐνθουσιώσας τῇ πυρώσει τῆς μέθης ἐπεξανῆπτον. ἀντὶ τοῦ ἐξανεγειρούσας, μαινομένας ("Possessed. As per Pisides: they kindled the lawless pleasures of Sarbaros, possessed by the burning of drunkenness. Instead of stirred up, maddened"; Adler 1967, E1367 in 2.286). On references to Corybantic *choreia* in the *Phaedrus*, see Belfiore 2006; Wasmuth 2015; cf. Périllié 2019, comparing Socratic midwifery to a Corybantic initiation. On references to Corybantic rites in the *Laws*, see Pfefferkorn 2022, 171 and 212; also, Wilson-Nightingale 2021, 195–197, arguing that "Plato brings together the telestic rites of Cybele and Dionysus in the *Laws*"; cf. chapter 3, pp. 79, 94–95.

161. Ustinova 2017, 119, 124, 134, 137 (on the use of wine in mystic rites) and 172, 174, 177, 182, 191 (on wine and Dionysus); Jiménez San Cristóbal 2002, 307–317; Dodds 1960, xiii, with Porres Caballero 2013, 173n85. On Orphic tablets listing wine as an afterlife delight for initiates, see Graf and Johnston 2007, 148–149, and 157; Bernabé and Jiménez San Cristóbal 2008, 84–89; cf. Wilson-Nightingale 2021, 144n59. On the rite of *kraterismos*, as part of the Corybantic rites at Erythrai, see Wankel 1979, 80, appreciating the rite as a kind of *sakramentalen Trank* ("sacramental drink"); cf. Graf 2010, for the epigraphic evidence of the cult. For other rituals involving alcohol consumption, such as the rite of the *kykeon* at the Eleusinian mysteries, see Webster et al. 2000; McGovern 2003, 267–268; Rinella 2010, 84–87, 117–119, 133–138, 222 (on how Socrates' use of mystic language

was mis-portrayed by his accusers to frame him as a profaner of the mysteries); for Dionysiac *ōmophagia* (esp. given the interchangeability of wine and blood), see Porres Caballero 2013, 179–180.

162. Socrates and Phaedrus share a Corybantic/Bacchic zeal for speeches: at *Phdr.* 228c1, Socrates describes Phaedrus as συγκορυβαντιῶντα (his "fellow celebrant of Corybantic rites"); at *Phdr.* 234d7–8, Socrates tells him: συνεβάκχευσα μετὰ σοῦ τῆς θείας κεφαλῆς ("I joined you in the divine frenzy"); cf. Belfiore 2006, 194; also, see her pp. 206–207 noting that satyr dance in the *Phaedrus* "is not merely poetic ornamentation but is essential to the meaning." Cf. Gorgias, *Hel.* 9 describing the symptoms of those who listen to poetry as φρίκη περίφοβος καὶ ἔλεος πολύδακρυς καὶ πόθος φιλοπενθής ("fearful fright and tearful pity and mournful longing"); cf. Anagnostou-Laoutides 2026.

163. *Ion* 533e5 and 7: ἐνθέους. Cf. Eur. *Hipp.* 141–144, where Phaedra is suspected of being possessed (ἔνθεος) by Pan, Hecate, the Corybants, or Cybele. Also, Suda s.v. Ἐνθουσιασμός: ὅταν ἡ ψυχὴ ὅλη ἐλλάμπηται ὑπὸ τοῦ θεοῦ ("Possession. When the whole soul is illuminated by the god"; Adler 1967, E1366 in 2.286). Notably, at *Phdr.* 245a3 the soul of inspired poets is also described as ἐκβακχεύουσα.

164. See Ustinova 2017, 269; cf. chapter 2, nn196 and 235; also, introduction, n8.

165. See introduction, n5; also, n160 above.

166. For example, Ustinova 2017, 116–126, notes that both rites involve collective *mania* and wine; cf. Graf 1985, 322–323.

167. Socrates was acknowledged as the inventor of inductive reasoning (τούς τ᾽ ἐπακτικοὺς λόγους) and holistic definitions (τὸ ὁρίζεσθαι καθόλου); Arist. *Met.* 1078b28–29.

168. The mystic motifs identified in the *Symposium* reflect the increasing importance of Dionysus (and Orpheus) at Eleusis; Zuntz 1971, 407–411; Graf 1974, 51–65; Burkert 1977; Cole 1980; Schmidt 1987, 162–165; Rinella 2010, 52–62; also, see his pp. 83–87 and 104–118 discussing the accusation that Socrates had profaned the Eleusinian mysteries. Similarly, Edmonds 2017, 206, argued that Plato invested Alcibiades' portrayal in the *Symposium* with phrases and symbols from the Eleusinian mysteries to allude to the accusation against him for blasphemy. For allusions to the Eleusinian mysteries in Plato, also see Linforth 1946; de Vries 1973; Levy 1979; Riedweg 1987, 2–69; (Wilson-)Nightingale 2005 and 2021, 88–95 and 148–155; Evans 2006; Ionescu 2007; Herrmann 2013. Cf. Mangieri 2016 for Dionysus as an initiate at the Eleusinian mysteries. The connection of Dionysus and Demeter is noted in *Bacch.* 274–278: δύο γάρ . . . , / τὰ πρῶτ᾽ ἐν ἀνθρώποισι: Δημήτηρ θεά/ . . . / ὃς δ᾽ ἦλθ᾽ ἔπειτ᾽ . . . ὁ Σεμέλης γόνος; cf. *Bacch.* 725–726; also, Ar. *Ran.* 336, 340–416, 886–887; Soph. *Ant.* 1118–1120; Diod. Sic. 5.75. On Platonic philosophy as initiation, see McGinn 1960; Adluri 2006; cf. Dunn 2012 (part a). Capra 2014, 95–114, argues that in the *Phaedrus* Plato revamps poetic

into Platonic initiation; also, Rinella 2000 and 2010, 131–138; see chapter 2, p. 50. Cf. Périllié 2019 (on *Euthyd.* 277e). Also, Adkins 1970 with Green 1979, 15n1, on the use of initiation language in the *Theaetetus* as a trope that Aristophanes recognized and alluded to in the *Clouds.* Cf. Wallace 2020, 15–16, 20–21, 93, 139, 185ff., arguing that for Plato (and Hegel), "mysticism" does not refer to extraordinary encounters of the divine but to being conscious about "our experience of trying to have an open mind" (p.15); Wallace explains the divine as the absolute experience of freedom, truth, love, and beauty that we choose based on reason.

169. Burkert 1987, 19–24 (on psychosomatic therapy in the cults of Dionysus and Meter), 69 with n14 and 72 (on mysteries and secret knowledge); Ustinova 2017, 119–121, 188–193. Segal 1997, 355 notes: "Mystic rites and initiation operate on another level through a close parallelism between initiatory and psychological meaning. Both tragedy and initiatory ritual use a dramatic enactment of symbolic events to bring to light a hitherto hidden reality and to lead the audience (spectator or initiand) to a knowledge or acceptance of an otherwise invisible power"; also, see Wilson-Nightingale 2021, 72–73 (with Platt 2011, 36–37), 203, 243–244, on the physical aspects of divine epiphanies (which for the philosopher would be experiencing the Forms), with emphasis on sight; cf. Wilson-Nightingale 2015 and Horky 2006.

170. Evans 2006, 3 and 11–13, argues that Diotima's story, reaching its climax with Erōs' birth, corresponds to the Eleusinian mysteries, where the birth of a child was celebrated; Burkert 1983, 289–290; Clinton 1992, 92–95. See Wilson-Nightingale 2021, 73–75, 80–88 and 105–106 (on Diotima's role as a mystagogue) and 31–36, 48, 85–88, 96, and 102–103 (on the Ladder of Love). As she notes (p. 19): "Only the philosopher who gets to the top of the Ladder of Love sees the epiphany of the divine Form of Beauty as an epoptês." Also see (Wilson-) Nightingale 2004, 115–116, for the soul as the receptive partner in its relationship with the Forms; after suffering labor pangs, the soul gives birth to intelligence and truth. Cf. Rinella 2010, 56, 174 (for Diotima as noetic flux), and 193.

171. See Wilson-Nightingale in nn121 and 170 above. For Socrates as the lover of wisdom par excellence, see Belfiore 2012, 82–88; cf. *Phdr.* 252e1–5 and 256a8–b, on the lover's philosophical inclination. At *Apol.* 20d10 Socrates explains his fame on account of his human wisdom (ἀνθρωπίνη σοφία), denying any knowledge of divine wisdom; cf. *Apol.* 23b1–3. In the same text, Socrates denies (1) that he is a sophist (20b–c) and (2) that he corrupts the Athenian youth (23c–24b).

172. According to Morgan 2010, 59–62, in the hands of the philosophers "mimēsis can be seen as compatible with a re-imagined inspiration" in a dialogue that requires a two-level reading: in the *Phaedrus*, Plato "uses conventional beliefs as a springboard for new thoughts. The vocabulary of inspiration is retained but developed and given different content"; thus, while rejecting mainstream forms of art, the philosopher claims to be a superior artist, able to produce exceptional copies of things much closer to the Forms.

173. Including storytelling. Hence, at *Phdr.* 253c8, Socrates admits that his theory of the soul's division in three parts, represented by two horses and their charioteer, was a story: . . . καθάπερ ἐν ἀρχῇ τοῦδε τοῦ μύθου (". . . just as in the beginning of this tale"). For the image of the winged charioteer in Parmenides, see the proem of his *On Nature* (fr.1.1–10; Gallop 1984, 48–49); cf. Morgan 2000, 185; also, Schiltz 2006 on the similarity between Plato and the Vedic Katha Upanishad (esp. 1:3:3–9), indicating that Plato was not averse to using mythic patterns provided they contributed to the ethical improvement of the listeners.

174. Also note the striking wording at *Phdr.* 249c8–9: τελέους ἀεὶ τελετὰς τελούμενος ("always performing perfect rites"), stressing the notion of bringing rites to fruition; cf. 250b7–c1: μακαρίαν ὄψιν τε καὶ θέαν . . . εἶδόν τε καὶ ἐτελοῦντο τῶν τελετῶν ἣν θέμις λέγειν μακαριωτάτην ("The blessed sight and vision . . . they witnessed and they performed what is rightly called the most blessed of rites"), 250e1, 251a3, referring to the newly initiated to the mysteries of Beauty as νεοτελὴς and ἀρτιτελής, both meaning "newly initiated," and 253c3: προθυμία . . . τῶν ὡς ἀληθῶς ἐρώντων καὶ τελετή ("the eagerness . . . and initiation of the true lovers").

175. For *phasmata* (visions, apparitions) in connection with the cult of Dionysus, see Petridou 2015, 71, with her nn225 and 226; for *phasmata* in the Eleusinian mysteries, see Burkert 1983, 286–288, and 1987, 92–93; Riedweg 1987, 55, 68, and Sourvinou-Inwood 2003, 33; cf. Bremmer 2014, 98 (with his nn77 and 78) and 107. For *epopteia* (or *theoria*) in the Eleusinian mysteries, see Mylonas 1961, 274–278; Kerényi 1967, 45–47 and 113; Dowden 1980; Burkert 1983, 275, 282–283; (Wilson-)Nightingale 2005, 173ff. and 2021, 21–22, 53, 100; 155, 188. Bremmer 2014, 11–16, and Dinkelaar 2020. Note the use of language in *Symp.* 210d4–6, where the philosopher contemplates the beautiful: (τοῦ καλοῦ . . . θεωρῶν); cf. *Phdr.* 250d4–e2: θεώμενος stressing the visibility of beauty and *Leg.* 650a1, where the "Test of the Wine" (see chapter 3) is described as Dionysus' Inspection (τῆς τοῦ Διονύσου θεωρίας), or as Bury translates it, "insight" (L187: 87). Cf. Eur. *Bacch.* 629–632 where Dionysus is said to have created a *phasma* that Pentheus eventually attacks in his madness.

176. Eur. *Bacch.* 34, 78–79 (where *orgia* is linked with the cult of Cybele), 262, 415–416, 470 and 471, 482, 998, 1080. On the connection of *mania* and truth in the *Phaedrus*, cf. Serranito 2020, 105–109. For beauty as healer of pain, see also *Phdr.* 252a9–252b1: τὸ κάλλος ἔχοντα ἰατρὸν ηὕρηκε μόνον τῶν μεγίστων πόνων; for love as a sickness, see *Phdr.* 228b6 and 231d2; cf. *Symp.* 193d with Wilson-Nightingale 2021, 79; also, see her pp. 149–150 (on Orpheotelists) and 195–198 (on Corybantic healing in the *Laws*).

177. Hsch. s.v. κορυβαντισμός: κάθαρσις μανίας (Schmidt 1867, 906) in line with *Phdr.* 244d9–e4, where Socrates refers to purification and rites as temporary means of tackling episodes of madness; furthermore, after praising the non-lover in the *Phaedrus*, Socrates delivers a palinode (*Phdr.* 243b2) to achieve purification

(243a2–5: ἐμοὶ . . . καθήρασθαι ἀνάγκη· ἔστιν δὲ τοῖς ἁμαρτάνουσι περὶ μυθο-λογίαν καθαρμὸς ἀρχαῖος); Wilson-Nightingale 2021, 183–191; cf. Annas 1999, 59–63; also, Capra 2014, 38–52, on Plato's structuring Socrates' two speeches in the *Phaedrus* as a unit containing an ode and a palinode. Note that in Eur. *Bacch.* 76–77, Bacchic rites are mentioned as *catharmoi* (βακχεύων ὁσίοις καθαρμοῖσιν).

178. The image is employed in schol. Ar. *Nub.* 604 s.v. σὺν πεύκαις (vis-a-vis the prologue of Euripides' *Hypsipyle*); on Delphic Bacchants, see Ar. *Nub.* 605 (s.v. Βάκχαις Δελφίσι) and Dübner 1841, 110b.26–36.

179. *Bacch.* 1270: γίγνομαι δέ πως ἔννους, μετασταθεῖσα τῶν πάρος φρενῶν ("I have somehow come to my senses, having changed from my previous state of mind").

180. *Phdr.* 250d6–8: "sight is the sharpest of the physical senses, though wisdom is not seen by it (ὄψις . . . ὀξυτάτη τῶν . . . αἰσθήσεων, ἣ φρόνησις οὐχ ὁρᾶται), for it could afford terrific loves, if such a clear image (ἐναργὲς εἴδωλον) of it were granted as would come through sight"; cf. *Phdr.* 250c5–7, where Socrates claims that the body is an impediment to our effort to restore the pure sight we had once experienced; on the philosopher's vision of the Form of Beauty in terms of a divine epiphany, see Wilson-Nightingale 2021, 30–31, 42, 56–57, 70–72 164–165, 96, 99–100, 109–111, 155, 161–167, 203–209, 216, 238–241; cf. *Ti.* 45b6–d4 on how the stream of vision connects daylight with the pure fire in us. On the metaphor of "seeing" divine beauty and its crucial role in effecting recollection, see Burnyeat 2011, 256; cf. (Wilson-)Nightingale 2004, 110; also, chapter 2, p. 44.

181. *Phdr.* 251e1–3: ἀδημονεῖ τε τῇ ἀτοπίᾳ τοῦ πάθους καὶ ἀποροῦσα λυττᾷ, καὶ ἐμμανὴς οὖσα οὔτε νυκτὸς δύναται καθεύδειν οὔτε μεθ᾽ ἡμέραν οὗ ἂν ᾖ μένειν . . .

182. *Bacch.* 1102: ἀπορίᾳ λελημμένος and 1391: τῶν δ᾽ ἀδοκήτων πόρον ηὗρε θεός. In addition, the Bacchants feel the sweet pain of Bromius (*Bacch.* 64: Βρομίῳ πόνον ἡδὺν), suffer in his name (189: ταῦτ᾽ ἐμοὶ πάσχεις), yearn for him (415–416 and 456: ἐκεῖ δὲ Πόθος· ἐκεῖ δὲ βάκχαις θέμις ὀργιάζειν; πόθου πλέως) and sense his rage (851, 977 and 981: ἐνεὶς ἐλαφρὰν λύσσαν; ἴτε θοαὶ Λύσσας κύνες ἴτ᾽ εἰς ὄρος; λυσσώδη κατάσκοπον μαινάδων). Also, see (Wilson-)Nightingale 2004, 113–115, on the feelings of *aporia* and *atopia* that the soul experiences after witnessing the Forms. Although Nightingale focuses on the *Republic*, Socrates is described as *atopos* both in the *Symposium* and the *Phaedrus*; cf. n14 above.

183. *Bacch.* 32–33: τοιγάρ νιν αὐτὰς ἐκ δόμων ᾤστρησ᾽ ἐγὼ μανίαις, 119: οἰστρηθεὶς Διονύσῳ, 664–665: βάκχας ποτνιάδας εἰσιδών, αἳ τῆσδε γῆς οἴστροισι λευκὸν κῶλον ἐξηκόντισαν, 979: ἀνοιστρήσατέ νιν, 999: μανεῖσα πραπίδι, 1093–1094: διὰ δὲ χειμάρρου νάπης ἀγμῶν τ᾽ ἐπήδων θεοῦ πνοαῖσιν ἐμμανεῖς, 1229: ἔτ᾽ ἀμφὶ δρυμοὺς οἰστροπλῆγας ἀθλίας, and 1295: ἐμάνητε, πᾶσά τ᾽ ἐξεβακχεύθη πόλις.

184. *Bacch.* 794–795: "I would rather sacrifice to the god than fight against his stings (πρὸς κέντρα λακτίζοιμι), getting angry, me a mortal against a god."

185. While growing its feathers the soul, according to *Phdr.* 251c4–5: "throbs with heat, and is irritated, and feels itchy as it grows the feathers"; see chapter 1, p. 33 and chapter 2, p. 45.

186. Porter 2016, 576. For the soul as winged in Greek eschatological beliefs, already in Homer (e.g., *Il.* 16.856–857 = 22.362–363; *Od.* 11.222 and 24.1–10), see Cairns 2013, 244n28. Erōs was often represented in archaic and classical art as a winged ephebe; see, for example, a red-figured vase painting from ca. 475–425 BCE at the Louvre (Inventory no: CA1798); Beazley 1963, 964.107 (https://www.beazley.ox.ac.uk/record/4AFBE033-4B75-41E9-A1AF-0DFC31E9D369). For cultic representations of Dionysus as winged at Amyclae, see Paus. 3.19.6; cf. the winged Dionysus from the House of Dionysus at Hellenistic Delos and, later, from the House of the Faun in Pompeii.

187. For Dionysus as a drink poured for the other gods to enjoy, see *Bacch.* 284: οὗτος θεοῖσι σπένδεται θεὸς γεγώς.

188. Cf. *Bacch.* 498 and 649 for Dionysus' ability to "release" (λύσει) his worshippers, and 651: ὃς τὴν πολύβοτρυν ἄμπελον φύει βροτοῖς ("he who brings forth the richly clustered vine for mortals").

189. Including composing poetry (*Phd.* 60e1–61b9) and engaging with natural philosophy (96a6–98b7).

190. Bordoy 2013, 391–394 and 398 (on *Phdr.* 244e5–6: λύσιν τῷ ὀρθῶς μανέντι τε καὶ κατασχομένῳ).

191. At *Phd.* 68c7–69c9, Socrates criticizes those who misinterpret *sōphrosynē* as an exchange of some pleasures for others, opting thus for a σκιαγραφία (*Phd.* 69b9: "rough painting") of virtue. Note that here Socrates uses the verb αἰνίττεσθαι (*Phd.* 69c5) ("to speak in riddles, hint") to describe the metaphorical language of the *mustai*, whom he compares to the philosopher; yet, by borrowing their language, Socrates also adopts their figurative style. Cf. Alcinous, *Didasc.* 25 (Whittaker 1990, 48.25–30); cf. *Ti.* 43c7–d2 in conclusion, n41.

192. See n136 above; also, see *Tht.* 187a3–8, where knowledge is defined as the thing that the soul encounters when engaging directly, alone, and by itself with realities (ἡ ψυχή, ὅταν αὐτὴ καθ᾽ αὑτὴν πραγματεύηται περὶ τὰ ὄντα).

193. Ustinova 2017, 316–317 on Socrates' "mental withdrawal"; Holmes 2010, esp. 366–367. Cf. *Soph.* 264a1: defining opinion as "that which arises in the soul silently by way of thought" (ὅταν οὖν τοῦτο ἐν ψυχῇ κατὰ διάνοιαν ἐγγίγνηται μετὰ σιγῆς, πλὴν δόξης ἔχεις ὅτι προσείπῃς αὐτό); cf. *Tht.* 190a5–6: ἀλλὰ σιγῇ πρὸς αὑτόν·.

194. *Bacch.* 636: ἥσυχος δ᾽ ἐκβὰς ἐγώ ("I left the house quietly"), 647: στῆσον πόδ᾽, ὀργῇ δ᾽ ὑπόθες ἥσυχον πόδα ("Hold on, calm your anger"), 789–790: οὔ φημι χρῆναί σ᾽ ὅπλ᾽ ἐπαίρεσθαι θεῷ, ἀλλ᾽ ἡσυχάζειν ("I advise you not to take up arms against a god but hold your peace"). On Plato's use of the wild music of Corybantic *choreia* (likely set to dithyrambic patterns) to superimposes its rhythm

on the disturbed souls of the manic, calming them down, see Belfiore 1986; also, Wilson-Nightingale 2021 in n160 above.

195. Chapter 2, pp. 42, 62.

196. Ustinova 2017, 116; Burkert 1987, 21–24; Trabattoni 2020, 148–149.

197. *Phd.* 99a7: ἄτοπον, 99a7 and 98c3: ἄτοπα. See nn14 and 181–182 above on Socrates' *atopia*. Here Socrates charges his enemies with an indictment typically applied to him, as in Xen. *Mem.* 1.1.11ff. (see chapter 2, p. 67). Cf. Müller 2017, 159–162.

198. The Loeb translation here (L36: 343) is "metaphor," but I chose "comparison" to avoid overinterpreting the text. According to the *Cambridge Greek Lexicon*, εἰκάζω means (1) represent (someone) by an image or likeness, portray; (2) give something or someone the likeness of something else; (3) see someone or something as being like something else. Kotwick 2019, 190, compares Plato's use of allegory in *Gorg.* 493b–d (based on the use of ἀπεικάζω in 493b2 and c1) and the Derveni Papyrus; while using the term "functional analogy" (https://www.britannica.com/topic/analogy-reason), she provides no theoretical discussion of it; cf. Kotwick 2020, 11–13. Morgan 2000, 66, on "allegory as a more 'philosophical' defence of myth," which transfers "the authority of interpretation from an author to a reader, while philosophy aims to communicate an authoritative vision."

199. Tate 1929, 147–154; Copeland and Struck 2010, 3. Morgan 2000, 89, notes: "The language of myth was not then expunged from philosophical vocabulary, but its reference was changed." Morgan acknowledges the role of the sophists in blurring the distinction between *mythos* and *logos* by appropriating traditional mythology with renewed zeal. Cf. Wdowiak 2017, 222–224, on Plato's attempt to put forward a theory for the educative use of myth and allegory; Wdowiak adopts the term εἰκὸς μῦθος, drawing on Brisson (with Naddaf) 1988, 130, who defined it as "a myth that bears upon the copies of intelligible things." Yet, at *Phdr.* 267a8 and 273b, εἰκὸς is understood as the less-than-certain probability that rhetoricians settle for. Cf. Brisson 2012a and n83 above.

200. At *Phdr.* 267c3, εἰκονολογία is listed alongside διπλασιολογία ("duplication") and γνωμολογία ("sententiousness") as known techniques of the art of speech (267b6: λόγων τέχνη). Gorgias, *Hel.* 10–11, compares powerful speeches to inspired incantations (αἱ γὰρ ἔνθεοι διὰ λόγων ἐπωιδαὶ) that "enchant and persuade the mind by intercourse with its *belief* (συγγινομένη γὰρ τῆι δόξηι τῆς ψυχῆς . . . ἔθελξε καὶ ἔπεισε). Gorgias claims that these are "deviations of mind and deceptions of belief" (αἵ εἰσι ψυχῆς ἁμαρτήματα καὶ δόξης ἀπατήματα); cf. Hartmann 2017, 130.

201. *Resp.* 376e2–383c7, 596b10–597e8, and 599c1–601b6.

202. In fact, Socrates accuses Thrasymachus in the *Republic* of wishing to put him on trial (336c–d, 337d) but failing to do so because of his own eagerness to speak (338a).

203. Also, see *Resp.* 390b1–2 and 395e7–396a1; cf. Plut. *Comp. Cim. Luc.* 1.2–4, where Cimon is praised for nor making "feastings and reveling the crowning

prize for arms and campaigns and trophies," with reference to Plato's criticism of the followers of Orpheus who declare that those who have lived rightly will enjoy everlasting intoxication in the afterlife (ὥσπερ Πλάτων ἐπισκώπτει τοὺς περὶ τὸν Ὀρφέα, τοῖς εὖ βεβιωκόσι φάσκοντας ἀποκεῖσθαι γέρας ἐν ᾅδου μέθην αἰώνιον); cf. *Resp.* 363c–d with Wilson-Nightingale 2021, 147. Plutarch recommends leisure and quiet, as well as gaining pleasure and perspective by spending time on arguments (σχολὴ μὲν οὖν καὶ ἡσυχία καὶ διατριβὴ περὶ λόγους ἡδονήν τινα καὶ θεωρίαν).

204. *Phdr.* 244a8–10: νῦν δὲ τὰ μέγιστα τῶν ἀγαθῶν ἡμῖν γίγνεται διὰ μανίας, θείᾳ μέντοι δόσει διδομένης, 244d6–7: μανίαν . . . τὴν ἐκ θεοῦ, and 245b1–2: μανίας γιγνομένης ἀπὸ θεῶν.

205. For what Merleau-Ponty referred to as "creative description," see chapter 1, n66.

206. Socratic love and unreason are filtered, according to Foucault ([2]1972, 103), by a "hierarchy of the sublime": "Throughout the development of Platonic culture, love had been distributed according to a hierarchy of the sublime that likened it, according to its level, either to a blind madness of the body or to the great intoxication of the soul where Unreason is able to know. In their different forms, love and madness were distributed across the various regions of knowledge. The modern age, after classicism, made a different choice: the love of reason and that of unreason."

207. The term has been used by Kierkegaard, who was deeply influenced by Socratic thought, in his pseudonymous works. See Kannany 1989; Muench 2010.

208. On Plato's use of rhetoric and the metaphorical use of myth across his dialogues but especially the *Phaedrus* and the *Timaeus*, see Hartmann 2017, esp. 274–279, 311, 339, 429, 432, 461–462, 486–487.

209. Cf. Hartmann 2017, 219–220, on Socrates' use of the vocabulary of *mania*, reason, and illness in the *Phaedrus*.

Chapter 2

1. See Rademaker 2005, esp. 251–356, who discusses the nuances of *sōphrosynē* across ancient Greek literature before discussing Plato's use of the concept. His work relies on North's seminal 1966 monograph on *sōphrosynē*; cf. Anagnostou-Laoutides 2022 on the Heraclitean and Pythagorean premises that Plato entertains in his attempt to work through the ethical dimensions of *sōphrosynē*; on *sōphrosynē* as a form of discipline especially manifested in the sympotic context, see Moore 2023, 4–5; also, see his pp. 32 and 339–340.

2. Woodruff 2000, 131–132; also, see his pp. 135–140, on Socrates' *elenchus* (and its role in *Crito* 46b). According to Woodruff (pp. 143–146), the Socratic *elenchus* relies on the irrational emotions of shame and honor, which Socrates attempts to re-accommodate in the ideal city in the *Laws*; Anagnostou-Laoutides 2021a, 4 and 12, with Baima 2018; cf. Baima 2017 and Pfefferkorn 2020. Woodruff

concludes that while rejecting traditional rationalism and blind belief in religion, Socrates champions instead "the moral conscience of a thoughtful individual" (p. 146). Also, Friesen 2015, 51–53, with North 1966, 83; cf. North 1948, 13, with n90 on "Euripides' much-quoted σώφρων ἐν βακχεύμασιν (*Bacch.* 317–18).

3. Also, *Phdr.* 237e1–238a1; *Charm.* 175e8–9; *Ti.* 71e7–72a6 (on applying reason to interpret divine omens) with Anagnostou-Laoutides 2021a, 7–8 and 15–21; *Phil.* 11b4–c2 with Warren 2014, 50–51. On Socratic *elenchus*, see *Apol.* 38a; *Laches* 189a–b; *Euthyd.* 272a–b, 293e, 295a, 303d–304d. On the importance of reasoning in Platonic and Socratic philosophy, see Klosko 1988a; McPherran 1991; Miller 2005; cf. Gocer 2000, 124–125, on the debate about Socrates' rationalism and his stance toward traditional religion. Cf. Moss 2014, 185 and 191–202, on Plato's understanding of *logos* as virtue-conferring reasoning (as in *Tht.* 201c–d, 202b–c; *Symp.* 202a; *Phd.* 76b; *Ti.* 51d–e; *Grg.* 465a, 501a; *Meno* 98a, 99e–100a; *Leg.* 653b, 645b, 659d, 696c, 835e, ff.); cf. Vogt 2013, 179–181, on Plato employing the drive of love in the *Symposium* as a kind of "rational madness."

4. See, for example, Foucault 1972, 24: "It is because it symbolizes a great worry that it [madness] suddenly rose on the horizon of European culture towards the end of the Middle Ages. Madness and the madman become major characters, in their ambiguity: threat and derision, the dizzying unreason of the world, and the thin ridicule of men"; Foucault admits that human societies have used madness metaphorically to determine socially unaccepted behavior(s); this is ironically most evident in his claim that our preoccupation with alienating the insane is *not* entirely metaphorical—in fact, institutionalization is an effort to act on our perception (1972, 118); cf. Scull 2015, esp. 35–36; Ustinova 2017, 7–8 with n60.

5. On the debate on whether Alcmaeon was a medical writer or philosopher, see Perilli 2001, esp. 56–57, criticizing Mansfeld 1975; more recently, see Camden 2023, 7, 35–37; cf. his pp. 44–46 noting that in Plato's *Symposium* Eryximachus employs Alcmaeon's theory of opposing humors.

6. The experience has been often described as a sudden flash of light; hence, Trabattoni 2007, 115 writes: "[T]he passage from not knowing to knowing occurs in an instant, identical to the moment when suddenly the spark explodes." Cf. Merleau-Ponty 1973, 121, on creating new meaning: "[I]n language significa- tion is fused with the juncture of signs; it is simultaneously tied to their bodily composition and blossoms mysteriously behind them. Signification bursts out above the signs and yet it is only their vibration, the way a cry carries outside and makes present to everyone the very breathing and pain of the man crying out"; cf. Candiotto and Politis 2020 in chapter 1, n157.

7. Hom. *Il.* 13.394 and 16.403, with Darcus Sullivan 1996, 34–35.

8. Plato also uses ἐκπλήττομαι in *Resp.* 576d8 and 577a5 to refer to the "astonishment" the tyrannical man tries to inspire to those around him with his extravagant lifestyle—though the tyrant always threatens violence.

9. Cf. Apollodorus, who narrates the events at Agathon's party: a fervent follower of Socrates at the time (*Symp.* 173b4: Σωκράτους ἐραστὴς ὢν ἐν τοῖς μάλιστα τῶν τότε), Apollodorus is described as "mad and out of his wits" (172e2: μαίνομαι καὶ παραπαίω). Vogt 2013, 180, draws attention on Apollodorus' nickname as *malakos*, meaning "weak-minded" or "soft in the head" (*Symp.* 173d7). Some manuscripts read *manikos* ("mad") instead of *malakos*, which agrees with Apollodorus' description of himself in 172e2, probably denoting Bacchic affliction.

10. Dübner 1841, xv.34–37, cites Platonius' *De diff. comoed.*, where the Athenian Crates is recorded as the first comic playwright to introduce drunken characters (πρῶτος μεθύοντας ἐν κωμῳδίᾳ προήγαγε).

11. Cf. Capra 2014, 150; also see Capra 2017 on the role of the *Clouds* in cementing Socrates' status as an aloof intellectual; cf. Anagnostou-Laoutides 2021b, 260–261. On the adverse impact of Aristophanes' portrayal of Socrates on the latter's trial, see Ziolkowski 2001a, 208; Socrates and Aristophanes seem to have shared in a fierce debate about civic education rather than mutual hostility; schol. Ar. *Nub.* 96 in Dübner 1841, 85.34–38; cf. Mus. Ruf. *Dis.* 10.12–16, in Lutz 1947, 78, on noble-mindedness (μεγαλόφρων): "Socrates . . . though publicly ridiculed by Aristophanes (δημοσίᾳ λοιδορηθεὶς ὑπ᾽ Ἀριστοφάνους), was not angry (οὐχ ὅπως ἀγανάκτησε)."

12. Ar. *Nub.* μανία (350, 832, 845, 926); μαίνομαι (660, 932, 1476); παραφρονέω (844, 1475); (παρανοῶ/παράνοια) 844, 1476, 1480; cf. (ἀνόητος) 858, 897, 920.

13. Thumiger 2013, 61, lists all the terms mentioned in n12 above, except ἀνόητος.

14. See Siegel 1973, 272–275, on Galen's reference to "garrulous and idiotic patients" whose character is betrayed by their "large and outstanding ears" (τὰ δὲ μεγάλα καὶ ἐπανεστηκότα μωρολογίας καὶ ἀδολεσχίας, *quod an. mor.* 4.797, Kühn 1822), arguably described by Hippocrates in the *Regimen*; cf. Arist. *Hist. an.* 492b2–3. In Galen's view, Hippocrates had defined madness "as a form of delirium (*paraphrosyne*) without fever"; on garrulity in Plutarch as betraying "a lack of the control of reason," see Nikolaidis 2011, 213–214; Athenaeus associates garrulity with drunkenness: *Deipn.* 2.38b4: οἴνου σε πλῆθος πόλλ᾽ ἀναγκάζει λαλεῖν; cf. Aretaeus, *Chron.* 6.1.2 (Hude 1958, 41.13). Aretaeus was likely writing in the second century CE but dating him has been challenging. Prioreschi 1996, 263–264, with Kudlien 1964, 23–32, placed him in the middle of the first century CE; cf. Oberhelman 1994, 946; Nutton 1996, 1051. Harris 1973, 235, in the late first century CE. Siegel 1968, 288, in the second century CE with Adams 1856, viii and 370n1. Finally, Wellmann 1895, 669, argued that Aretaeus should be dated in the late second or early third century CE.

15. The disorder described here—not to be confused with the sacred disease, is not given a name; the author relates its symptoms because, like the sacred disease, it affects the brain; Perczyk 2023, 262–263 with n45.

16. Note that some manuscripts read ἀγρυπνίαι ("insomnia").

17. Thumiger 2017, 305.

18. In L472 (Potter 1988) the reading φρενῖτις is preferred; Littré 7.108 read φροντὶς, like Jouanna 1983, 211, followed by Passavanti 2018, 14. On the dating of the Hippocratic works, see Jouanna 1999, 374–416.

19. Also see *Vict.* 4.93 (= 6.660 L.) for cases in which "bodies of alien form are seen in sleep and frighten a person" ἀλλόμορφα σώματα φαίνεται ἐν τοῖσιν ὕπνοισι καὶ φοβεῖ τὸν ἄνθρωπον) as indicating ". . . a bilious flux and a dangerous disease" (σημαίνει . . . ἀπόκρισιν καὶ χολέρην καὶ νοῦσον κινδυνώδεα). Thumiger 2017, 201–202.

20. Thumiger 2017, 34 and 145. Note that in the *Republic* Plato emphatically describes the tyrannical man and his city as "full of fear" (578a4: φόβου γέμειν); maddened by his desires and passions (378a11: μαινομένῳ ὑπὸ ἐπιθυμιῶν καὶ ἐρώτων); and again as "full of fear and lusts of every kind" (579b4: πολλῶν καὶ παντοδαπῶν φόβων καὶ ἐρώτων μεστός), the tyrant is riddled with suspicion of everyone around him (cf. chapter 3, n56). Furthermore, he is plagued by fear during his whole life (φόβου γέμων διὰ παντὸς τοῦ βίου), racked with convulsions and pains (σφαδασμῶν τε καὶ ὀδυνῶν πλήρης). For Plato's discussion of fear in the *Republic* and the *Laws*, see Anagnostou-Laoutides, forthcoming b.

21. Passavanti 2018, 14.

22. Thumiger 2013, 65–68, makes the point that mental disorders (i.e., *phrenitis, melancholy, mania*) should not be taken "as categorically homogeneous," despite being grouped as "types of insanity by the later medical tradition." On the differences of these affections as discussed in the ancient sources, see van der Eijk 2000, vol. 2, 144–160 and 214–225. According to Diocles of Carystus, "melancholy is characterized by mental derangement"; this view is reported in the Anonymous of Paris, *De morbis acutis et chroniis* 19.1, cited by van der Eijk 2000, fr. 108 in vol. 1, 188–189 (Garofalo 1997, 116.22–118.2); also, see van der Eijk 2000, vol. 2, 147. Diocles was likely active in Athens around 360 BCE and hence, a contemporary of Plato and Aristotle; Di Benedetto 1986, 50.

23. Cf. *Airs, Waters, Places* X.59–63, one of the oldest Hippocratic texts:"Ἢν δὲ (τὸ θέρος) βόρειόν τε ἦ καὶ ἄνυδρον . . . τοῖσι δὲ χολώδεσι τοῦτο πολεμιώτατον γίνεται· λίην γὰρ ἀναξηραίνονται· καὶ . . . αὐτοῖσιν ἐπιγίνονται . . . πυρετοὶ ὀξέες καὶ πολυχρόνιοι, ἐνίοισι δὲ καὶ μελαγχολίαι· ["But if the (sc. summer) weather is northerly and dry, . . . it is very harmful to the bilious: for these become excessively dry, and are attacked . . . by chronic acute fevers, in some cases by melancholies too"); Vinkesteijn 2022, 234. Cf. *Acut.* 50 (= 2.334 L.): ὁ μὲν γλυκὺς (sc. οἶνος) οὐκ ἐπιτήδειος δὲ οὐδὲ τοῖσι πικροχόλοισι. The connection derived (or perceived as originating in) Hippocratic medicine is also discussed by Galen; Stewart 2018, 88–100. Vinkesteijn 2022, 252 (who expands on van der Eijk 1990/2005) argues that, despite associating intellectual activity with hotness and yellow bile, Galen's views are closer to the *Problems* (which Galen accepted as genuinely Aristotelian)

than often assumed. Also, see Eubulus' fr. 94.9–10, where Dionysus is made to say that the ninth drinking cup is reserved for the bile, while upon drinking the tenth heavy drinkers become manic (ὁ δ' ἔνατος χολῆς·/ δέκατος δὲ μανίας; text and comm. Hunter 1983, 66 and 188 (= fr. 93 Kassel and Austin 1986, 244; Ath. *Deipn.* 2.36b–c); cf. Euenus fr. 2 (L258; *Anth. Gr.* 11.49). Aretaeus also explains melancholy with reference to black-bile irregularities (*Chron.* 5.1.1–2 = Hude 1958, 39.10–11); the melancholics, he says, often lose their sense of decency and do terrible and disgraceful things (*Chron.* 5.3.5–6 = Hude 1958, 39.31–40.1: ἀφρονέοντες καὶ δεινὰ καὶ αἰσχρὰ πρήσσοντες); further, they often suffer from unfounded fears (τάρβος ἔκτοπον) and tend to have vivid, terrifying dreams (ὄνειροι ἀληθέες, δειματώδεες, ἐναργέες); *Chron.* 5.6.1–2 = Hude 1958, 40.18–19; cf. Kotsopoulos 1986, 174–176. Also, see Caelius Aurelianus, *Acute Diseases* 1.11.99–1.12.103 (= CML VI 1, vol. 1, p. 76.25–80,8 Bendz), writing ca. the fifth century CE (Dysert 2006/2007, 162–163, with Sabbah 1998). Caelius disagrees with the views of Diocles of Carystus, who had prescribed venesection for those suffering from *phrenitis: atque ita etiam ex uinolentia in phreniticam passionem uenientes conuenit plerumque non phlebotomari, cum forte etiam solutio affuerit.* ("Moreover, in most cases it is better for people not to be venesected who have fallen into a phrenitic affection as a result of excessive drinking of wine, for then a loosening condition may be present"; text and trans. van der Eijk 2000, fr. 73; vol. 1, 144.23–24 and 145.)

24. *Acut.* 53 (= 2.336.15 L.): Μελίκρητον δὲ πινόμενον διὰ πάσης τῆς νούσου ἐν τῇσιν ὀξείῃσι νούσοισι τὸ ἐπίπαν μὲν τοῖσι πικροχόλοισι; cf. *Acut.* 54 (= 2.342 L.).

25. Cf. *Acut.* 63 (= 2.360.17 L.) specifying that "If a severe heaviness in the head or derangement of the mind is suspected in these [sc. acute] diseases (Ὑποπτεύσαντι μέντοι ἐν ταύτῃσι τῇσι νούσοισι καρηβαρίην ἰσχυρὴν ἢ φρενῶν ἅψιν), wine must be completely forbidden (παντάπασιν οἴνου ἀποσχετέον)."

26. See L473: 226 with Joly 1972, 11–14, on the relationship between the "genuine" and "spurious" parts of the *Regimen in Acute Diseases*; ancient authors, like Caelius Aurelianus, did not distinguish between the two parts.

27. Thumiger 2017, 38 and 121.

28. Thumiger 2017, 326–327; also, see her pp. 146, 291–292, 294, 314.

29. Suda s.v. Καρηβαρία: ἡ μέθη (K377 in Adler 1967, 3.32); also, K378: Καρηβαρῶν: τὴν κεφαλὴν βαρούμενος ἀπὸ μέθης οἴνου; cf. Hesch. s.v. καρη-βαρεῖ· βαρύνεται κεφαλήν. ἐξ οἴνου μεθύει κάρην δὲ κεφαλήν (Schmidt 1867, 813); Pollux, *Onom.* 2.41.1–8 (Dindorf 1824, 84): καὶ τὰ μὲν κεφαλῆς νοσήματα κεφαλαία καὶ κεφαλαλγία καὶ καρηβαρία καὶ ἡμικρανία, ἡμίκραιρα καὶ ἴλιγγος καὶ σκοτοδινίασις καὶ σκοτοδινία· Πλάτων (*Prt.* 339 E) δ' ἔφη 'ἐσκοτώθην καὶ ἰλιγγίασα' καὶ καρηβαρικὸν ποτὸν ἢ βρῶμα· τὸ δὲ τοῦτο ποιεῖν καροῦν Ἀντιφῶν φησίν. κεφαλαλγὲς σιτίον, ὡς 'τὸν τοῦ φοίνικος ἐγκέφαλόν' φησιν ὁ Ξενοφῶν (*Anab.* 2.3.16). καὶ καρηβαρικὸν τὸ πάθος Τηλεκλείδης (Plut. *Per.* 3.6 = fr. 47

in L515: 306). τὸ δὲ ὑπὸ μέθης τοῦτο πάσχειν καρηβαρᾶν Ἀριστοφάνης (fr. 832 in L502). ("And the diseases of the head are headache, heaviness of the head, and migraine, as well as vertigo and dizziness; Plato said, 'I was blinded, and I became dizzy.' And a heavy drink or food; this is said to cause heaviness by Antiphon. A food for headache, as Xenophon states, 'the brain of the phoenix.' And the condition of heaviness noted by Telecleides. And this suffering from drunkenness is referred to as heaviness by Aristophanes." Also, see Ath. *Deipn.* 2.54e–f: καὶ ὁ γλυκάζων δ᾽ οἶνος οὐ βαρύνει τὴν κεφαλήν, ὡς Ἱπποκράτης ἐν τῷ περὶ διαίτης φησίν . . . ὁ γλυκὺς ἧσσόν ἐστι καρηβαρικὸς τοῦ οἰνώδεος καὶ ἧσσον φρενῶν ἁπτόμενος . . . ("Sweet wine does not produce wooziness, according to Hippocrates *Acut.* 14 (= 2.332.5–8 L.) . . . Sweet wine goes to the head less than wine with a more vinous character; and it makes less of an assault on the rational faculties . . ."

30. Passavanti 2018, 16–17; cf. Metcalf 2023 on Plato staging in the *Theaetetus* and the *Gorgias* well-known sophistic doctrines so to undermine their performativity.

31. Cf. van der Eijk 2005, 155, who has argued that in his discussion of melancholy, Aristotle did not use the Hippocratic tradition in a systematic manner; rather his ". . . concept of the melancholic, with the associated psycho-physical and ethical characteristics seems to be a predominantly independent and genuine invention of Aristotelian philosophy."

32. Van der Eijk 2005, 144; Thumiger 2013, 62–63. Notably, the symptoms, including garrulity, accord with the memoirs of modern-day patients relating their experiences of mental illness; on this, see Hermsen 2011, 83 and 91.

33. See van der Eijk 2005, 141–143, who has challenged the view that Aristotle's representation of the dreams of the melancholics in his *On Dreams* differs from his treatment of the topic in the *On Divination in Sleep* (after all, the treatises *On Dreams, On Divination*, and *On Memory and Recollection* are included in the *Parva Naturalia*).

34. Van der Eijk 1990, 42 (the text is not fully cited in the English translation of his article = 2005, 144); cf. Camden 2023, 211n15 with *Vict.* 4.89.2 (= 6.644–646 L.) and 4.89.7 (= 6.648 L.) on "fiery" dreams perceived to have been caused by an excess of bile (εἰ δὲ πυροειδὲς τὸ ὑπεναντιούμενον δοκοίη εἶναι καὶ θερμόν, χολῆς ἀπόκρισιν σημαίνει·); if this condition is not cured, there is danger of being afflicted by *mania* (κίνδυνος μανῆναι τὸν ἄνθρωπον).

35. See L317: 274–275 on the authorship of book 30 of the *Problems*: although we cannot establish with certainty whether the chapter "was written by Aristotle or largely based on something he wrote," yet "the author was clearly familiar with Aristotle's scattered remarks on melancholy." Other possible sources for the treatise include Theophrastus' *On Melancholy* (DL 5.44), which did not survive, Diocles of Carystus, and the Hippocratic corpus.

36. Van der Eijk 2005, 161–168; cf. Vinkesteijn 2022, 250–251.

37. Ps.-Arist. *Pr.* 3.875b29–31: "Or is it because when drunk (ἐν ταῖς μέθαις), the soul, affected alongside the body, stumbles (συμπαθὴς γινομένη πταίει)? So, when the soul suffers this condition, it is reasonable (εἰκὸς) that the tongue also suffers the same." Cf. Hipp. *Morb.* 2.22 (= 7.36,14 L.). Thumiger 2017, 224. Galen draws on Plato's *Timaeus* (86e–87a) regarding the balance of our bodily humors and its impact on our psychic and mental state; cf. *Ti.* 83a–85e with Camden 2023, 25–26; also, *Suppl. Pr.* 2.91: Διὰ τί μεθυόντων μᾶλλον ἀπορρήγνυται ἡ φωνή, ἢ νηφόντων; ("Why is the voice of those who are drunk more fractured than of those who are sober?"; Kapetanaki and Sharples 2006 182–183).

38. Plut. *quaest. conv.* 645a4–9 in chapter 3, p. 91. For a description of bile as hot (and phlegm as cold), see ps.-Arist. *Pr.* 1.862b28–29: ἡ χολὴ μέν ἐστι θερμόν, τὸ δὲ φλέγμα ψυχρόν.

39. Van der Eijk 2005, 158–167; Camden 2023, 246; cf. Ahonen 2018a, 11 with n54. Interestingly, Merleau-Ponty (1964, 19) describes the experience prior to achieving creative speech as a "vague fever."

40. *Epid.* 4.15 (= 5.154,3–6, L.) and 5.2 (= 5.204,7 L.); *Vict.* 1.35,128–130 (= 6.520,20–522,1 L.). See Perdicoyianni-Paléologou 2009a, 314 with nn28 and 29, and Jouanna 2012b, 177–178. For fever resulting from drunkenness, see Hipp. *Loc.* 33.1–4 (= 6.324 L.: πρὸς δὴ τὸ ἀπὸ τοῦ πυρετοῦ θερμὸν τὸ ἀπὸ τοῦ φαρμάκου προσελθὸν μανίην ποιέει); *Cris.* 49.1–2. For wine causing a coma starting with loss of speech, see *Morb.* 2.22 (= 7.36,14 L.) and 3.8 (= 7.126,18 L.). If the patient vomits bile, he will suffer *mania* and die (ἢν . . . χολὴν ἐμέῃ, μαίνεται, καὶ ἀποθνῄσκει). Cf. Ustinova 2017, 93n88; also, see Ar. *Pax.* 66 with Olson 1998, *ad loc.* and *Acut.* 63 in n25 above.

41. Arist. *On Sleep and Waking* 457b8–10: μετὰ τὰ σιτία ἰσχυρότατος ὁ ὕπνος γίνεται, καὶ ἔστιν ὑπνωτικὰ οἶνος καὶ ἄλλα θερμότητα ἔχοντα τοιαῦτα ("sleep is deepest after food, and wine and other things which are naturally heating tend to produce sleep"). As Aristotle explains, sleep is produced when the heat is vaporized and reaches the head; when the vapors though are excessive, it leads to "loss of consciousness and imagination" (457b27: μὲν ἔκνοιαν ποιεῖ, ὕστερον δὲ φαντασίαν). On the soporific effects of wine, see chapter 3, n243.

42. Kapetanaki and Sharples 2006, 136–137 with n257, citing Arist. *Rhet.* 1389b31 for the coldness of the elderly and Plato, *Leg.* 666b where wine is discussed as a remedy for the dryness of old age; cf. chapter 3, pp. 86–87 and n49 below.

43. The books, containing material extracted from more continuous works dated as early as the third century BCE, were later appended to the ps.-Aristotelian *Problems*; Kapetanaki and Sharples 2006, 11.

44. Kapetanaki and Sharples 2006, 108–113: to expel this relaxation one must drink more wine, ideally the type of wine most mixed (with water). The author, then, cites Theognis' famous verses on moderate wine drinking, before discussing relevant mythological allegories, which relate the perceptual changes that wine drinking was commonly believed to cause: ". . . they say in the myths

that a Bacchant accompanies Dionysus because wine leads to dancing, the Satyrs because [it leads to] ease of movement; a Lydian female because some are relaxed by it; a leopard because of the variegated imagination of those who are drunk (for each of them takes on a different and variegated [mode of] reasoning when affected by the wine; and the skin of the animal too is variegated)" (. . . μυθεύ-ουσι τῷ Διονύσῳ βάκχην ἔπεσθαι, διὰ τὴν ἐκ τοῦ οἴνου χορείαν. Σατύρους δὲ διὰ τὴν εὐκινησίαν· Λύδην δὲ διὰ τό τινας ἐξ αὐτοῦ ἐκλύεσθαι· πάρδον δὲ διὰ τὴν ποικίλην φαντασίαν τῶν οἰνωμένων· διάφορον γὰρ ἕκαστος καὶ ποικίλον ἀναδέχεται λογισμὸν ὑπὸ τοῦ οἴνου κινούμενος). The text also refers to Agave, the Theban queen who murdered her son, Pentheus, under Bacchic *mania*; finally, it reiterates commonly held views about the drunk: they are unable to hide the truth (cf. chapter 3, p. 99) and they are desirous of women (τοῖς γὰρ οἰνωθεῖσι παρέπεται πλείστη γυναικῶν ἐπιθυμία).

45. Ps.-Arist. *Pr.* 30.953a10–15 and 26–29; cf. Camden 2023, 30 with n45. In DL 7.118 Zeno claims that great men (οἱ σπουδαῖοι) do not suffer drunkenness or madness but are prone to melancholy or delirium (προσπεσεῖσθαι . . . διὰ μελαγχολίαν ἢ λήρησιν). Aretaeus (*Chron.* 5.3.1–2 = Hude 1958, 39.27–28) considers melancholy—a temporary affliction—as the first stage of *mania*, which is permanent (τὸ δὲ ἔμπεδον ἡ μανίη ἴσχει; *Chron.* 6.2.1 = Hude 1958, 41.18). Plutarch (*Lys.* 2.3) quotes Aristotle on the melancholic nature of great minds such as Socrates, Plato, and Heracles. Plato compared Socrates' efforts to serve the gods to Heracles' labors repeatedly in his dialogues: see *Euthyd.* 297a–298b; *Phd.* 89c; *Cra.* 398d, with Bussanich 2006, 205. Indeed, Heracles offers an apt mythical/literary parallel for Socrates since they both pose as antithetical characters: in tragedy, Heracles was presented both as savior and destroyer, exemplifying Dionysus' dual power; Ruck 1976. He had a reputation as a mystic (while from the Hellenistic period onward he also acquired a philosophical profile as a Stoic and Epicurean hero) but also as a popular comic character, known for his excesses; see Stafford 2012, 105–130, on Herakles' comic profile, and 49, 108, 165–166, 172, on his initiation into the Eleusinian mysteries (with Xen. *An.* 6.3.6) cited in Anagnostou-Laoutides 2020c, 45n1; also, see Anagnostou-Laoutides 2016 with more references on Heracles' theological significance in Dionysiac and Orphic cult; cf. Colomo 2004, 91–92, 96–97; also, Moore 2017.

46. Heracles' fondness of wine and his lustful nature are amply recorded in the ancient sources: see Panyas. frs. 19–21 (L497 = frs. 12–14 Kinkel) with Matthews 1974, 76–87; cf. fr. 9 (= fr. 4 Kinkel); Soph. *Tr.* 268–29; Eur. *Alc.* 747–802; *Aug.* fr. 272b; Ar. *Ran.* 107–114, 503–518, 549–567; Dio Chrys. *Disc.* 32.94–95; Diod. Sic. 4.12.3–12; cf. Hes. *Wedding of Ceyx* frs. 203–204 and Menander's *False Heracles* (Kassel/Austin). On Heracles' melancholy, see Toohey 2004, 34–36; on his lovesickness, see Biggs 1966.

47. In the next sentence (*Phdr.* 251b1–2), Plato explains this process as such: δεξάμενος γὰρ τοῦ κάλλους τὴν ἀπορροὴν διὰ τῶν ὀμμάτων ἐθερμάνθη

("as the effluence of beauty enters him through the eyes he is warmed"). On the Empedoclean influences of the term ἀπορροαί (effluences), used in the singular (ἀπορροὴν) in the *Phaedrus* but in the plural in *Meno* 76c8–9 (. . . ἀπορροάς τινας τῶν ὄντων κατὰ Ἐμπεδοκλέα), see Yunis 2011, 153. The term is also linked to the Democritean concept of εἴδωλα (images); Long 1966, 260; cf. Cairns 2011, 45, on the "Platonic/Democritean terminology of *eidōla* and aporrho(i)ai," which "describe the onset of love as a result of the influx through the lover's eyes of emanations from the object of the gaze." On the influence Empedocles exercised on the theory of perception advanced in the Hippocratic *Regimen*, see Jouanna 2012a, esp. 212–222.

48. Cf. *Phdr.* 255d1–2: τὰς διόδους τῶν πτερῶν ἄρδει τε καὶ ὥρμησε πτεροφυεῖν . . .

49. Belfiore 1986, 433, notes that at *Leg.* 666b6–c1 "[T]he physical dryness, hardness and coldness of the old people . . . produces the psychic disorder of despondency (dysthymia)"; cf. Pfefferkorn 2022, 149–158, on wine as a tool needed to convince the virtuous members of the Dionysiac Choir to engage with younger people.

50. Notably, poetry was believed to cause similar effects; Pl. *Ion* 535c4–6: ἐγὼ γὰρ ὅταν ἐλεεινόν τι λέγω, δακρύων ἐμπίπλανταί μου οἱ ὀφθαλμοί· ὅταν τε φοβερὸν ἢ δεινόν, ὀρθαὶ αἱ τρίχες ἵστανται ὑπὸ φόβου καὶ ἡ καρδία πηδᾷ ("when I relate a tale of woe, my eyes are filled with tears; and when it is of fear or awe, my hair stands on end with terror, and my heart leaps"). Cf. *Phdr.* 251b9: ἀνακηκίει.

51. Cf. Vogt 2013, 189–190.

52. Cf. Erginel 2019, esp. 90–92, arguing that in the *Philebus* (but also across the dialogues) Plato discusses the mixed pleasures in terms of imbalance or disharmony, a concept he draws from the medical tradition.

53. For the role of *aporia* in Socrates' desire (*erōs*) for knowledge in the *Symposium* (esp. 203b9 on Penia's *aporia*), see Fine 2019; on the interplay between *aporia* and *euporia* in the dialogue, see Sheffield 2006a, 58–74, 122–127, 198; Ziolkowski 1999, 31; and Rowe 2000; on Socratic *aporia* overall, see Wolfsdorf 2008, 197–239, and (Wilson-)Nightingale 2010; also, see the papers by Szaif, Politis, Harte, and Brown in Karamanolis and Politis 2018; further, see Candiotto and Politis 2020, 32–34 (with Politis 2006), on *aporia* as the essence of the philosophical enterprise.

54. On itching as a symptom often associated with mental disorders, see Thumiger 2017, 55 and 177 (*Epid.* 1.23 = 2.670.5–9 L.), 131 (*Hum.* 2 = 5.478.6–13 L.), and 232–234.

55. The literature is extensive; indicatively, see Blood and Zattore 2001; Bernardi et al. 2009; Kulinski et al. 2022.

56. For example, see Anderson and Shivakumar 2013 on physical activity and mental disorders.

57. Spiers 1995; cf. Freund 1994 on the association of alcohol ingestion with exposure to cold temperatures.

58. Holmes 2010, 350–351.

59. See Camden 2023, 37–49 and 85, on contemporary medical views incorporated in Eryximachus' speech in the *Symposium* with n5 above; also, see n31 above (on Aristotle's unsystematic employment of the Hippocratic humoral theory).

60. Yet, cf. *Resp.* 382e3: "no one who is fool or mad is a friend of the gods" (οὐδείς . . . τῶν ἀνοήτων καὶ μαινομένων θεοφιλής).

61. Pl. *Apol.* 20d10 in chapter 1, n171. For drunkenness leading to madness, see also Eur. *Cycl.* 617–618 and esp. Hdt. 6.84.1, who regarded drunken madness as the opposite of divine madness; hence, he reports that, according to the Spartans, Cleomenes did not "suffer madness by any divine agent" (ἐκ δαιμονίου μὲν οὐδενὸς μανῆναι) but became addicted to strong wine (after becoming acquainted with the Scythians) and suffered madness as a result of this (ἀκρητοπότην γενέσθαι καὶ ἐκ τούτου μανῆναι)"; cf. Hdt. 6.84.3. Perdicoyianni-Paléologou 2009a, 314nn32 and 33, cites the sources. Cf. Arist. *Eth. Nic.* 1146a18–20, referring to a type of σπουδαία ἀκρασία (excellent unrestraint) as in the case of Neoptolemus in Sophocles' *Philoctetes*.

62. Jeffré 1922, 17; Schiefsky 2005, 67–71. Although Plato refers to Hippocrates, the Asclepiad (*Phdr.* 270c3–4), the authorship of the *VM* is doubtful.

63. On Plato's admiration of Hippocrates' holistic approach to the "nature of man," see *Phdr.* 270b–d; on his familiarity with the medical advances of his time, see Belfiore 1986, 431 with n36, citing among others Bertier 1972, 57–143; Tracy 1969, 77–156; Joly 1961, 435–451; and Jouanna 1978; also, Camden 2023, 5 and 161–162.

64. Littré adds the word ἀσθενέα ("ill") after ἄνθρωπον; thus, the meaning of the sentence would be "too much wine makes drinkers sick."

65. Cf. *Tht.* 158a6–7: Τίς . . . λείπεται λόγος τῷ τὴν αἴσθησιν ἐπιστήμην τιθεμένῳ καὶ τὰ φαινόμενα ἑκάστῳ ταῦτα καὶ εἶναι τούτῳ ᾧ φαίνεται ("What argument is left . . . for the man who says that perception is knowledge and that in each case the things which appear are to the one to whom they appear?"). Begodt 1915, 491. Theaetetus admits here that his opinion has been inspired by Protagoras' doctrines, which he had read some time ago (see n147 below); Passavanti 2018, 10; cf. Metcalf 2023, 2, with *Tht.* 161e–162a, admitting the similarities in the rhetorical performances of Protagoras and Socrates. Wisdom, Plato claims, can only be judged by its civic benefit; *Tht.* 166d–167d in Metcalf 2023, 5–6.

66. Van der Eijk 2005, 144–147.

67. Van der Eijk 2005, 144.

68. Van der Eijk 2005, 149–151, on Aristotle's theory that the melancholics are "characterized by a mixture of heat and cold (either too cold or too hot) that is permanently out of balance, something which Aristotle clearly regards as a sign of *disease*," and 161–163, on *Pr.* 954b1–5 claiming that the melancholics exhibit varying degrees of reason, according to the balance of hot and cold in them. Cf. *Pr.* 30.954b8–10 cited on p. 43; also see Toohey 2004, 55.

69. Van der Eijk 2005, 232n88; also, see Arist. *an. post.* 100b5–15, esp. 7–9, arguing that *nous* is the only faculty through which we can reliably grasp truth and come closer to knowing the first principles (ἀληθῆ δ᾽ ἀεὶ ἐπιστήμη καὶ νοῦς, καὶ οὐδὲν ἐπιστήμης ἀκριβέστερον ἄλλο γένος ἢ νοῦς, αἱ δ᾽ ἀρχαὶ τῶν ἀποδείξεων γνωριμώτερα).

70. Van der Eijk 2005, 165, with Tracy 1969, esp. 261–264.

71. Vinkesteijn 2022, 250 with n63, citing among others Flashar 1966, 62.

72. Here my translation follows van der Eijk 2005, 149. On the role of imagination in approximating the truth, see chapter 4, pp. 114 and 117.

73. For a further definition of the *ekstatikos* as the opposite of the unrestrained character, see Arist. *Eth. Nic.* 1151a20–27 where we read: ἔστι δέ τις διὰ πάθος ἐκστατικὸς παρὰ τὸν ὀρθὸν λόγον, ὃν ὥστε μὲν μὴ πράττειν κατὰ τὸν ὀρθὸν λόγον κρατεῖ τὸ πάθος, ὥστε δ᾽ εἶναι τοιοῦτον οἷον πεπεῖσθαι διώκειν ἀνέδην δεῖν τὰς τοιαύτας ἡδονὰς οὐ κρατεῖ· οὗτός ἐστιν ὁ ἀκρατής . . . ἄλλος δ᾽ ἐναντίος, ὁ ἐμμενετικὸς καὶ οὐκ ἐκστατικὸς διά γε τὸ πάθος ("But there is a person who undergoes ecstasy, against right reason, under the influence of passion, who is mastered by passion enough for him not to act according to right reason, but not so completely so as to believe that the reckless pursuit of pleasure is right. This is the man who lacks self-control. . . . Opposed to the unrestrained man is another character, who stands firm by his choice, and does not undergo ecstasy under the mere impulse of passion").

74. Cf. Vinkesteijn 2022, 247–248.

75. On Plato's use of our desire for wine as a metaphor for intemperance associated with bodily pleasures, see Palumbo and Motta 2020, mainly discussing the *Republic, Hippias Major, Protagoras,* and the *Timaeus;* cf. Bartels 2020 focusing on the *Laws.*

76. *Phil.* 61c; *Philebus* is one of Plato's later dialogues, dated to circa 360–347; Waterfield 1980, 199 with n4, suggests that the dialogue is earlier than the *Timaeus* (contra Owen 1953); cf. Sanmartín 2022, 189 with n23.

77. Arist. *Eud. Eth.* 1248a39–40: τοῦτο γὰρ εὖ ὁρᾷ καὶ τὸ μέλλον καὶ τὸ ὄν, καὶ ὧν ἀπολύεται ὁ λόγος οὗτοι. διὸ οἱ μελαγχολικοὶ καὶ εὐθυόνειροι· ("For this quality discerns aright the future as well as the present, and these are the men whose reason is disengaged. This is why the melancholic even have dreams that are true"). Aristotle makes this comment during a discussion about the starting point of motion in the spirit which is found in God and the divine element is us (1248a28–30: θεὸς . . . τὸ ἐν ἡμῖν θεῖον). Thus, Aristotle concludes, "the starting-point of reason is not reason but something superior to reason" (λόγου δ᾽ ἀρχὴ οὐ λόγος ἀλλά τι κρεῖττον).

78. See Rowe 2021, 212–213, discussing *Eud. Eth.* 1248a24–25: ἢ ἔστι τις ἀρχὴ ἧς οὐκ ἔστιν ἄλλη ἔξω, αὕτη δὲ [διὰ τί] τοιαύτη τῷ εἶναι τὸ τοιοῦτο δύναται ποιεῖν; ("Or shall we say that there is a certain starting-point outside which there is no other, and that this, because it is of such a nature, can produce a result of

such a nature?"); his argument is corroborated a few lines later (29–33), where Aristotle adds: λόγου δ' ἀρχὴ οὐ λόγος ἀλλά τι κρεῖττον. τί οὖν ἂν κρεῖττον καὶ ἐπιστήμης εἴη καὶ νοῦ πλὴν θεός; ("And the starting-point of reason is not reason but something superior to reason. What, then, could be superior even to knowledge and to intellect, except God?"); cf. Bussanich 2006, 206–209.

79. Also see *Eud. Eth.* 1248b4–7; van der Eijk 2005, 148; Vinkesteijn 2022, 244–245.

80. Here I follow the text reconstruction and translation by Rowe 2021, 210–211; cf. Vinkesteijn 2022, 249.

81. Rowe 2021, 208–209; van der Eijk 2005, 148; cf. Arist. *Eth. Nic.* 1099b9–23 insisting that it is better to be happy because of one's own efforts than good fortune. At *Eud. Eth.* 1249b16–24, Aristotle argues that "the noblest and finest way of acquiring goods is the one that promotes contemplation of the divine" (ἥτις οὖν αἵρεσις καὶ κτῆσις τῶν φύσει ἀγαθῶν ποιήσει μάλιστα **τὴν τοῦ θεοῦ θεωρίαν** . . . αὕτη ἀρίστη καὶ οὗτος ὁ ὅρος κάλλιστος·); cf. chapter 3, p. 108. A few lines later he adds: "the best spiritual standard is to be as far as possible unconscious of the soul's irrational part" (οὗτος τῆς ψυχῆς ὅρος ἄριστος, τὸ ἥκιστα αἰσθάνεσθαι τοῦ ἀλόγου μέρους τῆς ψυχῆς).

82. Van der Eijk 2005, 164–165.

83. Van der Eijk 2005, esp. 144–148; cf. Vinkesteijn 2022, 242–252. Also see Rowe 2021, 216, with *Eth. Nic.* 1179b7–16, where Aristotle claims that the truly *spoudaioi* (great men; cf. n45 above) are bound to be few.

84. Russell 2005, 106–137 (focusing on pleasure in the *Republic*); cf. Devereux 2017 (examining happiness mainly in the *Phaedo*, *Philebus*, and the *Laws*); also see Anagnostou-Laoutides 2022 drawing attention to *Resp.* 365c1: τὸ δοκεῖν . . . καὶ τὰν ἀλάθειαν βιᾶται καὶ κύριον εὐδαιμονίας, where Socrates protests that "appearance violates even the truth and rules our happiness," and 420d7–e1 where the guardians of the ideal city are expected to choose the kind of happiness that suits them, that is the happiness that promotes social harmony: μὴ ἀνάγκαζε ἡμᾶς τοιαύτην εὐδαιμονίαν τοῖς φύλαξι προσάπτειν, ἣ ἐκείνους πᾶν μᾶλλον ἀπεργάσεται ἢ φύλακας.

85. Cf. Kyriakou 2012, 119–120.

86. At *Her.* 889–893 Euripides notes that "the dances begin without the drums that add pleasure to the thyrsus of Dionysus" (κατάρχεται χορεύματ' ἄτερ τυπάνων/ οὐ Βρομίου κεχαρισμένα θύρσωι) because the libations involve pouring blood not wine (892–893: πρὸς αἵματ', οὐχὶ τᾶς Διονυσιάδος/ βοτρύων ἐπὶ χεύμασι λοιβᾶς). Cf. *ll.* 835–836 relating Lyssa's attack on Heracles; Lyssa, an agent of Dionysus, can inflict Bacchic *mania*. *Her.* 896–897: οὔποτ' ἄκραντα . . . / Λύσσα βακχεύσει; also see *Bacch.* 977 where Lyssa is invoked to afflict the Maenads with *oistros* against Pentheus whom they mistake him for an animal; Provenza 2013, 87–89.

87. Cf. Passavanti 2020, 206–210, who argues that Euripides' florid language of madness as employed in the *Orestes* may have influenced the description of a

clinical case in chapter 48 of the Hippocratic *Internal Affections*, dated between 400 and 390 BCE, that is shortly after the production of the play in 408 BCE. Earlier in the piece, Passavanti argues that Plato seems to be closer to Aeschylus' use of madness as godsent and able to reveal truth; however, as I discuss on p. 62, Euripides' defense of Bacchic *sōphrosynē* in the *Bacchae* indicates that he was aware of different types of madness and their different perceptual effects.

88. For example, see Hippoc. *Cris.* 28, 31, 33–34, on the effects of fevers, often in combination with sweating and/or palpitation. Also, Walshe 2016, 55, on Hippocrates' association of madness with moisture in the brain (Hipp. *morb. sacr.* 17.19–20: καὶ μαινόμεθα μὲν ὑπὸ ὑγρότητος [τοῦ ἐγκεφάλου]). Next, Hippocrates notes that madness can also originate in the phlegm, although these patients tend to be quieter (18.5–6: οἱ μὲν ὑπὸ φλέγματος μαινόμενοι ἥσυχοί τέ εἰσι καὶ οὐ βοηταὶ οὐδὲ θορυβώδεες). Walshe (2016, 165) discusses Praxagoras (fr. 72, Steckerl) who thought that *mania* occurred in the heart (which he accepted as the seat of thinking instead of the brain; see chapter 1, n3); cf. Longrigg 1998, 28–29; Mansfeld 1990, 3105. Plato's tripartite division of the soul places its constituent parts in the brain (λογιστικόν), the heart (θυμοειδές), and the liver (ἐπιθυμητικόν), respectively. Tracy 1976; cf. Crivellato and Ribatti 2007, 330–331, who identify a fourth kind of soul, that of sexual impulse, located under the umbilicus (cf. *Pr.* 30.953b24–25 and 31–34 on p. 44 on the importance of "breath" for sexual intercourse).

89. Galen, *Quod opt. med.* 1.58 (Kühn 1821): "In order to judge by experience what has been taught by words, one must become an eyewitness of all types of cities (παντοίων αὐτὸν πόλεων γενέσθαι αὐτόπτην)." Kühn writes πάντως . . . πόλεως, though the meaning is clearly either "of every city" (πασῶν τῶν πόλεων) or, more likely, "of every type of city," since Hippocrates refers here to different climatic factors that affect human health.

90. Yet see Perczyk 2023 for a negative interpretation of Cassandra's madness, associated with pain and death and presented as a disease. *Bacch.* 1105, 1112–1113, 1211–1212. Padel 1992, 73; cf. Padel 1981, 109, 126–129.

91. On Teiresias' profile as a sophist, see Roth 1984; Hilton 2022.

92. See Capra 2014, 1–3, noting that Plato's dialogues were included in Arist. *Poet.* 1447b and drawing attention to Albinus' brief mention of the similarities between tragedy and Plato in his second century CE *Prologue/Introduction* to Plato (1.2, Reis 1999).

93. See the reviews of O'Brien 2015; Platter 2017; cf. chapter 1, nn13 and 168.

94. On the Socratic notion of falsely led pedagogy, see Rudebusch 2011, 172, with *Apol.* 29e and *Laches*, 188a–b, on the Socratic *elenchus*; cf. n98 below.

95. Thus, at *Tht.* 158b1–4 we read: οὐκ ἂν δυναίμην ἀμφισβητῆσαι ὡς οἱ μαινόμενοι ἢ οἱ ὀνειρώττοντες οὐ ψευδῆ δοξάζουσιν, ὅταν οἱ μὲν θεοὶ αὐτῶν οἴωνται εἶναι, οἱ δὲ πτηνοί τε καὶ ὡς πετόμενοι ἐν τῷ ὕπνῳ διανοῶνται ("But really I cannot dispute that those who are insane or dreaming have false opinions,

when some of them think they are gods and others fancy in their sleep that they have wings and are flying"). Also, see Cooper 1990, 46–47 and 74.

96. Vogt 2013, 82, with *Phdr.* 236a1, 265e4, 266a3, and 245b4 (κεκινημέ-νος, stirred); cf. Hartmann 2017, 220–221. See n221 below on the longstanding association of the perfect tense participle κεκινημένος (and the verb κινέομαι) with Bacchic *mania*.

97. Cf. *Tht.* 157e4: ἐλέγχεσθαι δοκεῖ; Campeggianni 2020, 45–46.

98. Hartmann 2017, 289–302, compares Socrates' Hippocratic method with dialectic; cf. Bussanich 2006, 200, 202–203, on Socratic *elenchus* as therapy, which in the *Apology* is described as "coming to the aid of the god" (23b8: τῷ θεῷ βοηθῶν) and as "service to the god" (23c1: διὰ τὴν τοῦ θεοῦ λατρείαν, 30a6–7: τὴν ἐμὴν τῷ θεῷ ὑπηρεσίαν), with notable civic benefits (30a6–b5, 38a1–7). Bussanich also cites *Soph.* 230b8–c1: "The people who are being examined . . . grow angry with themselves (ἑαυτοῖς μὲν χαλεπαίνουσι) and gentle toward others (πρὸς δὲ τοὺς ἄλλους ἡμεροῦνται). Thus, they lose their high and obstinate beliefs about themselves" (τούτῳ δὴ τῷ τρόπῳ τῶν περὶ αὐτοὺς μεγάλων καὶ σκληρῶν δοξῶν ἀπαλλάττονται) and *Tht.* 210c1–2: βελτιόνων ἔσει πλήρης διὰ τὴν νῦν ἐξέτασιν. Drawing on (Ahbel-)Rappe 1995, 15, he further notes (p. 203): "Socratic elenctic therapy is a total assault on the ego, a radical depersonalization, which, combined with spiritual exercises, leads to the discovery of the true self."

99. Levin 2014, 73–211, compares the rivalry between medicine and philosophy in Plato to that between rhetoric and philosophy (vis-à-vis the larger debate on the hierarchy of the various *technai*); for Levin, the rivalry is resolved in the *Laws*; cf. Folch 2015, 10–20; Longrigg 1993, 82–103; also, see *VM* 20.1–17 with Aristotle's response in *Protr.* fr. 46–48.

100. Pigeaud 1989, 70; Gundert 2000, 35.

101. See Perdicoyianni-Paléologou 2009a and 2009b for a thorough list of the uses of μαίνομαι, βακχεύω, and λύσσα (and their compound forms) across ancient texts. Her diagrams in 2009b, 459–460, exemplify that the contexts in which these words were originally or fundamentally used could shift from strictly religious and related to Dionysus to civic in general, mainly to determine accept-able social behaviors.

102. Luhrmann 2011, 72, on cognition and hallucinations, with Geertz 2014, 40.

103. Foucault ²1972, 245–246; trans. Howard 1965, 88, with minor modifications.

104. For Socrates' meditation habits, which included standing on a spot for hours meditating, see *Symp.* 175a7–10 and 220c3–d5. Muramoto 2018, 448–450, applies retrospective diagnosis, a controversial methodology by his own admission, to argue that Socrates suffered from temporal lobe epilepsy; cf. Muramoto 2014. Although he does not consider Socrates' wine drinking patterns, the medical

community concurs that wine consumption, especially in large amounts, can trigger epileptic attacks; cf. Gordon 2001.

105. Catani and Mazzarello 2019, 1844–1845.

106. Gentile 2006; cf. Targum and Adler 2014, 58–59.

107. Vaidya and Stollstorff 2008; cf. Catani and Mazzarello 2019, 1844: "ADHD is . . . characterized by continuous procrastination, the inability to complete tasks, mind wandering and a restlessness of the body and mind."

108. See, for example, Ohlmeier et al. 2008, citing among others Biederman et al. 1998.

109. Schultz and Carron 2013 identify instances of Socratic meditation in Plato's works, arguing for its general neurological benefits. Cf. Mitchell et al. 2015 on meditation as an alternative way to manage ADHD. However, the practices described (i.e., detecting conflict by focusing on one object) do not correspond to Socrates' meditation practices.

110. Losh and Capps 2003.

111. Losh and Gordon 2014.

112. Davies and Dubie 2004; Bogdashina 2016, 86 (on hypotactility); Posar and Visconti 2018.

113. Marco et al. 2011; Thye et al. 2018.

114. At *Phdr.* 270b1–2, Plato compares medicine and rhetoric as arts using similar methodologies (ὁ αὐτός που τρόπος τέχνης ἰατρικῆς ὅσπερ καὶ ῥητορικῆς). Cf. Arist. *Protr.* frs. 2 and 4 on philosophy as a *techne* dedicated to the health of the soul. See Lidz 1995, 530–536, for a list of Plato's medical metaphors. For the importance of rhetoric in the Hippocratic corpus, see Jouanna 1984. On the use of medical language in the *Symposium* and *Philebus*, see Moes 2000, esp. 59–161 and 2001; Vegetti 1966; and esp. Lidz 1995 on its metaphorical value.

115. For example, see *Resp.* 444d–e; Moravcsik 1992, 100, with Lidz 1995, 527. Robinson 1995, 119–125 and 2000, with Ustinova 2017, 33n45; cf. Belfiore 1986, 431 and 433, citing Pl. *Ti.* 86b–87b; Bartoš 2015, esp. 175–181, for the body-soul analogy in Democritus; cf. Camden 2023, 45–47, 95–96, 161–163, 218.

116. On Alcmaeon's interest in human cognition and his contribution to promoting the brain as its center, see Walshe 2016, 117–119, 122–124; also, Lebedev 2017. On his influence on Plato, especially the *Timaeus* and the *Phaedo*, see Huffman 2021. Plato also draws on Alcmaeon's views in the *Laws*; see, for example, Longrigg 1993, 51–52 (on *Aët.* 5.30.1 = DK 24B4), 115, 121; Lidz 1995, 528; and Belfiore 1986, 431. For the political ramifications of Alcmaeon's definition of health as *isonomia* or balance of powers in the body (and its authenticity), see Mansfeld 2013, 85–86 with n38; Bartoš 2015, 78, 89, and 102; cf. Jouanna 1999, 327–328, and Kouloumentas 2014. Cf. Mansfeld 2013, 92, for a brief mention of Heraclitus' influence on the concept of opposite forces ruling the body, which is fully articulated by Alcmaeon. The view is also evocative of Parmenides' appreciation of human

intelligence. See D52 (L528: 80–81): "For when the hot or the cold dominates (ὑπεραίρῃ), thought becomes different (ἄλλην γίνεσθαι τὴν διάνοιαν). The better of the two and purer (βελτίω δὲ καὶ καθαρωτέραν) is the thought produced by what is hot; but this one too requires a certain proportionality"; cf. D40 (arguing that all things are constituted from hot and cold); D53a and b (identifying the soul and the intellect); and D54–55 (on the fiery nature of the soul); cf. D19–20 (on the fiery nature of heavens). On the influence of Heraclitus and Parmenides (but also Empedocles and Anaxagoras) on the author of the *Regimen*, see Bartoš 2015, esp. 111–112, 117–128, 163–164.

117. On Eryximachus' use of Hippocratic medicine as well as Alcmaeon's theory of opposites, see Camden 2023, 37–49.

118. Camden 2023, 18–37.

119. Jouanna 2012a, 200; Bartoš 2015, 191–192 (with n54); Lo Presti 2016; Camden 2023, 18–20 (with n20), 23; cf. Smith 1979, 47–48 (on Hippocrates as the author, a view largely outdated now).

120. On Heraclitean influences detected in the *Regimen*, see Camden 2023, 208, 219–221, 251, 255–256, and 259.

121. Camden 2023, 228–229.

122. Camden 2023, 234.

123. Camden 2023, 233–234; cf. Hüffmeier 1961, Jouanna 2007.

124. Camden 2023, esp. 245–249; Byl 2002; Bartoš 2015, 81–86 and 194–198; also see his pp. 185–187 (refuting the claim that the theory had a Pythagorean origin), 48–50, and 232n3 (on the *Regimen*'s author likely being a near contemporary of Plato, including the now obsolete suggestion that it was written by Eryximachus, Socrates' fellow diner in the *Symposium*), and 233–241 (on the influence of the *Regimen* on Plato's *Timaeus*); cf. Brisson 2013.

125. Cf. Hipp. *Acut.* 63 (= 2.362 L.): Ὑποπτεύσαντι μέντοι ἐν ταύτῃσι τῇσι νούσοισιν ἢ καρηβαρίην ἰσχυρὴν ἢ φρενῶν ἅψιν, παντάπασιν οἴνου ἀποσχετέον· ὕδατι δὲ ἐν τῷ τοιῷδε χρηστέον, ἢ ὑδαρέα καὶ κιρρὸν παντελῶς δοτέον οἶνον καὶ ἄοσμον παντάπασι, καὶ μετὰ τὴν πόσιν αὐτοῦ ὕδωρ μεταποτέον ὀλίγον· οὕτω γὰρ ἂν ἧσσον τὸ ἀπὸ τοῦ οἴνου μένος ἅπτοιτο τῆς κεφαλῆς καὶ γνώμης ("however, when the doctor suspects, in acute illnesses, either a strong heaviness in the head or a congestion to the brain, he will completely refrain from giving wine; he will prescribe water in this case, or at most he will administer a light wine, sparkling and lacking bouquet, and then the patient will drink a little water; thus, the effect of the wine will be less felt on the head and intellect"); Jouanna 2012b, 176; Bartoš 2020, esp. 22–23. Rufus of Ephesus, a first century CE doctor, also claimed that wine increases bodily heat; Jouanna 2012b, 173 with n1, citing Oribasius, *Coll. Med.* 5.7.1–2 (= 1.126, 26–33 Raeder).

126. Cf. Apul. *De Plat.* 1.17.1 (in Fowler 2016, 260, with reference to Beaujeu 1973) ascribing to Plato the view that a balance of wet and dry and hot and cold in the soul bestows health, strength, and beauty (*aequalitas ista sicci*

<atque> umidi, ferventis ac frigidi sanitatem, vires speciemque largitur), while an imbalanced mixture causes death.

127. *Vict.* 1.35, 103–104 (= 6.520,1–2 L.): ὀξυτέρην μὲν τοσούτῳ ἀνάγκη εἶναι τὴν ψυχὴν ὅσῳ θᾶσσον κινεῖται, καὶ πρὸς τὰς αἰσθήσιας θᾶσσον προσπίπτειν in Jouanna 2012a, 206–207 and 217. Cf. Camden 2023, 232–233.

128. *Vict.* 1.35, 104–106 (= 6.520,3–4 L.): ἧσσον δὲ μόνιμον τῶν πρότερον, διότι θᾶσσον ἐκκρίνεται τὰ παραγινόμενα καὶ ἐπὶ πλείονα ὁρμᾶται διὰ ταχυτῆτα.

129. Aretaeus, a close reader of the Hippocratic corpus (Roselli 2005) and Plato, esp. the *Timaeus* (King 1993, 26–28), recognized genius as a particular form of *mania*, which caused the afflicted to have odd visions (*Chron.* 6.5.8–9 = Hude 1958, 42.18–19: ἀλλόκοτοι φαντασίαι). Cf. *Phd.* 60e1–8 where Socrates claims he had recurrent dreams urging him "to cultivate the Muses" (. . . ἐνυπνίων τινῶν . . . πολλάκις ταύτην τὴν μουσικήν μοι ἐπιτάττοι ποιεῖν).

130. See n29 above. Cf. Telecleides in Ar. *Av.* 988 (= Tel. fr. 7 in L515) referring to the orator Diopeithes as ὑπομανιώδης ("crazy").

131. Thumiger 2017, 226.

132. Aretaeus listed astronomers, philosophers, and poets among the typical sufferers of this type of *mania*, noting that they tend to be very docile (*Chron.* 6.5.4–6 = Hude 1958, 42.15–16: τοῖσι μέν γε εὐφυέσι τε καὶ εὐμαθέσι ἀστρονομίη ἀδίδακτος, φιλοσοφίη αὐτομάτη, ποίησις δῆθεν ἀπὸ μουσέων. ἴσχει γάρ τι καὶ ἐν νούσοισι εὔχρηστον ἡ εὐπαιδευσίη). Still, this kind of *mania* can be found among less educated people (*Chron.* 6.5.6–7 = Hude 1958, 42.17–18: τοῖσι . . . ἀπαιδεύτοισι). Aretaeus makes here a categorical distinction between *mania* and delirium, which is temporary and aggravated by wine consumption (*Chron.* 6.1.4–5.1 = Hude 1958, 41.15–17: ἐκφλέγει γὰρ καὶ οἶνος ἐς παραφορὴν ἐν μέθῃ . . . ἀλλ' οὔ τί πω μανίη τάδε κικλήσκεται). Cf. Aretaeus, *Chron.* 5.4.6–5.5.1 and 6.2.2–3 (= Hude 1958, 40.10–11 and 41.20–21) where he attributes both melancholy and *mania* to dryness.

133. Henderson 1998, 9, ascribes the metaphor of wine as "the best of remedies" to Alcaeus fr. 335 (Lopel-Page/L142: 372 = Ath. *Deipn.* 10.430b–c: φαρμάκων . . . ἄριστον); Degani and Burzacchini 1977, 229; cf. *Cypria* fr. 10 (Kinkel 1877, 27 = Ath. *Deipn.* 1.35c = fr. 18: "Wine . . . is the best thing the gods have made for mortal men for dispelling cares (ἀποσκεδάσαι μελεδώνας)"; cf. Thgn. 883; Simonid. fr. 512; Alcaeus fr. 346 (= Ath. *Deipn.* 10.430c–d: "The son of Semele and Zeus gave men wine to forget their sorrows (οἶνον . . . λαθικάδεα ἔδωκ᾽)." Cf. Jouanna 2012b, 176: ". . . the medical writings of the Hippocratic Corpus never condemn intoxication. We must look to Plato's *Symposium* to find such condemnation from a doctor" (= *Symp.* 176d1–2; cf. *Leg.* 666a).

134. Aristotle notes that the *Laws* was written after the *Republic* (*Pol.* 1264b27–29). Sauvé-Meyer 2015, 1, with Kahn 2002, 107–108; cf. Zuckert 2009, 3–4.

135. Cf. Wilson-Nightingale 2013; cf. conclusion, p. 161.

136. On the educational role of "manic dancing" (*Leg.* 672b5–6: τὴν μανικὴν . . . χορείαν) and "raging wine" (773d1: μαινόμενος μὲν οἶνος) in the *Laws*,

see Pfefferkorn 2020, 259–260 and 262; 2021a; and 2022, 149–158 and 196; cf. Belfiore 1986, 431, citing Mnesitheus frs. 41 and 42 (Bertier = Ath. *Deipn.* 2.36a–b and 1.22e), where Dionysus poses as a great doctor, and fr. 45 (= Ath. *Deipn.* 11.484a), where excessive drinking is said to bring about "catharsis" of the body and relaxation of the mind. For the purifying effects of wine in Plutarch, see *quaest. conv.* 693a9–11 and b3. In Book 2 of the *Learned Banqueters*, Athenaeus champions moderation as the best way of drinking, while stressing the similarities of fire and wine (both excellent presents from the gods to humans) as well as the similarity between wine and the human nature (2.36e–37b); Jouanna 2012a, 193, and Austin 1985, 26. Cf. Jouanna 1978, 82–87, who argues that Plato modeled the legislator of the *Laws* on the example of the doctor, inspired by the doctor's need to persuade his patients to trust him; yet Plato still expects citizens to be enchanted by rhetoric, as Clark 2003, 149–152, notes; for rhetoric as another "drug," see Rinella 2010, esp. 210–223.

137. Ustinova 2017, 6; Ahonen 2018a, 5–6; cf. Walshe 2016, 124–128. For a comical version of this method, see Aristophanes' *Wasps* where Bdelycleon tries desperately to remand his deluded father, Philocleon, in the *oikos*. Ar. *Vesp.* 154–155, 200, 319, 337, 362, 380–383, 415–416, 442, and 452.

138. Anagnostou-Laoutides 2026, 282–283; in the *Republic* Plato claims that education instills in the guardians the virtues of "*sōphrosynē*, courage, liberality, and magnificence" (402c3–4: τὰ τῆς σωφροσύνης εἴδη καὶ ἀνδρείας καὶ ἐλευθεριότητος καὶ μεγαλοπρεπείας, 433d8: σωφροσύνης καὶ ἀνδρείας καὶ φρονήσεως . . . ἐγγενομένοις γε σωτηρίαν παρέχειν), virtues entrusted to the philosophizing members of the Nocturnal Council in the *Laws*, as I argue in chapter 3. At *Leg.* 643e5–9 education is defined as "the kind of training that makes someone desirous of becoming a perfect citizen, understanding both how to rule and be ruled righteously" (παιδείαν . . . ποιοῦσαν ἐπιθυμητήν τε καὶ ἐραστὴν τοῦ πολίτην γενέσθαι τέλεον, ἄρχειν τε καὶ ἄρχεσθαι ἐπιστάμενον μετὰ δίκης).

139. *Leg.* 934a2: πειθοῖ διὰ νεότητα.

140. *Leg.* 934a4–5: δι᾽ ἀκράτειαν ἡδονῶν ἢ λυπῶν, ἐν φόβοις δειλίας ἤ τισιν ἐπιθυμίαις ἢ φθόνοις ἢ θυμοῖς δυσιάτοις γιγνόμενος.

141. Jouanna 2013, 104; Simon 2008, 178; cf. Ustinova 2017, 6.

142. In the *Timaeus* (43d; 47d) Plato adopts the Hippocratic idea of humors mixing because of the revolutions of the soul. Jouanna 2012b, 220–225; Pigeaud 1989, 47–65. Also see Bartoš 2015, 239, who notes: "In agreement with the author of *On Regimen*, Timaeus holds that one can treat illnesses by moderating regimen in order to re-establish the equilibrium between the constitutive parts of man, although these are not fire and water, as we find in *On Regimen*, but rather soul and body." Also see Camden 2023, 25, 141 with n38, and esp. 207 (claiming that Plato's use of the *Regimen* in the *Timaeus* allows us to date the dialogue to 360 BCE).

143. Passavanti 2018, 18–19.

144. For clinical madness in the *Laws*, see 864d4 and esp. 934d5–7: μαίνονται μὲν οὖν πολλοὶ πολλοὺς τρόπους· οὓς μὲν νῦν εἴπομεν, ὑπὸ νόσων, εἰσὶν δὲ οἳ διὰ θυμοῦ κακὴν φύσιν ἅμα καὶ τροφὴν γενομένην ("There are many and various forms of madness: in the cases now mentioned it is caused by disease, but cases also occur where it is due to the natural growth and fostering of an evil temper"); for Plato's discussion of *amathia*, see *Leg.* 688e–689b and 691a (where *amathia* is said to cause disharmony in the soul and subsequently in the state); also see *Leg.* 732a, 734b, 737b, 784c, 831b, 886b, and 957e. The theme is reiterated in *Ti.* 86b2–4. Bossi 2000, 112–113; Jouanna 2013, 100. Cf. chapter 3, n156 (on Plato's objections to portraying clinically mad people in comedy).

145. Cf. *Ti.* 88b1–7: "When a large and overbearing body is united to a small and weak intellect (σμικρᾷ . . . ἀσθενεῖ τε διανοίᾳ) . . . the motions of the stronger part prevail and augment their own power, but they make that of the soul obtuse (κωφὸν) and dull of wit (δυσμαθὲς) and forgetful (ἀμνῆμόν), and so they produce in it the greatest disease, ignorance (τὴν μεγίστην νόσον ἀμαθίαν)"; cf. Xen. *Mem.*1.4.17; Pigeaud 1989, 52, and Robinson 1995, 107–110.

146. At *Leg.* 931e8, Plato claims that every right-minded man (πᾶς δὴ νοῦν ἔχων) respects his parents.

147. The bibliography on the dialogue is extensive and focuses on Plato's engagement with the theories of Protagoras and Heraclitus that underpin the definition of knowledge as perception but also tackles Socrates' definition of knowledge as true belief accompanied by a *logos* (an account; 201c–d); indicatively, see Giannopoulou 2013, 55ff.; Burnyeat 1990, esp. 9–10, 42–52; Cooper 1990; Bostock 1991, 40ff.; Lee 1999; Fine 1996; 1998a, 1998b, and 2017; Sedley 2004; Chappell 2005 and 2024; Thaler 2016. As Cooper noted (1970, 146), in the dialogue "knowledge is distinguished from other states of mind not by its objects but by how the knower is related to them."

148. For example, in *Resp.* 496c8–9 (τῶν πολλῶν . . . ἰδόντες τὴν μανίαν), Socrates describes as *mania* the obstinance of the many who find every excuse to avoid (and no doubt ridicule) philosophy; cf. chapter 3, pp. 96–97 on Socrates' definition of the ridiculous in the *Philebus* as someone unable to respond to his accusers.

149. Kahn 1985; Colvin 2007, 764–8; cf. Finkelberg 2017, 25 with n18, and 23–24 on Euripides' reported visit to the temple of the Ephesian Artemis, where Heraclitus had dedicated his book, making it accessible to visitors; cf. Arist. *Eth. Nic.* 1155b2–6. Heraclitus continued to be influential down the centuries: books were written about him by Heraclides Ponticus and Cleanthes in the fourth century BCE, and Plutarch in the second century CE. Hershbell 1977; cf. Finkelberg 2017, 26–33. For Heraclitus' influence on the theory of the Forms, see Arist. *Met.* 1078b13–17.

150. Kirk 1954, 150n1; Lebedev 2014, 27–42; Bartoš 2015, 118–129; also, Camden 2023 in nn120 and 124 above.

151. Finkelberg 2017, 48–50, with n36. I agree with Finkelberg that Diels' emendation in DK B67 is unnecessary (= D48: ἀλλοιοῦται δὲ ὅκωσπερ <πῦρ>

ὀκόταν συμμιγῇι θυώμασιν; ["God changes like (fire) when mixed with spices"]) and that reading B67 (= D48) through B65 (= D88) implies that god and fire are interchangeable.

152. = Her. fr. R88 (L526).

153. = Her. fr. R3b; cf. Simpl. *In de Cael.* 1,10 (Heiberg 1894, 294.13) claiming that "Heraclitus too conveyed his own wisdom through riddles (δι' αἰνιγμῶν τὴν ἑαυτοῦ σοφίαν ἐκφέρων) which did not mean what the many thought (οὐ ταῦτα, ἅπερ δοκεῖ τοῖς πολλοῖς, σημαίνει)"; Finkelberg 2017, 85. Cf. Käppel 2017, 214–222, who discusses Diodotus, the grammarian who wrote a commentary on Heraclitus and explains his understanding of the Heraclitus' philosophical paradigm in Saussurean terms.

154. Roig Lanzillotta 2018, 135; cf. Kahn 1981, 125, on Heraclitus' use of *hyponoia* (allegory); cf. Ael. Theon, *Prog.* 82.12–19 (on Heraclitus' use of ἀμφιβολία), with Finkelberg 2017, 35n70.

155. DK B123 (= D15 ap. Them. *Or.* 5.69b and Procl. *In Remp.* II. 107,5 (Kroll): φύσις κρύπτεσθαι φιλεῖ; cf. DK B54 (= D50 ap. Hippolytus, *Ref. omn. haer.* ix.9.5): ἁρμονίη ἀφανὴς φανερῆς κρείττων ("The invisible harmony is better than the visible").

156. ap. Plut. *De Pyth. or.* 404d; cf. Finkelberg 2017, 36n73.

157. Finkelberg 2017, 37–38.

158. Grey 2019, 190, with nn6 and 7.

159. DK B104 (= D10; ap. Cl. *Str.* 5.9.59.4/PG 9.92B6–9): "Which of them has reason or understanding (τίς γὰρ αὐτῶν νόος ἢ φρήν)? They are won over by popular singers and make the mob their teacher, without realizing that 'the many are bad, few are good' " (δήμων ἀοιδοῖσι πείθονται καὶ διδασκάλῳ χρείωνται ὁμίλῳ οὐκ εἰδότες ὅτι "οἱ πολλοὶ κακοί, ὀλίγοι δὲ ἀγαθοί"). Thus, Heraclitus anticipates Socrates' reference to the few true Bacchuses in *Phd.* 69d1–2 (ὥς φασιν οἱ περὶ τὰς τελετάς, 'ναρθηκοφόροι' μὲν πολλοί, 'βάκχοι' δέ τε παῦροι). Cf. DK B106 (= D25b), where Heraclitus reproaches Hesiod for his erroneous understanding of the nature of days (. . . ὡς ἀγνοοῦντι φύσιν ἡμέρας ἁπάσης μίαν οὖσαν); cf. DK A22 (= D23 ap. Arist. *Eth. Eud.* 1235a25) for his attack on Homer; cf. Hülsz Piccone 2015, 110–111. Probably because of his strong views, Heraclitus had a reputation for being arrogant: DK B78 (= D74), B101 (= D36), and B108 (= D43) in Finkelberg 2017, 21.

160. ap. Clem. *Str.* 5.14.115.23/PG 9.173A4–6.

161. Cf. DK B17 (= D3; ap. Clem. *Str.* 2.2.8.1/PG 8.937C12–14) castigating the many for lack of perception (οὐ . . . φρονέουσι) and inability to learn (οὐδὲ μαθόντες γινώσκουσιν), although they typically think (δοκέουσι) they know.

162. ap. Clem. *Protr.* 2.22.1–2/PG8.88A8–12; Finkelberg 2017, 133–134, following Babut 1994, 31–32, argues that the fragment targets not the mysteries per se, but the incorrect way they are celebrated.

163. ap. Cl. *Protr.* 2.34.5/PG8.112B11–14; also, Plut. *De Is. et Os.* 362a9–b4, with Finkelberg 2017, 97–98.

164. Finkelberg 2017, 135–136.

165. At *Resp.* 364a1–365c5, Plato despairs at the itinerant charlatans who profess to have knowledge of the gods based on Homeric poetry or perform rites allegedly instructed by Musaeus, Orpheus, Selene, or the Muses; the success of their deceit implies that injustice is rewarded; cf. *Resp.* 373b5–c1 relating how injustice takes root in an "unhealthy" polity swarmed by artists including "musicians, poets and their attendants, rhapsodes, actors, dancers, etc. ": οἵ τε μιμηταί . . . πολλοὶ δὲ οἱ περὶ μουσικήν, ποιηταί τε καὶ τούτων ὑπηρέται, ῥαψῳδοί, ὑποκριταί, χορευταί . . .); also see *Resp.* 606a4–7 claiming that poetry "satisfies and gratifies" (606a7: τοῦτο τὸ ὑπὸ τῶν ποιητῶν πιμπλάμενον καὶ χαῖρον) that part of our mind that "craves for tears and the release of a good cry" (606a4–5: τοῦ δακρῦσαί τε καὶ ἀποδύρασθαι ἱκανῶς καὶ ἀποπλησθῆναι . . . ἐπιθυμεῖν).

166. Shelton 2024, 255–256, on Socrates' reference to the Sibyl in *Phdr.* 244b4–5 as ἔνθεος.

167. Derived from the verb μάω/μά(ι)ομαι (desire/seek eagerly), *mania* is linked etymologically to the verbs μενεαίνω and μενοινάω, both meaning "to desire eagerly" and going back to the IE root *men-. This root is also related to the Homeric noun μῆνις (wrath) as well as to μένος (force/spirit/ardour) and μενοινή (eager desire); see Bomhard 2004, 33. Although Bomhard suggests that this root is different to the identical proto-IE root *men-, meaning "to think, to remember," in my view, the issue can be resolved by resorting to Meillet's etymology (1897, 10) according to which this root signifies "the mind to be set in motion (*mentem moueri*) . . . either for understanding (*ad intellegendum*) or for desiring or for getting angry or for warning (*ad monendum*)"; Muellner 1996, 177n1, translates the root *men- as "activate the mind." Ernout and Meillet 1951, 731–732, identify *men- ("*penser*") as the root of *moneo* ("advise, counsel, recommend"), also used to signify the act of predicting/prophesying (for example, see Tib. *El.* 2.4.51). Furthermore, Muellner observed that μῆνις is linked to the Avestan noun ma(i)niiu (good/bad spirit) and the Vedic Sanskrit noun manyú-, meaning "zeal, desire, anger"; Ustinova 2017, 220. Manyú also appears as an abstract noun in Hymns 10.83 and 10.84 of the *Rig Veda*. Malamoud 1968, 493–494; cf. Muellner 1996, 180. Muellner 1996, 182, and Malamoud 1968, 499, agree that the term represents a "permanent faculty in both humans and gods whose content varies in precise ways." Importantly, manyú, a faculty that exists "on the same plane as the essential forces of cosmic life" (Malamoud 1968, 499–500; Muellner 1996, 182) can be either negative or positive. Gods such as Indra and his associates but also (Mitra-)Varuṇa, Brahmaṇaspati and the fire-god Agni command a positive manyú (Muellner 1996, 183; Malamoud 1968, 500). In the case of the fire-god Agni, his manyú coincides with his fire quality. Muellner 1996, 183–184. Importantly, the

etymological association of *mania* and manyú allows for the articulation of both negative and positive aspects of *mania*.

168. See, for example, Kahn 1981, 298–299. Lambasting Dumézil's comparativist approach to which "even West seems to display an allergic reaction," Kahn argues that the intention to find comparisons smudges the inquiry with prejudice and "tends to produce historical fiction." Adding salt to the wound, he wonders: "[W]hy were Greek thinkers impressed by such Oriental wisdom, and how did they transform it?" Kahn 1981, 300. Nevertheless, we do know that by the second century BCE several works concerning eastern philosophical ideas were ascribed to Democritus (though they were possibly written by Bolus of Mendes); cf. Winiarczyk 2016, 88–90. In addition, see Duchesne-Guillemin 1963, esp. 45–47, on the notion of truth in connection with light; cf. Muellner 1996, 184, with Malamoud 1968, 502–505, discussing the adjective satyá ("sure to be realized") in connection with manyú. The latter is understood as the force that urges someone to fulfill "their desires, translate their thoughts into deeds." Cf. Wright 1998 on the meaning of satyá as "true," which is nonetheless debated.

169. West 1971, 183, on the Brihadaranyaka Upanishad; also see Seaford 2016, 209–211 and in the same volume, Chaturvedi 2016, esp. 52–53; furthermore, see Magnone 2016, 150–152 summarizing the discussions on "the hypothesis of influences between early Greek and Indian thought" (before arguing that Plato may have drawn his inspiration for the allegory of the soul chariot in the *Phaedrus* from the *Kaṭha Upaniṣad*). Still in the same volume, see Jurewicz 2016, 29 and Schlieter 2016, 169–172 on the role of conceptual metaphors in early Indian thought.

170. DK B30 (= D85) ap. Cl. *Str.* 5.14.104.2/PG 9.157B2–160A3; cf. DK22 B32 where the one wise thing has a fiery nature and is "both willing and not willing to be called by the name of 'Zeus' alone" (ἒν τὸ σοφὸν μοῦνον λέγεσθαι οὐκ ἐθέλει καὶ ἐθέλει Ζηνὸς ὄνομα) with Camden 2023, 252. On the role of heat and moisture in the human soul, see Bartoš 2020, 28; in the same volume, cf. Reece 2020, 119, and MacFarlane 2020, 317. Finkelberg 2017, 57–58. Cf. Betegh 2007 for an account of the soul as consisting of fire and air, the exhalations mentioned by Aristotle; DK B12 (= D65b); cf. DK A6 (= D65c = Pl. *Cra.* 402a) and DK A15 (= R43) ap. Arist. *De an.* 405a24.

171. Camden 2023, 249–256.

172. ap. Marcus Antoninus, *Adsemet ipsum* IV, 46. See Farquharson 1944, 68; cf. OF 437 ap. Cl. *Str.* 6.2.17.1/PG 9.229B4, discussed by Kahle 2011 and Finkelberg 2017, 84–85 with n3. According to Finkelberg 2013, 149–150, and 2017, 84, the change from plural "souls" to singular "soul" in this maxim indicates that while Heraclitus talks about individual souls to start with, he subsequently refers to the world-soul. Cf. DK B77 (= D101): καὶ Ἡράκλειτον ψυχῇσι φάναι τέρψιν ἢ θάνατον ὑγρῇσι γενέσθαι ("Heraclitus said that for the souls to become moist is pleasure or death"). On Porphyry's reading of this fragment and of *Ti.* 88b1–7 in allegorical terms with which Proclus disagrees, see Akçay 2019, 105–108. Also see, DK B118 = D103 cited on p. 69.

173. Heraclitus shows a notable disdain for Dionysiac revelry; see DK B14 and B15 discussed above. See Herrero de Jáuregui 2008, 142–3 and 156 (*ad loc.*); cf. Plutarch discussing Epicurus' views on the heat-producing atoms of wine: frs. 59–60 (Usener 1887, 116 = Plut. *adv. Coloten* 6; cf. *quaest. conv.* 651f) with Reesor 1983, 100.

174. DK B64 (= D82): τὰ δὲ πάντα οἰακίζει κεραυνός ("The thunderbolt guides all things"); DK B66 (= D84) we read: πάντα γὰρ τὸ πῦρ ἐπελθὸν κρινεῖ καὶ καταλήψεται ("For fire as it approaches will judge and conquer all things"). Finkelberg 2017, 43–44. Cf. Shelton 2024, esp. 257–258, who argues that in the *Phaedrus* the philosopher's ability to be godlike allows Socrates to claim philosophical inspiration as another form of beneficial madness. However, unlike the ἔνθεος Heraclitean Sibyl (p. 43 with n166 above) and other individuals who claim to be inspired when "invaded" by gods, "Socrates explains that the mind (διάνοια) of the recollecting philosopher comes close to the Forms through memory (πρὸς γὰρ ἐκείνοις ἀεί ἐστιν μνήμη κατὰ δύναμιν) and that it is the gods' closeness to the self-same Forms which makes them divine (πρὸς οἷσπερ θεὸς ὢν θεῖός ἐστιν, *Phdr.* 249c5–6)"; cf. Morgan 2010, 54, on the soul of the philosopher as "divinely occupied," unlike the souls that are "possessed" by *mania*. The concept agrees with *Leg.* 906a3–b4, discussed in chapter 3, p. 106, referring to the divine element in humans.

175. ap. Plut. *Conv. sept. sap.* 715e4–5; cf. ps.-Arist. *Pr.* 3.873a31–34 on wine, which being of a wet nature (ὑγρὸς . . . τὴν φύσιν), affects human intellect, adding: "Some who are melancholic by nature (μελαγχολικῶν τῇ φύσει) become totally dissipated in drunken excess (ἐν ταῖς κραιπάλαις ἐκλελυμένοι γίνονται πάμπαν)"; also see *Pr.* 3.873b11–12 (ὁ γὰρ οἶνος ὑγρὸς καὶ θερμός ἐστιν).

176. DK B112 (= D114): σωφρονεῖν ἀρετὴ μεγίστη καὶ σοφίη ἀληθέα λέγειν καὶ ποιεῖν κατὰ φύσιν ἐπαΐοντας ("To be of sound mind is the greatest virtue and to act and speak the truth is wisdom, perceiving things according to their nature"); Anagnostou-Laoutides 2022, 27.

177. Eur. *Alc.* 756–759: πίνει μελαίνης μητρὸς εὔζωρον μέθυ,/ ἕως ἐθέρμην᾽ αὐτὸν ἀμφιβᾶσα φλὸξ/ οἴνου ("he drinks in long drafts a pure and black wine, until the flame of this liquor has caused him to warm up"). On Euripides' interest in Hippocratic medicine, see Craik 2001 and Kosak 2004, esp. 131–192.

178. The three elements of Socrates' behavior at Potidaea that Alcibiades mentions (that is, being unaffected by wine, being unaffected by cold, and engaging in solitary inquiry) are in essence different aspects of his preoccupation with giving his own account instead of relying on the words of others; see Anagnostou-Laoutides and Payne 2021, 16–17 with n40, discussing *Phd.* 63d6–e2; cf. Xen. *Mem.* 1.2.1. Cf. chapter 3, p. 102.

179. Cf. Bartoš 2015, 182–183, with Xen. *Mem.* 3.14.7.1–5 where Socrates interprets the verb εὐωχεῖσθαι (feeling good) in connection with dietary practices.

180. Plato was familiar with solo reperformances of Pindar's poetry, praising the poet's wealthy patrons, typically represented as celebrating athletic victories in a symposiastic environment with notable komastic elements: as Agócs 2012,

205, has argued, Pindar already exemplifies the ambiguity between the solemn procession involving wreath dedications, known as *komos* in epinician poetry, and the fifth century drunken carousals also referred to as *komoi*; Rothwell 2006, 7–14; cf. Morrison 2012, 112, with Anagnostou-Laoutides 2020a, 127.

181. Corner 2005, 343–360 (drawing on Gentili 1988, 94), discusses homosexual and certain forms of heterosexual relationships (notably those with *hetaerai*) typically occurring at ancient *symposia*; in his view, the equality of the male participants is confirmed by sharing their objects of desire (slave boys and *hetaerai*), yet the symposiasts run the risk of becoming enslaved to their bodily desires thus excluding themselves from the symposiastic fellowship.

182. *Symp.* 177a6–c7. Socrates returns to the debate about the nature of Erōs' in the *Phaedrus* (237c10: περὶ ἔρωτος, οἷόν τ'ἔστι καὶ ἣν ἔχει δύναμιν); the answer comes a few lines later in 237d3–4, where love is defined as desire (ἐπιθυμία); according to Sheffield 2011, this definition forms the basis of Socrates' theory of friendship.

183. Cf. Aristotle's notion of *hexis* (*Eth. Nic.* 1105b25–6), the state of psychic equilibrium achieved by practicing virtue continuously. Cf. introduction, n12.

184. I summarize here Belfiore 1986, 424, who cites *Resp.* 398e6–7 and 403e4–6 (strictly forbidding drunkenness to the guardians) as well as *Resp.* 571c5 (where wine is charged with arousing the bestial and savage part of the soul).

185. Sauvé Meyer 2015, 330, s.v. 671e5–6.

186. Belfiore 1986, 430–431, with Boyancé 1951, 9–10, and Diod. Sic. 4.3.4 for a similar description of wine mixing; unmixed wine (οἶνον ἄκρατον), Diodorus claims, causes madness (πινόμενον μανιώδεις διαθέσεις ἀποτελεῖν), but when Dionysus' gift is mixed with "the rain of Zeus" (i.e., water), then it is most pleasant and corrects the manic and corrupting delusion (τὸ δὲ τῆς μανίας καὶ παραλύσεως βλάπτον διορθοῦσθαι); cf. Rinella 2010, 5–6, 27–28.

187. The *Symposium* is dated between 385 and 370 BCE; Thesleff 1978; on Plato's references to Euripides' *Bacchae*, see Sansone 1996 and O'Mahoney 2011a. Heraclitus too had effectively identified the Maenads with the Lenai; Valdés Guía 2013, 101–102, with Her. B14 and B15 (DK) (= D18 and 16); also see her n6 citing Hesch. s.v. λῆναι· Βάκχαι Ἀρκάδες (Schmidt 1867, 980) and the *scholia* to Clement of Alexandria, *Protr.* 16.25 (Stählin 1905/1972, 303): λήναις ταῖς Βάκχαις and 26.9 (Stählin 1905/1972, 307): ληναΐζουσιν βακχεύουσιν· Λῆναι γὰρ αἱ Βάκχαι.

188. Trans. modified from L495: 77; cf. l. 940: ὅταν . . . σώφρονας βάκχας ἴδῃς.

189. Roth 2005, 45–46. Pseudo-*baccheia* was often associated with tyrants; Anagnostou-Laoutides 2017 and 2020a.

190. Seaford 1994, 363–367, and 1996, 34–52; also, Seaford 2006, 27–30, and 2021.

191. Anagnostou-Laoutides 2021a, 14–15; Ustinova 2017, 123; and Folch 2015, 217–219. On Dionysiac dance as the result of the god's affliction with mad-

ness by Hera, see Boyancé 1951, 6–7, with Eur. *Cyclops* 1–3 (ὦ Βρόμιε . . . πρῶτον μὲν ἡνίκ᾽ ἐμμανὴς Ἥρας ὕπο); notably, in the play it is Silenus who relates this tradition. See Vickers 1987, 189–190 (with Plut. *Alc.* 1.7) arguing that Silenus likely pronounced Bromius as Blomius to hint at Alcibiades' mispronunciation of l/r. Cf. Belfiore 2006, 187–192 (on the satyr-like characteristics of the soul's unruly horse) and 196 (on the chariot as "a comic counterpart of the winged chariot of the gods"). Belfiore draws on Carpenter 1997, 25–26, who claimed that the satyr chariot, a popular theme in vase painting, ought to be understood as a parody of Zeus' chariot.

192. Euripides intends to draw attention to the theme of wisdom; thus, at *Bacch.* 178–179, Cadmus uses a wordplay to describe Teiresias who has "the wise voice of a wise man" (κλύων/ σοφὴν σοφοῦ παρ᾽ ἀνδρός). On Bacchic *sōphrosynē* in Euripides and Plato, see Anagnostou-Laoutides 2021a, 4–21, and chapter 3, pp. 72, 103–105.

193. At *Bacch.* 248–254, esp. 250, Cadmus is described as πολὺν γέλων, "totally ludicrous." The scene evokes Socrates' comparison with the funny-looking statues of the Silenoi that nevertheless contain statues of the gods at *Symp.* 215b.

194. Cf. Henrichs 1984, 235.

195. Mueller 2016, 63–64. Cf. Pentheus' superficial attempt to wear the Bacchic costume: obsessed with revealing the inappropriate conduct of the Bacchants, Pentheus misinterprets the Bacchic "alteration of consciousness" (*Bacch.* 944: μεθέστηκας φρενῶν) with the Bacchic attire, applying his usual hyperbole. In *ll.* 266–274 the opposition of appearances and essence is replayed: here Teiresias observes that despite appearing to speak *as* a wise person, Pentheus makes no sense (ὡς φρονῶν ἔχεις,/ ἐν τοῖς λόγοισι δ᾽ οὐκ ἔνεισί σοι φρένες); Rademaker 2005, 179–182.

196. Bussanich 2006, 210, notes in passing Socrates' calmness, a notable characteristic of "the virtuous man at peace with himself." And he continues: "Paradoxically, the picture of a calm and detached Socrates is combined with the Marsyas whose words cast a spell and intoxicate Alcibiades (215b–e), leading him to describe Socrates as a Corybant and surrogate for the god Dionysus." Cf. Kosman 1983, 216 (also cited by Bussanich), who refers to Socrates' calmness as "the virtue of the empty and mindless peace that belongs to the fully mindful and enlightened sage."

197. Cf. Eur. *Bacch.* 200–203, where Teiresias complains that οὐδὲν σοφιζόμεσθα τοῖσι δαίμοσιν . . . οὐδ᾽ εἰ δι᾽ ἄκρων τὸ σοφὸν ηὕρηται φρενῶν ("We do not act cleverly (οὐδὲν σοφιζόμεσθα) with regard to the gods . . . not even if the wise were found at the summit of the mind").

198. Xen. *Symp.* 2.1: ἔρχεται αὐτοῖς ἐπὶ κῶμον. See Hobden 2013, 217–222, on the ending of Xenophon's dinner party (*Symp.* 9.2–7), where the wedding of Dionysus and Ariadne is staged; the spectacle, performed with realistic sensuality, urges the banqueters to indulge their lustful side; this turn of the banquet cancels out Socrates' speech on Heavenly Aphrodite (*Symp.* 8.9–23); thus, Socrates and Callias decide to join Lycon and his son for a night walk.

199. At Ar. *Ran.* 218–219 (with Arata 2005, 66n19) Dionysus' drunken procession is described as a κραιπαλόκωμος . . . ὄχλος ("a drunken, crazed mob"); in the *scholia* κραιπαλόκωμος is identified as metonymy (μετωνυμικῶς ὁ κατὰ μέθην γινόμενος ὕμνος; schol. Ar. *Ran.* 216, s.v. Διὸς Διόνυσον ἐν Λίμναις; Dübner 1841, 281a.47–50); cf. Suda, s.v. κραιπαλόκωμος (Adler 1967, K2356 in 3.188). Arata 2005, 58–64, discusses the use of metonymy in ancient rhetoric and its vague association with metaphor. In my view, Aristophanes exchanges the expected ἐπικώμιος ὕμνος (Pind. *Nem.* 8.50–51; cf. Ar. *Thesm.* 985–988b) with κραιπαλόκωμος . . . ὄχλος, pointing to the drunken state of the worshippers. For Dionysus' association with κῶμος, as in Anacreon fr. 422, see Pires 2014, 87–88, 96–97, 211; also, Bierl 2009, with 320–321 with n137. Cf. Csapo 2013 on Dionysiac *pompai* and comedy.

200. Huss 1999a, 383–389. For a comparison of Plato's and Xenophon's *Symposia*, see Thesleff 1978 and Huss 1999b, 449–453; cf. Hdt. 6.129.2–4 on Hippocleides' symposiastic attitude, which included frenzied dancing (κως ἑωυτῷ . . . ἀρεστῶς; "in the way that pleased him"), which is firmly rejected by Cleisthenes of Sikyon; for the reception of these ideas about the appropriate symposiastic music and dancing in Plutarch, see de Jesus 2009.

201. Cf. Xen. *Symp.* 4.8. Immediately after, Callias suggests that they could even try some perfume, a suggestion sternly rejected by Socrates, who claims that the only odor suitable for free men is that of noble labor and *kalokagathia* (2.4). Interestingly, Socrates supports his view by citing Thgn. 35–36; cf. Germany 2016, 134–140; on Socratic *kalokagathia* in Xenophon, see Ollier 1961 and Dorion 2017a, 530–533.

202. Xen. *Symp.* 6.6: "The Syracusan, seeing that with such conversation going on the banqueters were paying no attention to his show, but were enjoying one another's company (ἀλλήλοις δὲ ἡδομένους), said spitefully (φθονῶν) to Socrates . . ." Cf. Socrates' complaint about being a victim of jealousy in *Apol.* 28a8–10 in n225 below.

203. At *Phdr.* 245b1–2 Socrates states that he limits himself to a few examples of godsent *mania*, though he could mention many more (καὶ ἔτι πλείω ἔχω μανίας γιγνομένης ἀπὸ θεῶν λέγειν καλὰ ἔργα). At *Phdr.* 242c5–d2 he poses as a prophet who senses his own error and figures out its expiation; on Socrates' palinode, see chapter 1, n177, and chapter 3, p. 85, with nn95–96; also, Hartmann in chapter 1, n209. At *Phdr.* 238d Socrates assumes the role of a poet of dithyrambs and at 241e of a rhetorician (note that Aristotle classifies dithyrambs with tragedy and comedy regarding their use of modes of musical mimesis; see, for example, *Poet.* 1447a14–16, 1447b25–26, and 1448a13–17, with Csapo 2004, 215–216). According to Asmis 1986, 160–161, 165, and 168, Socrates constructs here a new model of *psychagogia*; cf. Moore 2013 arguing that Plato also alludes here to Aristophanes' depiction of Socrates as *psychagogos* in the *Birds*. Cf. *Phd.* 60e1–8, where Socrates relates how, early on, he experienced recurrent dreams

urging him to "make music" (n129 above); apparently, before dedicating himself to philosophy, Socrates briefly dabbled "in composing ordinary poetry" (*Phd.* 61a8–9: ταύτην τὴν δημώδη μουσικὴν ποιεῖν); similar views are found in *Resp.* 591c1–d3 and *Laches* 188d3–9; with Anagnostou-Laoutides 2021c, 252–253, and forthcoming a1 and c.

204. Cf. *Phdr.* 242d7 with Rowe 1986, 163.

205. According to the text, these would be Apollo, the Muses, or Dionysus. Morgan 2010, 51; cf. Capra 2014, 255, with *Phdr.* 245b8–10: "The task is ours to prove the opposite, that such madness is given by the gods for our greatest happiness" (ὡς ἐπ᾽ εὐτυχίᾳ τῇ μεγίστῃ παρὰ θεῶν ἡ τοιαύτη μανία δίδοται). Equally, while Plato admits that prophetic *mania* (244b1) implies possession by the god (244b5: ὅσοι μαντικῇ χρώμενοι ἐνθέῳ), as in the case of mystai (244e6: μανέντι τε καὶ κατασχομένῳ) and poets (245a1–2: ἀπὸ Μουσῶν κατοκωχή τε καὶ μανία), in *Ion* 534e1–535a1, he adds: "For in his case especially [*viz.* Tynnichus the Chalcidian], it seems to me, the god meant to offer us proof . . . that the poets are nothing more but the interpreters of the gods, *possessed by whomever god each of them is possessed* (**κατεχόμενοι ἐξ ὅτου ἂν ἕκαστος κατέχηται**). To prove these things, the god intentionally sang the loveliest song through the basest of poets." So manic possession can reduce its avatars to mouthpieces of the relevant gods. Murray 1981, 93 (on *Ion* 535b–c) and 97–99 (on poetry as a craft incompatible with inspiration); cf. Aguirre 2016, 186–190 and 194–195, arguing that here Plato links divine inspiration with lack of judgement for the first time (cf. *Ion* 534b5: ἔνθεός τε γένηται καὶ ἔκφρων καὶ ὁ νοῦς μηκέτι ἐν αὐτῷ ἐνῇ).

206. *Phdr.* 265a9–10 and 242b10–c1: τὸ δαιμόνιόν τε καὶ τὸ εἰωθὸς σημεῖόν μοι γίγνεσθαι ἐγένετο.

207. Cf. *Symp.* 188c1–3 where Eryximachus observes that the interactions between humans and gods "concern nothing other than the preservation and healing of Erōs" (ταῦτα δ᾽ ἐστὶν ἡ περὶ θεούς τε καὶ ἀνθρώπους πρὸς ἀλλήλους κοινωνία—οὐ περὶ ἄλλο τί ἐστιν ἢ περὶ Ἔρωτος φυλακήν τε καὶ ἴασιν); Camden 2023, 46.

208. Havelock 1963, 152.

209. Cf. Parsons 1988, 8, on Pentheus' internal conflict, manifested in his hallucination during which he sees a double Thebes and two suns (*Bacch.* 918–919: καὶ μὴν ὁρᾶν μοι δύο μὲν ἡλίους δοκῶ,/ δισσὰς δὲ Θήβας καὶ πόλισμ᾽ ἑπτάστομον).

210. Chapter 1, p. 33. On the importance of silent reflection in the *Phaedo*, see Anagnostou-Laoutides 2023, discussing the philosopher's preoccupation with death (67e) and with attaining wisdom and truth (65e6–66a8) by relying on reason alone. Philosophers perceive truth with the eyes of the soul alone (66d10–e1: αὐτῇ τῇ ψυχῇ θεατέον αὐτὰ τὰ πράγματα). Socrates expounds here the theory of recollection, achieved in a state of quiet meditation (79d1–9): ὅταν δέ γε αὐτὴ καθ᾽ αὑτὴν σκοπῇ, ἐκεῖσε οἴχεται εἰς τὸ καθαρόν τε καὶ ἀεὶ ὂν καὶ ἀθάνατον καὶ ὡσαύτως ἔχον . . . τοῦτο αὐτῆς τὸ πάθημα φρόνησις κέκληται ("When the soul

inquires alone by itself, it departs into the realm of the pure, the everlasting, the immortal and the changeless . . . this state of the soul is called wisdom"). Cf. Pl. *Gorg.* 492e7–493a5. Plato implies that the theory is of Pythagorean origin; also see Finkelberg 2013, 154, who notes the similarity of this excerpt to Philo's *Leg. all.* 1.108.2–5 and Sextus Empiricus, *PH* 3.230.2–6.

211. Cf. Shelton 2024 in n174 above.

212. See Betegh 2021, 239–255.

213. See Merleau-Ponty 1962, 48–49, and 72, on understanding as reflection on an unreflective experience; cf. Karfík 2021, 214, 221–226, on Plato's discussion of perception in the *Timaeus* as "dependent on the encounter between things perceived and beings perceiving these things." Also see Renaut 2020, esp. 118–119, on emotions as "instruments of reason"; cf. Lorenz 2012, 256, also cited by Renaut, p. 112n23.

214. Called *himeros* at *Phdr.* 255c2: ὃν ἵμερον Ζεὺς . . . ὠνόμασε. At *Cra.* 406c4–6 Socrates proposes a novel etymology for Dionysus and wine: "Dionysus, the giver of wine, might be called in jest Didoinysus (ὁ διδοὺς τὸν οἶνον Διδοίνυσος ἐν παιδιᾷ καλούμενος), and wine, because it makes most drinkers *think* they have wit when they have not, might very justly be called Oionous (ὅτι οἴεσθαι νοῦν ἔχειν ποιεῖ . . . οἴόνους . . . καλούμενος)"; Plut. *quaest. conv.* 715a2: φησὶν ὁ Πλάτων 'ὅτι οἴεσθαι νοῦν ἔχειν ποιεῖ' τοὺς πίνοντας.

215. On the modern debate on phenomenological intentionality, that is, how we determine the outlook and content of mental states, see Horgan and Tienson 2002. Mendelovici 2018, 109–113, identifies intentionality with phenomenal consciousness (which relies on experience). On Merleau-Ponty's use of "second-generation cognitive science" to refer to language as an instrument of perceptual intention (more than representation), see Sambre 2009, 195–199.

216. Bussanich 2006, 212, argues that "the figure of Socrates represents Plato's refashioning of the Orphic-Pythagorean 'divine man' (*theios* or *daimonios anēr*) . . ." whose visionary reason draws on a transcendent source. By pursuing communion with the divine, immortal and eternal being (*Resp.* 611e2–3: τῷ τε θείῳ καὶ ἀθανάτῳ καὶ τῷ ἀεὶ ὄντι) in a state of purified mind (611c3–4: ἀλλ᾽ οἷόν ἐστιν καθαρὸν γιγνόμενον, τοιοῦτον ἱκανῶς λογισμῷ διαθεατέον), the soul is enabled to pursue self-knowledge; cf. *Ti.* 90a2–4, also in Bussanich, where the most sovereign part of our soul is defined as a gift given to us by god to be our guiding spirit (*daimon*) (τὸ δὲ δὴ περὶ τοῦ κυριωτάτου παρ᾽ ἡμῖν ψυχῆς εἴδους διανοεῖσθαι δεῖ τῇδε, ὡς ἄρα αὐτὸ δαίμονα θεὸς ἑκάστῳ δέδωκεν). Plato repeats the idea in *Laws* 906a3ff, cited in chapter 3, p. 106; cf. Moore 2015; also see Passavanti 2020, 187–190.

217. Socrates reiterates the need for constant training in his description of the chariot of the soul (*Phdr.* 254e7–8: ὅταν δὲ ταὐτὸν **πολλάκις** πάσχων ὁ πονηρὸς τῆς ὕβρεως λήξῃ . . .); cf. the "Test of the Wine," in chapter 3.

218. Cf. *Phdr.* 249d10–e1: τῶν κάτω δὲ ἀμελῶν, αἰτίαν ἔχει ὡς μανικῶς διακείμενος ("neglecting the things below, he is accused of being mad"); cf. Pl. *Tht.*

173c–e, where Socrates admits that the philosopher regards everyday concerns as σμικρὰ καὶ οὐδέν (173e3–4: "petty and non-existent") with Morgan 2000, 244–252.

219. Cf. *Phd.* 69b11–c3, where Socrates claims that truth, *sōphrosynē*, justice, courage, and wisdom (*phronēsis*) are a kind of purification (**κάθαρσίς τις . . . καθαρμός τις ἦ**). Cf. chapter 1, n177.

220. Although Socrates claims that *mania* is beneficial for the "rightly possessed" (244e6: τῷ ὀρθῶς μανέντι), which may even include poets (*Phdr.* 682a3–5 in Trabattoni 2012, 307–308), he is unforgiving of those who feign inspiration; *Phdr.* 245a5–9: ὃς δ' ἂν ἄνευ μανίας Μουσῶν . . . ἀτελὴς αὐτός τε καὶ ἡ ποίησις ὑπὸ τῆς τῶν μαινομένων ἡ τοῦ σωφρονοῦντος ἠφανίσθη ("Whoever arrives at the Muses' threshold without frenzy . . . remains unaccomplished, while the sane man's poetry vanishes before that of the frenzied").

221. See *Phdr.* 245b4 (κεκινημένος) in n96 above; also, the description of the drunken tyrannical man in *Resp.* 573c3 as μαινόμενος καὶ ὑποκεκινηκὼς ("a madman with a deranged mind") and *Pr.* 30.953b11–12 comparing the drunk to those who are by nature (and so permanently) "talkative, agitated, and prone to tears" (τοιοῦτος φύσει ἐστίν, ὁ μὲν λάλος, ὁ δὲ κεκινημένος, ὁ δὲ ἀρίδακρυς). Yet, cf. Pollux (*Onom.* 1.15; Dindorf 1824, 5) dated in the second century CE: Εἰ δέ που καὶ πνεῦμα εἴη μαντικόν, ὁ μὲν τόπος ἔνθεος καὶ ἐπίπνους καὶ κάτοχος καὶ ἐπιτεθειασμένος καὶ κατειλημμένος ἐκ θεοῦ, ὥσπερ καὶ ὁ χρῶν ἀνήρ· οὗτος δὲ καὶ ἐνθουσιῶν, καὶ κεκινημένος ἐκ θεοῦ, καὶ ἀναβεβακχευμένος, καὶ πλήρης θεοῦ, καὶ παραλλάττων ἐκ θεοῦ ("If indeed there is a prophetic spirit, the place is divine and inspired and possessed and added to and taken over by God, just as the man who speaks; this one is also enthusiastic, and stirred by God, and Bacchic, and full of God, and varying from God"). Once more, the vocabulary used to describe madness, intoxication, moral decadence, and genuine inspiration coincide dangerously, yet they are diametrically different experiences; cf. Wyss 2023, 192–193.

222. Philosophers were often regarded as madmen: at *Euthphr.* 3c an intellectual prophesying seems mad (μαινόμενος) to the crowds; Ustinova 2017, 320. At *Phil.* 46a2–4, Socrates refers to pleasures related to certain diseases; when pressed to explain which diseases he refers to, he says: "Repulsive diseases which the philosophers of dislike whom we mentioned utterly abominate" (Τὰς τῶν ἀσχημόνων, ἃς οὓς εἴπομεν δυσχερεῖς μισοῦσι παντελῶς). Cf. *Phil.* 51e7–52b9, where Socrates defends the pleasure derived from dialectic, since "the pleasures of knowledge are pure pleasures"; Delcomminette 2018, 50. Yet, he adds, these pleasures do not belong "to the many, but only to a very few" (οὐδαμῶς τῶν πολλῶν ἀνθρώπων ἀλλὰ τῶν σφόδρα ὀλίγων).

223. On sophists as deceptive imitators of philosophers, see Decolmminette 2018, 33–34, 38–39, 45.

224. On Socrates' teasing style and his rivalry with Aristophanes, see chapter 3, p. 72 with n15, and 91ff.

225. At *Apol.* 28a8–10 Socrates complains about the "prejudice and dislike of the many (ἡ τῶν πολλῶν διαβολή τε καὶ φθόνος) which has condemned many

other fine men"; cf. Morgan 2000, 172n37; Delcomminette 2018, 32–33. Socrates also relates the hostility he faces when he tries to dispel the misapprehensions of his audiences (ἐπειδάν τινα λῆρον αὐτῶν ἀφαιρῶμαι) at *Tht.* 151c5–d1; disinclined to believe his good intentions the "many" are "actually ready to bite" him (πολλοὶ γὰρ ἤδη . . . πρός με οὕτω διετέθησαν, ὥστε ἀτεχνῶς δάκνειν ἕτοιμοι εἶναι).

226. See the ps.-Hippocratic *Letter* (*Ep.*) 17 (= 9.348–380 L. = 75,25–92,12 Smith); Chitwood 2004, 125–126; Ustinova 2017, 341–342; cf. Kazantzidis 2018.

227. *Apol.* 26d–e; *Phd.* 72c4–6, 97c–100a; *Phdr.* 270a.

228. As Trabattoni 2012, 317, observed, for Plato, metaphysical reality refers "to any kind of reality that does not belong to the world of corporeal and movable things" and "to any kind of condition other than the present time, wherein men traditionally dwell." Accordingly, ". . . metaphysical knowledge coincides with that kind of knowledge that deems itself capable of uttering positive assertions about the classes of reality or situation I have just specified."

229. Ahonen 2014, 45, with Ustinova 2017, 33n48.

230. Xen. *Mem.* 1.1.13–14: ἐθαύμαζε δ᾽ εἰ μὴ φανερὸν αὐτοῖς ἐστιν, ὅτι ταῦτα οὐ δυνατόν ἐστιν ἀνθρώποις εὑρεῖν ("he was surprised it was not obvious to them that man cannot solve these riddles"). Cf. Eur. *Bacch.* 326, in chapter 1, p. 35.

231. Cf. *Crit.* 121a3: ἀλλ᾽ οὐ μεθύοντες ὑπὸ τρυφῆς διὰ πλοῦτον ἀκράτορες αὐτῶν ὄντες ἐσφάλλοντο and 121b7: πλεονεξίας ἀδίκου καὶ δυνάμεως ἐμπιμπλά-μενοι. On the issue of *akrasia* in the Platonic corpus, see the contributions in Bobonich and Destrée 2007; cf. Bobonich 1994. Socrates seems to identify *akrasia* with ignorance and lack of education (*Prt.* 359c–360d, esp. 360c1: θαρροῦσιν δὲ τὰ αἰσχρὰ καὶ κακὰ δι᾽ ἄλλο τι ἢ δι᾽ ἄγνοιαν καὶ ἀμαθίαν; cf. Xen. *Mem.* 3.9.4 and 4.5.6); Cooper 1999, 25; Callard 2014. The discussion on the paradox of *akrasia* (Arist. *Eth. Nic.* 1147a8–10), that is, the inconsistency between Socrates' belief that people choose what is beneficial for them (*Prt.* 332a–334a) and the fact that they clearly also succumb to the passions, is long-standing and I cannot do justice to it in a mere footnote. However, since, according to Plato, Socrates understands *akrasia* as the result of lacking proper education, it follows that such uneducated individuals are bound to have an imperfect appreciation of what is *truly* beneficial.

232. Xen. *Mem.* 1.3.6–8 in chapter 2, p. 60.

233. Belfiore 2006, 208. Cf. Sauvé Meyer 2015, 331 (s.v. *Leg.* 672c2–5) on the association of drunkenness and madness with "juvenile volatility."

234. Dionysus is invoked as Dithyrambos in the *Bacchae* (*l.* 526), and the dithyramb "was performed in satyr costume on some occasions." See Belfiore 2006, 205–206 with n59, with Pickard-Cambridge 1962, 4–7, 20, 33–35. In her analysis of the satyr dance motifs that Plato likely alludes to in the *Phaedrus'* image of the chariot of the soul, Belfiore (2006, 207) observes in passing that the philosopher's madness is *not* ordinary but involves "rational control." Thus, Socrates objects to disorderly *mania*, whether consciously ersatz or incomprehensible. Cf. Kurke 2013

on *choreia's* ability to connect its participants to the divine order of the *cosmos*; in the same volume, Kowalzig 2013 argues that *choreia* in the *Laws* functions as a model of achieving symmetry at the civic level; cf. Folch 2015, 219, arguing that "Bacchic and ecstatic performance programmatically undermines any meaning"; also, Pfefferkorn 2021a, 2021b, and 2022 on *choreia* as a symbol of *sōphrosynē*, Magnesia's core civic virtue.

235. Edmonds 2006, 349; cf. Belfiore 2006, 206, citing *Euthyd.* 277d6–e2 and *Laws* 790d–791a, where "initiation into the Corybantic rites is said to involve *choreia.*" This passage, on nursing mothers using Corybantic charms to settle their babies, is further discussed in chapter 3, pp. 79–80.

236. De Jonge 2015, 987–88. Cf. Pfefferkorn 2022, 235–236, noting that in the *Laws* Plato utilizes both sound and image in his semantics of mimesis to the point of referring to music as an image (669b5–8: λέγοντες τὸ περὶ τὴν μουσικὴν . . . ἐπειδὴ γὰρ ὑμνεῖται περὶ αὐτὴν διαφερόντως ἢ τὰς ἄλλας εἰκόνας); cf. Ruben 2016 on *Timaeus* (see, for example, pp. 25–29, 161–164, 179–182, 190, 204–205, 209–210, 294) and Hartmann 2017 across Plato's dialogues (for example, pp. 235, 405–411) both of whom discuss Plato's use of speech as an image.

237. Belfiore 2006, 210–211; Sauvé Meyer 2015, 323–329; Pfefferkorn 2022 in introduction, n39.

238. See Moss 2014 cited in n3 above. Cf. Papageorgiou 2004 on the competition (*agōn*) of *Kreitton* and *Ētton logos* in Aristophanes *Clouds*; despite the obvious homosexual references in the speech of *Kreitton logos*, Papageorgiou argues that Aristophanes stages an argument about desire in general rather than exclusively homosexual desire.

239. See, for example, Her. DK B14 (= D18); cf. Aguirre 2016, 94–95 (also discussed in n205 above) and Pl. *Resp.* 365a with Ustinova 2017, 114n9, noting that these rites do not induce madness.

240. Pl. *Leg.* 625a5.

241. ap. Stob. *Flor.* 3.5.8; cf. Ath. *Deipn.* 2.37b–c: νεανίσκους τινὰς ἐν αὐτῇ μεθυσκομένους ἐς τοσοῦτον ἐλθεῖν μανίας ἐκθερμανθέντας ὑπὸ τῆς μέθης. Cf. Betegh 2020.

242. This view is first expressed by Parmenides, fr. D51 (= B16.1–4 DK), cited by Arist. *Met.* 1009b22–25 and Theophr. *Sens.* 3; Sassi 2015, 460–466.

243. For Aristotle, recollection is linked with motions in the blood but also with moistness or dryness of the body; see *De an.* 450a27–b11; cf. Pl. *Phd.* 96b3–8, where Socrates wonders whether perception originates in the blood, the air, fire, or the brain; cf. Julião et al. 2016, 679–680, and Burnham 1888; also, see Pender 2014, esp. 99–102, who discusses the impact of these views on European thought well into the seventeenth century.

244. At *Phdr.* 238a–c Socrates argues that any excessive desire should be called *erōs*; Ustinova 2017, 304. For the tyrannical soul in the *Republic*, suffering in the grip of lust, drunkenness, and eventually madness, see n221 above.

245. Cf. Archil. fr. 11 (οἴνῳ δὲ καὶ παιδιᾷ πρὸς τὴν λύπην μάχεσθαι διανοούμενος) cited by Plut. *aud. poet.* 33a–b. Sauvé-Meyer 2015, 330 s.v. 671e5–6.

246. Also, *Leg.* 650b2–4: πεῖράν . . . ἐπιεικῆ ταύτην εἶναι, τό τε τῆς εὐτελείας καὶ ἀσφαλείας καὶ τάχους διαφέρειν πρὸς τὰς ἄλλας βασάνους ("This is a fair test . . . superior to all other tests because of its inexpensiveness, safety, and speed"). Cf. Lynch 2018b, 716–717 with n6, citing Prauscello 2014, 109–118; cf. Pfefferkorn 2022, 141.

247. Xen. *Mem.* 1.2.37–47 details Socrates' relationship with the politicians of his time.

248. Anagnostou-Laoutides 2026, 280–284.

249. For example, see Capra 2014, 150–155, on the importance of "terrible" rhetorical skill (δεινότης), which Socrates rates second to wisdom, and 175, on Plato's self-referential statement in *Leg.* 817a–c (with Gaiser 1984, 107–111, also discussed in Capra's appendix); here, Plato imagines responding to poets who wish to join the ideal city, stating that he is also a tragic poet and that his poetry is "the best and noblest" (817b1–3: ὅτι καλλίστης ἅμα καὶ ἀρίστης).

250. For example, Panaccio 2017, 11–107, claims that we have been bequeathed two traditions of mental language or interior discourse, one stemming from Greek philosophy and a theological one established by the early Christian Fathers.

251. Cf. De Vogel 1955; Prior 2001; Ustinova 2017, 2, 30.

252. Ustinova 2017, 30 with n287, citing among others Kahn 1992, 46, who defends the historicity of Socrates in the Platonic dialogues; cf. McKeon 1940, 73–91, on the use of history by Plato and Aristotle.

Chapter 3

1. "A grim and 'wineless drunkenness' is always lurking in the mind of an uncultured man."

2. On the association of truth and persuasion, see Morgan 2000, 69–70; cf. Morrow 1965 and Murray 1988a. Also, Hartmann 2017, 163–228, 310, 361, 397–399, 496–504; and Ruben 2016, 32, 71–75, 87, 112–117, 130–132, 153–155, 164–168, 176–177, 215–230, 237–238, 340, 361, 303, 318, 251–253, who focuses on *Timaeus-Critias*.

3. For Empedocles' association of tyranny with symposiastic conduct, see Timaeus *FGrH* 56 F134 and DL 8.64, discussed by Hobden 2013, 119–121.

4. In the *Republic*, Socrates' interlocutor observes that "everything that deceives appears to cast a spell upon the mind" (413c4: γοητεύειν πάντα ὅσα ἀπατᾷ), while later Socrates suggests that by rejecting poetry and its lies about the gods from a young age, the guardians are unlikely to be afraid of having been deceived in the soul about reality (382a8–382b3: ἑαυτῶν ψεύδεσθαι καὶ περὶ τὰ

κυριώτατα . . . πάντων μάλιστα φοβεῖται ἐκεῖ αὐτὸ κεκτῆσθαι . . . ὅτι τῇ ψυχῇ περὶ τὰ ὄντα ψεύδεσθαί τε καὶ ἐψεῦσθαι καὶ ἀμαθῆ εἶναι); cf. Delcomminette 2018.

5. See Murray 2018/2013, 252, on the centrality of the symposion in Plato's thought, also noting that much of Plato's "meaning is contained within context and metaphor"; also, Bartels 2017, 77, on the way the symposion "profoundly influences the conceptual structure of ἀρετή."

6. Eur. *Bacch.* 686: βαλοῦσαι σωφρόνως ("lying modestly"); cf. *Bacch.* 329: τιμῶν τε Βρόμιον σωφρονεῖς, μέγαν θεόν ("by honouring Dionysus, a great god, you act in accordance with *sōphrosynē*") and 504: αὐδῶ με μὴ δεῖν σωφρονῶν οὐ σώφροσιν ("I warn you not to tie me, as I am *sōphrōn* while you are not"). Cf. Schein 2016, 272. On Dionysus' role in disseminating civic *sōphrosynē*, see also Honestus' later epigram (*Athn. Gr.* 11.32, line 4: Βάκχος . . . χὦ μεθύων ἀστὸν ἐσωφρόνισεν). Anagnostou-Laoutides 2021a, 9 with nn36, and 37 and 11 with n43.

7. Murray 2018/1990a and 2018/1990b; Pellizer 1990 with Heirman 2013, 93n20; Corner 2010.

8. In the *Bacchae* Dionysus expects worship from every member of the community (see *ll.* 39–40 cited on p. 104 and 208–209: ἀλλ᾽ ἐξ ἁπάντων βούλεται τιμὰς ἔχειν/ κοινάς, διαριθμῶν δ᾽ οὐδέν᾽ αὔξεσθαι θέλει). For a recent appraisal of Dionysus' civic presence, see Isler-Kerényi 2021 and (in the same volume) Seaford 2021; also, Anagnostou-Laoutides 2021a, 11.

9. Davidson 1997, 59, cited by Corner 2005, 290.

10. Cf. Folch 2015, 79 with n60.

11. On the division of Platonic dialogues into early, middle, and late, see Rowe 2006, who claims that the *Symposium* (usually classified as a middle dialogue) is likely an early dialogue.

12. Plato appreciates poetry as a form of rhetoric; see *Grg.* 502a, with Griswold 2024.

13. Trans. Allen 1991, 117.

14. Aristophanes portrays Socrates as an arch-sophist. Cf. *Apol.* 18c9–d3: "The most irrational thing of all (πάντων ἀλογώτατον) is this, that it is not even possible to know and speak their names [i.e., of the accusers], except when one of them happens to be a writer of comedies (κωμῳδοποιὸς). And all those who persuaded you did so by means of envy and slander (φθόνῳ καὶ διαβολῇ χρώμενοι)"; at 18b8–9, Socrates is described as σοφὸς ἀνήρ, τά τε μετέωρα φροντιστὴς καὶ τὰ ὑπὸ γῆς πάντα ἀνεζητηκώς, drawing on Aristophanes' comic representations of him in the Thinkery; cf. *Nub.* 94–95: ψυχῶν σοφῶν τοῦτ᾽ ἐστὶ φροντιστήριον./ ἐνταῦθ᾽ ἐνοικοῦσ᾽ ἄνδρες οἳ τὸν οὐρανὸν, 102: μεριμνοφροντισταὶ καλοί τε κἀγαθοί, 154–155: Σωκράτους/ φρόντισμα, 266: τῷ φροντιστῇ μετέωροι, and 762: ἀλλ᾽ ἀποχάλα τὴν φροντίδ᾽ εἰς τὸν ἀέρα, where Strepsiades undergoes intellectual "labour pangs," evoking Socrates' psychic impregnation at *Symp.* 20c1–2; Edmonds 2000; for Socrates as a midwife at *Tht.* 151b, see Dypedokk Johnsen 2019, esp. 320n14, responding to Sheffield 2001a who reads

the two accounts of pregnancy independently; *Nub.* 192 (οὗτοι δ' ἐρεβοδιφῶσιν ὑπὸ τὸν Τάρταρον "[the pupils] study the darkness below Tartarus"). Following Aristophanes, Aeschines (*In Ti.* 1.173) refers to Socrates as a sophist condemned because of his association with the tyrannical Critias; see Fisher 2001, 319; also, Millett 2005, 23–24 and 28.

15. Before proclaiming that comedy should be strictly legislated; Folch 2015, 189–205, esp. 195 on *Laws* 816d3–817a1. Plato uses the verb παίζω in *Symp.* 216e5 to refer to Socrates' ironic and teasing stance toward his interlocutors (εἰρωνευόμενος δὲ καὶ παίζων πάντα τὸν βίον πρὸς τοὺς ἀνθρώπους διατελεῖ), which reflects the joyous ambiance of banquets (cf. *Symp.* 197e8 and 172a4); παίζω and the noun παιδιά (child's play) appear many times in the *Laws*, mainly vis-à-vis children's education but also drunkenness: 666b6, 667e8, 671e5–6 (τοιαύτη μὲν μέθη, τοιαύτη δὲ παιδιά), 673c9, d5, and e10, 685a8, 732d6, 761d6, 764e4, 769a1–3, 771e7, 789b6–7, 796d5, 797a8–c9 (on the importance of children's games for legislation), 803c6–7 (on being a plaything of god), 803d3 and e1, 819b2 and c3, 820d5, 829b8, 830e, 844d5 (παιδίαν Διονυσιάδα; "the plaything of Dionysus [= grapes]"), 864d6, 887d5, 936a4, 942a9 (I have omitted here references to military training or games as παιδιά); Ardley 1967; Pfefferkorn 2022, 214, on the false etymological association of χορός and χαρά in the *Laws*; cf. Hunnicutt 1990 and D'Angour 2013; also, Hartmann 2017, 335–339, on the use of παίζω to refer to the speech of the sophists.

16. Cf. *Leg.* 639c–e, where Socrates argues that most people react to hearing about drunkenness with praise or condemnation without thinking through the circumstances pertaining to it.

17. As Papakonstantinou has pointed out (2012, 1–7), wine drinking was employed in a variety of contexts (cultural and literary), which we cannot always reconstruct satisfactorily or presume to appreciate fully. Therefore, attention must be paid to the circumstances in which early poems about wine drinking were composed and received.

18. See Klooster 2018, 67–70, on the "speaker of words, doer of deeds" ideal (*Il.* 9.437–443), which stresses the importance of debating skills alongside military excellence; in the same volume, cf. de Jong 2018, 31. For models of wine drinking in the *Iliad* and the *Odyssey*, see Papakonstantinou 2009.

19. See introduction, n60.

20. Papakonstantinou 2012, 12–13; cf. Murray 2018/1983a, 17–21, and 2018/2008, 91–101.

21. Corner 2005, 4–46, esp. 13–18, criticizes Murray (esp. 2018/1983a, 1995a, 1983b, and 1995b; in agreement with Schmitt-Pantel 1992, esp. 46–48) for assuming an aristocratic structure for archaic Greek societies where symposia functioned as "private, escapist" events for the elites who focused on pleasure, having been politically defeated by the *demos*. But symposia were a major feature of the polis, not just of the embittered elites; Schmitt-Pantel counter-suggests the

notion of an aristocratic *polis* where elites claim political power. For Corner (2005, 188–197 and 235–258), the elitist aspects of the Greek symposion can be observed only by the end of the fifth century and have been anachronistically applied to the archaic period. In his view, (298) the symposion "constructs equality and is opposed to the productive and domestic spheres" (413–455). Cf. Wecowski 2014, 55–81, 318–328, who defends the fluidity of Greek aristocracy but regards its evolving character as one phenomenon.

22. See Alcaeus fr. 346 (Lobel-Page/L142) along with several other sources in Papakonstantinou 2012, 16–18, who notes that the material evidence also confirms that archaic feasts involved considerable consumption of wine. Cf. Corner 2005, 258ff., with Amouretti 1992, discussing the considerably more moderate wine consumption patterns of the average person, since wine production was a difficult, precarious, and expensive business.

23. For immoderate drinking in Homer, see Papakonstantinou 2009; see, for example, *Od.* 21.293–304, where Antinous suspects Odysseus, disguised as an old beggar and yet willing to compete with the suitors in the bow contest, of being drunk: οἶνός σε τρώει μελιηδής . . . ὅς ἄν μιν χανδὸν ἕλῃ μηδ᾽ αἴσιμα πίνῃ ("It is honey-sweet wine that wounds you, . . . : whoever takes it in great gulps, and drinks beyond measure"). Thus, Antinous tries to warn Odysseus off by relating the tale of the centaur Eurytion, who suffered madness (ὁ δ᾽ ἐπεὶ φρένας ἄασεν οἴνῳ,/ μαινόμενος) because of an excess of wine (οἰνοβαρείων). Here, both the social dimensions of drinking and the bestial aspects of intoxication are implied.

24. Cf. Thgn. 413–414.

25. See, for example, Thgn. 211–212, 509–510, 837–840; cf. Panyas. fr. 20, assigning the third cup of wine to Hubris, esp. 12–15: δείδια γὰρ τριτάτης μοίρης μελιηδέος οἴνου/ πινομένης, μή σ᾽ Ὕβρις ἐνὶ φρεσὶ θυμὸν ἀέρσῃ, . . . / ἀλλὰ πιθοῦ καὶ παῦε πολὺν πότον ("With the third round of the honey-sweet wine being drunk, I'm afraid of Hybris stirring up your spirits . . . So take my advice, and stop the excess drinking"); cf. fr. 22 and fr. 21, where he praises wine as the finest gift of the gods, which "expels every pain from men's hearts, provided it is drunk moderately; but beyond the measure, it is not so good" (4–5: πάσας δ᾽ ἐκ κραδίης ἀνίας ἀνδρῶν ἀλαπάζει/ πινόμενος κατὰ μέτρον· ὑπὲρ μέτρον δὲ χερείω).

26. Faraone 2008, 87–92, argues that this is not a complete poem but comprises five-couplet (ten-line) stanzas, which were originally independent but were joined together by Athenaeus much later. Nevertheless, the verses reflect popular views about wine drinking.

27. Corner 2005, 313–335, draws on Fehr 1990 and his analysis of the Homeric *ptōchos* (poor man) in discussing the connotations of bestiality and effeminacy associated with excessive drinking and represented in the comic figure of the pot-bellied wine-thirsty parasite; an early version of this figure can be glimpsed in Arch. fr. 124b West but also Alc. 129 (L142 and DL 1.81) where Pittakos' big belly is cast as a sign of his tyrannical character; see the sources cited by Corner

2005, 330. In classical Athens, unable to reciprocate dinner invitations, the poor man becomes parasitic and loses his equal status among his symposiastic peers; see Corner 2013a, 46–48 and 58ff., and 2013b, 227, 233–234.

28. Papakonstantinou 2012, 19; cf. Corner 2005, 191–197 (on the drinking habits of Scythians and the Cyclops); Murray 2009, 515–522; and Hobden 2013, 70–106 (on the drinking habits of foreigners in Herodotus).

29. Cf. Archil. fr. 120 in chapter 1, p. 25; Panyas. fr. 20.1–3 (= Ath. *Deipn.* 1.36d) pledging the first round of drinks to the Graces, the Horai, and Dionysus and the second to Aphrodite and Dionysus; fr. 21.2–3 (= Ath. *Deipn.* 1.37a), claiming that "every song, every dance and every delightful love harmonizes with wine." Cf. Panyas. fr. 19.10–19 in n32 below.

30. See Poem 4c (*Ath. Pol.* 5) where we read: ἦν δὲ ὁ Σόλων τῇ μὲν φύσει καὶ τῇ δόξῃ τῶν πρώτων ("Solon was by birth and reputation one of the foremost citizens"); cf. Solon 13.41 using the adjective ἀχρήμων ("he who lacks means"), also used by Pindar in fr. 124ab to refer to the liberatory effect of wine in connection with the self-illusion of the poor; Noussia 1999, 40. For Solon's use of the symposiastic setting to deliver a political cum martial exhortation, laden with epic connotations, see Steiner 2014. For Homer as part of Athenian education in the Classical period, see Ar. *Ran.* 1034–1036; Xen. *Symp.* 3.5 and 4.6; and Pl. *Resp.* 376e–378b, with Morgan 2011; cf. de Jong 2018, 20–22, who provides a more extensive bibliography.

31. Noussia 2010, 12 and 232; cf. Noussia 1999, 84 (= 2010, 277) on the concept of *koros* (surfeit, satiety) in Homer and archaic poetry.

32. Noussia 2010, 232, continues thus: "This idea is based upon the principle that the wisdom that produces a symposium without excess is the same wisdom that gives rise to the good government of a city." Noussia cites several Homeric and lyric examples advocating εὐφροσύνη ("joy," "delight") as the main quality that should characterize any successful symposion; on the history of *euphrosynē* in a symposiastic context, see Murray 2018/2005, esp. 267, citing Thgn. 1323–1326, where he advises his audience to replace *euphrosynē* with *sōphrosynē* as they grow in maturity; cf. *Od.* 2.310–311 and 9.5–10; Simon. 23; Xenophan. 1.4 and Anacr. 2 (West). The epic poet Panyassis 19.10–19 reminds us: "Wine is as much of a blessing as fire for us on earth (οἶνος γὰρ πυρὶ ἶσον): . . . . So, you must take the toasts at the feast and drink merrily (εὔφρονι θυμῶι), and not sit costive like a vulture after you have fed your face, oblivious of good cheer (λελασμένον εὐφροσυνάων)."

33. Plato names Solon in *Symp.* 209d7. On the familial relationship of Plato and Solon, see *Ti.* 20e (= Solon fr. 22); Apul. *De Plat.* 1.1; DL 3.1; and Proclus, *Ad Ti.* 1.81–82 (= Solon fr. 22a) in Flores 2013, 67–69. On Solon's reputation as the author of the Athenian democracy, see Schofield 2006, 76; Morgan 1998, 111–112 and 2015; Flores 2013, 34–38 and 189–190; and Anagnostou-Laoutides 2020a, 125–126, 130–131; also, Anagnostou-Laoutides and Payne 2021.

34. The bibliography is huge but see, indicatively, Long 2017. Plato discusses (and rejects) the possibility that virtue can be taught mainly in the *Protagoras* (Kahn 1997, 210–257; Nehamas 1999, 115–118; Gonzalez 2014) and the *Meno* (Rowe 1983; Weiss 2001). On the association of goodness with the nobility in archaic Greece, see Nietzsche's first essay in *The Genealogy of Morals*, on good and evil, with Clark and Swensen 1998, 13; on Plato's understanding of rational desires and his definition of intellectual virtues, see Kotsonis 2019.

35. Plato's excision of Homer and the arts from the ideal city in the *Republic* 10 has attracted undiminished scholarly attention; Nehamas 1982; Ferrari 1989; Urmson 1997; Moss 2007; Smith 2007; Clay 2011. Cf. Planinc 2003 arguing that the *Phaedrus*, the *Timaeus*, and the *Critias* draw on Homer's *Odyssey*; on Plato's use of Theognis, see Usher 2002, 211–212.

36. Plutarch juxtaposes fr. 25 (*Amat.* 751b) where Solon presents himself as a model of the erotic man, referring to his desire for young boys, with fr. 26 (*Amat.* 751e).

37. Beneker 2012, 35 with n75; Kochin 2002, 29.

38. Chapter 1, p. 27; Ustinova 2017, 29. Cf. Nathan 2020, 170n3, who takes *erōs* as "an ironic vehicle for philosophy."

39. Cf. *Phdr.* 242b9–243e4 on Socrates' humorous reaction upon realizing that he has delivered a speech against the lover as bad as the speech of Lysias that had so impressed young Phaedrus. Socrates immediately embarks on a *palinode*, assuming the role of a poet; Capra 2014, 66–71.

40. At *Symp.* 217e2–5, Alcibiades quotes the common proverb about truthfulness in wine, "whether you couple 'children' with it or no" (οἶνος ἄνευ τε παίδων καὶ μετὰ παίδων ἦν ἀληθής); cf. Aesch. fr. 393 (in L505) and Athen. *Deipn.* 2.37e (using the word *parrhēsia*) and f, and 2.38a–b. Although Socrates acknowledges Alcibiades' sincerity, which is encouraged by his drunkenness, this certainly differs from truth; cf. *Resp.* 523b–526b, where Socrates prescribes self-reflection as the only way to reach truth (προσαναγκάζον αὐτῇ τῇ νοήσει χρῆσθαι τὴν ψυχὴν ἐπ᾽ αὐτὴν τὴν ἀλήθειαν). See chapter 2, p. 65; cf. Sheppard 2008, 31–38, esp. 38: "Socrates and Alcibiades both display different versions of true rhetoric, a rhetoric which combines and transforms the styles of tragedy and comedy." G.A. Scott 2000, 138–139, compares Socratic irony to Alcibiades' intoxication as a way of telling the truth. Strauss 2003, 261: "This particular inspiration by wine is absent from the poetic representation of philosophy by Socrates or Diotima."

41. Destrée 2012, 112; Hobden 2013, 201–213; cf. Folch 2015, 68, 111–112, 137, 141–142, on Plato's use of metaphors to illustrate the imperfect performance of truth by mimetic arts.

42. Capra 2014, 61 with n10, on Socrates' tendency to associate jocular language with the truth as in *Phdr.* 265c2: μυθικόν τινα ὕμνον προσεπαίσαμεν (discussed in chapter 1, p. 31, with reference to Plato's use of metaphors). Trabattoni 2012, 318, notes that despite Plato's attempt to give metaphysical realities, as

determined through dialectics, some positive content, Aristotle is not convinced by his technique, noting instead that Plato fails "to outline anything other than poetic metaphors"; Socrates continues in *Phdr.* 265d1–2, admitting his whole discourse on *mania* was τῷ ὄντι παιδιᾷ πεπαῖσθαι ("a truly sportive jest").

43. Danzig 2014; Ober 2017; McBrayer 2017, 77–78; and Moore 2019a, 166–167, 176–189 (cf. his pp. 224–228 on Plato's *Charmides* where Socrates competes with Critias for influence over young Charmides); On Socrates' refusal to break the law in *Crito* and the *Apology*, see Kraut 1981; Domaradzki 2011a; cf. Lévystone 2019.

44. According to Flores 2018, Plato stages a gradual falling-out between Socrates and Critias who come to stand for opposed notions of virtue; Danzig 2014, 515–517; cf. Millett 2005, 23–24, 39–40.

45. See Hobden 2013, 105–107, on Critias' prose *Constitution of the Lacedaemonians* (DK 88 B3) and its elegiac version (DK 88 B6 = fr. 6 in L258: 466–467 ap. Ath. *Deipn.* 10.432d–433b). However, in DK 88 B1 (= fr. 1 ap. Ath. *Deipn.* 13.600d–e) Critias certainly praises Anacreon's symposiastic zest with reference to kottabos.

46. Critias, DK 88 B2 (= fr. 2 in L258 ap. Ath. *Deipn.* 1.28b–c); cf. Murray 2018/2016, 82 citing Anacreon fr. 415 (= Ath. *Deipn.* 10.427d) and Dicaearch. frs. 94–97 Wehrli (= Ath. *Deipn.* 11.479d); also, Pownall 2008b. On the association of Sicily with excessive tyrants and Alcibiades' reputation for striving to emulate them, see Anagnostou-Laoutides 2020a. Hence, Xenophon may well be here implying that despite Critias' public admiration for the strict Spartan life, he is in essence a tyrant like Dion I and his son, renowned for their drunken revelries; the comparison of Critias with the Sicilian tyrants is especially interesting given that Dionysius I was also a poet, like Critias; cf. n105 below and Alvino 2017, 548–558.

47. Danzig 2014, 522–523.

48. *Resp.* 561c–d, 571c4–5, and 573b–d details the symposiastic license that characterizes the tyrannical man, cited in n56 below; cf. Anagnostou-Laoutides 2020 and 2026, esp. 283.

49. See Rothstein 2007, 141, citing Aelian *VH* 2.13 (where Critias and Alcibiades appear together as two former disciples of Socrates turned villains) and 4.15 (where Critias is described as τυραννικώτατος δὲ καὶ φονικώτατος).

50. As Pownall (2012, 9) argued, "Xenophon (through Theramenes), not only labels Critias as a hypocrite, but also implies that his philo-Laconian views have no political or ideological basis but are confined to approval of Spartan social customs." Hobden 2013, 152–153. Although Hobden 2013, 153n73, is unconvinced by his argument, I would be inclined to revisit Usher 1979, who, pointing to the inconsistency between Critias' public advocation of *sōphrosynē* and his private penchant for drinking, regards the anecdote as designed to frame Critias' hypocrisy (cf. Pownall 2008a, 6–7, and 2008b, 20, also in Hobden).

51. See Jazdzewska 2018, 202–204, on Xenophon's *Cyr.* 2.2. Here, Cyrus defends those who cause laughter from the charge of arrogance, which he instead

applies to hypocrites, including those who "evidently do things for the sake of getting something or having some gain" (*Cyr.* 2.2.12: ὅτι τοῦ λαβεῖν τι ἕνεκα καὶ κερδᾶναι ποιοῦσιν). Cf. Aristotle's definition of the arrogant person at *Eth. Nic.* 1127a20–22 where we read: "An arrogant person (ὁ . . . ἀλαζὼν) is hypocritical (προσποιητικὸς) about having eminent qualities that he does not or to a greater degree than he does."

52. Pownall 2012, 11; Hobden 2004, 125, 132–135; Bevilacqua 2018, 475–476.

53. Rothstein 2007, 150, argues that Critias used Archilochus (whose name literally means "the leader of foot-soldiers") in political invective targeting Alcibiades or perhaps Cleon. Cf. Ar. *Ran.* 1053–1054 where Aeschylus reminds Euripides that "a poet ought to conceal wickedness (ἀποκρύπτειν χρὴ τὸ πονηρὸν τόν γε ποιητήν)—not to introduce it nor teach it (μὴ παράγειν μηδὲ διδάσκειν)."

54. *Prt.* 323b1–2. Morgan 2000, 140. Both Socrates *and* Protagoras are preoccupied with *paideia*; see Corradi 2017.

55. For the connection of wine and honey, especially mead, see chapter 1, p. 26.

56. At *Resp.* 573b10–c9, asked whether "a drunkard possesses a tyrannical mind to some extent (μεθυσθεὶς ἀνὴρ τυραννικόν τι φρόνημα ἴσχει;)," Socrates replies: "A man becomes a tyrant, precisely when through nature or habit, or both, he becomes drunk and lustful and gloomy (μεθυστικός τε καὶ ἐρωτικὸς καὶ μελαγχολικὸς)." On Plato's modeling of the tyrannical man in the *Republic* on Alcibiades, see Larivée 2012; Wohl 1999; Anagnostou-Laoutides 2020 and 2026, 283 and 287 with n96; cf. Finlay 1994, 58.

57. *Resp.* 439c5–d2; Belfiore 1986, 433.

58. Folch 2015, 71–82, esp. 82; Bartels 2017, 88, with *Leg.* 644d2–3: "The λογισμός that has become the shared conviction of a polis is called law (λογισμός . . . ὃς γενόμενος δόγμα πόλεως κοινὸν νόμος ἐπωνόμασται").

59. Folch 2015, 70, 75; Brisson 2012b.

60. Folch 2015, 78–79; as Bartels 2017, 88–90, explains, the three forces that influence the puppet (θάρρος, φόβος and λογισμός) are mythically represented as the cords or strings that pull the puppet. Also see Pfefferkorn 2022, esp. 35–37, 45–46, 50–68, 102, 113, 115–116, 122, 131,135, 138–140, 143, 147–155, 164, 175, 178–179, 253, 288–289, 293–294, 304–308; Pfefferkorn 2020; and Anagnostou-Laoutides 2026, 288–290; cf. Frede 2010.

61. Pfefferkorn 2020, 263–264 and 2021a, 354; cf. Pfefferkorn 2022, 35–37, 45–46, 50–60, 64–68, 113, 115, 138–143, 147–148, 152–155, 178–179, 288–296, 304–308; cf. Balot 2014, 38–43 who reads the episode as highlighting the limitations of human nature.

62. *Bacch.* 247: τόδ᾽ ἄλλο θαῦμα referring to old Teiresias dressed as a Bacchant, 449: ἀνὴρ θαυμάτων ἥκει and 1063: τοῦ ξένου τὸ θαῦμ᾽ ὁρῶ referring to Dionysus, 667: ὡς δεινὰ δρῶσι θαυμάτων τε κρείσσονα and 716: ὡς δεινὰ δρῶσι θαυμάτων τ᾽ ἐπάξια on the amazing achievements of the Bacchants, and 693: θαῦμ᾽ ἰδεῖν εὐκοσμίας on the orderly behavior of the Bacchants. Also, note

the association of wonder with philosophy as argued by Aristotle in *Met.* 982b with chapter 1, n157.

63. Pfefferkorn 2021b, 337–345, with n10 citing *Republic* 389d9–e2, 430e1–2, 6–9, 432a6–b1, where similar discussions were introduced.

64. This view is close to Thucydides' *Funeral Oration*, delivered in 431 BCE. See Thuc. 2.38.1: καὶ μὴν καὶ τῶν πόνων πλείστας ἀναπαύλας τῇ γνώμῃ ἐπορισάμεθα, ἀγῶσι μέν γε καὶ θυσίαις διετησίοις νομίζοντες, ἰδίαις δὲ κατασκευαῖς εὐπρεπέσιν, ὧν καθ᾽ ἡμέραν ἡ τέρψις τὸ λυπηρὸν ἐκπλήσσει ("And truly we provided plenty of respites for the mind from work, by holding games and sacrifices throughout the year, and we are also well accustomed to elegant homes, and every day the delight of these things expels our grief").

65. By staging his own show, Plato responds to his criticism (*Resp.* 599d–e; *Leg.* 858e) that Homer's poetry did not improve the legislation of any city. Griffith 2016, 76; also, Schöpsdau, 2003, 589; cf. Balot 2024, 337–353 on the "drama" of humans who "have no access to the truth" (on p. 348). For the overwhelming preference for Dionysiac *choros* in democratic Athens and Plato's objections, see Kowalzig 2004, 42–49.

66. *Leg.* 790e8–10: Δειμαίνειν ἐστίν που ταῦτ᾽ ἀμφότερα τὰ πάθη, καὶ ἔστι δείματα δι᾽ ἕξιν φαύλην τῆς ψυχῆς τινα. Also see Anagnostou-Laoutides 2026, 289.

67. Sauvé-Meyer 2015, 327 s.v. 671d5–7, translates ἀθορύβους as "undisturbed"; Bartels 2017, 85 with n39; cf. Pfefferkorn 2022, 43–44.

68. By using similar vocabulary in *Leg.* 671a (θορυβώδης), Plato guides the readers to a revision of his arguments in Book 1, now situated more explicitly in a civic context. Cf. Xen. *Symp.* 7.1: θορύβου δὲ ὄντος ὁ Σωκράτης αὖ πάλιν εἶπεν; also, see p. 98 for Alcibiades' noisy entrance into the house of Agathon, drunk and supported by a flute-girl. For the comparison between a symposiarch who ought to be ἀθόρυβος and a seasick steersman, see Bartels 2020, *passim* but esp. 154, where she notes: "In the metaphorical sense (referring to the soul), θόρυβος and θορυβεῖσθαι often refer to fear as a 'disturbance' of the soul's tranquillity." Accordingly, noisy banquets are associated with drunkenness and disorder, which reflects the cognitive state of the participants; also see Anagnostou-Laoutides 2026, 287.

69. *Resp.* 403e2–3: παντὶ γάρ που μᾶλλον ἐγχωρεῖ ἢ φύλακι μεθυσθέντι ("the guardian is the last person to whom getting drunk should be allowed") and 562d1–2: Ὅταν οἶμαι δημοκρατουμένη πόλις ἐλευθερίας διψήσασα κακῶν οἰνοχόων προστατούντων τύχῃ, καὶ πορρωτέρω τοῦ δέοντος ἀκράτου αὐτῆς μεθυσθῇ, τοὺς ἄρχοντας δή . . . κολάζει αἰτιωμένη ὡς μιαρούς τε καὶ ὀλιγαρχικούς ("when a democratic city athirst for liberty gets as its leaders bad cupbearers and becomes intoxicated by drinking too much of that unmixed wine . . . it chastises its governors accusing them of being foul oligarchs"). On the dangers of giving in to pleasure, see *Resp.* 561b1 (μὴ πέρα ἐκβακχευθῇ); cf. 426a7–8 on being unable to hear the truth before refraining from drunkenness and other excesses

(. . . τὸ πάντων ἔχθιστον ἡγεῖσθαι τὸν τἀληθῆ λέγοντα, ὅτι πρὶν ἂν μεθύων καὶ ἐμπιμπλάμενος καὶ ἀφροδισιάζων καὶ ἀργῶν παύσηται).

70. Belfiore 1986, 424; Sauvé-Meyer 2015, 326–327; for the identification of the symposiarch with the lawgiver in the *Laws*, see Bartels 2017, 95, 99, and 111. The identity of the Athenian Stranger has attracted much scholarly discussion; see indicatively, Gadamer 1980, 71; Klosko 1986, 198, who along with Cicero (*Leg.* 1.4.15), suggests that the Stranger is Plato himself; Morrow 1960, 9–11; Saunders 1992, 469; and Stalley 1983, 9, 14–15, 17–18, argued that here Plato reworks Socrates' positions from the *Republic*. Strauss 1975, 1–2; Pangle 1980, 378–379. Planinc 1991, 26, suggested that Plato imagines here what would happen if Socrates were engaged as a counselor by leading statesmen of his time. All sources are cited by Zuckert 2004, 374, who argues that the Athenian Stranger, distinct from both Plato and Socrates, is tasked in the *Laws* with outlining Socratic political philosophy.

71. *Leg.* 653a1–3: τούτου [= ὀρθῆς παιδείας] γάρ, ὥς γε ἐγὼ τοπάζω τὰ νῦν, ἔστιν ἐν τῷ ἐπιτηδεύματι τούτῳ καλῶς κατορθουμένῳ σωτηρία ("For the salvation of this [= of correct education] depends, as I now conjecture, upon the correct establishment of the institution mentioned [= that is the symposion]"), with Bartels 2017, 103–104 and 106–108. Cf. chapter 2, p. 69.

72. Schöpsdau 1994, 253–256; Pfefferkorn 2022, 110–112, 141–142 with n89, 209–210, 291–293; Pfefferkorn 2021b, 343–346; cf. Ford 2004, 314 and 331–333, on Aristotle's views on music as a means of ethical training.

73. For Socrates' argument in the *Laws* that education should include rational persuasion, see Bobonich 1991, expanding on the views of Morrow 1953 and Stalley 1983; cf. Murray 1988b cited by Bobonich 1991, 388n87. Also, *Symp.* 216a4, where Socrates asks Alcibiades to "lend him his ears" (παρέχειν τὰ ὦτα), in essence, an invitation to Alcibiades to be persuaded.

74. Pfefferkorn 2022, 112 and 142.

75. Bartels 2017, 92–99; Pfefferkorn 2022, esp. 55–58, 62–66, 113–131, 133–141, 145–154, 306–308, 310–311; cf. Pfefferkorn 2020, 258–260, arguing that Plato uses a *reverse analogy* of courage and moderation, "namely the confrontation of two potions (φάρμακον, 647e1), one generating fear in order to train courage, the other generating fearlessness, thus fostering moderation" (p. 259); in my view, the reverse results of employing fear (leading to courage) and boldness (leading to moderation) reflect Plato's conviction that everything can have two sides depending on its use (for example, music, pleasure etc.; cf. n81 below); also, see Militello 2020 in the same volume on the role of shame and its role in promoting moderation in the *Republic*.

76. Sauvé-Meyer 2015, 295 s.v. 667c6–7; Pfefferkorn 2022, 234; cf. *Leg.* 655b10, 657a8–10 and b3; cf. Calame 2013. Also, Folch 2015, 39–40, who notes Plato's punning between "**μέθης**, μεθ' ὧν, **μέθοδος**" aiming to effect "a convergence of the *Laws*' arguments with its literary soundscape."

77. Bartels 2017, 110; Pfefferkorn 2022, 145–146, 178, and 217–218; cf. *Resp.* 401d. At *Leg.* 655c9–d1 Plato disagrees with the uncritical opinion of the many that "the correctness of music lies in its power to afford pleasure to souls" (καίτοι λέγουσίν γε οἱ πλεῖστοι μουσικῆς ὀρθότητα εἶναι τὴν ἡδονὴν ταῖς ψυχαῖς πορίζουσαν δύναμιν); cf. *Leg.* 661a5–6: τὰ γὰρ ὑπὸ τῶν πολλῶν λεγόμεν᾽ ἀγαθὰ οὐκ ὀρθῶς λέγεται ("the things said by the many to be good are not identified correctly") and *Leg.* 670b8–c4 (on the crowd's inability to appreciate musical harmony; γελοῖος γὰρ ὅ γε πολὺς ὄχλος ἡγούμενος ἱκανῶς γιγνώσκειν τό τε εὐάρμοστον καὶ εὔρυθμον καὶ μή).

78. Note that at *Resp.* 607a–608b Socrates and Glaucon struggle to abstain from tragic performances for lack of education. Cf. Campeggiani 2020, esp. pp. 47–52, on Plato's appreciation of the impact of poetry on human perception. On p. 39 Campegianni lists the numerous references to Homer in the *Republic*: 377b5–9, 377c2–5, 378d7–e1, 386a6–7, 387b1–6, 395c3–d3, 401b1–d3, 401d5–402a4, 605b7–c4, 605c6–8, 606a2–b8, 606d1–7, 607a5–8, and 608a6–b2. On the concept of harmony in the *Laws*, see Pfefferkorn 2022, 93–97, 105–107, 180–181, 210–216, 231, 233, 238, 240, 246, 253, 293, 307, 309; also, see Anagnostou-Laoutides forthcoming c on the Pythagorean origins of Plato's concept of harmony and its application both in the *Republic* and the *Laws*; cf. Anagnostou-Laoutides 2024a, 2 with n10, and forthcoming a1; also see Chaturvedi 2016, 41–54 on the early uses of *harmonia* in Greek literature and the pre-Socratics, mainly Heraclitus, Empedocles and Philolaos, and their correspondence with the uses and meanings of ṛtá in the Rigveda hymns.

79. Pfefferkorn 2022, 25–26 and 221–222. At *Phil.* 36c–41b, Plato claims that there are "false pleasures" (cf. chapter 2, n222); see White 2001; Berman 1991 and Frede 2010, 120. Cf. Murray 2018/2005, 269, on the historical development of the word *euphrosynē* in connection with symposiastic pleasure; despite being associated with physical pleasure (*hēdonē*), as at Xen. *Mem.* 2.1.29, Aristotle defended *euphrosynē* as closest to philosophical life (*Protr.* 91.4).

80. Plut. *quaest. conv.* 704c–d compares a drunken group trying to sober up from dancing, "disgraceful for freeborn men" (συνεκινοῦντο κινήσεις ἀνελευθέρους), to those "recovering from madness" (ὥσπερ ἐκ μανίας). On Bacchic dancing and madness, see Xen. *Symp.* 2.19.5; cf. Artem. *Oneir.* 1.76, 2.37, and 4.39 where dreaming of dancing predicts mental derangement. Plato debates here (*Leg.* 775c4–8) the importance of being sober for the purposes of procreation, echoing popular medical lore; Hipp. *Steril.* 218 (= 8.422.18–20 L.) with Jouanna 2012b, 184; Arist. *Pr.* 3.871a24–26 and 872b15–24; Plut. *quaest. conv.* 623e, 652d, 655a–b, with Corvisier 2003, 130–131; cf. Plut. *Lyc.* 15.3–5; Soranus, *Gyn.* 1.36; 2.44.113.

81. See Sauvé-Meyer 2015, 317 s.v. *Leg.* 670b2–4; Folch 2015, 217–219; and Belfiore 1986, 431–432 with n40, on the Athenian politician Critias (fr. 6.20–21 West) who argued that moderate wine drinking produces health and *sōphrosynē*.

Plato made similar remarks in the *Republic*, that although poetry appears to be "pleasant . . . and beneficial to political systems and human life" (607d9–10: ἡδεῖα . . . καὶ ὠφελίμη), it is not beneficial (607e5: μὴ ὠφέλιμον). Also, see *Leg.* 816d4–8: τὰ δὲ τῶν αἰσχρῶν σωμάτων καὶ διανοημάτων καὶ τῶν ἐπὶ τὰ τοῦ γέλωτος κωμῳδήματα τετραμμένων, κατὰ λέξιν τε καὶ ᾠδὴν καὶ κατὰ ὄρχησιν καὶ κατὰ τὰ τούτων πάντων μιμήματα κεκωμῳδημένα, ἀνάγκη μὲν θεάσασθαι καὶ γνωρίζειν ("The actions of ugly bodies and ugly ideas and those who engage laugh-provoking comic-acting, through speech, song, and dance, and all these representations found in comedy—all this we must necessarily examine and get to know"); cf. n156 below.

82. Cf. *Leg.* 648d, 649a–b, 649e, 650a–b. Belfiore 1986, 433–434; Pfefferkorn 2022, 68–113, 306–311, and 2021, 347, 354–356; cf. Jouanna 2012d, 22–23, on earlier comparisons of political leaders to doctors, notably in Pindar.

83. Cf. *Leg.* 638d2–8, where Plato employs drunkenness as an example of debate among people, with some presenting "those who abstain as victorious in battle" (τοὺς μὴ χρωμένους αὐτῷ ὁρῶμεν νικῶντας μαχομένους). Plato insists that there is a "correct method" of judging all such things (περὶ ἁπάντων τῶν τοιούτων ὀρθὴν μέθοδον ἡμῖν δηλοῦν), echoing his views in *Symp.* 180e4–181a6.

84. Capra 2014, 150–155, with Pl. *Apol.* 17a–b; Capra traces the argument in the *Phaedrus*, where Socrates' young interlocutor expresses his unreserved admiration for Lysias, "the cleverest of present-day authors" (*Phdr.* 228a2: δεινότατος ὢν τῶν νῦν γράφειν); cf. Gonzalez 2011 juxtaposing the hermeneutics of poetry and philosophy in the *Phaedrus* and *Ion*, distinguished by the philosopher's ability to exercise *sōphrosynē*.

85. See Xen. *Men.* 1.1.11 cited in the chapter 2, p. 67.

86. Socrates made similar statements in the *Apology* (17b4–8, 20d5–6, 22b5–6, 24a4–5); Bussanich 2006, 203. Cf. Hartmann 2017, 72, 147–148, 265–266, on Socrates' rhetorical dexterity, which allows him to juxtapose his accusers' eloquent speeches to his own plain but truthful account of events, a trope also at play in the *Symposium*.

87. Hence, Plutarch argues in *quaest. conv.* 716a5–7 that wine stimulates the passions (κινοῦντα τὰ πάθη τὸν οἶνον) only in the wicked whose "deliberative faculty is never in a sober state" (οὐδέποτε νήφει τὸ βουλευόμενον). His view echoes that of Zeno in introduction, n96, and chapter 2, n45.

88. Cooper 1999, 79.

89. Cf. Demos 1999, 19, with the criticism of Yates 2000 who argues that, far from attempting to rescue Protagoras from the "ravages of sophistry," Socrates aims to use this analysis to attack both the poets and the sophists.

90. Anagnostou-Laoutides and Payne 2021, 10 (with n18 citing among others Trivigno 2013, 509; Frede 1986; Woodbury 1953, 150–159; Parry 1965, 315; and Babut 1975, 44) and 18–22; also see Corradi 2017, esp. 86–88; on Aristophanes' comic engagement with the poetry of Simonides, see Rawles 2013.

91. For νάμα as water, see esp. Aesch. fr. 304.2–3: πᾶσα δ᾽ εὐθαλὴς Αἴγυπτος ἁγνοῦ **νάματος πληρουμένη**. For the image of the water stream (and its variants) as metaphorically signifying poetic inspiration, see Crowther 1979, 2, citing *AP* 7.55, 9.64, 11.24 and Pind. *Ol.* 6.84–87; also, Nünlist 1998, 195–205.

92. Hes. *WD* 592–596: ἐπὶ δ᾽ αἴθοπα πινέμεν οἶνον,/ . . . / κρήνης τ᾽ ἀενάου καὶ ἀπορρύτου, ἥτ᾽ ἀθόλωτος,/ τρὶς ὕδατος προχέειν, τὸ δὲ τέτρατον ἱέμεν οἴνου. Bershadsky 2011, 9–10. Cf. Alcaeus fr. 347a (= Procl. *In Hes. WD* 584 ascribing a similar song to Alcaeus). Also, see Eur. *Bacch.* 278–283 crediting Dionysus with the discovery of wine, which lulls grief and daily cares with sleep reiterated in *Bacch.* 772; chapter 2, p. 63.

93. Also, *Phdr.* 238c7: θεῖον πάθος πεπονθέναι.

94. *Phdr.* 242d7: εὐήθη καὶ ὑπό τι ἀσεβῆ.

95. *Phdr.* 243a3–5: "for those who sin about mythology (τοῖς ἁμαρτάνουσι περὶ μυθολογίαν) there is an ancient purification (καθαρμὸς ἀρχαῖος), which Homer did not know, but Stesichorus did."

96. Thus, unlike Homer, Stesichorus grasped immediately that Helen was offended by the fallacy of his verses (*Phdr.* 243a10: οὐκ ἔστ᾽ ἔτυμος λόγος οὗτος; "This tale is not true"). Socrates, aligning with Stesichorus, repeats the phrase at the start of his second speech, at *Phdr.* 244a4: λεκτέος δὲ ὧδε, ὅτι οὐκ ἔστ᾽ ἔτυμος λόγος.

97. *Phdr.* 265a4–6: . . . ἐναντίω που ἤστην· ὁ μὲν γὰρ ὡς τῷ ἐρῶντι, ὁ δ᾽ ὡς τῷ μὴ δεῖ χαρίζεσθαι, ἐλεγέτην.

98. *Phdr.* 265c6–8: . . . λάβωμεν, ὡς ἀπὸ τοῦ ψέγειν πρὸς τὸ ἐπαινεῖν ἔσχεν ὁ λόγος μεταβῆναι; Hartmann 2017, 342–346.

99. *Phdr.* 259e–260a, 273b–274a. Bryan 2021 claims that Socrates responds here to Lysias' careless use of Socratic ethics. *Phdr.* 259e6–7: τὴν τοῦ λέγοντος διάνοιαν εἰδυῖαν τὸ ἀληθὲς ὧν ἂν ἐρεῖν πέρι μέλλῃ, 260a5–7: ἐκ γὰρ τούτων εἶναι τὸ πείθειν ἀλλ᾽ οὐκ ἐκ τῆς ἀληθείας, 272d5–6: οὐδὲν ἀληθείας μετέχειν δέοι δικαίων ἢ ἀγαθῶν πέρι πραγμάτων and 272d9–e1: οὐδὲν ἐν τοῖς δικαστηρίοις τούτων ἀληθείας μέλειν οὐδενί, ἀλλὰ τοῦ πιθανοῦ, and 273a1: πολλὰ εἰπόντα χαίρειν τῷ ἀληθεῖ. Cf. 261e and 275c1–2.

100. *Phdr.* 276d2: παιδιᾶς χάριν and 278b8: οὐκοῦν ἤδη πεπαίσθω μετρίως ἡμῖν τὰ περὶ λόγων. Socrates' comments may be a critique of Agathon, who focuses on entertainment, making only a weak attempt to examine the matter at hand; cf. *Symp.* 197e8–10, where Socrates insists on a praise of Erōs that "combines amusement with moderate examination" (τὰ μὲν παιδιᾶς, τὰ δὲ σπουδῆς μετρίας . . . μετέχων); on the role of παιδιά in the *Laws*, see n15 above.

101. *Phdr.* 266c1–5: "Tell me now what I ought to call the things taught by you and Lysias, or is this the art of speech (ἡ λόγων τέχνη) by the use of which Thrasymachus and the rest have become able speakers themselves, and make others so."

102. *Phdr.* 278d6–7.

103. *Symp.* 202e5–6: δαίμων μέγας, ὦ Σώκρατες: καὶ γὰρ πᾶν τὸ δαιμόνιον μεταξύ ἐστι θεοῦ τε καὶ θνητοῦ; cf. Pfefferkorn 2022, 294–295.

104. *Leg.* 662b5–6: ταύτῃ πειρῴμην ἂν τούς τε ποιητὰς ἀναγκάζειν φθέγγε-σθαι καὶ πάντας τοὺς ἐν τῇ πόλει ("I would try to force the poets and everyone in the city to speak in this sense"). Socrates explains his meaning a few lines further when he advises the heaviest penalties for those proclaiming that "things profitable and lucrative are other from just things" (662c2–3: λυσιτελοῦντα μὲν ἄλλα ἐστὶ καὶ κερδαλέα, δικαιότερα δὲ ἄλλα).

105. See Anagnostou-Laoutides 2020, 123–125, on Plato's relationship with the Sicilian tyrants Dionysius I and his son, Dionysius II, whose penchant for heavy drinking was notorious; cf. McKinlay 1939. According to Diodorus Siculus (15.74.1–2), Dionysius I, a competent tragic poet, died from excessive drinking when celebrating his dramatic victory at the Lenaia for his tragedy *The Ransom of Hector*; although there are other versions of Dionysius' death, this one offers a conspicuous parallel to Plato's *Symposium*, where Agathon too celebrates his dramatic victory at the Lenaia festival; Duncan 2012, 140–141. Also, see Anagnostou-Laoutides 2026, 284 with n61 noting the use of the verb ἐκπλήττω to describe the roar of the theatrical crowd that lacks education (*Leg.* 659a7–8: ἐκπληττόμενον ὑπὸ θορύβου τῶν πολλῶν καὶ τῆς αὑτοῦ ἀπαιδευσία).

106. In the *Republic* (386b6–10) Plato argues that the city must "take charge of those who attempt to talk about these fables" (ἡμᾶς ἐπιστατεῖν καὶ περὶ τούτων τῶν μύθων τοῖς ἐπιχειροῦσιν λέγειν) since "otherwise they would not be relating what is true or helpful for those destined to be warriors" (ὡς οὔτε ἀληθῆ ἂν λέγοντας οὔτε ὠφέλιμα τοῖς μέλλουσιν μαχίμοις ἔσεσθαι). Pfefferkorn 2022, 120–121. Cf. *Resp.* 372e6–7 where to illustrate "how justice and injustice take root in the cities," Socrates examines the case of a contemporary city steeped in luxury and artistic extravagance (373b1–c1). Also see Anagnostou-Laoutides 2024b, 279 and 2026, 280 with n36, on Plato's use of poetry in the *Republic* to highlight the ignorance of Socrates' interlocutors regarding the nature of justice: thus, Cephalus claims that the just life entails telling the truth and paying one's debts (331a–b); his son Pole-marchus, defines justice in Homeric terms as "helping friends and harming enemies" (332a–d). Thrasymachus demurs that justice "is nothing else but what is beneficial for the stronger" viz. those who pass legislation in cities (338c1–2; cf. 338e–339a), while injustice is more rewarding than justice (344c), as the example of the Homeric leaders suggests. Cephalus and Polemarchus often cite poetry (Pindar, Simonides, Homer) to justify their opinions, while Thrasymachus' discussion of unjust leaders as "shepherds" of the people is evocative of Homer's devious Agamemnon (cf. *Il.* 2.243; 4.413). Also citing poetry constantly (Aeschylus, Hesiod, Homer, Mousaeus, Orpheus, Archilochus), Glaucon claims that the unjust can ensure their posthumous happiness (364a–365c; cf. chapter 2, n84). In his response, Socrates introduces the example of a "healthy city" (372d) inviting us to juxtapose the role of justice in it versus the current political situation that Glaucon complains about. The comparison of two

cities, one that is a model of *eunomia*, versus one steeped in conflict and *dysnomia*, is a notable epic paradigm (Hom. *Il.* 18.489–495; Hes. *Sc.* 237–247; 270–285). On poetry's distortion of truth also see *Resp.* 602e4–603a8 (. . . ἡ γραφικὴ καὶ ὅλως ἡ μιμητικὴ πόρρω μὲν τῆς ἀληθείας . . . πόρρω δ᾽ αὖ φρονήσεως); cf. *Phil.* 38c5–7.

107. At *Leg.* 659e3–4, music can restore harmony in the soul, like medicine restores the harmony in the body. For the limits of the comparison, see Bartels 2017, 67–68, 135–140, 191–192; cf. chapter 2, p. 52.

108. The message is reiterated at *Leg.* 661b6–9; cf. 669b6–670a2 on the difficulty of deciphering musical representations, followed by a critique of contemporary composers, who despite their technical skills are not required to know "whether their representations are noble or ignoble" (670e5–6: εἴτε καλὸν εἴτε μὴ καλὸν τὸ μίμημα); cf. Ar. *Nub.* 547–548, cited on p. 93.

109. On the older age of the commanders, specified as 50 at *Leg.* 670b1 but 60 at 812b9–10, see Sauvé-Meyer 2015, 328–330, drawing on the views of England 1921 and Schöpsdau 1994; cf. Murray 2018/2013.

110. Pfefferkorn 2022, 120, 150–152, 190, 222n54, 241; cf. *Prt.* 347c–348a, discussed on p. 77. Also, Sauvé-Meyer 2015, 290 s.v. 666d11–e1. On theatrocracy, see also the conclusion of the book.

111. Sauvé Meyer 2015, 305 s.v. 669a7–9.

112. *Leg.* 671a3–4: ἣν τῷ τοῦ Διονύσου χορῷ βοήθειαν ἐπιδεῖξαι καλῶς λεγομένην.

113. Bartels 2017, 109, identifies the symposiasts with the Chorus of Dionysus; cf. Murray 2013, 116. Cf. Xen. *Symp.* 6.1–2 with Huss 1999b, 333–334, on Hermotimus' drunken silence.

114. Plato continues his argument at *Leg.* 666b3–c7 stipulating that only "when a man has reached the age of forty, he may join in the convivial gatherings (ἐν τοῖς συσσιτίοις εὐωχηθέντα) and invoke Dionysus (Διόνυσον παρακαλεῖν), above all other gods, inviting his presence at the rite (τελετὴν)." This rite is also the recreation (ἅμα καὶ παιδιάν) of the elders, a medicine (ἐδωρήσατο τὸν οἶνον φάρμακον) given to mankind against the grumpiness of old age. Thus relaxed, the participants to the banquet can make good merry and be prepared "to sing chants and incantations" (ᾄδειν τε καὶ . . . ἐπᾴδειν) in front of a few intimate friends; cf. Anagnostou-Laoutides 2020b, 85–86; Anagnostou-Laoutides and Payne 2021, 22; also, Pfefferkorn 2022, 149–158.

115. On the association of heat with enhanced intelligence (and wine), see chapter 2, pp. 53–55.

116. Note that Aristophanes is also included among those "soaked" in wine (*Symp.* 176b5, τῶν χθὲς βεβαπτισμένων) the night before.

117. My translation draws on Nehamas and Woodruff 1989, 13–14; cf. Anagnostou-Laoutides and Payne 2021, 2.

118. Chapter 2, pp. 45–46; cf. Xen. *Symp.* 2.26 where Socrates endorses moderate drinking, suggesting: ("But if the servants frequently 'besprinkle' us

(ἐπιψακάζωσιν)—if I too may use a Gorgian expression—with small cups, we shall thus not be driven on by the wine to a state of intoxication (οὐ βιαζόμενοι μεθύειν), but instead shall be brought by its gentle persuasion to a more sportive mood (ἀναπειθόμενοι πρὸς τὸ παιγνιωδέστερον)."

119. *Symp.* 177b1–2: τῷ δὲ Ἔρωτι . . . μηδὲ ἕνα πώποτε τοσούτων γεγονότων ποιητῶν πεποιηκέναι μηδὲν ἐγκώμιον and 177c2–3: ἔρωτα δὲ μηδένα πω ἀνθρώπων τετολμηκέναι εἰς ταυτηνὶ τὴν ἡμέραν ἀξίως ὑμνῆσαι. (Wilson-)Nightingale 1995, 158–162, argues that Socrates' philosophical definition of *erōs* is designed to invite comparison with the description of *erōs* in lyric poetry—despite his tendency to correct lyric *erōs*, Socrates maintains "the alteration of the boundaries of the psyche brought on by the assault of love."

120. Anagnostou-Laoutides and Payne 2021, 3–4. For Plato's view that music/poetry can still be useful for educational purposes, see *Resp.* 379b8–c1, 360e ff., and 606e1–5; cf. *Leg.* 886c and 941b; *Ion* 532c1–d2 and 532d6–e1.

121. Phaedrus draws on poets the most (see n122 below); Pausanias relates a tale about Heavenly Aphrodite found in Hesiod (*Th.* 188–200; cf. Sud. s.v. Pandemos Aphrodite; Adler 1967, vol. 4.19); Pausanias is also hinting at an epigram attributed to Simonides about the tyrannicides, Harmodios and Aristogeiton (Allen 1991, 122n184; also, see L476: 21; Page 1981, 188; and Day 1985, 33–34). Eryximachus speaks as a member of the Asclepiads; Asclepius is a hero, known to Homer (*Il.* 2.731, 4.219 and 193, 11.516–517) and a son of Apollo in the *Homeric Hymn to Asclepius*. Hesiod discussed the god's genealogy (Paus. 2.26.7 in Edelstein and Edelstein 1998, 1.18–19, 25–26, 53, and 2.26–27, 53–54) as did Pindar (*Pyth.* 3.5–10 and 40–46; Allen 1991, 126n187). Eryximachus also refers to Polymnia at *Symp.* 187e3 in relation to the Pandemos Erōs, where the muse is a metonymy for Pausanias' Pandemos Aphrodite (Allen 1991, 128). In his speech (189c–193e), Aristophanes names Homer and alludes to Hesiod (190c: Zeus' battle against the Giants) and possibly hints at tales told by comic playwrights (192a with Allen 1991, 132n199). Agathon names Hesiod, Parmenides, and Homer (195c1–d1) but also alludes to playwrights such as Sophocles (196d1 with Allen 1991, 138n209) and Euripides (196e2–3). In his own speech, Socrates insists on speaking the truth (199d8: ὡς εἰδὼς τὴν ἀλήθειαν τοῦ ἐπαινεῖν ὁτιοῦν) in his own voice (199b2: ἐθέλω εἰπεῖν κατ᾽ ἐμαυτόν). Cf. *Symp.* 198c, where in the interlude before his speech begins, Socrates admits knowledge of Gorgias' speeches and Homer's poems but in an ironic way (by portraying himself as vulnerable to the verbalistic overload of Agathon; the latter is compared to Gorgias who is in turn identified with the fearful Gorgon of *Od.* 11.632; see Allen 1991, 140n213). In the interlude, Socrates quotes a line from Euripides (*Symp.* 199a6); he also refers to the tales of Aclestis, Achilles, and Cadmus in 208d *but* in direct response to Phaedrus' speech.

122. In his speech (*Symp.* 178a–180b), Phaedrus names five poets (Hesiod, Acousileos, Parmenides, Homer, and Aeschylus) and refers to tales about Orpheus;

he also quotes lines from Hesiod's *Theogony* near the start of his speech, as well as a line from Parmenides' poem on being and non-being; further, he relates the tale of Alcestis, who is mentioned in Homer (*Il.* 2.715) but famously dramatized by Euripides in a play produced in 438 BCE. An allusion to Pindar may be found in Phaedrus' reference to the Isles of the Blessed (*Symp.* 179e2–3). Cf. Ihejirika 2012 arguing that Plato targets here the then prevalent theory that memory is knowledge.

123. Belfiore 2012, 121 with n10, tries hard to find merit in Phaedrus' complaint, arguing that ". . . while perhaps an exaggeration, is an accurate reflection of much of Greek literature, in which *erōs* is often represented as . . . , a destructive force causing sickness and madness."

124. Anagnostou-Laoutides and Payne 2021, 4.

125. Especially since his stellar example of a lover's ability to die for another is Alcestis (!) at 179b4–d2, and since his discussion of Achilles as the lover of Patroclus is cited as an objection (!) to Aeschylus' portrayal of him as the beloved at 179e1–18b8. Phaedrus also criticizes Orpheus for composing poetry instead of joining Eurydice in death; Dorter 1969, 216–217.

126. Eryximachus exempts Socrates from the agreement about drinking, since he can cope with whichever choice they make (*Symp.* 176c4–6: ἐξαιρῶ λόγου . . . ἱκανὸς . . . ἀμφότερα).

127. Sedley 2006b, 48–61, argues that Agathon has already made the connection between desire and creativity to which Diotima will add theoretical substance; cf. Hege 2012, 14–23, with Brisson 2006; Sheffield 2006a, 32, and 2006b; O'Brien 2012, 78–79; Anagnostou-Laoutides and Payne 2021, 5–7.

128. Nehamas and Woodruff 1989, 32n30 and 36n45; Belfiore 2012, 134–137.

129. Hence, at *Symp.* 198a1–3, Aristodemus reports that when Agathon concluded his speech, those present burst into applause (ἀναθορυβῆσαι τοὺς παρόντας).

130. Socrates uses the verb ἐκπλήττω to describe the effect of Agathon's speech, like Alcibiades used it earlier to refer to Socrates' effect on his audiences (*Symp.* 215d6 and 216d4); cf. Werner 2012, 138–147, esp. 145, on the use of the verb in the *Phaedrus* (esp. the cicada myth) noting that it does not have an unproblematically positive meaning. Cf. Plut. *aud. poet.* 17a on the mythic images that dramatists use to please and amaze their audiences (μυθοποίημα καὶ πλάσμα πρὸς ἡδονὴν ἢ ἔκπληξιν ἀκροατοῦ γέγονε; Hunter and Russell 2011, 92–93). On ἔκπληξις as a key component of tragic plays, see Arist. *Poet.* 1455a15 (πασῶν δὲ βελτίστη ἀναγνώρισις ἡ ἐξ αὐτῶν τῶν πραγμάτων, τῆς **ἐκπλήξεως** γιγνομένης δι' εἰκότων, οἷον ἐν τῷ Σοφοκλέους Οἰδίποδι καὶ τῇ Ἰφιγενείᾳ) and 1460b25 where the goal of poetry is to make the elements of the plot more striking (**ἐκπληκτι-κώτερον** ἢ αὐτὸ ἢ ἄλλο ποιεῖ μέρος). Yet, as Aristotle claims, playwrights can abuse ἔκπληξις: see *Rhet.* 1385b6: οὐ γὰρ ἐλεοῦσιν οἱ **ἐκπεπληγμένοι**, διὰ τὸ εἶναι πρὸς τῷ οἰκείῳ πάθει ("those who are awestruck are unable to feel pity

because they are preoccupied with their own condition") and 1408a4–5 where he comments on speakers who deceive their audiences that who speak the truth by using emotive language (παραλογίζεταί τε γὰρ ἡ ψυχὴ ὡς ἀληθῶς λέγοντος): "audiences always empathize with a character who speaks emotionally even if he really says nothing" (συνομοπαθεῖ ὁ ἀκούων ἀεὶ τῷ παθητικῶς λέγοντι, κἂν μηθὲν λέγῃ). "This is why many speakers confound the audience by mere noise" (διὸ πολλοὶ **καταπλήττουσι** τοὺς ἀκροατὰς θορυβοῦντες).

131. See *thelgein* in introduction, n35.

132. Equally, while Socrates is physically repulsive (215b4–6), and his speeches make people feel uncomfortable, yet they are necessary for anyone who wishes to live well (221d7–222b6). Our sources unanimously describe Socrates as ugly: Pl. *Tht.* 143e; Xen. *Symp.* 4.19 and 5.5–7; Ar. *Nub.* 362; cf. chapter 1, n151.

133. Dorter 1969, 217–218 also notes: "Pausanias uses this unwritten law as a criterion for evaluating written law. The laws of Elis and Boeotia are 'bad,' he says, due to laziness, and those elsewhere in Ionia are 'bad' due to cowardice (182b1–d4); the Athenian law is better, but 'not easy to understand' (184d4 f.). It does not, he admits, sanction the pederasty he advocates (183c4), and should be regarded not as a strict injunction but as a test (184a1 f.), a means for the lover and beloved to test each other's worth. It would not, therefore, regulate the actions of the lover and beloved and would allow them to apply their own (unwritten) law."

134. *Symp.* 181e4–5: οἱ μὲν οὖν ἀγαθοὶ τὸν νόμον τοῦτον αὐτοὶ αὑτοῖς ἑκόντες τίθενται ("Good men set this law to themselves of their own accord").

135. *Symp.* esp. 183c1–2: "Both gods and humans have given absolute license (πᾶσαν ἐξουσίαν) to the lover, as our Athenian law provides (ὁ νόμος . . . ὁ ἐνθάδε)."

136. *Symp.* 184c5–6: "Only one type of willing enslavement (δουλεία ἑκούσιος) is left without reproach: I mean the one regarding virtue."

137. Dorter 1969, 218; cf. Brisson 2006, 229, who argues that "the dialogue develops a critique of a specific form of education within the framework of *paiderastia*."

138. Cf. *Resp.* 503d12–e1: "we must put someone to the test (βασανιστέον) regarding pains, fears, and pleasures (πόνοις τε καὶ φόβοις καὶ ἡδοναῖς)."

139. *Leg.* 650a1–2, although the context is heterosexual.

140. Belfiore 2012, 126–127 with nn28–29; on Pausanias' views of Erōs, also see Xen. *Symp.* 8.32–33; cf. Neumann 1964; Ludwig 1996, 538–539; Hindley 1999, 77–78, 87, 89, 91, 97.

141. Dover 1968, liii–liv, notes that Aristophanes at *Nub.* 331ff. refers to seers, medical writers, and lyric poets under the general heading σοφισταί, as ἀργοί" ("idle"); cf. (Wilson-)Nightingale 1995, 62n9; Camden 2023, 37–49.

142. See chapter 2, p. 45 on medicine's rejection of divine causes for illnesses, a debate that Eryximachus ignores; cf. n145 below.

143. Belfiore 2012, 127–128.

144. Belfiore 2012, 129–130 with nn36–37, citing Kirk et al. 1995, 192–193.

145. Eryximachus exhibits gross lack of understanding of his own science, since several ancient doctors had adopted a Heraclitean appreciation of the body as *krasis* (blend) of opposing powers in the body; Belfiore 2012, 130–131. At *Symp.* 187a7–8 Eryximachus states: ἔστι δὲ πολλὴ ἀλογία ἁρμονίαν φάναι διαφέρεσθαι ἢ ἐκ διαφερομένων ἔτι εἶναι ("It is very illogical to speak of harmony as being at variance or as formed from varying things"); cf. McPherran 2006 on Plato trying to accommodate here piety into philosophy; also, O'Brien 2012, 77–78, with Edelstein 1945.

146. Blanckenhagen 1992, 58.

147. At *Symp.* 213c4 Aristophanes is described as someone who "is and wishes to be γελοῖος" (γελοῖος ἔστι τε καὶ βούλεται); Anagnostou-Laoutides 2021b, 264; cf. Hobden 2013, 204; for elements of parody in Aristophanes' speech, see Dover 1966, 45–48.

148. See Belfiore 2012, 133, on the similarities between Aristophanes' tale and that of Ares and Aphrodite, who caught naked in the act by Hephaestus, cause laughter among the gods who are invited to enjoy the spectacle (*Od.* 8.266–366). Cf. *Symp.* 190b9–c3 where Aristophanes compares his story with that of Ephialtes and Otus, related by Homer (*Od.* 11.305–320; *Il.* 5.385–6). Hooper 2013 argues that Aristophanes' tale ridicules an ideal kind of *erōs* that cannot be fulfilled. On the suggestion that Aristophanes' tale draws on the Hippocratic *Regimen* (chapter 28) to ridicule contemporary theories on the evolution of sex, see Bartoš 2015, 232, with Bury 1932, xxxii–xxxiii.

149. Eryximachus admits that he was persuaded by Aristophanes' speech (193e2: πείσομαί σοι) and praises him for his generous use of literary variety (193e5–7: διὰ τὸ πολλὰ καὶ παντοδαπὰ εἰρῆσθαι).

150. Piety (τὸ ὅσιον) is what is loved by the gods (φιλεῖται ὑπὸ τῶν θεῶν), as Socrates argues in *Euthphr.* 10a2. Cf. *Leg.* 712b5–8: Θεὸν δὴ πρὸς τὴν τῆς πόλεως κατασκευὴν ἐπικαλώμεθα· ὁ δὲ ἀκούσειέν τε, καὶ ἀκούσας ἵλεως εὐμενής τε ἡμῖν ἔλθοι συνδιακοσμήσων τήν τε πόλιν καὶ τοὺς νόμους ("Let us invoke the presence of the God in the establishment of the state; and may he hearken, and hearkening may he come, propitious and kindly to us, to help us in the fashioning of the state and its laws"); also, *Leg.* 713a2–5: χρῆν δ' εἴπερ του τοιούτου τὴν πόλιν ἔδει ἐπονομάζεσθαι, τὸ τοῦ ἀληθῶς τῶν τὸν νοῦν ἐχόντων δεσπόζοντος θεοῦ ὄνομα λέγεσθαι ("But if the State ought to be named after any such thing, the name it should be borne is that of the God who is the true ruler of rational men"); with Anagnostou-Laoutides 2024a, 2. For the association of piety with *sōphrosynē*, see pp. 90–91.

151. Belfiore 2012, 133; on the definition of piety in the *Euthyphro* (in n150 above), see Cohen 1971; Mann 1998.

152. Andrisano 2003; cf. Lombardini 2013, 209–213, discussing *eutrapelia* (wittiness) in Aristotle; Lombardini (p. 206) draws on Connolly 2002, 120, and his appreciation of laughter for achieving "ironic self-distancing"; cf. Bakola 2010, 13, on ancient comedy's self-reflexivity; also, Anagnostou-Laoutides 2021b. On Aristophanes' role in late fifth century debates about musical values, see Barker 2004 and in the same volume Csapo 2004, 215.

153. Jazdzewska 2018, 187 with n2.

154. Anagnostou-Laoutides 2021b. In the *Laws*, Socrates suggests that foreign poets should be rejected if their representations are deemed to undermine the city's notion of the best life (*Leg.* 817b3–4: πᾶσα οὖν ἡμῖν ἡ πολιτεία συνέστηκε μίμησις τοῦ καλλίστου καὶ ἀρίστου βίου). The reference to the foreign poets (817a4; 817b1) may be a hint to Aristophanes' non-native background. Cf. Bakola 2010, 39–40, citing Crat. fr. 361 addressed to a Ξενίας, taken as a reference to Aristophanes. Plato's idea of poets competing may be inspired by the motif, common in ancient comedy, of staging dramatic competitions, as in Cratinus' *Archilochoi* and Aristophanes' *Frogs*.

155. Carriére 2003, 178–179; in Aristophanes' *Wasps* (77–80), two slaves guard a madman locked in a house. When the audience is asked to guess what kind of madness he suffers from, a spectator offers as a possibility his love for wine (φιλοπότην), a suggestion refuted because "only gentlemen suffer from this affliction" (. . . αὕτη γε χρηστῶν ἐστιν ἀνδρῶν ἡ νόσος)—a joke that stresses the social class aspect of wine drinking at the time. Davidson 1997, 139–140. For the role of wine and symposia in comedy, see Wilkins 2000a, 202–256, and in the introduction, n34; also, Bakola 2010.

156. Cf. *Resp.* 396a1–2 where Plato criticizes comic representations portraying characters as "reviling and lampooning one another, speaking foul words in their cups or when sober" (κακηγοροῦντάς τε καὶ κωμῳδοῦντας ἀλλήλους καὶ αἰσχρολογοῦντας, μεθύοντας ἢ καὶ νήφοντας); Plato also notes that comic performances should not portray clinically mad people (οὐδὲ μαινομένοις ἐθιστέον ἀφομοιοῦν αὑτοὺς ἐν λόγοις οὐδὲ ἐν ἔργοις· γνωστέον μὲν γὰρ καὶ μαινομένους καὶ πονηροὺς ἄνδρας τε καὶ γυναῖκας, ποιητέον δὲ οὐδὲν τούτων οὐδὲ μιμητέον "nor should they make a habit of portraying madmen in word or even deed (cf. chapter 2, n144). They must of course recognize men and women who are mad and of low character, but they must not write about them nor imitate any of these"). See Jouët-Pastré 2005, 47 (on *Leg.* 816d–e with n81 above), and esp. 51–53 on Plato's objection to comedy as related in *Resp.* 606c2–9: indulging in embarrassing jokes, which one would not tolerate otherwise, unless presented in a comic imitation (ἐν μιμήσει . . . κωμῳδικῇ) or told in private, people give free reign to that part of them "that wants to play the fool (βουλόμενον γελωτοποιεῖν)," and which they had previously "repressed through reason for fear of being regarded as buffoons" (ὃ γὰρ τῷ λόγῳ αὖ κατεῖχες . . . φοβούμενος δόξαν

βωμολοχίας), eventually turning themselves into comedians (ὥστε κωμῳδοποιὸς γενέσθαι). In Jouët-Pastré's view, laughter functions as a resistance mechanism against artistic representations (tragic and comic) that threaten to corrupt our judgement; cf. Anagnostou-Laoutides 2021b, 266–267; Jouët-Pastré 2002 and 2003. Also see Prauscello 2013, 321–323, and esp. 341–342, on instances of comedy in the *Laws*, noting that the comic figure is typically conceived of as a madman in Aristophanes; cf. Folch 2015, 189–202 and 213–214, on *Leg.* 838b7–e1 arguing that in this passage "[T]he terms γελοίοις and πάσῃ τε σπουδῇ τραγικῇ λεγομένῃ may be understood to operate metaphorically, as representative of genres that, respectively, subvert or affirm civic norms."

157. On banquets and jokes in the *Laws*, see Jouët-Pastré 2003.

158. Hippocrates (*Aphr.* 5.58) associates hiccups with liver inflammation, a symptom observed in cases of cirrhosis, which is often attributed to ongoing excessive drinking; Barnett 2018. On the hiccups episode and its meaning, see Lowenstam 1986, 43, who notes that, while ancient commentators (in n2, Lowenstam cites Olymp. *Vit. Plat.*; Ael. *Arist.* 3.581 (Behr 1986) with Wilamowitz-Moellendorff 1920, 367n2, and Ath. *Deipn.* 187c) perceived the hiccups as an attempt to ridicule Aristophanes, modern scholars saw it as an attempt to ridicule Eryximachus; also see O'Mahoney 2011b.

159. On comic poets typically employing vulgar jokes to please their audiences, see Bakola 2010, 38; also, Farmer 2017, 225.

160. At Hom. *Od.* 17.541–542, Penelope predicts that if Odysseus ever returned to his palace, he and his son would take revenge on the suitors, upon which Telemachus sneezes loudly—a sign that these events will indeed unfold.

161. Thus, at Xen. *Anab.* 3.2.9, sneezing confirms an omen from Zeus Soter; Ar. *Pr.* 33.7 wonders why we associate sneezing with the divine, suggesting that perhaps it is because sneezing occurs in the head, the seat of reasoning.

162. Schröder 2010, 159–160, on Plut. *De gen. Soc.* 581a1–582c.

163. Levy 2020, 29.

164. On literary reflexivity as a unique feature of Old Comedy, see Bakola 2010, 13, with Slater 2002.

165. Bakola 2010, 14 with n4, citing Sommerstein 1992; Bremer 1993; and Silk 2000, 45–50. Cf. Bakola 2008 arguing that Aristophanes' persona of the isolated, heroic poet-reformer was a reworking of Solon's persona (frs. 1–11 and 31–7); with Rosen 2000 and Hubbard 1991. Also see Dobrov 1995, 50.

166. Sommerstein 2009, 130–132, with footnotes.

167. Sommerstein 2009, 129; the lines are spoken by Euripides during his theatrical *agōn* with Aeschylus, judged by Dionysus; Aeschylus asks why a poet must be admired (*Ran.* 1008: . . . τίνος οὕνεκα χρὴ θαυμάζειν ἄνδρα ποιητήν;). Perysinakis 2019, 251–252 with n9, points out the use of *elenchein*, which evokes the famous Socratic method of enquiry, in lines 857 (spoken by Dionysus), 894, 908, 922 (spoken by Euripides), and 1366 (spoken by Aeschylus).

168. Pl. *Euthphr.* 3c1–3: ὅταν τι λέγω ἐν τῇ ἐκκλησίᾳ περὶ τῶν θείων, προλέγων αὐτοῖς τὰ μέλλοντα, καταγελῶσιν ὡς μαινομένου ("When I say something in the assembly about divine matters, predicting the future to them, they laugh at me for being mad"); also in chapter 2, n222; cf. Delcomminette 2018.

169. We cannot ascertain whether Aristophanes refers here specifically to comedy or whether this is a comparison, for example, between Aeschylus and Sophocles. Sommerstein 2009, 127.

170. Telò 2016 claims that in the *Clouds* Aristophanes explains his metaphors to his audience (notably the metaphor of the cloak) to guide them to how they should interpret his poetry; for a constructive critique, see Peterson 2019b.

171. Kanellakis 2020, 96–97; Silk 2013, 36–39.

172. Bakola 2010, 16–23, on Aristophanes' attack on Cratinus in *Equ.* 526–536 and 275–285, on Cratinus' response in his *Pytine*; in the play, Cratinus played on his own reputation for heavy drinking by portraying his persona as married to Comedy and having problems with her due to his drinking habit. Cf. Biles 2002 cited by Bakola 2010.

173. Learned individuals are negatively compared to poets of true inspiration already in Pindar (*Ol.* 2.86–88); see Bakola 2008, 16.

174. Bakola 2008, 16–17, with Finkelberg 1998, 18n65.

175. Bakola 2008, 9; cf. Perysinakis 2019, 254.

176. Perysinakis 2019, 264–265; cf. Barker 2004, 198–199, on Aristophanes taking a stance against the "new music" that caused much controversy in late fifth century Athens.

177. Cf. Cratinus fr. 203 employing the contrast of drinking water versus drinking wine: ὕδωρ δὲ πίνων οὐδὲν ἂν τέκοις σοφόν ("You will never create anything brilliant by drinking water"). For the ascription of this verse to Cratinus' *Pytine*, see Luppe 2000, 19; also, Bakola 2010, 56–57, with Biles 2002, 173.

178. Rosen 2000, 41–49, with Bakola 2010, 18, citing Platon. *Diff. Char.* (*Prol. de com.* II, Koster 1978, 1 p.6 = Cratin. test. xxv in L513).

179. Bakola 2008, 18; cf. Hardie 2004, 20, noting that in contemporary Athens "the Muses are . . . identified with Dionysiac cult and choric activity and in that sense the *mvstai* engage with them too"; also, Kowalzig 2004 in n65 above.

180. Rosen 2007, 128; cf. his p. 136 on Homer's scene where Polyphemus admits that a prophecy had alerted him to his misfortune, but he always imagined a big, impressive opponent; *Od.* 9.515–516: "But now he who is tiny, and a nobody, and feeble has blinded my eye, after overpowering me with wine (ἐπεί μ' ἐδαμάσσατο οἴνῳ)."

181. Rosen 2007, 220 and 255–268.

182. Blundell 1987; Lévystone 2005 notes that despite Odysseus' terrible moral reputation, rhetorical eloquence was still admired among the Socratics.

183. Bakola 2010, 37, cites Aristophanes' *Women Claiming Tent-Sites* (fr. 488) where the poet admits (L502: 342–343): χρῶμαι γὰρ αὐτοῦ τοῦ στόματος

τῷ στρογγύλῳ,/ τοὺς νοῦς δ' ἀγοραίους ἧττον ἢ 'κεῖνος ποιῶ ("I make use of his polished, compact style, but my ideas are less vulgar than his are").

184. Aristophanes seems to admit as much in the *Thesmophoriazusae*, where he casts Agathon (the host of the *Symposium*) as claiming that a poet ought to use *mimesis* to get under the skin of every character he portrays (146–156, esp. 149–150: χρὴ γὰρ ποιητὴν ἄνδρα πρὸς τὰ δράματα/ ἃ δεῖ ποιεῖν πρὸς ταῦτα τοὺς τρόπους ἔχειν and 155–156: ἃ δ' οὐ κεκτήμεθα,/ μίμησις ἤδη ταῦτα συνθηρεύεται). Lauriola 2016, 76.

185. See DL 1.12: "Philosophers were also called sophists (οἱ δὲ σοφοὶ καὶ σοφισταὶ ἐκαλοῦντο); and not only these, but poets were also called sophists (ἀλλὰ καὶ οἱ ποιηταὶ σοφισταί), just as Cratinus praising those who follow Homer and Hesiod in his *Archilochoi* calls them"; Bakola 2010, 71.

186. Cratinus fr. 342. Lauriola 2016, 75 and 90–92; Bakola 2010, 19, with Ornaghi 2006, 87–93; Sidwell 1995; O'Sullivan 2006 (arguing that the fragment does not belong to the play *Pytine*).

187. See *Schol.* on Pl. *Apol.* 19c (Σ Areth. [B] with Lauriola 2016, 71 also in Bakola 2010, 37n65: ἐκωμῳδεῖτο δ' ἐπὶ τῷ σκώπτειν μὲν Εὐριπίδην, μιμεῖσθαι δ' αὐτόν. ("He was made fun of, for while he criticized Euripides, he imitated him.") For Euripides' influence on Aristophanes, see Silk 2000, 48–52, 322–6, and Bakola 2008, 4–10.

188. Perysinakis 2019, 259–261.

189. *Ran.* 814–825; cf. *l.* 1259 where Aeschylus is characterized as βακχεῖος. Lada-Richards 1999, 244, with Bakola 2008, 17–18. For Aeschylus as Cratinus' poetic model, see the anonymous *Prol. de com.* III (Koster 1978, 3.24, p. 8 = Cratin. Test. iii in L513): γέγονε δὲ ποιητικώτατος, κατασκευάζων εἰς τὸν Αἰσχύλου χαρακτῆρα ("He was most poetic, composing his plays in the style of Aeschylus"). Also see Ath. *Deipn.* 1.22a–b on Aeschylus' reputation for writing his poetry while drunk (in a pattern that evokes Archilochus' fr. 120 cited on p. 25); all sources are discussed in Bakola 2008, 18–19.

190. Cratinus probably referred to the Corybants in his *Idaioi*; Bowie 2010, 162. For a reference to the Corybants in Menander's *Theophorumene*, see Bowie 2010, 164–165. By the fourth century BCE, asking someone whether they were mad or possessed by the Corybants would be an ordinary, humorous response to someone uttering a strange phrase; Ustinova 2017, 118–119 with n56, citing Eur. *Hipp.* 141–144 and Ar. *Vesp.* 8.

191. Ustinova 2017, 119 with n57, citing Ar. *Vesp.* 119 with schol.: τὰ τῶν Κορυβάντων ἐποίει αὐτῷ μυστήρια ἐπὶ καθαρμῷ τῆς μανίας; Hsch. s.v. *korubantismos*.

192. Ustinova 2017, 116.

193. Ustinova 2017, 119.

194. *Euth.* 277d–e discussed in Ustinova 2017, 119 with n68.

195. Bakola 2010, 70 with n177, citing Bowie 1993, and Lada-Richards 1999.

196. Lada-Richards 1999, 159–215. For the traditional association of epic with tragic poetry, and (Archilochean) *iambos* with comedy, see Bakola 2010, 74–79. As Bakola discusses, Cratinus argued that *iambos* should be regarded as seriously as tragedy, if not more, because it fulfills the essentially duty of ψόγος or social critique. For Socrates' use of ψόγος and shaming in his axiological system, see Levy 2020. Cf. *Leg.* 829c–d, where Plato refers to the importance of such festivals involving public praise and blame but is adamant that the poets granted free speech in song must be strictly regulated by the state educators and law wardens.

197. Bakola 2010, 68 with n165, also citing Bierl 1991, 41–43; Padilla 1992; and Lada-Richards 1999, 216–311; cf. Barker in n176 above.

198. Bakola 2008, 4–6; Bakola 2010, 69.

199. Cf. Perysinakis 2019, 251–257.

200. The argument is analyzed further in Anagnostou-Laoutides 2021b.

201. At *Symp.* 203e6–7 Diotima describes Erōs as standing between wisdom and ignorance (σοφίας τε αὖ καὶ ἀμαθίας ἐν μέσῳ ἐστίν). Cf. *Phil.* 48c2 (κακὸν μὴν **ἄγνοια** καὶ ἣν δὴ λέγομεν ἀβελτέραν ἕξιν; "ignorance is certainly a bad thing, as is also what we call stupidity"), an arbitrary reading of Cornarius, a sixteenth century medical philosopher who changed the first 1513 edition by Aldus Pius Manutius. Manutius, relying on the extant manuscripts, had printed ἄνοια, not ἄγνοια. Although my argument is not influenced by either reading, I think Screech 2015, 62–67, is right to point out that Socrates probably refers here to madness, a symptom of ignorance. Cf. Arist. *Eth. Nic.* 1111a2–7: "Because he who acts in ignorance . . . is an involuntary agent (ἀγνοῶν ἀκουσίως πράττει). . . . Now no one, unless mad, could be ignorant of all these circumstances (ἅπαντα μὲν οὖν ταῦτα οὐδεὶς ἂν ἀγνοήσειε μὴ μαινόμενος); . . . —for a man must know himself."

202. In the *Sophist*, Socrates argues that ignorance is a kind of ugliness that affects the soul (228a–d) when it fails in its pursuit of the truth; Lott 2012, 41–42, 44–4, 51–52. On Socrates' ignorance as his core virtue, see Vlastos 1985, 6; also, Matthews 2003 on *Apol.* 21d; cf. *Charm.* 176a.

203. Thus, at *Symp.* 205e1–4 we read: "And certainly there runs a story, she continued, that all those who seek their other half are in love; though by my account (ὁ δ᾿ ἐμὸς λόγος), love is neither for half, nor for whole . . ."

204. *Symp.* 212c6–8: "After Socrates had thus spoken, there was applause from all except Aristophanes, who was beginning to comment (λέγειν τι ἐπιχειρεῖν) on the allusion which Socrates' speech had made to his own, when suddenly . . . "; Dorter 1969, 230–231. Although all other symposiasts are equally deprived of the chance to respond to Socrates' critique (198d1–201c1), only Aristophanes is accused of buffoonery.

205. Usher 2002, 213, 223 and 225, compares Alcibiades' erotic assault on Socrates (*Symp.* 214e2, 217c5–6) with "the monstrous threat posed by the

androgynes and same-sex creatures in Aristophanes' speech, who . . . would attempt a coup d'etat against Zeus in heaven."

206. Alongside genuine inspiration, comedy aesthetics were also reformulated during the fifth century; Bremmer 1997, 20: "First, buffoonery became less and less acceptable to the upper class as an expression of humour. Secondly . . . insulting others with jokes also became less acceptable."

207. As Aristotle observes at *Rhet.* 1419b7–8, there are different types of jokes (εἴδη γελοίων): Some suit a gentleman, while others do not (τὸ μὲν ἁρμόττει ἐλευθέρῳ τὸ δ᾽ οὔ). In his view, irony is more gentleman-like than buffoonery (ἡ εἰρωνεία τῆς βωμολοχίας ἐλευθεριώτερον), because while irony is employed on one's own account (αὐτοῦ ἕνεκα ποιεῖ τὸ γελοῖον), buffoonery is employed on account of another; see Anagnostou-Laoutides 2021b.

208. (Wilson-)Nightingale 1995, 111–115, argues that Plato here "attacks the expedient manipulation of the rhetoric of praise that was being taught to aspiring politicians in democratic Athens."

209. The concept is repeated at 201d9–11 where Socrates summarizes Diotima's speech "from the points which Agathon and I have agreed upon, on my own account, as well as I can" (ἐκ τῶν ὡμολογημένων ἐμοὶ καὶ Ἀγάθωνι, αὐτὸς ἐπ᾽ ἐμαυτοῦ, ὅπως ἂν δύνωμαι). Cf. *Phdr.* 229c7–8 where Socrates admits to being extraordinary (ἄτοπος) because he disbelieves ancient mythic accounts, while shortly after (*Phdr.* 230a) he adds that he finds the examination of such traditions irrelevant when he has not yet achieved a good understanding of himself. Thus, he uses customary views about myths as a strategy of pushing these matters aside so he can focus on examining himself (230a3–4: σκοπῶ οὐ ταῦτα ἀλλ᾽ ἐμαυτόν). On Socrates' ἀτοπία, cf. *Symp.* 215a4 and chapter 1, n14.

210. During Diotima's speech, Socrates often agrees that she relates the truth: see *Symp.* 202a11: ἀληθῆ . . . λέγεις, 205a5, 205c4, and 205c12: ἀληθῆ λέγεις, 205d9: κινδυνεύεις ἀληθῆ . . . λέγειν, and 206a15: ἀληθέστατα . . . λέγεις; furthermore, cf. 204c8–9: καλῶς . . . λέγεις and 208c1–2: εἶεν . . . ὦ σοφωτάτη Διοτίμα, ταῦτα ὡς ἀληθῶς οὕτως ἔχει;. On Socrates' preoccupation with the truth, see Hobden 2013, 198–201 and esp. 224–227, further discussing truth and symposiastic performances in Xenophon's *Symposium*; also, Wohl 2004, 358, also cited by Hobden; on the association of Socratic irony and Socratic "simplicity" with truth, see chapter 4, p. 130. Cf. Morgan 2000, esp. 157–179, on Plato's use of myth as a means of enhancing "well-intentioned philosophical persuasion" (p. 166), always tied to rational arguments.

211. Nussbaum 1986, 177 with n28; cf. chapter 1, n76. It may also be conjectured that Socrates is here assuming the role of the poet as envisaged by Plato in the *Laws*. More recently, see D'Angour 2019 arguing that Diotima was in fact Aspasia with whom Socrates fell in love at a young age.

212. Anagnostou-Laoutides and Payne 2021, 12–18. See D. Scott 2000, 25, on the correspondence between the speeches of Diotima and Alcibiades; besides

refuting the charge that Socrates corrupted the youth, Alcibiades illustrates how he applied the concepts he learned from Diotima; cf. White 2008; Wilburn 2015, 20–24; McBrayer 2017; also, Nehamas and Woodruff 1989, xxiv, who note that Alcibiades' "encomium of Socrates develops a number of themes from Diotima's speech."

213. Plato stresses the importance of persuading the citizens by suggesting that a preface should be added to each law (like the preludes that introduce musical *nomoi*) to explain their rationale (*Leg.* 722d–723a).

214. This raises the question of whether Plato speaks in his own voice; Nathan 2020, 4n3, with Frede 1992, 215–217; Gonzalez 2000; Clay 2000, 100–115; cf. Tarrant 2005 on the versions of Socrates projected by his students.

215. On Alcibiades' symposiastic insolence (ὑβριστικῶς καὶ ὑπερηφάνως) in a setting inspired by Plato's *Symposium* (for which also see Plut. *Alc.* 4.5–6), see Duff 2009, 42.

216. *Symp.* 214a9–b2: οὕτως οὔτε τι λέγομεν ἐπὶ τῇ κύλικι οὔτε τι ᾄδομεν, ἀλλ᾽ ἀτεχνῶς ὥσπερ οἱ διψῶντες πιόμεθα. Thus, Eryximachus' intervention responds to Alcibiades' resolve to make everyone drunk (*Symp.* 213e7–11).

217. See Anagnostou-Laoutides 2020a, 123, with Thuc. 6.15.3–4 on Alcibiades' reputation for antagonizing the profligate lifestyle of the Sicilian tyrants; cf. Thuc. 6.16.3 on Alcibiades' provision of choruses, which impressed his foreign acquaintances: πρὸς δὲ τοὺς ξένους καὶ αὕτη ἰσχὺς φαίνεται; also see the description of Dionysius II in Plato's *Ep.* 7, 326b; Monoson 2012, 158; Duncan 2012, 147; cf. the conclusion of the book.

218. Also, *Symp.* 214d3–11 and 214e2.

219. *Symp.* 222c1–3: εἰπόντος δὴ ταῦτα τοῦ Ἀλκιβιάδου γέλωτα γενέσθαι ἐπὶ τῇ παρρησίᾳ αὐτοῦ, ὅτι ἐδόκει ἔτι ἐρωτικῶς ἔχειν τοῦ Σωκράτους.

220. See Halperin 1986, 68–79, on Plato's gradual replacement of intercourse with discourse in the dialogue; cf. O'Byrne 2004 arguing that Aristophanes' speech accounts for the role of sex in the ideal city, which Plato failed to address in the *Timaeus*; also, Groneberg 2005.

221. Cf. *Symp.* 216a2 and 217e2–5. Holowchak 2003, 422–424. For Alcibiades' praise of Socrates through images, see Dominick 2013.

222. Murray 2018/2013, 254, cites Alcaeus fr. 366: παροιμία οἶνος καὶ ἀλήθεια, ἐπὶ τῶν ἐν μέθῃ τὴν ἀλήθειαν λεγόντων. ἔστι δὲ ἄσματος Ἀλκαίου ἀρχή· οἶνος, ὦ φίλε παῖ, καὶ ἀλάθεα, from the ancient scholia on Pl. *Symp.* 217e (Greene 1938, 65) and fr. 333: οἱ οἰνωθέντες τὰ τοῦ λογισμοῦ ἀπόρρητα ἐκφαίνουσιν· ὅθεν καὶ Ἀλκαῖός φησιν· οἶνος γὰρ ἀνθρώπῳ δίοπτρον/ ἀνθρώποις; Rösler 1995; Plut. *Art.* 15.3; cf. Ath. *Deipn.* 2.38b5: οὐκοῦν μεθύοντάς φασι τἀληθῆ λέγειν and Philochorus ap. Ath. *Deipn.* 2.37f (cf. n40 above) that "drinkers not only show who they really are themselves (οὐ μόνον ἑαυτοὺς ἐμφανίζουσιν οἵτινές εἰσιν) but also reveal other people's characters by speaking freely" (ἀλλὰ καὶ τῶν ἄλλων ἕκαστον ἀνακαλύπτουσι παρρησίαν ἄγοντες).

223. Folch 2015, 17 and 172–173.

224. Cf. Xen. *Symp.* 8.24 cited on p. 69. G.A. Scott 2000, 147–148; cf. Scott and Welton 2008, 166; for *parrhēsia* as the duty to tell the truth, see Pearson 2001, 19, who edited and published Foucault's 1983 lectures at the University of California in Berkeley. *Parrhēsia*, a core feature of fifth century BCE Athenian political culture, is first used by Euripides, as Foucault observed (in Pearson 2001, 11); for *parrhēsia* in the *Bacchae* (*ll.* 666–671), see Nikolopoulou 2011; cf. Gentile 2015 for *parrhēsia* in the *Hippolytus*; cf. Benitez 2003 for *parrhēsia* in Aeschylus' *Agamemnon*. For early premonitions of *parrhēsia* in Homer, see Golish 2013; Konstan 2012 distinguished two types of *parrhēsia*, one identified with frankness and one with insolence, in Euripides' *Phoenissae*; cf. Konstan 1995, esp. 334, on the way the concept evolved in later times from "freedom of speech to personal candor."

225. Cf. *Leg.* 694a4–5: "When the Persians, under Cyrus, maintained the due balance between slavery and freedom (τὸ μέτριον μᾶλλον δουλείας τε καὶ ἐλευθερίας), they became, first of all, free themselves" (πρῶτον μὲν ἐλεύθεροι ἐγένοντο); on the "Socratic" Cyrus in Xenophon, see Johnson 2017, 489–490.

226. For Socrates' appreciation of Cyrus as a model political figure, see *Alc.* 105d4–6; cf. *Alc.* 121c1–122a on the Persian education system, where one of the four teachers assigned to the Persian prince is the most moderate (ὁ δὲ σωφρονέστατος), entrusted with teaching him self-control, so that he can master above all "what is in himself" (122a7: τῶν ἐν αὑτῷ). Also, see Balot 2024, 72–75.

227. See Thuc. 8.45.2, claiming that Alcibiades became Tissaphernes' "instructor in everything" (διδάσκαλος πάντων), and 8.46.5, where he emphasizes their bond of trust based on their similar thinking. Vickers 1987 discusses the allusions to Alcibiades' sophistic ways in Sophocles' *Philoctetes* but Euripides' *Cyclops*; see esp. Vickers 1987, 191–192, on Alcibiades' drunkenness and womanizing; cf. Plut. *Alc.* 1.8 and *Symp.* 213e7–11.

228. See Foucault on Socratic *parrhēsia* as debated in the *Gorgias* and the *Apology*, edited and published by Pearson 2001, 96; cf. van Raalte 2004. For Foucault's appreciation of *parrhēsia* in *Alcibiades I* and *Laches*, see Kohan 2015, 14–16.

229. It is worth comparing here the case of Isocrates, also prosecuted for "corrupting the youth." Despite being a logographos, he refused the title of "sophist," insisting he was a philosopher; Schiappa 1995, 50; Murphy 2017. At *Antidosis* 15.285–286, Isocrates echoes Plato's concern about the moral crisis of contemporary Athenian society with reference to symposiastic manners. He criticizes the Athenians for their tendency to recognize as philosophers those who ignore practical matters opting for the wiles of the ancient sophists (τοὺς δὲ τῶν μὲν ἀναγκαίων ἀμελοῦντας, τὰς δὲ τῶν παλαιῶν σοφιστῶν τερατολογίας ἀγαπῶντας φιλοσοφεῖν φασιν) and ignore those who undertake philosophy for the benefit of ruling well both households and the state (καὶ τὸν ἴδιον οἶκον καὶ τὰ κοινὰ τὰ τῆς πόλεως καλῶς διοικήσουσιν). Their behavior has alienated the youth. As a result, "the most moderate young men wasted their youth in drinking-bouts, in parties,

in soft living and childish folly (τοὺς μὲν ἐπιεικεστάτους αὐτῶν ἐν πότοις καὶ συνουσίαις καὶ ῥᾳθυμίαις καὶ παιδιαῖς), indifferent to the prospect of improving themselves, while those of worse nature (τοὺς δὲ χείρω τὴν φύσιν) spent all their time in such dissipation (ἐν τοιαύταις ἀκολασίαις) that even slaves would despise; cf. *Antid.* 15.269; *Against the Sophists* 13.19–22; and *Encomium of Helen* 10.6–7. For the view that Isocrates attacked the Socratics in *Against the Sophists* and *Encomium of Helen*, see Villar 2019 and 2020—still, the antagonism between Isocrates and Plato reveals the extent of the debate at the time on what is philosophy (cf. *Antid.* 15.266, 271) and its relation to oratory, truth, and persuasion as well as its potential to serve the needs of the state; (Wilson-)Nightingale 1995, 13–59; cf. Ober 2004 arguing that Isocrates emulates Plato's Socrates to strengthen his claim of being a philosopher; cf. Kennedy 1963, 182; (Wilson-)Nightingale 1995, 192–194; Haskins 2004, 39–46. For Isocrates' attempt to link his understanding of virtue with Solon's ideas, see Konstan 2004, 115–117.

230. *Leg.* 699c6–7: ἧς ὁ δειλὸς ἐλεύθερος καὶ ἄφοβος· ("the coward is unfettered and unfrighten by it, i.e., by *aidōs*"); cf. 701a8–b3. On fear in the *Republic* and the *Laws*, see Anagnostou-Laoutides 2026; cf. Pfefferkorn 2020, 258–260.

231. Usher 2002, esp. 214–219; Sheffield 2001b; cf. Anagnostou-Laoutides 2021b, 258, with Sider 1980 (arguing that in the *Symposium* Plato alludes to activities associated with the City Dionysia) and Biles 2007, 24. The comic elements of the *Symposium*, long recognized in the bibliography, comprise Aristophanes' hiccups (185c3–e5, 188e3–189a6), the figure of the uninvited guest (Aristodemus at 174e), the drunken Alcibiades (212d4–213b4), teasing and banter among the guests, and finally Socrates' discussion of comedy (223d). For Aristophanes' hiccups, see Saxonhouse 1984, 16; Allen 1991, 20; Bloom 2001, 95–6; Nichols 2004, 188; and Nussbaum 2007, 172; cf. Jazdzewska 2016, 188–193. For the figure of the uninvited guest, see Puchner 2010, 17; cf. Platter 1993. For the association of comedy and excessive drinking, see Kidd 2014, 27–29 and 40–50; for Plato's introduction of comic elements in his dialogues, especially of motifs associated with satyr plays, see Erler 2017.

232. Pind. *Pyth.* 12.18–25; Arist. *Pol.* 1341b; Plut. *de cohib. ira* 456b and *quaest. conv.* 713d; Apollod. *Bibl.* 1.4.2; Hdt. 1.14.3 and 2.26.3; *A.P.* 7.696; Ov. *Met.* 6.392–395; Diod. Sic. 5.75.3; Str. 10.3.14 and 2.8.15; Ath. *Deipn.* 14.616e–617f citing among others Melanippides PMG 758 and Telestes PMG 805a–c and 806. For Marsyas' association with Phrygia, see Arist. *Pol.* 1341a21–23 and 1442b3; ps.-Plut. *Mus.* 1132e–f and 1133d–f. For further bibliography, see Weiss 2018a, esp. nn71–74, and 2018b. Plato also refers to Marsyas elsewhere in his dialogues, for example, in *Euthyd.* 285c and *Leg.* 677d; cf. Wilson 2004, 272–279 and 284–290, on a new myth of Marsyas invented in democratic Athens, according to which Marsyas was cast as playing not only the aulos but also the lyre, conventionally associated with Apollo and a symbol of musical and political conservatism; the myth possibly reflected a democratic tendency for inclusion. On the rise of "new

music" in democratic Athens and its political connotations, see in the same volume Csapo 2004, 213, 217–221, 229–230 and 235–240.

233. Trans. mainly from Nehamas and Woodruff 1989, 66–67; for Socrates' ability to mesmerize his audiences through his *elenchus*, see Hartmann 2017, 286–287, with Morrow 1953 and Gellrich 1994; cf. chapter 2, p. 37.

234. Cf. *Phdr.* 259a8–b2: "But if they see us conversing (διαλεγομένους) and sailing past them uncharmed as if passing by the Sirens (αραπλέοντάς σφας ὥσπερ Σειρῆνας ἀκηλήτους) . . . they would perhaps be pleased." The Sirens, known for their dangerous qualities, feature already in Homer, *Od.* 12.39–54 and 158–200; cf. Gresseth 1970, esp. 205–206, on their dangerous allure, a theme popular with comic playwrights. For the Sirens in Nicophon (probably an Old Comedy playwright), see Storey 2011, 407 (= L14) with Anagnostou-Laoutides 2021b, 266.

235. Marsyas supposedly engaged in a competition about wisdom with Apollo (and lost), a tradition Xenophon was apparently familiar with; see *Anab.* 1.2.8 with Buzzetti 2014, 18–20, 75, and 184; for the new version of the myth in fifth century Athens, see Wilson 2004 (in n232 above).

236. *Symp.* 216d8–9. Alcibiades' jesting style corresponds to Socrates' usual way of dealing with people, as Alcibiades notes in 216e5–6: εἰρωνευόμενος δὲ καὶ παίζων πάντα τὸν βίον πρὸς τοὺς ἀνθρώπους διατελεῖ; cf. 218d8–9: καὶ οὗτος ἀκούσας μάλα εἰρωνικῶς καὶ σφόδρα ἑαυτοῦ τε καὶ εἰωθότως ἔλεξεν. Socrates' humorous engagement with Alcibiades is an additional indication that he is talking metaphorically. For the affinity of metaphors and jokes (both operating at two levels of meaning), see Cohen 1978; for Aristotle's discussion of irony (esp. *Eth. Nic.* 1127b29–31 prescribing its measured use so as to avoid boasting) and humor (esp. in the lost part of the *Poetics*), see Lombardini 2013, 209–211; cf. Walker 2019 (with minimal bibliographical insights) and in the same volume Woodruff 2019, 170n13, with Cairns 2014, pars. 2–8 (Woodruff does not discuss the *Symposium* but touches upon the use of metaphor in Socrates' self-ridicule); also, Morreall 1987, 10–18; Krikmann 2009. D. Scott 2000, 30–31, argues that Alcibiades charges Socrates with *hubris* for scorning his charms; cf. the lyric poet Telestes, fr. 805 ap. Ath. *Deipn.* 14.616f–617a. Also, Sansone 2018, 80–81.

237. Ustinova 2017, 174–178; cf. the conclusion of the book.

238. Ustinova 2017, 174–179 and 182–183 (on the survival of these rites in later authors, such as Plutarch and Theophrastus); Wesselmann 2011, 144–159, on Herodotus' connection of Dionysus with the hubristic attitude of tyrants; cf. Bowie 2003; on tyranny and madness in Herodotus and Plato, see Bushnell 1990, 13–17.

239. Alcibiades compares his own "Socratic affliction" to a snake bite; *Symp.* 218a6–7: πληγείς τε καὶ δηχθεὶς ὑπὸ τῶν ἐν φιλοσοφίᾳ λόγων ("stricken and stung by philosophic discourses"). Euripides presents a snake-like Lyssa as the killer of Heracles' children in *Her.* 882–883: Νυκτὸς Γοργὼν ἑκατογκεφάλοις ὄφεων ἰαχήμασι Λύσσα μαρμαρωπός (Ustinova 2017, 31n27); also, Aesch. *TGF* fr. 169:

where Aeschylus compares Lyssa's attack to the stinging of a scorpion (. . . κέντημα γλώσσης [or Λύσσης], σκορπίου βέλος λέγω; with Ustinova 2017, 176n86).

240. Toohey 2004, 27–38, discusses the figures of Orestes, Ajax, and Heracles (cf. chapter 2, n46). At any rate, Toohey continues, from Euripides to Plutarch, melancholy is perceived as "a preeminently violent and angry condition." Cf. Kazantzidis 2018, 52–54.

241. Cf. Ustinova 2017, 176 on Aeschylus' description of the symptoms of being possessed by Lyssa (cf. n239 above).

242. Chapter 2, p. 63. Cf. Kazantzidis 2018, 50–52 with *Ep.* 12 (= 9.330–332 L.) where Hippocrates admits that when trying to meditate in isolation, one can still be misunderstood as melancholic.

243. On the soporific effect of wine, see Eur. *Bacch.* 380–385 and 772; cf. Ar. *On Sleep and Waking* 457b (cited in chapter 2, n41); Ath. *Deipn.* 1.26a; Plut. *Mar.* 45.3; *Thes.* 22.4–5; *quaest. conv.* 158f–159a, 652c–d, 657a and d, 686a–c, and 678b. Although wine is praised for its ability to facilitate sleep (cf. Galen, *De san. tuend.* 6.242–243 and 6.247 Kühn; Dioscorides 5.6.10 and 5.71; Pliny, *HN* 14.117, 23.38 and 23.41 on Hom. *Od.* 4.219–220), falling asleep at a symposion was perceived as a sign of intoxication; see, for example, *Od.* 9.345–399, 10.551–560, 11.59–65 relating the drunken stupors of Polyphemus and Elpenor; cf. Sen. *Ep.* 83.15, 16, and 24, with D'Arms 1995, 305; Suet. *Claud.* 8 and Lucian, *Symp.* 3 with König 2012, 250. In addition, sleep alongside cold water to induce sweating was recommended as hangover treatments; Celsus, pr. 69–70; 6.6.8c and f; Béguin 2002, 152. These references are discussed in Mudd 2015, who examines the medical and social benefits of wine in the Roman empire.

244. For Socrates, Agathon, and Aristophanes as representing their respective arts, that is, philosophy, drama, and comedy, see Erde 1976 and Duncan 1977; cf. Rosen 2005.

245. See *Resp.* 592b1–5 cited on p. 108.

246. *Symp.* 216e7–217a2 and 222a3–7. Chapter 1, p. 29 with n156.

247. For the *hermae* as a physical representation of the democratic male subject, see Winkler 1990, 35–36; also, Wohl 1999, 351: ". . . the mutilation of the herms speaks to an eroticized politics of democracy; cf. Murray 2018/1990b.

248. Also see the conclusion of the book.

249. Cf. Plut. *garr.* 503d ff., cited in chapter 4, p. 121.

250. Rademaker 2005, 340 with n69; cf. Pl. *Resp.* 439c5–d2. Also, Pfefferkorn 2022, 73–75, 96 with n81 with Xen. *Mem.* 1.5.4–5: ἆρά γε οὐ χρὴ πάντα ἄνδρα, ἡγησάμενον τὴν ἐγκράτειαν ἀρετῆς εἶναι κρηπῖδα, ταύτην πρῶτον ἐν τῇ ψυχῇ κατασκευάσασθαι, 98–105; on *sōphrosynē* as the primacy of reason in the soul, see conclusion, n64.

251. Cf. *Bacch.* 641, where Pentheus states ironically as he prepares to face Teiresias: πρὸς σοφοῦ γὰρ ἀνδρὸς ἀσκεῖν σώφρον᾽ εὐοργησίαν ("It is the duty

of the wise man to exercise self-controlled benignity"); on the many meanings of wisdom (*sophia*) in the *Bacchae*, see Schein 2016, esp. 268.

252. *Phd.* 69c9–d2; chapter 1, n199.

253. *Phd.* 66d3–e1: "If . . . we turn to philosophy, the body constantly interrupts our studies and bewilders us with noise and confusion (θόρυβον παρέχει καὶ ταραχὴν καὶ ἐκπλήττει), so that are unable to behold the truth (μὴ δύνασθαι ὑπ' αὐτοῦ καθορᾶν τἀληθές), and in fact it becomes obvious to us that if are ever to know anything clearly, we must be free from the body and must behold the realities themselves with our soul alone (αὐτῇ τῇ ψυχῇ θεατέον αὐτὰ τὰ πράγματα)." According to Socrates, the body is characterized by foolishness (67a8: τῆς τοῦ σώματος ἀφροσύνης); cf. *Phdr.* 250c5–7.

254. Socrates offers yet another definition of *sōphrosynē* in *Phdr.* 237e1–238a1, as "opinion (δόξης) that leads through reason toward the best" chapter 2, p. 37.

255. *Leg.* 631c5–d7 (on *phronēsis* and *sōphrosynē* as key civic virtues); cf. Her. B112 with Anagnostou-Laoutides 2022b.

256. Danzig 2021, 1–39; Anagnostou-Laoutides 2022b.

257. Pl. *Leg.* 665b and 666a2–c3; on the role of *choreia* in civic education, see Belfiore 1986; Prauscello 2014, 105–181, esp. 117–118; Folch 2015, 215–219; cf. Yu 2020.

258. Cf. Baima 2017, 67–73. Bartels 2017, 36, 98–99, and 105–107, identifies *sōphrosynē* with *aidōs* and *logismos* (the reasoning faculty) in the *Laws*, following Schöpsdau 1986, 122; the role of *sōphrosynē* in the moral and psychological framework of the *Laws* is further analyzed by Pfefferkorn 2022, 69–112. Rademaker 2005, 295–299 (cited by Bartels 2017, 82n29) associates *sōphrosynē* with *andreia*. Cf. Petrucci 2019, 167, on Plato's appreciation of nonphilosophical virtue as best exemplified in "popular and political virtue," with *Phd.* 82a11–b3 referring to the τὴν δημοτικὴν καὶ πολιτικὴν ἀρετὴν . . . ἣν δὴ καλοῦσι σωφροσύνην τε καὶ δικαιοσύνην.

259. Cf. Pfefferkorn 2022, 198.

260. Goldhill 1987 and 2000; Connor 1989; Seaford 2000 and 2021; Rhodes 2003; Carter 2004.

261. Cf. Eur. *Bacch.* 670–671 (δέδοικ', ἄναξ) and 775–776 (ταρβῶ . . . τὸν τύραννον) highlighting Pentheus' arrogant and tyrannical attitude. Thus, Pentheus appears closer to the tyrannical man of the *Republic* (see n56 above) who inspires fear in others and yet is also consumed by paranoid anxiety about losing his privileges.

262. Socrates begins his argument a few lines earlier at *Alc.* I 134b6–8: οὐκ ἄρα τειχῶν οὐδὲ τριήρων οὐδὲ νεωρίων δέονται αἱ πόλεις, ὦ Ἀλκιβιάδη, εἰ μέλλουσιν εὐδαιμονήσειν, οὐδὲ πλήθους οὐδὲ μεγέθους ἄνευ ἀρετῆς ("so it is not walls or warships or arsenals that cities need, Alcibiades, if they are to be happy, nor numbers, nor size, without virtue"); on virtue and happiness in the *Laws*, see Carone 2002 and Devereux 2017; cf. Hammond 1892, 133n3; and

Ahbel-Rappe 2010 refuting the view that Socratic ethics is an ancient version of egoistic eudaimonism.

263. Pfefferkorn 2022, 107, 110–112; Bartels 2017, 125. At *Leg.* 632c6–9 Socrates summarizes the lawgivers' mission thus: "the legislator will deliver his laws about all these matters to the guardians, some of whom will be guided by wisdom (διὰ φρονήσεως) and others by true opinion (δι' ἀληθοῦς δόξης), so that Reason, having bound all these things together, may declare them as according with *sōphrosynē* and justice (ὅπως πάντα ταῦτα συνδήσας ὁ νοῦς ἑπόμενα σωφροσύνῃ καὶ δικαιοσύνῃ ἀποφήνῃ)." Cf. 712a1–4: "Whenever the greatest power coincides in a man with wisdom and *sōphrosynē*, then the birth of the best polity and the best laws is brought forth" (ταὐτὸν τῷ φρονεῖν τε καὶ σωφρονεῖν ἡ μεγίστη δύναμις ἐν ἀνθρώπῳ συμπέσῃ, τότε πολιτείας τῆς ἀρίστης καὶ νόμων τῶν τοιούτων φύεται γένεσις); cf. *Leg.* 744a, 964b, 965c. Earlier, at *Leg.* 657b2–8, Plato entertained the idea of adapting the principle of correctness in tune into legal form; see Anagnostou-Laoutides forthcoming c. For *phronēsis* as practical wisdom in Plutarch, see *virt. mor.* 443e8–f2. On the mission of the "true lawgiver by nature" in the *Laws* (710e7–8: ὅταν ἀληθὴς μὲν νομοθέτης γένηται φύσει), who promotes a "virtuous philosophical tyranny" based on the rule of reason, see Balot 2024, 80–89 and 315–317.

264. Pfefferkorn 2022, 262–263.

265. Cf. *Cra.* 386a; *Tht.* 152a.

266. Carone 2005, 177–178; cf. Pl. *Phd.* 114d–115a, for *sōphrosynē* as an ornament of the soul.

267. Carone 2005, 183–184.

268. In the run-up to this argument, Plato compares the guardians with naval commanders (reworking the popular metaphor of the ship of state) who are, however, overwhelmed by their penchant for wine (*Leg.* 906e1–3: πότερον κυβερνήταις, λοιβῇ τε οἴνου κνίσῃ τε παρατρεπομένοις αὐτοῖς, ἀνατρέπουσι δὲ ναῦς τε καὶ ναύτας); Bartels 2017, 85 and 2020. The metaphor was famously introduced in *Resp.* 488c where the sailors of a ship who fight to take control of it try to incapacitate the steersman with drugs or by getting him drunk. Cf. n68 above.

269. Bartels 2017, 195–196 with *Leg.* 961d8–10: συλλήβδην δὲ νοῦς μετὰ τῶν καλλίστων αἰσθήσεων κραθείς . . . σωτηρία ἑκάστων δικαιότατ' ἂν εἴη καλουμένη; also see her p.192 on the "the intrinsic connection between νοῦς and σωτηρία: the natural object of νοῦς is σωτηρία; and conversely, aiming for σωτηρία requires νοῦς. This is the function of the nocturnal council." The inspectors are discussed at *Leg.* 945b–948b; the Nocturnal Council at 950d4–952d3, 961a1–968e6. Klosko 1988b, *passim* and Lewis 1998, 1–20, argue that Plato tries here to accommodate philosophical insight into the city rather than reiterate the importance of philosopher-kings as discussed in the *Republic*; Bartels 2017, 190–203; Anagnostou-Laoutides 2021a and forthcoming b.

270. See Rutherford 2004 on theoric song-dance and its political importance; cf. Rutherford, 2013, esp. 142–148 with n14, citing Ammonius' *Diff.* no. 226, where he distinguishes between a viewer (θεατὴς), preoccupied with theatrical performances and contests, and a *theōros* who is a man "sent to the gods:" θεωρὸς μὲν γάρ ἐστιν ὁ εἰς θεοὺς πεμπόμενος, θεατὴς δὲ ὁ ἀγώνων καὶ θεάτρων; cf. *Leg.* 950e1–952d3; Ker 2000, 308–309.

271. (Wilson-)Nightingale 2005, 153–154, 165–172 (for philosophical *theōria* in Plato's *Republic*); Rutherford 2013, 324–338.

272. *Leg.* 951a4–5. Verlinsky 2016, 182.

273. *Leg.* 961a5–9.

274. *Leg.* 951b5–8: εἰσὶ γὰρ ἐν τοῖς πολλοῖς ἄνθρωποι ἀεὶ θεῖοί τινες—οὐ πολλοί—παντὸς ἄξιοι συγγίγνεσθαι, φυόμενοι οὐδὲν μᾶλλον ἐν εὐνομουμέναις πόλεσιν ἢ καὶ μή, ὧν κατ᾽ ἴχνος ἀεὶ χρὴ τὸν ἐν ταῖς εὐνομουμέναις πόλεσιν οἰκοῦντα, ἐξιόντα κατὰ θάλατταν καὶ γῆν, ζητεῖν.

275. (Wilson-)Nightingale 2004, 63–64, notes that Herodotus refers to Solon's travels as "philosophizing" (1.30.2: ὡς φιλοσοφέων γῆν πολλὴν θεωρίης εἵνεκεν ἐπελήλυθας); the word probably refers to the intellectual vogue of gathering knowledge through extensive traveling, rather than to being a philosopher *stricto sensu*.

276. (Wilson-)Nightingale 2005, 173–179.

277. *Leg.* 966c1–5: "is it not one of the greatest the doctrine about the gods (τὸ περὶ τοὺς θεούς), which we thoroughly expounded (ὃ δὴ σπουδῇ διεπερανάμεθα), to know both that they exist and what power they seem to master (ὡς εἰσίν τε καὶ ὅσης φαίνονται κύριοι δυνάμεως, εἰδέναι) to the extent that man is able to understand these things." The Council ought to exclude from office anyone (966c8–9) "who does not strive find every proof about the existence of the gods" (ὃς ἂν μὴ διαπονήσηται τὸ πᾶσαν πίστιν λαβεῖν τῶν οὐσῶν περὶ θεῶν). Cf. Balot 2024, 237–238 and 243–254.

278. Cf. Bartels 2017, 192 with nn13 and 14. Furthermore, at 967d10 Plato claims that "reason controls what exists among the stars" (τόν . . . ἐν τοῖς ἄστροις νοῦν τῶν ὄντων), and that "the connection of these things follows the principles of music" (967e2: τά τε κατὰ τὴν μοῦσαν τούτοις τῆς κοινωνίας). Societies should apply these principles "by fitting together moral practices and customs" (967e3–5: χρήσηται πρὸς τὰ τῶν ἠθῶν ἐπιτηδεύματα καὶ νόμιμα συναρμοττόντως), "while being able to give a rational explanation of all that admits of rational explanation" (ὅσα τε λόγον ἔχει, τούτων δυνατὸς ᾖ δοῦναι τὸν λόγον).

279. Pfefferkorn 2022, 20–21.

280. Chapter 2, n191. Earlier in the dialogue Plato had noted that legislating the use of such music "would be the task of a god or godlike man" (657a10–11: τοῦτο δὲ θεοῦ ἢ θείου τινὸς ἀνδρὸς ἂν εἴη: cf. 669c–673d; 799a–b). Thus, Magnesia's legislators were also envisaged as philosophers since they were expected to engage in what philosophers typically dedicate their lives to—becoming godlike. See Anagnostou-Laoutides 2024a, 3.

281. Armstrong 2004, 174.

282. Verlinsky 2016, 192–194, interprets the Nocturnal Council as a philosophical school; cf. Anagnostou-Laoutides 2021a and forthcoming b; cf. Balot 2024, 276–277, 301–314, 321–329 and 330–336 who further argues (pp. 249–254) that the members of the Council will be recruited from young atheists with sound character (however, like Baima 2025, I do not see the Nocturnal Council as opposing the rule of law). On Aristotle's important recognition of levels of hierarchically ordered but interconnected levels of *theōria*, see Roochnik 2009; cf. Ward 2018 and 2021, esp. 162–183; also, (Wilson-)Nightingale 2004, 187–252.

283. Pl. *Leg.* 722d7–e5; also, *Phd.* 61a4–5; *Resp.* 591c1–592b; *Laches* 188d3–9; and cf. *Resp.* 424c5–7: οὐδαμοῦ γὰρ κινοῦνται μουσικῆς τρόποι ἄνευ πολιτικῶν νόμων τῶν μεγίστων, ὥς φησί τε Δάμων καὶ ἐγὼ πείθομαι; Power 2010, 335. Anagnostou-Laoutides 2024a and forthcoming a1 and c.

284. Anagnostou-Laoutides 2021c, 252–256, on the musical inclination of the philosopher; cf. Anagnostou-Laoutides 2023, 29–33; also, chapter 2, nn129 and 203. Note that in *Symp.* 215c6–8, as part of Socrates' comparison with Marsyas, we are told that his melodies are divine and able to reveal those ready for the god and his mysteries (τὰ οὖν ἐκείνου [i.e., of Marsyas] . . . αὐλῇ . . . μόνα κατέχεσθαι ποιεῖ καὶ δηλοῖ τοὺς τῶν θεῶν τε καὶ τελετῶν δεομένους διὰ τὸ θεῖα εἶναι); cf. Prior 2006, 153.

285. Cf. *Resp.* 500e–501e d1–e2 where Plato compares the philosopher with a verbal painter, able to render the ideal state as close to the divine visions he perceives as possible. Philosophers, Plato argues (500d1–e2), like painters, are compelled to do so (τις . . . αὐτῷ ἀνάγκη γένηται ἃ ἐκεῖ ὁρᾷ μελετῆσαι εἰς ἀνθρώπων ἤθη καὶ ἰδίᾳ καὶ δημοσίᾳ τιθέναι), posing as "craftsmen of sobriety and justice and all forms of ordinary civic virtue" (δημιουργὸν αὐτὸν οἴει γενήσεσθαι σωφροσύνης τε καὶ δικαιοσύνης καὶ συμπάσης τῆς δημοτικῆς ἀρετῆς); cf. Petraki 2015 arguing that Plato's preference to represent the ideal state as an individual (e.g., a statue or a painting of a single male figure, an *andreikelon*) aims to highlight the ability of the civic body to achieve unity and homogeneity. Importantly, the auxiliaries in the *Republic* are precisely characterized by manliness (ἀνδρεία), which they are encouraged to nourish and maintain through *sōphrosynē*. On this, see Anagnostou-Laoutides 2026, 282–283.

286. On Plato's use of mystic *epopteia*, see chapter 1, p. 32 with n175. For the use of *theōria* instead, see *Symp.* 210d4–6 where the philosopher contemplates the beautiful: (τοῦ καλοῦ . . . θεωρῶν); cf. *Phdr.* 250d4–e2: θεώμενος, stressing the visibility of beauty.

287. See, for example, *Tht.* 173d4–6 cited on p. 77.

288. Cf. Pl. *Alc.* I, 134s12–13 with Anagnostou-Laoutides 2022, 33–34. Plato here combines pleasure, as the criterion of music, with that of *sōphrosynē*.

289. *Leg.* 965c9–d3: ἔν τε ἀνδρείᾳ καὶ σωφροσύνῃ καὶ δικαιοσύνῃ καὶ ἐν φρονήσει ἓν ὄν, ἀρετὴν ἑνὶ δικαίως ἂν ὀνόματι προσαγορεύεσθαι; cf. 964b3–6.

290. See *Leg.* 828b; 871d; 885d–e for instances when the law-keepers get together with priests and divinators to examine matters of religious observance; cf. 908d; 913b; 933c–d for references to pseudo-divinators.

291. *Resp.* 532c: "all this discourse about the arts (ἡ πραγματεία τῶν τεχνῶν) which we have gone through, it has the ability to lead the best part of the soul (ταύτην ἔχει τὴν δύναμιν καὶ ἐπαναγωγὴν τοῦ βελτίστου ἐν ψυχῇ) toward the contemplation of the best among the realities (πρὸς τὴν τοῦ ἀρίστου ἐν τοῖς οὖσι θέαν)." Cf. Sermamoglou-Soulmaidi 2021, 110–111.

292. Cf. *Resp.* 523b3–4 where Plato refers to "summoners" as "those things that urge the mind to examine them in every way, since sense perception does not produce any sound outcome" (τὰ δὲ παντάπασι διακελευόμενα ἐκείνην [= τὴν νόησιν] ἐπισκέψασθαι, ὡς τῆς αἰσθήσεως οὐδὲν ὑγιὲς ποιούσης). The summoners, Plato explains, lead the soul to confusion by forcing it to consider the relativity of categories such as big and small, soft and hard, or thick and thin. Importantly, the process compels the soul to turn to "the contemplation of reality" (525a3–4; ἐπὶ τὴν τοῦ ὄντος θέαν), until eventually "the soul is forced to use intelligence itself to reach truth itself" (526b3–4: προσαναγκάζον αὐτῇ τῇ νοήσει χρῆσθαι τὴν ψυχὴν ἐπ᾿ αὐτὴν τὴν ἀλήθειαν). Cf. Plut. *garr.* 510c11–e10 arguing that to reject passion one "must grasp through reason the harm and shame that results from them" (τὰς βλάβας καὶ τὰς αἰσχύνας τὰς ἀπ᾿ αὐτῶν τῷ λόγῳ κατανοήσωμεν), adding: "the first remedy and medicine for curing excessive passion is reflection on the shameful and painful outcomes that come from them (τοῦτο πρῶτον ἴαμα καὶ φάρμακόν ἐστι τοῦ πάθους, ὁ τῶν ἀπ᾿ αὐτοῦ γινομένων αἰσχρῶν καὶ ὀδυνηρῶν ἐπιλογισμός); also, *de vit. pud.* 536c9–d5.

293. See Perysinakis 2019, 249–251, on aristocratic and handsome Alcibiades as the epitome of "*chrestos* or καλός τε κἀγαθός par excellence." Aristophanes' discussion in the *Frogs* (725–725; 730–733) of good and bad citizens relies on a metaphor about good and counterfeit money—on this, also see the Conclusion. Tordoff 2012, 264–270. Here, I am reminded of Socrates' famous coin metaphor in *Phd.* 69a6–b3, where he explicitly rejects the analogy between virtue and coins because the concept of exchange does not explain virtue adequately. Nathan 2020, 120–124. Cf. the conclusion, pp. 153 and 156 on wine as "cultural currency."

294. See *Life of Ar.* Test 1.39–40 Kassel/Austin (= L502) according to which Aristophanes "was especially praised and much loved by the citizens for taking pains to show in his plays how free the polity of the Athenians was and how unfettered by any tyrant (ὡς ἐλευθέρα . . . καὶ ὑπ᾿ οὐδενὸς τυράννου δουλαγωγουμένη), that it was on the contrary a democracy and that the people, being free, ruled themselves (ἐλεύθερος ὢν ὁ δῆμος ἄρχει ἑαυτοῦ)." As a result, he was crowned with a branch of sacred olive. Aristophanes commented on this honor in the *Frogs* in the lines cited on p. 109. Cf. Rosen 2015 on the Athenian decree on Aristophanes' second performance of the *Frogs*.

295. With n293 above, see Perysinakis 2019, 258, who points out that throughout the *Frogs*, Alcibiades is aligned with the *chrestoi* (good citizens) vs the *poneroi* (bad citizens); cf. Cohn 2013, 253–254 with n119.

296. Scott 2019, 249. On p. 234 Scott explains that he draws on joke theory as a response to cognitive theories of metaphor and their tendency to de-emphasize "the impossibilities of metaphorical language . . . in the process of cognition." This, of course, is precisely the problem that Socrates identifies with comedy: (what he regards as) the pretense of sincerity.

297. See Bartels 2017, 46–49, on the fifth century debate about the *technai* and their role in the sophistic movement (as well as the polemic against the definition of medicine as a *techne* on account of its inability to be precise); cf. n107 above.

298. Hardie 2004, 19, 21–22, and 25 with n87, on the prevalent role of *choreia* in Dionysian and Eleusinian rites that likely influenced Plato's representation of the chorus of the gods in the *Phaedrus*.

299. Scott 2019, 241–242, on Hom. *Il.* 1.247–249 and Nestor's rhetorical dexterity. On dialectics as *pharmakon*, see Rinella 2010, 242–248.

300. Sheppard 2008; cf. Crick and Poulakos 2008.

301. For example, see Clay 1975; Erde 1976.

302. Marren 2020; cf. Rinella 2010, 207–208.

303. Anagnostou-Laoutides 2020a; cf. *Resp.* 475a comparing the lovers and those covetous of honor (φιλοτίμους) to drunkards who "welcome any wine on any pretext" (τοὺς φιλοίνους . . . πάντα οἶνον ἐπὶ πάσης προφάσεως ἀσπαζομένους).

304. Stob. *Flor.* 1.18.25 (Meineke 1855, 1.295): Πυθαγόρας ἔλεγε τὴν μέθην μανίας εἶναι μελέτην. Cf. Stob. *Flor.* 1.18.24 (Meineke 1855, 1.294) for drunkenness as small-scale madness (μικρὰν μανία); Ahonen 2014, 121–122.

305. Stob. *Flor.* 1.18.34 (Meineke 1855, 1.296): Πυθαγόρας ἐρωτηθείς, πῶς ἂν οἰνόφλυξ τοῦ μεθύειν παύσαιτο· εἰ συνεχῶς, ἔφη, θεωροίη τὰ ὑπ' αὐτοῦ πρασσόμενα.

306. *Resp.* 479d11–e2: τοὺς ἄρα πολλὰ καλὰ θεωμένους, αὐτὸ δὲ τὸ καλὸν μὴ ὁρῶντας μηδ᾽ ἄλλῳ ἐπ᾽ αὐτὸ ἄγοντι δυναμένους ἕπεσθαι, καὶ πολλὰ δίκαια, αὐτὸ δὲ τὸ δίκαιον μή, καὶ πάντα οὕτω δοξάζειν φήσομεν ἅπαντα, γιγνώσκειν δὲ ὧν δοξάζουσιν οὐδέν ("Then those who see many beautiful things without seeing the beautiful itself and are unable to follow anyone who leads them toward it, and [see] many just things, not seeing the just itself, and so with everything else: these people, we shall say, have a belief about everything, but have no knowledge about that of which they have a belief"); the notion is reiterated in *Resp.* 476b4–8.

307. See DL 2.36 where Socrates is portrayed as defender of comedy and its ability to function as social corrective. Cf. Cohn 2013, 185 (with n109) and 253 (with n119), pointing out that in DL 2.38 Aristophanes is listed among Socrates' accusers; also, Muench 2009, 80.

308. Brisson 1998, 122–127, citing *Resp.* 378c3–e3.

309. Socratic irony is a much-discussed topic in the bibliography; Vlastos 1987; Ziolkowski 2001a; Wolfsdorf 2007; Muench 2009, esp. 81.

310. Cf. Barnden 2005, esp. 85, who draws on Lakoff 1993 to claim that "it is plausible that there is no practical alternative to metaphor for thinking about messy abstract domains, especially when matters are complex or subtle."

Chapter 4

1. "Drunkenness is nothing, but a condition of insanity purposely assumed."

2. Cf. introduction, nn54 and 56. Ath. *Deipn.* 10.435b–c (= Theopompus, fr. 115.282); cf. Burton 1992, 234–235. On the "famous Macedonian drunken brawls," see Amitay 2010, 24. On Alexander's proverbial drunkenness, including his emulation of Heracles, also reputed as a drunkard, see Amitay 2010, 36, 58, and appendix C on Alexander Alcoholicus (163–165) listing all the references to Alexander's unhealthy dependence on alcohol in Plutarch, Athenaeus, Justin/ Trogus, Strabo, Diodorus Siculus, and Arrian; cf. Gómez and Mestre 2009.

3. Eur. *Bacch.* 242–243: ἐκεῖνος εἶναί φησι Διόνυσον θεόν, ἐκεῖνος ἐν μηρῷ ποτ᾽ ἐρράφθαι Διός ("That one says that Dionysus is a god, that one [says] that he was once stitched in Zeus' thigh") and 247: ὅστις ἔστιν ὁ ξένος ("Whoever the stranger is") with Friesen 2015, 43.

4. See introduction, p. with nn68–74. Hellenistic poets rework the motif of Archilochus' drunken inspiration; see Callim. fr. 544 Pfeifer: τοῦ . . . μεθυ- πλῆγος φροίμιον Ἀρχιλόχου ("The wine-stricken mind of Archilochus"); cf. Ath. *Deipn.* 11.472f–473a citing an epigram of Hedylus with Floridi 2020, 121–124. However, cf. *Anth. Plan.* 306 and 307, criticizing Anacreon's drunkenness, and *Anth. Gr.* 11.24, contrasting water- and wine-inspired poetry; Knox 1985. Cf. Sens 2016 on "seizing the day" as a cross-generic trope drawing on symposiastic and sepulchral epigrams. On the importance of the symposion among Hellenistic intellectual elites, see Cameron 1995, 71–104; cf. Beneker 2009 on Plutarch's use of inebriation to discuss the broken relationship between Alexander and his father, which anticipated Alexander's transformation from a generous king to a murderous tyrant. Molina Marín 2009 argues that Plutarch sought to downplay the unsavory aspects of the Macedonian banquets, preoccupied with promoting Alexander as a model leader for the Romans; cf. *quaest. conv.* 623e1–624a3 on Alexander's drinking habits.

5. Friesen 2015, 28–39 and 72–85 (on Ptolemy Philadelphus and Theocritus' *Id.* 26, reworking many themes from Euripides' *Bacchae*), argues for the continuing importance of the religious and political aspects of Dionysiac drama in the Hellenistic world.

6. Chapter 1, n188. Friesen 2015, 49.

7. Pizzato 2011, 61–62.

8. Friesen 2015, 59–66.

9. See n24 below.

10. Weber 1946, 355.

11. While discussing *mimesis* in literature during the Second Sophistic, Whitmarsh 2001, 29, notes: "*mimēsis* . . . was not simply a means of marking a stable relationship between two fixed co-ordinates, the present and the past; it was a locus of conflict between various groups trying (vainly) to define that relationship in different ways"; with Friesen 2015, 67.

12. The views of Epictetus survived in Arius (see p. 120) and Stob. *Ecl.* 2.7.11m, 41–45 (Wachsmuth and Hense 1884, 109.5–9). Cf. Epict. fr. 115 (Schweighäuser 1799, 103): μέθυσός ἐστιν ὁ τριῶν πίνων πλέον· κἂν μὴ μεθύσῃ, ὑπερέβη τὸ μέτρον ("He who drinks over three units is a drunkard; even if he doesn't get drunk, he exceeded the limit"); Hobden 2013, 242–246; see DL 7.1 (on Zeno drinking liberally despite condemning drunkenness); Sen. *Ep.* 83.18–25; Lucan, *BC* 10.20–52 with Spencer 2002, 93–94. On the influence of Plato on Stoic ethics, see the contributions in Harte et al. 2010; in Bonazzi and Helmig 2007; and in Long 2013.

13. De Lacy 1974, 5. On Plutarch's association with the Second Sophistic, see Schmitz 2013.

14. On Plutarch's metaphorical connection between wine and conversation, see Lopes 2009, 417–419, with reference to *quaest. conv.* 613c1–2, 660b11–12, and 660c1–2; also, Flinterman 2002 and Goeken 2015 on Aelius Aristides. The greater metaphor at work here is that of speech as therapy, explicitly acknowledged by Gorgias in his *Encomium on Helen* (with Freeman 1948, 131–133).

15. Friesen 2015, 226.

16. Plut. *aud. poet.* 19f (= 19e, Hunter and Russell 2011, 39): "In Homer this form of instruction is given silently (σιωπώμενον), but it allows for useful reconsideration (ἀναθεώρησιν ὠφέλιμον) of the most discredited myths (τῶν διαβεβλημένων μάλιστα μύθων), which some people have abused (παραβιαζόμενοι) and distorted (διαστρέφοντες) through what was called 'undermeaning' by the then thinkers but nowadays allegories (ταῖς πάλαι μὲν ὑπονοίαις ἀλληγορίαις δὲ νῦν λεγομέναις)"; cf. Dem. *Eloc.* 99. Hunter 2009a, 177; Wdowiak 2017, 214. On allegory and *huponoia*, see Pépin 1958, 85–92. On Plato's use of the terms αἴνιγμα and σύμβολον in the context of allegory, see Wdowiak 2017, 215–218. Cf. chapter 1, pp. 33–34 with nn191, 198–199.

17. Niehoff 2010, 35 with introduction, n49.

18. Dillon 1996, 114–135; Bonazzi 2007 with introduction n49.

19. Dillon 1996, 366–379.

20. Again, see Niehoff 2010, 35n8, citing Eus. *Hist. Eccl.* 6.19 and Porph. *V. Plot.* 7–17. Saccas was born into a Christian family and perhaps remained a Christian later in life. On his Christianity, Eusebius (*HE* 6.19.7) and Porphyry (*C.Chr.* F39) disagree; their evidence is evaluated by Ramelli 2017, 7–8. On his

Platonism, see Ramelli 2009; cf. Dillon 1996, 381–383; O'Brien 1994, 137; O'Meara 1997, 113. On Saccas' belief that symbols are pointers to the path of wisdom, see Struck 2004, 102–103.

21. Gerson 2018, online; yet see Banner 2018, 86, noting that Plotinus probably just saw himself as a Platonist. On Plotinus' use of allegory, see *Enn.* 1.2 with Dillon 1996, 366, 372.

22. Collins 2000, 52–53; Fernández Marcos 2010; cf. *Letter of Arist.* 38 (Hadas 1951, 66–83, 114); trans. modified from Wright 2015, 157). The *Letter*, written by an Alexandrian Jew, albeit a hundred years later than it purports (Murray 1967; Wright 2011), celebrates Ptolemy's commission of the Septuagint (the translation of the Torah in Greek); Hacham 2005. On the symposium scene in the *Letter of Aristeas* (182–294) and its Platonic milieu, see Tcherikover 1958, 64–66. Wright 2015, 327–335, and Murray 1996/2018 believe that Aristeas adapts literary motifs in this part of the *Letter*; against this view, Zuntz 1959 argues that a treatise on kingship forms the backbone of the narration; cf. Capponi 2016. On Philo's awareness of the *Letter*, see *Mos.* 2.25–44 with Lim 2013, 77.

23. On Philo's familiarity with Plato, see Niehoff 2010, 36 with bibliography; cf. Yli-Karjanmaa 2018, esp. 122–128. On Philo's use of Euripides' *Bacchae* in the context of the racial tensions that troubled Alexandria during the reign of Caligula, see Friesen 2015, 86–87, noting that Philo, a theatrophile by his own admission, had watched Euripidian plays produced at the theatre of Alexandria (*Prob.* 141; *Ebr.* 177). On Philo's use of the language of the mysteries after Plato's example, see Riedweg 1987, 70–115. Philo, like Plato, is familiar with medical writings on inebriation, including the Hippocratic tradition; Runia and Geljon 2019, 257.

24. On *kataleptike phantasia*, see Sandbach 1971; on Arcesilaus' criticisms of the concept, see Ioppolo 1990, 437–441; Stevens 1996, 6; cf. Togni 2013 on the Stoics' reworking of Plato's *phantasia*, as negotiated mainly in the *Sophist*, the *Theaetetus*, and the *Philebus*. Ioppolo 1990, 442 notes: "For Zeno . . . the cognitive presentation, being a criterion of truth, is capable of recognizing things through the sense organs which grasp their special objects." On the feud of Arcesilaus and Zeno, see Num. fr. 25, *ll.* 83–148 (des Places 1973, 68–71) with Snyder 2018 and the discussion on p. 119. On the related concept of *epochē*, see Sext. Emp. *PH* I.28–29.

25. Obdrzalek 2006, 254–264, argues about the compatibility of Carneades' *pithanon* with the Skeptic concept of *epochē*, or suspension of judgement—which becomes important in Husserl's explanation of phenomenological reduction; cf. Luft 2004, 205–207 and 213. For Husserl, *epochē* is not a way of disengaging with the world but "a radical giving an account of this life" (p. 222).

26. Sext. Emp. *Math.* 7.166 (Bekker 1842, 227) argues that Carneades set out to prove the nonexistence of the criterion yet was compelled to frame a theory about it, as he needed a criterion for the conduct of life and the attainment of happiness (τὴν τοῦ βίου διεξαγωγὴν καὶ πρὸς τὴν τῆς εὐδαιμονίας περίκτησιν).

Thus, he adopted both the probable presentation and that which is at once probable and irreversible and tested (προσλαμβάνων τήν τε πιθανὴν φαντασίαν καὶ τὴν πιθανὴν ἅμα καὶ ἀπερίσπαστον καὶ διεξωδευμένην). On Antiochus of Ascalon's acceptance of the Stoic concept of *kataleptike phantasia,* see Dillon 1996, 64.

27. According to Flory 1996, 158, "the Stoical/rhetorical theory of *phantasia* . . . adheres much more closely to a model of human knowledge similar to the modern one than do Plato's or Aristotle's [theories]."

28. Brittain 2006, xxi.

29. Although Cicero identified himself as an Academic (*Nat. Deor.* 1.11; *Disp. Tusc.* 2.9; 3.7), his allegiance to both Academic Scepticism and Stoicism has been often criticized as hypocritical; for example, Nicgorski 1984; cf. DeGraff 1940; Burkert 1965; Boyancé 1970; Lévy 2008; Powell 2013, esp. 43; Renaud 2018, 73, 84, and 87–88.

30. To the point of questioning Socrates' famous alleged dictum claiming knowledge only of his ignorance (*Acad.* 1.12.45): *Arcesilas negabat esse quicquam quod sciri posset, ne illud quidem ipsum, quod Socrates sibi reliquisset ut nihil scire se sciret;* ("Arcesilaus said that there is nothing that can be known, not even that very thing Socrates had left for himself, that he knew he knew nothing"). The closest that Socrates comes to making the claim is in *Apol.* 21d7–10; cf. Symp. 175e2–4: ἡ μὲν γὰρ ἐμή (i.e., σοφία) φαύλη τις ἂν εἴη, ἢ καὶ ἀμφισβητήσιμος ὥσπερ ὄναρ οὖσα . . .

31. DL 2.8.90: πολὺ μέντοι τῶν ψυχικῶν τὰς σωματικὰς (i.e., ἡδονὰς) ἀμείνους εἶναι; cf. Xen. *Mem.* 2.1 with Dorion 2017b, 48, arguing for a distinction between the immediate pleasures that Aristippus craves for, and the greatest pleasure, which Socrates argues comes as the result of being self-controlled (*Mem.* 4.5.9–10).

32. Diogenes portrayed Carneades as asking for "honeyed wine" (οἰνό-μελι) to be released from his malady toward the end of his life (9.64–65), while Lacydes is said to have from drunkenness, like Arcesilaus (8.61: ἡ τελευτῇ δὲ αὐτῷ παράλυσις ἐκ πολυποσίας; cf. Ath. *Deipn.* 2.36b2–4: ἐὰν [i.e., πίνουσιν] δ' ἄκρατον, παράλυσιν τῶν σωμάτων; 10.438a–b; Ael. *VH* 2.41.

33. Chapter 3, p. 83; cf. Plut. *quaest. conv.* 644a4–645c2 and 716b6–c2 (the latter cited on p. 115); Ath. *Deipn.* 2.37e.

34. Sextus Empiricus compared Carneades' thesis that the "likely" (the *pithanon*) "reports true for the most part" to the tendency of the profligate (the *asōtoi*) to trust their flatterers (*PH* 1.230). Obdrzalek 2006, 275–277. The connection goes back to Plato's description of the tyrannical man as a drunkard in the *Republic* (chapter 3, n56); on flatterers in the *Republic,* see 538a–d; 575a and 575e–576a; 590d. Cf. Pl. *Resp.* 560e3 and 561a2 (on ἀσωτία) and *Leg.* 743b (on the ἄσωτος). Cf. Philo, *Contempl.* 5.47: ὑγρός γάρ και ἄσωτος βίος ἅπασιν ἐπίβουλος with specific reference to drunkenness.

35. DL 4.6.37 refers to Arcesilaus' unparalleled rhetorical skills, calling him εὑρεσιλογώτατος.

36. Numenius cites *Il.* 1.447–451, 131 and 471 in fr. 25 (des Places 1973, 68–69, *ll.* 88–94). Furthermore, Arcesilaus had reportedly taken up poetry; see DL 4.6.30: καὶ γὰρ ἐν τοῖς λόγοις ἐμβριθέστατος καὶ φιλογράμματος ἱκανῶς γενόμενος ἥπτετο καὶ ποιητικῆς. Cf. DL 4.6.31 on Arcesilaus' admiration for Homer and his praise of Pindar's eloquence.

37. Numenius is likely hinting here at Plato's definition of the just man as "simple and noble," by quoting Aesch. *Sept.* 577 (ἄνδρα ἁπλοῦν καὶ γενναῖον). Cf. *Resp.* 361b8 on the use of persuasion by the most unjust person, keen to detract attention from his indiscretions.

38. Num. fr. 27 (des Places 1973, 76, *ll.* 10–13): ἐξηγείρετο λάβρος οἷον ποταμὸς ῥοώδης, σφοδρῶς ῥέων, πάντα καταπιμπλὰς τὰ τῇδε καὶ τἀκεῖθι, καὶ εἰσέπιπτε καὶ συνέσυρε τοὺς ἀκούοντας διὰ θορύβου. In the symposiastic context, noise (θόρυβος) points to disorderly drunkenness (chapter 3, p. 80 with nn67 and 68); on garrulity as a symptom of madness or drunkenness, see chapter 2, p. 40. The metaphor of eloquence as a rushing current (cf. Luc. *Nigr.* 38 on p. 129) is common in Greco-Roman literature; Jones 2005, esp. 52–53 with nn4–5, citing Ar. *Equ.* 526–531; Quint. *Inst.* 5.14.31 and 9.4.7; and Sen. *Ep.* 100.1 and 115.18. Furthermore, the poetic description of wine as the gift of Dionysus that "flows" is well established in ancient literature; for example, Eur. *Bacch.* 142: ῥεῖ δ᾽ οἴνῳ; for the image of a river run with wine, see Luc. *VH* 1.7: ἐφιστάμεθα ποταμῷ οἶνον ῥέοντι ὁμοιότατον.

39. Arius Didymus, *Epitome* 10.1–3 (πάθος δ᾽ εἶναί φασιν ὁρμὴν πλεονά-ζουσαν καὶ ἀπειθῆ τῷ αἱροῦντι λόγῳ ἢ κίνησιν ψυχῆς <ἄλογον> παρὰ φύσιν; Pomeroy 1999, 56); cf. 10e23 (naming φιλοινία as one of the manifestations of having allowed the appetites to become ingrained and a source of illness).

40. Heil 2000, 364–366, lists Arius' excerpts preserved in Stobaeus and Eusebius but notes that we cannot be sure whether the Arius mentioned on three occasions by Clement of Alexandria is the same one.

41. Ar. Did. *Epit.* 11m9–13; Pomeroy 1999, 88.

42. On Arcesilaus' sarcasm, see DL 4.43.

43. Eus. *Prep. Evang.* 14.7.1–10 (= PG 21.1205D–1209B) discusses Lacydes' angry reaction to the practical jokes that his servants played against him but also his stinginess; cf. Ar. Did. *Epit.* 10c (on the Stoic rejection of anger) and 11d (claiming that the wise man ought to be skilled in household management), something that Lacydes so obviously lacked according to Eusebius.

44. DL 4.9.63–64 with Usher 2006, 194, on Carneades' mocking one of his students.

45. Ar. Did. *Epit.* 11s24–26; Pomeroy 1999, 98.

46. Heil 2000, 362; Colish 1985, 1.7–15. DL 7.121: πολιτεύσεσθαί φασι τὸν σοφὸν ἂν μή τι κωλύῃ, ὥς φησι Χρύσιππος ἐν πρώτῳ Περὶ βίων· καὶ γὰρ κακίαν ἐφέξειν καὶ ἐπ᾽ ἀρετὴν παρορμήσειν.

47. See n12 above with Ahonen 2014, 121.

48. Stob. *Flor.* 3.6.8 (= Epict. fr. 15): "At Rome the women have in their hands Plato's *Republic*, because he insists that women be shared"). On Plato's female readership during the Hellenistic and Roman periods, see Addey 2018, 418–422.

49. Plut. *quaest. conv.* 711b–d; Lakmann 2000; cf. Männlein-Robert 2006, 90–91; König 2019, 62–63.

50. Anagnostou-Laoutides 2017, 305; Desmond 2011, 61–81 (on Plutarch's popularity under the Flavians); Boys-Stones 2013, 128–146 (on Seneca and Plato); Manolaraki 2011, 173; Vasunia 2001, 216–288 (on Lucan's familiarity with *Critias* and *Timaeus*). On the familiarity of early Stoics, especially Chrysippus, with *Timaeus*, see Betegh 2003, 183–193. On Plutarch's place in Middle Platonism, see Dillon 2013. On his independent engagement with Platonic ideas, see Klotz 2007, 665. Cf. Bonazzi 2018, 133–142, and (in the same volume), Fowler 2018, 229–232. Chrysanthou 2019, 40–46 (on the influence of Plato's *Theaetetus* on Plutarch's self-representation as a philosopher-politician); also, Hunter 2012, 185–222; Kim 2009, 489.

51. Chapter 2, pp. 42–43. Jacob 2013, 109; Vamvouri Ruffy 2019, 18 with n5, citing Oikonomopoulou 2011, 108–112, and Meeusen 2016, 75–84. Cf. Karamanolis 2006, 89–109, where he claims that Plutarch tends to use Aristotle to support ideas that he believes to be Platonic; on Plutarch's Aristotelianism and his familiarity with Stoicism, see Becchi 1999 and 2013; also, Opsomer 2005 and 2013 (in the same volume as Becchi).

52. Nikolaidis 1999, 342–343.

53. Cf. Plut. *quaest. conv.* 704c–d in chapter 3, n80; cf. Teodorsson 2009, 4–7 and in the same volume, Martins de Jesus 2009; for Athenaeus and comic dancing, see Ceccarelli 2000.

54. Plut. *quaest. conv.* 715d1–5 in chapter 3, p. 103; cf. Philo, *Plant.* 165 on the relaxing effects of wine drunk by the wise, with Runia and Geljon 2019, 284–285; also, Boyancé 1936, 212, "on the etymological relation between μέθυ (wine) and μεθίημι (to relax)"; cf. Ath. *Deipn.* 363b.

55. On *adoleschia* and *lērēsin*, see chapter 2, p. 39.

56. Roskam 2017, 746–747; cf. his p. 756 noting that Plutarch cast Socrates as a " 'champion of the truth' . . . reliant on sober reason and a steadfast judgment"; cf. Moore 2019b, 19 with n31.

57. Teodorsson, Ingenkamp, Nikolaidis, and Stadter in the same 1999 volume; cf. Teodorsson 2009, 4 with n8, citing Tecuşan 1990, 238–243.

58. Teodorsson 2009, 5–6 and 10–15; König 2012, 30–32, 60–64; cf. Relihan 1992. On the symposiastic background of Hellenistic poems (cf. n4 above), see Burton 1992, 236–243 (on Theoc. *Id.* 14) and Cameron 1995, 71–103 (on Callimachus' *Aetia*); cf. Harder 2012, 1.35; 2.301–302 (on fr. 43.12–17 in 1. 182) and 955, 969–973 (on fr. 178.11–20 in 1.347–348).

59. An ancient Greek proverb maintained that people "hate a drinking companion with a memory" (μισῶ . . . μνάμονα συμπόταν); Luc. *Symp.* 3; Martial.

Ep. 1.27; Teodorsson 1989, 31–32. Philosophical symposia differed in this respect because one could remember what was said the night before, Plut. *quaest. conv.* 686b–d. Cf. Jacob 2013, 46 and 60, with Ath. *Deipn.* 11.503f where Plutarch is cast as offering a libation to the Muses and Mnemosyne; cf. Rösler 1990; Klotz 2007, 664, on *quaest. conv.* 745e–746a; Teodorsson 1989, 169, on Plut. *quaest. conv.* 629d; König 2007, 62; and Oikonomopoulou 2013, 148–149.

60. Plutarch's banquets promote the notions of *philanthropia* and friendship; see Becchi and Nikolaidis in the same 2009 volume; Teodorsson 1999, 66–69; cf. Martin 1961; De Romilly 1979, 275–308; also, Hubert 1961.

61. König 2019, 54–59.

62. See *Disc.* 38.38 on governors handing out titles instead of refraining from drunken violence and other types of corruption; cf. 64.22. Also, *Disc.* 6.11 on people who indulge in a luxurious lifestyle and drink too much wine, thus "having their souls steeped in drunken stupor" (κραιπάλης δὲ καὶ λήθης τὰς ψυχὰς γέμοντες).

63. *Disc.* 27.2–7: "since Dionysus is of a frenzied nature (διθύραμβος ὢν) and the child of lightning and thunder, as the poets say, he literally fills with fire (πυρὸς πίμπλησι) those who use him in too ignorant a way (τοὺς ἀμαθέστερον χρωμένους ἀτεχνῶς), and actually makes the majority of them thunderstruck (ἐμβροντήτους). Nay rather, his votaries, being practically crazed (μαινόμενοι), do many evil things, just as Homer says of the Centaur that in a fit of drunkenness he wrought evil in the home of Peirithoüs. And others, too, who are naturally loquacious (φύσει ἀδολέσχαι), feeling that they have got their table-companions for an audience, recite stupid and tedious speeches (ἀναισθήτους καὶ μακροὺς . . . λόγους); while still others sing in tune and out of tune, although they have no gift whatever for music; and one might almost say that they give more annoyance than those who quarrel and use abusive language. But there is another class of men who claim to be abstemious and temperate (αὐστηροὶ καὶ σώφρονες εἶναι λέγοντες), that bore people to death by their disagreeable manner (ἀποκναίουσιν ἀηδίᾳ), since they will not condescend either to drink moderately or to take part in the general conversation. But the man that is gentle (πρᾷος) and has a properly ordered character (τὸν τρόπον ἱκανῶς ἡρμοσμένος), easily endures the rudeness of the others, and acts like a gentleman himself, trying to the best of his ability to bring the ignorant chorus (τὸν ἀμαθῆ χορὸν) into a proper demeanour by means of fitting rhythm and melody. And he introduces appropriate topics of conversation (οἰκείους λόγους) and by his tact and persuasiveness (δεξιότητι καὶ πειθοῖ) attempts to get those present to be more harmonious and friendly in their intercourse with one another (ἐμμελέστερον καὶ φιλικώτερον ξυνεῖναι ἀλλήλοις)"; cf. *Disc.* 32.53–55, 62.

64. Vamvouri Ruffy 2019; on Plutarch and Athenaeus, see Jacob 2013, chapters 5 and 7; on Plutarch and Macrobius, Flamant 1977, 180 with n38 and

182–186 (also referring to Macrobius' relationship with Athenaeus, Apuleius, and Petronius); cf. Kaster 1980, 233 (on the metaphor of harmony in Book 7).

65. Oikonomopoulou 2019; on the influence of Plutarch on Apuleius, see DeFilippo 1990; Kirichenko 2008; Ní Mheallaigh 2009, Hunter 2009b; Van der Stockt 2012. For Plutarch and Gellius, see Holford-Strevens 2003, 110–114, 273–274 and 285; Van der Stockt 2003; González Delgado 2017; Setaioli 2020.

66. For the frequent use of the verb *zētein* and the word *zētēsis* in Plutarch's *quaest. conv.*, see Vamvouri Ruffy 2019, 18n5, citing 612e, 613c, 635b, 646a, 666a, 673b, 694d, 700c, and 701e.

67. Teodorsson 2009, 15, claims that "the writings of Athenaeus, Macrobius, Apuleius or Gellius have a quite different character and are not properly symposiac writings." In addition, apart from their knowledge of Plutarch's work, each of the authors mentioned here developed their own appreciation of Plato; for example, on Macrobius' reading of Plato, see Flamant 1977, 178–179; on Gellius and Plato, see Tarrant 1996 and Holford-Strevens 2003, esp. 95–97 and 268–269. On Plato's presence in Athenaeus, see Trapp 2000; cf. Trapp 2020 on Plato and Aelius Aristides. On Apuleius' use of Plato's *Phaedrus* and the *Republic* in his *Metamorphoses*, see Ulrich 2020; cf. Hunter 2012, 142–150, 187–188, and 226–255; also, see Roskam 2018, 156–159 on Apuleius' "vulgar Platonism," since Apuleius probably better qualifies as a sophist than a philosopher.

68. Klotz 2007, 653; Lopes 2009, 417–418. On Macrobius' use of Platonic drinking (in *Sat.* 2.8.5ff.), see Flamant 1977, 68–69; Aulus Gellius discusses Platonic drinking as expounded in *Laws* 1 and 2 in *N.A.* 15.2.3, with Holford-Strevens 2003, 266–267; Lakmann 1995, 157–160; Tarrant 1996, 177–178.

69. Klotz 2007, 656 on *quaest. conv.* 614d; Fowler 2018, 230–231; cf. Teodorsson 2009.

70. Klotz 2007, 652: "The Plutarchan narrator of the *quaest. conv.* presents himself, his friends and his family, as philosophical *paradeigmata* whose behaviour should be emulated. In many of the questions Plutarch poses as an idealized symposiarch, συμποσικώτατος (the opposite of Alcibiades in the *Symposium*), and as such, he is presenting his addressee (and the reader) with a template for sociable philosophical behaviour"; also, König 2011; cf. Van Hoof 2010, 261–265, with Mudd 2015, 29. On Plutarch's use of the concepts of time and space (with a summary of recent theoretical trends), see Georgiadou and Oikonomopoulou 2017, 16–19.

71. On Plutarch's didactic intentions in the *quaest. conv.*, see König 2007; Roskam 2009; Kechagia 2011; Beck 2019; cf. Stadter 1999. Also see Teodorsson 2009, 12, who claims that Plutarch balances his didactic tone with humorous interjections.

72. Also, Plut. *quaest. conv.* 612d, 660a–b, *Sept. sap. conv.* 156d; cf. Cicero's definition of the Roman *convivium* in *Fam.* 9.24.3, *Sen.* 45, with emphasis on "the

whole notion of a shared life"; Pelling 2009, iii; Frazier and Sirinelli 1996, 180–195; Scarcella 1998, 14–20; cf. Van der Stockt 2000, 94. On Plato's argument in the *Laws* that the purpose of the symposion is to induce friendship among fellow citizens, see Bartels 2017, 100 and 111–112 with n159, citing *Leg.* 671e5–672a3.

73. Chapter 1, p. 28, and chapter 2, p. 39.

74. Nikolaidis 2019 argues that Plutarch's sense of humor in the *quaest. conv.* draws on Plato; on Plutarch's use of humor in the *Conv. sept. sap.*, see Jazdzewska 2016. On his preference for Menander over Aristophanes because the latter had a penchant for "vulgarity, theatricality, and bad language," see Peterson 2019a, 30–31, on Plut. epit. of *Comp.* 853a with Xenophontos 2012, 618; also, Peterson 2019a, 34–35, on *Comp.* 854a and 38–40. On Athenaeus' use of humor and his adaptation of the comic elements of Plato's *Symposium* (notably his elision of drunkenness), see Wilkins 2000b, 29–33 and esp. 35; in the same volume, cf. Sidwell 2000, 137, 139, and 141, citing *Deipn.* 10.429a where Aristophanes appears along Alcaeus as composing his poetry while drunk—an indication that Athenaeus closely followed the rivalry of Aristophanes with Cratinus. See Whitmarsh 2000, 311–313, on Athenaeus' use of the figure of the jester, which we have also encountered in Xenophon's *Symposium*; cf. Olson 2018, 435–438. Anderson 2000, 322–323, compares Athenaeus' penchant for risqué jokes to Plutarch's conservative sense of humor, noting that Athenaeus attacks the hypocrisy of the philosophers like Lucian (for example, *Deipn.* 4.160d–165a); also see Milanezi 2000, esp. 411–412. For the later application of the theory of the four humors to people's characters and the association of pure blood with cheerful individuals, see Jouanna 2012c, esp. 338–343, who notes that it starts with Galen's commentary on the Hippocratic treatise *The Nature of Man*.

75. Chapter 2, pp. 81–82, 89.

76. Ingenkamp 1999, 277–90; Teodorsson 1999; Nikolaidis 1999; cf. Duff 1999, 15n6 and 32n56. Cf. Ath. *Deipn.* 14.613c on Xenophon's Agesilaus who tried to "avoid getting drunk and behaving manically" (μέθης μὲν ἀπέχεσθαι ὁμοίως ᾤετο χρῆναι καὶ μανίας). Athenaeus adopts the distinction between those who "get drunk in the crowded marketplace" (τῶν ἐξοίνων γινομένων πληθούσης ἀγορᾶς) and those who ought to attend what he refers to as "refined banquets" (τὰ μουσικὰ . . . συμπόσια). Cf. *Deipn.* 10.431f quoting Pl. *Laws* 775b–c. Olson 2018, 441–444. Brock and Wirtjes 2000, 462, note that Athenaeus is more interested in the wine's "impact on behaviour and character, and its value as a stimulus to artistic creativity."

77. The same theme is treated in *Disc.* 30.36 where Dio repeats that it is not wine but pleasure that makes people drunk, revealing their character that wine per se is not blameworthy as it just reveals the character of the people; cf. *Disc.* 8.21 and 27.1–2. Later in *Disc.* 30.37–39 Dio employs the metaphor of the Bowl of Sobriety, probably a reworking of Plato's mixing-bowl metaphor in *Leg.* 773c8–d4. Also, *Disc.* 9.10 on Diogenes being patient with those who were "drunken and crazed by reason of ignorance and stupidity" (μεθύοντας ἀνθρώπους

καὶ μαινομένους ὑπὸ ἀγνοίας καὶ ἀμαθίας); *Disc.* 11.42–43 quoting Stesichorus as arguing that just like the thirsty do not need wine but water, "so too seekers of truth have no need of verse (οὐδὲν δέονται μέτρων), but it is quite enough for them to hear the simple truth (ἁπλῶς ἀκοῦσαι). Poetry, however, tempts them to listen to falsehood (ἀναπείθει τὰ ψευδῆ ἀκούειν) just as wine leads to over-drinking (πίνειν μάτην)."

78. Millett 2005, 26–27, with Xen. *Mem.* 1.1–2 and DL 2.19–20; cf. Alesse 2018, 47.

79. Cf. Anagnostou-Laoutides 2021d.

80. Cf. Dem. *Eloc.* 183–185 on rhythm in Plato's speeches; cf. ps.-Long. *Subl.* 39.1 on harmony as a tool of "persuasion and pleasure" (πειθοῦς καὶ ἡδονῆς), but also of "magnificence and emotion" (μεγαληγορίας καὶ πάθους). Halliwell 2011b, 337–338. I am grateful to Harold Tarrant for sharing with me his suggestion that, based on a close reading of the disegno, we could read ἐντονίαν instead of εὐρυθμίαν, as in Plato's *Tht.* 173a1 (cf. *Resp.* 528c3: ἐντόνως ζητούμενα). Based on the sexual connotations of the word, a double entendre may be intended.

81. On the identity of the author (believed to be Aristotle's student, Demetrius of Phaleron) and the dating of the work (possibly as late as the first century BCE), see introductory notes in L199, 310–319.

82. See Dem. *Eloc.* 87 on metaphors that become so established that they often come to replace the proper term (μεμένηκεν ἡ μεταφορὰ κατέχουσα τὸν τοῦ κυρίου τόπον), and 89, where the author advises authors to avoid the use of ὥσπερ when turning a metaphor to a simile because it thus becomes a poetic comparison; cf. chapter 1, pp. 29–30 on Plato's use of εἰκάζω and ὥσπερ.

83. Halliwell 2011b, 359–367. See Trabattoni 2012 on Plato's definition of metaphysical reality, in chapter 2, n228; cf. chapter 3, n42 on Aristotle's criticism of Plato's metaphorical style.

84. Tieleman 2003, 166 (on Zeno); Plut. *De profect. in virt.* 84d reworking Alcibiades' praise of Socrates whose words make the heart "feel such anguish . . . that tears will flow" (καρδίαν στρέφεσθαι καὶ δάκρυα ἐκπίπτειν).

85. See Lucian, *Pisc.* 42 (with Peterson 2010, 130–131) where Philosophy admits that distinguishing between true philosophers and opportunist rhetoricians is challenging given "the similarity of their appearance" (τῇ ὁμοιότητι τῶν ἄλλων σχημάτων); in fact, often "the charlatans are often more convincing than the genuine philosophers" (πιθανώτεροι . . . οἱ γόητες . . . πολλάκις τῶν ἀληθῶς φιλοσοφούντων). Cf. *Phdr.* 261a, where Socrates characterizes rhetoric as an art, for evidence that he did not oppose rhetoric *per se* but its use by poets and *logographoi* who prioritize the aesthetic effect of speeches over moral grounding.

86. Plut. *De rect. rat. aud.* 44a–d discussing precisely the effect of philosophic reasoning, which "removes the wonder and amazement that springs from stalemate and ignorance" (44b9–10: ὁ γὰρ φιλόσοφος λόγος τὸ μὲν ἐξ ἀπορίας καὶ ἀγνοίας θαῦμα καὶ θάμβος ἐξαιρεῖ) and yet even Plutarch acknowledges that

there are speakers intent on impressing the audience who turn every eager listener "to a hypocrite, a flatterer or a boor in all matters regarding speeches" (44d6–7: εἴρων γὰρ ἢ κόλαξ ἢ περὶ λόγους ἀπειρόκαλος); his views are reiterated in Plut. *De profect. in virt.* 80e–81f; also, Cic. *Acad.* 1.17–19 and 33–34 in Karamanolis 2020 on the changes that Plato's heirs made to his unified philosophical system.

87. Suda, s.v. Καικίλιος (= Adler 1967, K1165 in 3.83); *BNJ* 1–3.

88. Cf. ps.-Long. *Subl.* 3.5 on writers who tend to exaggerate, as if drunk (ὥσπερ ἐκ μέθης), thus giving way to outbursts of emotion (παραφέρονται πάθη) beyond the scope of their subject. As a result, "while they (i.e., the poets) are in ecstasy, the audience is not" (ἐξεστηκότες πρὸς οὐκ ἐξεστηκότας). The comment echoes Plato's criticism in *Resp.* 606a4–7 in chapter 2, n165. Similarly, using Plato's metaphor of mixing wine with water, Plutarch (*aud. poet.* 15d–e) advises against overdramatic effects in poetry. On *Subl.* 32.7, see Walsh 1988, 262. For Plato's tendency to coin metaphors, see Caec. Cal. fr. 95 (Ofenloch 1967, 85.10–86.11). On the different approaches of ps.-Longinus and Caecilius to the role of sublimity in Plato, see Innes 2002. Cf. Dem. *Eloc.* 5 and 15 on rhetorical exaggeration making speakers appear drunk.

89. As we saw (chapter 1, n33), ps.-Longinus comments on the ability of the sublime to inspire wonder and amazement (ἐκπλήξει τοῦ πιθανοῦ καὶ τοῦ πρὸς χάριν ἀεὶ κρατεῖ τὸ θαυμάσιον). At *Subl.* 8.4, he argues that emotion is crucial to the success of the sublime because "it inspires the words, as if with a kind of frenzy, breathing divine spirit into them" (ὥσπερ ὑπὸ μανίας τινὸς καὶ πνεύματος ἐνθουσιαστικῶς ἐκπνέον καὶ οἱονεὶ φοιβάζον τοὺς λόγους); on ps.-Longinus' awareness of the distinction between persuasion and ecstasy, see Halliwell 2011b, 329–330.

90. Even Longinus is not oblivious to the tension between transformative ecstasy and the truth. Thus, he stresses the voluntary submission of the mind in experiencing ecstasy; Halliwell 2011b, 340: "Further evidence that the ecstasy of the Longinian sublime cannot be properly understood as an irrational 'possession' is the important statement in chapter 7 that a test of authentic *hupsos* is whether a piece of writing makes a cognitive impression which outlasts the immediate experience of hearing or reading."

91. See Asmis 2017, 136–137, on Plutarch's espousal of the Stoic theory of poetry in his *Quo. adol.*; cf. Peterson 2019a, 43 on Old Comedy quotations in Plutarch, which "often speak to the morality of the character and as such become exemplary of how Old Comedy's deployment of these traits could at times be harnessed for a larger moral and philosophical purpose." Cf. Dem. *Eloc.* 171: ἔστι δὲ καὶ τοῦ ἤθους τις ἔμφασις ἐκ τῶν γελοίων καὶ ἢ παιγνίας ἢ ἀκολασίας ("there is also some indication of character in jokes, either of playful wit or vulgarity"); cf. *Eloc.* 163–165 on the difference between charm and laughter (τὸ γελοῖον καὶ εὔχαρι). Both strategies used to rehabilitate the Socratic style rely on moral arguments, just as Plato's dismissal of poetry does; Relihan 1993, 181.

92. See Laird 2003 and Ní Mheallaigh 2014, 88–89, on Lucian's adaptation of Socratic ecstasy, as represented in Plato's *Symposium*, in his *Philopseudes*; There, the character that corresponds to Socrates, Eucrates, relies on his "august outer appearance [that] conceals his truly ludicrous nature." For Lucian's allusions to other Platonic dialogues, see Neef 1940, 18–38; cf. Hirzel 1895, 2.289–333; Bompaire 1958, 304–320, 372–374, and 607–613; also, Peterson 2010, 145–147, and Tarrant 2005, 229 (on the *Phaedrus*). Cf. *Bis acc.* 5 for a reference to the *Apology*, where Justice describes Socrates' accusers as "much superior to him" (παρὰ τοσοῦτον ὑπερέσχον) since, unlike Socrates, "they engaged with the philosophy about Injustice (περὶ τῆς Ἀδικίας φιλοσοφοῦντες). Peterson 2019a, 102–103. For Lucian's *Fisherman* and the *Apology*, see Whitmarsh 2001, 263–264; Peterson 2019a, 83n5.

93. Fowler 2018, 236–239, esp. 237: "Lucian's appropriation of Plato can be noticed on nearly every level: from thematic, structural, linguistic, allusive, down to the smallest quotation"; on the influence of Menippean satire on Lucian and Petronius, see Teodorsson 2009, 10; Anderson 1978, 372–373; Hunter 2012, 15–16; and Männlein-Robert 2021. For the various strands of Menippean satire, especially the tradition represented by Macrobius, Fulgentius, and Capella, see Fuchs 2006, 10–11. On Petronius' parody of Plato's *Symposium*, see Bessone 1993.

94. For the similarity of Lucian's *Lexiphanes* to Plato's *Symposium*, see Whitmarsh 2005, 46, with Weissenberger 1996, 68–84 and 151–283; cf. Kazantzidis 2019 on Lucian's use of the association between melancholy and irregular speech patterns (with n98 below).

95. Weissenberger 1996, 159–160.

96. Tarrant 2009, 20.

97. Lucian, *Lex.* 1: νέκταρος γάρ τινος ἔοικας οἰνοχοήσειν ἡμῖν ἀπ' αὐτοῦ ("I dare say you will properly 'wine us with nectar' out of it").

98. Weissenberger 1996, 72–74. Cf. Kazantzidis 2019, 291: ". . . just like black bile is said to 'cast its shadow,' literally and metaphorically, over the mind and to disrupt communication between the affected subject and the external environment, so does hyper-Atticism, a figurative sickness of language, obscure meaning by turning Lexiphanes into a user of recondite words which are no different from the babbling and raving of the insane."

99. In his own *Symposium* (par. 45), Lucian compares those philosophers who get drunk and attack each other to the mythical Lapiths and Centaurs, known for their drunken brawls. On Lucian's reception of Plato's *Symposium* in his *Double Indictment* and the *Dialogues of the Courtesans*, see Blondell and Boehringer 2014, 233–234; cf. Peterson 2018. On a revision of Socrates' rejection of rhetoric, which he mostly associates with the sophists, see Rossetti 1989.

100. Weissenberger 1996, 82–84, on Lucian's intention to identify Sopolis with Galen.

101. *Herm.* 60: "You take a self-evident thing (αὐθομολογούμενον), known to all, wine, and you compare to it most dissimilar things that everyone debates

about because they are obscure (τὰ ἀνομοιότατα καὶ περὶ ὧν ἀμφισβητοῦσιν ἅπαντες ἀφανῶν ὄντων). So, I surely cannot tell how in your view philosophy and wine are similar, except perhaps with regard to this, that philosophers sell their lessons as wine-merchants their wines (ὥσπερ οἱ κάπηλοι)—many indeed corrupting and cheating and giving bad measure (κερασάμενοί γε οἱ πολλοὶ καὶ δολώσαντες καὶ κακομετροῦντες)." The connection between philosophy and wine is also evident in Lucian's *VH* (cf. n38 above), as noted by Georgiadou and Larmour 1998, 316. For Plato's influence on *Hermotimus*, see Hunter 2012, 1–3 (cf. n92 above). For Lucian's influence on *Is.* 1:22, see Hafemann 1986, 123–124.

102. *Herm.* 63: "And now I don't understand why you are distressed (ὅ τι παθὼν ἀγανακτεῖς) if you cannot become a Chrysippus or a Plato or a Pythagoras today before sunset"; cf. Plut. *De profect. in virt.* 78e–f arguing that philosophical progress is typically reflected in one's speech: "for practically all beginners in philosophy are more inclined to pursue reputation with their speeches (πρὸς δόξαν διώκουσι); some of them, like birds, are attracted by vanity and ambition (τὸ ὕψος ὑπὸ κουφότητος καὶ φιλοτιμίας) to the brightness of the Natural Sciences; while others, 'like puppies that enjoy to play tug,' as Plato puts it, go in for the disputations, knotty problems, and quibbles (ἐπὶ τὰς ἔριδας καὶ τὰς ἀπορίας . . . καὶ τὰ σοφίσματα); but the majority choose dialectics, where they straightway stock themselves up for the practice of sophistry (πρὸς σοφιστείαν)."

103. *Herm.* 86: "I am going away to do just that—to make a change—of dress as well (μεταβαλοίμην καὶ αὐτὸ σχῆμα). You will soon see me without this big, shaggy beard. I shall not punish my daily life, but all will be liberty and freedom. Perhaps I shall even put on purple, to show everybody that I've no part in that nonsense now (μηκέτι μοι τῶν λήρων ἐκείνων μέτεστιν)." Cf. DL 2.78 on the life of Aristippus, where Diogenes reports how when ordered by Dionysius the Syracusan tyrant to wear purple at a dinner party, Plato refused, quoting a line from Euripides' *Bacchae* (*l.* 836) where purple is characterized as a woman's garment, but Aristippus conformed and retorted with another line from the play (*Bacch.* 317) arguing that modesty can be found even amid Bacchic revelry. On Alcibiades' penchant for luxurious, purple clothes, see Plut. *Alc.* 16.1; cf. *Symp.* 212e2 where Alcibiades barges into the banquet garlanded with ivy (known for its purple-black berries) and violets (which, as the name suggests, typically have a color close to purple).

104. On Lucian's critique of Platonic rhetoric (its misuse, at least), see Schlapbach 2010.

105. *Herm.* 63: περιέρχῃ με, ὦ Λυκῖνε, καὶ συνελαύνεις ἐς στενὸν . . . ἀλλ' οὐκ ἐᾷς σὺ βίαιος ὢν αἱρεῖσθαί τι . . . ("You surround me and push me in the corner . . . you don't give me a choice, being so forceful) and 65: οὐ μανθάνω τί σοι τὰ δίκτυα ταῦτα βούλεται· ἀτεχνῶς γάρ με περιβάλλεις αὐτοῖς ("I don't understand what these nets of yours mean; for you have clearly caught me in them"). The scene evokes Thrasymachus' disagreement with Socrates' style of

questioning his interlocutors in the *Republic*. Here, reworking the proverb "λύκον ἰδεῖν," about how dumbstruck people become upon seeing a wolf, Socrates describes Thrasymachus as a wild beast (ὥσπερ θηρίον; *Resp.* 336b6). Thrasymachus is about to disagree with Socrates (336c1) who notes at 336d6–7: "If I had not looked at him before he looked at me, I would have become speechless (ἄφωνος ἂν γενέσθαι)." On the Socratic style, cf. Dem. *Eloc.* 297: "What is particularly called the Socratic manner (εἶδος Σωκρατικόν) . . . Socrates unobtrusively drives the boy into a corner (εἰς ἀπορίαν)."

106. For a summary of scholarship on Lucian's *Nigrinus*, see Anderson 1978; also, Peterson 2010, 251–301.

107. Whitmarsh 2001, 267–269, 271, 274–276; Peterson 2010, 263–264 (on *amathia* and *erōs*).

108. The "recreation" of Platonic dialogues was trendy; see, for example, Cic. *De or.* 1.28.

109. For Socrates' description as θαυμάσιος in the *Symposium*, see chapter 1, n157; Alcibiades' heaping of adjectives at *Symp.* 217a1–2 evokes Lucian's description of Nigrinus' words on p. 129 (with two of them coinciding: θεῖα, θαυμαστά/θαυμάσια). The adverb σεμνῶς is found in both dialogues (*Symp.* 199a3: καὶ καλῶς γ' ἔχει καὶ σεμνῶς ὁ ἔπαινος), referring ironically to Agathon's speech; cf. *Phdr.* 258a1: λέγων μάλα σεμνῶς καὶ ἐγκωμιάζων ὁ συγγραφεύς, where Socrates makes fun of politicians and their speeches, although Phaedrus claims that they avoid the grand style, "for fear of being called sophists by posterity" (257d9–10: δόξαν φοβούμενοι τοῦ ἔπειτα χρόνου, μὴ σοφισταὶ καλῶνται).

110. Note the use of διέρχομαι (which is common otherwise) in *Phdr.* 273a3–7, where Socrates is said to have gone over the issues deemed important by professional rhetoricians who nevertheless care little about the truth: οἱ περὶ τοὺς λόγους τεχνικοὶ προσποιούμενοι εἶναι; on this, also see *Phdr.* 269b–c and 271a–c: here rhetoricians are criticized as "deceivers" (τέχνας λόγων πανοῦργοί) who "conceal the nature of the soul although they know it very well" (καὶ ἀποκρύπτονται, εἰδότες ψυχῆς πέρι παγκάλως) because they focus on the art of speech-making rather than its essence.

111. For the vocabulary of *mania* in the *Phaedrus*, including its pathological connotations, see chapter 2, pp. 44–45; cf. *Phdr.* 238c2 (ἡ . . . ἐπιθυμία πρὸς ἡδονὴν ἀχθεῖσα κάλλους) and 252c8 (τὸ τοῦ πτερωνύμου ἄχθος); on the use of the word *pathos* in the *Phaedrus*, see 238c7 (θεῖον πάθος πεπονθέναι), 250a9; 251c1; 251e1; 252b2; 252c4; 254e2; and 262b4.

112. Cf. *Symp.* 219b4 (**τετρῶσθαι** αὐτὸν ᾤμην) where Alcibiades hopes to have wounded Socrates erotically and 219e2 (χρήμασί γε πολὺ μᾶλλον **ἄτρωτος** ἦν πανταχῇ) where he concedes that Socrates is not tempted by money; at *Symp.* 220e1–2, τετρωσμένος is used literally to refer to Alcibiades' battle wounds.

113. Both the *Symposium* and the *Phaedrus* contain many references to *sōphrosynē* and its opposite (ἀφροσύνη); see, for example, ἄφρων, at *Symp.* 194b9–10

and 218d7 (about the foolish being many) and the noun τὸ ἄφρον (unreason), at *Phdr.* 236a2; 265e5; cf. *Ion* 533e7: οὐκ ἔμφρονες (on those dancing in Corybantic rites and enthused poets) in chapter 1, p. 30, and 534b5: ἔκφρων (cf. chapter 2, n205).

114. *Symp.* 217e7–218a: "I share the plight of the man bitten by the snake (τοῦ δηχθέντος): you know it is said that one in such a plight refused to describe his sensations to any but those who had been bitten themselves (πλὴν τοῖς δεδηγμένοις), since they alone would understand him and stand up for him if he should give way to wild words and actions in his agony. Now I have been bitten by a more painful, in the most painful way that one can be bitten (δεδηγμένος τε ὑπὸ ἀλγεινοτέρου καὶ τὸ ἀλγεινότατον ὧν ἄν τις δηχθείη): in my heart, or my soul, or whatever one is to call it, I am stricken and stung by his philosophical discourses (. . . πληγείς τε καὶ δηχθεὶς ὑπὸ τῶν ἐν φιλοσοφίᾳ λόγων), which adhere more fiercely than any adder when once they lay hold of a young and not ungifted soul, and force it to do or say whatever they will."

115. For example, see *Resp.* 464d9–e2 where Socrates claims that by having common families, the guardians would be "free of internal factions the sort that people quarrel over because of the possession of money, children, and relatives" (ὅσα γε διὰ χρημάτων ἢ παίδων καὶ συγγενῶν κτῆσιν ἄνθρωποι στασιάζουσιν). Cf. conclusion, n17.

116. Cf. *Phdr.* 250d6–8 in chapter 1, n180; also, *Vict.* 1.35,103–104 in chapter 2, n127.

117. Chapter 1, p. 58; on Galen's knowledge of the *Regimen*, see Bartoš 2015, 3, 92, 95, 102–110.

118. Cf. Caec. Cal. fr. 86 (Ofenloch 1967, 68 = ps.-Long. *Subl.* 7.2): "By nature our soul is somehow uplifted by true sublimity (τἀληθοῦς ὕψους ἐπαίρεται) and acquiring a kind of lofty stature (**γαῦρόν** τι ἀνάστημα λαμβάνουσα), it is filled with joy and pride (πληροῦται χαρᾶς καὶ με|γαλαυχίας) as if having created itself what it has heard."

119. For the use of the adjective μετέωρος to allude to both Aristophanes' *Clouds* and Plato's *Phaedrus* (269e6–270a7 on Anaxagoras), see Peterson 2010, 292–295; cf. Flores 2020 on Socrates' use of the study of nature, alongside rhetoric, as a tool for virtue; chapter 1, p. 67.

120. Clay 1992, 3420–3425.

121. Luc. *Nigr.*1: "But it is only my state of mind (τὴν ἐμὴν γνώμην) which I wish to reveal to you, how I feel now, and how deeply I have been moved (παρέργως εἴλημμαι) by your discourse . . . for clearly ignorance alone is not the reason (οὐχ ἡ ἀμαθία . . . αἴτιος) for such boldness on my behalf, but also my fondness for discourse (ὁ πρὸς τοὺς λόγους ἔρως)"; cf. Anderson 1978, 373.

122. Peterson 2010, 254–265, and 274–276.

123. Grethlein 2016, 272.

124. Peterson 2010, 266–271. According to Grethlein 2016, 272–273, Nigrinus' siren call originally helped the student allay the challenges of the Homeric

Sirens (nightingales and lotus) (*Nigr.* 3: τοσαύτην τινά μου λόγων ἀμβροσίαν κατεσκέδασεν, ὥστε καὶ τὰς Σειρῆνας ἐκείνας . . . καὶ τὰς ἀηδόνας καὶ τὸν Ὁμήρου λωτὸν ἀρχαῖον ἀποδεῖξαι).

125. Peterson 2010, 297–298, on Anderson 1978, 372–373n18.

126. Grethlein 2016, 268–276, esp. p. 275n45, on whether Lucian's *Nigrinus* responds to Plutarch's *De audiendo*.

127. Tarrant 2005, 226–228, with DL 4.16–20 on young Polemo being swayed to become a philosopher by Xenocrates.

128. Cf. Duff 2009, 44, on Plutarch's portrayal of Alcibiades based on Plato's *Symposium*; also see Landy 2007, 67–68, who claims that Alcibiades' ability to withstand Socrates' power is living proof that his theory of love is defective; cf. Anagnostou-Laoutides 2021b, 266.

129. Tarrant 2005, 230–232.

130. At Cic. *Brut.* 292 Socratic irony is defined as a witty and clever way of speaking (*facetam et elegantem*), which reveals a man free from conceit and at the same time witty (*minime inepti hominis et eiusdem etiam faceti*), as he playfully (*inludentem*) applies irony to those who pretend to be wise (*de sapientia disceptetur*). Cicero recognizes it as a technique that Socrates applied in many Platonic dialogues, where he is seen to praise his opponents (*ut apud Platonem Socrates in caelum effert laudibus Protagoram Hippiam Prodicum Gorgiam ceteros*) while representing himself as ignorant of everything and unrefined (*se autem omnium rerum inscium fingit et rudem*).

131. Lane 2010b, 239–242, 247–249 with n25; cf. Arist. *Eth. Nic.* 1127b23–26. Based on the similarities in the speeches of Lysias and Socrates in the *Phaedrus*, Bryan 2021, 5–9 and 18–21, claims that Socrates responds to Lysias' attempt to engage with Socratic ethics, which he misrepresents dangerously.

132. Strauss 1964, 51 (with Lane 2010b, 242), views Socratic irony as part of an allegorical strategy against those "capable of understanding neither the irony nor the philosophy which it protects."

133. Peterson 2010, 145–147; Tarrant 2005, 228: "The story presents a comic caricature of the effect of both Xenocrates' Academy on Polemo and Polemo on the Academy."

134. Cf. Weissenberger 1996, 9, 47, 73.

135. On Lucian's *Fisherman* especially, and its protagonist, Parrhesiades, see Peterson 2010, 129, who notes: "Through the *Fisherman*'s focus on parrhesia, a virtue that bridges the divide between Old Comedy and Philosophy, Lucian merges the parrhesia of comedy with that of the Cynics and in doing so, argues for its place in society." Also, Holland 2004, 263, and Branham 1989, esp. 33 (both cited by Peterson 2010, 111–112, and 129, respectively). On the civic importance of *parrhēsia* and Socrates' use of it, see chapter 3, pp. 99–100.

136. Cf. *Pisc.* 25 (with Peterson 2010, 127) where Parrhesiades attacks the Cynics for making Philosophy ridiculous and encouraging people to laugh at it: "The common people are such by nature; they delight in jesters and buffoons (τοῖς

ἀποσκώπτουσιν καὶ λοιδορουμένοις), and most of all when they criticize what is held in high reverence (τὰ σεμνότατα . . . διασύρηται). Just so in the past they took delight in Aristophanes and Eupolis, who brought Socrates on the stage to make fun of him (ἐπὶ χλευασίᾳ) and got up monstrous farces about him (ἀλλοκότους . . . κωμῳδίας)"; cf. Dem. *Eloc.* 170 and Eunap. *Vit. Soph.* 462 repeating this opinion vis-à-vis a plot against the philosopher Sopater.

137. Friesen 2015, 97–101 (citation from p. 101), summarizes the reception of the Bacchic religion and of Euripides' *Bacchae* in Rome. Cf. Mac Góráin and Perris 2020.

138. Hor. *Ep.* 1.1.3: *Maecenas, iterum antiquo me includere ludo.*

139. Hor. *Ep.* 1.1.11: *quid verum atque decens curo et rogo et omnis in hoc sum.*

140. Horace had studied at the Academy in Athens in his youth, but his studies were interrupted by the civil wars; see Günther 2013, 30; Friesen 2015, 101–102.

141. Hor. *Ep.* 1.1.30: *est quadam prodire tenus, si non datur ultra* ("It is worth taking some steps forward, even if it does not lead much further").

142. Pl. *Resp.* 364e–365a (βίβλων δὲ ὅμαδον παρέχονται Μουσαίου καὶ Ὀρφέως), echoed in Theophrast. *Char.* 16.11; cf. *Apol.* 41c5–d3 with reference to certain sayings (τὰ λεγόμενα) in the context of Orphic soteriology. For references to spells, see *Symp.* 202e13–203a2: ἡ τῶν ἱερέων τέχνη τῶν τε περὶ τὰς θυσίας καὶ τελετὰς καὶ τὰς ἐπῳδὰς καὶ τὴν μαντείαν πᾶσαν καὶ γοητείαν; of course, *Phd.* 69c1–d2 with reference to purification rites; cf. *Meno* 81b with Edmonds 2008.

143. Hor. *Ep.* 1.1.60: *rex eris . . . si recte facies*; also, 63 and 66.

144. Hor. *Ep.* 1.1.90: *quo teneam voltus mutantem Protea nodo?*

145. Hor. *Ep.* 1.1.53: *o cives, cives, quaerenda pecunia primum est.*

146. Hor. *Ep.* 1.1.16–17: *nunc agilis fio et mersor civilibus undis,/ virtutis verae custos rigidusque satelles* ("Now I become a man of action, and plunge into the tide of civil life, stern champion and follower of true virtue"). As L194: 253 notes, the adjective *agilis* translates the Stoic term πρακτικός, while *civilibus* translates the Greek πολιτικοῖς (political affairs).

147. On Heracles as a hero who was adopted by Stoic and Epicurean thinkers to stand for the man who remains a steadfast champion of virtue despite suffering many vicissitudes of fortune, see Anagnostou-Laoutides 2020c.

148. Which Seneca enthusiastically endorsed (see next section).

149. Cf. Hipp. *morb. sacr.* 1.2 (= 657iB L.): "My view is that those who first attributed a sacred character to this malady were like the magicians, purifiers, charlatans, and quacks of our own day (μάγοι τε καὶ καθάρται καὶ ἀγύρται καὶ ἀλαζόνες), men who claim great piety and superior knowledge (οὗτοι δὲ καὶ προσποιέονται σφόδρα θεοσεβέες εἶναι καὶ πλέον τι εἰδέναι). Being at a loss, and having no treatment which would help, they concealed and sheltered themselves behind superstition, and called this illness sacred, in order that their utter ignorance might not be manifest." The text goes on to specify purification rituals and incantations among the suggested cures (καθαρμοὺς προσφέροντες καὶ ἐπαοιδάς).

150. For *parrhēsia* as a duty of the Epicurean philosopher, see Konstan et al. 1998: 4; Glad 1996; Tsouna 2001, 247.

151. Mitsis 2005; cf. Yona 2018, 209.

152. Cf. Berno 2017; Edwards 2017 in the same volume.

153. As Roller has noted, Annaeus Serenus is addressed in three Senecan dialogues on "calm and equable states of mind: *De constantia sapientis, De tranquillitate animi* and (probably) *De otio*," which "play on the addressee's supposed lack of serenity, while Senecan therapy holds out the promise of harmonizing Serenus' disposition with his name." Roller 2015, 59; cf. Williams 2003, 12–13, on Serenus being addressed in Seneca's *De otio*.

154. Foucault 1999, 166 (also Foucault 2005, 33). The text reads: *non tempestate vexor, sed nausea* ("I am distressed, not by a tempest, but by seasickness"); cf. Luc. *Lex.* 16 (ἐγὼ γοῦν ἤδη μεθύω σοι καὶ ναυτιῶ) discussed on p. 126. The metaphor is also used extensively in Plutarch: see, for example, *Animine an corp.* 501d9–e4; *ad princ. iner.* 782d7–8; *de cohib. ira* 460b3–7.

155. *Tranq.* 1.10; cf. Pl. *Alc.* 105a–b.

156. In *Const.* 3.1 Serenus is cast as having "a fiery and ardent spirit" (*animum tuum incensum et effervescentem*).

157. For example, *Tranq.* 3.3; cf. *Ot.* 1.1–3; also, Pl. *Alc.* 127d–e and 134c.

158. For the Stoic idea of living in accordance with nature, see Colish 1985, 1.42; Reydams-Schils 2005, 43–44, 70–75.

159. This section reiterates the work of Anagnostou-Laoutides and Van Wassenhove 2020.

160. Cf. *Ep.* 104.6 where Seneca claims that traveling has healed him of a *marcor corporis dubii et male cogitantis* ("withering languor in my body and sloth in my brain"), restoring his physical and mental energy. Still, Seneca disapproves of a restless *iactatio* (cf. *Tranq.* 2.13–15). Chambert 2002; Montiglio 2006, esp. 563–4; Van Wassenhove 2016, 143n108.

161. In *Ep.* 95.36–38 Seneca argues that the soul must be freed (*solvendus est*) before it can benefit from philosophy.

162. Schiesaro 2003, 21; cf. Ustinova 2017, 272.

163. Chrysippus argues that virtue could be lost through drunkenness (SVF 3.237); Zeno of Citium crafted a syllogism establishing that a good man will not get drunk, quoted by Seneca in *Ep.* 83.9 = SVF 1.229.

164. See Richardson-Hay 2001 on Seneca's *Ep.* 83; cf. Motto and Clark 1990 for an overview of passages on drinking and drunkenness in Seneca.

165. Evenepoel 2014, 62.

166. Berger 1960, 366–368, argues that Seneca recommends a form of homeopathy (alluded in *Tranq.* 9.3), which derives from a Platonic theory reported in Plutarch and ultimately inspired by Democritus; cf. Gill 1994, 4616–4624, arguing that Seneca is here influenced by Democritean-Epicurean approaches to the concept of *euthumia/tranquillitas animi*. Seneca also makes seemingly un-Stoic statements in *De otio*, urging Serenus to occasionally withdraw from public life.

He defends his advice on the basis that he follows his teachers' example, rather than their instruction alone (*Ot.* 1.4–2.2). Later in *De otio* (esp. 3.1–2), he actively compares the doctrines of the Stoics and the Epicureans, arguing that the ability to reflect and adapt the views of one's teacher is a sign of healthy critical thinking.

167. Tieleman 2003, 162–166; cf. Ahonen 2018b, esp. 357–362.

168. SVF 1.285, consisting of very similar excerpts from Athenaeus, Galen, Eustathius, and Diogenes Laertius.

169. Tieleman 2003, 165–166; although Tieleman (p.165n100) appreciates that "the portrayal of Zeno as a melancholic is no doubt intended to mark him out as a man of genius, in accordance with current views as reflected by [Arist.] *Probl.* XXX.1"; on p. 166, he argues that the description is not necessarily completely apocryphal, before adding that Zeno's "general attitude to alcohol seems not to have differed all that much from Chrysippus."

170. Hipp. *Vict.* 1.33; also see *morb. sacr.* esp. par. 21.

171. Chapter 2, p. 53; cf. Belfiore 1986, 432.

172. Jouanna 2012b, esp. 194.

173. Chapter 2, p. 58; cf. Anagnostou-Laoutides and Payne 2021, 17n39; also, Herrero de Jauregui 2008, 142–143 and 156. For Epicurus' views on the heat-producing atoms of wine, see Plut. frs. 59 (*adversus Colotem*) and 60 (*quaest. conv.*) with Reesor (1983, 100). Cf. Xen. *Symp.* 2.24, cited on p. 59. Then, comparing plants to people, Socrates argues that they both flourish when "they drink only as much as they enjoy" (ὅσῳ ἥδεται τοσοῦτον πίνῃ).

174. *Tranq.* 17.9. Berger 1960, 351–352, notes that Seneca's careful wording here indicates his awareness that his recommendation is likely to surprise or even shock his readers; yet, at *Tranq.* 17.4 Seneca appears to prime the reader for this argument by noting that Cato used to relax his mind with wine when he was exhausted by public concerns (*Cato vino laxabat animum curis publicis fatigatum*). Notably, Seneca there compares Cato's appreciation of wine with Socrates' engagement with children (17.4: *cum puerulis Socrates ludere non erubescebat*), evoking Plato's description of the "Test of the Wine" as παιδιαί (child's play, pastimes; *Leg.* 649d11).

175. Seneca uses the expression *mota mens* and similar terms such as *motus animus* to refer to both rational and irrational states. In *Ep.* 94.36 it refers to a form of mild insanity, and in *De ira* 1.9.3 and 11.7.3 to a mind affected by emotions. In *Ep.* 39, however, Seneca claims that ardent enthusiasm sets our soul (*animus*) in motion (*in motu*), while in *Ep.* 109.11–12 he claims that even the souls of Stoic sages can be moved (*movere*) "skilfully" (*perite*), rationally (*rationaliter*), and "in accordance with nature" (*secundum naturam*). Seneca frequently describes mental tranquility and stability as involving a lack of movement. Cf. *De ira* 11.12.6 (*immota tranquillitas*) and *Ep.* 71.28, contrasting *mentis volutatio* with *immota stabilitas*.

176. Mazzoli 1970, 52.

177. Berger 1960, 365, refers to "[T]he difficulty of reconciling enthusiasm, in the actual meaning of the word, with the Stoic ideal of apathy."

178. Brennan 1998 and 2005a; Graver 2016 and 2017; cf. Graver 2007, 46, 103–104, 152–153, 163, 176, 206–210; cf. Konstan 2015; also, Gill 2016, esp. 150–152 and 157–159, on how joy as an emotion of the wise man (found in the doxographical tradition and Marcus Aurelius' *Meditations*) fits the profile of a Stoic; positive emotions, while they are not goals in themselves, facilitate the interpersonal relations of the wise man.

179. See, for a representative survey, Windt 2011, 238–248.

180. Plin. *NH* 14.137 and 14.150. Fleming 2001, vii. On viticulture and wine consumption in ancient Rome, see Seltman 1957 with Henderson 1824; Tchernia 1986; Purcell 1985; Austin 1985; Weeber 1993; Amouretti and Brun 1993; Murray and Tecuşan 1995; Jouanna and Villard 2002; Brun 2003; Russell 2003; Nelson 2005. François and Pittia 2000; the contributions in Slater 1991; also see McKinlay 1932, 1939, 1946, 1947, 1948a–d, 1949a–b; 1950, 1951, 1953a–b; 1953/1954. All these sources are extensively discussed in Mudd 2015, 16–24.

181. Cf. Dio Cass. *Hist.* 8.36.23, where the Roman general Papirius defended his wine drinking as a means of unwinding at the end of a difficult day. Roman doctors also emphasized the restorative aspects of wine; see Mudd 2015, 62–95.

182. On Roman alcoholism, see Jellinek 1976; Purcell 1985; Weeber 1993; Fleming 2001; and D'Arms 1995 who disagrees with the use of the term alcoholism; all are cited in O'Brien and Rickenbacker 1999; cf. Davidson 1997, 37–38, and Humphries 2002 with Mudd 2015, 51.

183. Ortiz de Landazuri 2015 discusses passages from *Charmides*, *Alcibiades* I, *Phaedo*, and the *Republic* on the notion of self-knowledge; cf. Kamtekar 2017; cf. chapter 2, pp. 77–78 on Socrates' speaking in his "own voice."

184. Foucault 2005, 494–495. Offering a perspective from social psychology, Algoe and Haidt 2009, 106, define *mania* as follows: "Elevation is elicited by acts of charity, gratitude, fidelity, generosity or any other strong display of virtue. It leads to distinctive physical feelings: a feeling of 'dilation' or opening in the chest, combined with the feeling that one has been uplifted or 'elevated' in some way. It gives rise to a specific motivation or action tendency: emulation, the desire 'of doing charitable and grateful acts also.' "

185. Foucault 2005, 495.

186. Sen. *Vit. beat.* 27.5.

187. The phrase alludes to *Phd.* 79d1–2, cited in chapter 1, p. 33; cf. chapter 2, n210.

188. *Ot.* 6.3: "Who will deny that virtue ought to test her progress (*profectus*) by deed, and should not only consider what ought to be done (*nec tantum quid faciendum sit cogitare*), but also at times apply her hand (*etiam aliquando manum exercere*) and bring into reality what she has conceived (*ea, quae meditate sunt, ad verum perducere*)?"

189. Plutarch compares the student of philosophy to sailors at sea, who consider the force of the wind in conjunction with the time spent on the task to calculate the distance they have covered. Furthermore, he rejects the Stoic view that passions ought to be extirpated and defends the usefulness of passions in making intellectual and moral progress: hence, at *virt. mor.* 451d11–e1 Plutarch writes: "the offsprings of passions are much more useful (πολὺ χρησιμώτερα τὰ τῶν παθῶν θρέμματα) when they are present alongside reason and reinforce the virtues (τῷ λογισμῷ συμπαρόντα καὶ συνεντείνοντα ταῖς ἀρεταῖς)"; cf. *virt. mor.* 452c5–6 where Plutarch draws on Homer to claim that the gods "added passion as an urge and vehicle to reason" ([τοὺς θεοὺς] . . . καθάπερ ὅρμημα τῷ λογισμῷ καὶ ὄχημα τὸ πάθος προστιθέντας), especially since in many people "reason is lazier and blunter" (452b2–3: ἐν πολλοῖς ἀργότερος ὁ λόγος καὶ ἀμβλύτερος); also, see *virt. mor.* 444e9–445a2 where he defines the concept of the mean in terms of a musical harmony (evoking thus Plato's *Laws*), before adding: "so virtue, being a movement and a force concerned with the irrational (αὕτη τε κίνησις οὖσα καὶ δύναμις περὶ τὸ ἄλογον), removes the shortcomings and over-exertions of the impulse and its excesses and defects altogether (τὰς ἐκλύσεις καὶ τὰς ἐπιτάσεις καὶ ὅλως τὸ μᾶλλον καὶ τὸ ἧττον ἐξαιρεῖ τῆς ὁρμῆς), and reduces each passion to moderation and flawlessness (εἰς τὸ μέτριον καὶ ἀναμάρτητον καθιστᾶσα τῶν παθῶν ἕκαστον)"; cf. Pl. *Resp.* 443d5–e2; also see conclusion, p. 160.

190. Plut. *virt. mor.* 452c6–8 accuses the Stoics of "often inciting young men with praise (πολλάκις μὲν ἐπαίνοις τοὺς νέους παρορμῶντας) and often chastising them with admonitions (νουθεσίαις κολάζοντας); and of these, in the first case pleasure is the consequence (ὧν τῷ μὲν ἔπεται τὸ ἥδεσθαι), in the second pain (τῷ δὲ τὸ λυπεῖσθαι)"; on dejection in Plutarch, cf. *Tim.* 6.1–5.

191. Long 1982, 36–40; Richardson-Hay 2009, 77–94, esp. 77–82.

192. Brennan 2005b, 127; Richardson-Hay 2009, 76n26; cf. Plut. *De profect. in virt.* 82a–e. For the important presence of doctors and the incorporation of medical knowledge in the sympotic tradition of the second sophistic, inspired of course by Plato's *Symposium*, see Flemming 2000, esp. 478–482; cf. Corvisier 2000, 494–497.

193. *De ira* 2.19.2; 2.20.4.

194. *De ira* 2.19.5; 2.20.2.

195. See *Ep.* 95.36–38 (with n161 above) where Seneca claims that while minds suffering from excessive *audacia* should be restrained, sluggish minds should be aroused and liberated from misguided fear.

196. Plutarch also discusses markers of progress in philosophy in his *De profectibus in virtute* where he advises the philosopher to read through philosophical treatises but also poetry and history with a focus on anything that is χρήσιμον καὶ σάρκινον καὶ ὠφέλιμον (79c: "useful, substantial, and beneficial").

197. Nevertheless, Seneca cautions that this method does not develop the sluggish person's virtues but only stands in for them (*De ira* 1.13.4–5: *nec virtutem instruunt . . . sed in vicem*).

198. See *Tranq.* 2.10 where Seneca identifies Serenus' condition as *inertia*; *taedium displicentia sui, animi volutatio*; *otii sui tristis atque aegra patientia*; *fastidium sui*; he also notes that he needs greater trust in himself (*Tranq.* 2.2: *fidem tibi*). See Van Wassenhove 2016, 145 with n116.

199. Seneca earlier defined tranquility as the equilibrium of a soul "neither rearing itself up nor thrusting itself down" (*Tranq.* 2.4: *nec adtollens se umquam nec deprimens*). Although this definition is contrary to his advice to Serenus to drink wine for relaxation (17.8: *ut deprimat nos*), Seneca's point here is that by relaxing, Serenus will recover the energy he wastes on worrying and feel invigorated. For Socrates' imperviousness not just to wine but also to cold, see *Symp.* 221c7–222d5; cf. 219e–220d; also, 174d4–e6; 175b1–4. Anagnostou-Laoutides and Payne 2021, 16–17.

200. Although Mazzoli cites this argument, he does not sufficiently differentiate between a false sense of sublimity inspired by emotions and Seneca's "real sublimity," which has nothing to do with the irrational and is instead associated with moral strength and greatness of soul.

201. See Reydams-Schils 2010, esp. 199–200, who discusses the Platonic influences of the passage. Graver 2016, 139–40, claims that Seneca often describes contemplation as "a form of relaxation of hard labor, as liberation for the mind from the imprisoning body, as raising the spirit to the level of the sublime, and as conferring pleasure." In her view, such associations "lend a sense of grandeur and excitement to the familiar message."

202. Also see *De ira* 1.21.4 and 3.6.1, *Ep.* 88.2, *Vit. beat.* 4.5 and 9.4.

203. Graver 2016, 131–132, citing Sen. *Ep.* 27.3: *sola virtus praestat audium perpetuum, securum* ("Only virtue brings about permanent, safe joy") and *Ep.* 59.16: *hunc esse sapientiae effectum, gaudii aequalitatem* ("This is the result of wisdom, stability of joy"). Cf. Plut. *virt. mor.* 452a1–4 approving emotions, including joy, provided they are moderate.

204. Graver 2016, 134–135.

205. Motto and Clark 1993, 144–147; also, Berger 1960, 353, and Porter 2016, 578.

206. Commentators who have observed the thematic correspondence between the two passages include Mazzoli 1970, 52; Cavalca Schiroli 1981, 140; and Porter 2016, 578. Setaioli 1985, 806–810, despite admitting the correspondences, argues that the concluding paragraphs cannot be intended to respond to Serenus' concerns. For a summary of Setaioli's position and a response, see Anagnostou-Laoutides and Van Wassenhove 2020, 12n58.

207. Note here the strong expression *lex* rather than a more neutral alternative such as *regula*.

208. Cf. *sublimius . . . ore iam non meo* (*Tranq.*1.14) and *cecinit grandius ore mortali. Non potest sublime quicquam . . .* (17.11). Both passages in turn echo *Aen.* 6.49 in which the Cumaean Sibyl is described as *maiorque videri / nec mortale sonans*. In addition, Seneca's argument that "nothing sublime and set on

high can come to [a mind] as long as it stays at home with itself (*apud se*)" may refer not only to Serenus' fear of speaking with an *ore non iam meo* but also to his tendency to confine his life to within his own walls (1.11: *placet intra parietes suos vitam coercere*). Also, Giusti 2017, 240–249.

209. Serenus refers here to his fears (1.2: *iis quae timebam et oderam*), which Seneca interprets as indicative of Serenus' dissatisfaction with himself (cf. 2.5); this dissatisfaction arises, according to Seneca, "from a badly tuned mind and desires that are either timid or unrealized" (2.7: *ab intemperie animi el cupiditatibus timidis aut parum prosperis*) and from a "fear of beginning something" (2.8: *incipiendi timor*).

210. *Phdr.* 246a8–248b5 and 253c8–254e.

211. For Seneca's allusions to *Phdr.* 245a, see Cavalca Schiroli 1981, 139. Cf. Gill 2006, 98, arguing that Seneca often exploits Platonic concepts "to make an essentially moral or ethical point." For Porter 2016, 578, "Seneca writes from the perspective of a moralist while dipping into Platonic and literary critical or rhetorical resources for enrichment." As Del Giovane 2015, 12, argues, in *Ep.* 108 Seneca "exploits the comparison between the students in ecstasy with the philosophical *res* and the Phrygians, without alluding to the theorization of poetic *mania*. He just avails himself of the strength and visual suggestiveness that were supposed to be carried by the metaphor." Reydams-Schils 2010 criticizes the tendency to read Platonic echoes in Seneca as "mere metaphors, or rhetoric in the service of practical moral philosophy," given that even if Seneca "explor[es] genuine affinities" with Plato, he "giv[e]s them a Stoic turn of thought" (p. 214) and "remains quite rooted in Stoic thought" (p. 196). Note that Plutarch also reworks the Platonic metaphor of the soul to discuss the passions as the wind in the sails of our rafters (*virt. mor.* 452b1–4).

212. Berger 1960, 364 concludes: "Surely this was to betray the ancient orthodoxy of the [Stoic] school rather than rally here to Plato and Aristotle" (my trans.) and describes Seneca's argument as an "an apology for movement and praise of unreason" despite noting that it is hard to believe that Seneca flagrantly contradicts his previous arguments without explanation (p. 366). Mazzoli 1970, 51–52, describes Seneca's definition of enthusiasm as a "condition . . . beyond the boundaries of rationality," noting Seneca "knew and followed the Democritean-Platonic theory of artistic inspiration" (my trans.). Schiesaro 2003, 23n39, claims that "these passages [*Tranq.* 17.10–11 along with *Ep.* 108.7] confirm quite explicitly that yielding to passions constitutes . . . a superior form of knowledge"; cf. Giusti 2017, 249–250.

213. Cavalca Schiroli 1981, 140, cautions against this hasty conclusion. Mazzoli 1970, 50–58, overlooks the fact that Seneca does not discuss poetics here, but a metaphor about the moral elevation of mind. Schiesaro 2003, 23, acknowledges that "Seneca is not engaged here in an explicit declaration of poetics and is addressing rather the issue of philosophical reflection," but still he reads the

passage as evidence for Seneca's poetics, arguing that "the presence of the Platonic quotation and the term *cecinit* (17.11) suggests that the same state of enthusiastic lack of control lies behind artistic creation and philosophical excitement." Overall, the Stoics paid close attention to poetry and its ability to portray emotional excess, albeit always in search of moral exempla, primarily ones to be avoided. Also, Mori 2005, 224–227.

214. Early on in his response, Seneca gently suggests that Serenus' main problem is his constant worrying about his moral shortcomings, which are hardly as bad as he thinks (*Tranq.* 1.2.1–5).

215. SVF 1.486; Sen. *Ep.* 75.3: *ieiuna esse et arida . . . neque enim philosophia ingenio renuntiat.* Note that Serenus' neologism *inelaborata oratio* in *Tranq.* 1.13 is echoed in *Ep.* 75.1 where Seneca describes his ideal for philosophical speech as *sermo . . . inlaboratus et facilis.* Cf. the stark contrast Seneca draws between the frivolous rhetoric of the itinerant preacher Serapio (*Ep.* 40) and the genuinely philosophical rhetoric of Fabianus (*Ep.* 100). Cf. the discussion above of Horace's *Epistle* 1 on pp. 131–133. Vogt 2016 suggests that instead of calling "Seneca an orthodox Stoic . . . we might want to say that he writes within the Stoic system"; cf. Inwood 2005, 23–64; also, Rist 1989, 1999–2003.

216. *Ot.* 5.6: *cogitatio nostra caeli munimenta perrumpit nec contenta est id, quad ostenditur, scire.* Seneca's language here evokes Plato's *Phdr.* 250a7–b5 in chapter 1, p. 31. Cf. Dionigi 1983, 242–243, citing among others ps.-Long. *Subl.* 35.3 where the author defends Plato's concept of contemplation, the result of nature's providence: διόπερ τῇ θεωρίᾳ καὶ διανοίᾳ τῆς ἀνθρωπίνης ἐπιβολῆς οὐδ ὁ σύμπας κόσμος ἀρκεῖ, ἀλλὰ καὶ τοὺς τοῦ περιέχοντος πολλάκις ὅρους ἐκβαίνουσιν αἱ ἐπίνοιαι ("Thus, even the whole world does not suffice for the contemplation and projection of the human mind, but our ideas often exceed the limits that contain us").

217. Armisen-Marchetti 2015, 156.

218. *Ep.* 59.6: *demonstrandae rei causa.* Armisen-Marchetti 2015, 155–157.

219. Corresponding to "the rhetorical notion of *evidential energeia*"; Armisen-Marchetti 2015, 157.

220. Ramelli 2018, par. 28–29, argues that in *Ben.* 1.3.8–10 Seneca is critical of Chrysippus and Cornutus, who look for truths in the mythological names and epithets of deities as found in poetry; cf. the objections of Picone 2013, 70–71, acknowledged by Ramelli 2018 n37. I am grateful to Prof. Ramelli for our email exchange on this point.

221. See Ramelli 2018, abstract. On the use of allegory in Stoicism and Platonism, see Ramelli 2011, 336–341; cf. Cornutus, *Compendium of Greek Theology* 75.17–76.16, and Porphyry, *Contr. Christ.* F39.30–5, Harnack 1916 (= Eus. *Hist. eccl.* 6.19.5–8); cf. Brisson 2004, 41–55, and Most 2010, 26–38. On the role of etymology in the allegorical analysis of poetic texts, see Most 2016. On the difference between allegory and allegoresis, the latter understood "as an interpretative mode," see Ford 2002, 67, also cited by Ramelli 2018 n16, alongside Naddaf

2009 and Domaradzki 2017, esp. 300–303; cf. Lamberton 2020. For Theagenes of Rhegium and his pivotal role in the development of allegoresis, see Svenbro 1984, 101–121, and Domaradzki 2011b.

222. Ramelli 2011, 341.

223. Cf. Num. 6:2 for the Nazirite vow, which involved abstaining from wine. Philo acknowledges this tradition in *Plant.* 165–166; Runia and Geljon 2019, 254.

224. For the proverb "enters wine, exit secrets" in the Talmud, see Antebi 2021, 366, who explains that there is a differentiation in the Talmud between wine that causes secrets to be revealed and wine that stimulates individuals to introspection, causing them to "have the mind of the Seventy Elders."

225. Cf. n114 above and chapter 3, n239; on descriptions of physical intoxication and its shameful results, see Jer 51:39 with Bacchiocchi 2001, 82; also, Is. 5:11–14 and 5:24.

226. Novak 2019, 107–139; on Philo's reception of Plato's *Timaeus*, see Reydams-Schils 1999, 14–15, 59, 135–166, and Runia 1986; on Philo as a Middle Platonist, see Runia 1993a, 124–139, arguing that Philo was rather "a Platonizing exegete of scripture"; also, Dillon 1993, 151 and 1996, 439, all cited in Gathercole 2014, 14–16; cf. Yli-Karjanmaa 2018 essentially agreeing with Runia's assessment of Philo.

227. On Philo's use of allegory, see *De Prov.* 2.40–1. Also, see Lamberton 1986, 44–54; Dawson 1992, 73–126; Long 1997; Borgen 2003, 114–143; Niehoff 2010; and Ramelli 2011, 346–348. Earlier Jewish authors such as Aristobulus and ps.-Aristeas used allegory but did not write allegorical commentaries, like Philo. Taylor 2020, xi–xii, 183–187.

228. Philo's ethics are essentially Stoic: at *Migr.* 128, he defines the goal of philosophy as "living in accordance with nature," achieved "when the mind traces the tracks of right reason and follows God" (τοῦτο δέ ἐστι τὸ παρὰ τοῖς ἄριστα φιλοσοφήσασιν ἀδόμενον τέλος, τὸ ἀκολούθως τῇ φύσει ζῆν . . . ὅταν ὁ νοῦς . . . κατ' ἴχνος ὀρθοῦ λόγου βαίνῃ καὶ ἕπηται θεῷ); cf. Taylor 2020, 6–7, 27–28. Clement of Alexandria (*Str.* 1.15.72.4/PG 8.1044B11) refers to the "Pythagorean" Philo; cf. Eus. *Hist. Eccl.* 2.4.2–3.

229. Standhartinger 2017, 144; cf. Runia and Geljon 2019, 255–256.

230. Philo appreciates the references to heavenly Love and Aphrodite as humorous interjections.

231. Cf. Philo *Plant.* 163 (Runia and Geljon 2019, 72) for the etymology of *methuein* as coming from the habit of drinking *meta to thuein* (after sacrificing)—the view is also found in Sud. s.v. Μέθη (Adler 1967, M420 in 3.347) and Ath. *Deipn.* 40d (τὸ δὲ μεθύειν φησὶν Ἀριστοτέλης τὸ μετὰ τὸ θύειν αὐτῷ χρῆσθαι).

232. Niehoff 2010; Lévy 2022; Novak 2019, 113; Taylor 2020, 7; cf. Schott 2013, 36.

233. Chapter 1, n3.

234. Cf. Sterling 2019, 35 with nn43 and 44, citing Lakoff and Johnson (*The Metaphors We Live By*).

235. Philo adopts the Plato's tripartite model of the soul; Dillon 2009; cf. the conclusion, pp. 162–163. For Philo's appreciation of heavenly love as a manifestation of God's *pneuma*, see Wyss 2023.

236. *Contempl.* 10: λέγω δὲ οὐ τὴν σώματος, ἀλλὰ τὴν ψυχῆς, ᾗ τὸ ἀληθὲς καὶ τὸ ψεῦδος μόνῃ γνωρίζεται ("I speak not of physical but of psychic sight, by which alone truth and falsehood are recognized"; trans. Taylor 2020, 76); cf. Taylor 2020, 136–137.

237. *Abr.* 57 with Taylor 2020, 147.

238. Inowlocki 2004 with Eus. *Hist. Eccl.* 2.17.

239. At *Leg.* 934a cited in chapter 2, n140.

240. Taylor 2020, 139–140, with Deutsch 2006, 293, on Philo's use of βλέπω alongside θεωρέω for psychic sight.

241. Standhartinger 2017, 145. For music as an antidote to strong wine, see ps.-Plut. *De mus.* 1146f–1147a, attributing this view to Aristoxenus. Cf. Pl. *Leg.* 790e–791a for the view that the flute of Pan was used to calm down the ecstatic dancers of Dionysus. Also, see Wyss 2023, 169, with *Questions on Genesis* 3:3 referring to the music that is perfected in heaven and rouses those who hear it to madness, producing in the soul "an indescribable and unrestrained pleasure." Philo compares here divine music to the singing of the Sirens.

242. Taylor 2020, 313 and 348. Cf. *Contempl.* 63, 76; on the enhanced sight of philosophically inclined lovers in Plato's *Phaedrus*, see chapter 1, pp. 32–33.

243. Cf. *Contempl.* 68 referring to "those who . . . spent their prime in pursuing the contemplative branch of philosophy, which indeed is the noblest and most god-like part (καὶ ἐνακμάσαντας τῷ θεωρητικῷ μέρει φιλοσοφίας, ὃ δὴ κάλλιστον καὶ θειότατόν ἐστι)," with Taylor 2020, 281.

244. On the liquid substance of emotions, which informs metaphors and metonymies about emotions in Greek antiquity, see Cairns 2016; on lovesickness expressed in terms that evoke melting and dripping from Homer onward, see Cyrino 1995. For Philo's use of the image of the fountain of God's wisdom from which the virtuous person drinks, see *Leg.* 2.87 with Runia and Geljon 2019, 199.

245. Chapter 1, p. 32.

246. *Phdr.* 255e5–256a7.

247. After death, Plato imagines the ideal lovers as "light and winged" (ὑπόπτεροι καὶ ἐλαφροὶ) similar only to Olympic victors; *Phdr.* 256b5–7. On the comparison of philosophical/moral progress to an athletic competition, see Reid 2011, 43–64.

248. *Anth. Gr.* 5.78: τὴν ψυχήν, Ἀγάθωνα φιλῶν, ἐπὶ χείλεσιν ἔσχον/ ἦλθε γὰρ ἡ τλήμων ὡς διαβησομένη ("While kissing Agathon, I had my soul on my lips/ for my poor soul came to cross over to him"); *Anth. Gr.* 5.171, esp. 3–4:

εἴθ' ὑπ' ἐμοῖς νῦν χείλεσι χείλεα θεῖσα/ ἀπνευστὶ ψυχὰν τὰν ἐν ἐμοὶ προπίοι ("If only she would now put her lips to my lips and drink down the soul within me without stopping to breathe"). Cf. Setaioli 2015 who traces the influence of this Platonic motif on Petronius and Gellius; for Sappho as the source of the motif, which has a long *Nachleben* (for example, in Paulus Silentiarius, the sixth century Byzantine epigrammatist), see Gosetti-Murrayjohn 2006.

249. See *Schol.* 245 (Wendel 1958).

250. In *Ebr.* 216–221, esp. 221, Philo castigates opulent feasts as inciting the passions of the soul. The reference to drinking from small cups evokes Socrates' advice in Xen. *Symp.* 2.26, while the reference to falling asleep after drinking alludes to the final scene of Plato's *Symposium.* Cf. *Plant.* 147 and *Agr.* 37 where Philo "presents madness (μανία) as a result of gluttony and drinking strong wine"; Runia and Geljon 2019, 267 and 279 (with further references to excessive food and drinking: *Agr.* 23–25, 36–37; *Somn.* 2.48–51, 115–168; *Ios.* 151–156).

251. Chapter 2, n55. Following Socrates' characterization of those who inflict harm on purpose as base people (see, for example, the use of πονηρὸς in *Grg.* 511b; 521b and d), Philo distinguishes two types of ignorance; one being the result of a lack of knowledge, the other of unfounded confidence in one's knowledge, which produces willful wrongdoing. On Socrates' understanding of intentional wrongdoing, see Weiss 2018a, esp. 281–282.

252. For drunkenness as a metaphor for ignorance, also see the Gospel of Thomas, *Logion* 28.2: "And I found all of them drunk, and I found none of them thirsting"; Gathercole 2014, 333; the Platonic influences of the so-called "fifth" Gospel and its similarities with Philo have been long noted in scholarship; see, for example, Miroshnikov 2018, 92, with Klijn 1962, 278, who argues that Philo and the Gospel of Thomas draw on "the same sources."

253. And he continues: *Plant.* 142: . . . ἔστι τοίνυν τὸ μεθύειν διττόν, ἓν μὲν ἴσον τι τῷ οἰνοῦσθαι, ἕτερον δὲ ἴσον τῷ ληρεῖν ἐν οἴνῳ ("Now, there are two ways of getting drunk; one is equivalent to wine drinking, the other to raving in your cups"); cf. Runia and Geljon 2019, 68 and 259–265; cf. Plut. *garr.* 503D (associating it with foolish talk) and *Epit.* 11m35–30, cited on p. 120.

254. Phillips 2008, 387 and 389; *Plant.* 176: "If one would not act reasonably (οὐκ . . . εὐλόγως) in entrusting a secret to a drunken man, and does entrust secrets to a good man, it follows that a good man does not get drunk." As Phillips notes (389n11), although Philo does not name the philosopher, Seneca attributes this opinion to Zeno (*Ep.* 83.9). Cf. Runia and Geljon 2019, 74.

255. Phillips 2008, 388–389.

256. Runia and Geljon 2019, 5.

257. Schürer 1973, 329–331; in the first book of *De ebrietate*, Philo recorded the views of many philosophers on drunkenness; his book, now lost, was still in circulation at the time of Eusebius (*HE* 2.18.2) and Jerome (*De vir. illustr.* 11).

Johannes Monachus (1250–1313) possessed an unedited copy of both books, probably in reverse order; Harris 1886, xix.

258. *Ebr.* 122–123: "for they act similarly to those who fill themselves up with wine intemperately to the pitch of intoxication (τοῖς ἐμφορουμένοις ἀπλήστως πρὸς μέθην οἴνου). Further, those people take the drink deliberately and under no compulsion, and so it is also deliberately that they eliminate soberness from their soul (τὸ μὲν νηφάλιον ἐκτέμνουσι τῆς ψυχῆς) and choose madness instead (τὸ δὲ παράληρον αἱροῦνται)." Cf. *Ebr.* 154–155: "drunkenness does not only denote raving (τὸ ληρεῖν), whose author is the lack of discipline (ὃ δημιουργὸν ἀπαιδευσίαν εἶχεν), but also complete insensibility (τὸ παντελῶς ἀναισθητεῖν). While in the body the cause of this is wine, in the soul it is ignorance of things of which we should naturally have acquired knowledge (τῆς δὲ κατὰ ψυχὴν ἄγνοια τούτων ὧν εἰκὸς ἦν ἐπιστήμην ἀνειληφέναι). . . . Now to what affection of the body can we compare what in the soul is called ignorance? (τίνι οὖν ἀπεικάσωμεν τῶν ἐν τῷ σώματι τὸ ἐν ψυχῇ πάθος ὃ κέκληται ἄγνοια)"; on the identification of drinking wine and getting drunk (*oinousthai* and *methuein*), cf. *Plant.* 154 in Runia and Geljon 2019, 71, 270, 273–275. Also, Hart 1904, 115–116.

259. Cf. Plato's use of εὐήθεια and εὐήθης (meaning both to have an innocent good disposition and/or being gullible) at *Leg.* 679d–e Plato refers to the εὐηθέστεροι as true icons of virtue.

260. See comments on L247: 503 s.v. 95; Lupieri 2018, 161 with n17, discusses Philo's use of ταῦρος both for Apis (whose name he does not use in the text), and for the golden calf of the Exodus (see Ex. 32). Cf. in the same volume, Tobin 2018.

261. *Ebr.* 127; on the structure of the Philo's *De ebrietate*, see Hart 1904, 111–118.

262. Cf. *Ebr.* 198 where Philo refers to the factions of the so-called philosophers, who can hardly agree on anything, evoking both Socrates' invective against other thinkers in Xen. *Mem.* 1.1.14 (chapter 2, p. 67) but also Lucian's representations of quarrelling intellectuals. Again, see Hart 1904, 115–116.

263. At *Ebr.* 138, Philo refers to lack of discipline: ἀπαιδευσίαν καὶ γάρ ἐστιν ἀμήχανον τὸ μέθης καὶ παροινίας ψυχῆς αἴτιον, ἀπαιδευσίαν, προσίεσθαι τὸν ταῖς γενικαῖς καὶ κατ᾽ εἶδος ἀρεταῖς ἐμμελετῶντα καὶ ἐγχορεύοντα ("For it is impossible for anyone, who studies and engages with the general and specific virtues, to let lack of discipline, the cause of drunkenness and debauchery of the soul, gain entry to him"); cf. *Plant.* 147 with Runia and Geljon 2019, 266; also, *Ebr.* 153–154: νηφόντων μὲν οὖν ὁ χορὸς οὗτος παιδείαν προστησαμένων ἡγεμονίδα, μεθυόντων δ᾽ ὁ πρότερος, οὗπερ ἦν **ἔξαρχος** ἀπαιδευσία ("This, then, is the company of the sober who have set before them education as their head, while the former was the company of the drunken, whose *leader* was indiscipline"). Philo's reference to the leaders of the sober and the drunken evokes Plato's

Symposium, where Alcibiades proclaims himself symposiarch though obviously drunk (213e9–10), and the *Laws*, where the need for sober symposiarchs is reiterated (*Leg.* 640d4–7); see chapter 3, pp. 80 and 99. Philo refers to drinking competitions using the word παροινία in *Plant.* 146, only found before in Plato (*Leg.* 666b1); Runia and Geljon 2019, 266 and 280.

264. Eventually succumbing to incest with them: *Ebr.* 162–164. Cf. Phil. *On Genesis* 4.56 where he tries to justify the actions of Lot's daughters, who allegedly thought that the whole world had been destroyed apart from the two of them and their father; the view is reiterated by Josephus (*JA* 1.205).

265. Cf. the discussion of Stoic joy on pp. 135, 139; in Sen. *Ep.* 106.7 philosophical joy is understood to confer calmness (*serenitatem laetitia [det]*?); also, Cic. *Tusc. Disp.* 3.24–25; on Augustine's adoption of the Stoic notion of *laetitia*, see Byers 2013, 61–69; cf. Brachtendorf 1997, 291–292.

266. Pl. *Phdr.* 249d1–4 discussed in chapter 2, p. 66.

267. (Ahbel-)Rappe 2000, 119.

268. Markovich 2022, 26–63 and 160–204; cf. Atkins 2013, esp. 29–30; McConnell 2019.

269. See, for example, Köster 2014.

Conclusion

1. "If only wisdom were a sort of thing that could flow out of the one of us who is fuller into him who is emptier, by our mere contact with each other . . ."; cf. Bussanich 2006, 209–210.

2. The topic is already introduced in the *Symposium*; see Halperin 1986 in chapter 3, n220.

3. Chapter 3, n105.

4. On whether the brain or the soul is the seat of cognition, see chapter 1, n3; cf. Lorenz 2024.

5. Introduction, n48.

6. See chapter 1, n29 on the role of poetic images in creating realities; cf. *Tht.* 186a10–b1.

7. On ongoing debates regarding the role of the senses in cognitive phenomenology, see Montague 2017 who discusses theories of "sensory" vs "cognitive" phenomenology; cf. Bayne and Montague 2011; also see Nes et al. 2021 and Chudnoff 2015, esp. 59, questioning that "a wholly sensory state can give you this sense [= of seeming awareness] with respect to abstract states of affairs," beyond one's spatiotemporal input.

8. Chapter 2, p. 46.

9. Cf. Fiske et al. 2007 on the universal association of warmth with competence and morality in interpersonal and intergroup social cognition.

10. Chapter 3, p. 86 with n106.

11. *Bacch.* 423 and 772 in chapter 2, p. 63; Pl. *Leg.* 666b3–c7 in chapter 3, n114, with Pfefferkorn 2022, 152–154.

12. On the concept of *epochē* in ancient Stoicism and phenomenology, see chapter 4, nn24–25.

13. Pfefferkorn 2022, 118–119; cf. Anagnostou-Laoutides 2026, 288.

14. See Thucydides 2.38.2, reporting Perikles' Funeral Oration, where the luxury of Athens is praised as a result of the city's growth after the Persian Wars (ἐπεσέρχεται δὲ διὰ μέγεθος τῆς πόλεως ἐκ πάσης γῆς τὰ πάντα, καὶ ξυμβαίνει ἡμῖν μηδὲν οἰκειοτέρᾳ τῇ ἀπολαύσει τὰ αὐτοῦ ἀγαθὰ γιγνόμενα καρποῦσθαι ἢ καὶ τὰ τῶν ἄλλων ἀνθρώπων); Tzanetou 2012, 89, 117; cf. Kallet 2003, 126–142, and id. 1998, esp. 54–58.

15. Thus, an impressive number of stamped Thasian wine amphoras have been found in the Athenian agora, dating from the fourth to the second century BCE. Tzochev 2016a and 2016b.

16. Sears 2013, 5; according to Plutarch (*Alc.* 1.22), Alcibiades was given a Thracian tutor named Zopyrus by his guardian Pericles; Sears 2013, 31. On the role of Thasos in the political career of Alcibiades and Thrasymachus, see Sears 2013, 32–39 and 90–139.

17. Cf. Demetriou 2014, 368. In the *Republic* Plato famously expressed his aversion to private property and wealth, adamant that possessions instill cowardice and fear of death in the guardians and the auxiliaries; cf. *Resp.* 372e6–7 in chapter 3, n106. Although private property is allowed in the *Laws*, there are extensive references to coinage and monetary policy, repeatedly warning the citizens about the dangers of monetization; see *Leg.* 705b4–7, 742a–743c6, 746d9–10, 849e, 916d1–5, 918a7–c7, 949c5–e6; cf. 764b. See Anagnostou-Laoutides 2026, 281, 283.

18. While Thasos was colonized early on (650 BCE) by Parian 'Greeks' (Graham 1978), archaeological evidence suggests that it was under Thracian cultural influence (Owen 2009); Thracians, however, were typically portrayed as savage barbarians in fifth century Greek literature; see Pache 2001, 3 with Parker 1996, 174; also, *Leg.* 637e with Sears 2013, 146 for Plato's reference to the Thracians as drunkards who take their wine unmixed, letting it drip all over the clothes (Θρᾷκες ἀκράτῳ παντάπασι χρώμενοι . . . καὶ κατὰ τῶν ἱματίων καταχεόμενοι). Plato is also familiar with the Athenian festival of Bendis, a Thracian goddess understood as an equivalent of Artemis. Sears 2013, 149–157, with *Resp.* 327a, 327c, 328a.

19. Although Athens forbade its allies from issuing coins in 450 BCE, Thasos was able to reissue coins after its revolt from Athens in 411 BCE; cf. Pleket 1963.

20. This iconography appears in a series of trihemiobols/hemihektes struck before 400 BCE; specimens of this small denomination were countermarked by the Athenians; Grigorova-Gencheva and Prokopov 2017, 43–45.

21. Cf. *Resp.* 487e4–6: "The question you ask requires a response through representation (δεόμενον ἀποκρίσεως δι᾽ εἰκόνος). 'But I thought,' he said, 'it was

not your habit to use images' (οὐκ εἴωθας δι᾽ εἰκόνων λέγειν)." In his response, Socrates says (488a1–2): "Therefore, listen to my representation (τῆς εἰκόνος) so you can see how painstakingly I form the parallel (ὡς γλίσχρως εἰκάζω)." See L276: 18–19 with n12 on the difficult translation of γλίσχρως for which I opted for "painstakingly" to render the apologetic tone of the phrase.

22. Chapter 3, n70.

23. Chapter 2, n222; cf. *Resp.* 489a4–b2 on the exclusion of "true" philosophers from the Greek states: (ταῖς πόλεσι πρὸς τοὺς ἀληθινοὺς φιλοσόφους), rendered through the metaphor (εἰκὼν) of the sailors who attack their ship captain. On the concept of truth, see (Wilson-)Nightingale 2004, 114–116 and 130; Trabattoni 2012, esp. 312–314 (on the relationship of myth and truth); and more recently Hartmann 2017, 310–312, who draws attention to *Resp.* 377a defending the use of myth for small children provided "there is truth in them" (ἔνι δὲ καὶ ἀληθῆ) and *Phdr.* 275bf. where Socrates again defends his invention of myths, provided he uses them to "only speak the truth" (εἰ μόνον ἀληθῆ λέγοιεν). Cf. Trabattoni 2020, 47–58 (on Plato's critique of religious and poetic "knowledge") and 153–157 (on *logos* and language as imitation of reality).

24. Isler-Kerényi 2015, 212.

25. See *Resp.* 350b9–d5, 351a6 (ἐστὶν ἀμαθία ἡ ἀδικία), 354b7, 382b3, 409d3, 411e2, 428b8, 444a3 and b9, 467c10, 518b1, 535e5–6, 609b11 (νυνδὴ διῆμεν πάντα, ἀδικία τε καὶ ἀκολασία καὶ δειλία καὶ ἀμαθία); see *Ti.* 88b1–7 in chapter 2, n145, on ignorance as the greatest illness; cf. *Apol.* 22b2 directly attacking the ignorance of poets; also, see *Apol.* 22d5–e6 and 29b1–2 (πῶς οὐκ ἀμαθία ἐστὶν αὕτη ἡ ἐπονείδιστος).

26. Billings 2021, 159–221.

27. Plato is worried about misguided versions of pleasure and fear that mesmerize people, urging them to change their minds (*Resp.* 413c1–3: τοὺς μὴν γοητευθέντας . . . κἂν σὺ φαίης εἶναι οἳ ἂν μεταδοξάσωσιν ἢ ὑφ᾽ ἡδονῆς κηληθέντες ἢ ὑπὸ φόβου τι δείσαντες); again, see Anagnostou-Laoutides 2026, 283–284.

28. Chapter 2, n231 and chapter 3, n69; cf. *Resp.* 426a8: μεθύων; 561c8–d1: χαριζόμενος τῇ προσπιπτούσῃ ἐπιθυμίᾳ, τοτὲ μὲν μεθύων καὶ καταυλούμενος.

29. *Resp.* 363c5–d1: συμπόσιον τῶν ὁσίων κατασκευάσαντες ἐστεφανωμένους ποιοῦσιν τὸν ἅπαντα χρόνον ἤδη διάγειν μεθύοντας, ἡγησάμενοι κάλλιστον ἀρετῆς μισθὸν μέθην αἰώνιον, 390b1–2: μέθυ δ᾽ ἐκ κρητῆρος ἀφύσσων/ οἰνοχόος φορέῃσι καὶ ἐγχείῃ δεπάεσσι . . . ; cf. chapter 1, n203 and chapter 3, n106.

30. Chapter 3, n156; *Resp.* 606a4–7 in chapter 2, n165.

31. At *Resp.* 607–608b Socrates and Glaucon admit that they struggle to abstain from tragic performances because of their lack of education.

32. In the *Frogs* Aeschylus claims that poets have a "duty to conceal what's wicked, not stage it or teach it. For children the teacher is the one who instructs, but grownups have the poet" (*ll.* 1053–1055: ἀλλ᾽ ἀποκρύπτειν χρὴ τὸ πονηρὸν τόν γε ποιητήν,/ καὶ μὴ παράγειν μηδὲ διδάσκειν/ τοῖς μὲν γὰρ παιδαρίοισιν/ ἐστὶ διδάσκαλος ὅστις φράζει, τοῖσιν δ᾽ ἡβῶσι ποιηταί).

33. *Poet.* 1453a9–10 insisting that tragedy seeks to inspire "pity and fear" by portraying heroes who "who fall into adversity not through evil and depravity, but through some kind of error" (μήτε διὰ κακίαν καὶ μοχθηρίαν μεταβάλλων εἰς τὴν δυστυχίαν ἀλλὰ δι᾽ ἁμαρτίαν τινά); cf. 1454b8 defining tragedy as the representation of characters better than us (ἐπεὶ δὲ μίμησίς ἐστιν ἡ τραγῳδία βελτιόνων ἢ ἡμεῖς).

34. *Symp.* 219d4–8 in chapter 1, n122.

35. Chapter 3, p. 102. On the coherence of Socrates' dramatic characterization in the first tetralogy, see Regali 2015.

36. Cf. Clay 2007, 214.

37. See, for example, Arist. *Poet.* 1454a4: ἡ ἀναγνώρισις ἐκπληκτικόν; 1455a15–17: πασῶν δὲ βελτίστη ἀναγνώρισις ἡ ἐξ αὐτῶν τῶν πραγμάτων, τῆς ἐκπλήξεως γιγνομένης δι᾽ εἰκότων, and 1460b25–26 defining the purpose of poetry as οὕτως ἐκπληκτικώτερον ἢ αὐτὸ ἢ ἄλλο ποιεῖ μέρος; cf. *Rhet.* 1385b6 cited on p. 248n130 above and 1408a5: διὸ πολλοὶ καταπλήττουσι τοὺς ἀκροατὰς θορυβοῦντες. Also see chapter 1, p. 20 with n58.

38. Chapter 3, p. 80 with nn67 and 68.

39. Chapter 1, n127 and chapter 3, p. 110.

40. Cf. *Tht.* 152c1: Τὸ δέ γε φαίνεται αἰσθάνεσθαί ἐστιν where Socrates claims that "seeming and perception" are identical, a view he rejects at 158a1–3: ὡς παντὸς μᾶλλον ἡμῖν ψευδεῖς αἰσθήσεις . . . καὶ πολλοῦ δεῖ τὰ φαινόμενα ἑκάστῳ ταῦτα καὶ εἶναι, ἀλλὰ πᾶν τοὐναντίον οὐδὲν ὢν φαίνεται εἶναι ("we certainly have false perceptions . . . and it is by no means true that everything is to each man as it appears to him; on the contrary, nothing is as it appears"). Cf. Morgan 2000, 242, who appreciates myth as a "synoptic view of reality."

41. Chapter 2, p. 44 and chapter 3, p. 80. Also, see *Phil.* 33e9–34a1 on the σεισμός of the body and the soul under the influence of perceptions: Ἀντὶ μὲν τοῦ λεληθέναι τὴν ψυχήν, ὅταν ἀπαθὴς αὕτη γίγνηται τῶν σεισμῶν τῶν τοῦ σώματος, ἣν νῦν λήθην καλεῖς, ἀναισθησίαν ἐπονόμασον ("Instead of saying that the soul forgets, when it is unaffected by the vibrations of the body, apply the term want of perception to that which you are now calling forgetfulness"); cf. *Ti.* 43c7–d2: . . . αἰσθήσεις . . . ἐνδελεχῶς ὀχετοῦ κινοῦσαι καὶ σφοδρῶς σείουσαι τὰς τῆς ψυχῆς περιόδους ("sensations . . . move and violently shake the revolutions of the Soul").

42. Hence, at *Leg.* 682e9–13 Plato explains how the discussion on music and drinking parties has afforded the interlocutors a fresh perspective on their original discussion about the settlement of Lacedaemon and its constitution, a new "grip" on the matter (περιπεσόντες μουσικῇ τε καὶ ταῖς μέθαις, νῦν ἐπὶ τὰ αὐτὰ πάλιν ἀφίγμεθα ὥσπερ κατὰ θεόν, καὶ ὁ λόγος ἡμῖν οἷον λαβὴν ἀποδίδωσιν).

43. Cf. *Phil.* 34a10–b8 where Socrates defines memory as the recovery of sensory perception (σωτηρίαν τοίνυν αἰσθήσεως τὴν μνήμην), and the difference between memory and recollection (μνήμης δὲ ἀνάμνησιν ἆρ᾽ οὐ διαφέρουσαν

λέγομεν) as the soul's ability to recover independently the things it experienced with the mediation of the body (Ὅταν ἃ μετὰ τοῦ σώματος ἔπασχέν ποθ' ἡ ψυχή, ταῦτ' ἄνευ τοῦ σώματος αὐτὴ ἐν ἑαυτῇ ὅτι μάλιστα ἀναλαμβάνῃ, τότε ἀναμιμνῄσκεσθαί που λέγομεν)—in other words, the ability of the soul to accurately recover sensory perception, which is then expected to carefully evaluate. On the soul's thinking processes, see chapter 1, nn136 and 192.

44. Renaut 2020, 115 with n27, citing Wilburn 2014; cf. Anagnostou-Laoutides 2024a and 2026; also chapter 1, pp. 31 and 34.

45. Chapter 3, n78. Of course, part of the problem is that poetry can at times be successful in grasping the truth, which is even more unsettling; *Leg.* 682a3–6: θεῖον γὰρ οὖν δὴ καὶ τὸ ποιητικὸν ἐνθεαστικὸν ὂν γένος ὑμνῳδοῦν, πολλῶν τῶν κατ' ἀλήθειαν γιγνομένων σύν τισιν Χάρισιν καὶ Μούσαις ἐφάπτεται ἑκάστοτε.

46. Cf. *Soph.* 240d1–4, 267e8–268a9; also, *Resp.* 602e4–603a8.

47. Plato is clearly referring here to the Homeric representation of Hades in *Od.* 11; cf. *Ap.* 29a5–b6; 40e10–41 a6. On the contrary, Plato argues, the poets should "praise the things in Hades" (τὰ ἐν Ἅιδου ἀλλὰ μᾶλλον ἐπαινεῖν, 386b10); cf. *Lg.* 660a4–9 in chapter 3, p. 86.

48. Chapter 1, p. 23 with nn82–83.

49. See Canfora 2002, 3, on Socrates as "a disturbing critic of the current political system."

50. See Plut. *max. cum princ.* 776c8–d3 where philosophy is said to "instil mobilizing impulses and judgments leading to what is beneficial (καὶ κινητικὰς ὁρμὰς ἐντίθησι καὶ κρίσεις ἀγωγοὺς ἐπὶ τὰ ὠφέλιμα), policies that strive for the good, aspiration and greatness accompanied by gentleness and safety (καὶ προαιρέσεις φιλοκάλους καὶ φρόνημα καὶ μέγεθος μετὰ πραότητος καὶ ἀσφαλείας), through which those engaged in politics interact more eagerly with the high and mighty (δι' ὧν τοῖς ὑπερέχουσι καὶ δυνατοῖς ὁμιλοῦσιν οἱ πολιτικοὶ προθυμότερον)."

51. See chapter 4, nn189–190. Cf. Plut. *virt. mor.* 443c10–d1: "by imposing a certain limit (ὅρον τινὰ) and order (καὶ τάξιν ἐπιτιθέντος)" on passion, reason "produces moral virtues, not as the result of apathy but of achieving a balance and an equilibrium of passions (τὰς ἠθικὰς ἀρετάς, οὐκ ἀπαθείας οὔσας ἀλλὰ συμμετρίας παθῶν καὶ μεσότητας, ἐμποιοῦντος)"; the notion is reiterated at *virt. mor.* 444b10–c6 and 444c6–9; also see *cons. Apol.* 102e2–8. At *Resp.* 441a2–3 Plato describes the spirited part of the soul as "a natural ally of the rational part" (τὸ θυμοειδές ἐπίκουρον ὂν τῷ λογιστικῷ φύσει); cf. *Resp.* 603e8–9.

52. See *Leg.* 645d7–646a5 in chapter 2, p. 60.

53. Chapter 2, p. 54.

54. Chapter 1, pp. 30, 32 and chapter 2, pp. 44–45.

55. See *Leg.* 644d2–3 in chapter 3, n58; also, Irwin 2010, 107–108.

56. Chapter 3, pp. 106–107.

57. Cimino 2024, 330–331.

58. Cimino 2024, 318 with Husserl 2003, 33.

59. Cimino 2024, 328–329 with Husserl 1973/1997, 289–290/250–251.

60. Cimino 2024, 330 with Husserl, 1973/1997, 289n1/ 250n2.

61. Cimino 2024, 331.

62. As Plato argued in the *Philebus* (29a–30d) and the *Timaeus* (35a–36e, 41d, 47b), individual souls participate in the cosmic soul, a theory further developed by the Stoics; Ademollo 2020, 127–133. Cf. *Resp.* 611b1–6 where Plato comments on the nature of the soul thus: "nor should we think that in its truest nature the soul is such (τῇ ἀληθεστάτῃ φύσει τοιοῦτον εἶναι ψυχήν) that teems with infinite diversity and unlikeness and contradiction in and with itself (ὥστε πολλῆς ποικιλίας καὶ ἀνομοιότητός τε καὶ διαφορᾶς γέμειν αὐτὸ πρὸς αὐτό). . . . It is not easy (οὐ ῥᾴδιον) . . . for a thing to be immortal that is composed of many elements not put together in the best way, as now appeared to us to be the case with the soul (ἀίδιον εἶναι σύνθετόν τε ἐκ πολλῶν καὶ μὴ τῇ καλλίστῃ κεχρημένον συνθέσει, ὡς νῦν ἡμῖν ἐφάνη ἡ ψυχή)"; also, Plut. *virt. mor.* 441e10–442b1.

63. See *Resp.* 580d3 where Plato discusses the structure of the soul, understood as a microcosm of the city: ὥσπερ πόλις . . . διῄρηται κατὰ τρία εἴδη, οὕτω καὶ ψυχὴ ἑνὸς ἑκάστου τριχῇ; on the variations among Plato's theories of the soul, see Finamore 2005; also, Gruber 2005 in the same volume.

64. At *Resp.* 442a4–c3 reason and the spirited part ought to "take control of the appetitive part" (προστήσεσθον τοῦ ἐπιθυμητικοῦ) and monitor it (τηρήσετον) in case it attempts to "enslave and rule" (καταδουλώσασθαι καὶ ἄρχειν ἐπιχειρήσῃ) the things it should not, "turning everyone's whole life upside down" (σύμπαντα τὸν βίον πάντων ἀνατρέψῃ). Reason and the spirited part are further tasked with "guarding against external enemies on behalf of the whole soul and the body" (τοὺς ἔξωθεν πολεμίους τούτω ἂν κάλλιστα φυλαττοίτην ὑπὲρ ἁπάσης τῆς ψυχῆς τε καὶ τοῦ σώματος), while the spirited part should be ". . . following its ruler, carrying out bravely its ruler's intentions" (. . . ἑπόμενον δὲ τῷ ἄρχοντι καὶ τῇ ἀνδρείᾳ ἐπιτελοῦν τὰ βουλευθέντα). The spirited and appetitive parts should not oppose reason (442d2: μὴ στασιάζωσιν αὐτῷ), while injustice is described as the result of "infighting among the three parts of the soul" (οὐκοῦν στάσιν τινὰ αὖ τριῶν ὄντων τούτων δεῖ αὐτὴν εἶναι). Notably, in the *Republic sōphrosynē* is defined as the acceptance of reason's rule in the soul (442d1–4). In the *Phaedrus*, the charioteer is often understood as reason, responsible for keeping the horses of the chariot under his control (yet see Plut. *Plat. quaest.* 1008c5–11 with Zaborowski 2018, esp. 199–200). In the *Timaeus* again, while acknowledging the presence of "irrational sensation and all-daring lust" in the soul (69d5: αἰσθήσει δὲ ἀλόγῳ καὶ ἐπιχειρητῇ παντὸς ἔρωτι), Plato insists that the spirited part ought to "violently subdue the tribe of desires" to reason (70a6: βίᾳ τὸ τῶν ἐπιθυμιῶν κατέχοι γένος) and that the gods appointed reason as "the best part" to rule over the others (70c1–2: καὶ τὸ βέλτιστον οὕτως ἐν αὐτοῖς πᾶσιν ἡγεμονεῖν ἐῷ); cf. Plut. *virt. mor.* 445c3–7; 448d7–10; *gen. Socr.* 584e8–f1; *Plat. quaest.* 1008b7–10, 1008c5–11; and *de profect. in virt.* 83a4–b8.

65. See n40 above. Karatzoglou 2021, 74–109; Nussbaum 1986, 216, and Lorenz 2006, 67–68; cf. Kamtekar 2010, 133–138; also, McCready-Flora 2018.

66. Chapter 3, p. 104 with n253.

67. Cf. Arist. *Eth. Nic.* 1102b29–32 and 1103a1–3; on types of madness in Stoic thought, see Ahonen 2018b.

68. See n63 above. Yet, see Ahonen 2018b, 154, on the divided stance of the Stoics towards *mania*.

69. Plut. *virt. mor.* 448a6–9: "for reason leans towards truth, gladly turning away from falsehood (διὸ πρὸς τὸ ἀληθὲς ὁ λογισμός, ὅταν φανῇ, προέμενος τὸ ψεῦδος ἀσμένως ἀπέκλινεν) since the ability to be persuaded and to change one's persuasion exists in reason and nothing else (ἐν αὐτῷ γὰρ ἔστιν, οὐκ ἐν ἑτέρῳ, τὸ πειθόμενον καὶ μεταπειθόμενον); cf. Plut. *rect. rat. aud.* 37f11–38b1.

70. The notion is reiterated in Plut. *virt. mor.* 443c8–10.

71. Plut. *soll. an.* 961a10–b1: "the impact on eyes and ears brings no perception if understanding is not present" (ὡς τοῦ περὶ τὰ ὄμματα καὶ ὦτα πάθους, ἂν μὴ παρῇ τὸ φρονοῦν, αἴσθησιν οὐ ποιοῦντος); cf. *virt. mor.* 440d4–9.

72. Trabattoni 2022, 271, 278–283; in the same volume, cf. Fronterotta 2022 and Bossi 2022, 190, on Arist. *Eth. Nich.* 1144b21–32; also, Cavini 2022, 309 and 319, on Arist. *APo.* 100b10: ἐπιστήμη δ' ἅπασα μετὰ λόγου ἐστί.

73. Trabattoni 2018, 235n318. Cf. Plut. *virt. mor.* 449c2–3 arguing that "passion intensifies some judgements, while opposing others (. . . ταῖς μὲν προστιθεμένου τοῦ πάθους κρίσεσι ταῖς δ' ἀπειθοῦντος).

74. Cf. Wallace 2020, 170, discussing the role of reason in inspiration in the Symposium; in his view, Plato "has shown that when we're inspired or intoxicated by a relationship, it's not because we've been hit by a purely random arrow from Cupid's bow. Rather, it's because we sense a kinship with the other person, which has something to do with a conception of value."

75. See Anagnostou-Laoutides 2021a, 2024b, 2025, and forthcoming a1.

76. Smith 2003, esp. 174. On the Platonic notions reworked in the Eucharist, see Anagnostou-Laoutides 2020b; cf. Gschwandtner 2019, 13–16, adopting a phenomenological approach.

77. Anagnostou-Laoutides, forthcoming a2.

78. See the contributions of Goulet and Reis, among others, in the same 2007 volume; also, Trizio 2013, 136–137 (summarizing our information on the Platonist Gaius); Pietruschka 2019 and Arzhanov 2019 (on the reception of Socrates in early Syriac Christianity).

79. Cf. the volumes by Anagnostou-Laoutides and Parry 2020 and 2023 and Anagnostou-Laoutides and Steiris forthcoming (listed under Anagnostou-Laoutides 2020b, 2023 and forthcoming a1/2 in the bibliography).

80. Karamanolis 2021, online, par. 2 and 3; cf. Dillon 1996, 361–378.

81. Klauck 1996, 124–143; cf. Brenk 1997 and id. 2014.

82. Introduction, p. 9.

83. The notion is first articulated in Stob. 2.7.3f (Wachsmuth and Hense 1884, 49.8–9) who cites Philo and Eudorus as his sources; see Bonazzi 2011; also, An. *In Th.* V.18–VI.31 with Bastianini and Sedley 1995, 495; Alc. *Did.* 28,1 with Torri 2017; cf. Baltzly 2004; Philo, *Op. mund.* 69 with Helleman 1990, esp. 56; and Plut. *De ser. num. vind.* 550d; cf. Dillon 1996, 184–304; van den Berg 2003; and Russell 2004.

84. See esp. Cl. *Str.* 5.12.78.1/PG 9.116B where Plato is mentioned as "φιλαλήθης."

85. See, for example, Cl. *Str.* 5.14.94.3–95.2/PG 9.140A–B; *Str.* 2.19.97.1–2/PG 8.1040B; *Str.* 4.22.137.1–2/PG 8.1348A; *Str.* 6.9.77.5/PG 9.297B; *Paed.* 1.12.98.2–3/PG 8.368B; and *Exc.* 3.50.1–2/PG 8.684A; cf. 3.54.1–2/PG 8.685A; for Clement's specific citation of Plato's *Tht.* 176b, see *Str.* 2.19.100.2–4/PG 8.1044B–1045A and 2.22.133.3–4/PG 8.1081B. Anagnostou-Laoutides 2020b, 96.

86. Lamberton 1986, 78–82; Runia 1993b, 134–156, and 340. In the *Stromata* Plato is portrayed as a key allegorist (Clement uses here the word παρακάλυμμα; *Str.* 5.9.82/PG 9.92A.8–10).

87. *Str.* 5.4.24.2/PG 9.44A; cf. 5.4.19.4–20.3/PG 9.37C–40B.

88. Lamberton 1983, 7.

89. Lamberton 1986, 185; cf. Uždavinys 2009, 16. Cf. Philo, *De gen.* 2.69 (discussing Gen 9:21), claiming that "the covering and screen of the soul is knowledge"; on virtue and vice as the clothing and cover of souls, cf. *Leg. all.* 2.53[76].15.

90. Bacchiocchi 2001, 63–87; cf. Anagnostou-Laoutides 2020, 82n5.

91. See Irvine 1987; cf. Dawson 2002, 231–232.

92. Cf. *Str.* 6.18.162.1–168.4/PG 9.395A–401A (on the Gnostic's use of pagan/Hellenic philosophy).

93. Chapter 4, nn5 and 8.

94. Anagnostou-Laoutides 2021a, 21–29, 2024a and 2024c, 2025, and forthcoming a1.

95. Adapting the metaphor of Platonic love, Origen interprets the *Song* as a celebration of the erotic union of the soul (or the church) with Christ; see *Comm. Cant.* 1.1 (Brésard et al. 1991); Biale 2007, 61.

96. Cf. Paul, 1 Corinthians 10:4. Also, see *Comm. Cant.* 1.2.8–9, 11 and 18–19; cf. 1.2.15 and 22; 1.6.5; 2.3.9 and 18; 3.6.2 and 4; 3.14.10 (Brésard et al. 1991) with Anagnostou-Laoutides 2025, esp. 43–59.

97. Cf. *Psalm,* 4.7 (PG 12.1165D13–1168A3): "Wine gladdens man's heart (οἶνος εὐφραίνει καρδίαν ἀνθρώπου), and bread sustains man's heart (καὶ ἄρτος καρδίαν ἀνθρώπου στηρίζει); we must understand the true bread which is nourishing for the mind (τὸν ἀληθινὸν ἄρτον νοητέον τροφιμώτα τον ὄντα τῇ διανοίᾳ), and the produce of the true vine which inebriates the best (καὶ τὸ γέννημα τῆς ἀληθινῆς ἀμπέλου μεθύσκον ὡς κράτιστον)." Origen starts here with a reference to *Psalm,* 104:15, draws on Mk. 14:25 and Jn. 15:1, and concludes with *Psalm,* 23:5.

98. Burns 1999, 193–203.

99. Burns 1999, 203–215. Gregory also reworks the *Song of Songs* systematically in his *Homilies*; Norris 2012, 169, 325–327; cf. Sferlea 2014 on the notion of spiritual *epectasis* (perpetual progress).

100. Gregory of Nyssa, Evagrius Ponticus, and the so-called Desert Fathers play a pivotal role in the development of hesychasm, the ascetic practice that involves quiet contemplation of God in uninterrupted prayer, a practice typically associated with Gregory Palamas in the fourteenth century. See Anagnostou-Laoutides 2021e, 2025, and forthcoming a1, focusing on the role of ps. Macarius in the hesychastic tradition.

101. Anagnostou-Laoutides 2020b.

102. See (Ahbel-)Rappe 2000, 93–114, on Plotinus' use of metaphors and their ritual investment in the *Enneads*; 170–196, on Proclus' use of metaphors in his *Platonic Theology*; and 208–229, on Damascius' use of figurative language to redefine the Neoplatonic identity thesis (that the intellect is identical with its object; see Plot. *Enn.* v.3.5.22.

103. Plot. *Enn.* vi.7.35.25; cf. *Enn.* iii.5.7.2. Harrington 2005; Clark 2016, 91–92, 97, 101–102; cf. Louth 2007, 35, and Gerson 1994, 190–192.

104. Callian 2013, 26–27 with n37 citing Sheppard 1980a, 145–161.

105. Struck 2001; on theurgy in ps.-Dionysius Areopagite and his Proclean influences, see Shaw 1999; Klitenic Wear and Dillon 2007, 102; also, Pavlos 2019 in introduction, n49.

106. De Andia 2006; Graham 2007; Klitenic Wear and Dillon 2007; Anagnostou-Laoutides 2020b; cf. König 2012, 123–129, on the importance of the symposiastic setting (and its dialogical format) for Christian writers (but not on the mystery of the Eucharist); also, König 2008, 95–113.

107. Anagnostou-Laoutides 2020b, 82 with nn7 and 8. On Proclus' influence on ps.-Dionysius, see Struck 2004, 257; Perczel 2003, 1195; Dodds 1933, xxvi.

108. Ziolkowski 2001b; Ziolkowski and Carruthers 2004; cf. Haskins 1927.

109. For the reception of Aristotle in Late Antiquity, see indicatively Elders, Mueller, and Anton in the same 1994 volume; similarly, see Sorabji, Erismann, and Karamanolis in a 2016 volume; for Aristotle's presence in Byzantine intellectual and theological debates, see, for example, Lankila and Bradshaw in a 2017 volume; The moralistic tenets of the Stoics appealed greatly to early Christians; see the volume by Rasinus et al. 2010.

110. For example, Ramelli 2009 and 2017; O'Meara 2003, 145–184; Louth 2007; cf. Colish 2005.

111. Colish 2005; cf. Pasnau 2002; also, Ramelli 2009, 2017, and 2023.

112. Hooker 1997, online.

113. *Sermo* 35.2.2–3: *secretos sacrosque veritatis ac sapientiae sensus dulciter haurire solebas* (Leclerq et al. 1957, 250); on Origen's influence on Bernard of Clairvaux, see Bruun 2007; Mews 2018.

114. *Conf.* 7.13; 8.3. Augustine probably read Plotinus and Porphyry; see O'Donnell 1992, 2.421–424, and Kany 2007, 50–61, cited by Tornau 2020. Augustine was also familiar with Plato through Cicero; see Bouton 2021.

115. *Sermo* 225.4/ PL 38.1098.

116. Vasilakis 2020.

117. Corrigan and Harrington 2018; on the influence ps.-Dionysius on Eriugena, see Titus 2021; cf. Rorem 2005.

118. Green 1957; Anagnostou-Laoutides 2015, 337 with n14 (for further bibliography), 339, 341–342.

119. Cf. Coleman 2022, 98–120.

120. Sheppard 1980b; Anagnostou-Laoutides forthcoming a1.

121. Landino, *DC* 17.21–18.6 (Lohe 1980).

122. Ficino also translated Plato's *Republic* and the *Laws* and understood the ideal city to represent "heavenly Jerusalem as manifested on earth for the benefit of men" (*coelestem quasi Hierusalem pro viribus in terris expressa*); see Ficino, *Opera omnia* 1576/1959, 1398.

123. Also see Anagnostou-Laoutides 2020b, 2020c, 2021a, 2021c, 2023, 2024a, 2024b, 2024c, 2025, forthcoming a1/2 and forthcoming c.

124. Roth 2005, xvi.

Bibliography

Adams, Francis. *The Extant Works of Aretaeus, the Cappadocian.* Sydenham Society, 1856.

Adams, Suzi. "Introduction to Post-Phenomenology." *Thesis Eleven: Critical Theory and Historical Sociology* 90, no. 1 (2007): 3–5.

Addey, Crystal. "Plato's Women Readers." In *Brill's Companion to the Reception of Plato in Antiquity*, ed. Harold Tarrant Danielle A. Layne, Dirk Baltzly, and François Renaud, 411–432. Brill, 2018.

Ademollo Francesco. "Cosmic and Individual Soul in Early Stoicism." In *Body and Soul in Hellenistic Philosophy*, ed. Brian Inwood and James Warren, 113–144. Cambridge University Press, 2020.

Adkins, Arthur W. H. "Clouds, Mysteries, Socrates and Plato." *Antichthon* 4 (1970): 13–24.

Adler, Ada. *Suidae Lexicon, Volumes 1–5.* Teubner, 1967.

Adluri, Vishwa. "Initiation into the Mysteries: The Experience of the Irrational in Plato." *Mouseion* 6, ser. 3 (2006): 407–423.

Aertsen, Jan A. "Truth as Transcendental in Thomas Aquinas." *Topoi* 11 (1992): 159–171.

Agócs, Peter. "Performance and Genre: Reading Pindar's κῶμοι." In *Reading the Victory Ode*, ed. Peter Agócs, Christopher Carey, and Richard Rawles, 191–223. Cambridge University Press, 2012.

Aguirre, Javier. "*Téchne* and *Enthousiasmós* in Plato's Critique of Poetry." *Revista Portuguesa de Filosofia* 72, no. 1 (2016): 181–197.

(Ahbel-)Rappe, Sara. "Socrates and Self-Knowledge." *Apeiron* 28 (1995): 1–24.

(Ahbel-)Rappe, Sara. *Reading Neoplatonism: Non-Discursive Thinking in the Texts of Plotinus, Proclus and Damascius.* Cambridge University Press, 2000.

Ahbel-Rappe, Sara. "Cross-Examining Happiness: Reason and Community in Plato's Socratic Dialogues." In *Ancient Modes of Mind: Studies in Human and Divine Rationality*, ed. Andrea Wilson-Nightingale and David Sedley, 27–44. Cambridge University Press, 2010.

Ahonen, Marke. *Mental Disorders in Ancient Philosophy.* Springer, 2014.

Ahonen, Marke. "Ancient Philosophers on Mental Illness." *History of Psychiatry* 30, no. 1 (2018a): 3–18.

Ahonen, Marke. "Making the Distinction: The Stoic View of Mental Illness." In *Mental Illness in Ancient Medicine: From Celsus to Paul of Aegina*, ed. Chiara Thumiger and Peter N. Singer, 341–364. Brill, 2018b.

Akçay, K. Nilüfer. *Porphyry's On the Cave of the Nymphs in its Intellectual Context.* Brill, 2019.

Alesse, Francesca. "The Influence of the Platonic Dialogues on Stoic Ethics from Zeno to Panaetius of Rhodes." In *Brill's Companion to the Reception of Plato in Antiquity*, ed. Harold Tarrant, Danielle A. Layne, Dirk Baltzly, and François Renaud, 46–57. Brill, 2018.

Algoe, Sara B., and Jonathan Haidt. "Witnessing Excellence in Action: The 'Other-praising' Emotions of Elevation, Gratitude, and Admiration." *Journal of Positive Psychology* 4, no. 2 (2009): 105–127.

Allen, Reginald E. "Anamnesis in Plato's *Meno* and *Phaedo*." *Review of Metaphysics* 13, no. 1 (1959): 165–174.

Allen, Reginald E. *Plato's Symposium.* Yale University Press, 1991.

Alper, Matthew. *The "God" Part of the Brain: Scientific Interpretation of Human Spirituality and God.* Rogue, 2001.

Alvino, Maria Consiglia. "*Aphroditê* and *Philophrosunê*: Xenophon's *Symposium* Between Athenian and Spartan Paradigms." In *Socrates and the Socratic Dialogue*, ed. Alessandro Stavru and Christopher Moore, 544–563. Brill, 2017.

Amitay, Ory. *From Alexander to Jesus.* University of California Press, 2010.

Amouretti, Marie-Claire. "Les boissons hors du symposion." In *La socialite à table. Commensalité et convivialité à travers les âges*, ed. Martin Aurell, Olivier Dumoulin, and Françoise Thélamon, 69–75. Publications de l'Université de Rouen, 1992.

Amouretti, Marie-Claire, and Jean-Pierre Brun. *La Production du vin et de l'huile en Méditerranée. Bulletin de correspondance hellénique suppl. 26.* De Boccard, 1993.

Anagnostou-Laoutides, Eva. *Eros and Ritual in Ancient Literature: Singing of Atalanta, Daphnis and Orpheus.* Gorgias Press, 2005.

Anagnostou-Laoutides, Eva. "*Vitae Vergili* and Florentine Intellectual Life to the Fifteenth Century." *Viator* 46, no. 2 (2015): 335–356.

Anagnostou-Laoutides, Eva. "Daphnis, *deus pastoralis*: the trail of his advent." *Giornale Italiano di Filologia* 68 (2016): 43–88.

Anagnostou-Laoutides, Eva. "Drunk with Blood: The Role of Platonic *Baccheia* in Lucan and Statius." *Latomus* 76, no. 2 (2017): 304–323.

Anagnostou-Laoutides, Eva. "A Toast to Virtue: Drinking Competitions, Plato, and the Sicilian Tyrants." In *Conflict and Competition: Agon in Western Greece: Selected Essays from the 2019 Symposium on the Heritage of Western Greece*, ed. Heather Reid, John Serrati, and Tim Sorg, 123–138. Parnassos Press, 2020a.

Anagnostou-Laoutides, Eva. "Drunk on New Wine (Acts 2:13): Drinking Wine from Plato to the Eucharist Tradition of Early Christian Thinkers." In *Eastern Christianity and Late Antique Philosophy*, ed. Ken Parry and Eva Anagnostou-Laoutides, 81–109. Brill, 2020b.

Anagnostou-Laoutides, Eva. "The Tides of Virtue and Vice: Augustine's Response to Stoic Herakles." In *Herakles Inside and Outside the Church*, ed. Emma Stafford, Arlene Allan, and Eva Anagnostou-Laoutides, 45–69. Brill, 2020c.

Anagnostou-Laoutides, Eva. "Beyond Human Reason: *Baccheia* and *Theōria* in Plato and Clement of Alexandria." *Journal of Hellenic Religion* 14 (2021a): 1–55.

Anagnostou-Laoutides, Eva. "Sócrates el sátiro sobrio y la posición de Platón respecto a la risa." In *Humor y filosofía en los diálogos de Platón*, ed. Jonathan Lavilla de Lera and Javier Aguirre Santos, 258–270. UAM-Iztapalapa, 2021b.

Anagnostou-Laoutides, Eva. "Attuning to the Cosmos: The Ethical Man's Mission from Plato to Petrarch." In *The Intellectual Dynamism of the High Middle Ages, A Festschrift in Honour of Professor Constant Mews*, ed. Clare Monagle, 249–278. Amsterdam University Press, 2021c.

Anagnostou-Laoutides, Eva. "Drunk with Wisdom: Metaphors of Ecstasy in Plato's *Symposium* and Lucian of Samosata." *Religions Special Issue* 12, no. 10 (2021d): 898. https://www.mdpi.com/2077-1444/12/10/898.

Anagnostou-Laoutides, Eva. "The Eye of the Soul in Plato and Pseudo-Macarius: Alexandrian Theology and the Roots of Hesychasm." In *Hymns, Homilies and Hermeneutics in Byzantium*, ed. Andrew Mellas and Sarah Gador-Whyte, 216–238. Brill, 2021e.

Anagnostou-Laoutides, Eva. "Sensing the Heat: Plato's Manic *Sōphrosynē* and the Meaning of Virtue in Heraclitus and Pythagoras." In *Aretē in Plato and Aristotle*, ed. Ryan M. Brown and Jay R. Elliott, 25–44. Parnassos Press, 2022.

Anagnostou-Laoutides, Eva. "Man Before God: Silence and Altered States of Consciousness in the *Phaedo* and Clement of Alexandria." In *Later Neoplatonists and Their Heirs: Christian, Jewish, and Muslim*, ed. Eva Anagnostou-Laoutides and Ken Parry, 25–60. Brill, 2023.

Anagnostou-Laoutides, Eva. "Theōria as Cure for Impiety and Atheism in Plato's Laws and Clement of Alexandria." *Religions* 15, no. 6 (2024a): 727. https://www.mdpi.com/2077-1444/15/6/727.

Anagnostou-Laoutides, Eva. "Plato." In *Research Handbook on the History of Political Thought*, ed. Cary J. Nederman and Guillaume Bogiaris, 278–289. Edward Elgar, 2024b.

Anagnostou-Laoutides, Eva. "Platonism." In *Research Handbook on the History of Political Thought*, ed. Cary J. Nederman and Guillaume Bogiaris, 76–88. Edward Elgar, 2024c.

Anagnostou-Laoutides, E. "Revelry and Reverie in Plato and Early Christian Thinkers: Platonic Metaphors of Ecstasy in Clement of Alexandria and Pseudo-Macarius." In *Encountering the Divine: The Soul's Communion with God in*

Western and Byzantine Christianity, Mediaevalia collection, ed. Luminița Diaconu and Andra Jugănaru, 43–74. University of Bucharest Press, 2025.

Anagnostou-Laoutides, Eva. "Puppets of Fear on the Stage of the Ideal City: Imbibing Civic Transformation in Plato's *Republic* and the *Laws*." In *The Rhetoric of Fear in Greek and Roman Literature and Beyond*, ed. Ian Worthington and Priscilla Gontijo Leite, 278–300. Routledge, 2026.

Anagnostou-Laoutides, Eva. "Gazing on the Gods and Trance Dancing with Them: Plato's Metaphors of Ideal Citizenship and Their Reception from Philo to Clement to ps-Macarius." In *Long Platonism: The Routes of Plato's Reception to the Italian Renaissance*, ed. Eva Anagnostou-Laoutides and George Steiris, tbc. De Gruyter Brill, forthcoming a1.

Anagnostou-Laoutides, Eva. "Plato's Nectar: Entranced Poet-Philosophers and the Making of New Jerusalem in Quattrocento Florence." In *Long Platonism: The Routes of Plato's Reception to the Italian Renaissance*, ed. Eva Anagnostou-Laoutides and George Steiris, tbc. De Gruyter Brill, forthcoming a2.

Anagnostou-Laoutides, Eva. "Plato on Euripides and *Baccheia* as a Metaphor of Higher Cognition." In *Plato and Cognition*, ed. Refik Güreman et al., tbc. Brill, forthcoming b.

Anagnostou-Laoutides, Eva. "Music and Theoretic Awakening from Plato to Augustine." In *Harmony of the Spheres*, ed. Ken Parry, Kim Cunio, and Dean Rickles, tbc. Bloomsbury, forthcoming c.

Anagnostou-Laoutides, Eva, and David Konstan. "Daphnis and Aphrodite: A Love Affair in Theocritus *Idyll* 1." *American Journal of Philology* 129, no. 4 (2008): 497–527.

Anagnostou-Laoutides, Eva, and Bart Van Wassenhove. "Drunkenness and Philosophical Enthusiasm in Seneca." *Scripta Classica Israelica* 39 (2020): 15–34.

Anagnostou-Laoutides, Eva, and Andrew Payne. "Drinking and Discourse in Plato." *Methexis* 33 (2021): 57–79.

Andén, Lovisa. "Literature and the Expressions of Being in Merleau-Ponty's Unpublished Course Notes." *Journal of the British Society for Phenomenology* 50, no. 3 (2019): 208–219.

Anderson, Elizabeth, and Geetha Shivakumar. "Effects of Exercise and Physical Activity on Anxiety." *Frontiers in Psychiatry* 4, article 27 (2013). https://doi.org/10.3389/fpsyt.2013.00027.

Anderson, Graham. "Lucian's *Nigrinus*: The Problem of Form." *Greek, Roman and Byzantine Studies* 19, no. 4 (1978): 367–374.

Anderson, Graham. "The Banquet of Belles-Lettres: Athenaeus and the Comic Symposium." In *Athenaeus and His World: Reading Greek Culture in the Roman Empire*, ed. David Braund and John Wilkins, 316–326. University of Exeter Press, 2000.

Anderson, James F. "Analogy in Plato." *Review of Metaphysics* 4, no. 1 (1950): 111–128.

Andrisano, Angela M. "Les performances du *Symposion* de Xénophon." In *Symposium: banquet et représentationsen Grèce et à Rome*, ed. Charalampos Orfanos and Jean-Claude Carrière, 287–302. Presses universitaires du Mirail, 2003.

Annas, Julia. *Platonic Ethics Old and New*. Cornell University Press, 1999.

Annas, Julia. *Virtue and Law in Plato and Beyond*. Oxford University Press, 2017.

Annus, Amar. "Drunkenness I. Ancient Near East." *Encyclopedia of the Bible and its Reception*, 7 (2013): 27–29.

Antebi, Mosheh. *Reflections and Introspection on the Torah Vayikra-Bamidbar I*. ZYA Publications, 2021.

Anton, John P. "The Aristotelianism of Photius's Philosophical Theology." In *Aristotle in Late Antiquity*, ed. Lawrence P. Schrenk, 158–183. Catholic University of America Press, 1994.

Apostolopoulos, Dimitris. *Merleau-Ponty's Phenomenology of Language*. Rowman & Littlefield, 2019.

Arata, Luigi. "The Definition of Metonymy in Ancient Greece." *Style* 39, no. 1 (2005): 55–70.

Ardley, Gavin. "The Role of Play in the Philosophy of Plato." *Philosophy* 42, no. 161 (1967): 226–244.

Arena, Valentina. "Roman Oratorical Invective." In *A Companion to Roman Rhetoric*, ed. William J. Dominik and Jon Hall, 149–160. John Wiley and Sons, 2007.

Armisen-Marchetti, Mireille. "Seneca's Images and Metaphors." In *The Cambridge Companion to Seneca*, ed. Shadi Bartsch and Alessandro Schiesaro, 150–160. Cambridge University Press, 2015.

Armstrong, John M. "After the Ascent: Plato on Becoming Like God." *Oxford Studies in Ancient Philosophy* 26 (2004): 171–183.

Arzhanov, Yury. "Plato in Syriac Literature." *Le Muséon* 132, no. 1/2 (2019): 1–36.

Asmis, Elizabeth. "Psychagogia in Plato's 'Phaedrus.'" *Illinois Classical Studies* 11, no. 1/2 (1986): 153–172.

Asmis, Elizabeth. "The Stoics on the Craft of Poetry." *Rheinisches Museum für Philologie* 160 (2017): 113–151.

Atack, Carol. "Xenophon and the Performativity of Kingship." In *How to Do Things with History*, ed. Danielle S. Allen, Paul Christesen, and Paul Millett, 109–135. Oxford University Press, 2018a.

Atack, Carol. "Plato's *Statesman* and Xenophon's *Cyrus*." In *Plato and Xenophon: Comparative Studies*, ed. Gabriel Danzig, David Johnson, and Donald Morrison, 510–543. Brill, 2018b.

Atack, Carol. *The Discourse of Kingship in Classical Greece*. Routledge, 2019.

Athanassiadi, Polymnia. "Numenius: Portrait of a Platonicus." In *Brill's Companion to the Reception of Plato in Antiquity*, ed. Harold Tarrant, Danielle A. Layne, Dirk Baltzly, and François Renaud, 183–205. Brill, 2018.

Atkins, Jed W. "Cicero on the Relationship Between Plato's 'Republic' and the 'Laws.'" *Bulletin of the Institute of Classical Studies Suppl*, 117 (2013): 15–34.

Austin, Gregory A. *Alcohol in Western Society from Antiquity to 1800.* ABC-Clio, 1985.

Austin, James H. *Zen and the Brain: Toward an Understanding of Meditation and Consciousness.* MIT Press, 1998.

Austin, James H. "Consciousness Evolves When the Self Dissolves." *Journal of Consciousness Studies* 7 (2000): 209–230.

Aygon, Jean-Pierre. "Le banquet tragique: le renouvellement du thème dans le Thyeste de Sénèque." In *Symposium: banquet et représentationsen Grèce et à Rome,* ed. Charalampos Orfanos and Jean-Claude Carrière, 271–284. Presses universitaires du Mirail, 2003.

Babut, Daniel. "Simonide moraliste." *Revue des Études Grecques* 88 (1975): 20–62.

Babut, Daniel. "Héraclite et la religion populaire." *Parerga* 24 (1994): 87–122.

Bacchiocchi, Samuele. *Wine in the Bible: A Biblical Study on the Use of Alcoholic Beverages.* Biblical Perspectives, 2001.

Bachelard, Gaston. *La poétique de l'espace.* Presses Universitaires de France, 1957.

Bachelard, Gaston. *La poétique de la rêverie.* Presses Universitaires de France, 1960.

Baima, Nicholas R. "Persuasion, Falsehood, and Motivating Reason in Plato's Laws." *History of Philosophy Quarterly* 33, no. 2 (2016): 117–134.

Baima, Nicholas R. "On the Value of Drunkenness in the *Laws.*" *History of Philosophy and Logical Analysis* 20, no. 1 (2017): 65–81.

Baima, Nicholas R. "Playing with Intoxication: On the Cultivation of Shame and Virtue in Plato's *Laws.*" *Apeiron* 51, no. 3 (2018): 345–370.

Baima, Nicholas R. "Review of Ryan K. Balot, *Tragedy, Philosophy, and Political Education in Plato's Laws.* Oxford University Press, 2024." *Bryn Mawr Classical Review* (2025): https://bmcr.brynmawr.edu/2025/2025.03.18/.

Bakola, Emmanuela. "The Drunk, the Reformer and the Teacher: Agonistic Poetics and the Construction of Persona in the Comic Poets of the Fifth Century." *Cambridge Classical Journal* 54 (2008): 1–29.

Bakola, Emmanuela. *Cratinus and the Art of Comedy.* Oxford University Press, 2010.

Baldwin, Thomas. "Speaking and Spoken Speech." In *Reading Merleau-Ponty: On Phenomenology of Perception,* ed. Thomas Baldwin, 87–103. Routledge, 2007.

Balot, Ryan K. *Tragedy, Philosophy, and Political Education in Plato's Laws.* Oxford University Press, 2024.

Baltzly, Dirk. "The Virtues and 'Becoming like God': Alcinous to Proclus." In *Oxford Studies in Ancient Philosophy 26,* ed. D. Sedley, 297–321. Oxford University Press, 2004.

Banner, Nicholas. *Philosophic Silence and the 'One' in Plotinus.* Cambridge University Press, 2018.

Baratz, Amit. "The Source of Divine Immortality in Archaic Greek Literature." *Scripta Classica Israelica* 34 (2015): 151–164.

Barker, Andrew. "Transforming the Nightingale: Aspects of Athenian Musical Discourse in the Late Fifth Century." In *Music and the Muses: The Culture of Mousikē in the Classical Athenian City*, ed. Penelope Murray and Peter Wilson, 185–204. Oxford University Press, 2004.

Barnden, John A. "Metaphor, Self-Reflection, and the Nature of Mind." In *Visions of Mind: Architectures for Cognition and Affect*, ed. Darryl N. Davis, 78–98. Information Science, 2005.

Barnett, Richard. "Liver Cirrhosis." *Lancet* 392, no. 10144 (2018): 275.

Bartels, Myrthe L. *Plato's Pragmatic Project. A Reading of Plato's Laws*. Steiner, 2017.

Bartels, Myrthe L. "Plato's Seasick Steersman: On (Not) Being Overwhelmed by Fear in Plato's *Laws*." In *Emotions in Plato*, ed. Laura Candiotto and Olivier Renaut, 147–168. Brill, 2020.

Bartoš Hynek. *Philosophy and Dietetics in the Hippocratic on Regimen: A Delicate Balance of Health*. Brill, 2015.

Bartoš, Hynek. "Heat, *Pneuma*, and Soul in the Medical Tradition." In *Heat, Pneuma, and Soul in Ancient Philosophy and Science*, eds. Hynek Bartoš and Colin Guthrie King, 21–31. Cambridge University Press, 2020.

Bartsch, Shadi. "'Wait a Moment, Phantasia': Ekphrastic Interference in Seneca and Epictetus." *Classical Philology* 102, no. 1 (2007): 83–95.

Bastianini, Guido and David N. Sedley. "Commentarium in Platonis 'Theaetetum.'" In *Corpus dei papiri filosofici greci e latini (CPF). Testi e lessico nei papiri di cultura greca e latina*. Parte III: Commentari, Florence, 227–562. Olschki, 1995.

Bateman, Anthony W., and Peter Fonagy. *Psychotherapy for Borderline Personality Disorder—Mentalization-Based Treatment*. Oxford University Press, 2004.

Baxter, Timothy M. S. *The Cratylus: Plato's Critique of Naming*. Brill, 1992.

Bayne, Tim, and Michelle Montague. "Introduction." In *Cognitive Phenomenology: An Introduction*, ed. Tim Bayne and Michelle Montague, 1–41. Oxford University Press, 2011.

Beaujeu, Jean. *Apulée: Opuscules philosophiques et fragments*. Les Belles Lettres, 1973.

Beazley, John D. *Attic Red-Figure Vase-Painters*. Clarendon Press, 1963.

Becchi, Francesco. "Plutarco tra Platonismo e Aristotelismo: la filosofia come παιδεία dell'anima." In *Plutarco, Platón y Aristóteles. Actas del V congreso de la I.P.S.* (Madrid-Cuenca, 4–7 de Mayo de 1999), ed. Aurelio Pérez Jiménez, Jose-Antonio García Lopez, and Rosa M. Aguilar, 25–43. Ediciones Clásicas, 1999.

Becchi, Francesco. "La Notion de *Philanthrōpia* chez Plutarque: Contexte Social et Sources Philosophiques." In *Symposion and Philanthropia in Plutarch*, ed. José Ribeiro Ferreira, Delfim Leão, Manuel Tröster, and Paula Barata Dias, 263–274. Imprensa da Universidade de Coimbra, Classica Digitalia, 2009.

Becchi, Francesco. "Plutarch, Aristotle and the Peripatetics." In *A Companion to Plutarch*, ed. Mark Beck, 73–87. Blackwell, 2013.

Beck, Mark. "Plutarch's Primary Use of the Socratic Paradigm in the *Lives*." In *Brill's Companion to the Reception of Socrates*, ed. Christopher Moore, 311–327. Brill, 2019.

Begodt, Georg. "Die Bedeutung des Begriffes φαντασία bei Plato." *Philosophisches Jahrbuch* 28 (1915): 490–502.

Béguin, Daniel. "Le vin médecin chez Galien." In V*in et santé en Grèce ancienne: actes du colloque organisé à l'Université de Rouen et à Paris* (Université de Paris IV Sorbonne et ENS) par l'UPRESA 8062 du CNRS et l'URLLCA de l'Université de Rouen, 28–30 septembre 1998), ed. Jacques Jouanna and Laurence Villard, 141–154. École française d'Athène, 2002.

Behr, Charles A. *P. Aelius Aristides, The Complete Works Translated into English, Vol. I: Orations I–XVI.* Brill, 1986.

Bekker, Immanuel. *Sextus Empiricus.* Reimer, 1842.

Belfiore, Elizabeth. "Wine and Catharsis of the Emotions in Plato's *Laws.*" *The Classical Quarterly* 36, no. 2 (1986): 421–437.

Belfiore, Elizabeth. "Dancing with the Gods: The Myth of the Chariot in Plato's 'Phaedrus.'" *American Journal of Philology* 127, no. 2 (2006): 185–217.

Belfiore, Elizabeth. "Poets at the *Symposium.*" In *Plato and the Poets*, ed. Pierre Destrée and Fritz-Gregor Herrmann, 155–174. Brill, 2011.

Belfiore, Elizabeth. *Socrates' Daimonic Art: Love for Wisdom in Four Platonic Dialogues.* Cambridge University Press, 2012.

Belt, Jaakko. "Phenomenological Skepticism Reconsidered: A Husserlian Answer to Dennett's Challenge." *Frontiers in Psychology* 11 (2020): 1–20.

Beneker, Jeffrey. "Drunken Violence and the Transition of Power in Plutarch's *Alexander.*" In *Symposion and Philanthropia in Plutarch*, ed. José Ribeiro Ferreira, Delfim Leão, Manuel Tröster, and Paula Barata Dias, 193–200. Imprensa da Universidade de Coimbra, Classica Digitalia, 2009.

Beneker, Jeffrey. *The Passionate Statesman: Erōs and Politics in Plutarch's Lives.* Oxford University Press, 2012.

Bendz, Gerhard. *Caelius Aurelianus. Celeres Passiones.* CML VI 1, vol. 1. Akademie Verlag, 1990.

Benitez, Rick. "Parrhesia, Ekmarturia and the Cassandra: Dialogue in Aeschylus' *Agamemnon.*" *Modern Greek Studies* 11 (2003): 334–346.

Beresford, Adam. *Aristotle. The Nicomachean Ethics.* Penguin, 2020.

Berg, George Olaf. *Metaphor and Comparison in the Dialogues of Plato.* Mayer and Müller, 1903.

Berg, Steven. *Eros and the Intoxications of Enlightenment: On Plato's Symposium.* State University of New York Press, 2010.

Berger, Marie-Paul. "Tristis sobrietas removenda (Sen., *De Tranq. an.*, XVII, 9)." *L'Antiquite Classique* 29, no. 2 (1960): 348–368.

Berman, Scott. "Socrates and Callicles on Pleasure." *Phronesis* 36, no. 2 (1991): 117–140.

Bernabé, Alberto, and Ana Isabel Jiménez San Cristóbal. *Instrucciones para el más allá. Las laminillas órficas de oro.* Ediciones Clásicas, 2001. Reprint, *Instructions for the Netherworld: The Orphic Gold Tablets.* Brill, 2008.

Bernardi, Luciano, Cesare Porta, Gaia Casucci, et al. "Dynamic Interactions Between Musical, Cardiovascular, and Cerebral Rhythms in Humans." *Circulation* 119 (2009): 3171–3180.

Berno, Francesca Romana. "Nurses' Prayers, Philosophical *otium*, and Fat Pigs: Seneca *Ep.* 60 versus Horace *Ep.* 1.4." In *Horace and Seneca: Interactions, Intersects, Interpretations*, ed. Martin Stöckinger, Kathrin Winter, and Andreas Thomas Zanker, 53–72. De Gruyter, 2017.

Bershadsky, Natasha. "A Picnic, a Tomb, and a Crow: Hesiod's Cult in the *Works and Days*." *Harvard Studies in Classical Philology* 106 (2011): 1–45.

Berti, Enrico. *In principio era la meraviglia: le grandi questioni della filosofia antica*. Laterza, 2007.

Bertier, Janine. *Mnésithée et Dieuchès*. Brill, 1972.

Bessone, Federica. "Discorsi dei liberti e parodia del 'Simposio' platonico nella 'Cena Trimalchionis.'" *Materiali e Discussioni* 30 (1993): 63–86.

Betegh, Gábor. "Cosmological Ethics in the *Timaeus* and Early Stoicism." *Oxford Studies in Ancient Philosophy* 24 (2003): 273–302.

Betegh, Gábor. "On the Physical Aspect of Heraclitus' Psychology." *Phronesis* 52 (2007): 3–32.

Betegh, Gábor. "Fire, Heat, and Motive Force in Early Greek Philosophy." In *Heat, Pneuma, and Soul in Ancient Philosophy and Science*, ed. Hynek Bartoš and Colin Guthrie King, 35–60. Cambridge University Press, 2020.

Betegh, Gábor. "Plato on Illness in the *Phaedo*, the *Republic*, and the *Timaeus*." In *Plato's Timaeus: Proceedings of the Tenth Symposium Platonicum Pragene*, ed. Chad Jorgenson, Filip Karfík, and Štěpán Špinka, 228–258. Brill, 2021.

Bettini, Maurizio. "*In Vino Stuprum*." In *In Vino Veritas*, ed. Oswyn Murray and Manuela Tecuşan, 224–235. British School at Rome, 1995.

Bevilacqua, Fiorenza. "Socrates' Attitude Towards Politics." In *Xenophon and Plato in Plato and Xenophon: Comparative Studies*, ed. Gabriel Danzig, David Johnson, and Donald Morrison, 461–486. Brill, 2018.

Biale, David. *Blood and Belief: The Circulation of a Symbol Between Jews and Christians*. University of California Press, 2007.

Biederman, Joseph, Timothy E. Wilens, Eric Mick, Stephen V Faraone, and Thomas Spencer. "Does Attention-Deficit Hyperactivity Disorder Impact the Developmental Course of Drug and Alcohol Abuse and Dependence?" *Biological Psychiatry* 44, no. 4 (1998): 269–273.

Bierl, Anton. *Dionysos und die griechische Tragödie: Politische und "metatheatralische" Aspekte im Text*. Narr, 1991.

Bierl, Anton. *Ritual and Performativity: The Chorus in Old Comedy*. Centre for Hellenic Studies, 2009.

Biggs, Penelope. "The Disease Theme in Sophocles' *Ajax*, *Philoctetes* and *Trachiniae*." *Classical Philology* 61, no. 4 (1966): 223–235.

Biles, Zachary. "Intertextual Biography in the Rivalry of Cratinus and Aristophanes." *American Journal of Philosophy* 123, no. 2 (2002): 169–203.

Biles, Zachary. "Celebrating Poetic Victory: Representations of *Epinikia* in Classical Athens." *Journal of Hellenic Studies* 127 (2007): 19–37.

Billings, Joshua. *The Philosophical Stage: Drama and Dialectic in Classical Athens.* Princeton University Press, 2021.

Black, Max. "Metaphor." In *Philosophical Perspectives on Metaphor,* ed. Mark Johnson, 63–82. University of Minnesota Press, 1981.

Blanckenhagen, Peter H. von. "Stage and Actors in Plato's *Symposium*." *Greek, Roman and Byzantine Studies* 33, no. 1 (1992): 51–68.

Block, Marvin A. *Alcohol and Alcoholism: Drinking and Dependence.* Wadsworth, 1970.

Blondell, Ruby, and Sandra Boehringer. "Revenger of the Hetairistria: The Reception of Plato's *Symposium* in Lucian's fifth *Dialogue of the Courtesans*." *Arethusa* 47, no. 2 (2014): 231–264.

Blood, Anne J., and Robert J. Zatorre. "Intensely Pleasurable Responses to Music Correlate with Activity in Brain Regions Implicated in Reward and Emotion." *Proceedings of the National Academy of Sciences of the United States of America* 98, no. 20 (2001): 11818–11823.

Bloom, Allen. "The Ladder of Love." In *Plato's Symposium,* ed. Seth Bernadete and Allen Bloom, 55–178. Chicago University Press, 2001.

Blundell, Mary Whitlock. "The Moral Character of Odysseus in *Philoctetes*." *Greek, Roman and Byzantine Studies* 28 (1987): 307–329.

Bobonich, Christopher. "Persuasion, Compulsion and Freedom in Plato's *Laws*." *The Classical Quarterly* 41, no. 2 (1991): 365–388.

Bobonich, Christopher. "*Akrasia* and Agency in Plato's *Laws* and *Republic*." *Archiv für Geschichte der Philosophie* 76, no. 1 (1994): 3–36.

Bobonich, Christopher, and Pierre Destrée. *Akrasia in Greek Philosophy: From Socrates to Plotinus.* Brill, 2007.

Bogdashina, Olga. *Sensory Perceptual Issues in Autism and Asperger Syndrome: Different Sensory Experiences—Different Perceptual Worlds.* Kingsley, 2016.

Bomhard, Allan R. "Indo-European *men- and *tel-." In *Studies in Baltic and Indo-European Linguistics: In Honor of William R. Schmalstieg,* ed. Philip Baldi and Pietro U. Dini, 33–36. Benjamins, 2004.

Bompaire, Jacques. *Lucien écrivain. Imitation et Creation.* De Boccard, 1958.

Bonazzi, Mauro. "Eudorus of Alexandria and Early Imperial Platonism." In *Greek and Roman Philosophy 100BC–200AD,* ed. Robert W. Sharples and Richard Sorabji, 365–377. Institute of Classical Studies, University of London, 2007.

Bonazzi, Mauro. "Il platonismo nel secondo libro dell'*Anthologium* di Stobeo: il problema di Eudoro." In *Thinking through Excerpts. Studies on Stobaeus,* ed. Gretchen Reydams-Schils, 441–456. Brepols, 2011.

Bonazzi, Mauro. "Plutarch of Chaeronea and the Anonymous Commentator on the *Theaetetus*." In *Brill's Companion to the Reception of Plato in Antiquity,* In

Brill's Companion to the Reception of Plato in Antiquity, ed. Harold Tarrant, Danielle A. Layne, Dirk Baltzly, and François Renaud, 130–142. Brill, 2018.

Bonazzi, Mauro. "Plutarch on Epicurus on Wine." In *Epicureanism and Scientific Debates. Epicurean Tradition and Its Ancient Reception*, vol. 2, ed. Francesca Masi, Pierre-Marie Morel, and Francesco Verde, 167–176. Peeters, 2024.

Bonazzi, Mauro, and Cristoph Helmig. *Platonic Stoicism, Stoic Platonism: The Dialogue between Platonism and Stoicism in Antiquity*. Peeters, 2007.

Bonitz, Hermann. *Index Aristotelicus*. Reimer, 1870.

Bordoy, Francesc Casadesús. "Dionysian Enthusiasm in Plato." In *Redefining Dionysos*, ed. Alberto Bernabé, Miguel Herrero de Jáuregui, Ana Isabel Jiménez San Cristóbal, and Raquel Martín Hernández, 386–400. De Gruyter, 2013.

Borgen, Peder. "Moses, Jesus, and the Roman Emperor. Observations in Philo's Writings and the Revelation of John." *Novum Testamentum* 38 (1996): 145–159.

Borgen, Peder. "Philo of Alexandria as Exegete." In *A History of Biblical Interpretation. Vol. 1. The Ancient Period*, ed. Alan J. Hauser and Duane F. Watson, 114–143. Eerdmans, 2003.

Bossi, Beatriz. "*Amathia, Akrasia* and the Power of Knowledge in the *Laws*: Break or Unity?" *Hermathena* 169 (2000): 99–114.

Bossi, Beatriz. "In What Sense Is the Philosopher Leader a 'Stranger' in the City? Notes on the "Digression" in *Theaetetus* (172c2–177c5)." In *New Explorations in Plato's Theaetetus*, eds. Diego Zucca. 177–198. Brill, 2022.

Bostock, David. *Plato's Theaetetus*. Oxford University Press, 1991.

Bougher, Lori D. "Cognitive Coherence in Politics: Unifying Metaphor and Narrative in Civic Cognition." In *Warring with Words: Narrative and Metaphor in Politics*, ed. Michael Hanne, William D. Crano, and Jeffrey Scott Mio, 150–271. Psychology Press, 2014.

Bouton, Anne-Isabelle. "Cicero and Augustine." In *The Cambridge Companion to Cicero's Philosophy*, ed. Jed W. Atkins and Thomas Bénatouïl, 252–267. Cambridge University Press, 2021.

Bowie, Angus M. *Aristophanes: Myth, Ritual and Comedy*. Cambridge University Press, 1993.

Bowie, Angus M. "Fate May Harm Me, I Have Dined Today: Near Eastern Royal Banquets and Greek Symposia in Herodotus." In *Symposium: banquet et représentationsen Grèce et à Rome*, eds. Charalampos Orfanos and Jean-Claude Carrière, 99–110. Toulouse: Presses universitaires du Mirail, 2003.

Bowie, Angus M. "Myth and Ritual in Comedy." In *Brill's Companion to the Study of Greek Comedy*, ed. Gregory Dobrov, 143–178. Brill, 2010.

Boyancé, Pierre. *Le culte des Muses chez les philosophes Grecs*. de Boccard, 1936. Reprint, 1972.

Boyancé, Pierre. "Platon et le vin." *Bulletin de l'Association Guillaume Budé* 3rd ser., 4 (1951): 3–19.

Boyancé, Pierre. "Le platonisme à Rome. Platon et Cicéron." In *Études sur l'humanisme cicéronien*, ed. Pierre Boyancé, 222–247. Latomus, 1970. Originally published, 1953.

Boys-Stones, George R. "Seneca against Plato: *Letters* 58 and 65." In *Plato and the Stoics*, ed. Anthony Arthur Long, 128–146. Cambridge University Press, 2013.

Brachtendorf, Johannes. "Cicero and Augustine on the Passions." *Revue des Études Augustiniennes* 43 (1997): 289–308.

Bradshaw, David. "The Presence of Aristotle in Byzantine Theology." In *The Cambridge Intellectual History of Byzantium*, ed. Anthony Kaldellis and Niketas Siniossoglou, 381–396. Cambridge University Press, 2017.

Branham, R. Bracht. *Unruly Eloquence: Lucian and the Comedy of Traditions*. Harvard University Press, 1989.

Breitenberger, Barbara. *Aphrodite and Eros: The Development of Greek Erotic Mythology in Early Greek Poetry and Cult*. Routledge, 2013.

Bremer, Jan N. "Aristophanes on His Own Poetry." In *Aristophane: Sept Exposés suivis de discussions*, ed. Jan N. Bremer and Eric W. Handley, 125–165. Fondation Hardt, 1993.

Bremer, Jan N. "Jokes, Jokers, and Jokebooks in Ancient Greek Culture." In *A Cultural History of Humour: From Antiquity to the Present Day*, ed. Jan N. Bremmer and Herman Roodenburg, 11–28. Cambridge University Press, 1997.

Bremer, Jan N. *Initiation into the Mysteries of the Ancient World*. de Gruyter, 2014.

Brennan, Tad. "The Old Stoic Theory of Emotions." In *The Emotions in Hellenistic Philosophy*, ed. Juha Sihvola and Troels EngbergPedersen, 21–70. Springer, 1998.

Brennan, Tad. "Socrates and Epictetus." In *A Companion to Socrates*, ed. Sara Ahbel-Rappe and Rachana Kamtekar, 285–298. Wiley-Blackwell, 2005a.

Brennan, Tad. *The Stoic Life: Emotions, Duties and Fate*. Oxford University Press, 2005b.

Brésard, Luc, Henri Crouzel, and Marcel Borret, *Origène: Commentaire sur le Cantique des Cantiques. Texte de la version latine de Rufin*, vol. 1. Paris, 1991.

Bringmann, Klaus. *Studien zu den politischen Ideen des Isokrates*. Vandenhoeck & Ruprecht, 1965.

Brenk, Frederick E. "Plutarch, Judaism and Christianity." In *Studies in Plato and the Platonic Tradition. Essays Presented to John Whitaker*, ed. Mark Joyal, 97–118. Routledge, 1997.

Brenk, Frederick E. "Philo and Plutarch on the nature of God." *Studia Philonica Annual* 26 (2014): 79–92.

Brisson, Luc. *Plato the Myth Maker*. Edited, translated, and Introduction by Gerard Naddaf. University of Chicago Press, 1998.

Brisson, Luc. *How Philosophers Saved Myths. Allegorical Interpretation and Classical Mythology*. Translated by Catherine Tihanyi. University of Chicago Press, 2004.

Brisson, Luc. "Agathon, Pausanias and Diotima in Plato's *Symposium*: *Paiderastia* and *Philosophia*." In *Plato's Symposium: Issues in Interpretation and Reception*, ed. James Lesher, Debra Nails, and Frisbee Sheffield, 229–251. Harvard University Press (on behalf of the Center for Hellenic Studies), 2006.

Brisson Luc. "Soul and State in Plato's *Laws*." In *Plato and the Divided Self*, ed. Rachel Barney, Tad Brennan, and Charles Brittain, 281–308. Cambridge University Press, 2012a.

Brisson, Luc. "Why Is the *Timaeus* Called an Eikôs Muthos and an Eikôs Logos?" In *Plato and Myth: Studies on the Use and Status of Platonic Myths*, ed. Catherine Collobert, Pierre Destrée, and Francisco J. Gonzalez, 369–391. Brill, 2012b.

Brisson, Luc. "Le *Timée* de Platon et le traité hippocratique *Du régime*, sur le mécanisme de la sensation." *Études Platoniciennes* 10 (2013). https://doi.org/10.4000/etudesplatoniciennes.367.

Brittain, Charles. *Cicero. On Academic Scepticism*. Hackett, 2006.

Brock, Roger, and Hanneke Wirtjes. "Athenaeus on Greek Wine." In *Athenaeus and His World: Reading Greek Culture in the Roman Empire*, ed. David Braund and John Wilkins, 455–465. Exeter, 2000.

Bromberg, Jacques A. "A Sage on the Stage: Socrates and Athenian Old Comedy." In *Socrates and the Socratic Dialogue*, ed. Alessandro Stavru and Christopher Moore, 31–63. Brill, 2017.

Brown, Eric. "Plato's Ethics and Politics in the *Republic*." In *Stanford Encyclopedia of Philosophy* (Fall 2017 Edition), ed. Edward N. Zalta. 2017. https://plato.stanford.edu/archives/fall2017/entries/plato-ethics-politics/.

Brown, Lesley. "*Aporia* in Plato's *Theaetetus* and *Sophist*." In *The Aporetic Tradition in Ancient Philosophy*, ed. George Karamanolis and Vasilis Politis, 91–111. Cambridge University Press, 2018.

Brun, Jean-Pierre. *Le vin et l'huile dans la Méditerranée antique: Viticulture, oléiculture et procédés de fabrication*. Errand, 2003.

Bruun, Mette Birkedal. *Parables: Bernard of Clairvaux's Mapping of Spiritual Topography*. Brill, 2007.

Bryan, Jenny. "The Role of Lysias' Speech in Plato's *Phaedrus*." *Cambridge Classical Journal* (2021): 1–24.

Burden, Robert. "Symbolisation in Psychoanalysis and Literature: Lacanian Readings of the Poetic Metaphor in D.H. Lawrence." *Hungarian Journal of English and American Studies* 4, no. 1/2 (1998): 91–104.

Burke, Edmund. *A Philosophical Enquiry into the Sublime and the Beautiful*. Dodsley, 1757. New edition, Routledge, 2008.

Burkert, Walter. "Cicero als Platoniker und Skeptiker." *Gymnasium* 72 (1965): 175–200.

Burkert, Walter. "Orphism and Bacchic Mysteries: New Evidence and Old Problems of Interpretation." In *Protocol of the 28th Colloquy of the Center for*

Hermeneutical Studies in Hellenistic and Modern Culture, ed. Wilhelm H. Wuellner, 1–8. Center for Hermeneutical Studies in Hellenistic and Modern Culture, 1977.

Burkert, Walter. *Homo Necans: The Anthropology of Ancient Greek Sacrificial Ritual and Myth*. Translated by Peter Bing. University of California Press, 1983.

Burkert, Walter. *Ancient Mystery Cults*. Harvard University Press, 1987.

Burnham, William H. "Memory, Historically and Experimentally Considered. I. An Historical Sketch of the Older Conceptions of Memory." *American Journal of Psychology* 2, no. 1 (1888): 39–90.

Burns, Stuart K. "Divine Ecstasy in Gregory of Nyssa and Pseudo-Macarius: Flight and Intoxication." *Greek Orthodox Theological Review* 44, no. 1–4 (1999), 309–327.

Burnyeat, Myles. *The Theaetetus of Plato*. Hackett, 1990.

Burnyeat, Myles. "The Passion of Reason in Plato's *Phaedrus*." In *Explorations in Ancient and Modern Philosophy*, 238–258. Cambridge University Press, 2011.

Burnyeat, Myles, and Michael Frede. *The Pseudo-Platonic Seventh Letter*, ed. Dominic Scott. Oxford University Press, 2015.

Burton, Joan B. "The Function of the Symposium Theme in Theocritus' *Idyll* 14." *Greek, Roman and Byzantine Studies* 33 (1992): 227–245.

Bury, Robert Gregg. *The Symposium of Plato*, 2nd ed. Heffer and Sons, 1932.

Bushnell, Rebecca W. *Tragedies of Tyrants: Political Thought and Theater in the English Renaissance*. Cornell University Press, 1990.

Bussanich, John. "Socrates and Religious Experience." In *The Blackwell Companion to Socrates*, ed. Sara Ahbel-Rappe and Rachana Kamtekar, 200–213. Wiley-Blackwell, 2006.

Buzzetti, Eric. *Xenophon the Socratic Prince: The Argument of the Anabasis of Cyrus*. Palgrave Macmillan, 2014.

Byers, Sarah Catherine. *Perception, Sensibility, and Moral Motivation in Augustine: A Stoic-Platonic Synthesis*. Cambridge University Press, 2013.

Byl, Simon. "Le vocabulaire de l'intelligence dans le chapitre 35 du livre I du traité du Régime." *Revue de philologie, de littérature et d'histoire anciennes* 76, no. 2 (2002): 217–224.

Cagnoli Fiecconi, Elena. *Ethics for Rational Animals: The Moral Psychology at the Basis of Aristotle's Ethics*. Oxford University Press, 2024.

Cairns, Douglas. "Looks of Love and Loathing: Cultural Models of Vision and Emotion in Ancient Greek Culture." *Métis* 9 (2011): 37–50.

Cairns, Douglas. "The Imagery of *Erôs* in Plato's *Phaedrus*." In *Erôs in Ancient Greece*, ed. Ed Sanders, Chiara Thumiger, Christopher Carey, and Nick J. Lowe, 233–250. Oxford University Press, 2013.

Cairns, Douglas. "Ψυχή, Θυμός, and Metaphor in Homer and Plato." *Études platoniciennes* 11 (2014). http://etudesplatoniciennes.revues.org/566.

Cairns, Douglas. "Mind, Body, and Metaphor in Ancient Greek Concepts of Emotion." *L'Atelier du Centre de recherches historiques* 16 (2016). http://journals.openedition.org/acrh/7416.

Cairns, Douglas. "The Tripartite Soul as Metaphor." In *Plato and the Power of Images*, ed. Pierre Destrée and Radcliffe G. Edmonds III, 219–238. Brill, 2017.

Cairns, Douglas. "Anchoring the Tripartite Soul." In *Resisting and Justifying Changes: How to Make the New Acceptable in the Ancient, Medieval and Early Modern World*, ed. Elisabetta Poddighe and Tiziana Pontillo, 193–221. Pisa University Press, 2021.

Calame, Claude. *The Craft of Poetic Speech in Ancient Greece.* Translated by Janice Orion. Cornell University Press, 1995.

Calame, Claude. *Myth and History in Ancient Greece: The Symbolic Creation of a Colony.* Translated by Daniel W. Berman. Princeton University Press, 2003.

Calame, Claude. "Choral Practices in Plato's *Laws*: Itineraries of Initiation?" In *Performance and Culture in Plato's Laws*, ed. Anastasia-Erasmia Peponi, 87–108. Cambridge University Press, 2013.

Calin, Rodolphe. "À la charnière de l'image et du langage. Deux approches du schématisme de l'imagination chez Paul Ricoeur." *Philosopiques* 41, no. 2 (2014): 253–273.

Callard, Agnes Gellen. "Ignorance and *Akrasia*-Denial in the *Protagoras*." *Oxford Studies in Ancient Philosophy* 47 (2014): 31–80.

Callian, Florin George. "'Clarifications of Obscurity:' Conditions for Proclus's Allegorical Reading of Plato's *Parmenides*." In *Obscurity in Medieval Texts*, ed. Lucie Doležalová, Jeff Rider, and Alessandro Zironi, 15–31. Institut für Realienkunde des Mittelalters und der frühen Neuzeit, 2013.

Camden, David H. *The Cosmological Doctors of Classical Greece. First Principles in Early Greek Medicine.* Cambridge University Press, 2023.

Cameron, Alan. *Callimachus and His Critics.* Princeton University Press, 1995.

Camp, Elisabeth. "Metaphor in the Mind: The Cognition of Metaphor." *Philosophy Compass* 1, no. 2 (2006): 154–170.

Campeggiani, Pia. "The Feel of the Real: Perceptual Encounters in Plato's Critique of Poetry." In *Emotions in Plato*, ed. Laura Candiotto and Olivier Renaut, 39–60. Brill, 2020.

Candiotto, Laura, and Vasilis Politis. "Epistemic Wonder and the Beginning of the Enquiry: Plato's *Theaetetus* (155d2-4) and Its Wider Significance." In *Emotions in Plato*, ed. Laura Candiotto and Olivier Renaut, 17–38. Brill, 2020.

Candiotto, Laura, and Olivier Renaut. "Introduction: Why Plato Comes First." In *Emotions in Plato*, ed. Laura Candiotto and Olivier Renaut, 1–16. Brill, 2020.

Canfora, Luciano. *Critica della retorica democratica.* Laterza, 2002.

Capponi, Livia. "The King in the Symposium Scene of the Letter of Aristeas." *Athenaeum* 104, no. 1 (2016): 31–49.

Capra, Andrea. *Plato's Four Muses. The Phaedrus and the Poetics of Philosophy.* Center for Hellenic Studies, 2014.

Capra, Andrea. "Aristophanes' Iconic Socrates." In *Socrates and the Socratic Dialogue,* ed. Alessandro Stavru and Christopher Moore, 64–83. Brill, 2017.

Carabine, Deirdre. *The Unknown God: Negative Theology in the Platonic Tradition: Plato to Eriugena.* Peeters, 1995.

Carone, Gabriela Roxana. "*Akrasia* in the Republic: Does Plato Change his Mind?" *Oxford Studies in Ancient Philosophy* 20 (2001): 107–148.

Carone, Gabriela Roxana. "Pleasure, Virtue, Externals, and Happiness in Plato's 'Laws.'" *History of Philosophy Quarterly* 19, no. 4 (2002): 327–344.

Carone, Gabriela Roxana. *Plato's Cosmology and Its Ethical Dimensions.* Cambridge University Press, 2005.

Carpenter, Thomas H. *Dionysian Imagery in Archaic Greek Art: Its Development in Black-figure Vase Painting.* Oxford University Press, 1986.

Carpenter, Thomas H. *Dionysian Imagery in Fifth-Century Athens.* Oxford University Press, 1997.

Carriére, Jean-Claude. "Les banquets de Démos dans les comédies d'Aristophane Stratégies poétiques et message politique." In *Symposium: banquet et représentationsen Grèce et à Rome,* ed. Charalampos Orfanos and Jean-Claude Carrière, 175–202. Presses universitaires du Mirail, 2003.

Carrigan, Matthew. "Hominoid Adaptation to Dietary Ethanol." In *Alcohol and Humans: A Long and Social Affair,* ed. Kimberley Hockings and Robin Dunbar, 24–44. Oxford University Press, 2020.

Carter, David. "Was Attic Tragedy Democratic?" *Polis* 21 (2004): 1–25.

Catani, Marco, and Paolo Mazzarello. "Grey Matter Leonardo da Vinci: A Genius Driven to Distraction." *Brain* 142, no. 6 (2019): 1842–1846.

Catoni, Maria Luisa, and Luca Giuliani. "Socrates Represented: Why Does He Look Like a Satyr?" *Critical Enquiry* 45, no. 3 (2019): 681–713.

Cavalca Schiroli, Maria Grazia. *De Tranquillitate Animi.* Cooperativa Libraria Universitaria Editrice Bologna, 1981.

Cavini, Walter. "Doxa and Epistēmē in Plato's *Theaetetus* and Aristotle's *Posterior Analytics.*" In *New Explorations in Plato's Theaetetus,* ed. Diego Zucca, 307–324. Brill, 2022.

Ceccarelli, Paolo. "Dance and Desserts: An Analysis of Book Fourteen." In *Athenaeus and His World: Reading Greek Culture in the Roman Empire,* ed. David Braund and John Wilkins, 172–291. University of Exeter Press, 2000.

Chambert, Régine. "Voyage et santé dans les Lettres de Sénèque." *Bulletin de l' Association Guillaume Bude* 6 (2002): 63–82.

Chappell, Sophie-Grace. "Plato on Knowledge in the *Theaetetus.*" In *Stanford Encyclopedia of Philosophy* (Fall 2024 Edition), ed. Edward N. Zalta and Uri Nodelman, 2024. https://plato.stanford.edu/archives/fall2024/entries/plato-theaetetus/.

Chappell, Timothy D. J. *Reading Plato's Theaetetus.* Hackett, 2005.

Chaturvedi, Aditi. "*Harmonia* and *r̥tá*." In *Universe and Inner Self in Early Indian and Early Greek Thought*, ed. Richard Seaford, 40–54. Edinburgh University Press, 2016.

Chesnut, Glenn F. "The Ruler and the *Logos* in Neopythagorean, Middle Platonic, and Late Stoic Political Philosophy." *Aufstieg und Niedergang der römischen Welt* II 16, no. 2 (1978): 1310–1332.

Chitwood, Ava. *Death by Philosophy: The Biographical Tradition in the Life and Death of the Archaic Philosophers Empedocles, Heraclitus, and Democritus.* University of Michigan Press, 2004.

Chroust, Anton-Hermann. "The Organization of the Corpus Platonicum in Antiquity." *Hermes* 93, no. 1 (1965): 34–46.

Chrysanthou, Chrysanthos S. "Orator-Politician vs. Philosopher: Plutarch's Demosthenes 1–3 and Plato's *Theaetetus*." *Classical World* 112, no. 2 (2019): 39–55.

Chudnoff, Elijah. *Cognitive Phenomenology.* Routledge, 2015.

Cimino, Andrea. "The Existence of the World as an Irrational and 'Rational' Fact." *Southern Journal of Philosophy* 62, no. 3 (2024): 277–402.

Clark, Maudemarie, and Alan J. Swensen (translation, introduction and notes). Friedrich Nietzsche. *On the Genealogy of Morality.* Hackett, 1998.

Clark, Randall B. *The Law Most Beautiful and Best: Medical Argument and Magical Rhetoric in Plato's Laws.* Oxford University Press, 2003.

Clark, Stephen R.L. *Plotinus: Myth, Metaphor, and Philosophical Practice.* University of Chicago Press, 2016.

Clay, Diskin. "The Tragic and Comic Poet of the *Symposium*." *Arion* 2, no. 2 (1975): 238–261.

Clay, Diskin. "Lucian of Samosata: Four Philosophical Lives (Nigrinus, Demonax, Peregrinus, Alexander Pseudomantis)." *Aufstieg und Niedergang der römischen Welt* II 36, no. 5 (1992): 3406–3450.

Clay, Diskin. *Platonic Questions: Dialogues with the Silent Philosopher.* University of Pennsylvania Press, 2000.

Clay, Diskin. "Plato Philomuthos." In *The Cambridge Companion to Greek Mythology*, ed. Roger D. Woodard, 210–236. Cambridge University Press, 2007.

Clay, Diskin. "Plato and Homer." In *Homer Encyclopedia*, vol. 2, ed. Margalit Finkleberg, 672–675. Wiley-Blackwell, 2011.

Clinton, Kevin. *Myth and Cult: The Iconography of the Eleusinian Mysteries.* The M.P. Nilsson Lectures on Greek Religion delivered at the Swedish Institute at Athens, November 19–21, 1990. P. Åstrom, 1992.

Coarelli, Filippo. "Vino e idelologia nella Roma Arcaica." In *In Vino Veritas*, ed. Oswyn Murray and Manuela Tecuşan, 224–235. British School at Rome, 1995.

Cohen, H. Hirsch. *The Drunkenness of Noah.* University of Alabama Press, 1974.

Cohen, S. Marc. "Socrates on the Definition of Piety: *Euthyphro* 10A–11B." In *The Philosophy of Socrates: A Collection of Critical Essays*, ed. Gregory Vlastos, 158–176. Palgrave Macmillan, 1971.

Cohen, Ted. "Metaphor and the Cultivation of Intimacy." *Critical Inquiry* 5, no. 1 (1978): 3–12.

Cohn, Matthew D. "The Admonishing Muse: Ancient Interpretations of Personal Abuse in Old Comedy." Unpublished PhD thesis, University of Michigan, 2013.

Cole, Susan Guettel. "New Evidence for the Mysteries of Dionysos." *Greek, Roman and Byzantine Studies* 21, no. 3 (1980): 223–238.

Cole, Susan Guettel. "Finding Dionysus." In *A Companion to Greek Religion*, ed. Daniel Ogden, 327–341. Wiley-Blackwell, 2007.

Coleman, James. K. *A Sudden Frenzy: Improvisation, Orality, and Power in Renaissance Italy*. University of Toronto Press, 2022.

Colish, Marcia. *The Stoic Tradition from Antiquity to the Early Middle Ages. Volume 1, Stoicism in Classical Latin Literature; volume 2, Stoicism in Christian Latin Thought through the Sixth Century*. Brill, 1985.

Colish, Marcia. *Ambrose's Patriarchs: Ethics for the Common Man*. University of Notre Dame Press, 2005.

Collins, Nina L. *The Library in Alexandria and the Bible in Greek*. Vetus Testamentum Supplements 82. Brill, 2000.

Colomo, Daniela. "Herakles and the Eleusinian Mysteries: P. Mil. Vogl. I 20, 18–32 Revisited." *Zeitschrift für Papyrologie und Epigraphik* 148 (2004): 87–98.

Colvin, Matthew. "Heraclitean Flux and Unity of Opposites in Plato's *Theaetetus* and *Cratylus*." *The Classical Quarterly* 57, no. 2 (2007): 759–769.

Connolly, William E. *Identity\Difference: Democratic Negotiations of Political Paradox*, expanded ed. University of Minnesota Press, 2002.

Connor, Walter R. "City Dionysia and Athenian Democracy." *Classica et Mediaevalia* 40 (1989): 7–32.

Cook, Arthur Bernard. "The Bee in Greek Mythology." *Journal of Hellenistic Studies* 15 (1895): 1–24.

Cooper, John. "Posidonius on Emotions." In *The Emotions in Hellenistic Philosophy*, ed. Juha Sihvola and Troels Engberg-Pedersen, 71–112. Kluwer, 1998. Also in Cooper 1999, 449–484.

Cooper, John. *Reason and Emotion: Essays on Ancient Moral Psychology and Ethical Theory*. Princeton University Press, 1999.

Cooper, John M. "Plato on Sense-Perception and Knowledge ('*Theaetetus*' 184–186)." *Phronesis* 15, no. 2 (1970): 123–146.

Cooper, John M. *Plato's Theaetetus*. Garland Publishing, 1990.

Copeland, Rita, and Peter T. Struck, P. "Introduction." In *The Cambridge Companion to Allegory*, ed. Rita Copeland and Peter T. Struck, 1–11. Cambridge University Press, 2010.

Corner, Sean. "*Philos* and *Polites*: The *Symposion* and the Origins of the *Polis*." PhD thesis, Princeton University, 2005.

Corner, Sean. "Transcendent Drinking: The Symposium at Sea Reconsidered." *The Classical Quarterly* 60 (2010): 352–380.

Corner, Sean. "The Politics of the Parasite (Part One)." *Phoenix* 67, no. 1/2 (2013a): 43–80.

Corner, Sean. "The Politics of the Parasite (Part Two)." *Phoenix* 67, no. 3/4 (2013b): 223–236.

Corradi, Michele. "Protagorean Socrates, Socratic Protagoras: A Narrative Strategy from Aristophanes to Plato." In *Socrates and the Socratic Dialogue*, ed. Alessandro Stavru and Christopher Moore, 84–104. Brill, 2017.

Corrigan, Kevin, and Michael Harrington. "Pseudo-Dionysius the Areopagite." In *Stanford Encyclopedia of Philosophy* (Summer 2018 Edition), ed. Edward N. Zalta, 2018. https://plato.stanford.edu/archives/sum2018/entries/pseudo-dionysius-areopagite/.

Corvisier, Jean-Nicolas. "Athenaeus, Medicine and Demography." In *Athenaeus and His World: Reading Greek Culture in the Roman Empire*, ed. David Braund and John Wilkins, 492–502. University of Exeter Press, 2000.

Corvisier, Jean-Nicolas. "*Hygieia*: Plutarch's Views on Good Health." *Nikephoros: Zeitschrift für Sport und Kultur im Altertum* 16 (2003): 115–146.

Craik, Elizabeth M. "Medical References in Euripides." *Bulletin of the Institute of Classical Studies* 45, no. 1 (2001): 81–95.

Crane, Gregory. "Bees without Honey, and Callimachean Taste." *American Journal of Philology* 108, no. 2 (1987): 399–403.

Crick, Nathan, and John Poulakos. "Go Tell Alcibiades: Tragedy, Comedy, and Rhetoric in Plato's *Symposium*." *Quarterly Journal of Speech* 94, no. 1 (2008): 1–22.

Crivellato, Enrico, and Domenico Ribatti. "Soul, Mind, Brain: Greek Philosophy and the Birth of Neuroscience." *Brain Research Bulletin* 71, no. 4 (2007): 327–336.

Crowther, Nigel B. "Water and Wine as Symbols of Inspiration." *Mnemosyne* 32 (1979): 1–11.

Crowther, Paul. "Literary Metaphor and Philosophical Insight: The Significance of Archilochus." In *Metaphor, Allegory, and the Classical Tradition*, ed. George R. Boys-Stones, 83–100. Oxford University Press, 2003.

Csapo, Eric. "The Politics of the New Music." In *Music and the Muses: The Culture of Mousikē in the Classical Athenian City*, ed. Penelope Murray and Peter Wilson, 207–248. Oxford University Press, 2004.

Csapo, Eric. "Comedy and the *Pompe*: Dionysian Genre Crossing." In *Greek Comedy and the Discourse of Genres*, ed. Emmanuela Bakola, Lucia Prauscello, and Mario Teló, 40–80. Cambridge University Press, 2013.

Cyrino, Monica. *In Pandora's Jar: Lovesickness in Early Greek Poetry*. University Press of America, 1995.

D'Angour, Armand. "Plato and Play: Taking Education Seriously in Ancient Greece." *American Journal of Play* 5, no. 3 (2013): 293–307.

D'Angour, Armand. *Socrates in Love: The Making of a Philosopher*. Bloomsbury, 2019.

Darcus Sullivan, Shirley. "Disturbances of the Mind and Heart in Early Greek Poetry." *L'antiquité Classique* 65 (1996): 31–51.

D'Arms, John H. "Heavy Drinking and Drunkenness in the Roman World." In *In Vino Veritas*, ed. Oswyn Murray and Manuela Tecuşan, 304–317. British School at Rome, American Academy in Rome, Istituto Universitario Orientale Napoli, Università di Salerno, and Svenska Institutet i Rom, 1995.

Danzig, Gabriel. "The Use and Abuse of Critias: Conflicting Portraits in Plato and Xenophon." *The Classical Quarterly* 64, no. 2 (2014): 507–524.

Danzig, Gabriel. "Teaching *Sophrosyne*: The Use of the Elenchos by Xenophon's Socrates." *Archai: Revista de Estudos Sobre as Origens Do Pensamento Ocidental* 31 (2021): 1–39.

Davidson, James. *Courtesans and Fishcakes: The Consuming Passions of Classical Athens*. Harper Collins, 1997.

Davies, Kim, and Melissa Dubie. "Sensory Integration: Tips to Consider." *Reporter* 9, no. 3 (2004): 3–8.

Dawson, David. *Allegorical Readers and Cultural Revision in Ancient Alexandria*. University of California Press, 1992.

Dawson, David. *Christian Figural Reading and the Fashioning of Identity*. University of California Press, 2002.

Day, Joseph W. "Epigrams and History: The Athenian Tyrannicides, A Case in Point." In *The Greek Historian: Literature and History: Papers Presented to A. E. Raubitschek*, ed. Michael Jameson, 25–46. Amna Libri, 1985.

De Andia, Ysabel. *Denys l'Aréopagite: Tradition et Métamorphoses*. Vrin, 2006.

DeBevoise Corcoran, Clinton. *Topography and Deep Structure in Plato: The Construction of Place in the Dialogues*. State University of New York Press, 2016.

DeFilippo, Joseph G. "Curiositas and the Platonism of the *Golden Ass*." *American Journal of Philology* 111, no. 4 (1990): 471–492.

Degani, Enzo, and Gabriele Burzacchini. *Lirici greci*. La Nuova Italia, 1977. Reprint, 1984.

DeGraff, Thelma B. "Plato in Cicero." *Classical Philology* 35 (1940): 143–153.

De Jesus, Carlos A. M. "Dancing with Plutarch. Dance and Dance Theory in Plutarch's *Table Talk*." In *Symposion and Philanthropia in Plutarch*, ed. José Ribeiro Ferreira, Delfim Leão, Manuel Tröster, and Paula Barata Dias, 403–414. Imprensa da Universidade de Coimbra, Classica Digitalia, 2009.

De Jong, Casper C. "Grammatical Theory and Rhetorical Teaching." In *Brill's Companion to Ancient Scholarship*, Vol. 2, ed. Franco Montanari, Stephanos Matthaios, and Antonios Rengakos, 981–1011. Brill, 2015.

De Jong, Irene J. F. "The Birth of the Princes' Mirror in the Homeric Epics." In *Homer and the Good Ruler in Antiquity and Beyond*, ed. Jacqueline Klooster and Baukje van den Berg, 20–38. Brill, 2018.

De Lacy, Philip. "Plato and the Intellectual Life of the Second Century A.D." In *Approaches to the Second Sophistic: Papers Presented at the 105th Annual Meeting of the American Philological Association*, ed. Glenn W. Bowersock, 4–10. University of Pennsylvania Press, 1974.

Delcomminette, Sylvain. "Plato on Hatred of Philosophy." *Review of Metaphysics* 72, no. 1 (2018): 29–51.

Del Giovane, Barbara. "Attalus and the Others: Diatribic Morality, Cynicism, and Rhetoric in Seneca's Teachers." *Maia* 67, no. 1 (2015): 3–24.

Demetriou, Denise. "Review of Sears, Athens, Thrace, and the Shaping of Athenian Leadership." *Classical Philology* 109, no. 4 (2014): 366–369.

Demos, Marian. *Lyric Quotation in Plato*. Rowman & Littlefield, 1999.

Dentzer, Jean-Marie. *Le motif du banquet couché dans le Proche-Orient et le monde grec du VIIe au IVe siècle avant J.-C.* Erma di Bretschneider, 1982.

De Romilly, Jacqueline. *La douceur dans la pensée grecque*. Les Belles Lettres, 1979.

Derrida, Jacques. *Marges de la philosophie*. Les Editions de Minuit, 1972.

Derrida, Jacques. "Plato's Pharmacy." In *Dissemination*, ed. Barbara Jones, 61–171. University of Chicago Press, 1981.

Derrida, Jacques. "White Mythology." In *Margins of Philosophy*, translated with notes by Alan Bass, 207–271. Harvester Press, 1982.

Desmond, William. *Philosopher-Kings of Antiquity*. Continuum, 2011.

Des Places, Edouard. *Numenius: Fragments*. Les Belles Lettres, 1973.

Destrée, Pierre. "The *Daimonion* and the Philosophical Mission—Should the Divine Sign Remain Unique to Socrates?" *Apeiron* 38, no. 2 (2005): 63–80.

Destrée, Pierre. "Spectacles from Hades. On Plato's Myths and Allegories in the Republic." In *Plato and Myth: Studies on the Use and Status of Platonic Myths*, ed. Catherine Collobert, Pierre Destrée, and Francisco J. Gonzalez, 109–126. Brill, 2012.

De Romilly, Jacqueline. 1979. La douceur dans la pensée grecque. Paris, 1979.

Deutsch, Celia. "The *Therapeutae*, Text Work, Ritual and Mystical Experience." In *Paradise Now: Essays on Early Jewish and Christian Mysticism*, ed. April DeConick, 287–312. Society of Biblical Literature, 2006.

Devereux, Daniel. "Virtue and Happiness in Plato." In *The Cambridge Companion to Ancient Ethics. Cambridge Companions to Philosophy*, ed. Christopher Bobonich, 53–71. Cambridge University Press, 2017.

De Vogel, Cornelia J. "The Present State of the Socratic Problem." *Phronesis* 1, no. 1 (1955): 26–35.

De Vries, Gerrit Jacob. "Colloquialisms in *Republic* and *Phaedrus*." In *Studia Platonica, Festschrift für Hermann Gundert*, ed. Klaus Döring and Wolfgang Kullmann, 87–92. Grüner, 1973.

Di Benedetto, Vincenzo. *Il medico e la malattia. La scienza di Ippocrate*. Einaudi, 1986.

Dietler, Michael. "Alcohol as Embodied Material Culture: Anthropological Reflections of the Deep Entanglement of Humans and Alcohol." In *Alcohol and*

Humans: A Long and Social Affair, ed. Kimberley Hockings and Robin Dunbar, 115–129. Oxford University Press, 2020.

Dietrich, Oliver, and Laura Dietrich. "Rituals and Feasting as Incentives for Cooperative Action at Early Neolithic Göbekli Tepe." In *Alcohol and Humans: A Long and Social Affair*, ed. Kimberley Hockings and Robin Dunbar, 93–114. Oxford University Press, 2020.

Dillon, John M. *Alcinous: The Handbook of Platonism: Translation with an Introduction and Commentary*. Oxford University Press, 1993.

Dillon, John M. *The Middle Platonists: A Study of Platonism 80 B.C. to A.D. 220*. Revised ed. with new afterword. Cornell University Press, 1996.

Dillon, John M. "Philo of Alexandria and Platonist psychology." In *The Afterlife of the Platonic Soul: Reflections of Platonic Psychology in the Monotheistic Religions*, ed. Maha Elkaisy-Friemuth and John M. Dillon, 15–24. Brill, 2009.

Dillon, John M. "The Ideas as Thoughts of God." *Études Platoniciennes* 8 (2011): 31–42.

Dillon, John M. "Plutarch and Platonism." In *A Companion to Plutarch*, ed. Mark Beck, 59–72. Wiley-Blackwell, 2013.

Dindorf, Wilhelm. *Pollux Julius of Naucratis. Onomasticon*. Kuehn, 1824.

Dinkelaar, Bianca M. "Plato and the Language of Mysteries." *Mnemosyne* 73, no. 1 (2020): 36–62.

Dionigi, Ivano. *Lucio Anneo Seneca. De Otio. Testo e apparato critico con introduzione, versione e commento*. Paedeia, 1983.

Dobrov, Gregory W. "The Poet's Voice in the Evolution of Dramatic Dialogism." In *Beyond Aristophanes: Transition and Diversity in Greek Comedy*, ed. Gregory Dobrov, 47–97. Oxford University Press, 1995.

Dodd, Emlyn K. *Roman and Late Antique Wine Production in the Eastern Mediterranean: A Comparative Archaeological Study at Antiochia ad Cragum (Turkey) and Delos (Greece)*. Archaeopress, 2020.

Dodds, Eric R. *Proclus. The Elements of Theology*. Clarendon Press, 1933.

Dodds, Eric R. *Euripides: Bacchae*. Clarendon Press, 1960.

Domaradzki, Mikołaj. "Defiance, Persuasion or Conformity? The Argument in Plato's *Apology* and *Crito*." *Peitho/Examina Antiqua* 1, no. 2 (2011a): 111–121.

Domaradzki, Mikołaj. "Theagenes of Rhegium and the Rise of Allegorical Interpretation." *Elenchos* 32, no. 2 (2011b): 205–227.

Domaradzki, Mikołaj. "The Beginnings of Greek Allegoresis." *Classical World* 110 (2017): 299–321.

Dominick, Yancy Hughes. "Images for the Sake of the Truth in Plato's *Symposium*." *The Classical Quarterly* 63, no. 2 (2013): 558–566.

Donald, Merlin. "Preconditions for the Evolution of Protolanguages." In *The Descent of Mind*, eds. Michael C. Corballis and Stephen E. G. Lea, 120–213. Oxford University Press, 1999.

Donald, Merlin. *A Mind So Rare: The Evolution of Human Consciousness*. W.W. Norton, 2001.

Dorion Louis-André. "Fundamental Parallels between Socrates' and Ischomachus' Positions in the *Oeconomicus*." In *Socrates and the Socratic Dialogue*, ed. Alessandro Stavru and Christopher Moore, 521–543. Brill, 2017a.

Dorion, Louis-André. "Xenophon and Greek Philosophy." In *The Cambridge Companion to Xenophon*, ed. Michael A. Flower, 37–56. Cambridge University Press, 2017b.

Dorter, Kenneth. "The Significance of the Speeches in Plato's *Symposium*." *Philosophy and Rhetoric* 2, no. 4 (1969): 215–234.

Dover, Kenneth J. "Aristophanes' Speech in Plato's *Symposium*." *Journal of Hellenic Studies* 86 (1966): 41–50.

Dover, Kenneth J. *Aristophanes: Clouds*. Oxford University Press, 1968.

Dow, Jamie. *Passions and Persuasion in Aristotle's Rhetoric*. Oxford University Press, 2015.

Dowden, Ken. "Grades in the Eleusinian Mysteries." *Revue de l'histoire des religions* 197, no. 4 (1980): 409–427.

Driscoll, Sean Donovan. "Metaphor as Lexis: Ricœur on Derrida on Aristotle." *Études Ricœuriennes/Ricœur Studies* 11, no. 1 (2020): 117–129.

Druckman, Daniel, and Robert A. Bjork. *Learning, Remembering, Believing: Enhancing Human Performance*. National Academy Press, 1994.

Dübner, Friedrich. *Scholia graeca in Aristophanem*. Firman-Didot, 1841.

Duchesne-Guillemin, Jacques. "Heraclitus and Iran." *History of Religions* 3, no. 1 (1963): 34–49.

Duff, Timothy E. *Plutarch's Lives: Exploring Virtue and Vice*. Oxford University Press, 1999.

Duff, Timothy E. "Plato's *Symposium* and Plutarch's *Alcibiades*." In *Symposion and Philanthropia in Plutarch*, ed. José Ribeiro Ferreira, Delfim Leão, Manuel Tröster, and Paula Barata Dias, 37–50. Imprensa da Universidade de Coimbra, Classica Digitalia, 2009.

Dunbabin, Katherine. *The Roman Banquet: Images of Conviviality*. Cambridge University Press, 2003.

Duncan, Anne. "A Theseus Outside Athens." In *Theater Outside Athens: Drama in Greek Sicily and South Italy*, ed. Kathryn Bosher, 137–155. Cambridge University Press, 2012.

Duncan, Roger. "Plato's *Symposium*. The Cloven Erōs." *Southern Journal of Philosophy* 15, no. 3 (1977): 277–291.

Dunkle, J. Roger. "The Rhetorical Tyrant in Roman History: Sallust, Livy, and Tacitus." *Classical World* 65, no. 1 (1971): 12–20.

Dunn, Carol. *Plato's Dialogues: Path to Initiation*. Portal Books, 2012.

Dypedokk Johnsen, Hege. "Socrates' Erotic Educational Methods." *Journal of Philosophy of Education* 53, no. 2 (2019): 309–322.

Dysert, Anna. "Capturing Medical Tradition: Caelius Aurelianus' on *Acute Diseases*." *Hirundo* 5 (2006/2007): 161–173.

Edelstein, Emma J., and Ludwig Edelstein. *Asclepius: Collection and Interpretation of the Testimonies*. John Hopkins University Press, 1998.

Edelstein, Ludwig. "The Role of Eryximachus in Plato's *Symposium*." *Transactions of the American Philological Association* 26 (1945): 85–103.

Edmonds, Radcliffe G. III. "Socrates the Beautiful: Role Reversal and Midwifery in Plato's *Symposium*." *Transactions of the American Philological Association* 130 (2000): 261–28.

Edmonds, Radcliffe G. III. "To Sit in Solemn Silence? 'Thronosis' in Ritual, Myth, and Iconography." *American Journal of Philology* 127, no. 3 (2006): 347–366.

Edmonds, Radcliffe G. III. "Extra-Ordinary People: *Mystai* and *Magoi*, Magicians and Orphics in the Derveni Papyrus." *Classical Philology* 103, no. 1 (2008): 16–39.

Edmonds, Radcliffe G. III. "Alcibiades the Profane: Images of the Mysteries in Plato's *Symposium*." In *Plato's Symposium: A Critical Guide*, eds, Pierre Destrée and Zina Giannopoulou, 194–215. Cambridge University Press, 2017.

Edwards, Catherine. "Saturnalian Exchanges: Seneca, Horace, and Satiric Advice." In *Horace and Seneca: Interactions, Intertexts, Interpretations*, ed. Martin Stöckinger, Kathrin Winter, and Andreas Thomas Zanker, 73–89. De Gruyter, 2017.

Ehrenberg, Victor. *The Greek State*. Methuen, 1969.

Elders, Leo J. "The Greek Christian Authors and Aristotle." In *Aristotle in Late Antiquity*, ed. Lawrence P. Schrenk, 111–142. Catholic University Press, 1994.

England, Edwin Bourdieu. *The Laws of Plato, Text ed. with Intr., Notes, etc.* 2 vols. Longmans, Green, 1921.

Erde, Edmund L. "Comedy and Tragedy and Philosophy in the *Symposium*: An Ethical Vision." *Southwest Journal of Philosophy* 7, no. 1 (1976): 161–167.

Erginel, Mehmet Metin. "Plato on Pleasures Mixed with Pains: An Asymmetrical Account." *Oxford Studies in Ancient Philosophy* 56 (2019): 73–122.

Erismann, Christophe. "Aristoteles Latinus: The Reception of Aristotle in the Latin World." In *Brill's Companion to the Reception of Aristotle in Antiquity*, ed. Andrea Falcon, 439–459. Brill, 2016.

Erler, Michael. "Crying for Help: Socrates as Silenus in the *Euthydemus*." In *Socrates and the Socratic Dialogue*, ed. Alessandro Stavru and Christopher Moore, 336–347. Brill, 2017.

Ernout, Alfred, and Antoine Meillet. *Dictionnaire étymologique de la langue latine*. Librairie C. Klincksieck, 1951.

Evans, Nancy. "Diotima and Demeter as Mystagogues in Plato's *Symposium*." *Hypatia* 21, no. 2 (2006): 1–27.

Evans, M. "The Blind Desires of *Republic IV*." In *Psychology and Value in Plato, Aristotle, and Hellenistic Philosophy: The Ninth Keeling Colloquium in Ancient*

Philosophy, ed. Fiona Leigh and Margaret Hampson, 82–96. Oxford University Press, 2022.

Evenepoel, Willy. "The Stoic Seneca on *virtus, gaudium* and *voluptas*." *L'Antiquite Classique* 83, no. 1 (2014): 45–78.

Faraone, Christopher A. *The Stanzaic Architecture of Early Greek Elegy*. Oxford University Press, 2008.

Farber, Marvin. *The Foundations of Phenomenology: Edmund Husserl and the Quest for a Rigorous Science of Philosophy*. State University of New York Press, 1967. Originally published by Harvard University Press, 1943.

Farmer, Matthew C. *Tragedy on the Comic Stage*. Oxford University Press, 2017.

Farquharson, Arthur Spencer Loat. *The Meditations of the Emperor Marcus Antoninus, Vol. 1: Text and Translation*. Clarendon Press, 1944.

Fauconnier, Gilles, and Mark Turner. *The Way We Think: Conceptual Blending and the Mind's Hidden Complexities*. Basic Books, 2002.

Fehr, Bernhard. "Entertainers at the Symposion: The *Akletoi* in the Archaic Period." In *Sympotica: A Symposium on the Symposium*, ed. Oswyn Murray, 185–195. Oxford University Press, 1990.

Fehr, Bernhard. "Bilderzählung und Handlungsmuster: Athena, Marsyas, der Aulos und die jungen Leute von Athen." *Komplexe Bilder*, ed. Martina Seifert, 129–150. Leonhard-Thurneysser, 2008.

Fernández Marcos, Natalio. "The Greek Pentateuch and the Library of Alexandria." In *Computer Assisted Research on the Bible in the 21st Century*, ed. Luis Vegas Montaner, Guadalupe Seijas de los Ríos-Zarzosa, and Javier del Barco, 25–42. Gorgias, 2010.

Ferrari, Giovanni R. F. "Plato and Poetry." In *The Cambridge History of Literary Criticism*, vol. 1, ed. George A. Kennedy, 92–148. Cambridge University Press, 1989.

Ficino, Marsilio. *Opera omnia*. Basel, 1576. Reprint, Bottega d'Erasmo, 1959. Reprint, Phénix Editions, 1999.

Finamore, John F. "The Tripartite Soul in Plato's *Republic* and *Phaedrus*." In *History of Platonism: Plato redivivus*, ed. John F. Finamore and Robert M. Berchman, 35–51. University Press of the South, 2005.

Fine, Gail. "Conflicting Appearances: *Theaetetus* 153D–154B." In *Form and Argument in Late Plato*, ed. Christopher Gill and Mary M. McCabe, 105–133. Oxford University Press, 1996.

Fine, Gail. "Plato's Refutation of Protagoras in the *Theaetetus*." *Apeiron* 32 (1998a): 201–234.

Fine, Gail. "Relativism and Self-Refutation in Plato's *Theaetetus*: Plato, Protagoras, and Burnyeat." In *Method in Ancient Philosophy*, ed. Jyl Gentzler, 138–163. Oxford University Press, 1998b.

Fine, Gail. "Plato on the Grades of Perception: *Theaetetus* 184–186 and the *Phaedo*." *Oxford Studies in Ancient Philosophy* 52 (2017): 65–109.

Fine, Jonathan. "The Guise of the Beautiful: *Symposium* 204d ff." *Phronesis* 65, no. 2 (2019): 129–152.

Finkelberg, Aryeh. "Heraclitus, the Rival of Pythagoras." In *Doctrine and Doxography. Studies on Heraclitus and Pythagoras*, ed. David Sider and Dirk Obbink, 147–162. De Gruyter, 2013.

Finkelberg, Aryeh. *Heraclitus and Thales' Conceptual Scheme: A Historical Study.* Brill, 2017.

Finkelberg, Margalit. *The Birth of Literary Fiction in Ancient Greece.* Oxford University Press, 1998.

Finlay, John. "The Night of Alcibiades." *Hudson Review* 47, no. 1 (1994): 57–79.

Fisher, Nicholas Ralph Edmund. *Aeschines, Against Timarchos.* Oxford University Press, 2001.

Fiske, Susan T., Amy J. C. Cuddy, and Peter Glick, "Universal Dimensions of Social Cognition: Warmth and Competence." *Trends in Cognitive Sciences* 11, no. 2 (2007): 77–83.

Flamant, Jacques. *Macrobe et le Néo-platonisme latin, à la fin du IVe siècle.* Brill, 1977.

Flashar, Hellmut. *Melancholie und Melancholiker in den Medizinischen Theorien der Antike.* De Gruyter, 1966.

Fleischer, Kilian. *Philodem Geschichte der Akademie. Einführung, Ausgabe, Kommentar.* Brill, 2023.

Fleming, Stuart James. *Vinum: The Story of Roman Wine.* Art Flair, 2001.

Flemming, Rebecca. "The Physicians at the Feast: The Place of Medical Knowledge at Athenaeus' *Dinner-Table*." In *Athenaeus and His World: Reading Greek Culture in the Roman Empire*, ed. David Braund and John Wilkins, 476–482. University of Exeter Press, 2000.

Flinterman, Jaap Jan. "'. . . largely fictions . . . .': Aelius Aristides on Plato's dialogues." *Ancient Narrative* 1 (2002): 32–54.

Flores, Samuel O. *The Roles of Solon in Plato's Dialogues.* PhD thesis, the Ohio State University, 2013.

Flores, Samuel O. "The Development of Critias in Plato's Dialogues." *Classical Philology* 113 (2018): 162–188.

Flores, Samuel O. "Returning to the Heavens: Plato's Socrates on Anaxagoras and Natural Philosophy." *Apeiron* 53, no. 2 (2020): 123–146.

Floridi, Lucia. *Edilo, ›Epigrammi‹: Introduzione, testo critico, traduzione e commento.* De Gruyter, 2020.

Flory, Dan. "Stoic Psychology, Classical Rhetoric, and Theories of Imagination in Western Philosophy." *Philosophy & Rhetoric* 29, no. 2 (1996): 147–167.

Folch, Marcus. *The City and the Stage: Performance, Genre, and Gender in Plato's Laws.* Oxford University Press, 2015.

Forbes, Robert James. *Studies in Ancient Technology.* 9 vols. Brill, 1955.

Ford, Andrew. *The Origins of Criticism: Literary Culture and Poetic Theory in Classical Greece*. Princeton University Press, 2002.

Ford, Andrew. "Catharsis: The Power of Music in Aristotle's *Politics*." In *Music and the Muses*, ed. Penelope Murray and Peter Wilson, 309–336. Oxford University Press, 2004.

Fortenbaugh, William W. *Aristotle on Emotion: A Contribution to Philosophical Psychology, Rhetoric, Poetics, Politics and Ethics*. 2nd ed. Duckworth, 2002. Originally published, 1975.

Fortenbaugh, William W., and Dimitris Gutas. *Theophrastus of Eresus Commentary Volume 6.1: Sources on Ethics*. Brill, 2011.

Foster, Jay, and Daryn Lehoux. "The Delphic Oracle and the Ethylene-Intoxication Hypothesis." *Clinical Toxicology* 45, no. 1 (2007): 85–89.

Foucault, Michel. *Madness and Civilization: A History of Insanity in the Age of Reason*. Translated by Richard Howard. Vintage, 1965.

Foucault, Michel. *Histoire de la folie à l'âge classique*. Gallimard, 1972. Revised edition.

Foucault, Michel. *Religion and Culture*, ed. and selection Jeremy R. Carrette. Routledge, 1999.

Foucault, Michel. *Fearless Speech*, ed. Joseph Pearson. Semiotext(e), 2001.

Foucault, Michel. *The Hermeneutics of the Subject: Lectures at the College de France 1981–1982*. Edited by Frédéric Gros. Translated by Graham Burchell. Palgrave Macmillan, 2005.

Fowler, Ryan C. *Imperial Plato: Albinus, Maximus, Apuleius: Text and Translation, with an Introduction and Commentary*. Parmenides, 2016.

Fowler, Ryan C. "Variations of Perceptions of Plato during the Second Sophistic." In *Brill's Companion to the Reception of Plato in Antiquity*, ed. Harold Tarrant, Danielle A. Layne, Dirk Baltzly, and François Renaud, 223–249. Brill, 2018.

François, Paul, and Sylvie Pittia. *Le vin de Rome/Denys D'Halicarnasse*. Pallas 53. Presses Universitaire du Mirail, 2000.

Franke, William. *On What Cannot Be Said: Apophatic Discourses in Philosophy, Religion, Literature, and the Arts: Vol. 1: Classic Formulations*. University of Notre Dame Press, 2007.

Frazier, Francoise, and Jean Sirinelli. *Plutarque. Propos de table, vol. 9, 3*. Les Belles Lettres, 1996.

Frede, Dorothea. "The Impossibility of Perfection: Socrates' Criticism of Simonides' Poem in the *Protagoras*." *Review of Metaphysics* 39 (1986): 729–753.

Frede, Dorothea. "The Soul's Silent Dialogue: A Non-Aporetic Reading of the *Theaetetus*." *Proceedings of the Cambridge Philological Society* 215 (1989): 20–49.

Frede, Dorothea. "Puppets on Strings: Moral Psychology in Laws Books 1 and 2." In *Plato's "Laws": A Critical Guide*, ed. Christopher Bobonich, 108–126. Cambridge University Press, 2010.

Frede, Michael. "Plato's Arguments and the Dialogue Form." In *Methods of Interpreting Plato and His Dialogues*, ed. James C. Klagge and Nicholas D. Smith, 201–219. Oxford University Press, 1992.

Freeman, Kathleen. *Ancilla to the Pre-Socratic Philosophers*. Harvard University Press, 1948.

Freidenberg, Olga. *Image and Concept: Mythopoetic Roots of Literature*. Edited by Nina Braginskaia. Translated by Kevin Moss. Harwood Academic Publishers, 1997.

Freund, Beau J., Catherine O'Brien, and Andrew J. Young. "Alcohol Ingestion and Temperature Regulation during Cold Exposure." *Journal of Wilderness Medicine* 5, no. 1 (1994): 88–98.

Friesen, Courtney. *Reading Dionysus: Euripides' Bacchae and the Cultural Contestations of Greeks, Jews, Romans, and Christians*. Mohr Siebeck, 2015.

Fronterotta, Francesco. "Two Remarks on False Opinion between Epistemology and Ontology in *Theaetetus* 187b–201c." In *New Explorations in Plato's Theaetetus*, ed. Diego Zucca. 249–270. Brill, 2022.

Fuchs, Dieter. *Joyce und Menippos: "A Portrait of the Artist as an Old Dog."* Königshausen & Neumann, 2006.

Gadamer, Hans-Georg. *Dialogue and Dialectic*. Yale University Press, 1980.

Gaiser, Konrad. *Platone come scrittore filosofico: Saggi sull'ermeneutica dei dialoghi platonici*. Bibliopolis, 1984.

Gallop, David. *Parmenides of Elea: Fragments: A Text and Translation with an Introduction*. University of Toronto Press, 1984.

Gardeil, Henri-Dominique. *Les étapes de la philosophie idéaliste*. Vrin, 1935.

Garnier, Nicolas, and Soultana M. Valamoti, "Prehistoric Wine-Making at Dikili Tash (Northern Greece): Integrating Residue Analysis and Archaeobotany." *Journal of Archaeological Science* 74 (2016): 195–206.

Garofalo, Ivan. *Anonymi medici de morbis acutis et chroniis*. Brill, 1997.

Garver, Newton. "Structuralism and the Challenge of Metaphor." *The Monist* 69, no. 1 (1986): 68–86.

Gathercole, Simon. *The Gospel of Thomas: Introduction and Commentary*. Brill, 2014.

Geertz, Armin W. "Brain, Body and Culture: A Biocultural Theory of Religion." *Method and Theory in the Study of Religion* 22, no. 4 (2010): 304–321.

Geertz, Armin W. "Whence Religion? How the Brain Constructs the World and What This Might Tell Us about the Origins of Religion, Cognition and Culture." In *Origins of Religion, Cognition and Culture*, ed. Armin Geertz, 17–70. Routledge, 2014.

Geertz, Clifford. "Religion as a Cultural System." In *The Interpretation of Cultures: Selected Essays*, 87–125. Basic Books, 1993.

Geldard, Richard. *Remembering Heraclitus*. Lindisfarne Books, 2000.

Gellrich, Michelle. "Socratic Magic: Enchantment, Irony, and Persuasion in Plato's Dialogues." *Classical World* 87 (1994): 275–307.

Gentile, Jill P. "Diagnosis, Differential Diagnosis, and Medication Management." *Psychiatry* 3, no. 8 (2006): 25–30.

Gentile, Jill P. "*Parrhesia*, Phaedra, and the *Polis*: Anticipating Psychoanalytic Free Association as Democratic Practice." *Psychoanalytic Quarterly* 84, no. 3 (2015): 589–624.

Gentili, Bruno. *Poetry and its Public in Ancient Greece: From Homer to the Fifth Century.* Translated by A. Thomas Cole. John Hopkins University Press, 1988.

Georgiadou, Aristoula, and David H. J. Larmour. "Lucian's 'Verae Historiae' as Philosophical Parody." *Hermes* 126 (1998): 310–325.

Georgiadou, Aristoula, and Katerina Oikonomopoulou. "Introduction: Reading Plutarch through Space, Time and Language." In *Time, Space, and Language in Plutarch*, ed. Aristoula Georgiadou and Katerina Oikonomopoulou, 15–28. De Gruyter, 2017.

Germany, Robert. *Mimetic Contagion: Art and Artifice in Terence's Eunuch.* Oxford University Press, 2016.

Gerson, Lloyd. *Plotinus.* Routledge, 1994.

Gerson, Lloyd. "Plotinus." In *The Stanford Encyclopedia of Philosophy* (Fall 2018 Edition), ed. Edward N. Zalta, 2018. https://plato.stanford.edu/archives/fall2018/entries/plotinus/.

Giannopoulou, Zina. *Plato's Theaetetus as a Second Apology.* Oxford University Press, 2013.

Gibbs, Raymond W. "Researching Metaphor." In *Researching and Applying Metaphor*, ed. Lynne Cameron and Graham Low, 29–47. Cambridge University Press, 1999.

Gibbs, Raymond W. "Multiple Constraints in Theories of Metaphor." *Discourse Processes* 48, no. 8 (2011): 575–584.

Gifford, Edwin Hamilton. *Eusebius of Caesarea: Praeparatio Evangelica.* Clarendon Press, 1903.

Gill, Christopher. "Peace of Mind and Being Yourself: Panaetius to Plutarch." *Aufstieg und Niedergang der römischen Welt* II 36, no. 7 (1994): 4599–4640.

Gill, Christopher. *The Structured Self in Hellenistic and Roman Thought.* Oxford University Press, 2006.

Gill, Christopher. "Positive Emotions in Stoicism: Are They Enough?" In *Hope, Joy and Affection in the Classical World*, ed. Ruth R. Caston and Robert A. Kaster, 143–162. Oxford University Press, 2016.

Giusti, Elena. "The Metapoetics of Liber-ty. Horace's Bacchic Ship in Seneca's *De Tranquillitate Animi*." In *Horace and Seneca: Interactions, Intertexts, Interpretations*, ed. Martin Stockinger, Kathrin Winter, and Andreas Thomas Zanker, 239–264. De Gruyter, 2017.

Glad, Clarence E. "Frank Speech, Flattery, and Friendship in Philodemus." In *Friendship, Flattery, and Frankness of Speech: Studies on Friendship in the New Testament World*, ed. John T. Fitzgerald, 21–59. Brill, 1996.

Glucksberg, Sam. "How Metaphors Create Categories—Quickly." In *The Cambridge Handbook of Metaphor and Thought*, ed. Raymond W. Gibbs Jr., 67–83. Cambridge University Press, 2008.

Gocer, Asli. "A New Assessment of Socratic Philosophy of Religion." In *Reason and Religion in Socratic Philosophy*, ed. Nicholas D. Smith and Paul Woodruff, 115–129. Oxford University Press, 2000.

Goddard, Justin. "The Tyrant at Table." In *Reflections of Nero: Culture, History, and Representation*, ed. Jaś Elsner and Jamie Masters, 67–82. University of North Carolina Press, 1994.

Goeken, Johann. "Aelius Aristide et le vin." *Food and History. Revue de l'Institut Européen d'Histoire de l'Alimentation* 13, no. 1–3 (2015): 235–253.

Gokcesu, Bahriye Selin. "Comparison, Categorization, and Metaphor Comprehension." *Proceedings of the Annual Meeting of the Cognitive Science Society* 31 (2009): 567–572.

Goldhill, Simon. "The Great Dionysia and Civic Ideology." *Journal of Hellenic Studies* 107 (1987): 58–76.

Goldhill, Simon. "Civic Ideology and the Problem of Difference: The Politics of Aeschylean Tragedy, Once Again." *Journal of Hellenic Studies* 120 (2000): 34–56.

Golish, Aaron. "*Parrhesia* before Παρρησία: Emerging Political Culture in the Iliad and Origins of the License to Speak Freely." *Hirundo* 11 (2013): 1–19.

Gómez, Pilar, and Francesca Mestre. "The Banquets of Alexander." In *Symposion and Philanthropia in Plutarch*, ed. José Ribeiro Ferreira, Delfim Leão, Manuel Tröster, and Paula Barata Dias, 211–222. Imprensa da Universidade de Coimbra, Classica Digitalia, 2009.

González Delgado, Ramiro. "Plutarco en las *Noctes Atticae* de Aulo Gelio/ Plutarch in *Noctes Atticae* by Aulus Gellius." *Humanitas* 70 (2017): 61–85.

Gonzalez, Francisco J. "The Eleatic Stranger: His Master's Voice?" In *Who Speaks for Plato? Studies in Platonic Anonymity*, ed. Gerald Alan Press, 161–181. Rowman & Littlefield, 2000.

Gonzalez, Francisco J. "The Hermeneutics of Madness: Poet and Philosopher in Plato's *Ion* and *Phaedrus*. In *Plato and the Poets*, ed. Pierre Destrée and Fritz-Grigor Herrmann, 93–110. Brill, 2011.

Gonzalez, Francisco J. "The Virtue of Dialogue, Dialogue as Virtue in Plato's *Protagoras*." *Philosophical Papers* 43, no. 1 (2014): 33–66.

Goodenough, Erwin Ramsdell. "The Political Philosophy of Hellenistic Kingship." *Yale Classical Studies* 1 (1928): 53–102.

Gordon, Elisabeth, and Orrin Devinsky. "Alcohol and Marijuana: Effects on Epilepsy and Use by Patients with Epilepsy." *Epilepsia* 42, no. 10 (2001): 1266–1272.

Goris, Wouter, and Jan Aertsen. "Medieval Theories of Transcendentals." In *The Stanford Encyclopedia of Philosophy* (Fall 2019 Edition), ed. Edward N. Zalta, 2019. https://plato.stanford.edu/archives/fall2019/entries/transcendentals-medieval/.

Gosetti-Murrayjohn, Angela. "Sappho's Kisses: Biographical Tradition and Intertextuality in 'AP' 5.246 and 5.236." *Classical Journal* 102, no. 1 (2006): 41–59.

Goulet, Richard. "La conservation et la transmission des textes philosophiques grecs." In *The Libraries of the Neoplatonists*, ed. Cristina D'Ancona Costa, 29–62. Brill, 2007.

Gourevitch, Danielle, and Gilles Demigneux. "Two Historical Case Histories of Acute Alcoholism in the Roman Empire." In *Disabilities in Roman Antiquity, Disparate Bodies A Capite ad Calcem*, ed. Christian Laes, Chris F. Goodey, and M. Lynn Rose, 73–87. Brill, 2013.

Graf, Fritz. *Eleusis und die orphische Dichtung Athens in vorhellenistischer Zeit.* De Gruyter, 1974.

Graf, Fritz. "Milch, Honig und Wein." *Perennitas* (Rome) (1980): 209–221.

Graf, Fritz. *Nordionische Kulte: Religionsgeschichtliche und epigraphische Untersuchungen zu den Kulten von Chios, Erythrai, Klazomenai und Phokaia.* Schweizerisches Institut in Rom, 1985.

Graf, Fritz. "The Kyrbantes of Erythrai." In *Studies in Greek Epigraphy and History in Honor of Stephen V. Tracy*, ed. Gary Reger, Francis X. Ryan, and Timothy F. Winters, 301–309. Ausonius Éditions, 2010.

Graf, Fritz, and Sarah Illes Johnston. *Ritual Texts for the Afterlife: Orpheus and the Bacchic Gold Tablets.* Routledge, 2007.

Graham, Anthony J. "The Foundation of Thasos." *Annual of the British School at Athens* 73 (1978): 61–98.

Graham, Gordon. "Liturgy as Drama." *Princeton Theological Seminary* 64, no. 1 (2007): 71–79.

Graver, Margaret. *Stoicism and Emotion.* University of Chicago Press, 2007.

Graver, Margaret. "Anatomies of Joy: Seneca and the *Gaudium* Tradition." In *Hope, Joy, and Affection in the Classical World*, ed. Ruth R. Caston and Robert A. Kaster, 123–142. Oxford University Press, 2016.

Graver, Margaret. "Pre-Emotions and Reader Emotions in Seneca." *Maia* 69 (2017): 281–296.

Green, Peter. "Strepsiades, Socrates and the Abuses of Intellectualism." *Greek, Roman, and Byzantine Studies* 20 (1979): 15–25.

Green, Richard Hamilton. "Dante's 'Allegory of Poets' and the Mediaeval Theory of Poetic Fiction." *Comparative Literature* 9, no. 2 (1957): 118–128.

Grenet, Paul. *Les origins de l'analogie philosophique dans les dialogues de Platon.* Boivin, 1948.

Gresseth, Gerard K. "The Homeric Sirens." *Transactions of the American Philological Association* 101 (1970): 203–218.

Grethlein, Jonas. "Lucian's Response to Augustine: Conversion and Narrative in *Confessions* and *Nigrinus*." *Religion in the Roman Empire* 2, no. 2 (2016): 256–278.

Grey, Safari. "Homer's *Odyssey* in the Hands of its Allegorists: Many Paths to Explain the Cosmos." In *Paths of Knowledge Interconnection (s) between

Knowledge and Journey in the Greco-Roman World, ed. Chiara Ferella and Cilliers Breytenbach, 189–215. Edition Topoi, 2019.

Griffith, Mark. "Greek Lyric and the Place of Humans in the World." In *The Cambridge Companion to Greek Lyric*, ed. Felix Budelmann, 72–94. Cambridge University Press, 2009.

Griffith Tom. *Plato: Laws*. Cambridge University Press, 2016.

Grigorova-Gentcheva, Valentina, and Ilya S. Prokopov. "New Hoards with Small Denomination Coins of the Island of Thasos (6th–5th BC): Context, Interpretation and Dating." In *Ex Nummis Lux: Studies in Ancient Numismatics in Honour of Dimitar Draganov*, ed. Diljana V. Boteva-Bojanova and Dimitar Draganov, 29–47. Bobokov Bros. Foundation, 2017.

Griswold, Charles. *Self-Knowledge in Plato's Phaedrus*. University of Pennsylvania Press, 1986.

Griswold, Charles L. "Plato on Rhetoric and Poetry." In *The Stanford Encyclopedia of Philosophy* (Spring 2024 Edition), ed. Edward N. Zalta and Uri Nodelman, 2024. https://plato.stanford.edu/archives/spr2024/entries/plato-rhetoric/.

Groneberg, Michael. "Myth and Science around Gender and Sexuality: Erōs and the Three Sexes in Plato's *Symposium*." *Diogenes* 208 (2005): 39–49.

Gruber, Gwen. "Immortality vs. Tripartition: The Soul in Plato." In *History of Platonism: Plato redivivus*, ed. John F. Finamore and Robert Berchman, 19–34. University Press of the South, 2005.

Gschwandtner, Christina M. "Mystery Manifested: Toward a Phenomenology of the Eucharist in Its Liturgical Context." *Religions* 10, no. 5 (2019): 315. https://doi.org/10.3390/rel10050315.

Gundert, Beate. "*Soma* and *Psyche* in Hippocratic Medicine." In *Psyche and Soma: Physicians and Metaphysicians on the Mind-Body Problem from Antiquity to Enlightenment*, ed. John P. Wright and Paul Potter, 13–36. Oxford University Press, 2000.

Guerra Doce, Elisa. "The Origins of Inebriation: Archaeological Evidence of the Consumption of Fermented Beverages and Drugs in Prehistoric Eurasia." *Journal of Archaeological Method and Theory* 22, no. 3 (2014): 751–782.

Guerra Doce, Elisa. "The Earliest Toasts: Archaeological Evidence of the Social and Cultural Construction of Alcohol in Prehistoric Europe." In *Alcohol and Humans: A Long and Social Affair*, ed. Kimberley Hockings and Robin Dunbar, 60–80. Oxford University Press, 2020.

Günther, Hans-Christian. "Horace's Life and Work." In *Brill's Companion to Horace*, ed. Hans-Christian Günther, 1–62. Brill, 2013.

Hacham, Noah. "The Letter of Aristeas: A New Exodus Story?" *Journal for the Study of Judaism* 36, no. 1 (2005): 1–20.

Hadas, Moses. *Aristeas to Philocrates*. Harper and Brothers, 1951.

Hadot, Pierre. *Philosophy as a Way of Life: Spiritual Exercises from Socrates to Foucault*. Edited and introduction by Arnold Davidson. Blackwell, 1995.

Hafemann, Scott J. *Suffering and the Spirit: An Exegetical Study of 2 Corinthians 2:4–3:3*. Mohr Siebeck, 1986.

Halliwell, Stephen. "The Theory and Practice of Narrative in Plato." In *Narratology and Interpretation*, ed. Jonas Grethlein and Antonios Rengakos, 15–41. De Gruyter, 2009.

Halliwell, Stephen. "Antidotes and Incantations: Is There a Cure for Poetry in Plato's *Republic*?" In *Plato and the Poets*, ed. Pierre Destrée and Fritz-Grigor Herrmann, 241–266. Brill, 2011a.

Halliwell, Stephen. *Between Ecstasy and Truth: Interpretations of Greek Poetics from Homer to Longinus*. Oxford University Press, 2011b.

Halperin, David M. "Plato and Erotic Reciprocity." *Classical Antiquity* 5, no. 1 (1986): 60–80.

Halperin, David M. *One Hundred Years of Homosexuality and Other Essays on Greek Love*. Routledge, 1990.

Hamilton, John T. *Music, Madness, and the Unworking of Language*. Columbia University Press, 2008.

Hammond, William A. "On the Notion of Virtue in the Dialogues of Plato, with Particular Reference to Those of the First Period and to the Third and Fourth Books of the *Republic*." *Harvard Studies in Classical Philology* 3 (1892): 131–180.

Harder, Annette. *Callimachus. Aetia. Vol. 1: Introduction, Text, and Translation, Vol. 2: Commentary*. Oxford University Press, 2012.

Hardie, Alex. "Muses and Mysteries." In *Music and the Muses*, ed. Penelope Murray and Peter Wilson, 11–37. Oxford University Press, 2004.

Harnack, Adolf von. *Porphyrius 'Gegen die Christen,' 15 Bücher. Zeugnisse, Fragmente und Referate*. Verlag der Königlichen Akademie der Wissenschaften, 1916.

Harrington, Michael. "The Drunken *Epibole* of Plotinus and its Reappearance in the Work of Dionysius the Areopagite." *Dionysius* 23 (2005): 117–138.

Harris, Rendel J., ed. *Fragments of Philo Judaeus*. Cambridge University Press, 1886.

Harris, Charles Reginald Schiller. *The Heart and Vascular System in Ancient Greek Medicine: From Alcmaeon to Galen*. Clarendon Press, 1973.

Hart, John Henry Arthur. "Philo of Alexandria." *Jewish Quarterly Review* 17, no. 1 (1904): 78–122.

Harte, Verity. "The Philebus on Pleasure: The Good, the Bad and the False." *Proceedings of the Aristotelian Society* 104 (2004): 111–128.

Harte, Verity. "Desire, Memory, and the Authority of Soul: *Philebus* 35cd." *Oxford Studies in Ancient Philosophy* 46 (2014): 34–72.

Harte, Verity. "*Aporia* in Plato's *Parmenides*." In *The Aporetic Tradition in Ancient Philosophy*, ed. George Karamanolis and Vasilis Politis, 67–90. Cambridge University Press, 2018.

Harte, Verity, Mary M. McCabe, Robert W. Sharples, and Anne Sheppard. *Aristotle and the Stoics Reading Plato*. Institute of Classical Studies, 2010.

Hartmann, Lucius. *Die grosse Rede des Timaios–ein Beispiel wahrer Rhetorik? Zu Theorie und Praxis philosophischer Rhetorik in Platons Dialogen Gorgias, Phaidros und Timaios.* Schwabe, 2017.

Haskins, Charles Homer. *The Renaissance of the Twelfth Century.* Harvard University Press, 1927.

Haskins, Ekaterina V. *Logos and Power in Isocrates and Aristotle.* University of South Carolina Press, 2004.

Havelock, Eric A. *Preface to Plato.* Belknap Press of Harvard University Press, 1963.

Hedreen, Guy Michael. *Silens in Attic Black-Figure Vase-Painting: Myth and Performance.* University of Michigan Press, 1992.

Hege, Sam. "Agathon's Unfulfilled Potential." *Aporia* 10 (2012). https://ojs.st-andrews.ac.uk/index.php/aporia/article/view/661.

Heiberg, Johan L. *Simplicii in Aristotelis De caelo commentaria.* Reimer, 1894.

Heil, Christoph. "Arius Didymus and Luke-Acts." *Novum Testamentum* 42, no. 4 (2000): 358–393.

Heirman, Jo. "Symbolic 'Lived Spaces' in Ancient Greek Lyric and the Heterotopia of the *Symposium.*" In *The Ideologies of Lived Space in Literary Texts, Ancient and Modern,* ed. Jo Heirman and Jacqueline Klooster, 83–93. Academia Press 2013.

Helleman, Wendy E. "Deification and Assimilation to God." *Studia Philonica Annual* 2 (1990): 51–71.

Henderson, Alexander L. *The History of Ancient and Modern Wines.* Baldwin Cradock and Joy, 1824.

Henderson, William John. "Greek Lyric Imagery: Problems of Interpretation." *Akroterion* 43 (1998): 3–14.

Henderson, William John. "Men Behaving Badly: Conduct and Identity at Greek Symposia." *Akroterion* 44 (1999): 3–13.

Henle, Paul. *Language, Thought, and Culture.* University of Michigan Press, 1958.

Henle, Paul. "Metaphor." In *Philosophical Perspectives on Metaphor,* ed. Mark Johnson, 83–104. University of Minnesota Press, 1981.

Henrichs, Albert. "Loss of Self, Suffering, Violence: The Modern View of Dionysos from Nietzsche to Girard." *Harvard Studies in Classical Philology* 88 (1984): 205–240.

Hermsen, Lisa M. *Manic Minds: Mania's Mad History and Its Neuro-Future.* Rutgers University Press, 2011.

Herren, Sabrina. "*Fueritne mulier pulcherrima specie Melissa, quam Iuppiter in apem convertit. Die Biene in der antiken Mythologie.*" In *Illum operum custos: Kulturgeschichtliche Beiträge zur antiken Bienensymbolik und ihrer Rezeption,* ed. David Engels and Carla Nicolaye, 40–59. G. Olms, 2008.

Herrero de Jauregui, Miguel. *The Protrepticus of Clement of Alexandria: A Commentary.* PhD thesis, Universita di Bologna, 2008.

Herrmann, Fritz-Grigor. "Dynamics of Vision in Plato's Thought." *Helios* 40 (2013): 281–307.

Hershbell, Jackson P. "Plutarch and Heraclitus." *Hermes* 105, no. 2 (1977): 179–201.

Heys, Alistair. *The Anatomy of Bloom: Harold Bloom and the Study of Influence and Anxiety.* Bloomsbury, 2014.

Hilton, Ita. "Reimagining the Prophet: Teiresias as Comedian and Sophist in Euripides' *Bacchae.*" *Philologia Classica* 17. no. 1 (2022): 4–21.

Hindley, Clifford. "Xenophon on Male Love." *The Classical Quarterly* 49, no. 1 (1999): 74–99.

Hirzel, Rudolf. *Der Dialog. Ein literarhistorischer Versuch.* 2 vols. S. Hirzel, 1895.

Hobden, Fiona. "How to Be a Good Symposiast and Other Lessons from Xenophon's *Symposium.*" *Proceedings of the Cambridge Philological Society* 50 (2004): 121–140.

Hobden, Fiona. *The Symposion in Ancient Greek Society and Thought.* Cambridge University Press, 2013.

Holford-Strevens, Leofranc. *Aulus Gellius: An Antonine Scholar and His Achievement.* Oxford University Press, 2003.

Holland, Glenn S. "Call Me Frank: Lucian's (Self-)Defense of Frank Speaking and Philodemus Περὶ Παρρησίας." In *Philodemus and the New Testament World*, ed. John Thomas Fitzgerald, Dirk D. Obbink, and Glenn S. Holland, 245–267. Brill, 2004.

Holmes, Brooke. "Body, Soul, and the Medical Analogy in Plato." In *When Worlds Elide: Classics, Politics, Culture*, ed. J. Peter Euben and Karen Bassi, 345–385. Rowman & Littlefield, 2010.

Holowchak, Andrew M. "Wisdom, Wine and Wonder-Lust in Plato's *Symposium.*" *Philosophy and Literature* 27, no. 2 (2003): 415–427.

Honorato, Diego E. "'Mythos' and 'Logos' as Forms of Figurative Discourse: A Critical Reading of Claude Calame's Semiotic Approach." *Ágora Estudos Clássicos em debate* 19 (2017): 437–465.

Hood, Ralph W. Jr. "The Mystical Self: Lost and Found." *International Journal for the Psychology of Religion* 12 (2002): 1–14.

Hooker, Richard. "The Platonic Tradition." *Hermetic Library*, 1997. http://hermetic.com/texts/neoplatonism.html.

Hooper, Anthony. "The Greatest Hope of All: Aristophanes on Human Nature in Plato's *Symposium.*" *The Classical Quarterly* 63, no. 2 (2013): 567–579.

Horgan, Terry, and John L. Tienson. "The Intentionality of Phenomenology and the Phenomenology of Intentionality." In *Philosophy of Mind: Classical and Contemporary Readings*, ed. David Chalmers, 520–532. Oxford University Press, 2002.

Horky, Philip S. "The Imprint of the Soul: Psychosomatic Affection in Plato, Gorgias, and the 'Orphic' Gold Tablets." *Mouseion: Journal of the Classical Association of Canada* 6, ser. 3 (2006): 371–386.

Hubbard, Thomas K. *The Mask of Comedy: Aristophanes and the Intertextual Parabasis.* Cornell University Press, 1991.

Hubert, Martin. "The Concept of *Philanthropia* in Plutarch's *Lives*." *American Journal of Philology* 82, no. 2 (1961): 164–75.

Hude, Karl. *Aretaeus.* CMG, vol. 2, 2nd ed. Akademie Verlag, 1958.

Huffman, Carl. "Alcmaeon." In *Stanford Encyclopedia of Philosophy* (Summer 2021 Edition), ed. Edward N. Zalta, 2021. https://plato.stanford.edu/archives/sum2021/entries/alcmaeon/.

Hüffmeier, Friedrich. "Phronesis in den Schriften des Corpus Hippocraticum." *Hermes* 89 (1961): 51–84.

Hughes, Glenn. *Transcendence and History: The Search for Ultimacy from Ancient Societies to Postmodernity.* University of Missouri Press, 2003.

Hülsz Piccone, Enrique. "Heraclitus, Plato, and the Philosophic Dogs (A Note on *Republic* II, 375E–376C)." *Revista Archai* 15 (2015): 105–115.

Humphries, Mark. "The Lexicon of Abuse: Drunkenness and Political Illegitimacy in the Late Roman World." In *Humour, History and Politics in Late Antiquity and the Early Middle Ages*, ed. Guy Halsall, 75–88. Cambridge University Press, 2002.

Hunnicutt, Benjamin K. "Leisure and Play in Plato's Teaching and Philosophy of Learning." *Leisure Sciences* 12, no. 2 (1990): 211–227.

Hunter, Richard L. *Eubulus. The Fragments.* Cambridge University Press, 1983.

Hunter, Richard L. *Plato's Symposium.* Oxford University Press, 2004.

Hunter, Richard L. *Critical Moments in Classical Literature. Studies in the Ancient View of Literature and its Uses.* Cambridge University Press, 2009a.

Hunter, Richard L. "The Curious Incident . . . : *Polypragmosyne* and the Ancient Novel." In *Readers and Writers in the Ancient Novel*, ed. Michael Paschalis, Stelios Panayotakis, and Gareth L. Schmeling, 51–63. Barkhuis, 2009b.

Hunter, Richard L. *Plato and the Traditions of Ancient Literature: The Silent Stream.* Cambridge University Press, 2012.

Hunter, Richard L., and Dan Russell *Plutarch. How to Study Poetry.* Cambridge University Press, 2011.

Huss, Bernhard. "The Dancing Socrates and Laughing Xenophon, or the Other *Symposium*." *American Journal of Philology* 120, no. 3 (1999a): 381–409.

Huss, Bernhard. *Xenophons Symposion: Ein Kommentar.* Teubner, 1999b.

Husserl, Edmund. *Ideas Pertaining to a Pure Phenomenology and to a Phenomenological Philosophy: First Book.* Translated by Frank Kersten. Kluwer, 1981. Originally published as *Ideen zu einer reinen Phänomenologie und phämenologischen Philosophie, I. Buch: Allgemeine Einfürung in die reine Phänomenologie.* Niemeyer, 1913.

Husserl, Edmund. *Thing and Space: Lectures of 1907.* Translated by Richard Rojcewicz. Kluwer, 1997. Originally published as *Ding und Raum. Vorlesungen 1907.* Husserliana vol. 16, ed. U. Claesges. Nijhoff, 1973.

Husserl, Edmund. *Transzendentaler Idealismus: Texte aus dem Nachlass (1908–1921).* Husserliana, vol. 36, ed. Robin D. Rollinger with Rochus Sowa. Springer, 2003.

Hutchinson, Darren S. *The Virtues of Aristotle*. Routledge, 1986.

Huxley, Aldous. *The Doors of Perception*. Harper Perennial, 2009. Originally published, 1954.

Ihejirika, Cardinal I. C. "Knowledge as Remembrance in Plato's *Symposium*: An Epistemic Interpretation." *Journal of Philosophy and Religion* 6, no. 1 (2012): 84–94.

Ingenkamp, Heinz Gerd. "Οὐ ψέγεται τὸ πίνειν. Wie Plutarch den übermäßigen Weingenuß beurteilte." In *Plutarco, Dioniso y el vino. Actas del VI Simposio Español sobre Plutarco: Cádiz, 14–16 de Mayo de 1998*, ed. J. Guillermo Montes Cala, Manuel Sánchez Ortiz de Landaluce, and Rafael J. Gallé Cejudo, 277–290. Ediciones Clásicas Madrid, 1999.

Innes, Doreen C. "Longinus and Caecilius: Models of the Sublime." *Mnemosyne* 55, no. 3 (2002): 259–284.

Innes, Doreen C. "Metaphor, Simile, and Allegory as Ornaments of Style." In *Metaphor, Allegory and the Classical Tradition*, ed. George R. Boys-Stones, 7–27. Oxford University Press, 2003.

Inowlocki, Sabrina. "Eusebius of Caesarea's Interpretatio Christiana of Philo's *De vita contemplativa*." *Harvard Theological Review* 97 (2004): 305–28.

Inwood, Brad. *Reading Seneca: Stoic Philosophy at Rome*. Oxford University Press, 2005.

Ionescu, Cristina. "The Transition from the Lower to the Higher Mysteries of Love in Plato's *Symposium*." *Dialogue* 46, no. 1 (2007): 27–42.

Ioppolo, Anna-Maria. "Presentation and Assent: A Physical and Cognitive Problem in Early Stoicism." *The Classical Quarterly* 40, no. 2 (1990): 433–449.

Irvine, Martin. "Interpretation and the Semiotics of Allegory in Clement of Alexandria, Origen, and Augustine." *Semiotica* 63, no. 1/2 (1987): 33–72.

Irwin, Terence. "Morality as Law and Morality in the *Laws*." In *Plato's Laws: A Critical Guide*, ed. Christopher Bobonich, 92–108. Cambridge University Press, 2010.

Isler-Kerényi, Cornelia. *Dionysos in Classical Athens: An Understanding Through Images*. Brill, 2015.

Isler-Kerényi, Cornelia. "Dionysos, the *Polis* and Power." In *Dionysus and Politics: Constructing Authority in the Graeco-Roman World*, ed. Filip Doroszewski and Dariusz Karłowicz, 9–17. Routledge, 2021.

Jacob, Christian. *The Web of Athenaeus*. Hellenic Studies Series 61. Translated by Arietta Papaconstantinou. Center for Hellenic Studies at Harvard University, 2013.

Jaworska-Wołoszyn, Magdalena. "Aristotle's Lost *Symposium* and *On Drunkenness*: The Content of the Extant Testimonies and Excerpts." *Peitho. Examina Antiqua* 7, no. 1 (2016): 205–216.

Jazdzewska, Katarzyna. "Laughter in Plutarch's *Convivium Septem Sapientium*." *Classical Philology* 111, no. 1 (2016): 74–88.

Jazdzewska, Katarzyna. "Laughter in Plato's and Xenophon's *Symposia*." In *Plato and Xenophon Comparative Studies*, ed. Gabriel Danzig, David Johnson, and Donald Morrison, 187–207. Brill, 2018.

Jeffré, Friedrich Bernhard. *Der Begriff τέχνη bei Plato*. PhD thesis, Christian-Albrechts University, 1922. https://chs.harvard.edu/book/der-begriff-tekhne-bei-plato/.

Jellinek, E. Morton. "Drinkers and Alcoholics in Ancient Rome." *Journal of Studies on Alcohol* 37, no. 11 (1976): 1718–1741.

Jensen, Jeppe Sinding. "Cognition and Meaning." In *Origins of Religion, Cognition and Culture*, ed. Armin W. Geertz, 241–257. Routledge, 2014.

Jessen, Mads D. "Religion and the Extra-Somatics of Conceptual Thought." In *Origins of Religion, Cognition and Culture*, ed. Armin W. Geertz, 319–340. Routledge, 2014.

Jiménez San Cristóbal, Ana Isabel. *Rituales órficos*. PhD thesis (edition on CDRom 2005). Universidad Complutense Madrid, 2002.

Jiménez San Cristóbal, Ana Isabel. "The Meaning of βάκχος and βακχεύειν in Orphism." In *Mystic Cults in Magna Graecia*, ed. Patricia A. Johnston and Giovanni Casadio, 46–60. University of Texas Press, 2009.

Johnson, David M. "From Generals to Gluttony: *Memorabilia* Book 3." In *Socrates and the Socratic Dialogue*, ed. Alessandro Stavru and Christopher Moore, 481–499. Brill, 2017.

Johnson, Mark. "Introduction: Metaphor in the Philosophical Tradition." In *Philosophical Perspectives on Metaphor*, ed. Mark Johnson, 3–47. University of Minnesota Press, 1981.

Johnson, Mark. "Philosophy's Debt to Metaphor." In *The Cambridge Handbook of Metaphor and Thought*, ed. Raymond W. Gibbs, 39–52. Cambridge University Press, 2008.

Joly, Robert. "Platon et la medicine." *Bulletin de l'Association Guillaume Budé: Lettres d'humanité* 20 (1961): 435–451.

Joly, Robert. *Hippocrate, Du régime des maladies aiguës, Appendice, De l'aliment, De l'usage des liquides*. Budé VI(2). Les Belles Lettres, 1972.

Jones, Prudence J. *Reading Rivers in Roman Literature and Culture*. Lexington Books, 2005.

Jouanna, Jacques. "Le Médecin Modèle du Législateur dans les *Lois* de Platon." *Ktema* 3 (1978): 77–91.

Jouanna, Jacques. *Hippocrate: Tome X, 2e partie: Maladies II*. Les Belles Lettres, 1983.

Jouanna, Jacques. "Rhétorique et Médecine dans la collection Hippocratique. Contribution à l'histoire de la rhétorique au Ve siècle." *Revue des Études Grecques* 97 (1984): 26–44.

Jouanna, Jacques. *Hippocrates*. Translated by Malcolm B. DeBevoise. John Hopkins University Press, 1999.

Jouanna, Jacques. "La théorie de la sensation, de la pensée et de l'âme dans le traité hippocratique du *Régime*: ses rapports avec Empédocle et le *Timée* de

Platon." *Annali dell'Università degli Studi di Napoli "L'Orientale"* 29 (2007): 9–39.

Jouanna, Jacques. "The Theory of Sensation, Thought and the Soul in the Hippocratic Treatise *Regimen*: Its Connections with Empedocles and Plato's Timaeus." In *Greek Medicine from Hippocrates to Galen. Selected Papers*, ed. Philip van der Eijk, 195–227. Brill, 2012a.

Jouanna, Jacques. "Wine and Medicine in Ancient Greece." In *Greek Medicine from Hippocrates to Galen: Selected Papers*, ed. Philip van der Eijk, 173–194. Brill, 2012b.

Jouanna, Jacques. "The Legacy of the Hippocratic Treatise *the Nature of Man*: The Theory of the Four Humours." In *Greek Medicine from Hippocrates to Galen: Selected Papers*, ed. Philip van der Eijk, 335–359. Brill, 2012c.

Jouanna, Jacques. "Politics and Medicine: The Problem of Change in *Regimen in Acute Diseases* and Thucydides (Book 6)." In *Greek Medicine from Hippocrates to Galen. Selected Papers*, ed. Philip van der Eijk, 21–38. Brill, 2012d.

Jouanna, Jacques. "The Typology and Aetiology of Madness in Ancient Greek Medical and Philosophical Writing." In *Mental Disorders in the Classical World*, ed. William V. Harris, 97–118. Brill, 2013.

Jouanna, Jacques, and Laurence Villard. *Vin et santé en Grèce ancienne: actes du colloque organisé à l'Université de Rouen et à Paris* (Université de Paris IV Sorbonne et ENS) par l'UPRESA 8062 du CNRS et l'URLLCA de l'Université de Rouen, 28–30 septembre 1998. Bulletin de correspondance hellénique suppl. 40. Ecole francaise d'Athenes, 2002.

Jouët-Pastré, Emmanuelle. "Les imitations comiques dans les *Lois* de Platon." *Kairos* 19 (2002): 97–109.

Jouët-Pastré, Emmanuelle. "Beuveries et comédies : deux expériences de bassesse dans la cité des *Lois*." In *Symposium: banquet et représentationsen Grèce et à Rome*, ed. Charalampos Orfanos and Jean-Claude Carrière, 303–311. Presses universitaires du Mirail, 2003.

Jouët-Pastré, Emmanuelle. "Le rire dans la comédie des *Lois* de Platon." *Pallas* 67 (2005): 45–57.

Julião Ricardo, Roberto Lo Presti, Dominik Perler, and Philip van der Eijk. "Mapping Memory. Theories in Ancient, Medieval and Early Modern Philosophy and Medicine." In *Space and Knowledge*, ed. Gerd Grasshoff and Michael Meyer. *Topoi Special Issue* 6 (2016): 678–702.

Jurewicz, Joanna. "The Concept of ṛtá in the Ṛgveda." In *Universe and Inner Self in Early Indian and Early Greek Thought*, ed. Richard Seaford, 28–39. Edinburgh University Press, 2016.

Kahle, Madayo. "OF 437 and the Transformation of the Soul." In *Tracing Orpheus: Studies of Orphic Studies*, ed. Miguel Herrero de Jáuregui, Ana Isabel Jiménez San Cristóbal, Eugenio R. Luján Martínez, Raquel Martín Hernández,

Marco Anotonio Santamaría Álvarez, and Sofía Torallas Tovar, 153–158. De Gruyter, 2011.

Kahn, Charles H. *The Art and Thought of Heraclitus: A New Arrangement and Translation of the Fragments with Literary and Philosophical Commentary (Edition of the Fragments with Translation and Commentary)*. Cambridge University Press, 1981.

Kahn, Charles H. "Plato and Heraclitus." *Proceedings of the Boston Area Colloquium in Ancient Philosophy* 1, no. 1 (1985): 241–258.

Kahn, Charles H. "Vlastos's Socrates." *Phronesis* 37, no. 2 (1992): 233–258.

Kahn, Charles H. *Plato and the Socratic Dialogue: The Philosophical Use of a Literary Form*. Cambridge University Press, 1997.

Kahn, Charles H. "On Platonic Chronology." In *New Perspectives in Plato: Ancient and Modern*, ed. Julia Annas and Christopher J. Rowe, 93–127. Harvard University Press, 2002.

Kahn, Charles H. "Review of Burnyeat, Myles and Frede, Michael. *The Pseudo-Platonic Seventh Letter*. Oxford University Press, 2015." *Notre Dame Philosophical Reviews: An Electronic Journal* (2015). https://ndpr.nd.edu/news/the-pseudo-platonic-seventh-letter/.

Kallet, Lisa. "Accounting for Culture in Fifth-Century Athens." In *Democracy, Empire and the Arts in Fifth–century Athens*, ed. Deborah Dickmann Boedeker and Kurt A. Raaflaub, 43–58. Harvard University Press, 1998.

Kallet, Lisa. "*Demos Tyrannos*: Wealth, Power and Economic Patronage." In *Popular Tyranny: Sovereignty and Its Discontents in Ancient Greece*, ed. Kathryn A. Morgan, 117–154. University of Texas Press: 2003.

Kamtekar, Rachana. "Psychology and the Inculcation of Virtue in Plato's *Laws*." In *Plato's Laws: A Critical Guide*, ed. Christopher Bobonich, 127–148. Cambridge University Press, 2010.

Kamtekar, Rachana. "Self-Knowledge in Plato." In *Self-Knowledge: A History*, ed. Ursula Renz, 25–43. Oxford University Press, 2017.

Kanellakis, Dimitrios. *Aristophanes and the Poetics of Surprise*. De Gruyter, 2020.

Kannany, Thomas. *Kierkegaard: The Philosopher of Meta-Reason. A Study on the Concept of Interest in his Pseudonymous Works*. PhD thesis, University of Leuven, 1989.

Kant, Immanuel. *Observations on the Feeling of the Beautiful and Sublime and Other Writings*, ed. Patrick Frierson and Paul Guyer. Cambridge University Press, 1764/2011.

Kany, Roland. *Augustins Trinitätsdenken. Bilanz, Kritik und Weiterführung der modernen Forschung zu "De trinitate."* Mohr Siebeck, 2007.

Kapetanaki, Sophia, and Robert W. Sharples. *Pseudo-Aristoteles (Pseudo-Alexander), Supplementa Problematorum: A New Edition of the Greek Text with Introduction and Annotated Translation*. De Gruyter, 2006.

Käppel, L. "Heraklits Kosmologie als Praxis von Modellierung." In *Heraklit im Kontext*, ed. Enrica Fantino, Ulrike Muss, Kurt Sier, and Charlotte Schubert, 211–230. De Gruyter, 2017.

Karamanolis, George. *Plato and Aristotle in Agreement? Platonists on Aristotle from Antiochus to Porphyry*. Oxford University Press, 2006.

Karamanolis, George. "Early Christian Philosophers on Aristotle." In *Brill's Companion to the Reception of Aristotle in Antiquity*, ed. Andrea Falcon, 460–479. Brill, 2016.

Karamanolis, George. "Plutarch." In *The Stanford Encyclopedia of Philosophy* (Summer 2020 Edition), ed. Edward N. Zalta, 2020. https://plato.stanford.edu/archives/sum2020/entries/plutarch/.

Karamanolis, George. "Numenius." In *The Stanford Encyclopedia of Philosophy* (Fall 2021 Edition), ed. Edward N. Zalta, 2021. https://plato.stanford.edu/archives/fall2021/entries/numenius/.

Karatzoglou, Orestis. *Embodied Self in Plato: Phaedo–Republic–Timaeus*. De Gruyter, 2021.

Karfík, F. "What is Perceptible in Plato's *Timaeus*?" In *Plato's Timaeus: Proceedings of the Tenth Symposium Platonicum Pragene*, ed. Chad Jorgenson, Filip Karfík, and Štěpán Špinka, 228–258. Brill, 2021.

Kassel Rudolf, and Colin Austin. *Poetae comici graeci*. De Gruyter, 1986.

Kaster, Robert A. "Macrobius and Servius: Verecundia and the Grammarian's Function." *Harvard Studies in Classical Philology* 84 (1980): 219–262.

Kazantzidis, George. "Between Insanity and Wisdom: Perceptions of Melancholy in the Ps.-Hippocratic *Letters* 10–17." In *Mental Illness in Ancient Medicine: From Celsus to Paul of Aegina*, ed. Chiara Thumiger and Peter N. Singer, 33–78. Brill, 2018.

Kazantzidis, George. "Pseudo-intellectualism and Melancholy: The Poetics of Black Bile in Lucian's *Lexiphanes*." *Araucaria. Revista Iberoamericana de Filosofía, Política y Humanidades* 21, no. 41 (2019): 289–307.

Kechagia, Eleni. "Philosophy in Plutarch's *Table Talk*. In Jest or in Earnest?" In *The Philosopher's Banquet: Plutarch's Table Talk in the Intellectual Culture of the Roman Empire*, ed. Frieda Klotz and Katerina Oikonomopoulou, 77–104. Oxford University Press, 2011.

Kelhoffer, James A. *The Diet of John the Baptist: "Locusts and Wild Honey" in Synoptic and Patristic Interpretation*. Mohr Siebeck, 2005.

Kennedy, Duncan F. "Aristotle's Metaphor." In *Derrida and Antiquity*, ed. Miriam Leonard, 267–288. Oxford University Press, 2010.

Kennedy, George A. *The Art of Persuasion in Greece*. Princeton University Press, 1963.

Kennedy, George A. *Aristotle on Rhetoric. A Theory of Civic Discourse*, 2nd ed. Oxford University Press, 2007.

Ker, James. "Solon's 'Theôria' and the End of the City." *Classical Antiquity* 19, no. 2 (2000): 304–329.

Kerényi, Karl. *Eleusis: Archetypal Image of Mother and Daughter.* Translated by Ralph Manheim. Bollingen Foundation, 1967.

Khachouf, Omar T., Stefano Poletti, and Giuseppe Pagnoni. "The Embodied Transcendental: A Kantian Perspective on Neurophenomenology." *Frontiers in Human Neuroscience* 7 (2013). https://doi.org/10.3389/fnhum.2013.00611.

Kidd, Stephen E. *Nonsense and Meaning in Ancient Greek Comedy.* Cambridge University Press, 2014.

Kidd, Stephen E. *Play and Aesthetics in Ancient Greece.* Cambridge University Press, 2019.

Kihlstrom, John F. "Conscious, Subconscious, Unconscious: A Cognitive Perspective." In *The Unconscious Reconsidered*, ed. Kenneth S. Bowers and Donald Meichenbaum, 149–211. Wiley, 1984.

Kim, Lawrence. "Historical Fiction, Brachylogy, and Plutarch's *Banquet of the Seven Sages.*" In *Symposion and Philanthropia in Plutarch*, ed. José Ribeiro Ferreira, Delfim Leão, Manuel Tröster, and Paula Barata Dias, 481–495. Imprensa da Universidade de Coimbra, Classica Digitalia, 2009.

King, Helen. "Once Upon a Text—Hysteria from Hippocrates." In *Hysteria Beyond Freud*, ed. Sander L. Gilman, Helen King, Roy Porter, George S. Rousseau, and Elaine Showalter, 3–90. University of California Press, 1993.

Kinkel, Gottfried. *Epicorum graecorum fragmenta.* Teubner, 1877.

Kirby, John T. "Aristotle on Metaphor." *American Journal of Philology* 118, no. 4 (1997): 517–554.

Kirichenko, Alexander. "Asinus Philosophans: Platonic Philosophy and the Prologue to Apuleius' *Golden Ass.*" *Mnemosyne* 61 (2008): 89–107.

Kirk, Geoffrey S. *Heraclitus: The Cosmic Fragments.* University Press, 1954.

Kirk, Geoffrey S., John E. Raven, and Malcolm Schofield, M. *The Presocratic Philosophers. A Critical History with a Selection of Texts.* Cambridge University Press, 1995. Originally published, 1983.

Klauck, Hans-Josef. *Die religiöse Umwelt des Urchristentums II. Herrscher-und Kaiserkult, Philosophie, Gnosis.* Kohlhammer, 1996.

Klijn, Albertus F. J. "The 'Single One' in the Gospel of Thomas." *Journal of Biblical Literature* 81 (1962): 271–278.

Klitenic Wear, Sarah, and John M. Dillon. *Dionysus the Areopagite and the Neoplatonist Tradition: Despoiling the Hellenes.* Ashgate, 2007.

Klooster, Jacqueline. "A Speaker of Words and a Doer of Deeds: The Reception of Phoenix' Educational Ideal." In *Homer and the Good Ruler in Antiquity and Beyond*, ed. Jacqueline Klooster and Baukje van den Berg, 65–85. Brill, 2018.

Klosko, George. *The Development of Plato's Political Theory.* Routledge, 1986.

Klosko, George. "The 'Rule' of Reason in Plato's Psychology." *History of Philosophy Quarterly* 5, no. 4 (1988a): 341–356.

Klosko, George. "The Nocturnal Council in Plato's *Laws*." *Political Studies* 36 (1988b): 74–88.

Klotz, Frieda. "Portraits of the Philosopher: Plutarch's Self-Presentation in the *Quaestiones Convivales*." *The Classical Quarterly* 57, no. 2 (2007): 650–667.

Knox, Peter E. "Wine, Water, and Callimachean Polemics." *Harvard Studies in Classical Philology* 89 (1985): 107–119.

Kochin, Michael Shalom. *Gender and Rhetoric in Plato's Political Thought*. Cambridge University Press, 2002.

Kohan, Walter. *Childhood, Education and Philosophy, New Ideas for an Old Relationship*. Routledge, 2015.

Komar, Paulina. *Eastern Wines on Western Tables Consumption, Trade and Economy in Ancient Italy*. Brill, 2021.

König, Jason. "Fragmentation and Coherence in Plutarch's *Sympotic Questions*." In *Ordering Knowledge in the Roman Empire*, ed. Jason König and Tim Whitmarsh, 43–68. Cambridge University Press, 2007.

König, Jason. "Sympotic Dialogue in the First to Fifth Centuries CE." In *The End of Dialogue in Antiquity*, ed. Simon Goldhill, 85–113. Cambridge University Press, 2008.

König, Jason. "Self-Promotion and Self-Effacement in Plutarch's *Quaestiones Convivales*." In *The Philosopher's Banquet: Plutarch's Table Talk in the Intellectual Culture of the Roman Empire*, ed. Frieda Klotz and Katerina Oikonomopoulou, 179–203. Oxford University Press, 2011.

König, Jason. *Saints and Symposiasts: The Literature of Food and the Symposium in Greco-Roman and Early Christian Culture*. Cambridge University Press, 2012.

König, Jason. "Representations of Intellectual Community in Plutarch, Pliny the Younger and Aulus Gellius." *Archimède: archéologie et histoire ancienne Special Issue* 1 (2019): 54–67.

Kosman, L. Aryeh. "Charmides' First Definition: *Sophrosyne* as Quietness." In *Essays on Ancient Greek Philosophy II*, ed. John P. Anton and Anthony Preus, 203–216. State University of New York Press, 1983.

Konstan, David. "Patrons and Friends." *Classical Philology* 90 (1995): 328–342.

Konstan, David. "Isocrates' 'Republic.'" In *Isocrates and Civic Education*, ed. T. Poulakos and D. Depew, 107–124. New York, 2004.

Konstan, David. *The Emotions of the Ancient Greeks: Studies in Aristotle and Classical Literature*. University of Toronto Press, 2006.

Konstan, David. "The Two Faces of *Parrhêsia*: Free Speech and Self-Expression in Ancient Greece." *Antichthon* 46 (2012): 1–13.

Konstan, David. "Senecan Emotions." In *The Cambridge Companion to Seneca*, ed. Shadi Bartsch and Alessandro Schiesaro, 174–184. Cambridge University Press, 2015.

Konstan, David, with Diskin Clay, Clarence Glad, Johan Thom, and James Ware, ed. *Philodemus, On Frank Criticism*. Society of Biblical Literature, 1998.

Kosak, Jennifer Clarke. *Heroic Measures: Hippocratic Medicine in the Making of Euripidean Tragedy*. Brill, 2004.

Köster, Isabel K. "Feasting Centaurs and Destructive Consuls in Cicero's *In Pisonem*." *Illinois Classical Studies* 39 (2014): 63–79.

Koster, Willem J. W. *Scholia in Aristophanem II.1 Scholia vetera et recentiora in Aristophanis Vespas*. Bouma's Boekhuis, 1978.

Kotarcic Ana. *Aristotle on Language and Style: The Concept of Lexis*. Cambridge University Press, 2021.

Kotsonis, Alkis. "The Platonic Conception of Intellectual Virtues: Its Significance for Virtue Epistemology." *Synthese* (2019): 1–16. https://doi.org/10.1007/s11229-019-02189-7.

Kotsopoulos, Sotiris. "Aretaeus the Cappadocian on Mental Illness." *Comprehensive Psychiatry* 27, no. 2 (1986): 171–179.

Kotwick, Mirjam E. "ANOHTOI AMYHTOI: Allegorical Interpretation in the Derveni Papyrus and Plato's *Gorgias*." *Classical Philology* 114, no. 2 (2019): 173–196.

Kotwick, Mirjam E. "Allegorical Interpretation in Homer: Penelope's Dream and Early Greek Allegoresis." *American Journal of Philology* 141, no. 1 (2020): 1–26.

Kouloumentas, Stavros. "The Body and the Polis: Alcmaeon on Health and Disease." *British Journal for the History of Philosophy* 22, no. 5 (2014): 867–887.

Kourakou-Dragona, Stavroula. *Vine and Wine in the Ancient Greek World*. Translated by Maria Relaki. Foinikas, 2015.

Kowalzig, Barbara. "Changing Choral Worlds: Song-Dance and Society in Athens and Beyond." In *Music and the Muses: The Culture of Mousikē in the Classical Athenian City*, ed. Penelope Murray and Peter Wilson, 39–65. Oxford University Press, 2004.

Kowalzig, Barbara. "Broken Rhythms in Plato's *Laws*: Materialising Social Time in the Chorus." In *Performance and Culture in Plato's Laws*, ed. Anastasia-Erasmia Peponi, 171–211. Cambridge University Press, 2013.

Kraut, Richard. "Plato's *Apology* and *Crito*: Two Recent Studies." *Ethics* 91, no. 4 (1981): 651–664.

Krikmann, Arvo. "On the Similarity and Distinguishability of Humour and Figurative Speech." *Trames-Journal of the Humanities and Social Sciences* 13, no. 1 (2009): 14–40.

Kroll, Wilhelm. *Procli Diadochi In Platonis Rem publicam commentarii*. Teubner, 1965.

Kudlien, Fridolf. *Untersuchungen zu Aretaios von Kappadokien*. Verlag der Akademie der Wissenschaften und der Literatur, 1964.

Kühn, Karl Gottlob. *Claudii Galeni opera omnia*. Knobloch, 1821–1833.

Kulinski, Jacquelyn, Ernest Kwesi Ofori, Alexis Visotcky, Aaron Smith, Rodney Sparapani, and Jerome L. Fleg. "Effects of Music on the Cardiovascular System." *Trends in Cardiovascular Medicine* 32, no. 6 (2022): 390–398.

Kurke, Leslie. "Imagining Chorality: Wonder, Plato's Puppets, and Moving Statues." In *Performance and Culture in Plato's Laws*, ed. Anastasia-Erasmia Peponi, 123–170. Cambridge University Press, 2013.

Kusch, Martin. *Language as Calculus and Universal Medium: A Study in Husserl, Heidegger, and Gadamer*. Dordrecht, 1989.

Kyriakou, Poulcheria. *A Commentary on Euripides' Iphigenia in Tauris*. De Gruyter, 2012.

Lada-Richards, Ismene. *Initiating Dionysus: Ritual and Theatre in Aristophanes' Frogs*. Clarendon Press, 1999.

Laird, Andrew. "Fiction as a Discourse of Philosophy in Lucian's *Verae Historiae*." In *The Ancient Novel and Beyond*, ed. Stelios Panayotakis, Maaike Zimmerman, and Wytse Hette Keulen, 115–127. Brill, 2003.

Lakmann, Marie-Luise. *Der Platoniker Tauros in der Darstellung des Aulus Gellius*. Brill, 1995.

Lakmann, Marie-Luise. "Dramatische Aufführungen der Werke Platons." In *Skenika. Beiträge zum antiken Theater und seiner Rezeption. Festschrift zum 65. Geburtstag von Horst-Dieter Blume*, ed. Susanne Gödde and Theodor Heinze, 277–289. WBG, 2000.

Lakoff, George. "The Contemporary Theory of Metaphor." In *Metaphor and Thought*, ed. Andrew Ortony, 202–251. Cambridge University Press, 1993. Originally published, 1979.

Lakoff, George, and Mark Johnson. *The Metaphors We Live By*. University of Chicago Press, 1980. Reprint, 2003.

Lamberton, Robert. *Porphyry, On the Cave of the Nymphs*. Station Hill Press, 1983.

Lamberton, Robert. *Homer the Theologian: Neoplatonist Allegorical Reading and the Growth of the Epic Tradition*. University of California Press, 1986.

Lamberton, Robert. "Allegory and Allegorical Interpretation." In *The Cambridge Guide to Homer*, ed. Corinne Ondine Pache, Casey Dué, Susan Lupack, and Robert Lamberton, 1090–1095. Cambridge University Press, 2020.

Lamberz, Erich. *Porphyry, Sententiae ad Intelligibilia ducentes*. Teubner, 1975.

Landy, Joshua. "Philosophical Training Grounds: Socratic Sophistry and Platonic Perfection in 'Symposium' and 'Gorgias.'" *Arion: A Journal of Humanities and the Classics* 15, no. 1 (2007): 63–122.

Lane, Melissa. "Persuasion et force dans la politique platonicienne." In *Aglaïa: autour de Platon. Mélanges offerts à Monique Dixsaut*, trans. Dimitri El Murr, ed. Aldo Brancacci and Dimitri El Murr et Daniela Patrizia Taormina, 133–166. Vrin, 2010a.

Lane, Melissa. "Reconsidering Socratic Irony." In *The Cambridge Companion to Socrates*, ed. Donald R. Morrison, 237–259. Cambridge University Press, 2010b.

Lankila, Tuomo. "The Byzantine Reception of Neoplatonism." In *The Cambridge Intellectual History of Byzantium*, ed. Anthony Kaldellis and Niketas Siniossoglou, 314–324. Cambridge University Press, 2017.

Larivée, Annie. "*Erōs Tyrannos*: Alcibiades as the Model of the Tyrant in Book IX of the *Republic*." *International Journal of the Platonic Tradition* 6, no. 1 (2012): 1–26.

Lauriola, Rosanna. "Euripides, Once Again: From *Hippolytus* 345 to *Knights* 16–18." *Prometheus* 5 (2016): 71–95.

Lebedev, Andrei V. *The Logos of Heraclitus: A Reconstruction of His Thought and Word (with a New Critical Edition of the Fragments)*. Nauka, 2014.

Lebedev, Andrei V. "Alcmaeon of Croton on Human Knowledge, the Seasons of Life, and Isonomia: A New Reading of B 1 DK and Two Additional Fragments from *Turba Philosophorum* and Aristotle." In *Physiologia: Topics in Presocratic Philosophy and its Reception in Antiquity*, ed. Christian Vassallo, 227–258. WVT Wissenschaftlicher Verlag, 2017.

Leclercq, Jean, Charles Hugh Talbot, and Henri Marie Rochais. *Bernard of Clairvaux: Sermones super Cantica canticorum 1–35. Ad fidem codicum recensuerunt*. Editiones Cistercienses, 1957.

Lee, Mi-Kyoung Mitzi. "Thinking and Perception in Plato's *Theaetetus*." *Apeiron* 32, no. 4 (1999): 37–54.

Lefkowitz, Jeremy B. "Fabulous Style: Learning to Compose Fables in the *Progymnasmata*." In *Overcoming Dichotomies: Parables, Fables, And Similes In The Graeco-Roman World*, ed. Albertina Oegema, Martijn Stoutjesdijk, and Jonathan Pater, 55–75. Mohr Siebeck, 2022.

Lehoux, Daryn. "Drugs and the Delphic Oracle." *The Classical World* 101, no. 1 (2007): 41–56.

Leibowitz, Joshua Otto. "Studies in the History of Alcoholism II: Acute Alcoholism in Ancient Greek and Roman Medicine." *British Journal of Addiction* 62 (1967): 83–86.

Leick, Gwendolyn. *Sex and Eroticism in Mesopotamian Literature*. Routledge, 1994.

Leigh, Matthew. "Varius Rufus and the Appetites of Antony." *Proceedings of the Cambridge Philological Society* 42 (1996): 171–97.

Levin, Susan B. *Plato's Rivalry with Medicine: A Struggle and Its Dissolution*. Oxford University Press, 2014.

Levinas, Emmanuel. *Totalité et Infini. Essai sur l'extériorité*. Martin Nijhoff, 1961.

Lévy, Carlos. "Cicéron, le moyen platonisme et la philosophie romaine: à propos de la naissance du concept latin de qualitas." *Revue de métaphysique et de morale* 57, no. 1 (2008): 5–20.

Lévy, Carlos. "Philo of Alexandria." In *The Stanford Encyclopedia of Philosophy* (Fall 2022 Edition), ed. Edward N. Zalta and Uri Nodelman, 2022. https://plato.stanford.edu/archives/fall2022/entries/philo/.

Levy, David. "The Definition of Love in Plato's *Symposium*." *Journal of the History of Ideas* 40, no. 2 (1979): 285–291.

Levy, David. "Socrates vs. Callicles: Examination and Ridicule in Plato's *Gorgias*." *Plato Journal* 13 (2020): 27–36.

Lévystone, David. "La figure d'Ulysse chez les Socratiques: Socrate polutropos." *Phronesis* 50 (2005): 181–214.

Lévystone, David. "What Rules and Laws Does Socrates Obey?" *Tópicos* (México) 57 (2019): 399–432.

Lewis, V. Bradley. "The Nocturnal Council and the Platonic Political Philosophy." *History of Political Thought* 19, no. 1 (1998): 1–20.

Lidz, Joel W. "Medicine as Metaphor in Plato." *Journal of Medicine and Philosophy* 20 (1995): 527–541.

Lieberoth, Andreas. "Religion and the Emergence of Human Imagination." In *Origins of Religion, Cognition and Culture*, ed. Armin W. Geertz, 160–177. Routledge, 2014.

Liebert, Rana Saadi. "Apian Imagery and the Critique of Poetic Sweetness in Plato's *Republic*." *Transactions of the American Philological Association* 140, no. 1 (2010): 97–115.

Lier, Tiago. *Reason, Rhetoric, and the Philosophical Life in Plato's Phaedrus.* Rowman & Littlefield, 2019.

Lim, Timothy H. *The Formation of the Jewish Canon.* Yale University Press, 2013.

Linforth, Ivan M. "The Corybantic Rites in Plato." *University of California Publications in Classical Philology* 13 (1946): 121–162.

Lissarrague, François. *The Aesthetics of the Greek Banquet: Images of Wine and Ritual.* Translated by A. Szegedy-Maszak. Princeton University Press, 2016.

Littré, Emile. *Oeuvres complètes d'Hippocrate.* J.-B. Baillière, 1839–1861.

Litwa, M. David. "The Deification of Moses in Philo of Alexandria." *Studia Philonica Annual* 26 (2014): 1–27.

Litwa, M. David. *Posthuman Transformation in Ancient Mediterranean Thought: Becoming Angels and Demons.* Cambridge University Press, 2021.

Lobel, Edgar, and Denys Page. *Poetarum lesbiorum fragmenta.* Clarendon Press, 1963.

Lohe, Peter. *Cristoforo Landino Disputationes Camaldulenses.* Sansoni, 1980.

Lombardini, John. "Civic Laughter: Aristotle and the Political Virtue of Humor." *Political Theory* 41, no. 2 (2013): 203–230.

Long, Alex G. *Plato and the Stoics.* Cambridge University Press, 2013.

Long, Anthony Arthur. "Thinking and Sense-Perception in Empedocles: Mysticism or Materialism." *The Classical Quarterly,* 16 (1966): 256–276.

Long, Anthony Arthur. "Allegory in Philo and Etymology in Stoicism: A Plea for Drawing Distinctions." *Studia Philonica Annual* IX (1997): 198–210.

Long, Anthony Arthur. "Soul and Body in Stoicism." *Phronesis* 27, no. 1 (1982): 34–57.

Long, Anthony Arthur. "Hellenistic Ethics and Philosophical Power." In *From Epicurus to Epictetus: Studies in Hellenistic and Roman Philosophy,* ed. Anthony Arthur Long, 3–22. Oxford University Press, 2006. First published in *Hellenistic History and Culture*, ed. Peter Green, 138–167. University of California Press, 1993.

Long, Anthony Arthur. "Socrates and Sophists." In *The Cambridge History of Moral Philosophy*, ed. Sacha Golob and Jens Timmermann, 15–27. Cambridge University Press, 2017.

Longrigg, James. *Greek Rational Medicine: Philosophy and Medicine from Alcmaeon to the Alexandrians*. Routledge, 1993.

Longrigg, James. *Greek Medicine: From the Heroic to the Hellenistic Age: A Source Book*. Routledge, 1998.

Lopes, Rodolfo. "The Omnipresence of Philosophy in Plutarch's *Quaestiones Convivales*." In *Symposion and Philanthropia in Plutarch*, ed. José Ribeiro Ferreira, Delfim Leão, Manuel Tröster, and Paula Barata Dias, 415–424. Imprensa da Universidade de Coimbra, Classica Digitalia, 2009.

Lo Presti, R. "Perceiving the Coherence of the Perceiving Body: Is There Such a Thing as a 'Hippocratic' View on Sense Perception and Cognition?" In *Ancient Concepts of the Hippocratic*, ed. Lesley Dean-Jones and Ralph M. Rosen, 163–194. Brill, 2016.

Lorenz, Hendrik. *The Brute Within: Appetitive Desire in Plato and Aristotle*. Oxford University Press, 2006.

Lorenz, Hendrik. "The Cognition of Appetite in Plato's *Timaeus*." In *Plato and the Divided Self*, ed. Rachel Barney, Tad Brennan, and Charles Brittain, 238–258. Cambridge University Press, 2012.

Lorenz, Hendrik. "Ancient Theories of Soul." In *The Stanford Encyclopedia of Philosophy* (Summer 2024 Edition), ed. Edward N. Zalta and Uri Nodelman, 2024. https://plato.stanford.edu/archives/sum2024/entries/ancient-soul/.

Losh, Molly, and Lisa J. Capps. "Narrative Ability in High-Functioning Children with Autism or Asperger's Syndrome." *Journal of Autism and Developmental Disorders* 33, no. 3 (2003): 239–251.

Losh, Molly, and Peter C. Gordon. "Quantifying Narrative Ability in Autism Spectrum Disorder: A Computational Linguistic Analysis of Narrative Coherence." *Journal of Autism and Developmental Disorders* 44, no. 12 (2014): 3016–3025.

Lössl, Josef. "Poets, Prophets, Critics, and Exegetes in Classical and Biblical Antiquity and Early Christianity." *Journal for Late Antique Religion and Culture* 1 (2007): 1–16.

Lott, Micah. "Ignorance, Shame and Love of Truth." *Phoenix* 66, no. 1 (2012): 36–56.

Louis, Pierre. *Les Métaphores de Platon*. Les Belles Lettres, 1945.

Louth, Andrew. *The Origins of the Christian Mystical Tradition: From Plato to Denys*. Oxford University Press, 2007.

Lowenstam, Steven. "Aristophanes' Hiccups." *Greek, Roman and Byzantine Studies* 27 (1986): 43–56.

Lu, Mathew T. "*Hexis* within Aristotelian Virtue Ethics." *Proceedings of the American Catholic Philosophical Association* 88 (2014): 197–206.

Ludwig, Paul W. "Politics and Erōs in Aristophanes' Speech: *Symposium* 191e–192a and the Comedies." *American Journal of Philology* 117, no. 4 (1996): 537–562.

Luft, Sebastian. "Husserl's Theory of the Phenomenological Reduction: Between Life-World and Cartesianism." *Research in Phenomenology* 34 (2004): 198–234.

Luhrmann, Tanya M. "Hallucinations and Sensory Overrides." *Annual Review of Anthropology* 40 (2011): 71–85.

Lukinovich, Alessandra. "The Play of Reflections between Literary Form and the Sympotic Theme in the *Deipnosophistae* of Athenaeus." In *Sympotica: A Symposium on the Symposium*, ed. Oswyn Murray, 263–271. Oxford University Press, 1990.

Lupieri, Eric F. "A Beast and a Woman in the Desert, or the Sin of Israel: A Typological Reflection." In *Golden Calf Traditions in Early Judaism, Christianity, and Islam*, ed. Eric F. Mason and Edmondo F. Lupieri, 157–175. Brill, 2018.

Luppe, Wolfgang. "The Rivalry between Aristophanes and Kratinos." In *The Rivals of Aristophanes: Studies in Athenian Old Comedy*, ed. F. David Harvey, John Wilkins, and Kenneth James Dover, 15–22. Duckworth and the Classical Press of Wales, 2000.

Lutz, Cora. *Musonius Rufus, "The Roman Socrates."* Yale University Press, 1947.

Lutz, Mark J. "Civic Virtue and Socratic Virtue." *Polity* 29, no. 4 (1997): 565–592.

Luyster, Robert. "Nietzsche/Dionysus: Ecstasy, Heroism, and the Monstrous." *Journal of Nietzsche Studies* 21 (2001): 1–26.

Lynch, Kathleen. "More Thoughts on the Space of the Symposium." In *Building Communities: House, Settlement and Society in the Aegean and Beyond: Proceedings of a Conference Held at Cardiff University, 17–21 April 2001*, ed. Ruth Westgate, Nick Fisher, and James Whitley, 243–249. British School at Athens, 2007.

Lynch, Kathleen. "The Hellenistic Symposium as Feast." In *Feasting and Polis Institutions*, ed. Floris van den Eijnde, Josine Blok, and Rolf Strootman, 233–256. Brill, 2018a.

Lynch, Tosca. "The Seductive Voice of the Aulos in Plato's *Symposium*: From the Dismissal of the Auletris to Alcibiades' Praise of Socrates-auletes." In *Music Cultures in Sounds, Words and Images*, ed. Antonio Baldassarre and Tatjana Markovic, 709–723. Hollitzer Wissenschaftsverlag, 2018b.

Mac Cormac, Earl R. *A Cognitive Theory of Metaphor*. MIT Press, 1985.

MacDowell, Douglas M. *Gorgias. Encomium of Helen*. Bristol Classical Press, 1982.

Mac Góráin, Fiachra, and Simon Perris. "The Ancient Reception of Euripides' *Bacchae* from Athens to Byzantium." In *Dionysus and Rome. Religion and Literature*, ed. Fiachra Mac Góráin, 39–84. De Gruyter, 2020.

MacFarlane, Patrick. "The Pathological Role of *Pneuma* in Aristotle." In *Heat, Pneuma, and Soul in Ancient Philosophy and Science*, ed. Hynek Bartoš and Colin Guthrie King, 310–330. Cambridge University Press, 2020.

Madsen, Mathias W. "Cognitive Metaphor Theory and the Metaphysics of Immediacy." *Cognitive Science* 40 (2016): 881–908.

Maehler, Herwig. *Pindarus*. Pars II. *Fragmenta. Indices*. K.G. Saur, 2001.

Magnone, Paolo. "Soul Chariots in Indian and Greek Thought: Polygenesis or Diffusion?" In *Universe and Inner Self in Early Indian and Early Greek Thought*, ed. Richard Seaford, 149–167. Edinburgh University Press, 2016.

Malamoud, Charles. "Manyúh Svayambhúh." In *Mélanges d'indianisme à la mémoire de Louis Renou*, 493–507. E. de Boccard, 1968.

Mangieri, Anthony F. "God as Cult Initiate: Dionysos and the Eleusinian Mysteries in Greek Vase-Painting." *Art Inquiries* 17, no. 1 (2016): 42–56.

Mann, William E. "Piety: Lending a Hand to Euthyphro." *Philosophy and Phenomenological Research* 58, no. 1 (1998): 123–142.

Männlein-Robert, Irmgard. "Die Aporien des Kritikers Longin. Zur Inszenierung der Platonexegese bei Proklos." In *Proklos. Methode, Seelenlehre, Metaphysik*, Akten der Konferenz in Jena am 18–20. September 2003, ed. Matthias Perkams and Rosa Maria Piccione, 71–97. Brill, 2006.

Männlein-Robert, Irmgard. "Between Conversion and Madness: Sophisticated Ambiguity in Lucian's *Nigrinus*." In *Strategies of Ambiguity in Ancient Literature*, ed. Martin Vöhler, Therese Fuhrer, and Stavros Frangoulidis, 237–250. De Gruyter, 2021.

Manolaraki, Eleni. "*Noscendi Nilum Cupido*: The Nile Digression in Book 10." In *Brill's Companion to Lucan*, ed. Paolo Asso, 153–182. Brill, 2011.

Mansfeld, Jaap. "Alcmaeon: 'Physikos' or Physician? With Some Remarks on Calcidius' 'On Vision' Compared to Galen, *Plac. Hipp. Plat.* VII." In *Kephalaion: Studies in Greek Philosophy and Its Continuation Offered to Professor C. J. de Vogel*, ed. J. Mansfeld and Lambertus M. de Rijk, 26–38. Van Gorcum, 1975.

Mansfeld, Jaap. "Doxography and Dialectic: the *Sitz im Leben* of the 'Placita.'" *Aufstieg und Niedergang der römischen Welt* II 36, no. 4 (1990): 3056–3229.

Mansfeld, Jaap. "The Body Politic: Aëtius on Alcmaeon on Isonomia and Monarchia." In *Politeia in Greek and Roman Philosophy Festschrift for Malcolm Schofield*, ed. Verity Harte and Melissa Lane, 78–95. Cambridge University Press, 2013.

Marasco, Gabriele. "Marco Antonio 'Nuovo Dioniso' e il 'De sua ebrietate.'" *Latomus* 51 (1992): 538–548.

Marco, Elysa J., Leighton B. N. Hinkley, Susanna S. Hill, and Srikantan S. Nagarajan. "Sensory Processing in Autism: A Review of Neurophysiologic Findings." *Pediatric Research* 69 (2011): 48–54.

Markovich, Daniel. *Promoting a New Kind of Education: Greek and Roman Philosophical Protreptic*. Brill, 2022.

Marren, Marina. "The Tragedy and Comedy of Tyranny: Plato's *Symposium* and Aristophanes's *Frogs*." *Philosophy and Literature* 44, no. 2 (2020): 207–225.

Martin, Hubert. "The Concept of Philanthropia in Plutarch's Lives." *American Journal of Philology* 82, no. 2 (1961): 164–175.

Martins de Jesus, Carlos A. "Dancing with Plutarch Dance and Dance Theory in Plutarch's *Table Talk*." In *Symposion and Philanthropia in Plutarch*, ed.

José Ribeiro Ferreira, Delfim Leão, Manuel Tröster, and Paula Barata Dias, 403–414. Imprensa da Universidade de Coimbra, Classica Digitalia, 2009.

Maso, Stefano. "Emotions in Context: 'Risk' as Condition for Emotion." In *Emotions in Plato*, ed. Laura Candioto and Olivier Renaut, 83–102. Brill, 2020.

Matthews, Gareth B. "Socratic Ignorance." *Philosophic Exchange* 33, no. 1 (2003): 5–16.

Matthews, Victor J. *Panyassis of Halikarnassos: Text and Commentary*. Brill, 1974.

Maturana, Humberto. *Emociones y lenguaje en educación y política*. J-C-Sáez, 1990.

Maturana, Humberto. *La objetividad, un argumento para obligar*. Dolmen Ediciones, 1997.

Maturana, Humberto, and Francisco Varela. *El árbol del conocimiento: Las bases biológicas del entendimiento humano*. Universitaria, 1984.

Mazzoli, Giancarlo. *Seneca e la Poesia*. Ceschina, 1970.

McBrayer, Gregory A. "Corrupting the Youth: Xenophon and Plato on Socrates and Alcibiades." *Kentron* 33 (2017): 75–90.

McCabe, Mary M. "Comments on Matthew Evans 'The Bling Desires of Republic IV' and Jessica Moss, 'Against Bare Urges and Good-Independent Desires: Appetites in Republic IV.'" In *Psychology and Value in Plato, Aristotle, and Hellenistic Philosophy: The Ninth Keeling Colloquium in Ancient Philosophy*, ed. Fiona Leigh and Margaret Hampson, 97–104. Oxford University Press, 2022.

McCall, Marsh H. Jr. *Ancient Rhetorical Theories of Simile and Comparison*. Harvard University Press, 1969.

McCloskey, Benjamin. "Xenophon's Democratic Pedagogy." *Phoenix* 71, no. 3/4 (2017): 230–249.

McConnell, Sean. "Cicero and Socrates." In *Brill's Companion to the Reception of Socrates*, ed. Christopher Moore, 347–366. Brill, 2019.

McCoy, Marina. "Socrates on Simonides: The Use of Poetry in Socratic and Platonic Rhetoric." *Philosophy and Rhetoric* 32, no. 4 (1999): 349–367.

McCready-Flora, Ian. "Affect and Sensation: Plato's Embodied Cognition." *Phronesis* 63, no. 2 (2018): 117–147.

McGinn, J. Bernard. "Plato as a Philosophical Theologian." *Phronesis* 5, no. 1 (1960): 23–31.

McGovern, Patrick E. *Ancient Wine. The Search for the Origins of Viniculture*. Princeton University Press, 2003.

McGovern, Patrick E. *Uncorking the Past: The Quest for Wine, Beer, and Other Alcoholic Beverages*. University of California Press, 2009.

McGovern, Patrick E. "Uncorking the Past: Alcoholic Fermentation as Humankind's First Biotechnology." In *Alcohol and Humans: A Long and Social Affair*, ed. Kimberley Hockings and Robin Dunbar, 81–92. Oxford University Press, 2020.

McGovern, Patrick E., Mindia Jalabadze, Stephen Batiuk, et al. "Early Neolithic Wine of Georgia in the South Caucasus." *Proceedings of the National Academy of Sciences of the United States of America* 114, no. 48 (2017): E10309–E10318.

McGovern, Patrick E., Stuart J. Fleming, and Solomon H. Katz. *The Origins and Ancient History of Wine.* Routledge, 1995.

McKeon, Richard. "Plato and Aristotle as Historians: A Study of Method in the History of Ideas." *Ethics* 51, no. 1 (1940): 66–101.

McKinlay, Arthur Patch. "Wine and Literary Inspiration" (abstract). *Proceedings of the American Philological Association* 63 (1932): 79.

McKinlay, Arthur Patch. "The 'Indulgent' Dionysius." *Transaction and Proceedings of the American Philological Association* 70 (1939): 50–61.

McKinlay, Arthur Patch. "The Wine Element in Horace (Part I)." *The Classical Journal* 42, no. 3 (1946): 161–167.

McKinlay, Arthur Patch. "The Wine Element in Horace (Part II)." *The Classical Journal* 42, no. 4 (1947): 229–235.

McKinlay, Arthur Patch. "Ancient Experience with Intoxicating Drinks: Non-Classical Peoples." *Quarterly Journal of Studies on Alcohol* 9 (1948a): 388–414.

McKinlay, Arthur Patch. "Christian Appraisal of Pagan Temperance." *Anglican Theological Review* 30 (1948b): 44–54.

McKinlay, Arthur Patch. "Early Roman Sobriety." *Classical Bulletin* 24 (1948c): 52.

McKinlay, Arthur Patch. "Temperate Romans." *Classical Weekly* 41 (1948d): 146–149.

McKinlay, Arthur Patch. "Ancient Experience with Intoxicating Drinks: Non-Attic Greek States." *Quarterly Journal of Studies on Alcohol* 10 (1949a): 298–315.

McKinlay, Arthur Patch. "Roman Sobriety in the Later Republic." *Classical Bulletin* 25 (1949b): 27–28.

McKinlay, Arthur Patch. "Roman Sobriety in the Early Empire." *Classical Bulletin* 26 (1950): 31–36.

McKinlay, Arthur Patch. "Attic Temperance." *Quarterly Journal of Studies on Alcohol* 12 (1951): 61–102.

McKinlay Arthur Patch. "Bacchus as Inspirer of Literary Art." *The Classical Journal* 49 (1953/1954): 101–110 and 135–136.

McKinlay, Arthur Patch. "New Light on the Question of Homeric Temperance." *Quarterly Journal of Studies on Alcohol* 14 (1953a): 78–93.

McKinlay, Arthur Patch. "Wine and the Law in Ancient Times." In *Studies Presented to David Moore Robinson on his Seventieth Birthday,* ed. George E. Mylonas and Doris Raymond, vol. 2, 858–867. Washington University, 1953b.

McLaughlin, John L. *The Marzēaḥ in the Prophetic Literature: References and Allusions in Light of the Extra-Biblical Evidence.* Brill, 2001.

McPherran, Mark L. "Socratic Reason and Socratic Revelation." *Journal of the History of Philosophy* 29, no. 3 (1991): 345–373.

McPherran, Mark L. "Medicine, Magic, and Religion in Plato's *Symposium.*" In *Plato's Symposium: Issues in Interpretation and Reception,* ed. James Lesher, Debra Nails, and Frisbee Sheffield, 71–95. Harvard University Press (on behalf of the Center for Hellenic Studies), 2006.

McTavish, Leigh. *Aspects of Wine and Drunkenness in Late Antiquity: Changes in a Changing world*. MPhil thesis, School of History, Philosophy, Religion and Classics, The University of Queensland, 2011.

Meeusen, Michiel. *Plutarch's Science of Natural Problems. A Study with Commentary on Quaestiones Naturales*. Peeters, 2016.

Meillet, Antoine. *De Indo-Europaea radice *men- "mente agitare."* Bouillon, 1897.

Melis, Valeria. "La Maladie d'Oreste." In *La Poésie dramatique comme discours de savoir*, ed. Marie-Laurence Desclos, 157–169. Classiques Garnier, 2020.

Mendelovici, Angela. *The Phenomenal Basis of Intentionality*. Oxford University Press, 2018.

Merleau-Ponty, Maurice. *Phenomenology of Perception*. Translated by Colin Smith. Routledge and Paul Kegan, 1962. Originally published by Gallimard, 1945.

Merleau-Ponty, Maurice. *Sense and Nonsense*. Translated by Hubert L. Dreyfus and Patricia Allen Dreyfus. Northwestern University Press, 1964.

Merleau-Ponty, Maurice. *The Prose of the World*. Translated by John O'Neill. Heinemann, 1973.

Metcalf, Robert. "What Performative Contradiction Reveals: Plato's *Theaetetus* and *Gorgias* on Sophistry." *Humanities* 12, no. 2 (2023): 33. https://doi.org/10.3390/h12020033.

Mews, Constant. "Intoxication and the Song of Songs: Bernard of Clairvaux and the Rediscovery of Origin in the Twelfth Century." In *Pleasures in the Middle Ages*, ed. Naama Cohen-Hanegbi and Piroska Nagy, 329–352. Brepols, 2018.

Milanezi, Silvia. "Laughter as Dessert: On Athenaeus' Book Fourteen, 613–616." In *Athenaeus and His World: Reading Greek Culture in the Roman Empire*, ed. David Braund and John Wilkins, 400–412. University of Exeter Press, 2000.

Miller, Fred D. Jr. "Plato on the Rule of Reason." *Southern Journal of Philosophy* 43, no. 1 (2005): 50–83.

Millett, Paul. "The Trial of Socrates Re-visited." *European Review of History* 12, no. 1 (2005): 23–62.

Militello, Chiara. "Αἰσχύνη and the Λογιστικόν in Plato's *Republic*." In *Emotions in Plato*, ed. Laura Candiotto and Olivier Renaut, 238–251. Brill, 2020.

Miroshnikov, Ivan. *The Gospel of Thomas and Plato: A Study of the Impact of Platonism on the "Fifth Gospel."* Brill, 2018.

Mitchell, John T., Lidia Zylowska, and Scott H. Kollins. "Mindfulness Meditation Training for Attention-Deficit/Hyperactivity Disorder in Adulthood: Current Empirical Support, Treatment Overview, and Future Directions." *Cognitive and Behavioral Practice* 22, no. 2 (2015): 172–191.

Mitsis, Philip. "The Stoics on Property and Politics." *Southern Journal of Philosophy* 43, no. 1 (2005): 230–249.

Moes, Mark M. *Plato's Dialogue Form and the Care of the Soul*. Cambridge University Press, 2000.

Moes, Mark M. "Plato's Conception of the Relations between Moral Philosophy and Medicine." *Perspectives in Biology and Medicine* 44 (2001): 353–367.

Molina Marín, Antonio Ignacio. "Política y Confrontación en los Banquetes Macedonios en la Obra de Plutarco." In *Symposion and Philanthropia in Plutarch*, ed. José Ribeiro Ferreira, Delfim Leão, Manuel Tröster, and Paula Barata Dias, 201–210. Imprensa da Universidade de Coimbra, Classica Digitalia, 2009.

Monoson, Sara. "Dionysius I and Sicilian Theatrical Traditions in Plato's *Republic*." In *Theater Outside Athens: Drama in Greek Sicily and South Italy*, ed. Kathryn Bosher, 156–172. Cambridge University Press, 2012.

Montague, Michelle. "Perception and Cognitive Phenomenology." *Philosophical Studies: An International Journal for Philosophy in the Analytic Tradition* 174, no. 8 (2017): 2045–2062.

Montiglio, Silvia. "Should the Aspiring Wise Man Travel? A Conflict in Seneca' s Thought." *American Journal of Philology* 127, no. 4 (2006): 553–586.

Moore, Christopher. "Socrates Psychagogos (*Birds* 1555, *Phaedrus* 261a7)." In *Socratica III: Studies on Socrates, the Socratics and the Ancient Socratic Literature*, ed. Alessandro Stavru and Fulvia de Luisa, 41–55. Akademie Verlag, 2013.

Moore, Christopher. "Socrates and Self-Knowledge in Aristophanes' *Clouds*." *The Classical Quarterly* 65, no. 2 (2015): 534–551.

Moore, Christopher. "Heracles the Philosopher (Herodotus, fr. 14)." *The Classical Quarterly* 67, no. 1 (2017): 27–48.

Moore, Christopher. *Calling Philosophers Names: On the Origin of a Discipline.* Princeton University Press, 2019a.

Moore, Christopher. "Socrates in Aristotle's History of Philosophy." In *Brill's Companion to the Reception of Socrates*, ed. Christopher Moore, 173–210. Brill, 2019b.

Moore, Christopher. *The Virtue of Agency: Sôphrosunê and Self-Constitution in Classical Greece.* Oxford University Press, 2023.

Moravcsik, Julius. *Plato and Platonism. Plato's Conception of Appearance and Reality in Ontology, Epistemology and Ethics, and Modern Echoes.* Blackwell, 1992.

Morgan, Kathryn A. "Designer History: Plato's Atlantis Story and Fourth-Century Ideology." *Journal of Hellenic Studies* 118 (1998): 101–118.

Morgan, Kathryn A. *Myth and Philosophy from the Presocratics to Plato.* Cambridge University Press, 2000.

Morgan, Kathryn A. "Inspiration, Recollection, and Mimesis in Plato's *Phaedrus*." In *Ancient Models of Mind: Studies in Human and Divine Rationality*, ed. Andrea Nightingale and David Sedley, 45–63. Cambridge University Press, 2010.

Morgan, Kathryn A. "Solon in Plato." In *Solon in the Making: The Early Reception in the Fifth and Fourth Centuries, Trends in Classics* 7, no. 1 (2015): 129–150.

Morgan, Teresa. "Homer in Education." In *Homer Encyclopedia*, ed. Margalit Finkelberg, 234–238. Wiley Blackwell, 2011.

Mori, Anatole. "Jason's Reconciliation with Telamon: A Moral Exemplar in Apollonius' *Argonautica* (1.1286–1344)." *American Journal of Philology* 126, no. 2 (2005): 209–236.

Morreall, John. *The Philosophy of Laughter and Humor*. State University of New York Press, 1987.

Morris, Michael. "Metaphor and Philosophy: An Encounter with Derrida." *Philosophy* 75, no. 292 (2000): 225–244.

Morrison, Andrew D. "Performance, Re-performance and Pindar's Audiences." In *Reading the Victory Ode*, ed. Peter Agócs, Christopher Carey, and Richard Rawles, 111–133. Cambridge University Press, 2012.

Morrow, Glenn R. "Plato's Conception of Persuasion." *Rheinisches Museum für philologie* 62 (1953): 234–250.

Morrow, Glenn R. *Plato's Cretan City*. Princeton University Press, 1960.

Morrow, Glenn. "Necessity and Persuasion in Plato's *Timaeus*." In *Studies in Plato's Metaphysics*, ed. Reginald E. Allen, 421–437. Routledge and Paul Keagan, 1965.

Mortensen, Daniel E. *Wine, Drunkenness, and the Rhetoric of Crisis in Ancient Rome*. University of Michigan Press, 2002.

Moss, Judith. "Pleasure and Illusion in Plato." *Philosophy and Phenomenological Research* 62 (2006): 503–535.

Moss, Judith. "What Is Imitative Poetry and Why Is It Bad?" In *The Cambridge Companion to Plato's Republic*, ed. Giovanni R.F. Ferrari, 415–444. Cambridge University Press, 2007.

Moss, Judith. "Appearances and Calculations: Plato's Division of the Soul." *Oxford Studies in Ancient Philosophy* 34 (2008): 35–68.

Moss, Judith. *Aristotle on the Apparent Good. Perception, Phantasia, Thought and Desire*. Oxford University Press, 2012a.

Moss, Judith. "Pictures and Passions in the *Timaeus* and *Philebus*." In *Plato and the Divided Self*, ed. Rachel Barney, Tad Brennan, and Charles Brittain, 259–280. Cambridge University Press, 2012b.

Moss, Judith. "Soul-Leading: The Unity of the Phaedrus, Again." *Oxford Studies in Ancient Philosophy* 43 (2013): 1–22.

Moss, Judith. "Right Reason in Plato and Aristotle: On the Meaning of *Logos*." *Phronesis* 59, no. 3 (2014): 181–230.

Moss, Judith. "Against Bare Urges and Good-Independent Desires: Appetites in *Republic* IV." In *Psychology and Value in Plato, Aristotle, and Hellenistic Philosophy: The Ninth Keeling Colloquium in Ancient Philosophy*, ed. Fiona Leigh and Margaret Hampson, 67–81. Oxford University Press, 2022.

Most, Glenn W. "Hellenistic Allegory and Early Imperial Rhetoric." In *The Cambridge Companion to Allegory*, ed. Rita Copeland and Peter T. Struck, 25–54. Cambridge University Press, 2010.

Most, Glenn W. "Allegoresis and Etymology." In *Canonical Texts and Scholarly Practices: A Global Comparative Approach*, ed. Anthony Grafton and Glenn Most, 52–74. Cambridge University Press, 2016.

Motto, Anna Lydia, and John R. Clark. "Seneca on Drunkenness." *Rivista di Cultura Classica e Medioevale* 32 (1990): 105–110.

Motto, Anna Lydia, and John R. Clark. "Serenity and Tension in Seneca's *De Tranquillitate Animi.*" In *Essays on Seneca,* ed. Anna Lydia Motto and John R. Clark, 133–154. Peter Lang, 1993.

Mudd, Shaun Anthony. *Constructive Drinking in the Roman Empire: The First to Third Centuries AD*. PhD thesis, University of Exeter, 2015.

Mueller, Ian. "Hippolytus, Aristotle, Basilides." In *Aristotle in Late Antiquity*, ed. Lawrence P. Schrenk, 143–157. Catholic University Press, 1994.

Mueller, Melissa. "Dressing for Dionysus: Statues and Material Mimesis in Euripides' *Bacchae.*" In *Gli oggetti sulla scena teatrale ateniese: Funzione, rappresentazione, comunicazione*, ed. Alessandra Coppola, Caterina Barone, and Monica Salvadori, 57–70. Cleup, 2016.

Muellner, Leonard. *The Anger of Achilles, Menis in Greek Epic*. Cornell University Press, 1996.

Muench, Paul. "Socratic Irony, Plato's Apology, and Kierkegaard's on the Concept of Irony." In *Kierkegaard Studies Yearbook 2009: Kierkegaard's Concept of Irony*, ed. Niels J. Cappelørn and Hermann Deuser, 71–125. De Gruyter, 2009.

Muench, Paul. "Kierkegaard's Socratic Pseudonym: A Profile of Johannes Climacus." In *Kierkegaard's 'Concluding Unscientific Postscript': A Critical Guide*, ed. Rick Anthony Furtak, 25–44. Cambridge University Press, 2010.

Müller, Jörn. "Socrates and Natural Philosophy: The Testimony of Plato's *Phaedo.*" In *Socrates and the Socratic Dialogue*, ed. Alessandro Stavru and Christopher Moore, 348–368. Brill, 2017.

Muramoto, Osamu. "Retrospective Diagnosis of a Famous Historical Figure: Ontological, Epistemic, and Ethical Considerations." *Philosophy, Ethics, and Humanities in Medicine* 9, no. 10 (2014): 1–15.

Muramoto, Osamu. "Solving the Socratic Problem—A Contribution from Medicine." *Mouseion* 15, no. 3 (2018): 445–473.

Murphy, David J. "Isocrates as a Reader of Socratic Dialogues." In *Socrates and the Socratic Dialogue*, ed. Alessandro Stavru and Christopher Moore, 105–124. Brill, 2017.

Murray, James S. "Disputation, Deception, and Dialectic: Plato on the True Rhetoric (Phaedrus 261–266)." *Philosophy and Rhetoric* 21 (1988a): 279–289.

Murray, James S. "Plato on Knowledge, Persuasion and the Art of Rhetoric: *Gorgias* 452e–455a." *Ancient Philosophy* 8 (1988b): 1–10.

Murray, Oswyn. *Sympotica: A Symposium on the Symposium*. Oxford University Press, 1990.

Murray, Oswyn. "The Culture of the *Symposion*." In *A Companion to Archaic Greece,* ed. Kurt A. Raaflaub and Hans van Wees, 508–523. Oxford University Press, 2009.

Murray, Oswyn. "The Greek *Symposion* in History." In *The Symposion: Drinking Greek Style,* ed. Vanessa Cazzato, 11–25. Oxford University Press, 2018. Originally published in *Tria Corda, Scritti in onore di Arnaldo Momigliano,* ed. Emilio Gabba, 257–262. New Press, 1983a.

Murray, Oswyn. "The Symposion as Social Organization." In *The Greek Renaissance of the Eighth Century BC,* ed. Robin Hagg, 195–199. P. Åström, 1983b.

Murray, Oswyn. "Sympotic History." In *The Symposion: Drinking Greek Style,* ed. Vanessa Cazzato, 31–42. Oxford University Press, 2018. Originally published in *Sympotica: A Symposium on the Symposium,* ed. Oswyn Murray, 3–13. Oxford University Press, 1990a.

Murray, Oswyn. "The Affair of the Mysteries: Democracy and the Drinking Group." In *The Symposion: Drinking Greek Style,* ed. Vanessa Cazzato, 237–250. Oxford University Press, 2018. Originally published in *Sympotica: A Symposium on the Symposium,* ed. Oswyn Murray, 149–161. Oxford University Press, 1990b.

Murray, Oswyn. "Histories of Pleasure." In *In Vino Veritas,* ed. Oswyn Murray and Manuela Tecuşan, 3–17. British School at Rome, American Academy in Rome, Istituto Universitario Orientale Napoli, Università di Salerno, and Svenska Institutet i Rom, 1995a.

Murray, Oswyn. "Forms of Sociality." In *The Greeks,* ed. Jean-Pierre Vernant, 218–253. University of Chicago Press, 1995b.

Murray, Oswyn. "Hellenistic Royal Symposia." In *The Symposion: Drinking Greek Style,* ed. Vanessa Cazzato, 271–282. Oxford University Press, 2018. Originally published in *Aspects of Hellenistic Kingship,* ed. Peter Bilde, Troels Engberg-Pedersen, Lise Hannestad, and Jan Zahle, 15–27. Aarhus Universitetsforlag, 1996.

Murray, Oswyn. "*Euphrosynē* and the Psychology of Pleasure." In *The Symposion: Drinking Greek Style,* ed. Vanessa Cazzato, 261–270. Oxford University Press, 2018. Previously unpublished in its current form but presented at a conference on *Cibo per gli uomini, cibo per i dei* at Piazza Armerina in 2005.

Murray, Oswyn. "The *Odyssey* as Performance Poetry." In *The Symposion: Drinking Greek Style,* ed. Vanessa Cazzato, 89–106. Oxford University Press, 2018. Originally published in *Performance, Iconography, Reception: Studies in Honour of Oliver Taplin,* ed. Martin Revermann and Peter Wilson, 161–179. Oxford University Press, 2008.

Murray, Oswyn. "The Chorus of Dionysus: Alcohol and Old Age in the *Laws.*" In *The Symposion: Drinking Greek Style,* ed. Vanessa Cazzato, 251–260. Oxford University Press, 2018. Originally published in *Performance and*

Culture in Plato's Laws, ed. Anastasia-Erasmia Peponi, 109–122, Cambridge University Press, 2013.

Murray, Oswyn. "The Symposion between East and West." In *The Symposion: Drinking Greek Style*, ed. Vanessa Cazzato, 77–88. Oxford University Press, 2018. Originally published in *The Cup of Song: Studies on Poetry and the Symposion*, ed. Vanessa Cazzato, Dirk Obbink, and Enrico Emanuele Prodi, 17–27. Oxford University Press, 2016.

Murray, Oswyn, and Manuela Tecuşan. *In Vino Veritas*. British School at Rome, American Academy in Rome, Istituto Universitario Orientale Napoli, Università di Salerno, and Svenska Institutet i Rom, 1995.

Murray, Penelope. "Poetic Inspiration in Early Greece." *Journal of Hellenic Studies* 101 (1981): 87–100.

Mylonas, George E. *Eleusis and the Eleusinian Mysteries*. Princeton University Press, 1961.

Naddaf, Gerard. "Allegory and the Origins of Philosophy." In *Logos and Muthos: Philosophical Essays on Greek Literature*, ed. William Wians, 99–131. State University of New York Press, 2009.

Nagy, Gregory. "Ancient Greek Poetry, Prophecy, and Concepts of Theory." In *Poetry and Prophecy: The Beginnings of a Literary Tradition*, ed. James L. Kugel, 56–64. Cornell University Press, 1990.

Nathan, Aidan R. *Plato's Use of Irony*. PhD thesis, Sydney University, 2020.

Nauck, Johann August. *Porphyrii philosophi Platonici opuscula selecta*. Georg Olms, 1963. Originally printed by Teubner, 1886.

Nawar, Tamer. "The Stoic Account of Apprehension." *Philosopher's Imprint* 14, no. 29 (2014): 1–21.

Neef, Eberhard. *Lukians Verhältnis zu den Philosophenschulen und seine μίμησις literarischer Vorbilder*. Dissertation Greifswald, Berlin, 1940.

Nehamas, Alexander. "Plato on Imitation and Poetry in *Republic* 10." In *Plato on Beauty, Wisdom, and the Arts*, ed. Julius Moravcsik and Philip Temko, 47–78. Rowman & Littlefield, 1982.

Nehamas, Alexander. *Virtues of Authenticity: Essays on Plato and Socrates*. Princeton University Press, 1999.

Nehamas, Alexander, and Paul Woodruff. *Plato, Symposium*. Hackett, 1989.

Nelson, Max. *The Barbarian's Beverage: A History of Beer in Ancient Europe*. Routledge, 2005.

Nes, Anders, Kristoffer Sundberg, and Sebastian Watzl. "The Perception/Cognition Distinction." *Inquiry* 66, no. 2 (2021): 165–195.

Neumann, Harry. "On the Sophistry of Plato's Pausanias." *Transactions and Proceedings of the American Philological Association* 95 (1964): 261–267.

Newberg, Andrew. *Neurotheology: How Science Can Enlighten Us About Spirituality*. Columbia University Press, 2018.

Newberg, Andrew, Eugene d'Aquilli, and Vince Rause. *Why God Won't Go Away: Brain Science and the Biology of Belief*. Ballantine Books, 2002.

Newman, Sara J. *Aristotle and Style*. Edwin Mellen Press, 2005.

Ní Mheallaigh, Karen. "Ec[h]oing the Ass-Novel: Reading and Desire in *Onos*, *Metamorphoses* and the *Name of the Rose*." *Ramus* 38, no. 1 (2009): 109–122.

Ní Mheallaigh, Karen. *Reading Fiction with Lucian: Fakes, Freaks, and Hyperreality*. Cambridge University Press, 2014.

Nicgorski, Walter. "Cicero's Paradoxes and His Idea of Utility." *Political Theory* 12, no. 4 (1984): 557–578.

Nichols, Mary P. "Socrates' Contest with the Poets in Plato's *Symposium*." *Political Theory* 32, no. 2 (2004): 186–206.

Nichols, Mary P. "Philosophy and Empire: On Socrates and Alcibiades in Plato's 'Symposium.'" *Polity* 39, no. 4 (2007): 502–521.

Niehoff, Maren R. "Philo's Role as a Platonist in Alexandria." *Etude Platoniciennes* 7 (2010): 35–62.

Nietzsche, Friedrich. *The Birth of Tragedy*. Translated by Walter Kaufmann. Vintage, 1872/1967.

Nikolaidis, Anastasios G. "Plutarch's Attitude to Wine." In *Plutarco, Dioniso y el vino. Actas del VI Simposio Español sobre Plutarco: Cádiz, 14–16 de Mayo de 1998*, ed. José Guillermo Montes Cala, Manuel Sánchez Ortiz de Landaluce, and Rafael J. Gallé Cejudo, 337–348. Ediciones Clásicas, 1999.

Nikolaidis, Anastasios G. "Philanthropia as Sociability and Plutarch's Unsociable Heroes." In *Symposion and Philanthropia in Plutarch*, ed. José Ribeiro Ferreira, Delfim Leão, Manuel Tröster, and Paula Barata Dias, 275–288. Imprensa da Universidade de Coimbra, Classica Digitalia, 2009.

Nikolaidis, Anastasios G. "Plutarch's 'Minor' Ethics: Some Remarks on *De garrulitate*, *De curiositate*, and *De vitioso pudore*." In *Virtues for the People: Aspects of Plutarchean Ethics*, ed. Geert Roskam and Luc van der Stockt, 205–222. Peeters, 2011.

Nikolaidis, Anastasios G. "*Quaestiones Convivales*: Plutarch's Sense of Humour as Evidence of his Platonism." *Philologus* 163, no. 1 (2019): 110–128.

Nikolitseas, Michael M. *Parmenides in Apophatic Philosophy*. CreateSpace, 2014.

Nikolopoulou, Kalliopi. "*Parrhesia* as Tragic Structure in Euripides' *Bacchae*." *Epoché: A Journal for the History of Philosophy* 15, no. 2 (2011): 249–261.

Nissinen, Martti. *Ancient Prophecy: Near Eastern, Biblical, and Greek Perspectives*. Oxford University Press, 2017.

Noël, Marie-Pierre. "La persuasion chez Gorgias." In *La rhétorique grecque: actes du colloque «Octave Navarre,»* ed. Jean-Michel Galy and Antoine Thivel, 89–105. Association des publications de la Faculté des lettres de Nice/C.I.D. Diffusion, 1994.

Norris, Richard A. *Gregory of Nyssa: Homilies on the Song of Songs*. Society of Biblical Literature, 2012.

North, Helen F. "The Concept of *Sophrosyne* in Greek Literary Criticism." *Classical Philology* 43, no. 1 (1948): 1–17.

North, Helen F. *Sophrosyne: Self-Knowledge and Self-Restraint in Greek Literature*. Cornell University Press, 1966.

Noussia, M. *A Commentary on Solon's Poems*. PhD thesis, University College London, 1999.

Noussia, Maria. *Solon of Athens: The Poetic Fragments*. Brill, 2010.

Novak, David. *Athens and Jerusalem. God, Humans, and Nature*. University of Toronto Press, 2019.

Nünlist, Rene. *Poetologische Bildersprache in der frühgriechischen Dichtung*. Teubner, 1998.

Nussbaum, Martha. *The Fragility of Goodness. Luck and Ethics in Greek Tragedy and Philosophy*. Cambridge University Press, 1986.

Nussbaum, Martha. *Plato's* Republic: *The Good Society and the Deformation of Desire*. Library of Congress, 1998.

Nussbaum, Martha. *The Fragility of Goodness: Luck and Ethics in Greek Tragedy and Philosophy*. Cambridge University Press, 2007.

Nutton, Vivian. "Aretaios." *Der Neue Pauly*, vol. 1, ed. Hubert Cancik and Helmuth Schneider, 1051–1052. Metzler, 1996.

O'Brien, Carl. "Dramatic Devices and Philosophical Content in Plato's *Symposium*." *Archai* 9 (2012): 73–84.

O'Brien, Carl. "Review of Andrea Capra, Plato's Four Muses: The "Phaedrus" and the Poetics of Philosophy. *Hellenic Studies*, 67. Center for Hellenic Studies, Trustees for Harvard University, 2014." *Bryn Mawr Classical Review* (2015). https://bmcr.brynmawr.edu/2015/2015.06.22/.

O'Brien, Denis. "Plotinus and the Secrets of Ammonius." *Hermathena* 157 (1994): 117–153.

O'Brien, John Maxwell, and Barney L. Rickenbacker. "Alcoholism." In *Oxford Classical Dictionary*, 3rd ed., ed. Simon Hornblower and Anthony Spawforth, 56. Oxford University Press, 1999.

O'Byrne, Anne. "The Excess of Justice: Timaeus and Aristophanes on Sex and the City." *International Studies in Philosophy* 36, no. 1 (2004): 129–142.

O'Donnell, James J. *Augustine: Confessions*. 3 vols. Oxford University Press, 1992.

O'Mahoney, Paul. "Alcibiades Epiphanes: On Two Remarks in Plato's 'Symposium.'" *Classics Ireland* 18 (2011a): 1–2.

O'Mahoney, Paul. "On the 'Hiccupping Episode' in Plato's "Symposium." *The Classical World* 104, no. 2 (2011b): 143–159.

O'Meara, Dominic J. P. *Pythagoras Revived: Mathematics and Philosophy in Late Antiquity*. Oxford University Press, 1997.

O'Meara, Dominic J. P. *Platonic Political Philosophy in Late Antiquity*. Oxford University, 2003.

O'Rourke, Fran, with commentary by Ioanna Patsioti-Tsacpounidi. "Aristotle and the Metaphysics of Metaphor." *Proceedings of the Boston Area Colloquium of Ancient Philosophy* 21, no. 1 (2006): 155–190.

O'Sullivan, Neil. "Aristophanes' First Critic: Cratinus FR. 342K-A." In *Special Issue: Institute of Classical Studies, Bulletin Supplement 49, S87: Greek Drama III: Essays in Honour of Kevin Lee*, ed. John Davidson, Frances Muecke, and Peter Wilson, 163–169. Institute of Classical Studies, 2006.

Ober, Josiah. "I, Socrates . . . The Performative Audacity of Isocrates' *Antidosis*." In *Isocrates and Civic Education*, ed. Takis Poulakos and David Depew, 21–43. Texas University Press, 2004.

Ober, Josiah. "The Trial of Socrates as a Political Trial: Explaining 399 BCE." In *Political Trials in Theory and History*, ed. Jens Meierhenrich and Devin O. Pendas, 65–87. Cambridge University Press, 2017.

Obbink, Dirk. "Early Greek Allegory." In *The Cambridge Companion to Allegory*, ed. Rita Copeland and Peter T. Struck, 15–25. Cambridge University Press, 2010.

Obdrzalek, Suzanne. "Living in Doubt: Carneades' Pithanon Reconsidered." *Oxford Studies in Ancient Philosophy* 31 (2006): 243–280.

Oberhelman, Steven M. "On the Chronology and Pneumatism of Aretaios of Cappadocia." *Aufstieg und Niedergang der römischen Welt* II 37, no. 2 (1994): 941–996.

Ofenloch, Ernst. *Caecilius Calactinus Fragmenta*. Teubner, 1967.

Ohlmeier, Martin D., Karsten Peters, Bert T. Te Wildt, Markus Zedler, Marc Ziegenbein, Birgitt Wiese, Hinderk M. Emrich, and Udo Schneider. "Comorbidity of Alcohol and Substance Dependence with Attention-Deficit/Hyperactivity Disorder (ADHD)." *Alcohol and Alcoholism* 43, no. 3 (2008): 300–304.

Oikonomopoulou, Katerina. "Peripatetic Knowledge in Plutarch's *Table Talk*." In *The Philosopher's Banquet: Plutarch's Table Talk in the Intellectual Culture of the Roman Empire*, ed. Frieda Klotz and K. Oikonomopoulou, 105–130. Oxford University Press, 2011.

Oikonomopoulou, Katerina. "Plutarch's Corpus of Quaestiones in the Tradition of Imperial Greek Encyclopaedism." In *Encyclopaedism from Antiquity to the Renaissance*, ed. Jason König and Greg Woolf, 129–153. Cambridge University Press, 2013.

Oikonomopoulou, Katerina. "Plutarch in Gellius and Apuleius." In *Brill's Companion to the Reception of Plutarch*, ed. Sophia Xenophontos and Katerina Oikonomopoulou, 37–55. Brill, 2019.

Ollier, François. *Xénophon Banquet, Apologie de Socrate*. Les Belles Lettres, 1961.

Olson, S. Douglas. *Aristophanes' Peace*. Oxford University Press, 1998.

Olson, S. Douglas. "Athenaeus' 'Fragments' of Non-Fragmentary Prose Authors and Their Implications." *American Journal of Philology* 139, no. 3 (2018): 423–450.

Opsomer, Jan. "Plutarch's Platonism Revisited." In *L'Eredità Platonica: Studi sul platonismo da Arcesilao a Proclo*, ed. Mauro Bonazzi and Vincenza Celluprica, 161–200. Bibliopolis, 2005.

Opsomer, Jan. "Plutarch and the Stoics." In *A Companion to Plutarch*, ed. Mark Beck, 88–103. Wiley-Blackwell, 2013.

Orfanos, Charalambos. "Ecclésia vs banquet." In *Symposium: banquet et représentationsen Grèce et à Rome*, ed. Charalampos Orfanos and Jean-Claude Carrière, 203–217. Presses universitaires du Mirail, 2003.

Orfanos, Charalambos, and Jean-Claude Carrière. *Symposium: banquet et représentationsen Grèce et à Rome*. Presses universitaires du Mirail, 2003.

Ornaghi, Massimiliano. "Note di onomastica comica: Cratino (POxy IV 663; PCG Cratinus Fr. 342; Fr. 502)." *Quaderni del Dipartimento di filologia linguistica e tradizione classica A. Rostagni* 5 (2006): 8–111.

Ortiz de Landazuri, Manuel C. "The Development of Self-Knowledge in Plato's Philosophy." *Logos: Anales del Seminario de Metafísica* 48 (2015): 123–140.

Owen, Gwilym Ellis Lane. "The Place of the Timaeus in Plato's Dialogues." *The Classical Quarterly* 3 (1953): 79–95.

Owen, Sara. "The 'Thracian' Landscape of Archaic Thasos." In *Inside the City in the Greek World: Studies of Urbanism from the Bronze Age to the Hellenistic Period*, ed. Sara Owen and Laura Preston, 85–98. Oxford University Press, 2009.

Pache, Corinne Ondine. "Barbarian Bond: Thracian Bendis among the Athenians." In *Between Magic and Religion: Interdisciplinary Studies in Ancient Mediterranean Religion and Society*, ed. Sulochana Ruth Asirvatham, Corinne Ondine Pache, and John Watrous, 3–11. Rowman & Littlefield, 2001.

Padel, Ruth. "Madness in Fifth Century (BC) Athenian Tragedy." In *Indigenous Psychologies: The Anthropology of the Self*, ed. Paul Heelas and Andrew Lock, 105–131. Academic Press, 1981.

Padel, Ruth. *In and Out of the Mind. Greek Images of the Tragic Self*. Princeton University Press, 1992.

Padilla, Mark. "Theatrical and Social Renewal in Aristophanes' *Frogs*." *Arethusa* 25 (1992): 359–381.

Page, Denys L. *Further Greek Epigrams*. Cambridge University Press, 1981.

Palumbo, Lidia, and Anna Motta. "On the Desire for Drink in Plato and the Platonist Tradition." In *Emotions in Plato*, ed. Laura Candiotto and Olivier Renaut, 123–146. Brill, 2020.

Panaccio, Claude. *Mental Language: From Plato to William of Ockham*. Translated by Joshua P. Hochschild and Meredith K. Ziebart. Fordham University Press, 2017.

Pangle, Thomas L. *The Laws of Plato: Translation with Notes and Interpretive Essay*. Basic Books, 1980.

Papageorgiou, Nikolaos. "Ambiguities in 'Kreitton Logos?'" *Mnemosyne* 57, no. 3 (2014): 284–294.

Papakonstantinou, Zinon. "Wine and Wine Drinking in the Homeric World." *L'Antiquité Classique* 78 (2009): 1–24.

Papakonstantinou, Zinon. "A Delight and a Burden (HES., *Sc.* 400): Wine and Wine-Drinking in Archaic Greece." *Ancient Society* 42 (2012): 1–32.

Parker, Robert. *Athenian Religion: A History.* Oxford University Press, 1996.

Parry, Hugh. "An Interpretation of Simonides 4 (Diehl)." *Transactions and Proceedings of the American Philological Association* 96 (1965): 297–320.

Parsons, Michael. "Self-knowledge Refused and Accepted: A Psychoanalytic Perspective on the *Bacchae* and the *Oedipus at Colonus.*" *Bulletin of the Institute of Classical Studies* 35 (1988): 1–14.

Pasnau, Robert. *The Cambridge Translations of Medieval Philosophical Texts: Volume 3, Mind and Knowledge.* Cambridge University Press, 2002.

Passavanti, Sandro. "Alterazioni sensoriali e delirio dai Presocratici al *Teeteto* di Platone. Medicina, sofistica, filosofia." In *Oeconomia Corporis: The Body's Normal and Pathological Constitution at the Intersection of Philosophy and Medicine,* ed. Chiara Beneduce and Denise Vincenti, 9–20. Edizioni ETS, 2018.

Passavanti, Sandro. "Crise de la mantique et pathologie de la perception dans l'*Oreste* d'Euripide." In *La Poésie dramatique comme discours de savoir,* ed. Marie-Laurence Desclos, 171–210. Classiques Garnier, 2020.

Paul, George. "*Symposia* and *Deipna* in Plutarch's *Lives* and in Other Historical Writings." In *Dining in a Classical Context,* ed. William J. Slater, 157–170. University of Michigan Press, 1991.

Pavlos, Panagiotis G. "Theurgy in Dionysius the Areopagite." In *Platonism and Christian Thought in Late Antiquity,* ed. Panagiotis G. Pavlos, Lars Fredrik Janby, Eyjólfur Kjalar Emilsson, and Torstein Theodor Tollefsen, 151–180. Routledge, 2019.

Payne, Andrew. "The Refutation of Agathon: *Symposium* 199c–201c." *Ancient Philosophy* 19 (1999): 53–74.

Pearson, Giles. *Aristotle on Desire.* Cambridge University Press, 2012.

Peirce, Sarah. "Visual Language and Concepts of Cult on the 'Lenaia Vases.'" *Classical Antiquity* 17, no. 1 (1998): 59–95.

Pelling, Christopher. "Introduction." In *Symposion and Philanthropia in Plutarch,* ed. José Ribeiro Ferreira, Delfim Leão, Manuel Tröster, and Paula Barata Dias, iii–viii. Imprensa da Universidade de Coimbra, Classica Digitalia, 2009.

Pellizer, Ezio. "Outlines of a Morphology of Sympotic Entertainment." In *Sympotica: A Symposium on the Symposium,* ed. Oswyn Murray, 177–184. Oxford University Press, 1990.

Pelosi, Francesco. *Plato on Music, Soul and Body.* Cambridge University Press, 2010.

Peltonen, Tuomo. "Transcendence, Consciousness and Order: Towards a Philosophical Spirituality of Organization in the Footsteps of Plato and Eric Voegelin." *Philosophy of Management* 18 (2019): 231–247.

Pender, Elizabeth E. "Plato on Metaphors and Models." In *Metaphor, Allegory and the Classical Tradition,* ed. George R. Boys-Stones, 55–81. Oxford University Press, 2003.

Pender, Elizabeth. "A Transfer of Energy: Lyric Eros in *Phaedrus*." In *Plato and the Poets*, ed. P. Destrée and Fritz-Gregor Herrmann, 327–348. Brill, 2011.

Pender, Stephen. "Heat and Moisture, Rhetoric and *Spiritus*." *Intellectual History Review* 24, no. 1 (2014): 89–112.

Pépin, Jean. *Mythe et Allégorie: Les Origines grecques et les contestations Judaeo-Chrétiennes*. Études Augustiniennes, 1958.

Perczel, Istvan. "God as Monad and Henad: Dionysus the Areopagite and the *Peri Archôn*." In *Origene e la Tradizione Alessandrina*, ed. Lorenzo Perrone, Paolo Bernardino, and Diego Marchini, 1193–1212. Peeters, 2003.

Perczyk, Cecilia J. "Cassandra's Madness in Aeschylus' *Agamemnon*." *Greek, Roman, and Byzantine Studies* 63 (2023): 245–266.

Perdicoyianni-Paléologou, Helen. "The Vocabulary of Madness from Homer to Hippocrates. Part 1: The Verbal Group of μαίνομαι." *History of Psychiatry* 20, no. 3 (2009a): 311–39.

Perdicoyianni-Paléologou, Helen. "The Vocabulary of Madness from Homer to Hippocrates. Part 2: The Verbal Group of βακχεύω, and the Noun λύσσα." *History of Psychiatry* 20, no. 4 (2009b): 457–67.

Perilli, Lorenzo. "Alcmeone di Crotone tra filosofia e scienza." *Quaderni Urbinati di Cultura Classica* 69 (2001): 55–79.

Périllié, Jean-Luc. "Corybantic Rituals of Socratic Mysteries and the Doctrine of Principles." *Revue de métaphysique et de morale* 103, no. 3 (2019): 267–285.

Persinger, Michael A. *Neurospsychological Bases of God Beliefs*. Bloomsbury, 1987.

Persinger, Michael A. "The Neuropsychiatry of Paranormal Experiences." *Neuropsychiatric Practice and Opinion* 13 (2001): 515–524.

Perysinakis, Ioannis N. "From the Ancient Quarrel Between Philosophy and Poetry: Archaic Moral Values and Political Behaviour in Aristophanes' *Frogs*." In *Poet and Orator: A Symbiotic Relationship in Democratic Athens*, ed. Andreas Markantonatos and Eleni Volonaki, 249–268. De Gruyter, 2019.

Peterson, Anna. *Laughter in the Exchange: Lucian's Invention of the Comic Dialogue*. PhD thesis, Ohio State University, 2010. https://etd.ohiolink.edu/.

Peterson, Anna. "Pushing Forty: The Platonic Significance of References to Age in Lucian's *Double Indictment* and *Hermotimus*." *The Classical Quarterly* 68, no. 2 (2018): 621–633.

Peterson, Anna. *Laughter on the Fringes: The Reception of Old Comedy in the Imperial Greek World*. Oxford University Press, 2019a.

Peterson, Anna. "Review of Mario Telò: Aristophanes and the Cloak of Comedy: Affect, Aesthetics, and the Canon, Chicago, 2016." *Comparative Drama* 53, no. 1/2 (2019b): 158–161.

Petraki, Zacharoula. "Painting, Ethics, and Ontology in Plato's *Republic 5*." *CHS Research Bulletin* 3, no. 2 (2015). http://nrs.harvard.edu/urn-3:hlnc.essay:-PetrakiZ.Painting_Ethics_and_Ontology.2015.

Petridou, Georgia. *Divine Epiphany in Greek Literature and Culture*. Oxford University Press, 2015.

Petrova, Maya. "Aristotle on Wine and Intoxication." In *Revisiting Aristotle's Fragments: New Essays on the Fragments of Aristotle's Lost Works*, ed. António Pedro Mesquita, Simon Noriega-Olmos, and Christopher John Ignatius Shields, 83–90. De Gruyter, 2020.

Petrucci, Federico Maria. "There Should Be a Virtue for Everyone. Non-Philosophical Virtue in the *Phaedo*." In *Phaedo: Selected Papers from the XI Symposium Platonicum*, ed. Gabriele Cornelli, Francisco Bravo, and Thomas M. Robinson, 166–171. Akademia Verlag, 2019.

Pfefferkorn, Julia. "Shame and Virtue in Plato's *Laws*: Two Kinds of Fear and the Drunken Puppet." In *Emotions in Plato*, ed. Laura Candiotto and Olivier Renaut, 252–269. Brill, 2020.

Pfefferkorn, Julia. "The Three Choruses of Plato's *Laws* and their Function in the Dialogue: A New Approach." *Phronesis* 66, no. 4 (2021a): 335–365.

Pfefferkorn, Julia. "Plato's Dancing City: Why is Mimetic Choral Dance so Prominent in the *Laws*?" In *Platonic Mimesis Revisited*, ed. Julia Pfefferkorn and Antonino Spinelli, 335–358. Academia Verlag, 2021b.

Pfefferkorn, Julia. *Platons tanzende Stadt. Moralpsychologie und Chortanz in den Nomoi*. Brill, 2022.

Pfeiffer, Rudolf. *The Fragments of Callimachus*. Clarendon Press, 1949.

Phillips, Thomas E. "'Will the Wise Person Get Drunk?' The Background of the Human Wisdom in Luke 7:35 and Matthew 11:19." *Journal of Biblical Literature* 127, no. 2 (2008): 385–396.

Pickard-Cambridge, Arthur Wallace. *Dithyramb, Tragedy and Comedy*. 2nd revised edition by Thomas Bertram Lonsdale Webster. Clarendon Press, 1962.

Picone, Giusto. *Le regole del beneficio. Commento tematico a Seneca, De beneficiis, libro I*. Palumbo, 2013.

Pietruschka, Ute. "Syriac Reception of Socrates." In *Brill's Companion to the Reception of Socrates*, ed. Christopher Moore, 518–544. Brill, 2019.

Pigeaud, Jackie. *La maladie de l'âme: étude sur la relation de l'âme et du corps dans la tradition médico-philosophique antique*. Les Belles Lettres, 1989.

Pires, Pobert Brose. *Epikomios Hymnos: investigações sobre a performance dos epinícios pindáricos*. PhD thesis, Faculdade de Filosofia, Letras e Ciências Humanas, Universidade de São Paulo, 2014.

Pizzato, Mark. *Ghosts of Theatre and Cinema in the Brain*. Palgrave Macmillan, 2006.

Pizzato, Mark. *Inner Theatres of Good and Evil: The Mind's Staging of Gods, Angels and Devils*. McFarland, 2011.

Planinc, Zdravko. *Plato's Political Philosophy: Prudence in the Republic and the Laws*. University of Missouri Press, 1991.

Planinc, Zdravko. *Plato Through Homer: Poetry and Philosophy in the Cosmological Dialogues*. University of Missouri Press, 2003.

Platt, Verity Jane. *Facing the Gods: Epiphany and Representation in Graeco-Roman Art, Literature and Religion*. Cambridge University Press, 2011.

Platter, Charles. "The Uninvited Guest: Aristophanes in Bakhtin's 'History of Laughter.'" *Arethusa* 26, no. 2 (1993): 201–216.

Platter, Charles. "Review: Plato's Four Muses: The *Phaedrus* and the Poetics of Philosophy by Andrea Capra." *Classical World* 110, no. 3 (2017): 430–431.

Pleket, Henri Willy. "Thasos and the Popularity of the Athenian Empire." *Historia* 12, no. 1 (1963): 70–77.

Pociña, Andrés. "Virtualités dramatiques d'un banquet effroyable: Thyeste dans la tragédie romaine." In *Symposium: banquet et représentationsen Grèce et à Rome*, ed. Charalampos Orfanos and Jean-Claude Carrière, 251–270. Presses universitaires du Mirail, 2003.

Politis, Vasilis. "Aporia and Searching in the Early Plato." In *Remembering Socrates: Philosophical Essays*, ed. Judson Lindsay and Vasilēs Karasmanis, 88–109. Clarendon Press, 2006.

Politis, Vasilis. "*Aporia* and Sceptical Argument in Plato's Early Dialogues." In *The Aporetic Tradition in Ancient Philosophy*, ed. George Karamanolis and Vasilis Politis, 48–66. Cambridge University Press, 2018.

Polito, Roberto. "Competence Conflicts between Philosophy and Medicine: Caelius Aurelianus and the Stoics on Mental Diseases." *The Classical Quarterly* 66, no. 1 (2016): 358–369.

Pomeroy, Arthur. *Epitome of Stoic Ethics Arius Didymus*. Society of Biblical Literature Press, 1999.

Pomeroy, Sarah B. *Xenophon Oeconomicus: A Social and Historical Commentary*. Clarendon Press, 1994.

Porres Caballero, Silvia. "Maenadic Ecstasy in Greece: Fact or Fiction?" In *Redefining Dionysos*, ed. Alberto Bernabé, Miguel Herrero de Jáuregui, Ana Isabel Jiménez San Cristóbal, and Raquel Martín Hernández, 159–184. De Gruyter, 2013.

Porres Caballero, Silvia. "La dionisización del dios Pan (The dionization of the god Pan)." *Synthesis* 19 (2012): 63–82.

Porter, James I. *The Sublime in Antiquity*. Cambridge University Press, 2016.

Posar, Annio, and Paola Visconti. "Sensory Abnormalities in Children with Autism Spectrum Disorder." *Jornal de Pediatria* (Rio J) 94 (2018): 342–350.

Pötscher, Walter. *Theophrastos. ΠΕΡΙ ΕΥΣΕΒΕΙΑΣ*. Brill, 1964.

Potter, Paul. *Hippocrates. Affections. Diseases 1. Diseases 2*. LCL 472. Harvard University Press, 1988.

Powell, Jonathan G. F. "Cicero's Reading of Plato's *Republic*." *Bulletin of the Institute of Classical Studies* Supplement, no. 117 (2013): 35–57.

Power, Timothy. *The Culture of Kitharôidia*. Centre for Hellenic Studies/Harvard University Press, 2010.

Pownall, Frances. "Critias' Commemoration of Athens." *Mouseion* 8 (2008a): 1–22.

Pownall, Frances. "Critias on the Aetiology of the Kottabos Game." In *L'étiologie dans la pensée antique*, ed. Martine Chassignet, 17–33. Brepols, 2008b.

Pownall, Frances. "Critias in Xenophons's *Hellenica*." *Scripta Classica Israelica* 31 (2012): 1–17.

Pragglejaz Group. "MIP: A Method for Identifying Metaphorically Used Words in Discourse." *Metaphor and Symbol* 22, no. 1 (2007): 1–39.

Pratt, Catherine E. *Oil, Wine, and the Cultural Economy of Ancient Greece: From the Bronze Age to the Archaic Era*. Cambridge University Press, 2021.

Prauscello, Lucia. "Comedy and Comic Discourse in Plato's *Laws*." In *Greek Comedy and the Discourse of Genres*, ed. Emmanuela Bakola, Lucia Prauscello, and Mario Teló, 319–342. Cambridge University Press, 2013.

Prauscello, Lucia. *Performing Citizenship in Plato's Laws*. Cambridge University Press, 2014.

Price, Anthony W. "Plato on the Object of Thirst: Comments on Jessica Moss, 'Against Bare Urges and Good-Independent Desires: Appetites in Republic IV.'" In *Psychology and Value in Plato, Aristotle, and Hellenistic Philosophy: The Ninth Keeling Colloquium in Ancient Philosophy*, ed. Fiona Leigh and Margaret Hampson, 105–113. Oxford University Press, 2022.

Prior, William J. "The Historicity of Plato's *Apology*." *Polis: The Journal for Ancient Greek and Roman Political Thought* 18, no. 1–2 (2001): 41–57.

Prior, William J. "The Portrait of Socrates in Plato's *Symposium*." *Oxford Studies in Ancient Philosophy* 31 (2006): 137–166.

Prioreschi, Plinio. *A History of Medicine: Roman Medicine*. Horatius Press, 1996.

Pritchard, James B. *The Ancient Near East. Vol. 2: A New Anthology of Texts and Pictures*. Princeton University Press, 1975.

Provenza, Antonietta. "Madness and Bestialization in Euripides' *Heracles*." *The Classical Quarterly* 63, no. 1 (2013): 68–93.

Puchner, Martin. *The Drama of Ideas: Platonic Provocations in Theater and Philosophy*. Oxford University Press, 2010.

Purcell, Nicholas. "Wine and Wealth in Ancient Italy." *Journal of Roman Studies* 75 (1985): 1–19.

Rademaker, Adriaan. *Sophrosyne and the Rhetoric of Self-Restraint. Polysemy and Persuasive Use of an Ancient Greek Value Term*. Brill, 2005.

Rákosi, Csilla. "On the Impact of Aptness, Conventionality and Familiarity on Metaphor Processing from a Meta-analytical Point of View." *Journal of Research Design and Statistics in Linguistics and Communication Science* 6, no. 1 (2020): 55–106.

Ramelli, Ilaria L. E. "Origen, Patristic Philosophy, and Christian Platonism: Re-Thinking the Christianization of Hellenism." *Vigiliae Christianae* 63 (2009): 217–263.

Ramelli, Ilaria L. E. "The Philosophical Stance of Allegory in Stoicism and its Reception in Platonism, Pagan and Christian: Origen in Dialogue with the Stoics and Plato." *International Journal of the Classical Traditions* 18 (2011): 335–371.

Ramelli, Ilaria L. E. "Origen and the Platonic Tradition." *Religions* 8, no. 2 (2017): 21. https://www.mdpi.com/2077-1444/8/2/21.

Ramelli, Ilaria L. E. "Annaeus Cornutus and the Stoic Allegorical Tradition: Meaning, Sources, and Impact." *Aetia* 8, no. 2 (2018). doi.org/10.4000/aitia.2882.

Ramelli, Ilaria L. E. "Some Aspects of the Reception of the Platonic Tradition in Origen." In *Later Platonists and their Heirs among Christians, Jews, and Muslims*, ed. Eva Anagnostou-Laoutides and Ken Parry, 61–86. Brill, 2023.

Ransome, Hilda M. *The Sacred Bee in Ancient Times and Folklore*. Allen and Unwin, 1939.

Rasinus, Tuomas, Troel Engberg-Pedersen, and Ismo Dunderberg. *Stoicism in Early Christianity*. Baker Academic, 2010.

Rawles, Richard. "Aristophanes' Simonides: Lyric Models for Praise and Praise." In *Greek Comedy and the Discourse of Genres*, ed. Emmanuela Bakola, Lucia Prauscello, and Mario Teló, 175–204. Cambridge University Press, 2013.

Reames, Robin, and Courtney Sloey. "Writing the Manic Subject: Rhetorical Passivity in Plato's *Phaedrus*." *Philosophy and Rhetoric* 54, no. 1 (2021): 1–24.

Reece, Bryan C. "Out of Thin Air? Diogenes on Causal Explanation." In *Heat, Pneuma, and Soul in Ancient Philosophy and Science*, ed. Hynek Bartoš and Colin Guthrie King, 106–121. Cambridge University Press, 2020.

Reesor, Margret E. "Anaxagoras and Epicurus." In *Essays in Ancient Greek Philosophy 2*, ed. John P. Anton and Anthony Preus, 93–106. State University of New York Press, 1983.

Regali, Mario. "The Mask of Dialogue: On the Unity of Socrates' Characterization in Plato's Dialogues." In *Second Sailing: Alternative Perspectives on Plato*, ed. Debra Nails and Harold Tarrant, 125–148. Societas Scientiarum Fennica, 2015.

Reid, Heather. *Athletics and Philosophy in the Ancient World: Contests of Virtue*. Routledge, 2011.

Reis, Burkhard. *Der Platoniker Albinos und sein sogenannter Prologos: Prolegomena, Überlieferungsgeschichte, kritische Edition und Übersetzung*. Reichert, 1999.

Reis, Burkhard. "Curricula vix mutantur. Zur Vorgeschichte der neuplatonischen Lektüreprogramme." In *The Libraries of the Neoplatonists*, ed. Cristina D'Ancona Costa, 99–120. Brill, 2007.

Relihan, Joel C. "Rethinking the History of the Literary Symposium." *Illinois Classical Studies* 17, no. 2 (1992): 213–244.

Relihan, Joel C. *Ancient Menippean Satire*. John Hopkins University Press, 1993.

Renaud, François. "Return to Plato and Transition to Middle Platonism in Cicero." In *Brill's Companion to the Reception of Plato in Antiquity*, ed. Harold Tarrant, Danielle A. Layne, Dirk Baltzly, and François Renaud, 72–89. Brill, 2018.

Renaut, Olivier. "Emotions and Rationality in the *Timaeus* (Ti. 42a–b, 69c–72e)." In *Emotions in Plato*, ed. Laura Candiotto and Olivier Renaut, 103–122. Brill, 2020.

Reydams-Schils, Gretchen. *Demiurge and Providence. Stoic and Platonist Readings of Plato's Timaeus*. Brepols, 1999.

Reydams-Schils, Gretchen. *The Roman Stoics: Self, Responsibility, and Affection*. University of Chicago Press, 2005.

Reydams-Schils, Gretchen. "Seneca's Platonism: The Soul and Its Divine Origin." In *Ancient Models of Mind: Studies in Human and Divine Rationality*, ed. Andrea Nightingale and David Sedley, 196–215. Cambridge University Press, 2010.

Rhodes, Paul. "Nothing to Do with Democracy: Athenian Drama and the Polis." *Journal of Hellenic Studies* 123 (2003): 104–119.

Rice, Ellen E. *The Grand Procession of Ptolemy Philadelphus*. Oxford University Press, 1983.

Richardson, Ernest Cushing. *Hieronymus, Liber de viris illustribus*. Hinrichs, 1896.

Richardson-Hay, Christine. "Drunk on False Argument—Seneca's *Epistulae Morales*, Epistle 83." *Prudentia* 33, no. 1 (2001): 12–40.

Richardson-Hay, Christine. "Dinner at Seneca's Table: The Philosophy of Food." *Greece & Rome*, 2nd series 56, no. 1 (2009): 71–96.

Richter, Gisela M. A. *The Portraits of the Greeks*. 3 vols. Phaidon Press, 1965.

Ricoeur, Paul. *La métaphore vive* [*The Living Metaphor*]. Editions du Seuil, 1975.

Ricoeur, Paul. *The Rule of Metaphor: The Creation of Meaning in Language*. Translated by Robert Czerny, Katheen McLaughlin, and John Costello. Toronto University Press, 1977.

Ricoeur, Paul. "The Metaphorical Process as Cognition, Imagination, and Feeling." *Critical Inquiry* 5, no. 1 (1978): 143–159.

Ricoeur, Paul. *Hermeneutics and the Human Sciences*. Edited and introduction by John B. Thompson. Cambridge University Press, 1981.

Ricoeur, Paul. *Fallible Man: Philosophy of the Will*. Fordham University Press, 1986.

Ricoeur, Paul. "Between Rhetoric and Poetics." In *Essays on Aristotle's Rhetoric*, ed. Amelie Oksenberg Rorty, 324–384. University of California Press, 1996.

Riedweg, Christoph. *Mysterienterminologie bei Platon, Philon und Klemens von Alexandrien*. De Gruyter, 1987.

Rinella, Michael A. "Supplementing the Ecstatic: Plato, the Eleusinian Mysteries, and the *Phaedrus*." *Polis* 17, no. 1/2 (2000): 61–78.

Rinella, Michael A. "Revisiting the Pharmacy: Plato, Derrrida, and the Morality of Political Deceit." *Polis* 24, no. 1 (2007): 134–153.

Rinella, Michael A. *Pharmakon: Plato, Drug Culture, and Identity in Ancient Athens*. Lexington Books, 2010.

Rist, John. "Seneca and Stoic Orthodoxy." *Aufstieg und Niedergang der romischen Welt* II 36, no. 3 (1989): 1993–2013.

Rix, Keith J. B. "'Alcohol Intoxication' or 'Drunkenness': Is There a Difference?" *Medicine, Science and the Law* 29, no. 2 (1989): 100–106.

Robinson, Thomas M. *Contrasting Arguments: An Edition of the Dissoi Logoi.* Arno Press, 1979.

Robinson, Thomas M. *Plato's Psychology.* University of Toronto Press, 1995.

Robinson, Thomas M. "The Defining Features of Mind-body Dualism in the Writings of Plato." In *Psyche and Soma: Physicians and Metaphysicians on the Mind-body Problem from Antiquity to Enlightenment*, ed. John P. Wright and Paul Potter, 37–56. Oxford University Press, 2000.

Rodrigo, Pierre. "The Dynamic of *Hexis* in Aristotle's Philosophy." *Journal of the British Society for Phenomenology* 42, no. 1 (2011): 6–17.

Roig Lanzillotta, Lautaro. "Ancient Greek Patterns of Knowledge Transmission and Their Continuity in Gnostic Esotericism." In *Sharing and Hiding Religious Knowledge in Judaism, Christianity and Islam*, ed. Mladen Popovic, Lautaro Roig Lanzillotta, and Clare Wilde, 121–144. De Gruyter, 2018.

Roller, Matthew. "The Dialogue in Seneca's Dialogues (and Other Moral Essays)." In *The Cambridge Companion to Seneca*, ed. Shadi Bartsch and Alessandro Schiesaro, 4–67. Cambridge University Press, 2015.

Rolleston, John Davy. "Alcoholism in Classical Antiquity." *British Journal of Inebriety (Alcoholism and Drug Addiction)* 24, no. 3 (1927): 100–120.

Roochnik, David. "What Is Theoria? *Nicomachean Ethics* Book 10.7–8." *Classical Philology* 104, no. 1 (2009): 69–82.

Roochnik, David. *Eat, Drink, Think What Ancient Greece Can Tell Us about Food and Wine.* Bloomsbury, 2020.

Rorem, Paul. *Eriugena's Commentary on the Dionysian Celestial Hierarchy.* Pontifical Institute of Medieval Studies, 2005.

Roscher, Wilhelm Heinrich. *Nektar und Ambrosia: Mit einem Anhang über die Grundbedeutung der Aphrodite und Athene.* Teubner, 1883.

Roselli, Amneris. "Areteo di Cappadocia lettore di Ippocrate." *Studies in Ancient Medicine* 31 (2005): 413–432.

Rosen, Ralph Mark. "Cratinus' *Pytine* and the Construction of the Comic Self." In *The Rivals of Aristophanes: Studies in Athenian Old Comedy*, ed. David Harvey and John Wilkins, 23–39. Duckworth and the Classical Press of Wales, 2000.

Rosen, Ralph Mark. "Aristophanes, Old Comedy and Greek Tragedy." In *A Companion to Tragedy*, ed. Rebecca W. Bushnell, 251–268. Wiley-Blackwell, 2005.

Rosen, Ralph Mark. *Making Mockery: The Poetics of Ancient Satire.* Oxford University Press, 2007.

Rosen, Ralph Mark. "Reconsidering the Reperformance of Aristophanes' *Frogs.*" *Trends in Classics* 7, no. 2 (2015): 237–256.

Roskam, Geert. "Educating the Young . . . Over Wine? Plutarch, Calvenus Taurus, and Favorinus as Convivial Teachers." In *Symposion and Philanthropia in*

Plutarch, ed. José Ribeiro Ferreira, Delfim Leão, Manuel Tröster, and Paula Barata Dias, 369–384. Imprensa da Universidade de Coimbra, Classica Digitalia, 2009.

Roskam, Geert. "Plutarch's 'Socratic Symposia'; The Symposia of Plato and Xenophon as Literary Models in the *Quaestiones convivales*." *Athenaeum* 98 (2010): 45–70.

Roskam, Geert. "Plutarch's Reception of Socrates." In *Socrates and the Socratic Dialogue*, ed. Alessandro Stavru and Christopher Moore, 744–759. Brill, 2017.

Roskam, Geert. "Cupid's Swan from the Academy (De Plat. 1.1, 183): Apuleius' Reception of Plato." In *Brill's Companion to the Reception of Plato in Antiquity*, ed. Harold Tarrant, Danielle A. Layne, Dirk Baltzly, and François Renaud, 156–170. Brill, 2018.

Roskam, Geert. "How to Date the Timeless? The Difficult Problem of the Pseudo-Pythagorean Treatises *On Kingship*." *Ktéma: civilisations de l'Orient, de la Grece et de Rome Antiques* 45 (2020): 125–141.

Rösler, Wolfgang. "Mnemosyne in the Symposion." In *Sympotica: a Symposium on Symposion*, ed. Oswyn Murray, 230–237. Oxford University Press, 1990.

Rösler, Wolfgang. "Wine and Truth in the Greek Symposion." In *In Vino Veritas*, ed. Oswyn Murray and Manuela Tecuşan, 106–112. British School at Rome, American Academy in Rome, Istituto Universitario Orientale Napoli, Università di Salerno, and Svenska Institutet i Rom, 1995.

Rossetti, Livio. "The Rhetoric of Socrates." *Philosophy and Rhetoric* 22, no. 4 (1989): 225–238.

Roth, Marty. *Drunk the Night Before: An Anatomy of Intoxication*. University of Minnesota Press, 2005.

Roth, Paul. "Teiresias as Mantis and Intellectual in Euripides' *Bacchae*." *Transactions of the American Philological Association* 114 (1984): 59–69.

Rothstein, Andrea. "Critias' Invective against Archilochus." *Classical Philology* 102, no. 2 (2007): 139–154.

Rothwell, Kenneth S. Jr. *Nature, Culture, and the Origins of Greek Comedy A Study of Animal Choruses*. Cambridge University Press, 2006.

Rouget, Gilbert. *La musique et la trance*. Éditions Gallimard, 1990.

Rowe, Christopher J. "Plato on the Sophists as Teachers of Virtue." *History of Political Thought* 4, no. 3 (1983): 409–427.

Rowe, Christopher J. *Plato Phaedrus*. Aris and Phillips, 1986.

Rowe, Christopher J. "The *Lysis* and the *Symposium*: Aporia and *Euporia*?" In *Plato: Euthydemus, Lysis Charmides: Proceeding of the V 'Symposium Platonicum,' Selected Papers*, ed. Thomas M. Robinson and Luc Brisson, 204–216. Akademia Verlag, 2000.

Rowe, Christopher J. "The *Symposium* as a Socratic Dialogue." In *Plato's Symposium: Issues in Interpretation and Reception*, ed. James Lesher, Debra Nails, and

Frisbee Sheffield, 9–22. Harvard University Press (on behalf of the Center for Hellenic Studies), 2006.

Rowe, Christopher J. "Aristotle and Socrates in the *Eudemian Ethics* on the Naturalness of Goodness." In *Ancient Ethics and the Natural World*, ed. Barbara M. Sattler and Ursula Coope, 203–217. Cambridge University Press, 2021.

Ruben, Tanja. *Le discours comme image. Énonciation, récit et connaissance dans le Hmée-Critias de Platon.* Les Belles Lettres, 2016.

Ruck, Carl. "Duality and the Madness of Herakles." *Arethusa* 9, no. 1 (1976): 53–75.

Rudebusch, George. "Socrates, Wisdom and Pedagogy." In *Socratic, Platonic and Aristotelian Studies: Essays in Honor of Gerasimos Santas*, ed. Georgios Anagnostopoulos, 165–184. Springer, 2011.

Runia, David. *Philo of Alexandria and the Timaeus of Plato.* Brill, 1986.

Runia, David. "Was Philo a Middle-Platonist? A Difficult Question Revisited." *Studia Philonica Annual* 5 (1993a): 112–140.

Runia, David. *Philo in Early Christian Literature: A Survey.* Fortress Press, 1993b.

Runia, David, and Albert Geljon. *Philo of Alexandria On Planting: Introduction, Translation, and Commentary.* Brill, 2019.

Russell, Daniel C. "Virtue as 'Likeness to God' in Plato and Seneca." *Journal of the History of Philosophy* 42, no. 3 (2004): 241–260.

Russell, Daniel C. *Plato on Pleasure and the Good Life.* Oxford University Press, 2005.

Russell, Brigette Ford. "Wine, Women, and the Polis: Gender and the Formation of the City-State in Archaic Rome." *Greece & Rome* 50, no. 1 (2003): 77–84.

Rutherford, Ian. "Theoria and Darśan: Pilgrimage and Vision in Greece and India." *The Classical Quarterly* 50, no. 1 (2000): 133–146.

Rutherford, Ian. "Song-Dance and State-Pilgrimage at Athens." In *Music and the Muses: The Culture of Mousikē in the Classical Athenian City*, ed. Penelope Murray and Peter Wilson, 67–90. Oxford University Press, 2004.

Rutherford, Ian. *State Pilgrims and Sacred Observers in Ancient Greece: A Study of Theoria and Theoroi.* Cambridge University Press, 2013.

Sabbah, Guy. "Noms et descriptions de maladies chez Cassius Felix." In *Maladie et maladies dans les textes latins antiques et médiévaux*, Actes du Colloque International "Textes médicaux latins" (Bruxelles, 4–6 septembre 1995), ed. Carl Deroux, 295–312. Latomus, 1998.

Sambre, Paul. "Fleshing out Language and Intersubjectivity: An Exploration of Merleau-Ponty's Legacy to Cognitive Linguistics." *Journal of Cognitive Semiotics* 4, no. 1 (2009): 189–224.

Sandbach, Francis Henry. "*Phantasia Katalēptikē.*" In *Problems in Stoicism*, ed. Anthony Arthur Long, 9–21. Athlone Press, 1971.

Sandilands, Joan Ruth. *Bacchus in Latin Love-Elegy.* Master's thesis, University of British Columbia, 1966.

Sanmartín, Nerea Terceiro. "The Dramatic Date of Plato's *Timaeus-Critias.*" *Greek, Roman, and Byzantine Studies* 62 (2022): 182–202.

Sansone, David. "Plato and Euripides." *Illinois Classical Studies* 21 (1996): 35–67.

Sansone, David. "Socrates, Satyrs, and Satyr-Play in Plato's *Symposium*." *Illinois Classical Studies* 43, no. 1 (2018): 58–87.

Sassi, Maria Michela. "Parmenides and Empedocles on *Krasis* and Knowledge." *Apeiron* 49, no. 4 (2015): 451–469.

Saunders, Trevor J. "Plato's Later Political Thought." In *Cambridge Companion to Plato*, ed. Richard Kraut. Cambridge University Press, 1992.

Sauvé-Meyer, Susan. *Plato Laws 1 and 2. Translation, Introduction, Commentary.* Oxford University Press, 2015.

Saxonhouse, Arlene. "The Net of Hephaestus: Aristophanes' Speech in Plato's *Symposium*." *Interpretation* 13, no. 1 (1984): 15–32.

Scarcella, Antonio M. *Conversazioni a tavola. Libro primo. Introduzione, testo critico, traduzione e commento.* D'Auria, 1998.

Schein, Seth L. "The Language of Wisdom in Sophokles' *Philoktetes* and Euripides' *Bacchae*." In *Wisdom and Folly in Euripides*, ed. Poulcheria Kyriakou and Antonios Rengakos, 257–274. De Gruyter, 2016.

Scheinberg, Susan. "The Bee Maidens of the Homeric *Hymn* to *Hermes*." *Harvard Studies in Classical Philology* 83 (1979): 1–28.

Schiappa, Edward. "Isocrates' Philosophia and Contemporary Pragmatism." In *Rhetoric, Sophistry, Pragmatism*, ed. Steven Mailloux, 33–60. Cambridge University Press, 1995.

Schiefsky, Mark. *Hippocrates: Ancient Medicine.* Brill, 2005.

Schiesaro, Alessandro. *The Passions in Play: Thyestes and the Dynamics of Senecan Drama.* Cambridge University Press, 2003.

Schlieter, Jens. "Master the Chariot, Master Your Self': Comparing Chariot Metaphors as Hermeneutics for mind, Self And Liberation In Ancient Greek and Indian Sources." In *Universe and Inner Self in Early Indian and Early Greek Thought*, ed. Richard Seaford, 168–185. Edinburgh University Press, 2016.

Schiltz, Elizabeth A. "Two Chariots: The Justification of the Best Life in the 'Katha Upanishad' and Plato's 'Phaedrus.'" *Philosophy East and West* 56, no. 3 (2006): 451–468.

Schlapbach, Karin. "The *Logoi* of Philosophers in Lucian of Samosata." *Classical Antiquity* 29, no. 2 (2010): 250–277.

Schmidt, Margot. "Beziehungen zwischen Eros, dem dionysischen und dem 'eleusinischen' Kreis auf apulischen Vasenbildern." In *Images et société en Grèce ancienne: Iconographie comme méthode d'analyse*, actes du colloque international, Lausanne, 8–11 février 1984, ed. Claude Bérard, Christiane Bron, Alessandra Pomari, 155–167. Institut d'archéologie et d'histoire ancienne, 1987.

Schmidt, Moritz. *Hesychii Alexandrini lexicon.* Dufft, 1867.

Schmitt-Pantel, Pauline. "Sacrificial Meal and Symposion: Two Models of Civic Institutions in the Archaic City?" In *Sympotica: A Symposium on the Symposium*, ed. Oswyn Murray, 14–33. Oxford University Press, 1990.

Schmitt-Pantel, Pauline. *La Cité au banquet: Histoire des repas publics dans les cités grecques.* École Française de Rome, 1992.

Schmitz, Thomas A. "Plutarch and the Second Sophistic." In *A Companion to Plutarch*, ed. Mark Beck, 32–42. Wiley-Blackwell, 2013.

Schofield, M. *Plato: Political Philosophy.* Oxford University Press, 2006.

Schofield, Malcolm. "The Noble Lie." In *The Cambridge Companion to Plato's Republic*, ed. Giovanni R. F. Ferrari, 138–164. Cambridge University Press, 2007.

Schofield, Malcolm. "Liberty, Equality, and Authority: A Political Discourse in the Later Roman Republic." In *A Companion to Greek Democracy and the Roman Republic*, ed. Dean Hammer, 113–127. Wiley-Blackwell, 2015.

Schofield, Malcolm. *Cicero: Political Philosophy.* Oxford University Press, 2021.

Schönfeld, Martin. *The Philosophy of the Young Kant: The Precritical Project.* Oxford University Press, 2000.

Schöpsdau, Klaus. "Tapferkeit, Aidos und Sophrosyne im ersten Buch der Platonischen *Nomoi*." *Rheinisches Museum* 129 (1986): 97–123.

Schöpsdau, Klaus. *Nomoi, Buch I–III. Werke / Platon, IX, 2.* Vandenhoeck & Ruprecht, 1994.

Schöpsdau, Klaus. *Nomoi IV–VII, übersetzt und kommentiert.* Vandenhoeck & Ruprecht, 2003.

Schott, Jeremy M. *Christianity, Empire, and the Making of Religion in Late Antiquity.* University of Pennsylvania Press, 2013.

Schröder, Stephan. "Plutarch on Oracles and Divine Inspiration." In *On the Daimonion of Socrates: Human Liberation, Divine Guidance and Philosophy*, ed. Heinz-Günther Nesselrath, 145–168. Mohr Siebeck, 2010.

Schultz, Anne-Marie, with Paul E. Carron. "Socratic Meditation and Emotional Self-Regulation: A Model for Human Dignity in The Technological Age." *Journal of Interdisciplinary Studies* 24 (2013): 1–29.

Schürer, Emil. *The Literature of the Jewish People in the Time of Jesus.* Schocken, 1973.

Schwartz, Stephan A. "Water, Wine and the Sacred, an Anthropological View of Substances Altered by Intentioned Awareness, Including Objective and Aesthetic Effects." *Explore* 15, no. 1 (2019): 13–18.

Schweighäuser, Johann. *Epicteti Dissertationum ab Arriano Digestarum libri 4. Eiusdem Enchiridion et ex deperditus sermonibus fragmenta.* Weidmann, 1799.

Scott, Dominic. "Socrates and Alcibiades in the 'Symposium.'" *Hermathena* 168 (2000): 25–37.

Scott, Gary Alan. *Plato's Socrates as Educator.* State University of New York Press, 2000.

Scott, Gary Alan, and William A. Welton. *Erotic Wisdom: Philosophy and Intermediacy in Plato's Symposium.* State University of New York Press, 2008.

Scott, Kenneth. "Octavian's Propaganda and Antony's *De sua ebrietate*." *Classical Philology* 24, no. 2 (1929): 133–141.

Scott, Naomi. "Metaphors and Jokes in the Fragments of Cratinus." *Arethusa* 52, no. 3 (2019): 231–251.

Screech, Michael A. *Laughter at the Foot of the Cross*. University of Chicago Press, 2015.

Scull, Andrew. *Madness in Civilization: A Cultural History of Insanity from the Bible to Freud, from the Madhouse to Modern Medicine*. Princeton University Press, 2015.

Seaford, Richard. *Reciprocity and Ritual: Homer and Tragedy in the Developing City State*. Oxford University Press, 1994.

Seaford, Richard. "Something to Do with Dionysos—Tragedy and the Dionysiac: Response to Friedrich." In *Tragedy and the Tragic: Greek Theatre and Beyond*, ed. Michael S. Silk, 284–294. Oxford University Press, 1996.

Seaford, Richard. "The Social Function of Attic Tragedy: A Response to Jasper Griffin." *The Classical Quarterly* 50 (2000): 30–44.

Seaford, Richard. *Dionysos*. Routledge, 2006.

Seaford, Richard. "The Interiorisation of Ritual in India and Greece." In *Universe and Inner Self in Early Indian and Early Greek Thought*, ed. Richard Seaford, 204–219. Edinburgh University Press, 2016.

Seaford, Richard. "The Politics of Euripides' *Bacchae* and the Preconception of Irresolveable Contradiction." In *Dionysus and Politics: Constructing Authority in the Graeco-Roman World*, ed. Filip Doroszewski and Dariusz Karłowicz, 18–31. Routledge, 2021.

Sears, Matthew A. *Athens, Thrace, and the Shaping of Athenian Leadership*. Cambridge University Press, 2013.

Sedley, David. "Zeno's Definition of *Phantasia Kataleptike*." In *Zeno of Citium and His Legacy: The Philosophy of Zeno*, ed. Theodore Scaltsas and Andrew S. Mason, 133–154. Municipality of Larnaca, 2002.

Sedley, David. *The Midwife of Platonism: Text and Subtext in Plato's Theaetetus*. Oxford University Press, 2004.

Sedley, David. *Plato's Cratylus*. Cambridge University Press, 2006a.

Sedley, David. "The Speech of Agathon in Plato's *Symposium*." In *The Virtuous Life in Greek Ethics*, ed. Burkhard Reis, 48–69. Cambridge University Press, 2006b.

Segal, Charles. "Greek Myth as a Semiotic and Structural System and the Problem of Tragedy." In *Interpreting Greek Tragedy: Myth, Poetry, Text*, 48–74. Cornell University Press, 1986. Originally published in *Arethusa* 16, no. 1/2 (1983): 173–198.

Segal, Charles. *Dionysiac Poetics and Euripides' Bacchae*. Princeton University Press, 1997.

Seltman, Charles. *Wine in the Ancient World*. Routledge, 1957.

Sens, Alexander. "Party or Perish: Death, Wine, and Closure in Hellenistic Sympotic Epigram." In *The Cup of Song Studies on Poetry and the Symposion*, ed. Vanessa Cazzato, Dirk Obbink, and Enrico Emanuele Prodi, 230–246. Oxford, 2016.

Sermamoglou-Soulmaidi, Georgia. "Love in Plato's *Alcibiades*." In *Wisdom, Love, and Friendship in Ancient Greek Philosophy Essays in Honor of Daniel Devereux*, ed. Georgia Sermamoglou-Soulmaidi and Evan Robert Keeling, 91–114. De Gruyter, 2021.

Serranito, Fábio. "*MANIA* and *ΑΛΗΘΕΙΑ* in Plato's *Phaedrus*." *The Classical Quarterly* 70, no. 1 (2020): 101–118.

Setaioli, Aldo. "Seneca e lo Stile." *Aufstieg und Niedergang der romischen Welt* II 32, no. 3 (1985): 776–858.

Setaioli, Aldo. "The Kiss and the Soul." *Giornale Italiano di Filologia* 67 (2015): 9–22.

Setaioli, Aldo. "Busybodies or Busy Bodies? Plutarch's de Curiositate and Gellius." *Prometheus* 46 (2020): 242–253.

Sferlea, Ovidiu. "On the Interpretation of the Theory of Perpetual Progress (epektasis): Taking into Account the Testimony of Eastern Monastic Tradition." *Revue d'histoire ecclésiastique* 109, no. 3–4 (2014): 564–584.

Shaw, Carl A. *Satyric Play: The Evolution of Greek Comedy and Satyr Drama*. Oxford University Press, 2014.

Shaw, Gregory. "Neoplatonic Theurgy and Dionysius the Areopagite." *Journal of Early Christian Studies* 7, no. 4 (1999): 573–599.

Sheffield, Frisbee C. C. "Psychic Pregnancy and Platonic Epistemology." *Oxford Studies in Ancient Philosophy* 20 (2001a): 1–30.

Sheffield, Frisbee C. C. "Alcibiades' Speech: A Satyric Drama." *Greece & Rome* 48, no. 2 (2001b): 193–209.

Sheffield, Frisbee C. C. *Plato's Symposium: The Ethics of Desire*. Oxford University Press, 2006a.

Sheffield, Frisbee C. C. "The Role of the Earlier Speeches in the *Symposium*: Plato's Endoxic Method?" In *Plato's Symposium: Issues in Interpretation and Reception*, ed. James Lesher, Debra Nails, and Frisbee Sheffield, 23–47. Harvard University Press (on behalf of the Center for Hellenic Studies), 2006b.

Sheffield, Frisbee C.C. "Beyond Eros: Friendship in the *Phaedrus*." *Proceedings of the Aristotelian Society* 111 (2011): 251–273.

Shelton, Matthew. "Divine Madness in Plato's *Phaedrus*." *Apeiron* 57, no. 2 (2024): 245–264.

Shen, Yeshayahu. "Aspects of Metaphor Comprehension: An Introduction." *Poetics Today* 13, no. 4 (1992): 567–574.

Sheppard, Anne. *Studies on the 5th and 6th Essays of Proclus' Commentary on the Republic*. Vandenhoeck & Ruprecht, 1980a.

Sheppard, Anne. "The Influence of Hermias on Marsilio Ficino's Doctrine of Inspiration." *Journal of the Warburg and Courtauld Institutes* 43 (1980b): 97–109.

Sheppard, Anne. "Rhetoric, Drama and Truth in Plato's *Symposium*." *International Journal of the Platonic Tradition* 2 (2008): 28–40.

Sider, David. "Plato's *Symposium* as a Dionysian Festival." *Quaderni Urbinati di Cultura Classica* 33 (1980): 41–56.

Sidwell, Keith. "Poetic Rivalry and the Caricature of Comic Poets: Cratinus' Pytine and Aristophanes' *Wasps*." In *Stage Directions: Essays in Ancient Drama in Honour of E.W. Handley*, ed. Alan Griffiths, 56–80. Institute of Classical Studies, 1995.

Sidwell, Keith. "Athenaeus, Lucian and Fifth-Century Comedy." In *Athenaeus and His World: Reading Greek Culture in the Roman Empire*, ed. David Braund and John Wilkins, 136–152. Exeter University Press, 2000.

Siegel, Rudolph E. *Galen's System of Physiology and Medicine*. S. Karger, 1968.

Siegel, Rudolph E. *Galen on Psychology, Psychopathology, and Function and Diseases of the Nervous System: An Analysis of His Doctrines, Observations and Experiments*. S. Karger, 1973.

Siikala, Anna-Leena. "The Siberian Shaman's Technique of Ecstasy." In *Studies on Shamanism*, ed. Anna-Leena Siikala and Mihály Hoppál, 26–40. Finnish Anthropological Society—Akademiai Kiado, 1992. Originally published in *Religious Ecstasy: Based on Papers Read at the Symposium on Religious Ecstasy Held at Åbo, Finland, on the 26th–28th of August 1981*, ed. Nils G. Holm, 103–121. Almqvist & Wiksell, 1982.

Silk, Michael. "Metaphor and Metonymy: Aristotle, Jakobson, Ricoeur, and Others." In *Metaphor, Allegory, and the Classical Tradition*, ed. George R. Boys-Stones, 115–148. Oxford University Press, 2003.

Silk, Michael S. *Aristophanes and the Definition of Comedy*. Oxford University Press, 2000.

Silk, Michael S. "The Greek Dramatic Genres: Theoretical Perspectives." In *Greek Comedy and the Discourse of Genres*, ed. Emmanuela Bakola, Lucia Prauscello, and Mario Teló, 14–39. Cambridge University Press, 2013.

Simon, Bennett. "Mind and Madness in Classical Antiquity." In *History of Psychiatry and Medical Psychology*, ed. Edwin R. Wallace and John Gach, 175–197. Springer, 2008.

Skinner, Quentin. "Meaning and Understanding in the History of Ideas." *History and Theory* 8, no. 1 (1969): 3–53.

Skinner, Quentin. "Hermeneutics and the Role of History." *New Literary History* 7, no. 1 (1975): 209–232.

Slater, Niall W. *Spectator Politics: Metatheatre and Performance in Aristophanes*. University of Pennsylvania Press, 2002.

Slater, William J. "Sympotic Ethics in the *Odyssey*." In *Sympotica: A Symposium on the Symposium*, ed. Oswyn Murray, 213–220. Oxford University Press, 1990.

Slater, William J. *Dining in a Classical Context*. University of Michigan Press, 1991.

Slingerland, Edward. *Drunk: How We Sipped, Danced, and Stumbled Our Way to Civilization*. Little Brown Spark, 2021.

Smith, Barry, and Woodruff David Smith. "Introduction." In *The Cambridge Companion to Husserl*, ed. Barry Smith and Woodruff David Smith, 1–44. Cambridge University Press, 1995.

Smith, Dennis E. *From Symposium to Eucharist: The Banquet in the Early Christian World*. Augsburg Fortress, 2003.

Smith, Nicholas D. "Socrates and Plato on Poetry." *Philosophic Exchange* 37, no. 1 (2007): 43–54.

Smith, Woodruff David. *The Hippocratic Tradition*. Cornell University Press, 1979.

Smith, Woodruff David. *Hippocrates: Pseudepigraphic Writings*. Brill, 1990.

Smith, Woodruff David. "Truth and Epoché: The Semantic Conception of Truth in Phenomenology." In *Beyond the Analytic-Continental Divide: Pluralistic Philosophy in the Twenty-First Century*, ed. Jeffrey A. Bell, Andrew Cutrofello, and Paul M. Linvingston, 111–128. Routledge, 2016a.

Smith, Woodruff David. "Husserl and Tarski: The Semantic Conception of Intentionality and Truth." In *Husserl and Analytic Philosophy*, ed. Guillermo E. Rosado Haddock, 143–174. De Gruyter, 2016b.

Snyder, Charles. "On the Teaching of Ethics from Polemo to Arcesilaus." *Études platoniciennes* 14 (2018): 1–25.

Sommerstein, Alan. "Old Comedians on Old Comedy." *Drama* 1 (1992): 14–33.

Sommerstein, Alan. *Talking about Laughter: And Other Studies in Greek Comedy*. Oxford University Press, 2009.

Sorabji, Richard. *Aristotle Re-Interpreted: New Findings on Seven Hundred Years of the Ancient Commentators*. Bloomsbury, 2016.

Sourvinou-Inwood, Christiane. "Aspects of the Eleusinian Cult." In *Greek Mysteries: The Archaeology and Ritual of Ancient Greek Secret Cults*, ed. Michael B. Cosmopoulos, 25–49. Routledge, 2003.

Spencer, Diana. *The Roman Alexander. Reading a Cultural Myth*. University of Exeter Press, 2002.

Sperger, Dan, Fabrice Clément, Christophe Heintz, Olivier Mascaro, Hugo Mercier, Gloria Origgi, and Deirdre Wilson. "Epistemic Vigilance." *Mind and Language* 25 (2010): 359–393.

Spiegelberg, Herbert. "The 'Reality Phenomenon and Reality.'" In *Philosophical Essays in Memory of E. Husserl*, ed. Marvin Farber, 84–105. Harvard University Press, 1940. Reprint, 2013.

Spiers Donald E. "Thermoregulation and Alcohol." In *Alcohol and Hormones: Drug and Alcohol Abuse Reviews 6*, ed. Ronald R. Watson, 193–208. Humana Press, 1995.

Spiller, Henry A., John R. Hale, and Jelle Z. de Boer. "The Delphic Oracle: A Multidisciplinary Defense of the Gaseous Vent Theory." *Clinical Toxicology* 40, no. 2 (2002): 189–196.

Stadter, Philip A. "Drinking, *Table-Talk*, and Plutarch's Contemporaries." In *Plutarco, Dioniso y el vino, Actas del VI Simposio Español sobre Plutarco*

(*Cádiz, 14–16 de Mayo, 1998*), ed. J. Guillermo Montes Cala, Manuel Sánchez Ortiz de Landaluce, and Rafael J. Gallé Cejudo, 481–490. Ediciones Clásicas Madrid, 1999.

Stafford, Emma. *Herakles*. Routledge, 2012.

Stählin, Otto with Ursula Treu, ed. *Scholia in Clementem Alexandrinum, in protrepticum et paedagogum* (scholia recentiora partim sub auctore Aretha). Clemens Alexandrinus, vol. 1, GCS 12. Akademie-Verlag, 1905. Reprint, 1972.

Stalley, Richard. *An Introduction to Plato's Laws*. Hackett Publishing House, 1983.

Stalley, Richard. "Persuasion in Plato's *Laws*." *History of Political Thought* 15, no. 2 (1994): 157–177.

Standhartinger, Angela. "Best Practice: Religious Reformation in Philo's Representation of the *Therapeutae* and *Therapeutrides*." In *Beyond Priesthood Religious Entrepreneurs and Innovators in the Roman Empire*, ed. Richard L. Gordon, Georgia Petridou, and J. Jörg Rüpke, 129–156. Brill, 2017.

Steckerl, Fritz. *Fragments of Praxagoras of Cos and His School*. Brill, 1958.

Steen, Gerard J. "Identifying Metaphor in Language: A Cognitive Approach." *Style* 36, no. 3 (2002): 386–406.

Steiner, Deborah T. "Solon fr. 1–3 W: The Poetics and Politics of a Gesture." *Cahiers Mondes anciens* 5 (2014): 1–19.

Sterling, Gregory E. "The Body as Metaphor: The Structure of a Human and the Meaning of Scripture." *Novum Testamentum* 61, no. 1 (2019): 26–39.

Stevens, John A. "Impulse and Animal Action in Stoic Psychology." *Society for Ancient Greek Philosophy Newsletter* 204 (1996). https://orb.binghamton.edu/sagp/204.

Stewart, Keith A. *Galen and Black Bile: Doxographical Strategies and Hippocratic Perspectives*. Brill, 2018.

Stoller, Silvia. "Phenomenology and the Poststructural Critique of Experience." *International Journal of Philosophical Studies* 17, no. 5 (2009): 707–737.

Storey, Ian C. *Fragments of Old Comedy II: Diopeithes to Pherecrates (LCL 14)*. Harvard University Press, 2011.

Stratton, Geoge Malcolm. *Theophrastus and the Greek Physiological Psychology before Aristotle*. Macmillan, 1917.

Strauss, L. *The City and Man*. University of Chicago Press, 1964.

Strauss, Leo. *The Argument and the Action of Plato's Laws*. University of Chicago Press, 1975.

Strauss, Leo. *On Plato's* Symposium. Edited and with a foreword by Seth Benardete. University of Chicago Press, 2003.

Striker, Gisela. "Emotions in Context: Aristotle's Treatment of the Passions in the *Rhetoric* and his Moral Psychology." In *Essays on Aristotle's Rhetoric*, ed. Amélie Rorty, 286–302. University of California Press, 1996. Also published in Stiker, Gisela. *From Aristotle to Cicero: Essays in Ancient Philosophy*, 112–127. Oxford University Press, 2022.

Strootman, Rolf. "The Return of the King: Civic Feasting and the Entanglement of City and Empire in Hellenistic Greece." In *Feasting and Polis Institutions*, ed. Floris van den Eijnde, Josine Blok, and Rolf Strootman, 273–296. Brill, 2018.

Struck, Peter T. "Pagan and Christian Theurgies: Iamblichus, Pseudo-Dionysius, Religion and Magic in Late Antiquity." *Ancient World* 32, no. 2 (2001): 25–38.

Struck, Peter T. *Birth of the Symbol: Ancient Readers at the Limits of their Texts*. Princeton University Press, 2004.

Svenbro, Jesper. *La parola e il marmo: Alle origini delle poetica greca*. Boringhieri, 1984. Revised and corrected edition, *La parole et le marbre: Aux origines de la poètique grecque*. Klassiska Institutionen, 1976.

Szaif, Jan. "Aporia in Plato's *Theaetetus* and *Sophist*." In *The Aporetic Tradition in Ancient Philosophy*, ed. George Karamanolis and Vasilis Politis, 29–47. Cambridge University Press, 2018.

Szaif, Jan. "Drunkenness as a Communal Practice: Platonic and Peripatetic Perspectives." *Frontiers of Philosophy in China* 14, no. 1 (2019): 94–110.

Szlezák, Thomas A. *Reading Plato*. Translated by Graham Zanker. Routledge, 1999. Originally published in *Platon lessen*. Frommann-Holzboog, 1993.

Tallis, Raymond. *Not Saussure: A Critique of Post-Saussurean Literary Theory*. Palgrave Macmillan, 1988.

Talmont-Kaminski, Konrad. "Epistemic Vigilance and the Science/Religion Distinction." *Journal of Cognition and Culture* 20, no. 1/2 (2020): 88–99.

Targum, Steven D., and Lenard A. Adler. "Our Current Understanding of Adult ADHD." *Innovations in Clinical Neuroscience* 11 (2014): 30–35.

Tarrant, Harold. "Myth as a Tool of Persuasion in Plato." *Antichthon* 24 (1990): 19–31.

Tarrant, Harold. "Platonic Interpretation in Aulus Gellius." *Greek, Roman and Byzantine Studies* 37 (1996): 173–193.

Tarrant, Harold. "Socratic *Synousia*: A Post-Platonic Myth?" *Journal of the History of Philosophy* 43 (2005): 131–155.

Tarrant, Harold. "Living by the *Cratylus*: Hermeneutics and Philosophic Names in the Roman Empire." *International Journal of the Platonic Tradition* 3 (2009): 1–25.

Tarrant, Harold. "Literal and Deeper Meanings in Platonic Myths." In *Plato and Myth*, ed. Catherine Collobert, Pierre Destrée, and Francisco J. Gonzalez, 47–65. Brill, 2012.

Tate, Jonathan. "Plato and Allegorical Interpretation." *The Classical Quarterly* 23, no. 3/4 (1929): 142–154.

Taylor, Joan, and David M. Hay. *Philo of Alexandria: On the Contemplative Life Introduction, Translation and Commentary*. Brill, 2020.

Tcherikover, Victor A. "The Ideology of the Letter of Aristeas." *Harvard Theological Review* 51, no. 2 (1958): 59–85.

Tchernia, André. *Le Vin de l'Italie Romaine: Essai d'histoire économique d'après les amphores.* École Française de Rome, 1986.

Tecuşan, Manuela. "Logos Sympotikos: Patterns of the Irrational in Philosophical Drinking: Plato Outside the Symposion." In *Sympotica: A Symposium on the Symposium,* ed. Oswyn Murray, 238–260. Oxford University Press, 1990.

Telò, Mario. *Aristophanes and the Cloak of Comedy: Affect, Aesthetics, and the Canon.* University of Chicago Press, 2016.

Teodorsson, Sven-Tage. *A Commentary on Plutarch's Table Talks, Vol. I (Books 1–3).* Göteborg: Acta Universitatis Gothoburgensis (University Press), 1989.

Teodorsson, Sven-Tage. "Dionysus Moderated and Calmed: Plutarch on the Convivial Wine." In *Plutarco, Dioniso y el vino. Actas del VI Simposio español sobre Plutarco (Cádiz, 14–16 de Mayo, 1998),* ed. J. Guillermo Montes Cala, Manuel Sánchez Ortiz de Landaluce, and Rafael J. Gallé Cejudo, 57–69. Ediciones Clásicas, 1999.

Teodorsson, Sven-Tage. "The Place of Plutarch in the Literary Genre of Symposium." In *Symposion and Philanthropia in Plutarch,* ed. José Ribeiro Ferreira, Delfim Leão, Manuel Tröster, and Paula Barata Dias, 3–16. Imprensa da Universidade de Coimbra, Classica Digitalia, 2009.

Thaler, Naly. "Perception and Knowledge in Plato's *Theaetetus.*" *Philosophy Compass* 11, no. 3 (2016): 160–167.

Theodoropoulou, Alexandra. *Επιβίωση και Ιερότητα. Η Πρώιμη Ανθρωπότητα, το Ελληνικό Κοσμοσύστημα και τα Μυστήρια της Ελευσίνας.* Papazisis, 2023.

Thesleff, Holger. "The Interrelation and Date of the "Symposia" of Plato and Xenophon." *Bulletin of the Institute of Classical Studies* 25 (1978): 157–170.

Thompson, John B. See Ricoeur Paul, 1981.

Thumiger, Chiara. "The Early Greek Medical Vocabulary of Insanity." In *Mental Disorders in the Classical World,* ed. William V. Harris, 61–96. Brill, 2013.

Thumiger, Chiara. "Mental Insanity in the Hippocratic Texts: A Pragmatic Perspective." *Mnemosyne* 68 (2015): 1–24.

Thumiger, Chiara. *A History of the Mind and Mental Health in Classical Greek Medical Thought.* Cambridge University Press, 2017.

Thye, Melissa D., Halry M. Bednarz, Abbey J. Herringshaw, Emma B. Sartin, and Rajesh K. Kana, "The Impact of Atypical Sensory Processing on Social Impairments in Autism Spectrum Disorder." *Developmental Cognitive Neuroscience* 29 (2018): 151–167.

Tieleman, Teun. *Chrysippus' On Affections: Reconstruction and Interpretation.* Brill, 2003.

Tietjen, Ruth Rebecca. "Religious Zeal, Affective Fragility, and the Tragedy of Human Existence." *Human Studies* 46 (2021): 1–19.

Titus, Alexander. "Some Dionysian Influences on John Scottus Eriugena's *On Predestination.*" In *Eriugena's Christian Neoplatonism and Its Sources in*

Patristic and Ancient Philosophy, Studia Patristica 122, ed. Ilaria Ramelli, 227–238. Peeters, 2021.

Tobin, Thomas H. "Philo of Alexandria's Interpretations of the Episode of the Golden Calf." In *Golden Calf Traditions in Early Judaism, Christianity, and Islam*, ed. Eric F. Mason and Edmondo F. Lupieri, 73–86. Brill, 2018.

Togni, Paolo. "Plato's Soul-Book Simile and Stole Epistemology." *Méthexis* 26, no. 1 (2013): 163–185.

Toohey, Peter. *Melancholy, Love, and Time: Boundaries of the Self in Ancient Literature.* University of Michigan Press, 2004.

Tordoff, Robert L. "Coins, Money, and Exchange in Aristophanes' 'Wealth.'" *Transactions of the American Philological Association* 142, no. 2 (2012): 257–293.

Tornau, Christian. "Saint Augustine." In *The Stanford Encyclopedia of Philosophy* (Summer 2020 Edition), ed. Edward N. Zalta, 2020. https://plato.stanford.edu/archives/sum2020/entries/augustine/.

Torri, Paolo. "Quale dio per quale vita?: Una interpretazione del τέλος platonico dell'assimilazione a dio nel *Didaskalikos* di Alcinoo." *Philologus* 161, no. 2 (2017): 216–242.

Trabattoni, Franco. *Scrivere nell'anima. Verità, dialettica e persuasione in Platone.* La Nuova Italia, 1993.

Trabattoni, Franco. *Platone.* Carocci, 1998.

Trabattoni, Franco. *La verità nascosta. Oralità e scrittura in Platone e nella Grecia Classica.* Carocci, 2007. First edition, 2002.

Trabattoni, Franco. "Myth and Truth in Plato's *Phaedrus*." In *Plato and Myth: Studies on the Use and Status of Platonic Myths*, ed. Catherine Collobert, Pierre Destrée, and Francisco J. Gonzalez, 305–322. Brill, 2012.

Trabattoni, Franco. *Platone. Teeteto.* Einaudi, 2018.

Trabattoni, Franco. *La filosofia di Platone. Verità e ragione umana.* Carocci, 2020.

Trabattoni, Franco. "Knowledge, Opinion, and Recollection in the Theaetetus." In *New Explorations in Plato's Theaetetus*, ed. Diego Zucca, 271–283. Brill, 2022.

Tracy, Theodore James. *Physiological Theory and the Doctrine of the Mean in Plato and Aristotle.* Mouton, 1969.

Tracy, Theodore James. "Plato, Galen, and the Center of Consciousness." *Illinois Classical Studies* 1 (1976): 43–52.

Trapp, Michael. "Plato in Athenaeus' *Deipnosophists*." In *Athenaeus and His World: Reading Greek Culture in the Roman Empire*, ed. David Braund and John Wilkins, 353–364. University of Exeter Press, 2000.

Trapp, Michael. "With All Due Respect to Plato: The *Platonic Orations* of Aelius Aristides." *Transactions of the American Philological Association* 150, no. 1 (2020): 85–113.

Trawny, Peter. "Tragic or Philosophic Eros in Sophocles and Plato." In *Phenomenology of Eros*, ed. Jonna Bornemark and Marcia Sá Cavalcante Schuback, 19–32. Södertörns Högskola University Press, 2012.

Trivigno, Franco V. "Childish Nonsense? The Value of Interpretation in Plato's *Protagoras*." *Journal of the History of Philosophy* 51, no. 4 (2013): 509–543.

Trizio, Michele. "A New Testimony on the Platonist Gaius." *Greek, Roman, and Byzantine Studies* 53 (2013): 136–145.

Trusso, Dana. *The Erotic Charms of Platonic Discourse: Mythmaking, Love Potions, and Role Reversals*. PhD thesis, Duquesne University, 2015. https://dsc.duq.edu/etd/1294.

Tsouna, Voula. "Philodemus on the Therapy of Vice." *Oxford Studies in Ancient Philosophy* 21 (2001): 233–258.

Turner, Mark. *Death Is the Mother of Beauty: Mind, Metaphor, Criticism*. University of Chicago Press, 1987.

Turner, Mark. *The Literary Mind*. Oxford University Press, 1996.

Tzanetou, Angeliki. *City of Suppliants: Tragedy and the Athenian Empire*. University of Texas Press, 2012.

Tzochev, Chavdar. *Amphora Stamps from Thasos: The Athenian Agora XXXVII*. Oxford University Press, 2016a.

Tzochev, Chavdar. "Markets, Amphora Trade and Wine Industry: The Case of Thasos." In *The Ancient Greek Economy: Markets, Households and City-States*, ed. Edward M. Harris, David M. Lewis, and Mark Woolmer, 230–253. Cambridge University Press, 2016b.

Ulrich, Jeffrey P. "Hermeneutic Recollections: Apuleius' Use of Platonic Myth in the Metamorphoses." *Classical Philology* 115, no. 4 (2020): 677–704.

Unwin, Naomi Carless. *Caria and Crete in Antiquity. Cultural Interaction between Anatolia and the Aegean*. Cambridge University Press, 2017.

Urmson, James O. "Plato and the Poets." In *Plato's Republic: Critical Essays*, ed. Richard Kraut, 223–234. Rowman & Littlefield, 1997.

Usener, Hermann. *Epicurea*. Teubner, 1887.

Usher, Mark David. "Satyr Play in Plato's *Symposium*." *American Journal of Philology* 123, no. 2 (2002): 205–228.

Usher, Mark David. "Carneades' Quip: Orality, Philosophy, Wit, and the Poetics of Impromptu Quotation." *Oral Tradition* 21, no. 1 (2006): 190–209.

Usher, Stephen. "This to the Fair Critias." *Eranos* 77 (1979): 39–42.

Ustinova, Yulia. *Divine Mania: Alteration of Consciousness in Ancient Greece*. Routledge, 2017.

Uždavinys, Algis. *The Heart of Plotinus: The Essential Enneads Including Porphyry's On the Cave*. World Wisdom, 2009.

Vaidya, Chandan J., and Melanie Stollstorff. "Cognitive Neuroscience of Attention Deficit Hyperactivity Disorder: Current Status and Working Hypotheses." *Developmental Disabilities Research Reviews* 14, no. 4 (2008): 261–267.

Valamoti, Soultana-Maria, Maria Mangafa, Chaido Koukouli-Chrysanthaki, and Dimitra Malamidou. "Grape-Pressings from Northern Greece: The Earliest Wine in the Aegean?" *Antiquity* 81 (2007): 54–61.

Valdés Guía, Miriam. "Redefining Dionysos in Athens from the Written Sources: The Lenaia, Iacchos and Attic Women." In *Redefining Dionysos*, ed. Alberto Bernabé, Miguel Herrero de Jáuregui, Ana Isabel Jiménez San Cristóbal, and Raquel Martín Hernández. 100–119. Brill, 2013.

Vamvouri Ruffy, Maria. "Symposium, Physical and Social Health in Plutarch's Table Talk." In *The Philosopher's Banquet: Plutarch's Table Talk in the Intellectual Culture of the Roman Empire*, ed. Frieda Klotz and Katerina Oikonomopoulou, 130–157. Oxford University Press, 2011.

Vamvouri Ruffy, Maria. *Les vertus thérapeutiques du banquet: Médecine et idéologie dans les Propos de Table de Plutarque*. Les Belles Lettres, 2012.

Vamvouri Ruffy, Maria. "Plutarch in Macrobius and Athenaeus." In *Brill's Companion to the Reception of Plutarch*, ed. Sophia Xenophontos and Katerina Oikonomopoulou, 17–36. Brill, 2019.

van de Grift, Jon. "De Lycurgo Insano: The Dionysiac Frieze on a Silver Kantharos." *Journal of the Walters Art Gallery* 42 (1984): 6–15.

van den Berg, Robert. " 'Becoming Like God' According to Proclus' *Interpretations of the Timaeus*, the Eleusinian Mysteries, and the Chaldaean Oracles." *Bulletin of the Institute of Classical Studies* 46 (2003): 189–202.

van der Eijk, Philip J. "Aristoteles Über Die Melancholie." *Mnemosyne* 43, no. 1/2 (1990): 33–72. Translated and printed with minor changes in van der Eijk 2005, 139–168.

van der Eijk, Philip J. *Diocles of Carystus. A Collection of the Fragments with Translation and Commentary*. 2 vols. Brill, 2000.

van der Eijk, Philip J. *Medicine and Philosophy in Classical Antiquity: Doctors and Philosophers on Nature, Soul, Health and Disease*. Cambridge University Press, 2005.

van der Stockt, Luc. "Aspects of the Ethics and Poetics of the Dialogue in the Corpus Plutarcheum." In *I Generi Letterari in Plutarco. Atti del VIII Convegno Plutarcheo (Pisa, 2–4 Giugno, 1999)*, ed. Italo Gallo and Claudio Moreschini, 93–116. D'Auria, 2000.

van der Stockt, Luc. "Plutarch's Anger in Aulus Gellius, *Noctes Atticae* I, 26." *Humanitas* 55 (2003): 143–156.

van der Stockt, Luc. "Plutarch and Apuleius: Laborious Routes to Isis." In *Aspects of Apuleius' Golden Ass, vol. III: The Isis Book. A Collection of Original Papers*, ed. Wytse H. Keulen and Ulrike Egelhaaf-Gaiser, 168–182. Brill, 2012.

Vander Waerdt, Paul A. "Kingship and Philosophy in Aristotle's Best Regime." *Phronesis* 30 (1985): 249–273.

van Hoof, Lieve. *Plutarch's Practical Ethics: The Social Dynamics of Philosophy*. Oxford University Press, 2010.

van Raalte, Marlein. "Socratic *Parrhesia* and Its Afterlife in Plato's *Laws*." In *Free Speech in Classical Antiquity*, ed. Irene Sluiter and Ralph Rosen, 279–312. Brill, 2004.

van Wassenhove, Bart. *Moral Admonition and the Emotions in Seneca's Philosophical Works.* PhD thesis, University of Chicago, 2016.

Vasilakis, Dimitris A. *Eros in Neoplatonism and its Reception in Christian Philosophy: Exploring Love in Plotinus, Proclus and Dionysius the Areopagite.* Bloomsbury, 2020.

Vasunia, Phiroze. *The Gift of the Nile: Hellenizing Egypt from Aeschylus to Alexander.* University of California Press, 2001.

Vegetti, Mario. "La Medicina in Platone." *Rivista Critica di Storia della Filosofia* 21, no. 1 (1966): 3–39.

Verlinsky, Alexander. "The Nocturnal Council in Plato's *Laws.*" *Philologia Classica* 11 (2016): 180–222.

Vetta, Massimo. "Plutarco e il 'Genere Simposio.'" In *I Generi Letterari in Plutarco. Atti del VIII Convegno Plutarcheo (Pisa, 2-4 Giugno, 1999),* ed. Italo Gallo and Claudio Moreschini, 217–229. D'Auria, 2000.

Vickers, Michael. "Alcibiades on Stage: *Philoctetes* and *Cyclops.*" *Historia* 36 (1987): 171–197.

Villa, Dana Richard. *Socratic Citizenship.* Princeton University Press, 2001.

Villar, Francisco. "Critica de Isocrates a los Socraticos en Contra los Sofistas y Encomio de Helena." *Signos Filosóficos* 21, no. 42 (2019): 8–35.

Villar, Francisco. "Isócrates y el crítico anónimo del Eutidemo de Platón." *AGORA Papeles de Filosofía* 39, no. 2 (2020): 169–191.

Vinkesteijn, Robert. *Philosophical Perspectives on Galen of Pergamum: Four Case-Studies on Human Nature and the Relation between Body and Soul.* Brill, 2022.

Vlastos, Gregory. "The Historical Socrates and Athenian Democracy." *Political Theory* 11, no. 4 (1983): 495–516.

Vlastos, Gregory. "Socrates' Disavowal of Knowledge." *Philosophical Quarterly* 35 (1985): 1–31.

Vlastos, Gregory. "Socratic Irony." *The Classical Quarterly* 37, no. 1 (1987): 79–96.

Voegelin, Eric. *Order and History, Volume III.* Louisiana State University Press, 1957.

Vogiatzi, Melpomeni. *Byzantine Commentaries on Aristotle's "Rhetoric": Anonymous and Stephanus, "In Artem Rhetoricam Commentaria."* De Gruyter, 2019.

Vogt, Katja M. "Plato on Madness and the Good Life." In *Mental Disorders in the Classical World,* ed. William V. Harris, 177–192. Brill, 2013.

Vogt, Katja M. "Plato on Hunger and Thirst." *History of Philosophy & Logical Analysis* 20, no. 1 (2017): 103–119.

Vogt, Katja Maria. "Seneca." In *The Stanford Encyclopedia of Philosophy* (Winter 2016 Edition), ed. Edward N. Zalta, 2016. https://plato.stanford.edu/archives/win2016/entries /seneca/.

Wachsmuth, Curt, and Otto Hense. *Ioannis Stobaei anthologium: Libri duo priores qui inscribi solent eclogae physicae et ethicae.* Weidmann, 1884.

Walker, Matthew D. "Aristotle on Wittiness." In *Laughter, Humor, and Comedy in Ancient Philosophy*, ed. Pierre Destrée and Franco V. Trivigno, 103–121. Oxford University Press, 2019.

Wallace, Robert M. *Philosophical Mysticism in Plato, Hegel, and the Present.* Bloomsbury, 2020.

Walsh, George B. "Sublime Method: Longinus on Language and Imitation." *Classical Antiquity* 7, no. 2 (1988): 252–269.

Walshe, Thomas M. III. *Neurological Concepts in Ancient Greek Medicine.* Oxford University Press, 2016.

Wankel, Hermann. "I. Erythrai 206, 6–12 und Demosth. 18, 259." *Zeitschrift für Papyrologie und Epigraphik* 34 (1979): 79–80.

Ward, Julia. "Theoria as Practice and as Activity." In *Aristotele e le Sfide del Suo Tempo*, ed. Roberto Radice and Marcello Zanatta, 235–250. Editioni Unicopli, 2018.

Ward, Julia. *Searching for the Divine in Plato and Aristotle.* Cambridge University Press, 2021.

Warren, James. *The Pleasures of Reason in Plato, Aristotle, and the Hellenistic Hedonists.* Cambridge University Press, 2014.

Warren, James. "Memory, Anticipation, Pleasure." In *Psychology and Value in Plato, Aristotle, and Hellenistic Philosophy: The Ninth Keeling Colloquium in Ancient Philosophy*, ed. Fiona Leigh and Margeret Hampson, 141–169. Oxford University Press, 2022.

Wasmuth, Ellisif. "ΩΣΠΕΡ ΟΙ ΚΟΡΥΒΑΝΤΙΩΝΤΕΣ: The Corybantic Rites in Plato's Dialogues." *The Classical Quarterly* 65, no. 1 (2015): 69–84.

Waterfield, Robin Anthony Herschel. "The Place of the 'Philebus' in Plato's 'Dialogues.'" *Phronesis* 25, no. 3 (1980): 270–305.

Wdowiak, Magdalena. "Allegorical Interpretation and Place of Myth in Plato." *Classica Cracoviensia* 20 (2017): 213–226.

Weber, Max. *From Max Weber: Essays in Sociology.* Translated, edited, and with an introduction by Hans Heinrich Gerth and Charles Wright Mills. Oxford University Press, 1946.

Webster, Peter, Carl Ruck, and Daniel M. Perrine. "Mixing the *Kykeon*." *Eleusis: Journal of Psychoactive Plants and Compounds* 4 (2000): 1–8.

Wecowski, Marek. *The Rise of the Greek Aristocratic Banquet.* Oxford University Press, 2014.

Weeber, Karl-Wilhelm. *Die Weinkultur der Römer.* Artemis & Winkler, 1933.

Wehrli, Fritz. *Dikaiarchos.* Schwabe, 1944.

Wehrli, Fritz. *Die Schule des Aristoteles. Texte und Kommentar: Heft VI: Lykon und Ariston von Keos.* Schwabe, 1952.

Weiss, Naomi A. *The Music of Tragedy: Performance and Imagination in Euripidean Theater.* University of California Press, 2018a.

Weiss, Naomi A. "Hearing the Syrinx in Euripidean Tragedy." In *Music, Text, and Culture in Ancient Greece*, ed. Tom Phillips and Armand D'Angour, 139–162. Oxford University Press, 2018b.

Weiss, Roslyn. *Virtue in the Cave: Moral Inquiry in Plato's Meno*. Oxford University Press, 2001.

Weiss, Roslyn. "Pity or Pardon: Plato, Xenophon and Aristotle on the Appropriate Response to Intentional Wrongdoing." In *Plato and Xenophon; Comparative Studies*, ed. Gabriel Danzig, David Johnson, and Donald Morrison, 277–317. Brill, 2018.

Weissenberger, Michael. *Literaturtheorie bei Lukian. Untersuchungen zum Dialog Lexiphanes*. Teubner, 1996.

Wellmann, Max. "Aretaios." In *Paulys Realencyclopädie der Classischen Altertumswissenschaft* II.1, ed. Georg Wissowa, 669–670. Metzler, 1895.

Wendel, Karl. *Scholia in Apollonium Rhodium vetera*. Georg Olms, 1958.

Wentura, Dirk. "Cognition and Emotion: On Paradigms and Metaphors." *Cognition and Emotion* 33 (2019): 85–93.

Werner, Daniel S. *Myth and Philosophy in Plato's Phaedrus*. Cambridge University Press, 2012.

Wesselmann, Katharina. *Mythische Erzählstrukturen in Herodots "Historien."* De Gruyter, 2011.

West, Martin Litchfield. *Early Greek Philosophy and the Orient*. Clarendon Press, 1971.

West, Martin Litchfield. *Iambi et elegi Graeci ante Alexandrum cantati*. 2 vols. Oxford University Press, 1989–1992.

West, Martin Litchfield. *Indo-European Poetry and Myth*. Oxford University Press, 2007.

White, David A. *Derrida on Being as Presence: Questions and Quests*. De Gruyter, 2017.

White, Francis. "Love and Beauty in Plato's *Symposium*." *Journal of Hellenic Studies* 109 (1989): 149–157.

White, Francis. "Plato's Last Words on Pleasure." *The Classical Quarterly* 51, no. 2 (2001): 458–476.

White, Francis. "Beauty of Soul and Speech in Plato's '*Symposium*.'" *The Classical Quarterly* 58, no. 1 (2008): 69–81.

Whiteford-Damerall, Alison, and Ronald T. Kellogg. "Familiarity and Aptness in Metaphor Comprehension." *American Journal of Psychology* 129, no. 1 (2016): 49–64.

Whitehorn, John. "Aristophanes' Representations of 'Intellectuals.'" *Hermes* 130, no. 1 (2002): 28–35.

Whitmarsh, Tim. "The Politics and Poetics of Parasitism: Athenaeus on Parasites and Flatterers." In *Athenaeus and His World: Reading Greek Culture in the*

Roman Empire, ed. David Braund and John Wilkins, 304–315. University of Exeter Press, 2000.

Whitmarsh, Tim. *Greek Literature and the Roman Empire: The Politics of Imitation.* Oxford University Press, 2001.

Whitmarsh, Tim. *The Second Sophistic.* Oxford University Press, 2005.

Whittaker, John. *Alcinoos, Enseignement des doctrines de Platon.* Translated by Pierre Louis. Les Belles Lettres, 1990.

Wilamowitz-Moellendorff, Ulrich von. *Plato.* Weidmann, 1920.

Wilburn, Joshua. "The Spirited Part of the Soul in Plato's *Timaeus*." *Journal of the History of Philosophy* 52, no. 4 (2014): 627–652.

Wilburn, Joshua. "The Problem of Alcibiades: Plato on Moral Education and the Many." *Oxford Studies in Ancient Philosophy* 49 (2015): 1–36.

Wilkins, John. *The Boastful Chef: The Discourse of Food in Ancient Greek Comedy.* Oxford University Press, 2000a.

Wilkins, John. "Dialogue and Comedy: The Structure of the *Deipnosophistae*." In *Athenaeus and His World: Reading Greek Culture in the Roman Empire*, ed. David Braund and John Wilkins, 23–37. University of Exeter Press, 2000b.

Wilkins, John. "Banquets sur la scène comique ou tragique." In *Symposium: banquet et représentations Grèce et à Rome, Pallas* 61, ed. Charalampos Orfanos and Jean-Claude Carrière, 167–174. Presses universitaires du Mirail, 2003.

Williams, Gareth D. *Seneca De Otio, De Brevitate Vitae.* Cambridge University Press, 2003.

Williams, David Lay. "Plato's Noble Lie: From Kallipolis to Magnesia." *History of Political Thought* 34, no. 3 (2013): 363–392.

(Wilson-)Nightingale, Andrea. *Genres in Dialogue: Plato and the Construct of Philosophy.* Cambridge University Press, 1995.

(Wilson-)Nightingale, Andrea. *Spectacles of Truth in Classical Greek Philosophy: Theoria in its Cultural Context.* Cambridge University Press, 2004.

(Wilson-)Nightingale, Andrea. "The Philosopher at the Festival: Plato's Transformation of Traditional *Theōria*." In *Seeing the Gods: Pilgrimage in Graeco-Roman and Early Christian Antiquity*, ed. Jaś Elsner and Ian Rutherford, 151–180. Oxford University Press, 2005.

(Wilson-)Nightingale Andrea. "Plato on *Aporia* and Self-Knowledge." In *Ancient Models of Mind: Studies in Human and Divine Rationality*, ed. Andrea Nightingale and David Sedley, 8–26. Cambridge University Press, 2010.

Wilson-Nightingale, Andrea. "The Orphaned Word: The Pharmakon of Forgetfulness in Plato's *Laws*." In *Performance and Culture in Plato's Laws*, ed. Anastasia-Erasmia Peponi, 243–264. Cambridge University Press, 2013.

Wilson-Bightingale, Andrea. "Sight and the Philosophy of Vision in Classical Greece: Democritus, Plato and Aristotle." In *Sight and the Ancient Senses*, vol. 4 of *The Senses in Antiquity*, ed. M. Squire, 54–67. Routledge, 2015.

Wilson-Nightingale, Andrea. *Philosophy and Religion in Plato's Dialogues*. Cambridge University Press, 2021.

Wilson, Peter. "Athenian Strings." In *Music and the Muses: The Culture of Mousikē in the Classical Athenian City*, ed. P. Murray and P. Wilson, 269–306. Oxford University Press, 2004.

Windt, Jennifer M. "Altered Consciousness in Philosophy." In *Altering Consciousness. Multidisciplinary Perspectives, Volume 1: History, Culture, and the Humanities*, ed. Etzel Cardeña and Michael Winkelman, 229–254. Praeger ABC-CLIO, 2011.

Winiarczyk, Marek. *Diagoras of Melos: A Contribution to the History of Ancient Atheism*. De Gruyter, 2016.

Winkler, John. "*Phallos Politikos*: Representing the Body Politic in Athens." *Differences* 2, no. 1 (1990): 29–44.

Wittgenstein, Ludwig. *Remarks on Colour*. Edited by Gertrude E. M. Anscombe. Translated by Linda L. McAlister and Margarete Schättle. Oxford University Press, 1977.

Witzel, Michael E. J. *The Origins of the World's Mythologies*. Oxford University Press, 2012.

Wohl, Victoria. "The *Erōs* of Alcibiades." *Classical Antiquity* 18, no. 2 (1999): 349–385.

Wohl, Victoria. "Dirty Dancing: Xenophon's *Symposium*." In *Music and the Muses: The Culture of Mousikē in the Classical Athenian City*, ed. Penelope Murray and Peter Wilson, 337–364. Oxford University Press, 2004.

Wolfsdorf, David. "The Irony of Socrates." *Journal of Aesthetics and Art Criticism* 65, no. 2 (2007): 175–187.

Wolfsdorf, David. *Trials of Reason: Plato and the Crafting of Philosophy*. Oxford University Press, 2008.

Wolfsdorf, David. *Pleasure in Ancient Greek Philosophy*. Cambridge University Press, 2012.

Woodbury, Leonard. "Simonides on Aretē." *Transactions and Proceedings of the American Philological Association* 84 (1953): 135–163.

Woodruff, Paul. "Socrates and the Irrational." In *Reason and Religion in Socratic Philosophy*, ed. Nicholas D. Smith and Paul Woodruff, 130–150. Oxford University Press, 2000.

Woodruff, Paul. "Self-Ridicule: Socratic Wisdom." In *Laughter, Humor, and Comedy in Ancient Philosophy*, ed. Pierre Destrée and Franco V. Trivigno, 165–181. Oxford University Press, 2019.

Wright, Benjamin G. III. "The Letter of Aristeas and the Question of Septuagint Origins Redux." *Journal of Ancient Judaism* 2, no. 3 (2011): 304–326.

Wright, Benjamin G. III. *The Letter of Aristeas 'Aristeas to Philocrates' or 'On the Translation of the Law of the Jews.'* De Gruyter, 2015.

Wright, J. Clifford. "Ṛgvedic satyá." *Bulletin of the School of Oriental and African Studies* 61, no. 3 (1998): 519–526.

Wyss, Beatrice. "Philon aus Alexandreia: Himmlische Liebe, Gottes Pneuma und Ekstasis." In *Der Mensch als Bild des unergründlichen Gottes. Von der Theologie zur Anthropologie und zurück*, ed. Georgiana Huian, Beatrice Wyss and Rainer Hirsch-Luipold, with the help of Ilya Kaplan, 159–193. De Gruyter, 2023.

Xenophontos, Sophia. "Comedy in Plutarch's *Parallel Lives*." *Greek, Roman, and Byzantine Studies* 52 (2012): 603–631.

Yaden, David B., Khoa D. Le Nguyen, Margaret Kern, Alexander B. Belser, Johannes C. Eichstaedt, Jonathan Iwry, Mary E. Smith, Nancy A. Wintering, Ralph W. Hood, and Andrew B. Newberg. "Of Roots and Fruits: A Comparison of Psychedelic and Nonpsychedelic Mystical Experiences." *Journal of Humanistic Psychology* 57, no. 4 (2017): 338–353.

Yardley, John C. "The Symposium in Roman Elegy." In *Dining in a Classical Context*, ed. William J. Slater, 149–156. Michigan University Press, 1991.

Yates, Velvet. "Review of Marian Demos, Lyric Quotation in Plato. Rowman & Littlefield, 1999." *Bryn Mawr Classical Review* (2000). https://bmcr.brynmawr.edu/2000/2000.06.16/.

Yli-Karjanmaa, Sami. "Philo of Alexandria." In *Brill's Companion to the Reception of Plato in Antiquity*, ed. Harold Tarrant, Danielle A. Layne, Dirk Baltzly, and François Renaud, 115–129. Brill, 2018.

Yona, Sergio. *Epicurean Ethics in Horace: The Psychology of Satire*. Oxford University Press, 2018.

Yoos, George E. "A Phenomenological Look at Metaphor." *Philosophy and Phenomenological Research* 32, no. 1 (1971): 78–88.

Yu, Kenneth W. "The Politics of Dance: Eunomia and the Exception of Dionysus in Plato's *Laws*." *The Classical Quarterly* 70, no. 2 (2020): 605–619.

Yunis, Harvey. *Plato: Phaedrus*. Cambridge University Press, 2011.

Zaborowski, Robert. "Plato's *Phaedrus* 253e5–255a1 Revisited: A Reappraisal of Plato's View on the Soul." *Organon* 50 (2018): 165–207.

Zanker, Paul. *The Mask of Socrates: The Image of the Intellectual in Antiquity*. Translated by Alan Shapiro. University of California Press, 1995.

Ziolkowski, Jan M., and Mary Carruthers. *The Medieval Craft of Memory: An Anthology of Texts and Ideas*. University of Pennsylvania Press, 2004.

Ziolkowski, John E. "The Bow and the Lyre: Harmonizing Duos in Plato's 'Symposium.'" *The Classical Journal* 95, no. 1 (1999): 19–35.

Ziolkowski, John E. "From *Clouds* to Corsair: Kierkegaard, Aristophanes, and the Problem of Socrates." In *The Concept of Irony*, ed. Robert L. Perkins, 193–234. Mercer University Press, 2001a.

Ziolkowski, John E. "The Highest Form of Compliment: Imitation in Medieval Latin Culture." In *Poetry and Philosophy in the Middle Ages: A Festschrift for Peter Dronke*, ed. John Marenbon, 293–307. Brill, 2001b.

Zlatev, Jordan. "Embodiment, Language and *Mimesis*." In *Body, Language and Mind. Vol. 1: Embodiment*, ed. Tom Ziemke, Jordan Zlatev, and Roslyn, M. Frank, 297–338. De Gruyter, 2007.

Zlatev, Jordan. "The Dependence of Language on Consciousness." *Journal of Consciousness Studies* 15, no. 6 (2008): 34–62.

Zlatev, Jordan. "Phenomenology and Cognitive Linguistics." In *Handbook of Phenomenology and Cognitive Science*, ed. Shaun Gallagher and Daniel Schicking, 415–446. Springer, 2010.

Zlatev, Jordan. "Turning Back to Experience in Cognitive Linguistics via Phenomenology." *Cognitive Linguistics* 27, no. 4 (2016): 559–572.

Zuckert, Catherine H. "Plato's *Laws*: Postlude or Prelude to Socratic Political Philosophy?" *Journal of Politics* 66, no. 2 (2004): 374–395.

Zuckert, Catherine H. *Plato's Philosophers: The Coherence of the Dialogues*. University of Chicago Press, 2009.

Zuntz, Gunther. "Aristeas Studies I: 'The Seven Banquets.'" *Journal of Semitic Studies* 4 (1959): 21–36.

Zuntz, Gunther. *Persephone*. Clarendon Press, 1971.

Index *Locorum*